INTERNATIONAL BANKING LAW

■ ■ ■

V. Gerard Comizio

Partner and Chair,
Global Banking Practice Group, Paul Hastings LLP

AMERICAN CASEBOOK SERIES®

WEST
ACADEMIC
PUBLISHING

American Casebook Series is a trademark registered in the U.S. Patent and Trademark Office.

© 2016 LEG, Inc. d/b/a West Academic
    444 Cedar Street, Suite 700
    St. Paul, MN 55101
    1-877-888-1330

West, West Academic Publishing, and West Academic are trademarks of West Publishing Corporation, used under license.

Printed in the United States of America

ISBN: 978-1-63459-761-6

For my wife Debra, and Allison, Joseph,
Christine and Michael Comizio

V.G.C.

ACKNOWLEDGMENTS

We are indebted to the following authors, publishers, government agencies and international organizations for their generosity in permitting us to reprint excerpts, including from copyrighted materials:

The Bretton Woods System: Cooperation and Reconstruction, The International Monetary Fund: History (2015).

Patricia A. McCoy, The Moral Hazard Implications of Deposit Insurance: Theory and Evidence, 5 Current Developments in Monetary and Financial Law 417–41, International Monetary Fund (2008). Reprinted with permission.

International Association of Deposit Insurers, Core Principles for Effective Deposit Insurance Systems (November 2014).

Antonio Mendoza, International Business Planning, Chapter 5, pp. 362–367, West Group (2001).

Ross P. Buckley & Xiang Gao, The Development of the Fraud Rule in Letter of Credit Law, 664 U. Pa. J. Int'l Econ. L. 23 (2002).

Hong Kong Monetary Authority Fraud Cases Related to Letters of Credit (August 2011).

Xiang Gao and Ross P. Buckley, A Comparative Analysis of the Standard of Fraud Required Under the Fraud Rule, Oxford U. Comparative L. Forum 3 (2003). Reprinted with permission.

David J. Bederman, International Law Frameworks, Foundation Press, Chapter 17 (2001).

Jonathan Jones, William W. Lang, and Peter Nigro, OCC Economics Working Paper 2000–10, Recent Trends in Bank Loan Syndications, Office of the Comptroller of the Currency (December 2000).

U.S. Office of the Comptroller of the Currency Banking Circular, 181 (August 7, 1984).

Interagency Guidance on Leveraged Lending, The Board of Governors of the Federal Reserve System, the Office of the Comptroller of the Currency, The Federal Deposit Insurance Corporation (March 21, 2013).

Interagency Statement on Sales of 100% Loan Participations, The Board of Governors of the Federal Reserve System, the Office of the Comptroller of the Currency, The Federal Deposit Insurance Corporation (April 10, 1997).

V. Gerard Comizio and Ryan Chiachiere, Ringfencing U.S. Bank Foreign Branch Deposits: Working Toward a Clearer Understanding of Where Deposits Are Payable in the Midst of Chaos, 3 Amer. Univ. Bus. L. Rev. 2 (2014). Reprinted with permission.

U.K. Financial Services Authority: Addressing the Implications of Non-EEA National Depositor Preference Regimes (September 2012).

Thomas C. Baxter, Jr. and Jet Joseph De Saram BCCI: The Lessons for Banking Supervision, International Monetary Fund, Current Legal Issues Affecting Central Banks, Vol. 4 (1997).

HM Treasury, U.K., Designation of Payment Systems for Regulation by the Payment Systems Regulator (October 14, 2014).

Basel Committee on Banking Supervision, Working Paper No. 13, Bank Failures in Mature Economies (April 2004).

Paul Lewis, Italy's Mysterious, Deepening Bank Scandal, New York Times (1982).

Basel Committee on Banking Supervision, History of the Basel Committee and Its Membership (2009).

Principles for the Supervision of Banks' Foreign Establishments, The Basel Committee on Banking Supervision (May 1983).

Minimum Standards for the Supervision of International Banking Groups and Their Cross-Border Establishments, The Basel Committee on Banking Supervision (July 1992).

The Supervision of Cross-Border Banking, The Basel Committee on Banking Supervision (October 1996).

Core Principles for Effective Banking Supervision, The Basel Committee on Banking Supervision (September, 1997).

Peter Coy, How New Global Banking Rules Could Deepen the U.S. Crisis, Bloomberg Businessweek (April 16, 2008) © Bloomberg LP 2008. Reprinted with permission.

Group of Governors and Heads of Supervision Announces Higher Global Minimum Capital Standards, Basel Committee on Banking Supervision (September 12, 2010).

United Kingdom House of Commons, Treasury Committee, The Run on the Rock, Volume I (January 26, 2008).

The Financial Crisis Inquiry Report, Final Report of the National Commission on the Causes of the Financial and Economic Crisis in the United States, The U.S. Financial Crisis Inquiry Commission (January 2011).

President Bush's Speech to the Nation on the Economic Crisis (September 24, 2008).

Conclusions of the Financial Crisis Inquiry Commission (January 2011).

G20 Declaration: Summit on Financial Markets and the World Economy (November 15, 2008).

G20 Leaders Statement: The Pittsburgh Summit (September 24, 2009).

Global Systemically Important Banks, Basel Committee on Banking Supervision (July 2013).

Randall D. Guynn, Mark E. Plotkin, and Ralph Reisner, Regulation of Foreign Banks & Affiliates in the United States, 6th Edition. © 2012 Thomson Reuters. Reprinted with permission.

U.S. General Accounting Office: Foreign Banks (February, 1996).

Federal Reserve Board, Industrial and Commercial Bank of China, Beijing, People's Republic of China, Order Approving Establishment of a Representative Office (January 27, 1997).

Federal Reserve System, Industrial and Commercial Bank of China Limited, Beijing, People's Republic of China, Order Approving Establishment of a Branch (August 5, 2008).

Legal Interpretative Letter, Request for Exemption Under Section 4(c) 9 of the Bank Holding Company Act, Federal Reserve Board (August 5, 2008).

Federal Reserve System, Industrial and Commercial Bank of China Limited, Board Order No. 2012–4 (May 9, 2012).

Tharak Chacko, Case Study: Daiwa Bank.

The Daiwa Bank Limited, Osaka, Japan, Federal Reserve Board (February 28, 2003).

European Banking Authority, EBA Opinion on Virtual Currencies (July 4, 2014).

European Banking Authority, Warning to Consumers on Virtual Currencies (December 12, 2013).

Bank of England, The Prudential Regulation Authority's Approach to Bank Supervision (June 2014).

Andrea Enria, Chairman, European Banking Authority, Challenges for the Future of EU Banking, Banking Forum of IESE Business School, Barcelona, Spain (November 26, 2014).

The White House Office of the Press Secretary (December 17, 2014).

US Department of the Treasury, The Office of Foreign Assets Controls: Frequently Asked Questions Related to Cuba (January 15, 2015).

Department of Treasury, Washington, D.C. 20220, Compl-2013-193659 (June 30, 2014).

Robert E. Lutz, Ethics and International Practice: A Guide to the Professional Responsibility of Practitioners, 16 Fordham Int'l L.J., 1 (1992). Reprinted with permission.

Laurence Ethertington and Robert Lee, Ethical Codes and Cultural Context: Ensuring Legal Ethics in the Global Law Firm, 14 Indiana Journal of Global Legal Studies, 1 (2007). Reprinted with permission.

American Bar Association: *Law Firms And Associations*, Rule 5.5 Unauthorized Practice of Law; Multijurisdictional Practice of Law.

International Bar Association, International Principles on Conduct for the Legal Profession (May 28, 2011).

Commentary on IBA International Principles on Conduct for the Legal Profession, Adopted by the International Bar Association at the Warsaw Council Meeting (May 28, 2011).

Final Call: Section Won't Accredit Non-US Law Schools, but Foreign Lawyers Can Be Admitted, American Bar Association Journal Online (October 1, 2012).

American Bar Association, Voluntary Good Practices Guidance for Lawyers to Detect and Combat Money Laundering and Terrorist Financing (April 23, 2010).

Anonymous, The History of Banks, The Gotham City Insider Blog (October 30, 2007).

Also thanks to the American Banker, BBC News, Bloomberg News, Coin Desk, Daily Mail, Financial Times, the Guardian, New York Times, U.S. News and World Report, Market Watch, National Law Review, The New York Review of Books, The Telegraph, Los Angeles Times, Tass Russia News Agency, The Wall Street Journal, Time Magazine, Quorum Books, World Bank Publications, Columbia University Press, Business Pundit Blog and the Washington Post for the many interesting and informative books and articles cited in this book.

I also want to thank Jon Harkness and Greg Olson at West Academic for their many important, useful and thoughtful suggestions needed to ensure the successful completion of a quality casebook on international banking law.

Finally, I would like to thank my outstanding legal assistant Sandy Day for her tireless work in assisting me in the drafting and completion of this book.

SUMMARY OF CONTENTS

TABLE OF CONTENTS

TABLE OF CASES

The principal cases are in bold type.

———

INTERNATIONAL
BANKING LAW

CHAPTER 1

INTRODUCTION: OVERVIEW OF INTERNATIONAL BANKING LAW

■ ■ ■

1. INTRODUCTION

This book examines the developments in international banking law, and the business and structural means by which banks conduct international activities—the business of international banking. In doing so, the book highlights the fact that, as international banking has grown and increasingly plays a key role in the international economy, so has there been increasing need and support for international banking laws.

It also presents the practical aspects of legal issues that arise in the most common international banking transactions, including the legal role of international banks in letters of credit transactions (Chapter 2), international loan syndications (Chapter 3) and international deposit transactions (Chapter 4). In so doing, the book will seek to engage the students to understand the respective roles, responsibilities and liabilities of banks associated with these transactions, and the related regulatory concerns reflected in banking laws, regulations and policies.

Chapter 5 explores international banking regulation, including an analysis of the international principles of bank supervision and the evolving work and influence of the Basel Committee on Bank Regulation and Supervision and regulation of U.S. banks in foreign markets.

Chapter 6 examines critical international banking legal issues and policies addressing the recent global financial crisis and reform initiatives responding to the crisis. The Chapter will focus on the causes of the recent global financial crisis, government reaction to the crisis and perceived weaknesses in the international financial regulatory system, and regulatory reform.

Chapter 7 will examine the regulation of foreign banking organizations in the U.S. Chapter 8 analyzes developments in anti-terrorism, money laundering, and embargo laws as relates to international banking operations. Chapter 9 analyzes the banking regulation of the European Monetary Union—the first transnational regulation of international banking.

Finally, Chapter 10 presents emerging ethical considerations in international banking law practice, and the implications of relevant ethical guidance by the American Bar Association and the International Bar Association.

2. WHAT IS A BANK?

It is important to our understanding of international banking law principles to understand generally what a bank is and does in terms of its business operations.

In summary, a bank is a financial intermediary that creates money by lending money to a borrower, thereby creating a corresponding deposit on the bank's balance sheet. Lending activities can be performed directly by loaning or indirectly through capital markets. Due to their importance in the financial system and influence on national economies, banks are highly regulated in most countries. Most nations have institutionalized a system known as fractional reserve banking discussed below, under which banks hold liquid assets equal to only a portion of their current liabilities.

A bank can generate revenue in a variety of different ways including interest, transaction fees and financial advice. The main method is via charging interest on the capital it lends out to customers in the form of commercial i.e., business, residential and consumer loans. The bank profits from the difference between the level of interest it pays for deposits and other sources of funds, and the level of interest it charges in its lending activities.

This difference is referred to as the "spread" between the cost of funds and the loan interest rate. Historically, profitability from lending activities has been cyclical and dependent on the needs and strengths of loan customers and the stage of the economic cycle. Fees and financial advice constitute a more stable revenue stream and banks have therefore placed more emphasis on these revenue lines to smooth their financial performance.

Banks act as payment agents by conducting checking or current accounts for customers, paying checks drawn by customers on the bank, and collecting checks deposited to customers' current accounts. Banks also enable customer payments via other payment methods such as Automated Clearing House (ACH), wire transfers or telegraphic transfer, and automated teller machine (ATM).

Banks borrow money by accepting funds deposited on current accounts, by accepting term deposits, and by issuing debt securities such as bank notes and bonds. Banks lend money by making advances to customers on current accounts, by making installment loans, and by investing in marketable debt securities and other forms of money lending.

Banks provide different payment services, and a bank account is considered indispensable by most businesses and individuals. Non-banks that provide payment services such as remittance companies are normally not considered as an adequate substitute for a bank account.

Activities undertaken by international banks include investment banking, corporate banking, private banking, insurance, consumer finance, foreign exchange trading, commodity trading, trading in equities, futures and options trading and money market trading. National laws however, often place limits on bank activities and investments that may limit banks to a narrow range of lending, checking and deposit activities while permitting a broader range of financial activities in parent companies, affiliates and/or subsidiaries.

Banks face a number of risks in order to conduct their business, and how well these risks are understood, managed and mitigated is a key driver behind profitability.

Some of the main risks faced by banks include:

- Sovereign risk: also known as country risk, risk of dealing with a sovereign borrower.

- Credit risk: risk of loss arising from a borrower who does not make payments as promised.

- Liquidity risk: risk that a given security or asset cannot be traded quickly enough in the market to prevent a loss, or make the required profit, or meet depositor withdrawal/demands.

- Market risk: risk that the value of a portfolio, either an investment portfolio or a trading portfolio, will decrease due to the change in value of the market risk factors.

- Regulatory risk: risk related to penalties and sanctions related to failure to comply with applicable banking laws.

- Operational risk: risk arising from execution of a company's business functions.

The risk of data breaches, cyberattacks and other cybercriminal and cyberterrorist threats:

- Reputational risk: a type of risk related to the trustworthiness of business.

- Macroeconomic risk: risks related to the aggregate economy the bank is operating in.

Banks are susceptible to many forms of risk which have triggered occasional systemic crises. These include liquidity risk (where many depositors may request withdrawals in excess of available funds), credit risk (the chance that those who owe money to the bank will not repay it), and interest rate risk (the possibility that the bank will become unprofitable, if rising interest rates force it to pay relatively more on its deposits than it receives on its loans).

Certain aspects of the expansion of international banking in the last forty years have concerned international banking regulators. Two examples will suffice. One example involves the number of special risks in international lending. First, there is the common risk of the credit-worthiness of the borrower. But in addition, there are risks involving the clearing of payments between nations and the risk of foreign exchange fluctuations. The most recent aspect of risk, raising substantial concern, is country risk. Country risk is the possibility that sovereign borrowers of a particular country may be unable or unwilling to fulfill their foreign obligations for reasons beyond the usual risks of lending. It may be based on socio-political changes in the borrowing country generated by largely unpredictable events. A final risk of international lending is the possibility of foreign impediments that might endanger the ability to enforce repayment of the bank's loans.

A second concern of international regulators has to do with a nation's responsibility for the international banking activities of a bank either headquartered in, or operating in its country, and how multinational supervision should occur. It has gradually become evident that international banking is related to the safety and soundness of the home and host countries' banking systems and to their economies.

Banking crises have developed many times throughout history, when one or more risks have emerged for a banking sector as a whole. Prominent examples include the bank runs that occurred during the Great Depression, the U.S. savings and loan crisis in the 1980s and early 1990s, the Japanese banking crisis during the 1990s, and the recent U.S. sub-prime mortgage crisis and global financial crisis in the 2000s. Further, a number of international bank failures, including some notable ones discussed in Chapter 5, have highlighted perceived weaknesses in international regulation of banking organizations.

3. HISTORY OF INTERNATIONAL BANKING

THE HISTORY OF BANKS

The Gotham City Insider Blog (October 30, 2007)

I've often wondered how the first banks got started.

How or why would you trust someone else with your money? Back during Late Antiquity and the Middle Ages, how did you build trust like that?

* * *

Naturally, these days we think nothing of it. We dump our money into banks because we *know* it'll be safe; safer than keeping it stuffed under our mattress. We have time on our side and the history of the past to trust. We have hindsight. But what about in the days before there were giant banks on every corner? How did the concept ever get off the ground in the frontier days?

Well, I learned the history of banking is closely related to the history of money. As monetary payments became important, people looked for ways to safely store their money and just as trade grew, merchants looked for ways of borrowing money to fund expeditions.

The first banks were probably the religious temples of the ancient world, and were probably established sometime back in the 3rd millennium B.C.

Some say banks may have predated the invention of money. Deposits initially consisted of grain and later other goods including cattle, agricultural implements, and eventually precious metals such as gold, in the form of easy-to-carry compressed plates.

Temples and palaces were the safest places to store gold as they were constantly attended and well built. As sacred places, temples presented an extra deterrent to would-be thieves.

There are extant records of loans from the 18th century BC in Babylon that were made by temple priests to merchants. And by the time of Hammurabi's Code, banking was well enough developed to justify the promulgation of laws governing banking operations.

* * *

Ye Ol' Ancient Greece holds further evidence of banking. Greek temples, as well as private and civic entities, conducted financial transactions such as loans, deposits, currency exchange, and validation of coinage. There is evidence too of credit, whereby in return for a payment from a client, a moneylender in one Greek port would write a credit note for the client who could "cash" the note in another city, saving the client the danger of carting coinage with him on his journey.

Pythius, who operated as a merchant banker throughout Asia Minor at the beginning of the 5th century B.C., is the first individual banker of whom we have records. Many of the early bankers in Greek city-states were "metics" or foreign residents. Around 371 B.C., Pasion, a slave, became the wealthiest and most famous Greek banker, gaining his freedom and Athenian citizenship in the process.

The fourth century B.C. saw increased use of credit-based banking in the Mediterranean world. In Egypt, from early times, grain had been used as a form of money in addition to precious metals, and state granaries functioned as banks. When Egypt fell under the rule of a Greek dynasty, the Ptolemies (330–323 B.C.), the numerous scattered government granaries were transformed into a network of grain banks, centralised in Alexandria where the main accounts from all the state granary banks were recorded. This banking network functioned as a trade credit system in which payments were effected by transfer from one account to another without money passing.

In the late third century B.C., the barren Aegean island of Delos, known for its magnificent harbour and famous temple of Apollo, became a prominent banking center. As in Egypt, cash transactions were replaced by real credit receipts and payments were made based on simple instructions with accounts kept for each client. With the defeat of its main rivals, Carthage and Corinth, by the Romans, the importance of Delos increased. Consequently it was natural that the bank of Delos should become the model most closely imitated by the banks of Rome.

Naturally, ancient Rome perfected the administrative aspect of banking and saw greater regulation of financial institutions and financial practices. Charging interest on loans and paying interest on deposits became more highly developed and competitive. The development of Roman banks was limited, however, by the Roman preference for cash transactions. During the reign of the Roman emperor Gallienus (260–268 CE), there was a temporary breakdown of the Roman banking system after the banks rejected the flakes of copper produced by his mints. With the ascent of Christianity, banking became subject to additional restrictions, as the charging of interest was seen as immoral. After the fall of Rome, banking was abandoned in western Europe and did not revive until the time of the crusades.

Most early religious systems in the ancient Near East, and the secular codes arising from them, did not forbid interest. These societies regarded inanimate matter as alive, like plants, animals and people, and capable of reproducing itself. Hence if you lent 'food money', or monetary tokens of any kind, it was legitimate to charge interest.

"Food money" in the shape of olives, dates, seeds or animals was lent out as early as c. 5000 BC, if not earlier. Among the Mesopotamians, Hittites, Phoenicians and Egyptians, interest was legal and often fixed by the state.

* * *

By 1200 there was a large and growing volume of long-distance and international trade in a number of agricultural commodities and manufactured goods in western Europe, including corn, wool, finished cloth, wine, salt, wax and tallow, leather and leather goods, and weapons and armour.

* * *

OK, let's skip a few hundred years because I'm getting bored . . .

Modern Western economic and financial history is usually traced back to the coffee houses of London. The London Royal Exchange was established in 1565. At that time moneychangers were already called bankers, though the term "bank" usually referred to their offices, and did not carry the meaning it does today. There was also a hierarchical order among professionals; at the top were the bankers who did business with heads of state, next were the city exchanges, and at the bottom were the pawn shops or "Lombard's". Some European cities today have a Lombard street where the pawn shop was located.

After the siege of Antwerp trade moved to Amsterdam. In 1609 the Amsterdamsche Wisselbank (Amsterdam Exchange Bank) was founded which made Amsterdam the financial centre of the world until the Industrial Revolution.

Banking offices were usually located near centers of trade, and in the late 17th century, the largest centers for commerce were the ports of Amsterdam, London, and Hamburg. Individuals could participate in the lucrative East India trade by purchasing bills of credit from these banks, but the price they received for commodities was dependent on the ships returning (which often didn't happen on time) and on the cargo they carried (which often wasn't according to plan). The commodities market was very volatile for this reason, and also because of the many wars that led to cargo seizures and loss of ships.

Around the time of your boy Adam Smith (circa 1776) there was a massive growth in the banking industry. Within the new system of ownership and investment, the State's intervention in economic affairs was reduced and barriers to competition were removed. Smith was a Scottish moral philosopher and a pioneering political economist. He is a major contributor to the modern perception of free market economics.

Fast forward about 200 years . . .

In the 1970's, a number of smaller crashes tied to the policies put in place following the depression, resulted in deregulation and privatisation of government-owned enterprises in the 1980's, indicating that governments of industrial countries around the world found private-sector solutions to problems of economic growth and development preferable to state-operated, semi-socialist programs. This spurred a trend that was already prevalent in the business sector, large companies becoming global and dealing with customers, suppliers, manufacturing, and information centres all over the world.

Global banking and capital market services proliferated during the 1980's and 1990's as a result of a great increase in demand from companies, governments, and financial institutions, but also because financial market conditions were buoyant and, on the whole, bullish. Interest rates in the United States declined from about 15% for two-year U.S. Treasury notes to about 5% during the 20-year period, and financial assets grew then at a rate approximately twice the rate of the world economy. Such growth rate would have been lower, in the last twenty years, were it not for the profound effects of the internationalization of financial markets especially U.S. Foreign investments, particularly from Japan, who not only provided the funds to corporations in the U.S., but also helped finance the federal government; thus, transforming the U.S. stock market by far into the largest in the world.

THE BRETTON WOODS SYSTEM: COOPERATION AND RECONSTRUCTION
The International Monetary Fund: History (2015)

During the Great Depression of the 1930s, countries attempted to shore up their failing economies by sharply raising barriers to foreign trade, devaluing their currencies to compete against each other for export markets, and curtailing their citizens' freedom to hold foreign exchange. These attempts proved to be self-defeating. World trade declined sharply (see chart below), and employment and living standards plummeted in many countries.

This breakdown in international monetary cooperation led the IMF's founders to plan an institution charged with overseeing the international monetary system—the system of exchange rates and international payments that enables countries and their citizens to buy goods and services from each other. The new global entity would ensure exchange rate stability and encourage its member countries to eliminate exchange restrictions that hindered trade.

The IMF was conceived in July 1944, when representatives of 45 countries meeting in the town of Bretton Woods, New Hampshire, in the

Northeastrn United States, agreed on a framework for international economic cooperation, to be established after the Second World War. They believed that such a framework was necessary to avoid a repetition of the disastrous economic policies that had contributed to the Great Depression.

The IMF came into formal existence in December 1945, when its first 29 member countries signed its Articles of Agreement. It began operations on March 1, 1947. Later that year, France became the first country to borrow from the IMF.

The IMF's membership began to expand in the late 1950s and during the 1960s as many African countries became independent and applied for membership. But the Cold War limited the Fund's membership, with most countries in the Soviet sphere of influence not joining.

The countries that joined the IMF between 1945 and 1971 agreed to keep their exchange rates (the value of their currencies in terms of the U.S. dollar and, in the case of the United States, the value of the dollar in terms of gold) pegged at rates that could be adjusted only to correct a "fundamental disequilibrium" in the balance of payments, and only with the IMF's agreement. This par value system—also known as the Bretton Woods system—prevailed until 1971, when the U.S. government suspended the convertibility of the dollar (and dollar reserves hold by other governments) into gold.

NOTES

1.   The Bretton Woods system of monetary management established the rules for commercial relations among the world's major industrial states in the mid-20th century. On August 5, 1971, due to complex balance of payment issues, President Nixon announced that the U.S. had unilaterally terminated convertibility of the U.S. dollar to gold effectively ending the Bretton Woods system, creating a situation where the U.S. dollar became the reserve currency for most of the world's currency. See also Michael D. Bordo, The Bretton Woods International Monetary System: A Historical Overview, National Bureau of Economic Research, University of Chicago Press, (January 1993); Robert L. Hetzel, Overview of Bretton Woods, Federal Reserve Board History (1958).

2.   The Bretton Woods conference led to the establishment of two powerful financial institutions in the world economy: 1) the IMF and 2) the International Bank for Reconstruction and Development (IBRD)—now part of the World Bank. Although their respective missions are often confused—and often criticized by developing countries in their dealings with them—their missions are distinct, albeit complementary. The World Bank, component of the World Bank Group, which is comprised of the World Bank, IBRD and International Development Association is an international financial institution that has the mission of providing loans to developing countries for capital programs, with the official goal as the reduction of poverty. Under its charter all its decisions mut be guided by a commitment to the promotion of

foreign investment and international trade and the facilitation of capital investment. See About Us, World Bank (August 14, 2011).

The IMF promotes international monetary cooperation and technical assistance to help countries build and maintain strong economies, and makes loans and design policies programs to solve balance of payments issues. See the IMF at a Glance, International Monetary Fund (March 27, 2015).

While the IMF and World Bank share the same goal of raising living standards as institutions in the United Nations system, the IMF focuses on macroeconomics issues, while the World Bank concentrates on long term economic development and poverty reduction. See Factsheet: the IMF and the World Bank, International Monetary Fund (March 27, 2015).

The complex role of these international financial institutions in the world economy is beyond the scope of this book, but their existence and preeminent role in international sovereign lending is worth noticing in a discussion of international banking.

4. CROSS-BORDER BANKING AND BANKING REGULATION

Important questions of international law arise when banks engage in cross-border activities.

To what extent does a bank which operates in another country only through correspondent banks (banks in the host country at which the foreign bank has one or more deposit accounts) or representative offices (physical locations of the foreign bank in the host country, much like loan production offices) submit itself to the jurisdiction of that host country? Is it a forbidden exercise of extraterritorial jurisdiction for a government agency to demand to examine the books of the foreign head office of a bank which maintains an agency or branch in that country? Is it improper to apply a country's regulatory standards to the activities of a foreign holding company wishing to do business in that country? What rights does a government have to seize the assets of a foreign bank? These questions may be presented in some of the matters we consider here, but we will not deal with them directly.

International banking is an economic interface between nations. As such it is a good place for governments to regulate their nations' activities in the international economy. The policies of governments relating to the money supply, foreign investment, foreign exchange, and the balance of payments are applied directly to banking and are calculated to encourage or control such economic activity by all businesses.

Foreign entry into "retail" banking has stimulated additional regulation. Some foreign banks have found it profitable to compete with local banks for local deposits and to offer a full range of services.

To accomplish these ends several forms of organization have been adopted. Establishing a relationship with a correspondent bank is the simplest and most popular means of transacting banking business in a foreign country. A correspondent relationship usually consists of accounts held by each bank in the other and contracts which specify the services to be performed and the fees to be charged. Negotiating or paying letters of credit, accepting drafts, providing credit information, and investing in short-term local government funds are common correspondent services. The advantage of doing business through a correspondent bank is that there are no significant commitments of capital or transfers of bank personnel. Because there is no physical or legal presence in the other country, there is no exposure to its jurisdiction and are few assets to be seized. While correspondent bank relationships are large in number (a large bank will have a correspondent in most of the world's major cities), they are not as important as other foreign business forms that are fewer in number. Generally, the scale of the transactions going through a correspondent is small and recent growth of international banking has rested on more active and direct establishments such as branches or subsidiaries.

A representative office is a physical presence in the foreign country but the office does not perform any banking activities. Because they perform no banking activity, such offices are usually not licensed or examined by the foreign banking authorities. Their chief purposes are to seek business for their parent banks and to transmit information to and from the host country. The representative may supervise relations with correspondent banks in the host country and direct clients to those banks or to branches of the parent bank elsewhere. He may also act as a commercial ambassador for some of the parent's large clients. He will take a more active interest in long run opportunities in that country for the parent bank and is often a forerunner for a branch or subsidiary. Some banks maintain both branches or other direct presences and representative offices. Although it is physically present within the jurisdiction the representative office is usually not "legally present" and therefore not subject to suit or taxation because it does not do business within the host country. To protect this status a representative may leave the country to transact business which might expose it to local jurisdiction and regulation.

There are limitations to the representative office. Having found new customers, it cannot transact business with them but must refer the new customers elsewhere—to a correspondent or to an office of the parent in another city. Sometimes the establishment of a representative office in another country will be viewed as unwanted competition and can harm profitable correspondent relationships. Finally, usual representative offices are small and cannot provide the depth of research required for decisions about major commitments of money.

No
depositors/
fiduciary
relationship"

A banking "agency" is a licensed establishment which can perform all banking functions except receiving deposits and undertaking fiduciary obligations. Agencies can hold credit balances for money received from another office of the parent bank. The credit balances may then be spent (for limited purposes) as easily as if they were deposits held by the agency itself. The primary usefulness of agencies has been to finance and service trade between host and parent countries. Accordingly, they issue and service letters of credit; buy, sell, and collect bills of exchange; and are regularly active in both the foreign exchange and short-term government funds markets of the host nation. An agency may also buy and sell securities for its parent and clients. Agencies are not subject to many of the regulatory limitations that branches suffer. However agencies are clearly "doing business" for jurisdictional purposes.

Short of the ownership of a fully chartered and regulated subsidiary in that country, branches are the fullest possible extension of the bank of one country into another. Creditors of a branch may or may not be creditors of the foreign parent. Branches are usually the functional equivalents of local domestic banks with deposit taking and trust powers. They are licensed by the host country and their assets are more closely examined than agency assets because they often represent funds of local origin. They are also generally subject to greater regulation, including potential capital, reserves and other regulatory requirements applicable to have country banks. A branch has the advantage of allowing very extensive banking operations while still being directly controlled and owned by the head office. However, a branch is usually subject to examination and licensing in both countries.

The number of international branch banks has grown phenomenally. However, a large number of these branches are only "shells"—offices which provide no local services and are in fact only communications centers on foreign soil directly controlled by their head offices and used only for access to the Euro-currency markets. The real growth of branching has been substantial nonetheless. London has seen the arrival of banks from all over the capitalist world to participate in its Euro-dollar market. The number of international branch banks has also grown in the United States, Europe, Asia and Latin America. Branching has been the most widely used means of expansion in international banking.

A subsidiary is a wholly or partially owned bank which is chartered, regulated, and examined in the host jurisdiction. The foreign parent may be a bank or it may be a holding company which is not itself a bank. Because they are locally organized and wholly within the jurisdiction, such subsidiaries will usually be treated like any other local bank and may face fewer limitations on their activities and less rigorous examinations than a similarly situated branch. The separate legal entity also helps to isolate the parent from liability on contracts entered into and torts committed by the subsidiary. Major disadvantages are that there may be citizenship requirements on ownership and directorship; that establishing a full service bank can be very costly; and that loan limits are a set percentage of the capital of the subsidiary, not of the parent.

A foreign bank will establish a subsidiary in another country for any of several reasons. It may find the limitations placed on branches and agencies in that country too prohibitive for its purposes. It may wish to establish a special type of operation such as investment banking or corporate trust work. Large clients of the parent bank may have substantial business operations which require the services of a complete banking operation in the host country. Or it may estimate that the domestic "retail" market offers an opportunity for profits. Some subsidiaries of foreign banks may carry an ethnic appeal which will attract deposits.

Joint ventures, or consortia, are multibank and often multinational arrangements intended to meet specific large-scale objectives. Examples of such objectives are entering the medium-term Euro-dollar lending market, creation of a securities affiliate, or the organization of a merchant or investment bank. Sometimes only temporary alliances and sometimes permanent institutions, banking joint ventures have become common.[1]

The reasons for the rise of consortia are many but boil down to two—the pooling of resources and the pooling of risks. The capital demands of some large enterprises—large utilities, nationalized industries, and the bigger multinational corporations—may exceed the resources of any single bank. While a bank faced with a large request might be willing to fund a loan by borrowing in the interbank market, it might also wish to limit the possibility of large losses resulting from default. It must balance potential returns against potential risk. By organizing a consortium or other joint venture bankers can put together large amounts of money, realize economies of scale on the cost of administering loans, share costs and expertise, and limit risk to a known amount; in return profits must be shared. In addition, a joint venture may result in an ongoing business with roots in several countries large enough to have countervailing power in relation to its large customers. The other side of the balance is that a bank will often keep the most profitable undertakings to itself while it passes the less promising jobs to its consortium partners, that any joint decision making process is bound to be clumsy, and that a change of the original purpose may quickly cause the consortium to become obsolete.

As suggested above, international banking performs the same payments and financing functions as domestic banking, but because

---

[1]   A consortium has been defined as "a partnership of two or more independent banks which organize or acquire control of a separate bank or financial institution." See, e.g., Charles Ganoe, Banking Consortia: "Are They Here to Stay?", Columbia J. of World Business (July/Aug. 1972).

national borders intervene risks are increased. The value of the payments contracted for may change in a short period of time through foreign exchange fluctuations, devaluations, and revaluations. Shipping strikes or unexpected economic conditions can leave the importer unable to pay for goods long out of the exporter's hands. The fact that the importer lives in a distant country with a legal system in which standing is difficult or expensive to establish and which may recognize the importer's defenses can make legal recourse on a defaulted instrument difficult. To define and limit these risks certain practices, usages, and instruments—such as letters of credit, discussed in Chapter 2—have evolved. Of those practices that are prevalent in international banking, some are unique while others are adaptations of familiar domestic practices. Foreign exchange transactions are completely unique to international banking.

Banks buy and sell most major currencies to provide customers with cash or balances in whatever nation's currency they may need to make direct payments for goods or travel. Who shall bear the risk of exchange variation in a sale of goods is determined by the agreement between the buyer and seller which states in whose currency final payment is to be made. Banks also maintain inventories of foreign currencies in accounts in correspondent banks to be able to settle the obligations of their customers by simple deposit transfers. To meet customer demands and to provide for the needs of their own obligations, banks enter both the spot and forward foreign exchange markets. Traditionally, banks have attempted continually to adjust their present and future foreign exchange positions by buying or selling forward funds as soon as future obligation in a foreign currency would be recognized as due from or to them. Risks are avoided because the amount to be paid or received is immediately known and realized. The difference between the spot and forward prices is a function of current interest rates and the premonitions of those who undertake the risk about which way a given currency will move. Some major banks have been criticized for adopting the risk-taking strategy by speculating on their own accounts in foreign exchange. The collapses of Bankhaus I.D. Herstatt, discussed in Chapter 5, has been attributed at least in part to unsuccessful speculation in foreign exchange.

The larger a bank, the more likely it is to have international operations. Although there has been some increase in international banking activity by regional and smaller banks in recent years, there have been years in which more than half of the profits of some of the largest United States banks have come from international operations. In practice, international banking is a field for giant banks. The larger American banks generally have foreign branches as well as an "Edge corporation," a domestic corporation, often with foreign subsidiaries, organized to conduct international or foreign banking operations from within the United States (discussed in Chapter 7).

* * *

In addition to international supervision problems, there are international currency problems. Foreign exchange has become a major aspect of international banking. Much of this activity evolves out of correspondent banking, which is simply banks opening accounts with one another. For example, a United States bank may open an account in Swiss francs in a Swiss bank at the same time that the Swiss bank opens an account with the United States bank by depositing dollars in a checking account. When one of the United States bank's customers desires to pay an obligation in Swiss francs, the customer goes to its United States bank and pays an appropriate sum in U.S. dollars, asking the bank to accomplish the transfer. The United States bank will direct the Swiss bank to pay the payee the appropriate amount in Swiss francs. The Swiss bank will reimburse itself by taking that amount of Swiss francs out of the United States bank's account with it.

In addition to individual exchange transactions, banks may generally engage in foreign exchange, exchanging of one country's currency for the currency of another. There are numerous regulations in many countries with respect to exchange rates and the convertibility of the currency of that country. Generally, exchange rates are determined by a free market system. However, the ability to purchase foreign currencies may be subject to licensing and taxation limitations, and the requirement that foreign exchange go through the central bank of the country.

One way that such general foreign exchange activities can be utilized is to lessen the risk of an obligation to pay in a foreign currency at a future date. It is possible to go to a United States bank and have that bank purchase a particular foreign currency for delivery at a future date at a promised exchange rate, known as a forward contract. This shifts the risks of exchange fluctuations from the United States business to either a United States or a foreign bank that is more knowledgeable of foreign exchange and capable of assuming the risks of fluctuation.

Another aspect of international banking is international deposits and loans, commonly called Eurodollar activities. Eurodollars are obligations denominated in dollars, even though all the activity is outside the United States. Any attempt to explain Eurodollar activities is guaranteed to be oversimplified. Nonetheless, Eurodollars may be created when a European exporter accepts payment for his goods in dollars and deposits those dollars with a bank in his country. In turn, that bank lends the dollars in the international money markets. Just as a few dollars in the United States can be multiplied by the recurrent lending and depositing of those funds, the same can occur in the Eurodollar market.[2]

5. THE INTERNATIONAL BANK'S BALANCE SHEET

In order to better understand both the activities that constitute international banking and some of the concerns of international banking law, it is important to have a basic understanding of a bank's primary financial statement, the balance sheet.

A working knowledge of a bank's balance sheet can provide valuable insight into a bank's operations, financial health and regulatory profiles.

A balance sheet, also known as a statement of financial condition, can be described as a financial report that shows the value of a bank's assets, liabilities and shareholders' equity at a specific period in time, typically at the end of an accounting period, such as quarterly, or annually, i.e., the fiscal year end. As such, a balance sheet is often described as a "snapshot" of a bank's financial condition at a specific point in time of a bank's fiscal year.

A standard bank balance sheet sets out three primary components: 1) assets, 2) liabilities, and 3) shareholders equity. An asset is anything owned by the bank that can be sold for value. The main categories of assets are usually listed first, generally in order of liquidity, i.e., the ability of an asset to be quickly turned in cash. Assets earn revenue for a bank and include cash, securities, other investments, loans it has made, property and equipment.

A bank must hold some cash as reserves, which is the amount held in a bank's account with its central bank. Generally, banking regulation will establish the minimum amount of cash that a bank must hold in their accounts to ensure the safety of a bank. To do business at its branches and ATMs, a bank also needs vault cash, which includes not only cash in its vaults, but also cash elsewhere on a bank's premises, such as in teller drawers, and the cash in its ATM machines.

Loans are the major asset for most banks. They earn more interest than banks have to pay on deposits, and thus, are a major source of revenue for a bank. Often banks will sell the loans, such as mortgages, credit card and auto loan receivables, to be securitized into asset-backed securities which can be sold to investors. This allows banks to make more loans while also earning origination fees and/or servicing fees on the securitized loans.

---

[2]   Many thanks to Professors Edward L. Symons and James J. White for the discussion in this section taken from their seminal textbook *Banking Law*, West (1991).

Loans include the following major types:

- business loans, usually called commercial and industrial loans and small business loans

- real estate loans
    - residential mortgages
    - home equity loans
    - commercial mortgages

- consumer loans
    - credit cards
    - auto loans

- interbank loans[3]

Assets are followed by liabilities. A liability is an obligation that must eventually be paid-in essence, the bank debts. A bank liability may also be considered a claim on its assets, since liabilities are generally paid from a bank's assets.

A bank's primary liabilities are its customer deposits. Checkable deposits are deposits where depositors can withdraw the money at will. These include all checking accounts. Some checkable deposits, such as money market accounts pay interest, but most checking accounts pay very little or no interest. Instead, depositors use checking accounts for payment services, which, nowadays, also includes electronic banking services.

Before the 1980s, checkable deposits were a major source of cheap funds for banks, because they paid little or no interest on the money. But as it became easier to transfer money between accounts, people started putting their money into higher yielding accounts and investments, transferring the money when they needed it.[4]

The difference between the assets and liabilities is generally known as shareholders equity or net worth; a bank's net worth, however, is referred to as its bank or regulatory capital.

Regulatory capital is the amount of capital a bank or other financial institution has to hold as required by its financial regulator. This is usually expressed as a capital adequacy ratio of equity that must be held as a percentage of so-called risk-weighted assets. These requirements are put into place to ensure that these institutions do not take on excess leverage and become insolvent. Capital requirements govern the ratio of equity to debt, recorded on the assets side of a firm's balance sheet. They should not be confused with reserve requirements, which govern the liabilities side of

---

[3]   See http://thismatter.com/money/banking/bank-balance-sheet.htm.

[4]   *Id.*

a bank's balance sheet—in particular, the proportion of its assets it must hold in cash or highly-liquid assets.

Capital serves as a buffer to absorb unexpected losses as well as to fund ongoing activities of the bank. As more fully discussed in Chapter 5, the main international effort to establish rules around capital requirements has been the Basel Accords, published by the Basel Committee on Banking Supervision. This sets a framework on how banks and depository institutions must calculate their capital in "Tier 1" and "Tier 2" categories as a percentage of their risk weighted assets.

The basic formula for a bank's balance sheet is as follows:

$$\text{assets} - \text{liabilities} = \text{equity/regulatory capital}$$

The following balance sheet illustrates this formula and a bank's balance sheet components:

ABC Bank

Balance Sheet
(Dollar figures in thousands)
December 31, 2014

Assets and Liabilities

Total assets	**1,474,077,383**
Cash and due from depository institutions	114,276,595
Interest-bearing balances	88,003,829
Securities	329,538,402
Federal funds sold & reverse repurchase agreements	14,692,165
Net loans & leases	738,934,365
Loan loss allowance	17,063,054
Trading account assets	87,319,703

Bank premises and fixed assets (including foreign offices)	10,147,374
Other real estate owned	3,267,735
Goodwill and other intangibles	63,741,602
All other assets	112,159,442
Total liabilities and capital	1,474,077,383
Total liabilities	**1,296,579,018**
Total deposits	1,117,622,296
Interest-bearing deposits	724,757,179
Deposits held in domestic offices	1,045,280,007
% insured	54.27%
Federal funds purchased & repurchase agreements	68,662,096
Trading liabilities	35,192,257
Other borrowed funds	32,738,338
Subordinated debt	15,240,775
All other liabilities	27,123,256
Total equity capital	**117,498,365**

Total bank equity capital	117,457,631
Perpetual preferred stock	0
Common stock	3,020,043
Surplus	145,000,334
Undivided profits	29,437,254
Noncontrolling interests in U.S. and foreign consolidated subsidiaries	40,734

QUESTIONS AND NOTES

1.   Regulatory capital, in addition to constituting a buffer to absorb losses, is used in many countries as part of a formula for other regulatory limitations. See, e.g., U.S. Federal Reserve Board transactions with affiliates regulations (Section 23H of the Federal Reserve Act generally prohibits a bank from initiating a "covered transaction" with its affiliates if, after the transaction the aggregate amount of the bank's capital would exceed 10 percent of the bank's capital, see 12 USC 37(c); U.S. Office of Comptroller of the Currency loans to one borrower limits (rules establishing limit on various types of loans to any one borrower to specified percentages of capital). See also 12 CFR Part 32. Regulatory capital standards will be more fully discussed in Chapter 5.

6.   THE ROLE OF DEPOSIT INSURANCE

Deposit insurance is a measure implemented in many countries to protect bank depositors, in full or in part, from losses caused by a bank's inability to pay its debts when due. Deposit insurance systems are one component of a financial system safety net that promotes financial stability.

Banks are allowed (and usually encouraged) to lend or invest most of the money deposited with them instead of safe-keeping the full amounts (see fractional-reserve banking). If many of a bank's borrowers fail to repay their loans when due, the bank's creditors, including its depositors, risk loss. Because they rely on customer deposits that can be withdrawn on little or no notice, banks in financial trouble are prone to bank runs, where depositors seek to withdraw funds quickly ahead of a possible bank insolvency. Because banking institution failures have the potential to trigger a broad spectrum of harmful events, including economic recessions, policy makers maintain deposit insurance schemes to protect depositors and to give them comfort that their funds are not at risk.

Many national deposit insurers are members of the International Association of Deposit Insurers (IADI), an international organization established to contribute to the stability of financial systems by promoting international cooperation and to encourage wide international contact among deposit insurers and other interested parties. According to the AIDI, as of 31 January 2014, 113 countries have instituted some form of explicit deposit insurance up from 12 in 1974. Another 41 countries are considering the implementation of an explicit deposit insurance system.[5]

Deposit insurance institutions are for the most part government run or established, and may or may not be a part of a country's central bank, while some are private entities with government backing or completely private entities. There are a number of countries with more than one deposit insurance system in operation including Austria, Canada (Ontario & Quebec), Germany, Italy, and the United States. On the other hand, one deposit insurance system can cover more than one country: for example, many banks in the Marshall Islands, the Federated States of Micronesia, and Puerto Rico are insured by the U.S. Federal Deposit Insurance Corporation. Cameroon, the Central African Republic, Chad, Congo, Equatorial Guinea, and Gabon will also soon be covered by a single system.[6]

PATRICIA A. MCCOY, THE MORAL HAZARD IMPLICATIONS OF DEPOSIT INSURANCE: THEORY AND EVIDENCE

5 Current Developments in Monetary and Financial Law 417–41,
International Monetary Fund (2008)

* * *

There are several reasons for the recent widespread adoption of explicit deposit insurance. Explicit guarantees have immense political appeal because they assuage citizens' concerns about the safety of their deposits and thus increase the flow of funds into banks without requiring fiscal expenditures. Financial experts from international financial institutions and elsewhere have also counseled developing countries to adopt explicit systems in recent years. Finally, the European Union's adoption of explicit deposit insurance in its 1994 Directive on Deposit Insurance helped fuel the surge in explicit deposit insurance.

---

[5]   http://www.iadi.org/di.aspx.

[6]   *Id.*

II. Rationales for Deposit Insurance

As the preceding discussion suggests, explicit deposit guarantees are an increasingly common response to the problem of bank runs and contagion. Banks are uniquely prone to runs because they borrow "short" (by taking in demand deposits) and lend "long" (by making loans with longer maturities). This results in a "term mismatch" that makes the balance sheets of banks inherently unstable. If depositors descend en masse and insist on withdrawing more cash than the bank has in the vault, the bank will not be able to liquidate its assets fast enough to satisfy depositors' demands and a bank run can ensue. Furthermore, bank runs can have a ripple effect and trigger full-blown contagion.

The unstable balance sheet of banks is not a quirk. Rather, it is inherent to a key economic function of banks, which is providing financial liquidity. As financial intermediaries, banks accept liquid deposits from the public and reinvest those funds in long-term, illiquid loans. In the process, banks provide borrowers with liquidity by allowing them to post their illiquid land or machinery as collateral and convert those assets into cash in the form of loan proceeds. Similarly, banks provide depositors with liquidity by giving them immediate access to their funds via demand deposits. Demand deposits, in turn, are integral to the payment system because they permit buyers to make payments via bank drafts and sellers to clear the drafts quickly.[10]

When banks make loans, they assume the risk of holding illiquid assets. Under international capital standards today, generally eighty percent or more of a bank's funds are tied up in illiquid loans and only a small fraction of a bank's deposits are on hand at any one time to satisfy withdrawals. Banks have confidence that they actually can honor depositors' demands based on the principle of fractional reserves, which holds (1) that depositors will normally withdraw only a small fraction of deposits on any given day and (2) that this fraction is statistically ascertainable. If the unexpected strikes, however, and withdrawals exceed cash on hand, then the bank will not be able to honor all demands for withdrawal because its funds are tied up in loans that cannot be easily

---

[10]   See, e.g, Douglas W. Diamond & Philip H. Dybvig, *Bank Runs, Deposit Insurance, and Liquidity*, 91 J. POL. ECON. 401, 402–03 (1983); Daniel R. Fischel, Andrew M. Rosenfield & Robert S. Stillman, *The Regulation of Banks and Bank Holding Companies*, 73 Va. L. Rev. 301, 307 (1987); Jonathan R. Macey & Geoffrey P. Miller, *Deposit Insurance, the Implicit Regulatory Contract, and the Mismatch in the Term Structure of Banks' Assets and Liabilities*, 12 YALE J. On Reg. 1, 3–4, 7–8 (1995).

converted to cash. Unless the bank can tap backup sources of liquidity,[11] it will have to sell off its assets at fire-sale prices or close its doors.[12]

Absent deposit guarantees, once rumors start that a bank is on the brink of failure (whether those rumors are true or false), its depositors face a collective action problem. In an ideal world, if depositors stood firm and all refrained from withdrawing their deposits, then the bank could escape immediate liquidation and preserve the value of its asset portfolio. Rational depositors know, however, that the world is not ideal and that nothing stops other depositors from demanding withdrawal of their funds in full. Furthermore, rational depositors know that if they wait to withdraw their funds, the bank may run out of money before they get to the head of the line. Thus, they will rush to the head of the line and immediately withdraw their funds in order to avoid losing their life savings. The resulting stampede will trigger a bank run, spelling the bank's demise.[13]

In other type of industries, exit by investors, in the form of mass sell-offs of shares, exerts valuable market discipline. Bank runs also exert market discipline, at least when they are based on accurate information. However, the hair-trigger nature of bank runs makes them susceptible to false rumors, which can accidentally topple solvent banks. When this happens, depositors are unnecessarily harmed and funds are shifted to less efficient uses.[14]

Whether the rumors behind bank runs are true or false, runs inflict severe social costs. Bank runs pose a classic prisoner's dilemma[15] that results in two types of harm to depositors, absent deposit guarantees. The first is a matter of distributive justice. Depositors at the end of the line lose their deposits altogether, while depositors at the front of the line receive their deposits in full. Second, depositors have a smaller pie to divide because the bank must liquidate assets at distress sale prices to try to satisfy the demand for withdrawals en masse.

---

[11]   Those sources include the market for interbank credit and resort to the discount window of the central bank as the lender of last resort. In the United States, discount window access is limited and strictly administered for institutions that are financially unsound. See BOARD OF GOVERNORS OF THE FEDERAL RESERVE, THE FEDERAL RESERVE SYSTEM: PURPOSES & FUNCTIONS 45–48 (9th ed. 2005); Walker F. Todd, *Central Banking in a Democracy: The Problem Of The Lender of Last Resort*, in FINANCIAL MODERNIZATION AFTER GRAMM-LEACH-BLILEY 135 (Patricia A. McCoy, ed., Lexis 2002).

[12]   See, e.g., Jonathan R. Macey & Geoffrey P. Miller, *Bank Failures, Risk Monitoring, and the Market for Bank Control*, 88 COLUM. L. REV. 1153, 1156 (1988).

[13]   See, e.g., Fischel, Rosenfield & Stillman, *supra* note 10, at 307–09.

[14]   See *Helen A. Garten, Banking on the Market: Relying On Depositors to Control Bank Risks*, 4 YALE J. ON REG. 129, 154–55 (1986); Robert E. Litan, *Evaluating and Controlling the Risks of Financial Product Deregulation*, 3 YALE J. ON REG. 1, 35 (1985); R. Mark Williamson, *Regulatory Theory and Deposit Insurance Reform*, 42 CLEV. ST. L. REV. 105, 114 (1994).

[15]   In a prisoner's dilemma, individuals rationally refuse to cooperate, even though cooperation would maximize everyone's benefit, because they cannot trust others to cooperate and they will suffer the worst result if they cooperate and others do not.

In the worst case, a bank run can ripen into a panic. If a run at one bank causes depositors at other banks to fear for the safety of their own deposits, the run can spread into generalized contagion. As public trust in banks evaporates, depositors will pull their funds out of banks and hide them under the proverbial mattress, sending the banking system into severe disintermediation. As the money supply contracts, credit will dry up, resulting in deflation, production cutbacks, and widespread unemployment.[16] Bank runs and panics can further paralyze the payment system by causing failed banks to default on payments in transit, thereby disrupting commerce.[17]

* * *

Deposit insurance seeks to reverse the psychology of bank runs by reassuring depositors that if their banks fail for any reason, their funds will be protected up to the limits on coverage.[21] This goal is deemed so important that numerous countries require depositors to have deposit insurance, whether or not they want it. Such widespread protection makes deposit insurance highly popular and resistant to reforms.

In the United States, federal deposit insurance has had remarkable success in stemming bank runs and losses to depositors. Even during the massive U.S. bank and thrift failures in the 1980s and early 1990s, runs were the exception, not the rule.[22]

---

[16] See Fischel, Rosenfield & Stillman, *supra* note 10, at 311–12; Thomas M. Hoenig, *Financial Modernization: Implications for the Safety Net*, 49 MERCER L. REV. 787, 788 (1998).

[17] See, e.g., Hoenig, *supra* note 16, at 788–89; Macey & Miller, *Deposit Insurance*, *supra* note 10, at 15. Harm to the payment system from bank runs has declined as nonbank payment providers have gained market power.

[21] See Carter H. Golembe, *The Deposit Insurance Legislation of 1933: An Examination of Its Antecedents and Its Purposes*, 75 POL. SCI. Q. 181, 189, 192, 194 (1960).

[22] Despite federal deposit insurance, in 1983, Continental Illinois National Bank and Trust Company, a wholesale bank in Chicago, Illinois, with mostly large, uninsured deposits, did experience a bank run. * * * Otherwise, practically all of the other runs during the 1980s crisis took place at savings and loan institutions that were insured by state deposit insurance systems in Ohio, Maryland and Rhode Island, and not by the federal government. In the aftermath, all of the state deposit insurance systems that had not already failed closely their doors. See, e.g., Kenneth E. Scott, *Deposit Insurance—The Appropriate Roles for State and Federal Governments*, 53 BROOK. L. REV. 27, 27–28 (1987).

INTERNATIONAL ASSOCIATION OF DEPOSIT INSURERS, CORE PRINCIPLES FOR EFFECTIVE DEPOSIT INSURANCE SYSTEMS

(November 2014)

* * *

III. Moral Hazard, Operating Environment and Other Considerations

Minimising Moral Hazard

A well-designed financial safety-net contributes to the stability of the financial system. However, if poorly designed, it may increase risks notably moral hazard, Moral hazard arises when parties have incentives to accept more risk because the costs are borne, in whole or in part, by others. In the context of deposit insurance, protecting depositors from the threat of loss (e.g. through explicit limited deposit insurance or the belief that banks will not be allowed to fail) insulates them from the consequences of unsafe and unsound bank practices, and can lead to greater risk-taking by banks than might otherwise be the case.

Deposit insurance, like any insurance system, must be designed to mitigate the impact of moral hazard on the behavior of shareholders, bank management and depositors, while recognizing that most depositors are typically less able to differentiate between safe and unsafe banks. Such mitigation is a function of the overall design of the system. Moral hazard is also mitigated by other safety-net participants.

The assessment of the extent to which moral hazard affects a deposit insurance system is based on an overall evaluation of the effectiveness of supervision, the legal framework, and the early warning, intervention and resolution regimes.

Operating Environment

The effectiveness of a deposit insurance system is influenced not only by its design features but also by the environment within which it operates. The operating environment includes macroeconomic conditions, the strength of the sovereign, the financial system structure, prudential regulation and supervision, the legal and judicial framework, and the accounting and disclosure system.

* * *

3. Prudential regulation, supervision and resolution

The strength of prudential regulation, supervision and the resolution regime influences the functions and effectiveness of a deposit insurance system. Strong prudential regulation and supervision ensure that an institution's weaknesses are promptly identified and corrected.

Implementation of corrective measures is monitored and, where deficient, early intervention and an effective resolution regime help to lower the costs associated with bank failures.

The strength of prudential regulation and supervision is a critical factor in mitigating moral hazard. If shareholders and management of an institution feel they can operate their institution in an unsafe or unsound manner without effective market discipline, supervisors become the last defense against poor practices. In the absence of strong regulation and supervision, the risks to the deposit insurer cannot be fully understood or mitigated. Intervention in weak banks comes late, increasing the cost of resolution and the cost to the deposit insurer. The supervisory authority should have an effective licensing or chartering regime for new institutions, conduct regular and thorough examinations of individual banks, and have an effective early warning system. All banks within the safety-net should be subject to an effective resolution regime. Sound governance of agencies comprising the safety-net should also be in place, to strengthen the financial system's architecture and contribute directly to financial stability.

The system of prudential regulation, supervision and resolution should be in compliance with international standards, including the Basel Committee's Core Principles for Effective Banking Supervision.[*]

* * *

NOTES

1.   If you were advising a government on the need for a federal deposit insurance scheme, what would you describe as the relative considerations? Other than the AIDI, what other international organizations would you take into account that address issues related to deposit insurance systems? See, e.g., Basel Committee on Banking Supervision, Bank for International Settlement, Core Principles for Effective Deposit Insurance Systems (June 18, 2009); The Financial Stability Board, Thematic Review of Deposit Insurance Systems (February 8, 2012); The European Banking Authority, Consultation Guidelines as to methods for calculating contributions to Deposit Guarantee Schemes (October 11, 2014).

2.   Directive 94/19/EC of the European Parliament and of the Council of 30 May 1994 on deposit-guarantee schemes requires all member states to have a deposit guarantee scheme for at least 90% of the deposited amount, up to at least 20,000 euros per person. On October 7, 2008, the Ecofin meeting of EU's ministers of finance agreed to increase the minimum amount to 50,000 euros. Timelines and details on procedures for the implementation, which is likely to be a national matter for the member states, was not immediately available. The increased amount followed on Ireland's move, in September 2008, to

---

[*]   [The work of the Basel Committee will be covered in Chapter 5].

increase its deposit insurance to an unlimited amount. Many other EU countries, starting with the United Kingdom, reacted by increasing limits to avoid people transferring savings to Irish banks.

In November 2007 a comprehensive report was published by EU, with a description and comparison of each Insurance Guarantee Scheme in place for all EU member states. The report concluded, that many of the schemes (but not all) had restricted the appliance of guarantees to retail consumers, usually private individuals, although Small or Medium-sized (SME) businesses sometimes also were placed into the retail category. Common for all schemes are, that they do not apply to big wholesale customers. The argument behind this decision is, that the big wholesale customers often are in a better position than retail customers to assess the financial risks of particular firms with whom they engage, or even able to their own hand to reduce their risk by using several financial banks/institutes. The report recommended that this practice continue, as the limiting of the scheme's to "retail customers" help reduce the cost of the scheme while also helping to increase its available funds towards those who really depend on the guarantee—when being activated for protection of claimants in a certain case. See Oxera Consulting, Ltd., Insurance guarantee schemes in the EU, Final report prepared for the European Commission (November 2007).

CHAPTER 2

THE BANK'S ROLE IN INTERNATIONAL LETTER OF CREDIT TRANSACTIONS

■ ■ ■

1. INTRODUCTION

With the exponential growth of international commerce since the end of World War II, letters of credit have emerged as the primary means of facilitating trillions of dollars of international trade each year. Banks are the key—and indispensable—players in these multi-faceted transactions. Issuing a letter of credit serves essentially as a guarantee to the seller that it will be paid by a buyer in another country, and can also be used to ensure that all agreed upon standards and quality of goods and services are met by the seller, provided that these requirements are reflected in the documents described in the letter of credit. In understanding international banking law, it is critical to understand the business, legal and regulatory issues related to letters of credit—perhaps the most important business transactions engaged in by banks in facilitating international commerce and trade.

In addressing the role and duties of banks in letter of credit transactions, the Chapter addresses the basic structure of letters of credit, and the bank's legal responsibilities and liability to the three standard parties to such transactions: 1) the bank issuing the letter of credit, 2) the seller, and 3) the buyer. In addition, the materials in this Chapter introduce the primary international legal standards governing such instruments, the Uniform Commercial Code and the International Chamber of Commerce's Uniform Custom and Practices, focusing on the role of banks under these standards.

Further, the chapter will explore a cross-section of relevant case law analyzing the circumstances under which banks must enforce or dishonor letters of credit and the primary role of bank custom and usage in interpreting letters of credit. In emphasizing the high presumption reflected in relevant case law internationally for banks to perform in these transactions, the Chapter will explore the limited circumstances in which a court may be called upon to enjoin a bank's performance under a letter of credit in situations involving fraud either in the underlying sales transaction, or the documentary evidence required to be presented to a bank under a letter of credit.

Finally, the chapter will examine letters of credit in which performance may be prevented due to potential—as opposed to actual—fraud. The unique context for this analysis will be a series of litigation arising among U.S. banks, U.S. companies, the Iranian government and Iranian banks in the wake of the Iranian revolution in 1979, and the related force majeure and state succession doctrine issues presented.

ANTONIO MENDOZA, INTERNATIONAL BUSINESS PLANNING
Chapter 5, pp. 362–367, West Group (2001)

* * *

* * * Among the many issues between a buyer and seller that the Sales Contract should address is the payment obligation. The Sales Contract should state how and when the payment will be required under the contract. Each party faces some risk in agreeing to the payment terms.

The risk to the buyer is to pay for the goods but not to receive the quantity and quality of the goods promised by the seller. If the buyer receives non-conforming goods it would have to sue the seller, probably in the seller's home country with the seller already having the buyer's money—not a very good prospect. Conversely, the risk to the seller is to send the goods abroad and to not get paid. Even if the seller maintains control over the goods, they will be in a foreign country. If the product is not sold to the original buyer, the goods will have to be shipped hack or sold abroad, perhaps at an unfavorable price.

The seller can avoid this risk by converting the transaction into a domestic sale. In this scenario, the buyer comes to the seller's place of business, orders the goods, and pays cash on delivery. This puts the onus on the buyer. If the seller has the economic and market position dominance over the buyer, it should compel the seller to buy the goods domestically. The buyer can likewise avoid risk by insisting that the seller bring the goods to the buyer and then, only after inspection, be obligated to pay for the goods.

The shifting of risk creates a dilemma. In order for one party to totally avoid risk the other must bear it all. Under these conditions, the business transaction will likely never occur. Neither party will trust the other, especially if they have had no prior dealings with each other. The key is in formulating a transaction where each party assumes part of the risk.

The documentary transaction financed with a letter of credit, hereafter, the 'Documentary Transaction' is the business solution to the risk segmentation issue. The Documentary Transaction divides the risk between the buyer, seller, and one or more banks. By using banks to assume part of the risk, each party can proceed with the transaction with a manageable share of risk. The Documentary Transaction enjoys wide acceptance in the international business community.

1.　The Parties, Their Roles and the Contractual Undertakings

* * *

In a Documentary Transaction, the Buyer causes a bank—the Buyer's Bank—also known as the Issuing Bank, to emit a Documentary Letter of Credit naming the Seller as a third party beneficiary. The Letter of Credit defines the relationship between the Buyer's Bank as Issuer and the Seller as beneficiary and controls the payment for the international sale of goods. It informs the Seller of the requirements it must meet to get paid. Typically, payment is conditioned upon Seller's delivery of conforming documents to the Issuing Bank during a pre-scribed period of time.

The Issuing Bank's obligations are predicated on receiving conforming documents—not on the buyer receiving conforming goods—hence the term Documentary Transaction. As mentioned above, although issued pursuant to the Sales Contract, the rights and obligations flowing from—the letter of credit are independent from it. This is known as the Independence Principle and it is strictly adhered to except in those cases where there is fraud in the transaction.

Assume the following documents are called for in a letter of credit—bank draft, commercial invoice, negotiable bill of lading, certificate of insurance, inspection report, packing list, and shippers export declaration. How are they assembled? In the typical case, the Inspector inspects the goods and prepares her report at the time the goods that are delivered to the carrier. The insurance company issues the Certificate of Insurance. The Carrier executes and delivers the negotiable Bill of Lading when the goods are physically delivered to it. The Seller and/or Customs Agent receives the various documents described above and prepares the shippers export license or other export license as needed, the hank draft, the commercial invoice, and the packing list.

Once assembled, the Seller takes the documents to the Seller's Bank. If the Seller's Bank is a confirming bank and if the documents are in conformance with the letter of credit, the bank pays the Seller. At this point the Seller's Bank has possession of the documents including a properly endorsed Bill of Lading. The Seller's Bank owns the goods and has the risk of loss. The Seller has been paid and is now out of the loop. The risk is now transferred to the Seller's Bank. If the Seller's Bank is an advising bank, it merely opines on the conformity of the documents as required by the letter of credit but does not pay the Seller. In this case the Seller has not been paid since the Seller's Bank is serving as a collection agent for the Seller.

The Seller's Bank then presents the documents to the Buyer's Bank. If the Buyer's Bank finds them conforming it will pay the Seller's Bank. The Seller's Bank, if it is a confirming bank, will receive and keep the payment. If the Seller's Bank is serving in an advisory rote it will remit the funds to Seller. At this point the Seller and Seller's Bank are out of the loop and the Buyer's Bank is in possession of the documents, owns the goods, and has the risk of loss. The Buyer's Bank then takes the documents to the Buyer.

The Buyer receives the documents from the Buyer's Bank and pays the amount due. The Buyer's Bank is now out of the loop. The Buyer has possession of the documents that represent the ownership of the goods. At this point the Buyer has the risk of loss but does not have physical possession of the goods. During the time the documents are winding their way from party to party the Carrier is transporting the goods physically to their destination. Upon arriving at the destination the Carrier is obligated to deliver the goods to the holder of the property endorsed negotiable Bill of Lading.

The flow of documents, payment, and goods described above assumes that every party does what they ought and that no problem areas emerge. Unfortunately there are many moving parts to the documentary transaction and points of contention frequently arise. For example, what obligations are the banks assuming? What law applies? What if the documents presented are not conforming? What if the carrier delivers the goods to the wrong person? What if the goods are lost? What if the buyer goes bankrupt? What if there is fraud in the transaction?

* * *

NOTES

1.   As discussed in the excerpt from Professor Mendoza's excellent book on international business, in a documentary letter of credit, the Issuing Bank replaces the financial strength and integrity of the buyer. The bank's promise to pay, evidenced by the letter of credit, can be either revocable or irrevocable. In a revocable letter of credit, the Issuing Bank can revoke its promise to pay at any time. In an irrevocable letter of credit the issuing Bank cannot revoke its promise to pay prior to the expiration date of the letter of credit. The bank's promise to pay is of critical importance in these transactions; thus, the irrevocable letter of credit is typically used in international trade.

2. STANDARDS FOR REVIEW: STRICT V. SUBSTANTIAL COMPLIANCE

BEYENE V. IRVING TRUST COMPANY

United States Court of Appeals
762 F. 2d 4 (2nd Cir. 1985)

KEARSE, CIRCUIT JUDGE.

Plaintiffs Dessaleng Beyene and Jeau M. Hanson appeal from a final judgment of the United States District Court for the Southern District of New York, Morris E. Lasker, Judge, dismissing their complaint seeking damages for the alleged wrongful refusal of defendant Irving Trust Company ("Irving") to honor a letter of credit. The district court granted Irving's motion for summary judgment dismissing the complaint on the ground that, since the bill of lading presented to Irving misspelled the name of the person to whom notice was to be given of the arrival of the goods and thereby failed to comply with the terms of the letter of credit, Irving was under no duty to honor the letter of credit. On appeal, plaintiffs contend, inter alia, that the mere misspelling of a name should not relieve a bank of its duty to honor a letter of credit. We agree with the district court that the misspelling in this case was a material discrepancy that relieved Irving of its duty to pay the letter of credit, and we affirm the judgment.

FACTS

The material undisputed facts may be stated briefly. In March 1978, Beyene agreed to sell to Mohammed Sofan, a resident of the Yemen Arab Republic ("YAR"), two prefabricated houses. Sofan attempted to finance the purchase through the use of a letter of credit issued by the Yemen Bank for Reconstruction and Development ("YBRD") in favor of Beyene. YBRD designated Irving as the confirming bank for the letter of credit and Irving subsequently notified Beyene of the letter's terms and conditions. Beyene designated the National Bank of Washington ("NBW") as his collecting bank.

In May 1979, NBW sent Irving all of the documents required under the terms of the letter of credit. Thereafter, Irving telephoned NBW to inform it of several discrepancies in the submitted documents, including the fact that the bill of lading listed the party to be notified by the shipping company as Mohammed Soran instead of Mohammed Sofan. The NBW official contacted testified at deposition that Irving never waived the misspelling discrepancy and continued to assert that it was a discrepancy, though it undertook to request authorization from YBRD to pay the letter of credit despite the discrepancy. Such authorization was not forthcoming, and Irving refused to pay.

Plaintiffs instituted the present suit seeking damages for Irving's failure to pay the letter of credit. Irving moved for summary judgment dismissing the complaint on a variety of grounds. The district court, in an opinion reported at 596 F.Supp. 438 (1984), granted the motion on the sole ground that the misspelling of Sofan's name in the bill of lading constituted a material discrepancy that gave Irving the right to dishonor the letter of credit. This appeal followed.

DISCUSSION

On appeal, plaintiffs contend principally that (1) the district court's ruling is unsound as a matter of precedent and of policy, and (2) Irving should be required to pay the letter of credit on grounds of waiver and estoppel. We find merit in none of plaintiffs' contentions. We need discuss only the first.

The nature and functions of commercial letters of credit have recently been explored by this Court, see Voest-Alpine International Corp. v. Chase Manhattan Bank, N.A., 707 F.2d 680, 682–83 (2d Cir.1983); Marino Industries Corp. v. Chase Manhattan Bank, N.A., 686 F.2d 112, 114–15 (2d Cir.1982), and will not be repeated in detail here. The terms of a letter of credit generally require the beneficiary of the letter to submit to the issuing bank documents such as an invoice and a bill of lading to provide "the accredited buyer [with] some assurance that he will receive the goods for which he bargained and arranged payment." H. Harfield, Bank Credits and Acceptances 57 (5th ed. 1974). The issuing bank, or a bank that acts as confirming bank for the issuer, takes on an absolute duty to pay the amount of the credit to the beneficiary, so long as the beneficiary complies with the terms of the letter. In order to protect the issuing or confirming bank, this absolute duty does not arise unless the terms of the letter have been complied with strictly. Literal compliance is generally "essential so as not to impose an obligation upon the bank that it did not undertake and so as not to jeopardize the bank's right to indemnity from its customer." Voest-Alpine International Corp. v. Chase Manhattan Bank, 707 F.2d at 683; see H. Harfield, Letters of Credit 57–59 (1979).

While some variations in a bill of lading might be so insignificant as not to relieve the issuing or confirming bank of its obligation to pay, see, e.g., H. Harfield, Bank Credits and Acceptances 75–78, we agree with the district court that the misspelling in the bill of lading of Sofan's name as "Soran" was a material discrepancy that entitled Irving to refuse to honor the letter of credit. First, this is not a case where the name intended is unmistakably clear despite what is obviously a typographical error, as might be the case if, for example, "Smith" were misspelled "Smithh." Nor have appellants claimed that in the Middle East "Soran" would obviously be recognized as an inadvertent misspelling of the surname "Sofan." Second, "Sofan" was not a name that was inconsequential to the document, for Sofan was the person to whom the shipper was to give notice of the arrival of the goods, and the misspelling of his name could well have resulted in his nonreceipt of the goods and his justifiable refusal to reimburse Irving for the credit. (Indeed, the record includes a telex from Beyene, stating that Sofan had not been notified when the goods arrived in YAR and that as a result demurrage and other costs had been incurred.) In the circumstances, the district court was entirely correct in viewing the failure of Beyene and NBW to provide documents that strictly complied with the terms of the letter of credit as a failure that entitled Irving to refuse payment.

Plaintiffs do not contend that there was any issue to be tried as to the fact of the misspelling of Sofan's name. Their assertions that Irving waived the admitted discrepancy or was estopped from relying on it were not supported sufficiently to withstand a motion for summary judgment and were properly rejected by the district court for the reasons stated in its opinion, 596 F.Supp. at 439–41. * * *

The judgment of the district court is affirmed.

MARINE MIDLAND TRUST COMPANY OF N.Y. v. BANCO DEL PAIS, SA

United States District Court S.D. New York
261 F.Supp. 884 (S.D.N.Y. 1966)

* * *

Both plaintiff and defendant move for summary judgment in this action. The complaint seeks recovery of $256,153.84 upon an overdraft resulting from the fact that plaintiff paid checks drawn by defendant upon its account with plaintiff, although there were no funds on deposit in the account to cover the checks. Defendant's answer alleges that there were sufficient funds on deposit. It is apparent from the motion papers that defendant means that there should have been adequate funds, but that plaintiff wrongfully failed to credit defendant's account with the amount of certain drafts presented by defendant to plaintiff under four letters of credit issued by plaintiff. The question thus turns upon whether plaintiff properly refused to honor the drafts.

Many of the facts are undisputed. They may be summarized as follows:

On August 26, 1965, August 30, 1965, September 3, 1965 and September 7, 1965, plaintiff issued its letters of credit numbered respectively 146531, 146576, 146723 and 59425, in the respective amounts of $26,738, $51,000, $53,382 and $120,000, each in favor of Ricardo Nevares Ocampo, Mexico, D. F. Each letter of credit stated that the credit was transferable by Ocampo. In each letter of credit plaintiff undertook to pay drafts presented under it when accompanied by certain specified documents pertaining to shipments of mercury. Three letters of credit specified that the documents should include "full set clean on board truckers bills of lading." The fourth letter of credit, No. 146576 dated August 30, 1965, specified "Full Set Clean On board ocean bills of lading issued to the order of MARINE MIDLAND GRACE TRUST COMPANY OF NEW YORK, N.Y., marked notify:—J. CLETON & CO. N.V., P.O. BOX 193, ROTTERDAM, HOLLAND.

[261 F.Supp. 886]

This letter of credit specified that the goods were to be shipped "PER S/S 'SCHAVENBURG' (OZEAN STINNES LINES)."

Three of the letters of credit stated that the credit was subject to the "Uniform customs and practice for Commercial Documentary Credits fixed by the Thirteenth Congress of the International Chambers of Commerce" ("Thirteenth Congress Rules"). One, No. 59425, dated September 7, 1965, stated that it was subject to "THE UNIFORM CUSTOMS AND PRACTICE FOR DOCUMENTARY CREDITS 1962 REVISION INTERNATIONAL CHAMBER OF COMMERCE BROCHURE NO. 222" ("1962 Revision").

These two sets of rules for letter of credit transactions contain two provisions which are pertinent here. The first relates to the procedure to be followed by the issuing bank when a draft drawn under its letter of credit is presented to it for payment and the issuing bank claims that the documents accompanying the draft do not conform to the terms of the credit. Article 10 of the Thirteenth Congress Rules provides:

> "If such claim is to be made, notice to that effect, stating the reasons therefor, must be given by cable or other expeditious means to the Bank demanding reimbursement and such notice must state that the documents are being held at the disposal of such Bank or are being returned thereto. The issuing Bank shall have a reasonable time to examine the documents."

Article 8 of the 1962 Revision contains a substantially identical provision.

The second relates to on board bills of lading. Article 23 of the Thirteenth Congress Rules provides:

> "When a shipment is stipulated "On Board", the loading on board can be evidenced by means of a notation signed or initialed on behalf of the carrier. If the Bill of Lading is presented after the ultimate shipment date specified in the credit, the said notation must be dated and this date shall be considered as the date of loading on board and shipment."

Defendant further contends, as to all four letters of credit, that plaintiff did not comply with the Thirteenth Congress Rules (or in the one case, with the 1962 Revision) because it did not assert its position as to the documents within a reasonable time after they were presented. This contention breaks down into two parts: (a) under the Rules, in order to make a valid rejection of the documents, the issuing bank, i.e., plaintiff, must use the identical words mentioned in the Rules, and must expressly state "we are holding the documents at your disposal"; (b) defendant did not use these words until its cable of September 27, which was ten days after the first three drafts were presented, and seven days after the presentation of the fourth draft. This period, says defendant, is not a reasonable time.

There is a sharp dispute in the affidavits as to the custom followed by bankers in interpreting and applying the so-called uniform rules. As to the first point raised by defendant, plaintiff's affidavit states that it is normal banking practice to use the word "instruct," which "bankers understand to indicate that the retained defective documents are being 'held at the disposal' of the presenting bank." Defendant, on the other hand, has submitted an affidavit which states "the issuing bank must *specifically* inform the negotiating bank that it is holding the documents at its disposal or that they are being returned."

As to defendant's second point, plaintiff's affidavit states that "New York banks normally consider a 'reasonable time' to be a period of approximately ten working days or two calendar weeks." Defendant's affidavit, on the contrary, asserts that a reasonable time is, at most, three business days.

Of course, as to three letters of credit, we do not reach this question of interpretation of the Rules if, as defendant claims, the documents complied with the terms of the credits. Hence that question must first be considered.

In my opinion, the documents did not comply. The truckers bills of lading did not state that the goods were "on board" the trucks. They bore no such notation signed, initialed or stamped by the carrier. This was an essential requirement of the letter of credit and these requirements must be strictly complied with. Anglo-South American Trust Co. v. Uhe, 261 N.Y. 150, 184 N.E. 741 (1933); Lamborn v. Lake Shore Banking & Trust Co., 196 App.Div. 504, 188 N.Y.S. 162 (1st Dept. 1921), aff'd mem. 231 N.Y. 616, 132 N.E. 911 (1921); North Woods Paper Mills Ltd. v. National City Bank of New York, 121 N.Y.S.2d 543 (Sup.Ct. 1953), aff'd mem. 283 App. Div. 731, 127 N.Y.S.2d 663 (2d Dept. 1954).

Defendant's affidavits say that in Mexico it is not customary for truckers bills of lading to specify that the goods are "on board." They say that these bills of lading were in the customary Mexican form. I believe that the Mexican custom is immaterial. Dixon, Irmaos & Cia., Ltda. v. Chase Nat. Bank of City of New York, 144 F.2d 759 (2d Cir. 1944), cert. denied, 324 U.S. 850, 65 S.Ct. 687, 89 L.E.d. 1410 (1945); Vietor v. National

City Bank of New York, 200 App. Div. 557, 193 N.Y.S. 868 (1st Dept. 1922), aff'd mem. after remand, 237 N.Y. 538, 143 N.E. 733 (1923).

* * *

NOTES

1.   The *Beyene* and *Marine Midland* cases highlight the doctrine of *strict compliance*, followed by the vast majority of jurisdictions. This doctrine basically refers to the fact that, in determining compliance with the terms of a letter of credit, the documents tendered by the beneficiary to the bank shall on their face "strictly" comply with the terms and conditions stipulated in the documentary credit, so that even the smallest discrepancy can be sufficient for the banks to reject the documents tendered. This principle was first formulated in a 1927 decision handed down by an English court in Equitable Trust Co. v. Dawson Partners Ltd., 27 Lloyds List L.R. 52 (H.L. 1927):

> There is no room for documents which are almost the same, or which will do just as well . . . [t]he bank which knows nothing officially of the details of the transactions financed cannot take upon itself to decide what will do well enough, and what will not. If it does as it is told it is safe; if it declines to do anything else, it is safe; if it departs from the conditions laid down, it acts at its own risk.

The rationale for the strict compliance rule is rooted in the need to preserve the commercial vitality of letters of credit by fostering certainty to the greatest extent possible. In exploring this rationale, one commentator cited a U.S. federal appellate court which observed that, if banks deviate or are allowed to deviate from the term of a letter of credit, "the certainty that makes this device so attractive and useful may well be undermined, with the result that banks may become reluctant to assume the additional risks of litigation." See Daniel M. Kolko, Strict Compliance Applies to Letter of Credit Issuers, Too, 237 N.Y.L.J. 46 (March 19, 2007); Insurance Co. of North America v. Heritage Bank, 595 F.2d 171, 176 (3rd Cir. 1979).

On the other hand, other commentators have noted that it is very easy to discover even minimal discrepancies between the letter of credit and the documents; legitimizing the rigid strict compliance doctrine would allow banks to refuse *a priori*; some payments and this might lead to abuses of the parties involved in the transactions. Further, it may allow bad faith behavior contrary to the expectations of the beneficiary. See, e.g., Erika Arban, The Doctrine of Strict Compliance in the Italian Legal System, 84 Ariz. J of Int'l and Comp. Law 23 No. 1 (2005).

Further, a strictly literal approach by issuing banks may lead to criticisms by parties to the transaction that they are being too nit-picking i.e., pointing out miniscule errata or discrepancies of little or no materiality or relevance to the transaction.

Courts in the U.S. and some common law jurisdictions have adopted a different approach: substantial compliance. Substantial compliance means that not all documentation and conditions to payment involved in presentment to the issuing bank need not comply in a strict literal sense. The U.S. judicial approach has been described as follows: "Where a letter of credit is substantially complied with every reasonable effort should be made by the courts to uphold its validity particularly where the objections are technical in nature and made only in an effort to escape from the legal effect of business bargain." Folsom, Ralph H., Gordon, Michael Wallace and Spanogle, John A. Jr., International Business Transactions, West (2d Ed. 1991) at 162.

This approach, however, is designed to overcome purely technical issues and not substantive defects. The U.S. Uniform Commercial Code ("UCC") and the International Chamber of Commerce's Uniform Customs and Practices ("UCP"), which are principal sources of U.S. and international letter of credit standards, respectively, provide for the ability of parties to a letter of credit to waive defects raised by the issuing bank. See UCC § 5 and UCP § 500. The UCC and UCP are discussed in more detail below.

2.   Please note that in the *Marine Midland* case the court concluded that, in determining compliance with the documentary requirements at issue, the fact that in Mexico "it is not customary for truckers bill of lading to say that the goods are "on board" is "immaterial;" citing Dixon, Irmaos & Cia, Ltda. V. Chase National Bank of City of New York, 144F.2d 759 (2d Cir.1944), cert. denied 342 U.S. 850 (1945).

In that case, a Brazilian exporter had contracted to sell cotton to a Belgian purchaser. Chase (at the request of a Belgian bank) had issued two letters of credit on behalf of the purchaser. The terms of the credit required Chase to honor drafts accompanied by specified documents, including "a full set of bills of lading." The seller shipped the goods and received two original bills of lading for each shipment, but only one of the two sets of bills of lading was presented to Chase by the due date. In lieu of the other set, the exporter's New York representative, another New York bank, gave Chase an indemnity agreement against loss. Chase dishonored the drafts on the grounds that both full sets of bills of lading had not been presented. The plaintiff introduced evidence that New York banks that financed international sales with letters of credit customarily accepted a guaranty in place of a missing document when the letter of credit required a "full set of bills of lading." The court found that Chase was bound by the custom, and had failed to follow it in this instance only because the German invasion of Belgium had intervened. Since Chase was a confirming bank, entitled to recover from the purchaser's Belgian bank once it honored the drafts, Chase may have been concerned about its ability to obtain reimbursement rather than with the adequacy of the presented documents. The court, in short, believed that Chase was simply acting opportunistically. See Clayton P. Gillette, Harmony and Statis in Trade Usage for International Sales, 39 Virg. J. Int'l L. at 715–716 (Spring 1999).

3. FRAUD

ROSS P. BUCKLEY & XIANG GAO, THE DEVELOPMENT OF THE FRAUD RULE IN LETTER OF CREDIT LAW

664 U. Pa. J. Int'l Econ. L. 23 (2002)

The doctrine of autonomy is one of the foundation stones of the law of letters of credit. Under this doctrine, the obligation of an issuing bank of a letter of credit is independent from the underlying sale of goods contract for which the credit will provide payment. An exception to this doctrine may arise in a case of fraud.

Under the fraud rule, although the documents presented may comply strictly on their face with the terms and conditions of the letter of credit, payment under the credit may be stopped if fraud is found to have been committed before payment is made, provided the presenter or party demanding payment does not belong to a protected class.

The policy tension behind the fraud rule was well expressed by Justice Le Dam in the leading Canadian case of *Bank of Nova Scotia v. Angelica-Whitewear Ltd.*, in these terms:

> The potential scope of the fraud exception must not be a means of creating serious uncertainty and lack of confidence in the operation of letter of credit transactions; at the same time the application of the principle of autonomy must not serve to encourage or facilitate fraud in such transactions.[1]

The fraud rule allows an issuer or a court to view the facts behind the face of conforming documents and to halt the payment of a letter of credit when fraud is involved. The raison d'etre of letters of credit is to provide an absolute assurance of payment to a seller, provided the seller presents the right documents. The fraud rule thus goes to the very heart of the letter of credit obligation and has been described as "the most controversial and confused area" in the law governing letters of credit.[2]

Why, then, is it necessary to have such a rule? There are at least three reasons: (1) to close a loophole in the law; (2) to uphold the public policy of limiting fraud; and (3) to maintain the commercial utility of letters of credit. Each will be considered.

1. CLOSING A LOOPHOLE

In accordance with the principle of autonomy, all parties under a letter of credit arrangement are dealing in documents, not the goods or services to which the documents relate. If the documents tendered appear on their

---

[1]   [1987] D.L.R. 161,168 (Can.).

[2]   Note, *"Fraud in the Transaction": Enjoining Letters of Credit During the Iranian Revolution*, 93 HARV. L. REV. 992, 995 (1980).

face to be in strict compliance with the terms and conditions stipulated in the credit, the issuer must make the payment, irrespective of any disputes or claims with regard to other related transactions. The issuer is entitled to full recourse against the applicant, even if the documents received turn out to be forgeries or include fraudulent statements. The issuer's only duty is to exercise reasonable care to ensure that the documents tendered comply on their face with the terms and conditions of the credit. This doctrine normally serves commerce well and facilitates the commercial utility of letters of credit.

However, "[a]s is the case with any rule that paints human conduct with a broad brush, an overly rigid application" of the autonomy principle may in some cases produce harsh results, which can undermine the original purpose of the principle.[3] This happens when fraud is involved in the transaction. Because of the document-oriented nature of the letter of credit operation, beneficiaries demanding payment do not have to show that they have properly performed their duties in the underlying transaction; they need only produce conforming documents. The separation in law of the documents from the actual performance of the underlying transaction is absolutely necessary for credits to fulfill their essential commercial function and creates a loophole for unscrupulous beneficiaries to abuse the system. Perpetrators of fraud ("Fraudsters") may thus utilize letters of credit to obtain others' money by presenting forged or fraudulent documents. The classic example is where the seller gets paid under a letter of credit by presenting forged documents that comply in form with the requirements in the credit, yet the buyer receives only a shipment of worthless rubbish instead of the expected goods. With the fraud rule in place, this loophole in the letter of credit system has shrunk: even if every injustice fraud can cause is not prevented, its effects are at least minimized.

2. PUBLIC POLICY FOR THE CONTROL OF FRAUD

The fraud rule fills a gap in the law of letters of credit and a public policy requirement. As an American judge has stated, "[T]here is as much public interest in discouraging fraud as in encouraging the use of letters of credit."[4] Thus the fraud rule is part of a sound legal system that upholds the public policy of limiting fraud.

* * *

---

[3]   Herbert A. Getz, Comment, *Enjoining the International Standby Letter of Credit: The Iranian Letter of Credit Cases*, 21 HARV. INT'L L.J. 189, 204 (1980).

[4]   Dynamics Corp. of Am. v. Citizens & S. Nat'l Bank, 356 F. Supp. 991, 1000 (N.D. Ga. 1973) (Edenfield, J.).

3. MAINTAINING THE UTILITY OF LETTERS OF CREDIT

Fraud in the letter of credit not only violates the public policy against fraud, but also poses "an equally serious potential threat to the commercial utility of letters of credit."[6] The popularity of the letter of credit lies in the fact that it provides a fair balance of competing interests among the parties involved. The normal operation of the letter of credit not only provides the beneficiary with safe and rapid access to the purchase price or a sum of money when the applicant defaults, but also provides the applicant with credit and/or other commercial benefits, protects the applicant against improper calls on the credit by requiring the beneficiary to present documents indicating that it has properly performed its obligations under the underlying transaction, and most importantly, assists the applicant to realize its commercial goal.

* * *

A. FRAUD RELATING TO GOODS

SZTEJN V. J. HENRY SCHRODER BANKING CORPORATION ET AL.
New York Supreme Court
31 N.Y.S.2d 631 (1941)

SHIENTAG, JUSTICE.

[* * *] On January 7, 1941, the plaintiff and his coadventurer contracted to purchase a quantity of bristles from the defendant Transea Traders, Ltd. (hereafter referred to as Transea) a corporation having its place of business in Lucknow, India, In order to pay for the bristles, the plaintiff and Schwarz contracted with the defendant J. Henry Schroder Banking Corporation (hereafter referred to as Schroder), a domestic corporation, for the issuance or an irrevocable letter of credit to Transea which provided that drafts by the latter for a specified portion of the purchase price of the bristles would be paid by Schroder upon shipment of the described merchandise and presentation of an invoice and a bill of lading covering the shipment, made out to the order of Schroder.

The letter of credit was delivered to Transea by Schroder's correspondent bank in India, Transea placed fifty cases of material on board a steamship, procured a bill of lading from the steamship company and obtained the customary invoices. These documents describe the bristles called for by the letter of credit. However, the complaint alleges that in fact Transea filled the fifty crates with cowhair, other worthless material and rubbish with intent to simulate genuine merchandise and

---

[6]   Guy W. Lewin Smith, *Irrevocable Letters of Credit and Third Party Fraud: The* American Accord, 24 Va. J. INT'L L. 55, 96 (1983).

defraud the plaintiff and Schwarz. The complaint then alleges that Transea drew a draft under the letter of credit to the order of the Chartered Bank and delivered the draft and the fraudulent documents to the "Chartered Bank at Cawnpore, India, for collection for the account of said defendant Transea". The Chartered Bank has presented the draft along [*721] with the documents to Schroder for payment, The plaintiff prays for a judgment declaring the letter of credit and draft thereunder void and for injunctive relief to prevent the payment of the draft.

For the purposes of this motion, the allegations of the complaint must be deemed established and "every Intendment and fair inference is in favor of the pleading" Madole v. Gavin, 215 App.Div. 299, at page 300, 213 N.Y.S. 529, at page 530; McClare v. Massachusetts Bonding & Ins. Co., 266 N.Y. 371, 373, 195 N.E. 15. Therefore, it must be assumed that Transea was engaged in a scheme to defraud the plaintiff and Schwarz, that the merchandise shipped by Transea is worthless rubbish and that the Chartered Bank is not an innocent holder of the draft for value but is merely attempting to procure payment of the draft for Transea's account.

It is well established that a letter of credit is independent of the primary contract of sale between the buyer and the seller. The issuing bank agrees to pay upon presentation of documents, not goods. This rule is necessary to preserve the efficiency of the letter of credit as an instrument for the financing of trade. One of the chief purposes of the letter of credit is to furnish the seller with a ready means of obtaining prompt payment for his merchandise. It would be a most unfortunate interference with business transactions if a bank before honoring drafts drawn upon it was obliged or even allowed to go behind the documents, at the request of the buyer and enter into controversies between the buyer and the seller regarding the quality of the merchandise shipped, If the buyer and the seller intended the bank to do this they could have so provided in the letter of credit itself, and in the absence of such a provision, the court will not demand or even permit the bank to delay paying drafts which are proper in form. * * * Of course, the application of this doctrine presupposes that the documents accompanying the draft are genuine and conform in terms to the requirements of the letter of credit. Lamborn v. Lake Shore Banking & Trust Co., 196 App.Div. 504, 188 N.Y.S, 162; affirmed 231 N.Y. 616, 132 N.E. 911; Bank of Montreal v. Recknagel, 109 N.Y. 482, 17 N.E. 217; 38 Y.L.J. 111, 112.

However, I believe that a different situation is presented in the instant action. This is not a controversy between the buyer and [* * *] seller concerning a mere breach of warranty regarding the quality of the merchandise; on the present motion, it must be assumed that the seller has intentionally failed to ship any goods ordered by the buyer. In such a situation, where the seller's fraud has been called to the bank's attention before the drafts and documents have been presented for payment, the

*Fraud
exception
applies*

*Bank
had
knowledge
of payment*

principle of the independence of the bank's obligation under the letter of credit should not be extended to protect the unscrupulous seller, It is true that even though the documents are forged or fraudulent, if the issuing bank has already paid the draft before receiving notice of the seller's fraud, it will be protected if it exercised reasonable diligence before making such payment. Bank of New York & Trust Co. v. Atterbury Bros., Inc., 226 App.Div. 117, 234 N.Y.S. 442, affirmed 253 N.Y. 569, 171 N.E. 786; I., 120 Misc. 787, 200 N.Y.S. 491, affirmed 208 App.Div, 799, 203 N.Y.S. 922. However, in the instant action Schroder has received notice of Transea's active fraud before it accepted or paid the draft. The Chartered Bank, which under the allegations of the complaint stands in no better position than Transea, should not be heard to complain because Schroder is not forced to pay the draft accompanied by documents covering a transaction which it has reason to believe is fraudulent.

Although our courts have used broad language to the effect that a letter of credit is independent of the primary contract between the buyer and seller, that language was used in cases concerning alleged breaches of warranty; no case has been brought to my attention on this point involving an intentional fraud on the part of the seller which was brought to the bank's notice with the request that it withhold payment of the draft on this account. The distinction between a breach of warranty and active fraud on the part of the seller is supported by authority and reason. As one court has stated: "Obviously, when the issuer of a letter of credit knows that a document, although correct in form, is, in point of fact, false or illegal, he cannot be called upon to recognize such a document as complying with the terms of a letter of credit." Old Colony Trust Co. v, Lawyers' Title & Trust Co., 2 Cir., 297 F. 152 at page 158, certiorari denied 265 U.S. 585, 44 S.Ct. 459, 68 L.Ed. 1192. * * *

No hardship will be caused by permitting the bank to refuse payment where fraud is claimed, where the merchandise is not merely inferior in quality but consists of worthless rubbish, where the draft and the accompanying documents are in the hands of one who stands in the same position as the fraudulent seller, where the bank has been given notice of the fraud before being presented with the drafts and documents for payment, and where the bank itself does not wish to pay pending an adjudication of the rights and obligations of the other parties, While the primary factor in the issuance of the letter of credit is the credit standing of the buyer, the security afforded by the merchandise is also taken into account. In fact, the letter of credit requires a bill of lading made out to the order of the bank and not the buyer. Although the bank is not interested in the exact detailed performance of the sales contract, it is vitally interested in assuring itself that there are some goods represented by the documents. Finkelstein, Legal Aspects of Commercial Letters of Credit, p, 238; O'Meara v. National Park Bank of New York, 239 N.Y. 386, 401, 146 N.E.

636, 39 A.L.R. 747, opinion of Cardozo, J., dissenting; Thayer, Irrevocable Credits in International Commerce, 37 C.L.R. 1326, 1335.

* * *

NOTES

1.   As discussed in the following case, the doctrine of holder in due course presents further challenges for issuing banks in letter of credit transactions when presented with evidence of fraud relating to either the goods or services that are the subject of the underlying business contract, or the documents required to be presented by the customer i.e., seller pursuant to the terms of the letter of credit.

UNITED BANK LTD. V. CAMBRIDGE SPORTING GOODS CORP.

New York Court of Appeals
41 N.Y.2d 254 (1976)

GABRIELLI, JUSTICE.

* * *

On this appeal, we must decide whether fraud on the part of a seller-beneficiary of an irrevocable letter of credit may be successfully asserted as a defense against holders of drafts drawn by the seller pursuant to the credit. If we conclude that this defense may be interposed by the buyer who procured the letter of credit, we must also determine whether the courts below improperly imposed upon appellant buyer the burden of proving that respondent banks to whom the drafts were made payable by the seller beneficiary of the letter of credit were not holders in due course. The issues presented raise important questions concerning the application of the law of letters of credit and the rules governing proof of holder in due course status set forth in article 3 of the Uniform Commercial Code. * * *

In April, 1971 appellant Cambridge Sporting Goods Corporation (Cambridge) entered into a contract for the manufacture and sale of boxing gloves with Duke Sports (Duke), a Pakistani corporation. Duke committed itself to the manufacture of 27,936 pairs of boxing gloves at a sale price of $42,576.80; and arranged with its Pakistani bankers, United Bank Limited (United) and The Muslim Commercial Bank (Muslim), for the financing of the sale. Cambridge was requested by these banks to cover payment of the purchase price by opening an irrevocable letter of credit with its bank in New York, Manufacturers Hanover Trust Company (Manufacturers). Manufacturers issued an irrevocable letter of credit obligating it, upon the receipt of certain documents indicating shipment of the merchandise pursuant to the contract, to accept and pay, 90 days after acceptance, drafts drawn upon Manufacturers for the purchase price of the gloves.

Following confirmation of the opening of the letter of credit, Duke informed Cambridge that it would be impossible to manufacture and deliver the merchandise within the time period required by the contract, and sought an extension of time for performance until September 15, 1971 and a continuation of the letter of credit, which was due to expire on August 11. Cambridge replied on June 18 that it would not agree to a postponement of the manufacture and delivery of the gloves because of its resale commitments and, hence, it promptly advised Duke that the contract was canceled and the letter of credit should be returned. Cambridge simultaneously notified United of the contract cancellation.

Despite the cancellation of the contract, Cambridge was informed on July 17, 1971 that documents had been received at Manufacturers from United purporting to evidence a shipment of the boxing gloves under the terms of the canceled contract. The documents were accompanied by a draft, dated July 16, 1971, drawn by Duke upon Manufacturers and made payable to United, for the amount of $21,288.40, one half of the contract price of the boxing gloves. A second set of documents was received by Manufacturers from. Muslim, also accompanied by a draft, dated August 20, and drawn upon Manufacturers by Duke for the remaining amount of the contract price.

An inspection of the shipments upon their arrival revealed that Duke had shipped old, unpadded, ripped and mildewed gloves rather than the new gloves to be manufactured as agreed upon, Cambridge then commenced an action against Duke in Supreme Court, New York County, joining Manufacturers as a party, and obtained a preliminary injunction prohibiting the latter from paying drafts drawn under the letter of credit; subsequently, in November, 1971 Cambridge levied on the funds subject to the letter of credit and the draft, which were delivered by Manufacturers to the Sheriff in compliance therewith. Duke ultimately defaulted in the action and judgment against it was entered in the amount of the drafts, in March, 1972.

The present proceeding was instituted by the Pakistani banks to vacate the levy made by Cambridge and to obtain payment of the drafts on the letter of credit. The banks asserted that they were holders in due course of the drafts which had been made payable to them by Duke and, thus, were entitled to the proceeds thereof irrespective of any defenses which Cambridge had established against their transferor, Duke, in the prior action which had terminated in a default judgment. The banks' motion for summary judgment on this claim was denied and the request by Cambridge for a jury trial was granted. Cambridge sought to depose the petitioning banks, but its request was denied and, as an alternative, written interrogatories were served on the Pakistani banks to learn the circumstances surrounding the transfer of the drafts to them. At trial the banks introduced no evidence other than answers to several of the written interrogatories which were received over objection by Cambridge to the effect that the answers were conclusory, self-serving and otherwise inadmissible. Cambridge presented evidence of its dealings with Duke including the cancellation of the contract and uncontested proof of the subsequent shipment of essentially worthless merchandise.

The trial court concluded that the burden of proving that the banks were not holders in due course lay with Cambridge, and directed a verdict in favor of the banks on the ground that Cambridge had not met that burden; the court stated that Cambridge failed to demonstrate that the banks themselves had participated in the seller's acts of fraud, proof of which was concededly present in the record. The Appellate Division affirmed, agreeing that while there was proof tending to establish the defenses against the seller, Cambridge had not shown that the seller's acts were 'connected to the petitioners (banks) in any manner.' * * *

We reverse and hold that it was improper to direct a verdict in favor of the petitioning Pakistani banks. We conclude that the defense of fraud in the transaction was established and in that circumstance the burden shifted to petitioners to prove that they were holders in due course and took the drafts for value, in good faith and without notice of any fraud "on the part of Duke (Uniform Commercial Code, § 3–302). Additionally, we think it was improper for the trial court to permit petitioners to introduce into evidence answers to Cambridge's interrogatories to demonstrate their holder in due course status.

This case does not come before us in the typical posture of a lawsuit between the bank issuing the letter of credit and presenters of drafts drawn under the credit seeking payment [* * *]. Because Cambridge obtained an injunction against payment of the drafts and has levied against the proceeds of the drafts, it stands in the same position as the issuer, and, thus, the law of letters of credit governs the liability of Cambridge to the Pakistani banks. Article 5 of the Uniform Commercial Code, dealing with letters of credit, and the Uniform Customs and Practice for Documentary Credits promulgated by the International Chamber of Commerce set forth the duties and obligations of the issuer of a letter of credit. A letter of credit is a commitment on the part of the issuing bank that it will pay a draft presented to it under the terms of the credit; and if it is a documentary draft, upon presentation of the required documents of title (See Uniform Commercial Code) § 5–103) Banks issuing letters of credit deal in documents and not in goods and are not responsible for any breach of warranty or nonconformity of the goods involved in the underlying sales contract * * * Subdivision (2) of section 5–114, however indicates certain limited circumstances in which an issuer may properly refuse to honor a draft drawn under a letter of credit or a customer may enjoin an issuer from honoring such a draft. Thus, where 'fraud in the transaction' has been shown and the holder has not taken the draft in circumstances that would make it a holder in due course, the customer may apply to enjoin the issuer from paying drafts drawn under the letter of credit. * * * This rule represents a codification of precode case law most eminently articulated in the landmark case of Sztejn v. Schroder Banking Corp., 177 Misc. 719, 31 N.Y.S.2d 631, Shientag, J., where it was held that the shipment of cowhair in place of bristles amounted to more than mere breach of warranty but fraud sufficient to constitute grounds for enjoining payment of drafts to one not a holder in due course. * * * Even prior to the Sztejn case, forged or fraudulently procured documents were proper grounds for avoidance of payment of drafts drawn under a letter of credit [* * *] and cases decided, after the enactment of the code have cited Sztejn with approval [* * *].

The history of the dispute between the various parties involved in this case reveals that Cambridge had in a prior, separate proceeding successfully enjoined Manufacturers from paying the drafts and has attached the proceeds of the drafts. It should be noted that the question of the availability and the propriety of this relief is not before us on this appeal. The petitioning banks do not dispute the validity of the prior injunction nor do they dispute the delivery of worthless merchandise. Rather, on this appeal they contend that as holders in due course they are entitled to the proceeds of the drafts irrespective of any fraud on the part of Duke. * * * Although precisely speaking there was no specific finding of fraud in the transaction by either of the courts below, their determinations were based on that assumption. The evidentiary facts are not disputed and we hold upon the facts as established, that the shipment of old, unpadded, ripped and mildewed gloves rather than the new boxing gloves as ordered by Cambridge, constituted fraud in the transaction within the meaning of subdivision (2) of section 5–114. It should be noted that the drafters of section 5–114, in their attempt to codify the Sztejn case and in utilizing the term 'fraud in the transaction', have eschewed a dogmatic approach and adopted a flexible standard to be applied as the circumstances of a particular situation mandate. It can be difficult to draw a precise line between cases involving breach of warranty (or a difference of opinion as to the quality of goods) and outright fraudulent practice on the part of the seller. To the extent, however, that Cambridge established that Duke was guilty of Fraud in shipping, not merely nonconforming merchandise, but worthless fragments of boxing gloves, this case is similar to Sztejn.

* * *

Even though section 3–307 is contained in article 3 of the code dealing with negotiable instruments rather than letters of credit, we agree that its provisions should control in the instant case. Section 5–114 (subd. (2), par. (a)) utilizes the holder in due course criteria of section 3–302 of the code to determine whether a presenter may recover on drafts despite fraud in the sale of goods transaction. It is logical, therefore, to apply the pleading and practice rules of section 3–307 in the situation where a presenter of drafts

under a letter of credit claims to be a holder in due course. In the context
of section 5–114 and the law of letters of credit, however, the 'defense'
referred to in section 3–307 should be deemed to include only those
defenses available under subdivision (2) of section 5–114, i.e.,
noncompliance of required documents, forged or fraudulent documents or
fraud in the transaction. In the context of a letter of credit transaction and,
specifically subdivision (2) of section 5–114, it is these defenses which
operate to shift the burden of proof of holder in due course status upon one
asserting such status. * * * Thus, a presenter of drafts drawn under a letter
of credit must prove that it took the drafts for value, in good faith and
without notice of the underlying fraud in the transaction * * *.

Turning to the rules of section 3–307 as they apply to this case,
Cambridge failed to deny the effectiveness of the signatures on the draft in
its answer and, thus, these are deemed admitted and their effectiveness is
not an issue in the case. However, this does not entitle the banks as holders
to payment of the drafts since Cambridge has established 'fraud' in the
transaction'. The courts below erroneously concluded that Cambridge was
required to show that the banks had participated in or were themselves
guilty of the seller's fraud in order to establish a defense to payment. But,
it was not necessary that Cambridge prove that United and Muslim
actually participated in the fraud, since merely notice of the fraud would
have deprived the Pakistani hanks of holder in due course status.

In order to qualify as a holder in due course, a holder must have taken
the instrument 'without notice * * * of any defense against * * * it on the
part of any person' (Uniform Commercial Code, § 3–302, subd. (1), par. (c)).
Pursuant to subdivision (2) of section 5–114 fraud in the transaction is a
valid defense to payment of drafts drawn under a letter of credit. Since the
defense of fraud in the transaction was shown, the burden shifted to the
banks by operation of subdivision (3) of section 3–307 to prove that they
were holders in due course and took the drafts without notice of Duke's
alleged fraud. As indicated in the Official Comment to that subdivision,
when it is shown that a defense exists, one seeking to cut off the defense by
claiming the rights of a holder in due course 'has the full burden of proof
by a preponderance of the total evidence' on this issue. This burden must
be sustained by 'affirmative proof of the requisites of holder in due course
status * * * . It was error for the trial court to direct a verdict in favor of
the Pakistani banks because this determination rested upon a
misallocation of the burden of proof; and we conclude that the banks have
not satisfied the burden of proving that they qualified in all respects as
holders in due course, by any affirmative proof. * * * The failure of the
banks to meet their burden is fatal to their claim for recovery of the
proceeds of the drafts and their petition must therefore be dismissed.

* * *

NOTES

1.   The following are the texts of Sections 5–114 and 3–302 discussed in the *United Bank* case:

Uniform Commercial Code, Article 5, Letters of Credit

§ 5–114. Issuer's Duty and Privilege to Honor; Right to Reimbursement

(1) An issuer must honor a draft or demand for payment, which complies with the terms of the relevant credit regardless of whether the goods or documents conform to the underlying contract for sale or other contract between the customer and the beneficiary. The issuer is not excused from honor of such a draft or demand by reason of an additional general term that all documents must be satisfactory to it.

(2) Unless otherwise agreed when documents appear on their face to comply with the terms of a credit but a required document does not in fact conform to the warranties made on negotiation or transfer of a document of title (Section 7–507) or of a certified security (Section 8–108) or is forged or fraudulent or there is fraud in the transaction:

> (a) the issuer must honor the draft or demand for payment if honor is demanded by a negotiating bank or other holder of the draft or demand which has taken the draft or demand under the credit and under circumstances which would make it a holder in due course (Section 3–302) and in an appropriate case would make it a person to whom a document of title has been duly negotiated (Section 7–503) or a bona fide purchaser of a certified security (Section 8–302); and

> (b) in all other cases as against its customer, an issuer acting in good faith may honor the draft or demand for payment despite notification from the customer of fraud, forgery or other defect not apparent on the face of the documents but a court of appropriate jurisdiction may enjoin such honor.

Uniform Commercial Code, Revised Article 3 Negotiable Instruments Part 3. Enforcement of Instruments

§ 3–302. Holder in Due Course

(a) Subject to subsection (c) and Section 3–103(d), "holder in due course" means the holder of an instrument if:

> (1) the instrument when issued or negotiated to the holder does not bear such apparent evidence of forgery or adulteration or is not otherwise so irregular or incomplete as to call into question its authenticity; and

> (2) the holder took the instrument (i) for value, (ii) in good faith, (iii) without notice that the instrument is overdue or has been dishonored or that there is an uncured default with respect to payment of another instrument issued as part of the same series, (iv) without notice that the instrument contains an unauthorized

signature or has been altered, (v) without notice of any claim to the instrument described in Section 3–306, and (vi) without notice that any party has a defense or claim in recoupment described in Section 3–305(a).

2. The holder in due course provisions of Section 3–302 are premised on the notion that it would be unjust to permit a holder to enforce a letter of credit that he knew at the time he acquired it to be defective, subject to claims or defenses, or had been dishonored. Thus, under Section 3–302 the holder must receive the letter of credit without notice of such defect. Proving knowledge is difficult, so Section 3–302(2) lists several types of notice that presumptively defeat any entitlement to status as a holder in due course.

However, as noted in the *United Bank* case, once a defense of fraud is proven, the burden shifts to the asserted holder to prove "by a preponderance of the total evidence" that they have the right of a holder in due course. *Id.* at 263.

B. FRAUD RELATING TO DOCUMENTS PRESENTED

HONG KONG MONETARY AUTHORITY FRAUD CASES RELATED TO LETTERS OF CREDIT

(August 2011)

The Chief Executive
All authorized institutions

* * *

Fraud cases relating to letter of credit

In view of the significant number of letter of credit ("L/C") related fraud cases received by the Commercial Crime Bureau ("CCB"), I am writing to draw your attention to the schemes commonly used to deceive banks and their trade customers and the precautionary measures which may help prevent such frauds.

According to CCB's statistics, it has received reports on 45 L/C related fraud cases since January 1998, involving a total of $1.2 billion. These cases involved bills drawn under L/Cs negotiated with authorized institutions ("AIs") in Hong Kong using false negotiation documents. While most of the L/Cs concerned were issued by banks on the Mainland, the number of local L/Cs is also quite significant. In addition, there are cases involving L/C kiting (see below). Details of these schemes are given below.

Use of false negotiation documents

1. The culprit lured unwary buyers to open L/Cs (local L/Cs on some occasions) to buy goods from him by offering very attractive terms, e.g. below market pricing,

2.   or

> The culprit ("company A") requested another company ("company B") to apply for L/Cs on its behalf from a bank on the Mainland. Company B received a certain amount as commission. In some cases, A and B were both companies on the Mainland and Company B was actually an associate of Company A.

* * *

5.   The buyer and the negotiating bank later on discovered that the goods did not exist.

* * *

Preventive measures

While some of the reported cases are still under investigation, CCB observes that some of the fraud cases mentioned above could have been avoided, or at least the scale of the problem could be significantly reduced, if the following preventive measures were adopted by AIs concerned.

1.   In the credit assessment and approval process, AIs should pay particular attention to the nature and history of the customer's business, including any recent change in the ownership and management of the company, major trading partners and its trading pattern.

2.   Credit lines should be approved having regard to, among other factors, the business need of the borrower, the value of underlying collateral and proven track record of repayment. Request for drastic increase in credit facilities within a short period of time should be carefully examined.

3.   Drastic increase in L/C outstanding balances should be closely monitored. It would be useful to visit the borrower's office or factory to ensure that business and production are normal and can cope with the increased volume.

* * *

5.   In handling the L/C documentation, negotiating banks should ensure that L/Cs presented have been authenticated by the advising bank. Where necessary, they should confirm the authenticity of the L/C with the issuing bank. It should also review carefully the terms of L/Cs and any subsequent amendments and where necessary, follow up with the issuing bank. For L/Cs of substantial amount or in case of doubt, shipping documents should be authenticated before negotiation. As far as possible spot checks should be arranged on suppliers and inspection certificates should be obtained from independent surveyors. These steps could help ensure the authenticity of L/Cs and the shipping documents.

6.   If the beneficiary of the L/C is not a well-established company or the bank is not familiar with the beneficiary, extreme care should be taken to discount the relevant bills. If not sure of the background of the beneficiary, AIs should avoid negotiating the documents but to send them to the L/C issuing bank for collection only.

* * *

NOTES

1.   If you are counsel to an issuing bank, what steps would you advise your client to take in avoiding fraudulent letter of credit transactions in light of the *Siderius* case below, and the Hong Kong Monetary Authority's 2011 guidance? How about potential customers i.e., buyers in business agreements secured with letters of credit?

SIDERIUS, INC. V. WALLACE CO., INC.

Texas Court of Civil Appeals
583 S.W.2d 852 (1979)

* * *

SUMMERS, JUSTICE.

* * *

Originally, Siderius was going to sell 5,000 net tons of foreign steel pipe to Melton for approximately $715.00 per net ton. Melton, in back-to-back transaction, intended to then sell the same pipe to Wallace. This agreement was conditioned upon Wallace's obtaining a letter of credit for Melton's benefit for approximately $4.1 million. Wallace was unable to obtain the letter of credit, and as a result, the deal fell through. Siderius then approached Wallace and offered to sell the pipe to Wallace directly for $715.00 per net ton, conditioned on Wallace's obtaining a letter of credit for Siderius' benefit.

Based upon Wallace's application, Texas Commerce Bank issued an irrevocable documentary letter of credit for Siderius' benefit on August 1, 1974. The terms of the letter of credit specified that: "GENTLEMEN: WE HEREBY OPEN OUR IRREVOCABLE LETTER OF CREDIT IN YOUR FAVOR FOR THE ACCOUNT OF Wallace Company, Inc. P.O. Box 2597 Houston, Texas 77001 FOR A SUM OR SUMS NOT EXCEEDING IN THE AGGREGATE THE SUM OF Three Million Seven Hundred Fifty-Three Thousand Seven Hundred Fifty and No/100 U.S. Dollars ($3,753,750.00). AVAILABLE BY YOUR DRAFTS ON us AT _____ sight _____ TO BE ACCOMPANIED BY:–Commercial Invoice,–Customs Invoice,–Certificate of Origin,–Packing List (Including Tallies) Dock Delivery Order.– Negotiable Insurance Certificate of Policy covering Marine and War risks

including All Risk Warehouse to Warehouse for 110% of full invoice value.–
Full set of On Board Ocean Bills of Lading to the order of Texas Commerce
Bank National Association, Notify: W.A. Sammis, Wallace Co., Inc., Box
2597, Houston, Texas 77001, Telephone Number 713–675–2661, showing
'Freight Prepaid,' EVIDENCE SHIPMENT from 1. Italian Port, 2. & 3.
Israel Port to Port of Houston, Texas U.S.A., not later than November 30,
1974

* * *

The terms of the letter of credit were amended by letters of amendment
five times, each of which stated "ALL OTHER CONDITIONS REMAINED
UNCHANGED." The shipping deadlines for all three shipments of steel
pipe, as specified originally in the letter of credit, were amended by
agreement of the parties. In early November, 1974, Siderius requested an
extension of the shipping deadline in regards to the pipe to be
manufactured in Italy; Wallace consented. In order to reflect this
modification, the letter of credit was amended on November 18, 1974, to
allow the bills of lading pertaining to the Italian pipe to be dated no later
than January 15, 1975. In addition, the expiration date of the letter of
credit was postponed to February 28, 1975. Subsequently, Siderius
requested that the shipping deadline for the Israeli pipe also be extended.
Wallace agreed, and the letter of credit was amended to change the
shipping deadline for these portions of the pipe from November 30, 1974,
to December 15, 1974. In late December or early January, a request was
once again made by Siderius seeking a further extension for shipment of
the Italian pipe. Wallace refused to agree to anymore extensions and the
January 15, 1975, deadline remained in force. The two shipments of pipe
manufactured in Israel were shipped, delivered in Houston, and Siderius'
first and second drafts on the letter of credit in regards to these two
shipments were honored by the Bank. The dispute in the instant case
pertains to the shipment of the portion of pipe manufactured in Italy. * * *

The pipe in question was to be shipped form the Italian port of
Ravenna on board the M/V Slavonija. On February 20, 1975, Siderius
presented to the Bank a bill of lading and other documents along with the
third draft for payment in an amount in excess of $1.8 million. The bill of
lading was dated January 15, 1975, and on its face appeared to conform to
the terms of the letter of credit. Wallace notified the Bank that it suspected
that the bill of lading presented by Siderius in the third draft was
fraudulent because the shipping requirements had not been met and
informed the Bank that it declined to waive any defects. The Bank
dishonored Siderius' first presentation of the third draft on February 24,
1975, as nonconforming because the bill of lading was issued under and
subject to a charter party, the insurance certificate was short, and the dock
delivery order was improper. In addition, Wallace notified Siderius that it
was rejecting the Italian pipe on the grounds that the shipment of such

pipe failed to conform to the contract terms. It is undisputed that on January 15, 1975, the Slavonija had not yet arrived in the Italian port of Ravenna and did not reach that port until January 24, 1975. The loading of the pipe on board the Slavonija was not completed until January 29, 1975.

Although the letter of credit expired on February 28, 1975, Siderius returned to the Bank and made a second presentation of the third draft on March 7, 1975. A new dock delivery order and copy of the bill lading with charter party language removed were submitted to the Bank by Siderius. The insurance certificate remained short and the bill of lading continued to be dated January 15, 1975. Wallace refused to waive any defects, including late presentation, and the Bank dishonored Siderius' second presentation of the third draft. Subsequently, Wallace applied for a temporary injunction in order to enjoin the Bank from honoring Siderius' third draft because it was allegedly accompanied by false and fraudulent documents. On March 24, 1975, the trial court so enjoined the Bank. * * *

Letter of Credit

In the case at hand, we are presented with a documentary letter of credit; the issuer agrees to honor a timely draft accompanied by the documents specified in the letter of credit. The issuer deals only in documents and is not concerned with the merchandise, which is the subject of the underlying contract between the buyer and the seller. If the beneficiary presents documents which precisely and strictly conform to the requirements of the letter of credit, the issuer must honor the draft. * * * The rule of strict conformity is necessary because the issuer, dealing solely in documents, should not be required to examine the performance of the underlying transaction to determine if the terms of the letter of credit have been fulfilled. * * *

An exception to this general rule, requiring an issuer to honor a draft which is conforming on its face, is found in Subdivision (b)(2) of sec. 5–114, supra. Under the limited circumstances established by section 5–114(b)(2), supra, the issuer has the option to honor or dishonor, or the customer may enjoin the issuer form honoring such a draft. * * * This rule has be recognized as a codification of the pre-code case law as articulated in Sztejn v. J Henry Schroder Banking Corporation, 177 Misc. 719, 31 N.Y.S.2d 631 (NY.Sup.Ct.1941) and Old Colony Trust Company v. Lawyers' Title and Trust Company, 297 F. 152 (2d Cir.) cert. denied, 265 U.S. 585, 44 S.Ct. 459, 68 L.Ed. 1192 (1924). It is undisputed that Siderius was not an innocent third party as defined in subsection (b)(1) of section 5–114, supra. * * *

The letter of credit, as amended, required that the draft in connection with the Italian shipment be accompanied by a copy of an "onboard" bill of lading dated no later than January 15, 1975. * * * The bill of lading presented by Siderius represented that the pipe was so loaded, even though the ship had not yet arrived in the Italian port and wasn't loaded until two weeks later. * * *

In the instant case, the ship arrived in to the port of Ravenna after January 15, 1975. The lack of formal notification by the Bank of any fraud in the bill of lading did not prejudice Siderius or prevent cure on the part of Siderius. No cure was possible; therefore the Bank has not waived its right to assert fraud as a defense under section 5–114(b), supra, to Siderius' action for wrongful dishonor.

In the alternative, Siderius asserts that the alleged fraud was insufficient to justify dishonor of the third draft. We disagree. The issuer of a documentary letter of credit, dealing in documents and not merchandise, must be able to rely on the accuracy and integrity of the documents presented by the beneficiary. * * * In the instant case, the fraud related to the documents themselves and not the pipe which was the subject of underlying contract of sale; therefore the fraud was sufficient, upon notification by the customer, to give the Bank the option to honor or dishonor. * * *

4. NOTICE INJUNCTIONS ON LETTERS OF CREDIT: THE IRANIAN CASES

XIANG GAO AND ROSS P. BUCKLEY, A COMPARATIVE ANALYSIS OF THE STANDARD OF FRAUD REQUIRED UNDER THE FRAUD RULE

Oxford U. Comparative L Forum 3 (2003)

* * *

Iranian Cases

The Iranian Revolution of 1979 gave rise to considerable litigation in the United States over standby letters of credit. These cases are known as the Iranian cases. The Iranian cases raised novel legal questions and prompted heated discussion upon a range of issues, especially the standard of fraud of the fraud rule, not only at that time but also thereafter.

The Iranian cases can be divided into two groups: pre-hostage cases and post-hostage cases. The pre-hostage cases were decided before hostages were taken at the US Embassy in Teheran in November 1979. The post-hostages cases were decided after that date. The post-hostages cases are extreme examples of how the fraud rule, if the standard or concept of fraud is not clearly defined, can be misused by the parties and misapplied by the courts.

The facts of the Iranian cases were similar one to another. Prior to the Iranian Revolution, the Imperial Government of Iran spent billions of dollars modernising the country. Many US companies poured into Iran on this "gold rush" and were awarded lucrative contracts by the Imperial Government. At the same time, they were required to procure independent guarantees, counter-guaranteed by standby letters of credit, to secure the good performance of those contracts or the return of advance payments. All transactions involved four parties—a US company, an Iranian government agency, an Iranian bank, and a US Bank. The US company contracted with the Iranian government agency to provide goods or services in Iran. The contract required the US company to provide for the Iranian agency independent guarantees as above. The independent guarantees were issued by the Iranian bank and counter-guaranteed by standby letters of credit issued by the US bank in favour of the Iranian Bank at the request of the US company. In the event of a dispute the Iranian government agency would demand payment under the guarantee from the Iranian bank, the Iranian bank would demand payment under the standby letter of credit from the US bank, and the US bank would in turn look to the US company for reimbursement.

In the wake of the Iranian Revolution US companies, fearing that the new Iranian regime would arbitrarily demand payment under the letters of credit, flocked to US courts, in most of the cases on the ground of fraud, to prevent the letters of credit from being paid and their accounts from being charged.

* * *

NOTES

1.   Unlike a conventional letter of credit, which is premised on the bank's performance, a standby letter of credit typically imposes an obligation on a bank to perform *only* when a designated party to the transaction has failed to perform. In that case, a standby letter of credit acts as a surety or guaranty. See Jim L. Banks, The Standby Letter of Credit: What it is and How to Use It, 45 Mont. L. Rev. 1 (Winter 1984). However, compare this description to the events in the *American Bell* case, below.

UNITED TECHNOLOGIES CORP. v. CITIBANK, N.A.

United States District Court, S.D. New York
469 F. Supp. 473 (S.D. N.Y. 1979)

GAGLIARDI, DISTRICT JUDGE.

Plaintiffs United Technologies Corporation and United Technologies International, Inc. (hereinafter collectively "United") commenced this action in New York Supreme Court seeking to enjoin defendant Citibank, N.A. ("Citibank") from making payments on two letters of credit to defendant Iranians' Bank ("Iranians"). The state court issued a temporary restraining order against Citibank's payment on March 5, 1979. Citibank removed the case to this court pursuant to 12 U.S.C. § 632 on the following day. This court subsequently extended the duration of the restraining order to permit the parties to brief the difficult issues raised by this case. United has moved for an order remanding the action to state court, or, in the alternative, for a preliminary injunction. For the reasons stated below, both motions are denied.

Statement of Facts

* * *

The letters of credit which are the subject of this action were both issued in connection with certain contracts pursuant to which United agreed to sell $20 million worth of telephone cable to defendant Telecommunication Company of Iran ("TCI"). The contracts of sale required United, as seller, to procure from Iranians' performance bonds in an amount approximately equal to 10% of the contract price. The contracts also provided for proportionate reductions of the amounts due under the performance bonds within two months of the delivery of each shipment of telephone cable. As an inducement to Iranians' to issue the performance bonds, United procured the issuance by Citibank of two irrevocable letters of credit in the original aggregate amount of $2,003,295 in favor of Iranians'. Letter of Credit No. CK–656061 was issued in the amount of $1,861,245, and letter of credit No. K–312190 was subsequently issued in the amount of $142,050. Iranians', in turn, issued the performance bonds to TCI required by the underlying contracts of sale.

United contends, and it is not disputed, that the contracts of sale have been fully performed on both sides, *i.e.*, that United has delivered all of the cable ordered by TCI and that TCI has paid United the full purchase price of over $20 million. The last shipment under the contracts was allegedly made in August, 1978. TCI has apparently never claimed that there was any failure to perform on United's part. In May, 1977, TCI agreed to a reduction of the performance bonds and of letter of credit No. CK–650061 from $1,861,245 to $1,128,245. No further reduction in the performance bonds or in either of the letters of credit has ever been made, notwithstanding TCI's contractual commitment to reduce and ultimately discharge the bonds to reflect completion of the underlying contracts.

Under the terms of the letters of credit, Iranians' is entitled to draw against Citibank by notifying Citibank by cable either that:

> "(A) YOU [Iranians'] WERE REQUIRED TO DISBURSE THE AMOUNT UNDER YOUR UNDERTAKING OR (B) YOUR UNDERTAKING IS STILL OUTSTANDING AT EXPIRATION DATE OF OUR [Citibank's] LETTER OF CREDIT.

The letters of credit further provide that if Citibank is required to pay out any amount to Iranians' under the terms of the letters, Citibank is entitled to be reimbursed by United for that amount. With the consent of all parties the expiration of both letter of credit No. CK–650061 and Iranians' guarantee thereunder was extended to January 9, 1979. Letter of credit No. K–312190 was similarly extended by consent to February 24, 1979.

On December 23, 1978, Iranians' sent the following cable to Citibank with respect to letter of credit No. CK–650061:

> OUR GUARANTEE IS ON CALL TO BE EXTENDED UP TO 9. JUNE, 1979 OR PAYMENT TO BE MADE IN FULL STOP PLEASE EITHER EXTEND YOUR COUNTER GUARANTEE/CREDIT IN OUR FAVOUR ACCORDINGLY OR CREDIT OUR ACCOUNT FOR THE TOTAL AMOUNT WITH YOURSELVES DLRS 1,128,245.

At United's request, Citibank responded to Iranians' that United had fulfilled its contractual obligations and that the performance bond upon which TCI was making its call should have been cancelled. The January 9, 1979 expiration date came and went. Apparently because of the civil disturbances in Iran, Citibank received no tested messages from Iranians' from December 27, 1978 through February 19, 1979. No further word came from Iranians' on letter of credit No. CK–650061 until February 27, 1979 when Citibank received the following telex dated the previous day:

> RE YOUR TELEX JAN 5. PLEASE NOTE WE CANNOT CANCEL OUR GTEE PRIOR TO BENEFICIARIES APPROVAL AND SINCE THEY HAVE DEMANDED EITHER EXTENSION UNTIL 9. JUNE 1979 OR FULL PAYMENT THEREFORE TO HONOUR OUR UNDERTAKINGS WE CALL GTEE AMOUNT PLEASE CREDIT OUR ACCOUNT WITH YOURSELVES $1,128,245.

United again refused to extend the expiration date notwithstanding Citibank's warning that this cable could be construed as a demand for payment under the letter of credit.

As to letter of credit No. K–312190, scheduled to expire on February 24, 1979, Citibank received a cable from Iranians' in late February which read as follows:

> OUR GUARANTEE IS ON CALL TO BE EXTENDED UP TO MAY 24, 1979 OR PAYMENT TO BE MADE IN FULL STOP PLEASE EITHER EXTEND YOUR CREDIT IN OUR FAVOUR ACCORDINGLY OR CREDIT OUR ACCOUNT WITH YOURSELVES DLRS 142,050.

Citibank contends that this cable was received on February 23; United argues that it was received on February 26. United has refused to agree to any further extension of time as to this letter of credit.

On March 14, 1979, Iranians' informed Citibank by telex that Iranians' had given written assurance to TCI of an extension or payment within a reasonable time on the performance bond and that Citibank's "prompt action" would be appreciated.

DISCUSSION

* * *

II. *The Motion for a Preliminary Injunction*

The standard which governs the issuance of preliminary injunctive relief is well established in this circuit. The movant must show:

* * *

> possible irreparable injury *and* either (1) probable success on the merits *or* (2) sufficiently serious questions going to the merits to make them a fair ground for litigation *and* a balance of hardships tipping decidedly toward the preliminary relief.

Caulfield v. Board of Education, 583 F.2d 605, 610 (2d Cir. 1978); *Triebwasser & Katz v. American Telephone & Telegraph Co.,* 535 F.2d 1356, 1358 (2d Cir. 1976). On the merits, United raises three distinct theories in support of its claim for injunctive relief which will be discussed *seriatim*.

A. *The Merits*

1. *"Fraud in the Transaction"*

A letter of credit is a commitment on the part of the issuing bank that it will pay a draft or demand for payment presented to it under the terms of the credit. United Bank Ltd. v. Cambridge Sporting Goods Corp., 41 N.Y.2d 254, 392 N.Y. S.2d 265, 270, 360 N.E.2d 943 (1976). There are usually three distinct contracts involved in a letter of credit transaction: the contract of the bank with its customer by which it undertakes to issue the letter of credit; the letter of credit itself; and the underlying contract of sale ordinarily between the buyer who has procured the issuance of the letter and the seller who is given the right to present drafts thereunder. Venizelos, S.A. v. Chase Manhattan Bank, 425 F.2d 461, 465 (2d Cir. 1970). In this case, unlike the usual pattern, the seller [United] procured the issuance of the letter as a guarantee of its contractual performance. See Dynamics Corp. of America v. Citizens & Southern National Bank, 356 F.Supp. 991, 996 (N.D.Ga.1973). Moreover, the beneficiary of the letter here is not a party to the sales contract but a foreign bank [Iranians'] which has issued a performance bond as security to the buyer [TCI] for United's contractual performance.

It is axiomatic that the issuing bank's obligations under its letter of credit is independent of its customer's obligations under the contract of sale. "Banks issuing letters of credit deal in documents and not in goods and are not responsible for any breach of warranty or nonconformity of the goods involved in the underlying sales contract." *United Bank, supra,* 392 N.Y.S.2d at 270, 360 N.E.2d at 948. New York's Uniform Commercial Code, which the parties agree is applicable here, nevertheless provides for certain limited circumstances in which the issuing bank may be enjoined by its customer from honoring a demand for payment. UCC § 5–114(2) states in pertinent part:

> (2) Unless otherwise agreed when documents appear on their face to comply with the terms of a credit but a required document . . . is forged or fraudulent or there is fraud in the transaction

> (a) the issuer must honor the draft or demand for payment if honor is demanded by a negotiating bank or other holder of the draft or demand which has taken the draft or demand under the credit and under circumstances which would make it a holder in due course (Section 3–302) . . .; and

> (b) in all other cases as against its customer, an issuer acting in good faith may honor the draft or demand for payment despite notification from the customer of fraud, forgery or other defect not apparent on the face of the documents but a court of appropriate jurisdiction may enjoin such honor.

Citibank contends that it must honor Iranians' demand for payment pursuant to § 5–114 (2) (a) and that this court is powerless to issue an injunction against payment because Iranians' is a "holder in due course." When Iranians' accepted the letter of credit in 1975, Citibank argues, it had no notice of any "fraud in the transaction" or any defense to the underlying contract. UCC § 3–302(1) (c). Under UCC § 3–302(2), a payee on a note may be a holder in due course and, it might be argued, the named beneficiary on a letter of credit should enjoy similar status. UCC § 5–114(2) (a), however, renders the issuing bank's obligation enforceable, and non-enjoinable, only where the holder "of the draft or demand has *taken the draft or demand* under the credit and under circumstances which would make it a holder in due course." This section thus protects one who takes a draft or demand issued pursuant to a letter of credit, rather than the beneficiary of the letter of credit who issues the demand. A letter of credit itself is not a negotiable instrument; thus, Iranians' good faith at the time it accepted the letter would appear irrelevant. At least one commentator has stated that the issuing bank may lawfully refuse honor (and may be enjoined against making payment) if there is "fraud in the transaction" and the party presenting the draft "is the beneficiary or some other party who is not . . . a holder in due course." White & Summers, Uniform Commercial Code, § 18–6 at 624 (1972 ed.).

The question remains whether the statutory standard of "fraud in the transaction" has been established here. The statute is a codification of the landmark case of Sztejn v. Schroder Banking Corp., 177 Misc. 719, 31 N.Y.S.2d 631 (Sup.Ct.1941). In *Sztejn,* the purchaser under a contract of sale sued to enjoin a bank from honoring drafts under a letter of credit issued to secure the purchase price. The complaint alleged that the seller delivered fifty crates of cowhair and rubbish in place of the bristles called for in the contract. Although the court acknowledged the general principle that the issuer's obligation under its letter of credit is independent of the primary contract of sale, it held that the issuer may be restrained from honoring a demand when it has received notice of the seller's "active fraud." 31 N.Y.S.2d at 634. The *Sztejn* case has been recently cited with approval by the New York Court of Appeals which stated that the framers of § 5–114 (2) "eschewed a dogmatic approach and adopted a flexible standard to be applied as the circumstances of a particular situation mandate." *United Bank, supra,* 392 N.Y.S.2d at 271, 360 N.E.2d at 949. The Court of Appeals acknowledged, however, that "[i]t can be difficult to draw a precise line between cases involving breach of warranty (or a difference of opinion as to the quality of goods) and outright fraudulent practice on the part of the seller." *Id.* This court must conclude that on the limited record before it, United has failed to show that fraud rather than a mere dispute as to performance is involved.

United contends that it has fully performed its contracts and has not been informed by TCI of any claim for breach. Of course, TCI is not before the court at this time and the court cannot judge the bona fides of any claim TCI may have on the contracts. The contracts do not contain any deadline by which TCI must determine whether a shipment of tendered cable is non-conforming nor do they limit the time within which TCI must make a claim under its performance bond with Iranians' in the event of United's breach. Even after the date upon which United claims that it made the last delivery of cable called for under the contracts, United agreed to extend the terms of both letters of credit until January 9, 1979 and February 24, 1979 respectively. Although it is not apparent from the record why United acceded to the requests for extensions, it may be inferred that United was, at least, put on notice of the possibility of a claim by TCI under the performance bond with Iranians'. The limited facts available to the court on this record are more indicative of a dispute as to performance than of an outright fraud.

2. *Political Turmoil*

United next contends that payment under the letters of credit should be enjoined on the ground that political unrest in Iran may account for TCI's demand for payment on Iranians' performance bond when the underlying contract has been fully performed. As a matter of substantive law, United argues, New York will suspend the usual obligation of an issuing bank to honor demands for payment on a letter of credit where international political developments hinder economic performance.

Arg.

There is undoubtedly support in the case law for this proposition. Thus, in Nadler v. Mei Loong Corp. of China, 177 Misc. 263, 30 N.Y.S.2d 323 (Sup.Ct.1941), purchasers of fur who had procured the issuance of letters of credit in favor of the New York agent of the Chinese seller brought suit to enjoin the issuing bank from honoring drafts and bills of lading that had been presented to it. The plaintiffs alleged that the fur had not yet arrived and, due to the disruption of Chinese shipping and the American and Japanese embargoes in effect at the time, the bills of lading had been either fraudulent in their inception or that the furs had subsequently been removed from the ships. The New York Supreme Court granted the injunction stating:

> In normal times bills of lading and drafts of the kind in suit cannot be questioned and must be honored; but these are extraordinary times in which ordinary business standards and strict legal rules must be specially examined and perhaps disregarded in the interest of justice and equity. . . . Consider the effect of denying plaintiffs' motion. The trust company could then honor the drafts; the moneys would leave this jurisdiction and the plaintiffs would have neither furs nor money. In any subsequent litigation plaintiffs might bring against the trust company, the latter might well argue that its conduct in paying was approved by the court's denial of this motion. On the other hand, the money is here; the contracts were all made here; the respective rights of all the parties should be determined here, and the plaintiffs should not have to go to China for their furs or their moneys.

30 N.Y.S.2d at 324.

A scant three weeks before *Nadler* was decided, the same court presented with the virtually identical claim denied the requested injunctive relief. In Grob v. Manufacturers Trust Co., 177 Misc. 45, 29 N.Y.S.2d 916 (Sup.Ct.1941), the purchaser of egg yolk powder from a Chinese seller sought to enjoin the bank which had issued letters of credit in the seller's behalf from accepting drafts drawn under the letters. The court acknowledged that the plaintiffs apprehension that the Japanese ships which were likely to issue the bills of lading would fail to bring the powder to the United States was well founded. Nevertheless, the Court denied the motion for injunctive relief.

* * *

These cases reflect two irreconcilable approaches to the same problem: the allocation of risk among the parties to a letter of credit transaction when the uncertainties of events abroad disrupt normal commercial enterprise. * * *

3. *Untimeliness of the Demand*

United's final theory on the merits is that the demands made by Iranians' for payment pursuant to the letters of credit, were untimely. Strict compliance with the terms of a letter of credit must generally be established to create liability on the part of the issuing bank, *Venizelos, S.A., supra,* 425 F.2d at 465; *Dynamics Corp., supra,* 356 F.Supp. at 995; *Sztejn, supra,* 31 N.Y.S.2d at 634, and an untimely demand under the terms of the letter excuses the bank's obligation to honor it. See Banco Tornquist v. American Bank & Trust Co., 71 Misc.2d 874, 337 N.Y.S.2d 489 (1972).

The cable sent by Iranians' to Citibank on December 23, 1978 was somewhat equivocal: Citibank was given the option to pay or to extend the expiration date of letter No. CK–650061. It was not until February 27, 1979 some seven weeks after the expiration of that letter of credit that Iranians' demanded payment in an unconditional manner. Citibank does not contend that the December 23, 1978 cable should be construed to be a substantive request for payment, but that Iranians' was permitted a commercially reasonable period of time past the expiration date of the letter of credit in which to determine that its performance bond in favor of TCI remained outstanding. In light of the civil unrest in Iran during the weeks in question and Iranians' resultant inability to transmit any telexes to Citibank at that time, Citibank argues that this seven week hiatus was not a commercially unreasonable delay.

Citibank, however, points to no provision of the letter of credit agreement which expressly permits Iranians' to wait *any* period of time beyond the specified expiration date in order to notify Citibank. Nor has Citibank shown that the course of dealing between these parties or the usage of the trade is to permit the beneficiary in Iranians' position to delay a reasonable period of time before certifying that the conditions *481 permitting it to draw upon the letter of credit exist. The court must thus conclude that United has shown sufficiently serious questions going to the merits of the issue of timeliness to make it a fair ground for litigation.

B. *Balance of Equities and Possible Irreparable Harm*

In light of Citibank's right of reimbursement from United for amounts disbursed under the letters of credit, this court has little trouble concluding that the equities tip decidedly in United's favor. Citibank's fears that the failure to honor Iranians' demands will subject it to possible recriminations in Iran are wholly speculative. The chance that an Iranian court might fail to recognize this court's injunction against payment and thereby subject

Citibank to liability without the right to reimbursement from United is also conjectural.

A prime requisite for the issuance of preliminary injunctive relief, however, is the existence of possible irreparable harm. Rondeau v. Mosinee Paper Corp., 422 U.S. 49, 57, 95 S.Ct. 2069, 45 L.Ed.2d 12 (1975). An adequate remedy at law exists for United's claim of untimely demand. Although Article 5 of the Uniform Commercial Code does not expressly state a measure of damages for "wrongful honor," damages are nonetheless recoverable against the issuing bank when it honors a demand that fails to conform to the terms of the letter of credit. Interco, Inc. v. First National Bank of Boston, 560 F.2d 480, 484–86 (1st Cir. 1977). United's motion for a preliminary injunction must, therefore, be denied.

* * *

NOTES

1.   Article 5 of the UCC "deals with some but not all of the rules and concepts of letters of credit." UCC § 5–102(3). Precode case law continues to govern where Article 5 is not controlling. See the *United Bank* case, at note 2.

2.   The Iranian letter of credit cases generally involved so-called "suicide" standby letters of credit, where customers and beneficiaries both engaged banks, respectively, to act as bank guarantors of the down payment for an underlying contract, and for performance under the contract. As such, the respective banks also typically had a confirming and advising bank, respectively, for a total of at least four banks in each transaction. For a discussion generally of standby letters of credit and bank guarantees, see Agasha Mugasha, The Law of Letters of Credit and Bank Guarantees at 75, Federation Press (2003).

AMERICAN BELL INTERNATIONAL
V. ISLAMIC REPUBLIC OF IRAN
474 F. Supp. 420 (S.D.N.Y 1979)

* * *

MacMAHON, DISTRICT JUDGE.

Plaintiff American Bell International Inc. ("Bell") moves for a preliminary injunction pursuant to Rule 65(a), Fed.R.Civ.P. and the All Writs Act, 28 U.S.C. § 1651, enjoining defendant Manufacturers Hanover Trust Company ("Manufacturers") from making any payment under its Letter of Credit No. SC 170027 to defendants the Islamic Republic of Iran or Bank Iranshahr or their agents, instrumentalities, successors, employees and assigns. We held an evidentiary hearing and heard oral argument on August 3, 1979. The following facts appear from the evidence presented:

The action arises from the recent revolution in Iran and its impact upon contracts made with the ousted Imperial Government of Iran and upon banking arrangements incident to such contracts. Bell, a wholly-owned subsidiary of American Telephone & Telegraph Co. ("AT & T"), made a contract on July 23, 1978 (the "Contract") with the Imperial Government of Iran Ministry of War ("Imperial Government") to provide consulting services and equipment to the Imperial Government as part of a program to improve Iran's international communications system.

The Contract provides a complex mechanism for payment to Bell totalling approximately $280,000,000, including a down payment of $38,800,000. The Imperial Government had the right to demand return of the down payment at any time. The amount so callable, however, was to be reduced by 20% of the amounts invoiced by Bell to which the Imperial Government did not object. Bell's liability for return of the down payment was reduced by application of this mechanism as the Contract was performed, with the result that approximately $30,200,000 of the down payment now remains callable.

In order to secure the return of the down payment on demand, Bell was required to establish an unconditional and irrevocable Letter of Guaranty, to be issued by Bank Iranshahr in the amount of $38,800,000 in favor of the Imperial Government. The Contract provides that it is to be governed by the laws of Iran and that all disputes arising under it are to be resolved by the Iranian courts.

Beil obtained a Letter of Guaranty from Bank Iranshahr. In turn, as required by Bank Iranshahr, Bell obtained a standby Letter of Credit, No. SC 170027, issued by Manufacturers in favor of Bank Iranshahr in the amount of $38,800,000 to secure reimbursement to Bank Iranshahr should it be required to pay the Imperial Government under its Letter of Guaranty.

The standby Letter of Credit provided for payment by Manufacturers to Bank Iranshahr upon receipt of:

"Your [Bank Iranshahr's] dated statement purportedly signed by an officer indicating name and title or your Tested Telex Reading: (A) 'Referring Manufacturers Hanover Trust Co. Credit No. SC170027, the amount of our claim $represents funds due us as we have received a written request from the Imperial Government of Iran Ministry of War to pay them the sum of under our Guarantee No. issued for the account of American Bell International Inc. covering advance payment under *422 Contract No. 138 dated July 23, 1978 and such payment has been made by us'. . . ."

In the application for the Letter of Credit, Bell agreed guaranteed by AT & T immediately to reimburse Manufacturers for all amounts paid by Manufacturers to Bank Iranshahr pursuant to the Letter of Credit.

Bell commenced performance of its Contract with the Imperial Government. It provided certain services and equipment to update Iran's communications system and submitted a number of invoices, some of which were paid.

In late 1978 and early 1979, Iran was wreaked with revolutionary turmoil culminating in the overthrow of the Iranian government and its replacement by the Islamic Republic. In the wake of this upheaval, Bell was left with substantial unpaid invoices and claims under the Contract and ceased its performance in January 1979. Bell claims that the Contract was breached by the Imperial Government, as well as repudiated by the Islamic Republic, in that it is owed substantial sums for services rendered under the Contract and its termination provisions.

On February 16, 1979, before a demand had been made by Bank Iranshahr for payment under the Letter of Credit, Bell and AT & T brought an action against Manufacturers in the Supreme Court, New York County, seeking a preliminary injunction prohibiting Manufacturers from honoring any demand for payment under the Letter of Credit. The motion for a preliminary injunction was denied in a thorough opinion by Justice Dontzin on March 26, 1979, and the denial was unanimously affirmed on appeal by the Appellate Division, First Department.

On July 25 and 29, 1979, Manufacturers received demands by Tested Telex from Bank Iranshahr for payment of $30,220,724 under the Letter of Credit, the remaining balance of the down payment. Asserting that the demand did not conform with the Letter of Credit, Manufacturers declined payment and so informed Bank Iranshahr. Informed of this, Bell responded by filing this action and an application by way of order to show cause for a temporary restraining order bringing on this motion for a preliminary injunction. Following argument, we granted a temporary restraining order on July 29 enjoining Manufacturers from making any payment to Bank Iranshahr until forty-eight hours after Manufacturers notified Bell of the receipt of a conforming demand, and this order has been extended pending decision of this motion.

On August 1, 1979, Manufacturers notified Bell that it had received a conforming demand from Bank Iranshahr. At the request of the parties, the court held an evidentiary hearing on August 3 on this motion for a preliminary injunction.

Criteria for Preliminary Injunctions

The current criteria in this circuit for determining whether to grant the extraordinary remedy of a preliminary injunction are set forth in

Caulfield v. Board of Education, 583 F.2d 605, 610 (2d Cir. 1978): [citing the three criteria for preliminary injunctions discussed in the United Technologies case, supra.]

* * *

We are not persuaded that the plaintiff has met the criteria and therefore deny the motion.

A. *Irreparable Injury*

Plaintiff has failed to show that irreparable injury may possibly ensue if a preliminary injunction is denied. Bell does not even claim, much less show, that it lacks an adequate remedy at law if Manufacturers makes a payment to Bank Iranshahr in violation of the Letter of Credit. It is too clear for argument that a suit for money damages could be based on any such violation, and surely Manufacturers would be able to pay any money judgment against it.

Bell falls back on a contention that it is without any effective remedy unless it can restrain payment. This contention is based on the fact that it agreed to be bound by the laws of Iran and to submit resolution of any disputes under the Contract to the courts of Iran. Bell claims that it now has no meaningful access to those courts.

There is credible evidence that the Islamic Republic is xenophobic and anti-American and that it has no regard for consulting service contracts such as the one here. Although Bell has made no effort to invoke the aid of the Iranian courts, we think the current situation in Iran, as shown by the evidence, warrants the conclusion that an attempt by Bell to resort to those courts would be futile. *Cf.* Stromberg-Carlson Corp. v. Bank Melli, 467 F.Supp. 530 (Weinfeld, J.) (S.D.N.Y. 1979). However, Bell has not demonstrated that it is without adequate remedy in this court against the Iranian defendants under the Sovereign Immunity Act which it invokes in this very case. 28 U.S.C. §§ 1605(a) (2), 1610(b) (2) (Supp. 1979).

Accordingly, we conclude that Bell has failed to demonstrate irreparable injury.

B. *Probable Success on the Merits*

Even assuming that plaintiff has shown possible irreparable injury, it has failed to show probable success on the merits. Caulfield v. Board of Education, supra, 583 F.2d at 610.

In order to succeed on the merits, Bell must prove, by a preponderance of the evidence, that either (1) a demand for payment of the Manufacturers Letter of Credit conforming to the terms of that Letter has not yet been made, see, *e.g.,* Venizelos, S.A. v. Chase Manhattan Bank, 425 F.2d 461, 465 (2d Cir. 1970); North American Foreign Trading Corp. v. General Electronics Ltd., App.Div., 413 N.Y.S.2d 700 (1st dep't 1979), or (2) a demand, even though in conformity, should not be honored because of fraud in the transaction, see, *e. g.*, N.Y. UCC § 5–114(2); United Bank Ltd. v. Cambridge Sporting Goods Corp., 41 N.Y.2d 254, 392 N.Y.S.2d 265, 360 N.E.2d 943 (1976); Dynamics Corp. v. Citizens & Southern Nat'l Bank, 356 F.Supp. 991 (N.D.Ga.1973). It is not probable, in the sense of a greater than 50% likelihood, that Bell will be able to prove either nonconformity or fraud.

As to nonconformity, the August 1 demand by Bank Iranshahr is identical to the terms of the Manufacturers Letter of Credit in every respect except one: it names as payee the "Government of Iran Ministry of Defense, Successor to the Imperial Government of Iran Ministry of War" rather than the "Imperial Government of Iran Ministry of War." *Compare* defendants' Exhibit A *with* Complaint Exhibit C. It is, of course, a bedrock principle of letter of credit law that a demand must strictly comply with the letter in order to justify payment. See, *e.g.*, Key Appliance, Inc. v. First Nat'l City Bank, 46 A.D.2d 622, 359 N.Y.S.2d 866 (1st dep't 1974), *aff'd*, 37 N.Y.2d 826, 377 N.Y.S.2d 482, 339 N.E.2d 888 (1975). Nevertheless, we deem it less than probable that a court, upon a full trial, would find nonconformity in the instant case.

At the outset, we notice, and the parties agree, that the United States now recognizes the present Government of Iran as the legal successor to the Imperial Government of Iran. That recognition is binding on American Courts. Guaranty Trust Co. v. United States, 304 U.S. 126, 137–38, 58 S.Ct. 785, 82 L.Ed. 1224 (1938). Though we may decide for ourselves the consequences of such recognition upon the litigants in this case, *id.* , we point out that American courts have traditionally viewed contract rights as vesting not in any particular government but in the state of which that government is an agent.

Accordingly, the Government of Iran is the successor to the Imperial Government under the Letter of Guaranty. As legal successor, the Government of Iran may properly demand payment even though the terms of the Letter of Guaranty only provide for payment to the Government of Iran's predecessor, see Pastor v. National Republic Bank, 56 Ill.App.3d 421, 14 Ill.Dec. 74, 371 N.E.2d 1127 (1977), *aff'd,* 76 Ill.2d 139, 28 Ill.Dec. 535, 390 N.E.2d 894 (1979), and a demand for payment under the Letter of Credit reciting that payment has been made by Bank Iranshahr to the new government is sufficient. We are fortified in this conclusion and made confident that a court, upon full trial, would reach the same result by Justice Dontzin's decision in the New York Supreme Court earlier this year that the Government of Iran was the legal successor to the Imperial Government of Iran. See American Bell Int'l, Inc. v. Manufacturers Hanover Trust Co., No. 3157/79 (Sup.Ct. Mar. 26, 1979).

Finally, an opposite answer to the narrow question of conformity would not only elevate form over substance, but would render financial arrangements and undertakings worldwide wholly subject to the vicissitudes of political power. A nonviolent, unanimous transformation of the form of government, or, as this case shows, the mere change of the name of a government agency, would be enough to warrant an issuer's refusal to honor a demand. We cannot suppose such uncertainty and opportunity for chicanery to be the purpose of the requirement of strict conformity.

If conformity is established, as here, the issuer of an irrevocable, unconditional letter of credit, such as Manufacturers normally has an absolute duty to transfer the requisite funds. This duty is wholly independent of the underlying contractual relationship that gives rise to the letter of credit. Shanghai Commercial Bank, Ltd. v. Bank of Boston Int'l, 53 A.D.2d 830, 385 N.Y.S.2d 548 (1st dep't 1976). Nevertheless, both the Uniform Commercial Code of New York, which the parties concede governs here, and the courts state that payment is enjoinable where a germane document is forged or fraudulent or there is "fraud in the transaction." N.Y.U.C.C. § 5–114(2); *United Bank Ltd. v. Cambridge Sporting Goods Corp., supra.* Bell does not contend that any documents are fraudulent by virtue of misstatements or omissions. Instead, it argues there is "fraud in the transaction."

The parties disagree over the scope to be given as a matter of law to the term "transaction." Manufacturers, citing voluminous authorities, argues that the term refers only to the Letter of Credit transaction, not to the underlying commercial transaction or to the totality of dealings among the banks, the Iranian government and Bell. On this view of the law, Bell must fail to establish a probability of success, for it does not claim that the Imperial Government or Bank Iranshahr induced Manufacturers to extend the Letter by lies or half-truths, that the Letter contained any false representations by the Imperial Government or Bank Iranshahr, or that they intended misdeeds with it. Nor does Bell claim that the demand contains any misstatements.

Bell argues, citing equally voluminous authorities, that the term "transaction" refers to the totality of circumstances. On this view, Bell has some chance of success on the merits, for a court can consider Bell's allegations that the Government of Iran's behavior in connection with the consulting contract suffices to make its demand on the Letter of Guaranty fraudulent and that the ensuing demand on the Letter of Credit by Bank Iranshahr is tainted with the fraud.

There is some question whether these divergent understandings of the law are wholly incompatible since it would seem impossible to keep the Letter of Credit transaction conceptually distinct. A demand which facially conforms to the Letter of Credit and which contains no misstatements may, nevertheless, be considered fraudulent if made with the goal of mulcting the party who caused the Letter of Credit to be issued. Be that as it may, we need not decide this thorny issue of law. For, even on the construction most favorable to Bell, we find that success on the merits is not probable. Many of the facts alleged, even if proven, would not constitute fraud. As to others, the proof is insufficient to indicate a probability of success on the merits.

Bell, while never delineating with precision the contours of the purported fraud, sets forth five contentions which, in its view, support the issuance of an injunction. Bell asserts that (1) both the old and new Governments failed to approve invoices for services fully performed; (2) both failed to fund contracted-for independent Letters of Credit in Bell's favor; (3) the new Government has taken steps to renounce altogether its obligations under the Contract; (4) the new Government has made it impossible to assert contract rights in Iranian courts; and (5) the new Government has caused Bank Iranshahr to demand payment on the Manufacturers Letter of Credit, thus asserting rights in a transaction it has otherwise repudiated. Plaintiff's Memorandum (Aug. 2, 1979) at 17–18.

As to contention (4), it is not immediately apparent how denial of Bell's opportunity to assert rights under the Contract makes a demand on an independent letter of credit fraudulent.

Contentions (1), (2), (3) and the latter part of (5) all state essentially the same proposition that the Government of Iran is currently repudiating all its contractual obligations with American companies, including those with Bell. Again, the evidence on this point is uncompelling.

Bell points to (1) an intragovernmental order of July 2, 1979 ordering the termination of Iran's contract with Bell, and (2) hearsay discussions between Bell's president and Iranian officials to the effect that Iran would not pay on the Contract until it had determined whether the services under it had benefited the country. Complaint Exhibit E; Kerts Affidavit ¶ 3. Manufacturers, for its part, points to a public statement in the Wall Street Journal of July 16, 1979, under the name of the present Iranian Government, to the effect that Iran intends to honor all legitimate contracts. Defendant's Exhibit C. Taken together, this evidence does not suggest that Iran has finally and irrevocably decided to repudiate the Bell contract. It suggests equally that Iran is still considering the question whether to perform that contract.

Even if we accept the proposition that the evidence does show repudiation, plaintiff is still far from demonstrating the kind of evil intent necessary to support a claim of fraud. Surely, plaintiff cannot contend that every party who breaches or repudiates his contract is for that reason culpable of fraud. The law of contract damages is adequate to repay the economic harm caused by repudiation, and the law presumes that one who repudiates has done so because of a calculation that such damages are cheaper than performance. Absent any showing that Iran would refuse to pay damages upon a contract action here or in Iran, much less a showing that Bell has even attempted to obtain such a remedy, the evidence is ambivalent as to whether the purported repudiation results from non-fraudulent economic calculation or from fraudulent intent to mulct Bell.

Plaintiff contends that the alleged repudiation, viewed in connection with its demand for payment on the Letter of Credit, supplies the basis from which only one inference fraud can be drawn. Again, we remain unpersuaded.

Plaintiffs argument requires us to presume bad faith on the part of the Iranian government. It requires us further to hold that that government may not rely on the plain terms of the consulting contract and the Letter of Credit arrangements with Bank Iranshahr and Manufacturers providing for immediate repayment of the down payment upon demand, without regard to cause. On the evidence before us, fraud is no more inferable than an economically rational decision by the government to recoup its down payment, as it is entitled to do under the consulting contract and still dispute its liabilities under that Contract.

While fraud in the transaction is doubtless a possibility, plaintiff has not shown it to be a probability and thus fails to satisfy this branch of the *Caulfield* test.

C. *Serious Questions and Balance of Hardships*

If plaintiff fails to demonstrate probable success, he may still obtain relief by showing, in addition to the possibility of irreparable injury, both (1) sufficiently serious questions going to the merits to make them a fair ground for litigation, and (2) a balance of hardships tipping decidedly toward plaintiff. *Caulfield v. Board of Education, supra.* Both Bell and Manufacturers appear to concede the existence of serious questions, and the complexity and novelty of this matter lead us to find they exist. Nevertheless, we hold that plaintiff is not entitled to relief under this branch of the *Caulfield* test because the balance of hardships does not tip *decidedly* toward Bell, if indeed it tips that way at all.

To be sure, Bell faces substantial hardships upon denial of its motion. Should Manufacturers pay the demand, Bell will immediately become liable to Manufacturers for $30.2 million, with no assurance of recouping those funds from Iran for the services performed. While counsel represented in graphic detail the other losses Bell faces at the hands of the current Iranian government, these would flow regardless of whether we ordered the relief sought. The hardship imposed from a denial of relief is limited to the admittedly substantial sum of $30.2 million.

But Manufacturers would face at least as great a loss, and perhaps a greater one, were we to grant relief. Upon Manufacturers' failure to pay, Bank Iranshahr could initiate a suit on the Letter of Credit and attach $30.2 million of Manufacturers' assets in Iran. In addition, it could seek to hold Manufacturers liable for consequential damages beyond that sum resulting from the failure to make timely payment. Finally, there is not guarantee that Bank Iranshahr or the government, in retaliation for Manufacturers' recalcitrance, will not nationalize additional Manufacturers' assets in Iran in amounts which counsel, at oral argument, represented to be far in excess of the amount in controversy here.

Apart from a greater monetary exposure flowing from an adverse decision, Manufacturers faces a loss of credibility in the international banking community that could result from its failure to make good on a letter of credit.

Conclusion

Finally, apart from questions of relative hardship and the specific criteria of the *Caulfield* test, general considerations of equity counsel us to deny the motion for injunctive relief. Bell, a sophisticated multinational enterprise well advised by competent counsel, entered into these arrangements with its corporate eyes open. It knowingly and voluntarily signed a contract allowing the Iranian government to recoup its down payment on demand, without regard to cause. It caused Manufacturers to enter into an arrangement whereby Manufacturers became obligated to pay Bank Iranshahr the unamortized down payment balance upon receipt of conforming documents, again without regard to cause.

Both of these arrangements redounded tangibly to the benefit of Bell. The Contract with Iran, with its prospect of designing and installing from scratch a nationwide and international communications system, was certain to bring to Bell both monetary profit and prestige and good will in the global communications industry. The agreement to indemnify Manufacturers on its Letter of Credit provided the means by which these benefits could be achieved.

One who reaps the rewards of commercial arrangements must also accept their burdens. One such burden in this case, voluntarily accepted by Bell, was the risk that demand might be made without cause on the funds constituting the down payment. To be sure, the sequence of events that led up to that demand may well have been unforeseeable when the contracts were signed. To this extent, both Bell and Manufacturers have been made the unwitting and innocent victims of tumultuous events beyond their control. But, as between two innocents, the party who undertakes by contract the risk of political uncertainty and governmental caprice must bear the consequences when the risk comes home to roost.

* * *

NOTES

1.   How would you compare the rationale in addressing preliminary injunction, respectively, in the *United Technologies* and *American Bell* cases?

2.   In the *American Bell* case, is it fair to say the court was asked by plaintiff to take a strict compliance view of the name of the Iranian government agency it had contracted with prior to the Iranian revolution? Was the plaintiff's motivation in this regard to avoid payment under the letter of credit or avoiding paying multiple parties? If the latter, why was plaintiff unable to prove it met the standards for injunction?

3.   The letter of credit cases arising between U.S. companies and the post-revolution Iranian government involved concerns about whether U.S. companies would be paying the correct party and/or responding to a request for payment from someone with appropriate authority to do so. As such, the case law involved as so-called "notice" injunction cases i.e., where courts granted temporary injunctions—usually 10 days—once a demand on a letter of credit was made. Ostensibly, this gave U.S. companies a limited period of time to seek to authenticate the identity and authority of parties seeking letter of credit payment.

4.   The *American Bell* case, while considered a key case in injunction precedent related to the Iranian cases, is somewhat aberrational insofar as the Iranian government could trigger return of its down payment for essentially no reasons at all as long as it gave notice. In its conclusion, the court derided the plaintiff—and its counsel—for drafting such an open ended agreement.

5.   The *American Bell* court noted that, while relegation of the matter to Iranian courts may have been perceived as futile given anti-American xenophobia in post-revolutionary Iran, the plaintiff may have had recourse to the Foreign Sovereign Immunities Act, codified at 28 U.S.C. §§ 1330, 1332, 1391(f), 1441d and 1602–1611, discussed in the following excerpt:

DAVID J. BEDERMAN, INTERNATIONAL LAW FRAMEWORKS

Foundation Press, Chapter 17 (2001)

* * *

[Discussion of the evolution of the doctrine of Sovereign Immunity]

Beginning after the Second World War—at a time when the role and conception of the State was changing in any event—absolute sovereign immunity came under intense attack. Some European courts began to adopt a "restrictive" form of foreign sovereign immunity, one which did not immunize the commercial activities of foreign governments.[2] The United States began to move towards this position with the 1952 issuance of a State Department opinion on this subject, known as the "Tate Letter." The

---

    [2]   See, *e.g., Drolie v. Republic of 3.* 2G Dept of State Bulletin 984 Czechoslovakia, 1950 Int'l L. Rep. 155 (1952).

letter pragmatically concluded that "the Department feels that the widespread and increasing practice of governments of engaging in commercial activities makes necessary a practice which will enable persons doing business with them to have their rights determined in the courts."

Within a few decades, State practice—as largely reflected in the views of Foreign Ministries and domestic tribunals around the world—had shifted to a theory of restrictive immunity for foreign sovereigns, one which carved-out extensive exceptions to claims of immunization from proceedings in other nations' courts. The socialist and Eastern European nations were the last holdouts for absolute foreign sovereign immunity, not surprising in view of their centrally-planned economies structured around State-run enterprises. With the dismantling of such structures in the 1980's and 1990's those countries also embraced restrictive theories of foreign sovereign immunity.

2. *The U.S Foreign Sovereign Immunities Act of 1976.* To a surprising degree, questions of foreign sovereign immunity remain a problem for customary International law and domestic case law. Attempts to fully codify this subject in multilateral treaties have failed notably. A 1972 European Convention on State Immunity received little attention, and a project by the U.N. International Law Commission (ILC) to draft a comprehensive treaty on this subject has languished in the United Nations. A handful of countries—particularly those from common law traditions— have set-forth the contours of foreign sovereign immunities in statutory form.

The United States adopted such a law in 1976, the Foreign Sovereign Immunities Act (FSIA). The FSIA is an immensely significant statute in many respects. It purports to codify international law on an important subject. It also seeks to convert questions of granting foreign sovereign immunity—which had previously been regarded as matters for political and diplomatic expediency—into judicial and legal questions. Indeed, prior to 1976, the only time that a litigant could initiate a suit against a foreign sovereign in a U.S. court was by first procuring the permission of the State Department. This resulted in threshold proceedings in which State Departmental lawyers would review potential claims, check for potential diplomatic fall-out, and only then grant a "pass" to file suit. The explicit intent of Congress in legislating the FSIA was to largely remove the role of the Executive Branch from these foreign sovereign immunity determinations.

The last point to be considered about the FSIA is that it is a subtle and complex piece of legislation. It has often been criticized by lawyers, judges, and commentators as difficult to understand and apply, and, even after a quarter-century of experience, many problematic issues continue to arise under the Act. If one reads the FSIA and keeps a few basic points in mind, it should become more comprehensible.

The FSIA is the mechanism for gaining jurisdiction over a foreign sovereign, its officials and agents, its political subdivisions and government offices, and its agencies and instrumentalities. Perhaps the most difficult issue raised under the FSIA is whether a particular entity being sued in a U.S. court is even notionally covered under the Act. This is obvious if a plaintiff's complaint lists the "Republic of France" as a defendant, but it becomes more problematic if the entity being sued is a company in which France owns a 51 percent stake (or, even more tenuously, a company owned by a company owned by the French government). Courts have ruled that individuals working within the scope of their employment or official authority with a foreign State may also be covered in some situations.

It is vital to realize that the FSIA is that *exclusive* avenue for gaining jurisdiction over a foreign sovereign entity in a United States court (whether, federal or state). It previously had been suggested that the Alien Tort Claims Act, which gives district courts' jurisdiction over torts in violation of international law, would also extend to foreign sovereigns included as defendants in such suits. In 1989, the U.S. Supreme Court squelched such arguments in a case where and American company complained that Argentina had illegally destroyed its ship during the Falkiands War. The Courts rules that a suit against a foreign sovereign may only be brought under the restrictive rules of the FSIA. This decision has, in large measure, blunted the thrust of much human rights litigation in U.S. courts (discussed in Chapter 9(B)), because such suits can only be initiated against private parties, and not the abusing States themselves.

Once it is clear that a particular defendant is covered by the FSIA (and the foreign sovereign entity bears the burden of proof in this regard), the critical provision is 28 U.S.C 9 1604 which indicates that such an entity is presumptively *immune* from the adjudicatory jurisdiction of U.S. courts, *unless* one of the exceptions to immunity (set forth in section 1605) is satisfied. This effectively means that it is the plaintiff in foreign sovereign immunity cases that carries that burden of showing that a U.S. court has jurisdiction over the matter. If this showing cannot be made, the case is dismissed.

The heart of the FSIA is thus the enumerated exceptions to presumptive foreign sovereign immunity. In rough order of importance they are the commercial activity exception (section 1605(a)(2)), waivers of immunity, (section 1605(a)(1)), tortious acts (section 1605(a)(5)), and the newly-legislated terrorist States exception (1605(a)(7)). These will be discussed in turn. (Other exceptions covering admiralty claims, expropriated property, real property situated in the U.S., and arbitration agreements have less impact and will be discussed only tangentially in the following discussion.)

The commercial activity exception is the most-litigated exclusion of foreign sovereign immunity under the Act, and also one of the most confusingly drafted. In many respects, the key phrase—"commercial activity"—is inadequately defined by the FSIA to mean "either a regular course of commercial conduct or a particular commercial transaction or act. The commercial character of an activity shall be determined by reference to the nature of the course of conduct or particular transaction or act, rather than by reference to its purpose. If this sounds simple, it is not. Just because a particular course of conduct can be engaged-in by a private business party, does not make that same act a "commercial activity". If performed by a foreign sovereign.

* * *

It is not enough, however, to show that a foreign sovereign or instrumentality has engaged in a commercial activity. A plaintiff must also show some connection in a commercial activity. A plaintiff must also show some connection between that activity and the United States. Section 1605(a)(2) allows for a withdrawal of immunity where an

(i) action is based upon a commercial activity carried on in the United States by the foreign state; (ii) or upon an act performed in the United States in connection with a commercial activity of the foreign state elsewhere; (iii) or upon an act outside the territory of the United States in connection with a commercial activity of the foreign state elsewhere and that act causes a direct effect in the United States.

The three "prongs" of the commercial activity exception can be used by plaintiffs singularly or in combination to persuade a court that a foreign sovereign entity had engaged in commercial conduct meriting an exclusion of immunity.

* * *

NOTES

1.   A number of FSIA exceptions give scope to the idea that a foreign sovereign can consent by *waiver* to jurisdiction in U.S. courts. Sometimes this kind of waiver can be manifested in Friendship, Commerce and Navigation (FCN) treaties concluded between the U.S. and other nations, and are encompassed in section 1604's reference to pre-existing international agreements to which the United States is a party. More typically, foreign governments or instrumentalities may consent to the jurisdiction of U.S. courts in forum selection clauses found in contracts or arbitration agreement (contemplated in section 1605(a)(1)). Implied waivers are also possible, but only in very narrow circumstances. If a foreign sovereign enters an appearance

in a U.S. proceeding, without invoking its immunity, that will be taken as a waiver. Furthermore, if that foreign sovereign files a counterclaim in a pending suit (within the meaning of section 1607), that is also a waiver.

* * *

ITEK CORPORATION V. THE FIRST NATIONAL BANK OF BOSTON

United States Court of Appeals
730 F.2d 19 (1984)

BREYER, CIRCUIT JUDGE.

The First National Bank of Boston ("FNBB"), at the request of Itek Corp., issued several letters of credit running in favor of Bank Melli Iran ("Melli"). Melli demanded payment from FNBB of the money that the letters promised. Itek obtained a federal district court injunction (see 12 U.S.C. Sec. 632) prohibiting FNBB from paying Melli, 566 F.Supp. 1210. Melli, the true party in interest, appeals. The basic question that Melli's appeal presents is whether its effort to obtain the money by calling the letters is "fraudulent." We find the district court's affirmative answer to this question adequately supported. And we therefore affirm its decision to issue the injunction.

The following, somewhat simplified, account provides the necessary factual background:

> a. The basic contract. The letters of credit arise out of promises made in a 1977 contract between Itek and Iran's Imperial Ministry of War. The contract provided that Itek would make and sell high-technology optical equipment to the War Ministry at a price of $22.5 million. Iran was to make a twenty percent down payment ($4.5 million). It would pay Itek sixty percent of the total price ($13.5 million) as work progressed; it would pay the remaining forty percent upon satisfactory completion. The down payment amount would be deducted gradually from the payments due under Itek's "work-in-progress" invoices. See Contract, Appendix 3, paragraphs 1.1, 1.4.

> b. The contract's bank guarantees. The contract required Itek to provide two types of bank guarantees. The first, the "down payment" guarantee, was for $4.5 million, the amount of the down payment. Its object apparently was to give the Ministry the right to obtain return of the down payment (or portions of the down payment) until Itek produced work of sufficient value to have "earned" the down payment. The second, the "good performance" guarantee was for $2.25 million, ten percent of the contract price. Its object was to protect the Ministry against a breach of contract

as might occur, for example, if the goods produced were defective. These guarantees were to be issued in favor of the Ministry by an approved Iranian bank. The Ministry could call for payment under the guarantees simply by submitting a written request for payment to the bank.

Bank Melli, an instrumentality of the Iranian government, issued the guarantees in the form of five "guarantee letters." One letter was for $2.25 million; it backed "good performance." The other four letters were each for $1,125 million; they backed the down payment. Melli, as a condition for issuing them, required Itek to provide it with five similar "standby" letters of credit, issued by an American bank in Melli's favor, and payable on Melli's certification that the Ministry had required it to pay under its letters to the Ministry. The "standby" letters are the FNBB letters at issue here.

      c.   The contract's procedures for cancelling the guarantees. The contract contains specified procedures and conditions governing the termination of the guarantees. It states that the Ministry is to release "down payment" guarantees "within 4 weeks after the clearance of down-payments amount." Contract p 9.5. It states that the Ministry is to release the "good performance" guarantee four weeks after its final acceptance of the goods.

The contract provided for another circumstance, directly relevant here, under which the Ministry was to release the "good performance" guarantee. If the contract "is cancelled due to Force Majeure . . ., all Bank Guarantees of good performance of work will be immediately released." Contract p 9.4. The contract defines "Force Majeure" to include cancellation by the United States of necessary export licenses. If force majeure occurs—if, for example, there is a war or a natural disaster, or if the United States cancels the export license—either party can cancel the contract. A party can cancel the contract on this basis, however, only if it has notified the other party of the occurrence of force majeure, the parties have been unable to agree to some resolution of the force majeure difficulty, and three months have passed since notification. The contract also stipulates that, if force majeure leads to cancellation of the contract, Itek will be paid for equipment shipped, for equipment then being manufactured, and for all services rendered to date.

The guarantee letters and the letters of credit backing them had various expiration dates. But both provided for extension upon the request of their respective beneficiaries. And some of them were apparently extended as their expiration dates approached, so that they would remain valid until the completion of the work they guaranteed. The standby letters of credit stated that they were extendable on request and that, if the issuer was "unwilling to extend" a letter, it became immediately payable. See, e.g., Record App. at 31.

    d.   The circumstances of cancellation. Itek's work proceeded uneventfully until Iran's government collapsed in early 1979. At that time Itek's performance was ahead of schedule, but it had not yet delivered any equipment to Iran. By February 1979, Itek had billed Iran for more than $20 million. It had received the original down payment of $4.5 million and additional payments of $6.6 million—a total of $11.1 million. Iran had consequently released the down payment guarantees to the point where there remained outstanding but one full down payment letter in the amount of $1,125 million and one partial down payment letter in the amount of $70,753.

The change of government in Iran, however, brought with it a deterioration in Iranian/American relations. In April 1979 the United States suspended Itek's export license. In May Itek notified Iran's new Ministry of National Defense about this "force majeure" problem, and, in accordance with the contract's terms, it called for consultations. These took place in Iran in August. Subsequently Itek applied for renewal of the suspended export license.

* * *

    e.   The court proceedings. In January 1980, before Itek cancelled the contract, it brought this suit against FNBB seeking an order requiring FNBB to tell it if Melli tried to call the letters and then to delay for several days before paying. The district court granted this order on January 19. On March 11, after Itek cancelled the contract, it asked the court to enjoin FNBB from honoring any call on the letters. The court granted a temporary restraining order. Itek then joined Melli as a defendant. In April 1981, after hearings and fact finding, the court entered a preliminary injunction forbidding FNBB to pay Melli. It accompanied the injunction with extensive findings of fact and a published opinion. Itek Corp. v. First National Bank of Boston, 511 F.Supp. 1341 (D.Mass.1981). A year later, in May 1982, it made the injunction permanent. We had to vacate the permanent injunction, however, because of a change in Treasury Department regulations that had the effect of preventing American courts from entering final judgments in Iranian letter of credit cases. Itek Corp. v. First National Bank of Boston, 704 F.2d 1 (1st Cir.1983). The district court then reinstated its preliminary injunction; and Bank Melli now appeals that decision.

Melli raises two sets of arguments. First, it claims that Itek has not shown the "irreparable harm" requisite to the award of an injunction. Second, it claims that Itek has not shown the "fraud" here necessary to stop a beneficiary from calling a letter of credit. The record before us supports the district court's rejection of these arguments. See Massachusetts Association of Older Americans v. Sharp, 700 F.2d 749, 751–52 (1st Cir.1983); National Tank Truck Carriers, Inc. v. Burke, 608 F.2d 819, 823 (1st Cir.1979).

II   Irreparable Harm

Itek and Melli are fighting over money. To allow Melli to call the letters of credit will put the money in Melli's—and ultimately in the Iranian Ministry of Defense's—hands and require Itek to sue to recover it. Itek's harm is "irreparable" and warrants an injunction only if Itek has no adequate remedy at law to reclaim money in the Ministry's hands that rightfully belongs to Itek. See Rockwell International Systems, Inc. v. Citibank, N.A., 719 F.2d 583, 586 (2d Cir. 1983); Inter co, Inc. v. First National Bank of Boston, 560 F.2d 480, 484–85 (1st Cir.1977).

The contract provides a remedy at law. It provides that Itek can sue the Ministry to resolve disputes under the contract. But it stipulates that any such disputes shall be decided in Iran's courts applying the law of Iran. The recent history of relations between Iran and the United States indicates that this remedy is inadequate. Itek's efforts to recover money that Itek is legally owed through the Iranian courts would be futile. The district court found as much. Other courts have ruled similarly. See, e.g., Rockwell International Systems, Inc. v. Citibank, N.A., 719 F.2d at 587–88; Harris Corp. v. National Iranian Radio & Television, 691 F.2d 1344, 1356–57 (11th Cir.1982). And Melli does not disagree.

The Iranian-American Hostage Agreements may have provided Itek with another remedy. An American firm can ask the Iran-United States Claims Tribunal (established under the Agreements) to adjudicate a dispute between it and Iran. This legal remedy is presently inadequate, however, for Itek missed the filing deadline of January 1982. See Declaration of the Government of the Democratic and Popular Republic of Algeria Concerning the Settlement of Claims by the Government of the United States of America and the Government of the Islamic Republic of Iran, Art. III, p 4, (Jan. 19, 1981), reprinted in Dep't St. Bull., Feb. 1981, at 3, 4. Thus, if the letter of credit money belongs to Itek but is given to Melli, Itek now seems without any adequate legal method to recover it.

Melli argues that the Claims Tribunal route—though now inadequate—formerly was adequate. Itek might have applied to the tribunal before January 1982. Itek should not, in Melli's view, obtain relief from a court of equity when Itek itself placed an alternative adequate remedy beyond its power to invoke. See Commissioner v. Shapiro, 424 U.S. 614, 634 n. 15, 96 S.Ct. 1062, 1074 n. 15, 47 L.Ed.2d 278 (1976); Laino v. United States, 633 F.2d 626, 629–30 (2d Cir.1980).

The fatal flaw in this argument, however, rests in the district court's finding that Itek was not unreasonable in failing to invoke the Claims

Tribunal's jurisdiction before January 1982. Before that time Itek might reasonably have concluded that the Tribunal lacked jurisdiction. The Tribunal's mandate stated that it could not hear claims arising under a binding contract between the parties specifically providing that any disputes thereunder shall be within the sole jurisdiction of the competent Iranian courts. . . .

Declaration, supra, at Art. II, p 1. The Itek-Ministry contract appears to fit within this jurisdictional bar. At the very least, this language rendered the availability of the Tribunal uncertain. And that uncertainty prevents the Tribunal from standing as an obstacle to injunctive relief. See Rockwell International Systems, Inc. v. Citibank, N.A., 719 F.2d at 586–87; cf. General Electric Co. v. Callahan, 294 F.2d 60, 64 (1st Cir.1961) (availability of remedy at law must be "clear"), cert, dismissed, 369 U.S. 832, 82 S.Ct. 851, 7 L.Ed.2d 840 (1962).

Melli replies that a Tribunal case, Ford Aerospace & Communications Corp. v. Air Force of the Islamic Republic of Iran, Case No. 159 (Iran-U.S. Claims Tribunal, Nov, 5, 1982), interprets the jurisdictional bar so narrowly that in fact the contract's "Iranian court" language would not have deprived the Tribunal of jurisdiction. This Tribunal case, however, was decided in November 1982, nearly ten months after the January 1982 filing deadline. The record supports the district court's conclusion that the November 1982 interpretation was far from obvious ten months earlier. See Itek Corp. v. First National Bank of Boston, 511 F.Supp. at 1349 n. 17; see also Itek Corp. v. First National Bank of Boston, 704 F.2d at 11 n. 9 (noting that Tribunal had appeared to lack jurisdiction, before Ford Aerospace decision). Thus, we accept its conclusion that the Tribunal remedy reasonably appeared inadequate before January 1982 and plainly was inadequate after January 1982. We need not consider the other problems Itek raises about the adequacy of a Tribunal remedy, for this jurisdictional problem alone sufficiently spoils this "alternative" legal route. There is sufficient risk that, without an injunction, Itek would be without means to recover its money from the Ministry to warrant a finding of "irreparable harm." That is to say, if Itek is otherwise entitled to the injunction, there is no "alternative legal remedy" that would bar a court from issuing the injunction.

III Fraud

The basic legal question in this case is whether the circumstances surrounding Melli's calls on FNBB's letters of credit establish "fraud in the transaction" within the meaning of this U.C.C. provision.

We answer this question fully aware of the need to interpret the "fraud" provision narrowly. The very object of a letter of credit is to provide a near foolproof method of placing money in its beneficiary's hands when he complies with the terms contained in the letter itself—when he presents, for example, a shipping document that the letter calls for or (as here) a simple written demand for payment. Parties to a contract may use a letter of credit in order to make certain that contractual disputes wend their way towards resolution with money in the beneficiary's pocket rather than in the pocket of the contracting party. * * *

Thus, courts typically have asserted that such letters of credit are "independent" of the underlying contract. See, e.g., Pringle-Associated Mortgage Corp. v. Southern National Bank, 571 F.2d 871 (5th Cir.1978); Venizelos, S.A. v. Chase Manhattan Bank, 425 F.2d 461, 464–65 (2d Cir.1970); Intraworld Industries, Inc. v. Girard Trust Bank, 461 Pa. 343, 336 A.2d 316, 323–24 (1975); see also U.C.C. Sec. 5–114(1); Note, "Fraud in the Transaction:" Enjoining Letters of Credit During the Iranian Revolution, 93 Harv.L.Rev. 992, 1001 (1980). And they have recognized that examining the rights and wrongs of a contract dispute to determine whether a letter of credit should be paid risks depriving its beneficiary of the very advantage for which he bargained, namely that the dispute would be resolved while he is in possession of the money. See, e.g., KMW International v. Chase Manhattan Bank, N.A., 606 F.2d 10, 15–17 (2d Cir.1979); Note, "Fraud in the Transaction", supra, at 1008–09; Note, Letters of Credit: Injunction as a Remedy for Fraud in U.C.C. Section 5– 114, 63 Minn.L.Rev. 487, 489–90 (1979).

Despite these reasons for hesitating to enjoin payment of a letter of credit, the need for an exception is apparent. Suppose the document for which a letter calls has been forged. Or suppose that the beneficiary has knowingly failed to comply with an important term contained in the underlying contract—a term that the parties intended as a precondition for the beneficiary's exercise of his right to call the letter. Courts have not hesitated to examine the documents that the letter calls for to see if they show fraud. See, e.g., Harris Corp. v. National Iranian Radio & Television, 691 F.2d at 1355–56; Shaffer v. Brooklyn Park Garden Apartments, 311 Minn. 452, 250 N.W.2d 172, 180–81 (1977); cf. Banco Espanol de Credito v. State Street Bank & Trust Co., 409 F.2d 711 (1st Cir.1969). And courts have also enjoined payment where there was relevant fraud in the underlying transaction. Thus, in a leading case, a seller, contractually committed to ship bristles to a buyer, shipped rubbish instead. The court refused to allow the seller to call the letter, put the money in his pocket, and let the buyer sue him, for in the court's view, the seller did not even have a colorable claim that he had done what the contract called for as a precondition to obtaining the money, namely, ship the bristles. Sztejn v. J. Henry Schroder Banking Corp., 177 Misc. 719, 31 N.Y.S.2d 631 (Sup.Ct. 1941).

The Uniform Commercial Code provision here at issue embodies this "fraud" exception. The exception recognizes the unfairness of allowing a beneficiary to call a letter of credit under circumstances where the underlying contract plainly shows that he is not to do so. See, e.g., Dynamics Corp. of America v. Citizens & Southern National Bank, 356 F.Supp. 991 (N.D.Ga.1973); United Bank Ltd. v. Cambridge Sporting Goods Corp., 41 N.Y.2d 254, 360 N.E.2d 943, 392 N.Y.S.2d 265 (1976); O'Grady v. First Union National Bank, 296 N.C. 212, 250 S.E.2d 587, 598–602 (1978). Yet, it also recognizes the need for courts to tread with care lest they deprive the letter's beneficiary of the very benefit for which he bargained. Thus, courts have stated that the "fraud in the transaction" exception is available only where the beneficiary's conduct has "so vitiated the entire transaction that the legitimate purposes of the independence of the issuer's obligation would no longer be served." Roman Ceramics Corp. v. Peoples National Bank, 714 F.2d 1207, 1212 n. 12, 1215 (3d Cir.1983) (quoting Intraworld Industries, Inc. v. Girard Trust Bank, 461 Pa. at 359, 336 A.2d at 324–25 (1975)); see also Comment, Enjoining the International Standby Letter of Credit: The Iranian Letter of Credit Cases, 21 Harv.Intl.L. J. 189, 241–43 (1980) (focus should be on parties' original allocation of risks and responsibilities).

In applying these principles to this case, we assume that Melli presented to FNBB the simple document (a written request asserting that the Ministry had required Melli to pay the associated guarantee letters) that the letters called for. We also assume that at least one purpose of the parties in arranging for the letters was to give the Ministry control of the money during the pendency of underlying contractual disputes. We take as a given that the parties intended the contract's express terms concerning the guarantees to govern the Ministry's right to call the letters from Melli to the Ministry. (The parties do not dispute this point.) And we take as given that these same contract terms limit the rights of Melli to call the FNBB letters; Melli could only legitimately call the FNBB letters if the Ministry had legitimately called the Melli guarantees. (The parties do not dispute this point either, perhaps because, as the district court found, see 511 F.Supp. at 1350–51, Melli and the Ministry are both part of, or owned by, Iran's government, and they were equally aware of the relevant events. See Touche Ross & Co. v. Manufacturers Hanover Trust Co., 107 Misc.2d 438, 434 N.Y.S.2d 575 (Sup.Ct. 1980), aff'd mem., 86 App.Div.2d 990, 449 N.Y.S.2d 125 (1982).) We conclude that the issue before us is whether, given the terms of the contract, the Ministry and in turn Melli have a colorable right to call the "guarantees," or whether Itek has successfully shown that, in light of the contractual terms governing the guarantees, the beneficiaries' demands for payment have "absolutely no basis in fact." See Dynamics Corp. of America v. Citizen's & Southern Bank, 356 F.Supp. at 999; see also Harris Corp. v. National Iranian Radio & Television, supra; United Technologies Corp. v. Citibank, N.A., 469 F.Supp. 473 (S.D.N.Y.1979). If Melli has no plausible or colorable basis under the contract to call for payment of the letters, its effort to obtain the money is fraudulent and payment can be enjoined. The district court found that Itek had met this standard and shown fraud. Opinion of June 28, 1983, at 17–18 (finding likelihood of success); Opinion of May 25, 1982, at 9–10 (finding success on merits). We agree.

* * *

QUESTIONS AND NOTES

1.   In KMW International v. Chase Manhattan Bank, NA, 606 F.2d 10 (2d Cir. 1979), the court held that preliminary injunctive relief was inappropriate. In the *KMW* case the relief requested was essentially declaratory; no demands had been made on the letters of credit and any future damage was, at that time, "purely conjectural." The court also found that allegations regarding the then "unsettled situation in Iran" were insufficient to justify an injunction. Other courts were willing to grant "a more limited form of relief," in the form of a notice requirement which would allow the plaintiff "to provide evidence of fraud or to take such other action" as might be appropriate in the event of a call. See also Rockwell International Systems v. Citibank, NA, 719 F.2d 583 (1983) where the court viewed fraud as a likely problem).

2.   The Iranian letter of credit cases were identified early on as an interesting case study in this area. See "Fraud in the Transaction" Enjoining Letters of Credit During the Iranian Revolution, 93 Harv. L. Rev. 5 May (1980).

3.   Multiple Choice Questions:

a.   The purpose of the letter of credit is to facilitate trade, typically international trade, by substituting the known credit worthiness of a bank for the buyer, which may be unknown to the seller. a) True or b) False.

b.   The three parties to a conventional letter of credit are: the issuer of the letter of credit (typically a bank), the issuer's customer (typically a buyer of goods), and the beneficiary of the letter of credit (the seller of goods). a) True or b) False.

c.   Under the holding in the *Marine Midland* case, a bank issuing a letter of credit should: a) be very familiar with the particular customs of truckers in South America; b) not read the terms of a letter of credit it issues literally; c) refer disgruntled beneficiaries to the *American Bell* case; or d) be aware that issuers are not held accountable for commercial and trade usage of terms particular to the shipping of goods involved in a letter of credit.

d.   In determining document conformity in letters of credit, some courts apply the "strict compliance" standard, which contemplates that an issuing bank: a) perform a comprehensive review of the underlying contract; b) research letter of credit case law; c) perform clerical functions only by comparing the presented documents with those called for in the letter of credit; or d) assess the commercial impact of a discrepancy in the documents.

e.   Under the holding in the *American Bell* case decision, a U.S. computer company which has entered into a letter of credit in connection with the sale of computers to the national government of the nation of Backwardia is unlikely to get a preliminary injunction against performance by the issuing bank under the letter of credit solely by proving to a U.S. federal court that resort to the courts of Backwardia would be futile. a) True orb) False.

f.   As issuers of letters of credit, banks are primarily held accountable for understanding: a) commercial and trade usage of terms particular to the goods involved; b) bill of lading contract practices; or c) knowledge of banking industry practices.

g.   In a letter of credit transaction, a party may: a) intentionally waive the right to receive perfectly conforming documents; b) lose the right to assert objections to the documents that it did not assert promptly; or c) all of the above.

h.   As legal counsel to a company that has entered into a contract with a construction company to build an office building in a foreign country, you would be most concerned about the following relating to a standby letter of credit entered into by the construction company in connection with its performance on the project: a) was it in the primary language of the home country; b) does it comply with the Basel Concordats; c) does it provide an objective standard of documentary evidence for the issuing bank to pay out in the event the construction company fails to perform; or d) a and b only.

i.   In the *Alaska Textile Co.* case, the U.S. Court of Appeals found that the consequences of an issuer's untimely action on a beneficiary's demand for payments are significantly different under Section 5 of the Uniform Commercial Code and Section 14 of the Uniform Customs and Practice standards. a) True or b) False.

j.   Under the holdings in the *United Bank* and *Siderius* cases, a court may enjoin performance of a letter of credit if: a) only where there has been a breach of the underlying sales contract; b) the buyer under the underlying contract has been defrauded; c) the parties seeking performance are not holders in due course; d) it is proven that certain documentary evidence has been fabricated, i.e., fraudulent; or e) b, c and d.

CHAPTER 3

INTERNATIONAL BANK
LOAN SYNDICATIONS

■ ■ ■

1. INTRODUCTION

This Chapter explores the legal and bank regulatory issues associated with international bank loan syndications. A new development in the late 1970s, the use of syndicated loans has emerged over the last 30 years as a primary international business funding transaction, and a major source of large project financing. Further, there has been a recent marked increase in non-bank financial organizations and corporate entities participating in this lending market.

The Chapter will explore the development, structure and implications of syndicated loan transactions. The chapter will also analyze the business and legal differences between loan syndication and participation agreements. In cases where syndicated borrowers default on loans, case law developments establish liability favoring so-called "participating" banks in such transactions—and defenses for so-called "lead" banks— under emerging theories implicating the disclosure requirements of the securities laws to loan syndications, as well as the regulatory issues associated with so-called "leveraged" lending syndications.

JONATHAN JONES, WILLIAM W. LANG, AND PETER NIGRO,
OCC ECONOMICS WORKING PAPER 2000–10,
RECENT TRENDS IN BANK LOAN SYNDICATIONS
Office of the Comptroller of the Currency (December 2000)

* * *

1. Introduction

Syndicated loans increasingly have become the financing choice of large firms. As a result, syndicated lending has become a major component of today's financial landscape. Syndicated loan commitments totaled $1.05 trillion in 1999, and syndicated lending now represents approximately 51 percent of new corporate financing, generating more underwriting revenue than either the equity or bond market.[2] Perhaps more importantly, the

---

[2]   See "The Biggest Secret of Wall Street," PaineWebber Equity Research, May 1999.

leveraged lending component of the syndicated loan market has been growing rapidly, as commercial borrowers have increasingly displayed a preference for leveraged borrowing over junk bond financing.[3]

A loan syndicate is a group of banks that jointly makes or underwrites a loan to a single borrower. Loan syndicates are led typically by an agent bank that initially underwrites the credit, and finds participants willing to purchase shares of the credit and to share the associated pro rata losses. The shift towards syndicated lending over other forms of financing can be attributed to the fact that the syndicated loan market combines some of the best features of both commercial and investment banking. First, syndicated loans, like other types of bank loans, can be of any maturity, possess numerous covenants, and most importantly, provide the flexibility of changing and renegotiating contract features during the life of the loan.[4] Similar to public debt contracts, however, syndicated loans are typically longer term, possess loose covenants, and are rarely restructured.[5]

* * *

The syndicated loan market has gradually been developing qualities typically exhibited by public capital markets. This progression is most readily apparent in the individual loan ratings assigned by both Moody's and Standard and Poor's (S&P). These ratings were initiated in 1995, and during the past five years, corporations have actively solicited and paid for loan ratings, which has greatly enhanced their liquidity.

* * *

Banks are benefiting from this broadening of the syndicated loan market and the increased ability to sell and securitize syndications in a number of ways. Loan syndications are a costeffective method for participating banks to achieve diversification in their banking books and to exploit any funding advantages relative to agent banks.[9] Syndicated lending also allows banks to compete more effectively with public debt markets for corporate borrowers. To a considerable extent, the development of the loan syndication market has stemmed, if not reversed, the trend toward "disintermediation" of corporate debt.[10] Finally, the

---

[3]   The Loan Pricing Corporation defines leveraged loans as those with all-in-drawn pricing of the London interbank offered rate (Libor) plus 125 basis points or more, and highly leveraged loans as those with all-in-drawn spreads in excess of (Libor) plus 250 basis points. These loans are the high-risk portion of the market and are typically senior-secured. Libor-based floating rate, quarterly coupon instruments that typically have strong covenant and collateral protection.

[4]   See "Leveraged Loans: The Plot Thickens," Bank of America Securities Syndicated Finance Research, November 1999.

[5]   The Characteristics of the public debt markets have been examined in Berlin and Mester (1992) and Rajan and Winton (1995).

[9]   Pennachi (1988) argues that loan purchasers may have funding advantages relative to some originators.

[10]   Of course, this is accomplished by reducing the differences between intermediated and public debt markets.

syndicated loan market enables agent banks to leverage their expertise in loan origination and fee collection for structuring, distributing, and servicing the larger credits that are part of Shared National Credit (SNC) program. At the same time, agent banks shed much of the credit risk, thus providing a mechanism to manage interest rate risk and avoid current capital requirements on loans held in portfolio.

Besides the benefits of syndications, however, there are also costs. One of these costs is the increased portfolio credit risk that participant banks might mistakenly assume if an agent bank does not disclose all relevant credit information about particular borrowers to syndicate members.

* * *

For junior banks, participating in a syndicated loan may be advantageous for several reasons. These banks may be motivated by a lack of origination capability in certain types of transactions, geographical areas or industrial sectors, or indeed a desire to cut down on origination costs. While junior participating banks typically earn just a margin and no fees, they may also hope that in return for their involvement, the client will reward them later with more profitable business, such as treasury management, corporate finance or advisory work * * * .[7]

* * *

2. ARRANGER LIABILITY

IN RE COLOCOTRONIS TANKER SECURITIES LITIGATION

Judicial Panel on Multidistrict Litigation
420 F.Supp. 998 (S.D.N.Y. 1976)

OPINION AND ORDER

PER CURIAM.

This litigation involves six actions pending in three districts: three in the Southern District of New York, two in the Eastern District of Pennsylvania and one in the Southern District of Texas. These actions arise from the default on loans made by European-American Banking Corporation to a number of companies engaged in the charter-hire of oil tankers. Each company operated one tanker, and the companies were jointly managed by the Colocotronis family. The plaintiff in each action is a bank that extended funds as a participant in European-American's loans to the Colocotronis companies. Five of the six plaintiffs were involved in loans to two or more of the borrowers.

---

[7] In practice, though, these rewards fail to materialise in a systematic manner. Indeed, anecdotal evidence for the United States suggests that, for this reason, smaller players have withdrawn from the market lately and have stopped extending syndicated loans as a loss-leader.

The actions basically allege that European-American violated various federal and state securities laws by false and misleading representations and omissions of material facts in connection with sales of the loan participations. In addition, each action charges European-American with common law fraud and breach of common law fiduciary duties allegedly owed to plaintiffs with regard to the participations. European-American is a defendant in all six actions and is the sole defendant in five of them. One of the New York actions also includes as a defendant Deutsche Bank, a German banking institution that owns approximately twenty percent of the stock of European-American. This action alleges that Deutsche Bank conspired with and aided and abetted European-American in violating federal and state securities statutes and additionally seeks to hold Deutsche Bank liable by virtue of its alleged control over European-American.

* * *

IN RE COLOCOTRONIS TANKER SECURITIES LITIGATION
449 F.Supp. 828 (S.D.N.Y. 1978)

TENNEY, DISTRICT JUDGE.

At the center of this litigation is a series of transactions in which EABC entered into loans with the Colocotronis group of shipping companies and then established agreements whereby the various plaintiff banks took "participations" in these loans. The loans began in 1972; by late-1975 it became apparent that the financial condition of the Colocotronis group was deteriorating. Thus, in December 1975 there began the "workout," an attempt, which continues to this day, to salvage as much as possible from the loans. The workout was discussed in a series of meetings which began on December 16, 1975 and were attended by the participant banks. By May 1976 several of the banks had concluded that they had grounds for legal action against EABC; the first action was filed on May 7, 1976, and six more ultimately followed, one of which has been settled.

U.S. OFFICE OF THE COMPTROLLER OF THE CURRENCY BANKING CIRCULAR
181 (August 7, 1984)

* * *

SUMMARY

The purchase of loans and participations in loans may constitute an unsafe or unsound banking practice in the absence of satisfactory documentation, credit analysis, and other controls over risk.

* * *

SCOPE

This Circular describes prudent purchases of loans and loan participations. A participation, as distinguished from a multibank loan transaction (syndicated loan),[1] is an arrangement in which a bank makes a loan to a borrower and then sells all or a portion of that loan to a purchasing bank.[2] All documentation of the loan is drafted in the name of the selling bank. Generally, the purchasing bank's share of the participated loan is evidenced by a certificate which assigns an interest in the loan and any related collateral.

BACKGROUND

The purchase and sale of loans and participation in loans are established banking practices. These transactions serve legitimate needs of the buying and selling banks and the public interest. However, recent abuses have highlighted the need for the Office to remind banks of prudent banking practices for these transactions.

POLICY

The absence of satisfactory controls over risk may constitute an unsafe or unsound banking practice and thus cause for the OCC to seek appropriate corrective action through its administrative remedies. Satisfactory controls over the purchase of loans and participations in loans ordinarily include, but are not limited to, the following:

- written lending policies and procedures governing these transactions;

- an independent analysis of credit quality by the purchasing bank;

- agreement by the obligor to make full credit information available to the selling bank;

- agreement by the selling bank to provide available information on the obligor to the purchaser; and

- written documentation of recourse arrangements outlining the rights and obligations of each party.

---

[1]   This Circular was drafted to address safety and soundness concerns arising from the purchase of loans and participations in loans. Nevertheless, the practices outlined in this Circular are illustrative of those principles of prudent banking which generally apply to any multibank lending transaction. For example, a prudent member of a loan syndication would obtain full and timely credit information to conduct an informed and independent analysis of the credit in a manner consistent with its formal lending policies and procedures.

[2]   For the purposes of this Circular, a "loan" includes any binding agreement to advance funds on the basis of an obligation to repay the funds.

NOTES

1. Like public debt markets, syndicated lenders have found it advantageous not only to participate, but also to sell or securitize highly leveraged syndicated loans, in order to satisfy a growing institutional demand for the risk/return profile of these investments. More than 140 institutional investors bought leveraged syndicated loans by year-end 1999, as compared to only 20 institutional investors in 1993. See David Weidner, "Syndicated Loans Gaining Leverage on Junk Bonds," American Banker, February 11, 2000. These nonbank investors typically purchase a different tranche of the credit than their bank counterparts. The primary distinction between the tranches involves differences in spread, fees, and maturity. The institutional tranche is typically back-end loaded, which permits bank lenders to continue to specialize in loan monitoring early in the life cycle of the credits when it is most vital. Most importantly, however, the tranches are pari-passu in the case of restructuring and default, which greatly reduces any strategic motivations on the part of participants that may occur during the default or restructuring process. *Id.*

2. The information asymmetry between agent banks and syndicate members could allow agent banks to engage in opportunistic behavior, such that they would retain a larger share of high-quality loans and a smaller share of low-quality loans than would be retained if there were no information asymmetries. Banks that engage in this type of behavior, however, may suffer from some form of reputation risk that would impede their ability to do this on a long-term basis, and legal risk.

IFE FUND SA v. GOLDMAN SACHS INTERNATIONAL

U.K. High Court of Justice
EWHC 2887 (Com Ct.)
(21 November 2006)

THE HON. MR. JUSTICE TOULSON.

* * *

2. IFE claims damages for its loss on the transaction against Goldman Sachs on the grounds of misrepresentation, pursuant to section 2(1) of the Misrepresentation Act 1967, and negligence. The claim in negligence is put in alternative ways, either negligent misstatement or breach of a duty of care to inform. The essence of IFE's complaint is that it was induced to enter into the transaction by information provided by Goldman Sachs, which presented a picture that was in fact misleading and which was not corrected or qualified after Goldman Sachs had cause to doubt its reliability as a result of receiving two reports (dated 19 and 26 May 2000) from investigating accountants, Arthur Andersen. At the outset of the case Mr Nash QC made it plain that no allegation of dishonesty was made against Goldman Sachs or any of its employees.

3.   Goldman Sachs's grounds of defence to the claim under the Misrepresentation Act are in summary as follows:

1) It did not make the pleaded representations;

2) If it did, such representations were confined to Goldman Sachs's state of knowledge at the time when they were made and did not give rise to any duty to disclose information subsequently acquired by it;

* * *

48. In summary Mr Nash submitted that by issuing the SIM [Syndicate Information Memorandum] and procuring that the Arthur Andersen reports were sent to IFE for the purpose of enabling IFE to consider whether to take part in the syndication, Goldman Sachs impliedly represented that it knew nothing which showed that the information in the SIM or in the reports was or might be materially incorrect, and that this representation continued until completion of the syndication.

* * *

53.   In Photo Production Ltd v Securicor Transport Ltd [1980] AC 827, 843, Lord Wilberforce said:

After this Act [the Unfair Contract Terms Act 1977], in commercial matters generally, when the parties are not of unequal bargaining power, and when risks are normally borne by insurance, not only is the case for judicial intervention undemonstrated, but there is everything to be said, and this seems to have been Parliament's intention, for leaving the parties free to apportion the risks as they think fit and for respecting their decisions.

54.   Similarly, in the specialised world of syndicated finance there is everything to be said for leaving the participants to determine the respective responsibilities and risks of the sponsors, the debtor, the arranger and the investors, and for respecting their decisions. The SIM has to be read as a whole in order to see what a reasonable participant would understand was the scope of the responsibility undertaken by the arranger in relation to its contents.

55.   In addressing the effect of the notice at the beginning of the SIM, Mr Nash highlighted the opening words of paragraph (ii):

"The Arranger $\lceil$has not independently verified the information$\rceil$ set out in this Memorandum. $\lceil$Accordingly, no representation . . . is made and no responsibilities accepted by Goldman Sachs$\rceil$. . . as to or in relation to the accuracy or completeness or otherwise of this Memorandum . . ." (His emphasis).

56. Mr Nash drew an analogy between this case and Hummingbird Motors Ltd v Hobbs [1986] RTR 276, where the seller of a car gave an express warranty that to the best of his knowledge and belief the odometer reading was correct. Kerr LJ said at page 281 that:

> " . . . it is clear from Smith v Land and House Property Corporation (1884) 28 Ch D 7 that this statement imports something further by way of implication. It imports an implied assertion that the defendant knew of no facts leading to the conclusion that the odometer reading was or might be incorrect."

57. Mr Nash submitted that the fact that Goldman Sachs had not independently verified the information in the SIM made it understandable that it was not prepared to give a positive representation as to its accuracy or completeness, but this did not preclude an implied representation that it was unaware of any facts showing that the information was or might be materially incorrect.

58. In Hummingbird Motors Ltd v Hobbs the seller of the car made an express representation that the odometer reading was true to the best of his knowledge and belief, whereas in the present case Goldman Sachs expressly stated that it made no representation as to the accuracy of the information provided. Of equal or greater significance is the difference in the nature and circumstances of the transaction. An implied representation that Goldman Sachs did not know of any facts showing that the statements in the SIM "were or might be incorrect in any material way", or that the opinions in the Arthur Andersen reports "were not or might not be reasonable", would open up wide and uncertain territory.

59. The Arthur Andersen pre-acquisition reports had made it clear that it had limited information about Finelist. It could therefore be difficult to judge whether some particular piece of information "might" make the statements about Finelist's financial performance incorrect, and, if so, "in a material way" (whether by reference to the materiality test applied by PWC as Finelist's auditors, materiality in the view of Arthur Andersen or materiality in the view of a potential investor). An implied representation of the scope contended for by IFE would potentially require Goldman Sachs to carry out an evaluation in order to decide what information it was required to disclose, inconsistent with the express language of the SIM ("The Arranger expressly does not undertake to review the financial condition, status or affairs of . . . Finelist . . . at any time or to advise any potential or actual participant in the Facilities of any information coming to the attention of the Arranger").

60. Mr Mitjavile's evidence did not support IFE's case that a reasonable person would have understood that Goldman Sachs was making any such implied representation, and I do not accept that there was any such implied representation. That is not to say that Goldman

Sachs made no representations at all. I do not doubt that there was an implied representation that in supplying the SIM it was acting in good faith, that is, not knowingly putting forward information likely to mislead; or that this was a continuing representation, so that if, after the issue of the SIM but before a recipient acted on it, Goldman Sachs became aware that the information which it had supplied in good faith was misleading, it would be under a duty to disclose this (at all events unless it honestly believed that the error was a matter of no importance). There is, however, a difference between actual knowledge that the information previously supplied was misleading and acquisition of information which merely gave rise to a possibility that the information previously supplied was misleading. In the latter case, Goldman Sachs would not be under a duty to the prospective participant to investigate the matter further, or to advise the participant, in view of the terms of the SIM.

* * *

NOTES

1.   Note the legal obligations owed to syndicate members by banks that arrange syndicated loans in various jurisdiction, particularly as relates to the syndicate information memorandum provided by the arranger to participating Lenders. In the *IFE Fund SA* case, for example, under English law arranger liability can generally arise in four ways:

- the tort of negligence;

- the Misrepresentation Act 1967;

- the tort of deceit; and

- a claim for breach of fiduciary duty.

Market convention is for arrangers to use extensive disclaimers to fend off such risks and potential liabilities. See Denis Petkovic, Arranger Liability in The Euro Markets, 125 Banking L.J 49 (2008); but see UBAF Ltd v. European American Banking Corporation, 1 QB 713 (1984) (arranger owed fiduciary duties to syndicate members to disclose inadequacies in the security arrangement); Sumitomo Bank Ltd. v. Banque Bruxelles, 1 Lloyd's Rep. 487 (1997) (U.K. Commercial Court held that arranging bank owed the participating lenders a duty of care when disclosing information to insurers of security for the syndicate loan).

2.   What if IFE Fund had asked whether the arranger had received any new information regarding the financial status of the target which indicated that previous reports of investigating accountants were materially incorrect or that might otherwise be detrimental to syndication? IFE Fund would, no doubt, have received an answer making the Fund pause before investing.

Indeed, arrangers' responses to requests for information by syndicate members may be an area of potential risk under U.K. law since representations may be made in such responses without the benefit of disclaimers and notwithstanding that loan documentation may state otherwise. See the Petkovic article at 65.

3.   With the U.S. market climbing toward a trillion dollars in record volume in 2015, from a regulatory perspective, syndicated loans may present oversight difficulties, particularly for large and/or complex lending syndicates and cross border participants. The U.S. Shared National Credit Program, established in 1977, is an interagency program administered by the major U.S. federal banking regulatory agencies that provides a periodic credit risk assessment of the largest and most complex syndicating lending credit arrangements involving U.S. regulated banking institutions. The SNC Program is designed to provide "uniformity and efficiency" in analyzing and rating the credit quality of the most complex credit facilities. It also is intended to avoid redundant regulatory reviews of the same credit in multiple banks. See, e.g., Shared National Credit Program Annual Review, Board of Governors of the Federal Reserve System, Federal Deposit Insurance Corporation, Office of Comptroller of the Currency, (November 7, 2014).

In recent years, the SNC Program has paid increased attention to the continuing growth of the U.S. leveraged loan market and in international impact, See Fed Scrutiny of Leveraged Loans Grows, Along with Bubble Concern, http://www.bloomberg.com/news/articles/2014-10-01/fed-scrutiny-of-leveraged-loans-grows-along-with-bubble-concern); Peter Eavis, A Recent Surge of Leveraged Loans Rattles Regulators, N.Y. Times (November 4, 2014); Board of Governors of the Federal Reserve System press release dated November 7, 2014, Credit Risk in Shared National Credit Portfolio is High; Leveraged Lending Remains A Concern (concern expressed about credit quality of large loan commitments by U.S. and foreign banking organizations).

INTERAGENCY GUIDANCE ON LEVERAGED LENDING
(March 21, 2013)

Purpose

The Office of the Comptroller of the Currency (OCC), Board of Governors of the Federal Reserve System (Board), and Federal Deposit Insurance Corporation (FDIC) (collectively the "agencies") are issuing this leveraged lending guidance to update and replace the April 2001 Interagency guidance regarding sound practices for leveraged finance activities (2001 guidance).[2] The 2001 guidance addressed expectations for the content of credit policies, the need for well-defined underwriting standards, the importance of defining an institution's risk appetite for

---

[2]   For the purpose of this guidance, references to leveraged finance, or leveraged transactions encompass the entire debt structure of a leveraged obligor (including loans and letters of credit, mezzanine tranches, senior and subordinated bonds) held by both bank and non-bank investors. References to leveraged lending and leveraged loan transactions and credit agreements refer to all debt with the exception of bond and high-yield debt held by both bank and non-bank investors.

leveraged transactions, and the importance of stress-testing exposures and portfolios.

Leveraged lending is an important type of financing for national and global economies, and the U.S. financial industry plays an integral role in making credit available and syndicating that credit to investors. In particular, financial institutions should ensure they do not unnecessarily heighten risks by originating poorly underwritten loans. For example, a poorly underwritten leveraged loan that is pooled with other loans or is participated with other institutions may generate risks for the financial system. This guidance is designed to assist financial institutions in providing leveraged lending to creditworthy borrowers in a safe-and-sound manner.

* * *

Definition of Leveraged Lending

The policies of financial institutions should include criteria to define leveraged lending that are appropriate to the institution. For example, numerous definitions of leveraged lending exist throughout the financial services industry and commonly contain some combination of the following:

- Proceeds used for buyouts, acquisitions, or capital distributions.

* * *

- A borrower recognized in the debt markets as a highly leveraged firm, which is characterized by a high debt-to-net-worth ratio.

- Transactions when the borrower's post-financing leverage, as measured by its leverage ratios (for example, debt-to-assets, debt-to-net-worth, debt-to-cash flow, or other similar standards common to particular industries or sectors), significantly exceeds industry norms or historical levels.

A financial institution engaging in leveraged lending should define it within the institution's policies and procedures in a manner sufficiently detailed to ensure consistent application across all business lines. A financial institution's definition should describe clearly the purposes and financial characteristics common to these transactions, and should cover risk to the institution from both direct exposure and indirect exposure via limited recourse financing secured by leveraged loans, or financing extended to financial intermediaries (such as conduits and special purpose entities (SPEs)) that hold leveraged loans.

Reputational Risk

Leveraged lending transactions are often syndicated through the financial and institutional markets. A financial institution's apparent failure to meet its legal responsibilities in underwriting and distribution transactions can damage its market reputation and impair its ability to compete. Similarly, a financial institution that distributes transactions which over time have significantly higher default or loss rates and performance issues may also see its reputation damaged.

* * *

3. STANDING FOR PARTICIPATING BANKS TO SUE

An issue litigated with some frequency is the right of an individual lender in a multi-lender loan arrangement to bring suit on its own to enforce contractual remedies against the borrower or related parties, such as guarantors. As often is the case, the issue would not arise in the first place if the loan documents dealt with it directly. In the absence of direct language, the determination of this issue generally turns on the court's view of the intent of the parties as gleaned from other, less direct, language.[1]

BEAL SAVINGS BANK V. SOMMER
(N.Y. Ct. of App. 2007)
8 N.Y. 3d 318

We are asked to determine whether one lender in a syndicated loan arrangement has standing to sue for breach of contract, contrary to the will of the other 36 lenders to forbear from taking action. The specific, unambiguous language of several provisions, read in the context of the agreements as a whole, convinces us that, in this instance, the lenders intended to act collectively in the event of the borrower's default and to preclude an individual lender from disrupting the scheme of the agreements at issue.

Facts

On February 26, 1998, a lending syndicate, originally comprised of 13 institutions (the Lenders), invested in the construction of Aladdin Gaming, LLC (the Borrower), to develop the Aladdin Resort and Casino in Las Vegas, Nevada. The Lenders advanced 410 million dollars through the Bank of Nova Scotia (succeeded by BNY Asset Solutions, LLC), the Administrative Agent. A Credit Agreement was the primary loan document

---

[1]   For a detailed analysis of this area, *See* Thomas Joseph Hall, The Rights of Individual Lenders in Multi-Lender Loans to Enforce Remedies Banking L.J (May 2007).

governing the loan. A Keep-Well Agreement, which plaintiff-appellant Beal Savings Bank alleges was breached, was one of the many ancillary instruments evidencing the loan. Both the Credit Agreement and the Keep-Well were dated February 26, 1998.

The Credit Agreement

The title page of the Credit Agreement shows Aladdin Gaming, LLC, as the Borrower, "Various Financial Institutions" as the Lenders, the Bank of Nova Scotia as the Administrative Agent and two other institutions, the syndication agent and the documentation agent. The Lenders are not individually named.

Under section 9.1 of the Credit Agreement, the Lenders authorize the Administrative Agent to act on their behalf pursuant to the Loan Documents and, "in the absence of other written instructions from the Required Lenders to exercise such powers as are specifically delegated to or required of the Administrative Agent by the terms [of the Loan Documents], together with such powers as may be reasonably incidental thereto." The term "Required Lenders" is defined as those holding at least 66 2/323% of the outstanding principal and the participation interests in the outstanding Letters of Credit (Credit Agreement § 1.1). Among those powers delegated to the Administrative Agent are that it set the Base Rate of interest and the London Interbank Offer (LIBO) Rate (Credit Agreement §§ 1.1, 3.2), collect payments from the Borrower for the pro rata account of the Lenders (§ 4.7), and review financial statements of the Borrower and other Aladdin Parties (§§ 5.1.4, 6.5).

Article 8 of the Credit Agreement addresses Events of Default. Section 8.1.4 provides that the Borrower defaults if, after the Administrative Agent gives notice, the nonperformance continues for 30 days. Section 8.3 states that the Administrative Agent, at the direction of the Required Lenders, may "exercise any or all rights and remedies at law or in equity," including the right to recover judgment on the Keep-Well. The Credit Agreement includes a section providing that if a Lender receives any payment, such as by setoff, it must share any excess of its pro rata share of payments with the other Lenders (§ 4.8). Section 10.20 is a cumulative remedies provision that "[n]o right or remedy conferred upon the Administrative Agent or the Lenders in this Agreement is intended to be exclusive" and "every such right and remedy shall be cumulative to every other right or remedy contained in the other Loan Documents."

The Keep-Well Agreement

The Keep-Well Agreement was made, as the title pages state, "in favor of each of the Administrative Agent and the Lenders and their respective successors, transferees and assigns." The Sponsors agreed in section 2 of the Keep-Well to make Equity Contributions to the Borrower if the financial ratio fell below a certain minimum. Section 4 states that in the event of acceleration under section 8.2 and section 8.3 of the Credit Agreement the Sponsors guarantee payment of the accelerated amount to the Administrative Agent for the benefit of the Lenders.

The Keep-Well is not a stand-alone document but is to be read in accordance with the Credit Agreement. Section 18, "Miscellaneous Provisions," provides in subsection (a) that the Keep-Well is a "Loan Document executed pursuant to the Credit Agreement and shall (unless otherwise expressly indicated herein) be construed, administered and applied in accordance with the terms and provisions thereof." The next subsection, 18(b), states that the Keep-Well is binding upon the Sponsors and their successors and shall "be enforceable by the Administrative Agent and each Lender" and their assigns. Section 18(e), like section 10.20 of the Credit Agreement, is a cumulative remedies provision.

Enter the Plaintiff

In July 2000, the Borrower obtained a 50 million dollar increase in loan funds, and the Sommer Trust, one of the Borrower's parent companies, agreed to become a Sponsor along with other organizations under the Keep-Well Agreement. The Aladdin casino began operations, but just after September 11, 2001, the Borrower sought bankruptcy protection. Neither plaintiff-appellant Beal nor its assignor, BFC Capital, Inc., was an original Lender, and neither held any interest in the loan when the Borrower petitioned for bankruptcy protection. BFC acquired a 4.5% interest in the bank debt after the Borrower filed for bankruptcy.

* * *

The Litigation

On April 6, 2005, Beal filed a claim under section 4 of the Keep-Well and sought 90 million dollars to share with the other Lenders or, in the alternative, Beal's pro rata share. The Trust, moving to dismiss, contended that Beal lacked standing, for no individual member of the consortium was empowered to enforce the agreements in the event of default, and only the Administrative Agent, at the behest of a supermajority of Lenders, could do so. Beal argued that while the agreements authorized the Agent to act administratively, no provision in the agreements precluded a Lender from otherwise proceeding individually. The Supreme Court granted the Trust's motion under CPLR 3211(a)(1) and (7) to dismiss the complaint on the grounds that the Loan Documents explicitly and implicitly precluded Beal from recovering a judgment under the Keep-Well. Affirming, the Appellate Division concluded that the Keep-Well is to be administered in accordance with the terms of the Credit Agreement, which sets forth the procedures in the event of default, and that those procedures provide for collective action. We agree with the trial court and Appellate Division, and now affirm.

Analysis

* * *

In Credit Francais Intl. v. Sociedad Fin. de Comercio, 128 Misc.2d 564, 490 N.Y.S.2d 670 [Sup.Ct., N.Y. County 1985], the court analyzed a situation similar to the one presented here. A syndicate of banks lent money to a Venezuelan financial institution. When the government of Venezuela called on financial institutions to suspend payments of principal, the borrower sought to delay its payments. The majority of the banks in the consortium chose to allow delayed payment, and only one member sought to proceed against the borrower. The court noted that the loan transaction was between the borrower and a consortium, not individual banks. Even the title page-that the lenders were not named but were called "Depositors"-indicated that the nature of the agreement was that the lenders act collectively. The agent was authorized to act on behalf of the lenders collectively by its own initiative or at the direction of a majority of lenders: the agent determined the rate of interest, collected repayments for the pro rata account of each depositor, collected advances to be made to the borrower and received the borrower's financial statements to provide to the lenders. Concerning the provision on acceleration, the court wrote:

"The actual acceleration of the entire amount due does not occur, however, until the agent, 'with the consent or at the direction of the Majority Depositors', declares the entire amount due and payable. Thus, while the agent has the power to declare the entire amount due if an event of acceleration occurs, he also has the power to refrain from accelerating the entire amount unless otherwise directed by the majority depositors. No individual bank is given those rights" (*id.* at 578, 490 N.Y.S.2d 670).

The court also noted that a sharing provision was included to prevent a bank from obtaining an undue preference so that were an individual institution to obtain any payment, that bank would act as agent on behalf of all the depositors. The parties thus contemplated that the agent take collective action on behalf of all members pursuant to the direction of the majority depositors. Such a plan was intended to prevent the possibility of a multiplicity of suits by individual banks perhaps working at cross-purposes-a situation that could be chaotic.

* * *

Similarly, in New Bank of New England, N.A. v Toronto-Dominion Bank, 768 F.Supp. 1017 [S.D.N.Y. 1991], the majority of lenders in a syndicate wished to negotiate with the defaulting borrower, and one lender refused to consent to a waiver of default. An Intercreditor Agreement provided that "the agent may act in certain circumstances in accordance with the directions of the majority lenders" (*id.* at 1020). The court determined that the discretionary language allowed a majority to direct acceleration but also authorized it to refrain from doing so. No provision permitted a minority lender to compel acceleration. The meaning of the agreement between sophisticated parties was unambiguous, even if one party asserted a different interpretation (*id.* at 1021, 1022; see also In re Enron Corp., 302 B.R. 463, 473 [Bankr. S.D.N.Y.2003], affd. 2005 WL 356985, 2005 U.S. Dist LEXIS 2134 [S.D.N.Y.2005]).

Here, of course, neither the Credit Agreement nor the Keep-Well contains an explicit provision stating that a Lender may-or may not-take individual action in the event of default, and thus we are compelled to look to other specific clauses and the agreements as a whole to ascertain the parties' intent. The examination leads us to conclude that the agreements have an unequivocal collective design.

Section 18 (a) of the Keep-Well states that it was "executed pursuant to the Credit Agreement" and, unless otherwise expressly indicated, must be "construed, administered and applied" in accordance with the Credit Agreement. No express provision in the Keep-Well sets forth the actions to be taken in the event of default. Only article 8 of the Credit Agreement articulates these procedures. Section 8.3 provides:

"If any Event of Default . . . shall occur for any reason, whether voluntary or involuntary, and be continuing, the Administrative Agent, upon the direction of the Required Lenders, shall by notice to the Borrower declare all or any portion of the outstanding principal amount of the Loans and other Obligations . . . to be due and payable or the Commitments . . . to be terminated, whereupon . . . the Borrower shall automatically and immediately be obligated to deposit with the Administrative Agent cash collateral in an amount equal to all Letter of Credit Outstandings. . . . In addition to the foregoing, the Administrative Agent upon direction of the Required Lenders may, without further notice of default, presentment or demand for payment, protest or notice of non-payment or dishonor, or other notices or demands of any kind., exercise any or all rights and remedies at law or in equity (in any combination or order that the Lenders may elect, subject to the foregoing), including, without prejudice to the Lenders' other rights and remedies, the following":

"(h) recover judgment on the Completion Guaranty or the Keep-Well Agreement either before, during or after any proceedings for the enforcement of the Lenders' rights and remedies hereunder or under the other Loan Documents."

Thus, under section 8.3, the Administrative Agent acts upon the direction of the Required Lenders a two-thirds majority-to give notice to the Borrower and, if required, the Borrower must deposit the outstanding principal with the Administrative Agent. In addition, it is the Administrative Agent that, upon direction of the Required Lenders, may exercise any or all rights and remedies as the Lenders elect, including recovering judgment on the Keep-Well Agreement "for the enforcement of the Lenders' rights and remedies."

Section 18(b) of the Keep-Well, on which Beal relies to assert standing, is a general section that provides:

"This Agreement shall be binding upon the Sponsors and their permitted successors, transferees and assigns and shall inure to the benefit of and be enforceable by the Administrative Agent and each Lender and their respective successors, transferees and assigns; provided, however, that the Sponsors may not assign any of their obligations hereunder without the prior written consent of the Required Lenders."

* * *

An interpretation favoring Beal's view would render section 8.3 meaningless because there would be no reason to provide that the Required Lenders could enforce the agreements by a supermajority directing the Administrative Agent to act (see Excess Ins. Co., 3 N.Y.3d at 582, 789 N.Y.S.2d 461, 822 N.E.2d 768). Nor does the language of section 8.3 support Beal's contention that, if the Administrative Agent does not move to enforce the Keep-Well, any individual Lender may do so. As the court in Credit Francais construed a similar provision, the Administrative Agent, at the direction of the Required Lenders, has the power to declare the entire amount due and the power to refrain from accelerating—no individual institution is given those rights (128 Misc.2d at 578, 490 N.Y.S.2d 670). Here, the Required Lenders—with 95.5% of the interest, well over a supermajority—made an election by directing the Administrative Agent not to pursue legal action (see New Bank of New England, 768 F.Supp. at 1020). Section 18(b) of the Keep-Well, as analyzed in the context of an event of default, does not contravene the Required Lenders' decision to act collectively (see Westmoreland Coal, 100 N.Y.2d at 358, 763 N.Y.S.2d 525, 794 N.E.2d 667).

* * *

BANCO ESPANOL DE CREDITO V. SECURITY PACIFIC NATIONAL BANK

United States Court of Appeals
973 F.2d 51 (2d Cir. 1992)

ALTIMARI, CIRCUIT JUDGE.

Plaintiffs-appellants, purchasers of various "loan participations" sold by defendants-appellees Security Pacific National Bank and Security Pacific Merchant Bank (collectively "Security Pacific"), appeal from a judgment entered in the United States District Court for the Southern

District of New York (Milton Policek, Judge), granting summary judgment for Security Pacific and dismissing plaintiffs' complaints, In the two underlying actions, which were consolidated for appeal, plaintiffs charged that Security Pacific had withheld material information on the financial solvency of Integrated Resources, Inc. ("Integrated") when Security Pacific sold plaintiffs portions of loan notes owed by Integrated to Security Pacific. Plaintiffs sought to rescind their purchase agreements based on an alleged violation of Section 12(2) of the 1933 Securities Act and sought damages for Security Pacific's alleged breach of various common law duties.

Plaintiffs moved for summary judgment on the securities claim and Security Pacific cross-moved for summary judgment on all claims. In granting defendants' motion for summary judgment, the district court first rejected plaintiffs' securities claim, holding that the loan participations at issue were not "securities" within the meaning of the 1933 Act, and were therefore not governed by the federal securities laws.

The district court also rejected plaintiffs' common law claims, finding that Security Pacific had no duty to disclose information on Integrated's financial condition under either the terms of the loan participation agreements signed by plaintiffs or under general principles of common law.

On appeal, plaintiffs contend that the district court erred in: (1) determining that loan participations sold by Security Pacific were not securities; and (2) determining that Security Pacific owed no duty to disclose negative financial information about Integrated.

For the reasons set forth below, we affirm the judgment of the district court.

BACKGROUND

In 1988, Security Pacific extended a line of credit to Integrated permitting Integrated to obtain short-term unsecured loans from Security Pacific, Security Pacific subsequently made a series of shortterm loans to Integrated, Security Pacific sold these loans, in whole or in part, to various institutional investors at differing interest rates. Resales of these loans were prohibited without Security Pacific's express written consent. The practice of selling loans to other institutions is known as "loan participation," Short-term loan participation permits a primary lender such as Security Pacific to spread its risk, while at the same time allowing a purchaser with excess cash to earn a higher return than that available on comparable money market instruments. Security Pacific, as manager of the loans, earned a fee equal to the difference between the interest paid by the debtor and the lower interest paid to the purchaser.

Security Pacific assumed no responsibility for the ability of Integrated to repay its loans. Indeed, each purchaser of loan participations was required to enter into a Master Participation Agreement ("MPA"), which contained a general disclaimer providing, in relevant part, that the purchaser "acknowledges that it has independently and without reliance upon Security [Pacific] and based upon such documents and information as the participant has deemed appropriate, made its own credit analysis."

In late 1988, Integrated began to encounter financial difficulties, In April 1989, Security Pacific refused a request by Integrated to extend further credit. Despite this refusal, Security Pacific continued to sell loan participations on Integrated's debt. Indeed, from mid-April through June.9, 1989, Security Pacific sold seventeen different loan participations to plaintiffs-appellants. Unable to obtain enough working capital, Integrated began defaulting on its loans on June 12, 1989. Integrated subsequently declared bankruptcy.

As a result of Integrated's default, two sets of investors, who had purchased the seventeen loan participations, initiated separate actions against Security Pacific in the United States District Court for the Southern District of New York, Contending that the loan participations were "securities" within the meaning of the Securities Act of 1933 ("the 1933 Act"), plaintiffs sought to rescind their purchase agreements by alleging that Security Pacific had failed to disclose to them material' facts about Integrated's financial condition in violation of § 12(2) of the 1933 Act. 15 U.S.C. 5 77/(2). Plaintiffs also claimed that Security Pacific's failure to disclose constituted a breach of Security Pacific's implied, and express contractual duties under its MPA's, and a breach of Security Pacific's duty to disclose material information based on superior knowledge. Based on these common law claims, plaintiffs sought to recover their investment plus unpaid interest, Plaintiffs in each of the two actions moved for partial summary judgment on the securities claim. Security Pacific cross-moved for summary judgment on all claims. The cases were consolidated for argument.

In ruling on these motions, the district court concluded that the loan participations were not "securities" within the meaning of the Securities Act of 1933, and that, therefore, plaintiffs could not assert a violation under § 12(2) of this Act In addition, the district court held that the express disclaimer provisions in the MPA precluded plaintiffs' common law claims. Accordingly, the district court granted summary judgment to Security Pacific and dismissed the complaints. See Banco Espanol de Credito v. Security Pacifia National Bank 763 F.Supp. 36 (S.D.N.Y.1991.). Plaintiffs now appeal.

DISCUSSION

* * *

Section 2(1) of the 1933 Act provides in pertinent part:

> [U]nless the context otherwise requires—(1) the term "security" means any note . . . evidence of indebtedness, . . . investment contract, . . . or any certificate of interest or participation in . . . any of the foregoing.

15 U.S.C. § 77b(1). It is well-settled that certificates evidencing loans by commercial banks to their customers for use in the customers' current operations are not securities, See, *e.g.,* Reves v. Ernst & Young, 494 U.S. 56, 61 110 S.Ct. 945, 951, 108 L.Ed.2d 47 (1990) (citing Chemical Bank v. Arthur Andersen & Co. 726 F.2d 930, 939 (2d Cir.), *cert, denied,* 469 U.S. 884, 105 S.Ct. 253, 83 L.Ed.2d 190 (1984)). However, as the district court noted, a participation in an instrument might in some circumstances be considered a security even where the instrument itself is not. See *Banco Espanol de Credito,* 763 F.Supp. at 41.

With respect to loan participations, the district court reasoned that "because the plaintiffs did not receive an undivided interest in a pool of loans, but rather purchased participation in a specific, identifiable short-term Integrated loan, the loan participation did not have an identity separate from the underlying loan." *Id.* at 42. Thus, Judge Pollack reasoned, because under *Chemical Bank* the loans to Integrated were not securities, the plaintiffs1 purchase of discrete portions of these loans could not be considered securities.

On appeal, plaintiffs concede that traditional Joan participations do not qualify as securities. Instead, plaintiffs contend that the peculiar nature of Security Pacific's Joan participation program-which aimed at the sale of 100% of its loans through high speed telephonic sales and often pre-paid transactions qualified these loan participations as securities. Specifically, plaintiffs argue that the loan participations sold by Security Pacific are more properly characterized as securities—in the nature of "notes"—as enumerated in § 2(1) of the 1933 Act.

In examining whether the loan participations could be considered "notes" which are also securities, the district court applied the "family resemblance" test set forth by the Supreme Court in *Reves. 494* U.S. at 63–67, 110 S.Ct. at 950–952. Under the family resemblance test, a note is presumed to be a security unless an examination of the note, based on four factors, reveals a strong resemblance between the note and one of a judicially-enumerated list of instruments that are not securities, 110 S.Ct at 951. If the note in question is not sufficiently similar to one of these instruments, a court must then consider, using the same four factors, whether another category of non-security instruments should be added to the list. *Id.* at 67, 110 S.Ct. at 951. The four *Reves* factors to be considered in this examination are: (1) the motivations that would prompt a reasonable buyer and seller to enter into the transaction; (2) the plan of distribution of the instrument; (3) the reasonable expectations of the investing public; and (4) whether some factor, such as the existence of another regulatory scheme, significantly reduces the risk of the instrument, thereby rendering application of the securities laws unnecessary.

In addressing the first *Reves* factor, the district court found that Security Pacific was motivated by a desire to increase lines of credit to Integrated while diversifying Security Pacific's risk, that Integrated was motivated by a need for short-term credit at competitive rates to finance its current operations, and that the purchasers of the loan participations sought a short-term return on excess cash. Based on these findings, the district court concluded that "the overall motivation of the parties was the promotion of commercial purposes" rather than an investment in a business enterprise. *Banco Espanol de Credito.* 763 F.Supp. at 42–43,

Weighing the second *Reves* factor—the plan of distribution of the instrument—the district court observed that only institutional and corporate entities were solicited and that detailed individualized presentations were made by Security Pacific's sales personnel. The district court therefore concluded that the plan of distribution was "a limited solicitation to sophisticated financial or commercial institutions and not to the general public." We agree.

The plan of distribution specifically prohibited resales of the loan participations without the express written permission of Security Pacific. This limitation worked to prevent the loan participations from being sold to the general public, thus limiting eligible buyers to those with the capacity to acquire information about the debtor. This limitation also distinguishes Gary Plastic Packaging v. Merrill Lynch. Pierce. Fenner & Smith. Inc. 756 F.2d 230 (2d Cir. 1985), which involved a secondary market for the instruments traded in that case.

With regard to the third factor—the reasonable perception of the instrument by the investing public—the district court considered the expectations of the sophisticated purchasers who signed MPA's and determined that these institutions were given ample notice that the instruments were participations in loans and not investments in a business enterprise.

Finally, the district court noted that the Office of the Comptroller of the Currency has issued specific policy guidelines addressing the sale of loan participations. Thus, the fourth factor—the existence of another regulatory scheme—indicated that application of the securities laws was unnecessary.

Thus, under the *Reves* family resemblance analysis, as properly applied by the district Court, we hold that the loan participations in the instant case are analogous to the enumerated category of loans issued by banks for commercial purposes and therefore do not satisfy the statutory definition of "notes" which are "securities." Since the loan participations do not meet the statutory definition of securities, plaintiffs may not maintain their action for relief under § 12(2) of the 1933 Act.

We rule only with respect to the loan participations as marketed in this case. We recognize that even if an underlying instrument is not a security; the manner in which participations in that instrument are used, pooled, or marketed might establish that such participations are securities, See *Gary Plastic Packaging.* 756 F.2d at 240–42.

Turning to plaintiffs' contractual and other common-law claims, we agree with the district court that the waiver provision in the MPA's signed by the loan participants specifically absolved Security Pacific of any responsibility to disclose information relating to Integrated's financial condition. Moreover, as an arms length transaction between sophisticated financial institutions, the law imposed no independent duty on Security Pacific to disclose information that plaintiffs could have discovered through their own efforts, See, *e.g.,* Aaron Ferer & Sons v. Chase Manhattan Bank. 731 F.2d 112.122 (2d Cir. 1984).

CONCLUSION

Based on the foregoing, and on Judge Pollack's well-reasoned opinion, we affirm the judgment of the district court.

OAKES, CHIEF JUDGE, dissenting.

I believe that the majority opinion mistakenly assumes that the debt instruments—which Security Pacific terms "loan notes"—were sold in a "loan participation" and hence were not "securities." In doing so, I fear that the majority opinion misreads the facts, makes bad banking law and bad securities law, and stands on its head the law of this circuit and of the. Supreme Court in Reves y. Ernst & Young. 494 U.S. 56. 110 S.Ct. 945. 108 L.Ed.2d 47 (1990). Accordingly, I dissent.

For reasons that I will explain in detail, I agree with the Securities and Exchange Commission, which submitted a brief amicus curiae, a brief which is not mentioned in the majority opinion, that these so called loan notes were purchased in investment transactions and are securities accordingly, and that the loan note program engaged in by Security Pacific, while bearing a superficial resemblance to traditional loan participations, differs from those traditional participations in several important respects, including (1) who the participants are; (2) what the purposes of the purchasers or participants are; and (3) what the promotional basis used in marketing the loan notes is. The participants, rather than being commercial lenders who engage in traditional loan participations, were instead in many cases non-financial entities not acting as commercial lenders but making an investment, and even though there were some banks that purchased the so-called loan notes, they generally did so not through their lending departments but through their investment and trading departments. These participants were motivated not by the commercial purpose of operating a lending business in which participations are taken as an adjunct to direct lending operations, but were motivated by an investment purpose. The promotional literature put out by Security Pacific advertised the so-called loan note's as competitive with commercial paper, a well-recognized security under the Securities Act, and on the basis of the return that they offered over that of other investments.

Beyond that, and importantly to the Securities Act aspect of the case, these loan notes differ from traditional loan participations in the scope of information available to the purchasers, In the traditional loan participation, participants generally engage in one-to-one negotiation with the lead lender, and at times with the borrower, and can inspect all information, public and non-public, that is relevant, and consequently are able to do their own credit analysis, Here, Security Pacific did not provide the participants with non-public information it had, provided only publicly-available documents or ratings, and the purchasers were not in a position to approach the hundred or more possible borrowers in the program and conduct their own examinations. This is important for, as emphasized in *Reves.* 494 U.S. at 60, 1.10 S.Ct. at 949, "[t]he fundamental purpose undergirding the Securities Acts is 'to eliminate serious abuses in a largely unregulated securities market' United Housing Foundation, Inc. v. Forman, 421 U.S. 837, 849 [95 S.Ct, 2051, 2059, 44 L.Ed.2d 621] (19751)." It is for this reason—overlooked by the majority—that "because the Securities Acts define 'security' to include 'any note,' we begin with a presumption that every note is a security." *Reves,* 494 U.S. at 65. 110 S.Ct. at 951.

* * *

According to Security Pacific's promotional literature,

> Security Pacific's strong trading capabilities afford *investors* a large selection of issuers, maturities, and amounts from which to choose. Our traders and sales professionals work closely with *investors* In order to match their individual *investment* needs. (Emphasis supplied.)

It also promoted the liquidity of the instrument, stating that Security Pacific would "make a bid on a Security Pacific-originated loan note on a best efforts basis and represented that although it did not 'fully commit to make a secondary market in loan notes,' its 'trading and distribution capabilities should afford [purchasers] liquidity in most cases.'" From 1986 through October 1990, a total of 843 entitles purchased one or more loan notes in the program, and as of 1989 Security Pacific had approximately six to seven hundred investors and approximately one hundred to two hundred fifty active borrowers. Nor was this a program limited to Security

Pacific, As pointed out in the SEC amicus brief, the 1980s, in addition to seeing the era of "junk bonds," saw a vast expansion of sales by large money center banks of participations in short-term loans made to corporate buyers, sort of an evolution out of old-style banking into investment banking, in an effort to compete with the borrowing of money through debt instruments, such as commercial paper, rather than through traditional bank loans. The SEC estimates that the total market for these loan notes is considerable, with annual sales by all sellers estimated in excess of 100 billion dollars a year. This case, therefore, is not exactly about chicken feed.

* * *

BOARD OF GOVERNORS OF THE FEDERAL RESERVE SYSTEM FEDERAL DEPOSIT INSURANCE CORPORATION OFFICE OF THE COMPTROLLER OF THE CURRENCY OFFICE OF THRIFT SUPERVISION

INTERAGENCY STATEMENT ON SALES OF 100% LOAN PARTICIPATIONS

April 10, 1997

INTRODUCTION

A loan participation is a sharing or selling of interests in a loan. Depository institutions use loan participations as an integral part of their lending operations. Participations in underlying loans may be sold to enhance an institution's liquidity, interest rate risk management, capital, and earnings; diversify its loan portfolio; and serve the credit needs of its borrowers. When depository institutions reach internal or legal lending limits for particular borrowers, loan participations enable the institutions to continue providing needed credit to borrowers. This statement does, not apply to the vast majority of loan participations typically engaged in by insured depository institutions, as described below.

In some cases, depository institutions structure loan originations and participations with the intention of Selling off 100% of the underlying loan amount. Certain 100% loan participation programs raise unique safety and soundness issues that should be addressed by an institution's policies, procedures and practices.[1] The "100% loan participation programs" that are the subject of this statement include only programs involving the sale of participations like those involved in Banco, that are short-term loans

---

[1]   Banco Espanol de Credito v. Security Pacific National Bank, 973 F.2d 51 (2nd Cir. 1992), cert. denied, 113 S. Ct. 2992 (1993) ("Banco"), provides relevant information for institutions structuring 100% loan participation programs. * * *

originated-by an institution that sells off, without recourse, 100% participation under a continuing program, and retains no further interest in the originated loan. The four federal banking agencies—the Board, of Governors of the Federal Reserve System, the Federal Deposit Insurance Corporation, the Office of the Comptroller of the Currency, and the Office of Thrift Supervision—are issuing this statement to provide uniform guidance for depository institutions that structure these 100% loan participation programs. This statement does not apply to other sales of participations or assignments of entire loans, such as sales of 100% participation in problem loans from the bank's portfolio, or sales in connection with loan trading activities.

SAFETY AND SOUNDNESS CONSIDERATIONS

If not appropriately structured, a 100% participation program can present unwarranted risks to the originating institution, including legal, reputation and compliance risks. The policies of a depository institution engaged in the origination of 100% loan participations should address safety and soundness concerns and include criteria for these programs. This criteria should address (1) the program's objectives, (2) the plan of distribution, (3) the credit requirements applicable to the borrower, and (4) the access afforded program participants to financial information on the borrower. In addition, the institution should establish procedures for ensuring compliance with applicable regulations and consistency with the institution's policies and procedures.

ADOPTION OF POLICIES AND PROCEDURES

Participation Agreements. The originating institution should use written participation agreements to set forth the rights and obligations of the parties participating in the program. The agreements should clearly state the limitations the originating and participating institutions impose on each other and the rights all parties retain. The originating institution should state, unequivocally, that loan participants are participating in loans and are not investing in a business enterprise.

Program Objectives. A 100% loan participation program should be structured to accommodate commercial objectives and not objectives geared primarily to investment in a business enterprise. Therefore, the motivations of the parties involved in the program (the originating institution, the borrower, and the participants) should be of a commercial nature,[2] For example, banks may structure 100% loan participation programs to provide borrowers with short-term credit to finance their current operations, and to provide parties with excess cash the opportunity to obtain a short-term return by purchasing interests in these loans.

---

[2]   For additional discussion on this issue see the underlying district court decision in Banco Espanol de Credito v. Security Pacific National Bank, 763 F.Supp. 36 (S.D.N.Y. 1991) at 42–43.

Plan of Distribution. The originating institution should take reasonable steps to ensure that the general public does not become the target of marketing efforts as a result of resales by loan participants. For example, the originating institution should have a program in place to ensure that participants are limited to sophisticated financial and commercial entities, and sophisticated persons, and that the participations are not sold directly to the general public. Steps that might be taken by the originating institution include retaining a right of first refusal on any bona-fide offer to a participant from a third party, or requiring the originating institution's permission, not to be unreasonably withheld, before a participant could sell or pledge a loan participation interest.

Credit Condition of the Borrower. The originating institution should structure 100% loan participation programs only for borrowers who meet the originating institution's credit requirements. Loan participations will also have to meet the credit requirements of the loan participants. In the event the originating institution decides to terminate its credit relationship with a borrower, or materially downgrades its relationship with the borrower, the institution should reevaluate whether originating new loans for that borrower for 100% loan participations is appropriate.

Access to Credit Information, The originating institution should allow potential loan participants to obtain and review appropriate credit and other information on the borrower to enable the participants to make an informed credit decision. Promotional materials should clearly state that the participants and not the originating depository institution are responsible for making the ultimate credit decision through the participant's own review of information pertaining to the borrower.

QUESTIONS AND NOTES

1.   As the *Beal* case makes clear, the language adopted in the loan documents will likely determine whether an individual lender has the right to enforce remedies. Without a provision directly establishing or negating such a right, the courts will resort to distilling the intent of the parties from other contractual provisions. See Hall Article at 395.

2.   A fundamental element of a loan syndication is that all payments made by the borrower must be distributed pro rata to each syndicate member according to their individual participation percentages. This is usually achieved through the mechanism of a 'sharing clause' in the loan agreement.

A sharing clause aims to: (a) prohibit the borrower from discriminating against the lenders by making payments to only some and not all the lenders; and (b) discourage a syndicate member from unilaterally enforcing its rights under the loan syndication since it will be liable to share the proceeds of the litigation. See Dawn Tong, Sharing Clauses in Loan Syndication Documentation, http://www.lawgazette.com.sg/2002-2/Feb02-focus3.htm.

3. A syndicate arranger performs many roles regarding a syndicated loan, both with respect to the borrower as well as the participating banks in the syndicate. These respective roles often place the lead bank in a position fraught with potential conflicts of interests. Why?

4. Multiple Choice Questions

a. As counsel to a bank managing a syndicated loan deal, you would be most concerned that a loan participation interest not be deemed a "security" under the U.S. securities laws because: a) it may potentially result in greater liability exposure for the managing bank if the loan goes bad; b) it significantly increases the costs and expenses of the deal because it may have to comply with the U.S. securities laws registration and disclosure requirements; c) the borrower may assert the "lex monetae" doctrine against the lenders; or d) a and b only.

b. You are counsel to Large Bank, a lead bank in connection with an international loan syndication to finance construction by the Mickey Corporation ("Mickey") of a futuristic amusement park in the United States. Which of the following steps should Large Bank take that are likely to reduce its exposure under the U.S. securities laws? a) require all participating banks to have previous experience in financing similar projects; b) pick only participating banks headquartered outside the U.S.; c) bring only participating banks into the syndication that have an existing lending relationship with Mickey; d) include a provision in the placement memorandum stating that it has been unable to verify information supplied by Mickey regarding the profitability of certain of its operations; e) a, b and c only; or f) a, c and d only.

c. Under the holding in the *Banco Espanol* case, a bank structuring a loan participation will potentially cause the participation interests to be deemed "securities" rather than loans, if: a) the participation interests meet the *Reves* "family resemblance" test; b) the bank does not follow the *U.S. Interagency Policy Statement on Sales of 100% loan participations*, c) the participation interests are marketed to the general public; or d) all of the above.

CHAPTER 4

"RING FENCING" OF INTERNATIONAL DEPOSITS: U.S. HOME OFFICE LIABILITY FOR FOREIGN BRANCH DEPOSITS

■ ■ ■

This Chapter explores the legal and regulatory issues associated with international deposits in foreign branches of U.S. banks. With more than $1 trillion in deposits in foreign branches of U.S. banks, the main question for consideration in this Chapter is: when is a depositor in a foreign branch of a US bank able to obtain the return of their deposit in a foreign branch from the home office of the US bank when they cannot access their deposit in the foreign branch. The answer to this question—in terms of the obligations of the home offices of US banks to be responsible for foreign deposits—has profound legal and financial implications for both US banks and their overseas depositors, and raises important bank regulatory issues under U.S. law.

This Chapter will analyze case law and federal and state banking regulations regarding the respective legal rights of US banks and depositors when a foreign branch is not in a position to pay its depositors due to extraordinary circumstances: war, civil unrest, government decree, or force majeure that otherwise renders payment at the branch impossible. This Chapter explores case law in this area arising from events ranging from the Russian and Cuban revolutions to the Vietnam war and beyond, analyzing the regulatory and legal implications for depositors of a U.S. bank closing a foreign branch.

1. INTERNATIONAL DEPOSITS: DEVELOPMENT AND ISSUES

A. DEVELOPMENT OF INTERNATIONAL DEPOSITS

V. GERARD COMIZIO AND RYAN CHIACHIERE, RING FENCING U.S. BANK FOREIGN BRANCH DEPOSITS: WORKING TOWARD A CLEARER UNDERSTANDING OF WHERE DEPOSITS ARE PAYABLE IN THE MIDST OF CHAOS

3 Amer. Univ. Bus. L. Rev. 2 (2014)

* * *

In the second half of the Twentieth Century, the investment of U.S. companies abroad grew dramatically as the United States emerged as a world economic power. The number of foreign offices of U.S. banks skyrocketed commensurate with new U.S. investment, and new challenges to the understanding and regulation of banking deposits abroad accompanied this growth.[1]

In 1960, eight U.S. banks maintained offices abroad; in 1984, there were 163; and by 1987, 902 U.S. banks had offices abroad.[2] In 1985, there were over 2,000 foreign offices of American banks, with Citibank and Chase Manhattan together accounting for nearly 1,200 offices at the end of 1983.[3] At that time, more than half of the total assets of both banks were foreign.[4] As of 2013, Citibank claims to operate over 4,000 branches overseas,[5] including offices in 160 countries across North and South America, Europe, the Middle East, and the Asia-Pacific region.[6] According to the Federal Deposit Insurance Corporation (FDIC), foreign branch deposits have doubled since 2001 alone, totaling approximately $1 trillion.[7]

The U.S. bank regulatory environment has generally been favorable for foreign branches.[17] For instance, Regulation D, which pertains to

---

[1]   See M. Ann Hannigan, United States Home Bank Liability for Foreign Branch Deposits, 1989 U. ILL. L. REV. 735, 737 (1989).

[2]   Adam Telanoff, Comment, American Parent Bank Liability for Foreign Branch Deposits: Which Party Bears Sovereign Risk?, 18 PEPP. L. REV., 561,568 (1991).

[3]   Ethan W. Johnson, Comment, Reducing Liability of American Banks for Expropriated Foreign Branch Deposits, 34 EMORY L.J. 201, 201 (1985).

[4]   *Id.*

[5]   Citibank Branches, CITIGROUP, http://www.citigroup.com/citi/about/countrypresence/

[6]   See Citi Mission & Principles, CITIGROUP, http://www.citigroup.com/citi/about/mission_principles.html (last visited Apr. 9, 2014); see generally Citi Country Presence, Citigroup, http://www.citigroup.com/citi/about/countrypresence/ (last visited Apr. 9, 2014).

[7]   FDIC Deposit Insurance Regulations; Definition of Insured Deposit, 78 Fed. Reg. 11604, 11605 (proposed Feb. 19, 2013) (to be codified at 12 C.F.R. pt. 330).

[17]   Telanoff, supra note 2, at 569.

reserves that depository institutions are required to maintain for "the purpose of facilitating the implementation of monetary policy," does not apply to any deposit that is payable only at an office located outside the United States.[18] The rule's impact is significant—U.S. banks do not have to hold reserves against the large amount of deposits at foreign branches of their banks.

Further, the overwhelming majority of foreign deposits are not dually payable; that is, they are not payable at the U.S. home office in addition to being payable at the foreign branch.[19] Significantly, recent events have made it less costly for banks to hold dually payable deposits.[20] The Dodd-Frank Act, as one such event, altered the deposit insurance assessment such that all liabilities are included, so dual-payability no longer increases the assessment base.[21] Additionally, the Federal Reserve now pays interest on reserves.[22] Nonetheless, banks have been hesitant to make deposits in foreign branches dually payable because they have concerns that dual-payability would mean they would no longer be protected from sovereign risk under Section 25(c) of the Federal Reserve Act.[23]

While domestic branches of U.S. banks are not considered separate legal entities, *foreign* branches of U.S. banks *have* been treated by courts as separate entities, and accordingly banks have traditionally not been compelled to incorporate as a subsidiary abroad to shield the parent from liability.[24] This is known as the "Separate Entity Doctrine," but courts have not treated it as an ironclad principle, resulting in a great deal of uncertainty regarding liability for foreign branch deposits.

* * *

In general, foreign branch banking is beneficial to all parties involved, as foreign countries obtain investment capital and U.S. financial services and U.S. companies reap the profitable rewards of foreign operations. Further, corporations may use foreign bank deposits as a means of minimizing U.S. tax consequences. Problems can arise, however, when tumultuous social and political events in countries where U.S. bank branches are located result in questions as to whether risk of political upheaval ("political risk") is borne by depositors or by the U.S. offices of the

---

[18]   See 12 C.F.R. § 204.1(c)(4)–(5) (2014). Furthermore, before its repeal, Regulation Q's establishment of a ceiling for interest paid on deposits did not apply to deposits payable only outside the United States. Telanoff, supra note 2, at 569 n.62.

[19]   See FDIC Deposit Insurance Regulations; Definition of Insured Deposit, 78 Fed. Reg. 11604, 11605 (proposed Feb. 19, 2013) (to be codified at 12 C.F.R. pt. 330).

[20]   *Id.*

[21]   See *id.* (citing Dodd-Frank Wall Street Reform and Consumer Protection Act, 12 U.S.C. § 5301 (2012)).

[22]   *Id.*

[23]   *Id.*

[24]   See Hannigan, supra note 1, at 739.

branch. Accordingly, banks have attempted to "ringfence" foreign deposits; to wall them off so that they are not payable in the U.S. The U.S. government and state governments have sought, in various ways, to "ringfence" foreign deposits as well, either by attempting to ensure that banks are not liable for the deposits or by mandating that deposits payable outside the U.S. are not, unlike deposits payable exclusively in the U.S., backed by the full faith and credit of the U.S. government.

* * *

NOTES

1.   A U.S. bank may establish a foreign presence in a number of ways, including through representative agency or branch offices, correspondent banking relationships, affiliates, subsidiaries (See Chapter 1 discussion), or Edge Act corporations (see Chapter 7 for a discussion of Edge Act corporations). The Federal Reserve Act of 1913 grants banks the authority to open foreign branches, and the branch office is the most common form of foreign presence. See 12 U.S.C. § 601 (2012). Nationally chartered banks operate the majority of foreign branches. See M. Ann Hannigan, United States Home Bank Liability for Foreign Branch Deposits, 1989 U.ILL.L.REV. at 758. A foreign branch is subject to both American law and the laws and regulations of the country in which it is located. See Francis D. Logan & Mark A. Kantor, Deposits at Expropriated Foreign Branches of U.S. Banks, 1982 U. ILL L. REV. 333, 334 (1982). Host country law may apply to capital requirements, reserves, submission to local courts and laws, and assurances from the parent bank.

2.   As with U.S. banks, foreign banks can accept two broad types of deposits: special deposits and general deposits. In a special deposit, the deposited funds are kept separate from the bank's funds, and the same bills deposited must be returned. They are, however, less common than the general deposit, in which the funds deposited become the property of the bank, and thus, the depositor can demand payment from general assets of the bank.

B. DEVELOPMENT OF DEPOSIT LIABILITY DOCTRINES: WAR AND CIVIL UNREST

The Russian Revolution

SOKOLOFF V. NATIONAL CITY BANK OF NEW YORK
New York Supreme Court
224 N.Y.S. 102 (1927)

ALFRED R. PAGE, OFFICIAL REFEREE.

* * * The defendant is a national banking corporation organized under the laws of the United States, and having its principal place of business in the city of New York. A branch of the defendant was opened at Petrograd

in Russia pursuant to permission granted by the Federal Reserve Act (38 Stat. 251) and by the Federal Reserve Board. Before opening its branch in Petrograd, the defendant was required to and did obtain the permission of the Imperial Government of Russia, the then existing government, to operate the branch, which permission was given in the form of a charter, prescribing 'rules for the operation of the Russian branches of the National City Bank of New York.'

* * *

In the month of March, 1917, the Imperial Government of Russia was overthrown and was superseded by the Provisional Government of Russia, popularly known as the Kerensky Government, which was recognized by the government of the United States as a government de facto and de jure, and was the last government of Russia recognized by the United States. On June 27, 1917, the plaintiff, a Russian citizen, who was then residing in the city of New York, paid to the defendant at its head office in the city of New York, the sum of $30,225 and of $883.50, respectively, for which he received the following receipts, dated on that day and signed in the name of the defendant by a duly authorized employee:

[handwritten margin note: Made deposit in U.S.]

'Received from Boris N. Sokoloff thirty thousand two hundred twenty-five dollars representing the cost of Rs. 130,000 at 23 1/4 cents which are to be transferred to our Petrograd Branch to open his account.'

And:

'Received from Boris N. Sokoloff eight hundred eighty-three 50/xx dollars, representing the cost of rubles 3,800 00/xx at 23 1/4 cents for transfer to our Petrograd Branch.'

Upon the receipt of the sums aggregating $31,108.50 from the plaintiff and the delivery to him of the above mentioned receipts, the defendant credited to its record of its ruble account with its Petrograd branch 133,800 rubles, and simultaneously or immediately thereafter the head office of the defendant advised its Petrograd branch by letter which read in part as follows:

[handwritten margin note: Credit account in Petrograd rubles]

'Kindly charge our account 133,800 rubles and open an account on your books for a like amount in the name of Boris Nikolaevitch Sokoloff.'

The specimen signature of the plaintiff was transmitted by the defendant's head office to its Petrograd branch with the letter of advice.

On or about August 21, 1917, the Petrograd branch debited its record of the ruble account with it of the head office with 133,800 rubles and opened a new account on its books in the name of the plaintiff, to which it made a corresponding credit of 133,800 rubles.

* * *

On November 7, 1917, the Provisional Government of Russia was overthrown by the Bolshevik Revolution, which established the so called Soviet Government, which has been in control of the city of Petrograd ever since its establishment, and still controls the said city and all territories of the former Russian Empire as the same was constituted after the Brest-Litovsk Peace.

* * *

While the American personnel was in Vologda during the month of March, 1918, a letter was mailed to the depositors in which they were asked to withdraw any balance that they might have to their credit with the defendant's Petrograd branch, in view of the unsettled conditions then prevailing in Russia, and the uncertainty of the defendant's continuance in Russia. In May, 1918, another letter was sent to all the depositors who had not answered the previous letter, stating that they would have to withdraw their balances. From September 1, 1918, until December 16, 1918. One Heuts, a subject of Holland, was in charge of the Petrograd branch. On December 16, 1918, there appeared a squad of soldiers with an order from the head of the committee on conflict between labor and capital, to the effect that the premises had all been requisitioned by the Fifth Army Corps of the Red army, with the exception of one small room, which Mr. Heuts occupied until January 20, 1919, when he was forcibly ejected by the soldiers, and they moved their barracks into the premises.

* * *

On December 29, 1918, the Soviet Government purported to issue a decree 'nationalizing' all private banks, and merged them into the People's (State) Bank, and thereby confiscated all the assets of the Petrograd branch of the defendant. The defendant claims that, under the contract made with the plaintiff, the defendant's head office in New York undertook only two things, (1) to sell the plaintiff rubles at 23 1/4 cents, and (2) to transmit them to its Petrograd branch, which was completely performed; that, when the plaintiff received a passbook from the defendant's Petrograd branch, a new contract relation between himself and the Petrograd branch was made to be performed in Russia; that the plaintiff only had such rights against defendant as he would have against any Russian bank.

* * *

There was no further opportunity to make an effective demand. The promulgation of the decree by the Soviet authorities on December 27, 1917; the occupation of premises of the Petrograd branch by Soviet soldiers on that day; their withdrawal on the understanding that the bank would abide by the regulations which were imposed by the chief of the commissary of the State Bank of Russia, among which was the inhibition of payment to any of the depositors, except Americans, of more than 150 rubles a week—

all of these happenings rendered it impossible for the defendant to pay on demand, at its banking office in Petrograd, 120,370 rubles. Therefore during this time such a demand would have been futile. The letters written to depositors, urging them to withdraw their deposits, do not affect the plaintiff's claim, because at no time had the defendant signified its willingness to pay to the plaintiff the 120,000 rubles or in any manner reversed its position that it had theretofore taken, that it was not liable for that amount. In my opinion, therefore, there was no necessity for plaintiff to prove a more formal demand than that contained in his letter presented by his sister to the Petrograd branch in order to enable him to bring his action.

The defendant pleads, first, as a complete defense, and, second, as a partial defense, that the agreement between the plaintiff and defendant was made and to be performed in Russia; that the laws of Russia then and now provide that, where the performance of a contract is prevented by superior force, which it is impossible for that party to resist, and which was caused by no fault of his, that party is excused from performance in Russia, and is not responsible in damages for failure to perform; that such superior force excusing performance may consist in popular or political disturbances; and that the Bolshevik Revolution and the superior force exercised by the revolutionists rendered it impossible for the defendant to maintain its branches in Russia or to pay to the plaintiff in Russia any rubles to which he may have been entitled.

In support of this defense, there was offered in evidence section 684 of the General Code of the Russian Empire, two decisions of the Civil Cassation Department of the Ruling Senate of Russia, the highest court of appeal of the empire, known as decision No. 1 of 1906 and decision No. 1 of 1907. Boris Brasol, an eminent Russian lawyer, whose qualification was admitted, testified that the decisions of this court have the force of binding precedents in Russia, that these decisions extend the provisions of section 684 of the General Code of Russia to cover riots, revolutions, and civil commotions; and he also testified, in response to a hypothetical question, that, under this statute, force majeure would be a defense to a bank against any claim from a depositor for damages owing to the inability of the bank to pay deposits to a depositor during the existence of the revolutionary conditions. He further testified that, after the condition of force majeure ceased to exist, the bank would be liable to the depositor for the amount of his deposit. In other words, that while force majeure would excuse a debtor from liability for damages for delay caused thereby, it would not discharge the debt.

* * *

The action, however, is not brought to recover damages alleged to have been caused by the delay in paying the money, and the only damage that could be recovered for withholding the money would be interest. Plaintiff's waiver of any claim to interest prior to September 1, 1918, disposes of this defense, and it is not necessary to determine the effect of the Russian law. This action is brought to recover the debt and not for damages for failure to pay during a period when it is claimed the defendant's Petrograd branch was prevented from paying by an alleged force majeure. In this case the Court of Appeals has held (239 N. Y. 158, 145 N.E. 917, 37 A. L. R. 712) that the decrees of the Soviet Government nationalizing the banks of Russia, with the accompanying seizure of their assets, have no force and effect as act of sovereignty, in our courts, for the reason that the government of the United States has refused to recognize the Soviet Republic as the government of Russia de facto or de jure. The confiscation of the assets in Russia by this unrecognized government has no other effect, in law, than seizure by bandits or by other lawless bodies.

* * *

QUESTIONS AND NOTES

1.   The *Sokoloff* court did not place any emphasis on the fact that the deposit account at the Petrograd branch of National City Bank at issue in the case was opened by the plaintiff in New York City. Should it have in light of the court's decision? What about the court's discussion of the role of the U.S. government at the time of the *Sokoloff* decision in not recognizing the new Soviet government, as having no "other effect in law, than seizure by bandits or by other lawless bodies." In light of the U.S. government subsequently recognizing the Soviet government as a diplomatic matter, does this render in question any of the court's rationale for its decision?

2.   In other contexts involving international banking issues, U.S. courts have placed emphasis on U.S. diplomatic recognition of a new government as successor in interest to the prior regime in resolving the obligations of both U.S. and foreign banks. See, e.g., American Bell International Inc. v. The Islamic Republic of Iran, 474 F. Supp 420 (1979) (notice injunction denied for U.S. bank to perform on letter of credit in favor of Iranian government, in part because U.S. government had previously recognized the new government), discussed in Chapter 3.

The Cuban Revolution

GARCIA V. CHASE MANHATTAN BANK, N.A.
United States Court of Appeals
735 F.2d 645 (2nd Cir 1984)

MESKILL, CIRCUIT JUDGE.

* * * Garcia and her late husband Jose Lorenzo Perez Dominguez, a wealthy businessman, were Cuban citizens prior to the Cuban revolution.

Dominguez also served in the Cuban Senate from 1954–1958 and retired from the Cuban army with the rank of colonel in 1949. Dominguez and Garcia became concerned for the safety of their money in 1958 in light of the ongoing Cuban revolution. At the recommendation of a friend, they visited Chase's Vedado branch on March 10, 1958 and spoke to two bank officers. Dominguez expressed his fears over the safety of his money and stated that he wanted to make a fixed term deposit of 100,000 pesos. The Chase officials responded that he was doing the right thing "because it was an insurance, security for the money." They explained that the deposit was a "private contract" between the bank and Dominguez and Garcia. They stated that Chase's main office in New York would guarantee the certificate and that they could be repaid by presenting the certificate at any Chase branch worldwide. The officials said that repayment could be made in dollars in New York since "that is the money that the bank used." Pesos were equal in value to dollars at the time.

Dominguez and Garcia gave Chase 100,000 pesos that day and received a non-negotiable certificate of deposit (CD) which by its terms was returnable on March 10, 1959 and bore an interest rate of three and one-half percent.

As the political situation in Cuba worsened during 1958, Dominguez and Garcia became increasingly worried about the safety of their money. They returned to the Vedado branch on September 16, 1958 and spoke with two Chase officers, one of whom was present during the March 10 discussion. The Chase officials again told them that they were doing the right thing by securing their money. The officers reaffirmed that payment could be had in dollars at any Chase branch, Dominguez and Garcia gave Chase 400,000 pesos this time. The CD they received would mature on March 16, 1959 and was otherwise identical to the first CD except that it bore an interest rate of three percent and was for six months rather than a year.

* * *

When Fidel Castro entered Havana on January 1, 1959, Dominguez took refuge in the El Salvadorian Embassy and subsequently went to El Salvador. Garcia left Cuba for Spain in 1964. Dominguez died in Puerto Rico in 1975. The CDs were found after his death in his safe deposit box in a Chase branch in Puerto Rico.

In February 1959 the revolutionary Cuban government enacted Law No. 78 which enabled the Ministry of Recovery of Misappropriated Property, *inter alia,* to freeze bank accounts. The Ministry subsequently ordered Chase to freeze the Garcia/Dominguez "account." On July 16, 1959, the Ministry ordered the "account" closed and demanded that Chase remit its value. Chase complied by sending a sum equal to the debts owed Garcia and Dominguez to the Ministry.

* * *

Chase argues that a demand is unnecessary to start the statute of limitations running where there is a repudiation of the obligation prior to the demand. We need not decide whether a clear and unequivocal repudiation of the debt obligation would commence the imitations period, see Tillman v. Guaranty Trust Co., 253 N.Y. 295, 297, 171 N.E. 61 (1930) (per curiam), because we agree with the court below that no such repudiation occurred in this case.

* * *

Chase maintains that the events of 1959 and 1960 and its communication of those facts to Garcia and Dominguez by letters in 1964 and 1968 constituted a clear and unequivocal repudiation. We disagree. Repudiation must be clear and unequivocal to constitute an anticipatory breach of contract. Gittlitz v. Lewis, 28 Misc.2d 712, 713, 212 N.Y.S.2d 219 (N.Y.Sup.Ct.), *appeal dismissed,* 14 A.D.2d 783 (1961); 11 W, Jaeger, Williston on Contracts § 1322 (3d ed. 1968). Chase's 1964 letter did not unequivocally indicate that it would not honor its obligations. The letter merely recounted the actions of the Cuban government and referred inquiries to the National Bank of Cuba. Chase did not definitely state that it would not pay the debt, although this could be inferred from the letter, *Cf, Tillman,* 253 N.Y at 297, 171 N.E. 61. Chase's 1968 letter was not introduced into evidence. Presumably it was similar in substance to both the 1964 and 1970 letters. As such, we cannot say as a matter of law that Chase clearly and unequivocally repudiated its contractual obligations to Dominguez and Garcia. Therefore, the statute of limitations did not begin to run until a demand was made. Chase's statute of limitations argument thus fails.

Chase seeks to avoid liability to Garcia on the basis of the Cuban government's actions. It argues that while the CDs could be repaid at any Chase branch worldwide, Cuba's closing of Garcia's "account" and its appropriation of Chase's funds in a sum equal to the amount of its debt to Dominguez and Garcia prior to their presentment of the CDs canceled the debt. It then asserts that we may not question the validity of the Cuban government's action under the act of state doctrine. Chase's arguments on both of these issues must fail.

* * *

Chase would not argue that its debt was extinguished if an armed gunman had entered its Vedado branch and demanded payment of a sum equal to the amount of its debt to Dominguez and Garcia. Yet in effect, this is what transpired. The Cuban government did nothing more than "enter" Chase's Vedado branch armed with Law No. 78 and demand depositors' money. Chase turned over funds without requiring the surrender of the

CDs, without notice to the holder of the CDs and without a fight, As in the case of a bank robbery, the bank itself must bear the consequences. See Michie on Banks and Banking, § 326a at 317–18 (1983) ("[A] bank cannot be compelled to pay a certificate of deposit issued by it, without the production and surrender of the certificate . . . [U]pon its payment by the bank of issue the certificate should be surrendered for cancellation. A bank acts at its peril in paying a certificate without surrender thereof and endorsement. . . .") (footnotes omitted). Where, as here, the debtor creditor relationship was created primarily to ensure the safety of the creditors' funds, a debtor's payment to a third party of a sum equal to that owed the creditors does not extinguish the original debt. Thus, the actions of the Cuban government did not accomplish the cancellation of Chase's obligation to ensure the safety of Garcia's funds.

* * *

Thus, if the situs of Chase's debt to Garcia were in Cuba, the Cuban government could validly seize it. But even if what occurred was a seizure of the debt and not merely payment of a sum equal to it, the facts in the instant case call for a result favoring Garcia. The purpose of the agreement between Chase and Dominguez and Garcia was to ensure that, no matter what happened in Cuba, including seizure of the debt, Chase would still have a contractual obligation to pay the depositors upon presentation of their CDs, Garcia and Dominguez selected Chase because of its international reputation. Chase was aware of their desire to safeguard their money and assured them that their funds were protected. Chase "accepted the risk that it would be liable elsewhere for *obligations* incurred by its branch." Vishipco Line v. Chase Manhattan Bank, N.A., 660 F.2d 854, 863 (2d Cir.1981), *cert, denied,* 459 U.S. 976, 103 S.Ct. 313, 74 L.Ed.2d 291 (1982). If the understanding was that the debt to the Cuban government if it should win the race to the bank, it is apparent that the deposits would never have been made.

Today's decision is predicated on Chase's contractual undertaking to ensure the safety of Dominguez's and Garcia's money by agreeing to honor its obligations in dollars at any of its branches. Our decision is not inconsistent with the policy considerations underlying the act of state doctrine. "The major underpinning of the act of state doctrine is the policy of foreclosing court adjudications involving the legality of acts of foreign states on their own soil that *might* embarrass the Executive Branch of our Government in the conduct of our foreign relations." Alfred Dunhill of London, Inc. v. Republic of Cuba, 425 U.S. 682, 697, 96 S.Ct. 1854, 1862, 48 L.Ed.2d 301 (1976) (plurality opinion) (citing *Sabbatino,* 376 U.S. at 427–28, 431–33, 84 S.Ct. at 941–2); see also Banco Nacional de Cuba v. Farr, 383 F,2d 166, 180 (2d Cir. 1967), *cert, denied,* 390 U.S. 956, 88 S.Ct. 1038, 19 L.Ed.2d 1 151 (1968). We are not challenging the validity of the Cuban government's actions here and Cuba has shown no interest in the outcome of this case. We are simply resolving a private dispute between an American bank and one of its depositors. The result we reach will have no international repercussions. Chase cannot use the act of state doctrine as a defense because the doctrine is not implicated. See Texas Trading & Milling Corp. v. Federal Republic of Nigeria, 647 F.2d 300, 316 n. 38 (2d Cir. 1981), *cert, denied,* 454 U.S. 1148, 102 S.Ct. 1012, 71 L.Ed.2d 301 (1982) ("Act of state analysis depends upon a careful case-by-case analysis of the extent to which the separation of powers concerns on which the doctrine is based are implicated by the action before the court").

The judgment of the district court is affirmed.

KEARSE, CIRCUIT JUDGE, dissenting:

With all due respect to the majority, I must dissent since I believe the act of state doctrine relieves defendant Chase Manhattan Bank, N.A. ("Chase"), of liability in this case. The majority correctly recognizes that that doctrine, see Banco Nacional de Cuba v. Sabbatino, 376 U.S. 398, 416, 84 S.Ct. 923, 934, 11 L.Ed.2d 804 (1964), precludes our questioning the validity of acts of the Republic of Cuba within its borders (Majority opinion, *ante* at 650), and that "if the situs of Chase's debt to Garcia were in Cuba, the Cuban government could validly seize it" *(id)*. However, it appears to me that the majority gives insufficient recognition to the facts that the debts in question were collectible in Cuba; that the contract was not intended to guarantee the safety of plaintiff's funds against seizure by the Cuban government; and that, independently of the Cuban government's subsequent seizure of Chase's own assets and liabilities, that government in fact seized the assets of the plaintiff that are at issue here.

* * *

PEREZ V. CHASE MANHATTAN BANK N.A.

Court of Appeals of New York
61 N.Y.2d 460 (1984)

KAYE, JUDGE.

* * *

Rosa Manas y Pineiro (Manas), a Cuban national, in 1958 purchased five certificates of deposit from the Marianao, Cuba branch of defendant Chase Manhattan Bank (Chase), and first presented them for payment at Chase's New York office in 1974. The issue on this appeal is whether Chase is excused from payment to Manas because, in September, 1959, the Cuban government confiscated Manas' accounts and Chase surrendered the funds representing the certificates. Because the certificates were payable in Cuba and Chase at the time of the confiscation was present there, the Cuban government had the power to enforce and collect Chase's debt to Manas in

Cuba, and the Act of State doctrine precludes inquiry by this court into the propriety of a confiscation directed particularly at Manas' assets in Cuba. Having once made payment, Chase is not liable to pay on the certificates of deposit a second time.

* * *

By Law No. 78 of February 13, 1959, the Cuban government created the Ministry of Recovery of Misappropriated Property "to recover property of any type which has been removed from the National Wealth and obtain the complete restoration of the proceeds of unjust enrichments obtained under the cover of the Public Power." The minister was given the power to conduct investigations, freeze bank accounts, take possession of property, and enact "final decisions" returning the confiscated property to the "National Wealth." Chase was thereafter directed to freeze accounts belonging to certain former government officials and their families, and in September, 1959 the ministry ordered Chase to close such frozen accounts—including specifically those represented by Manas' certificates which had by then reached maturity—and remit the proceeds to the ministry. In compliance with that directive Chase turned funds in the amount of Manas' certificates over to the government. Approximately a year after the confiscation of Manas' assets, on May 6, 1960, the Castro government enacted Law No. 851, providing for nationalization of United States firms in Cuba, and by Resolution No. 2 of September 17, 1960, the government nationalized all of Chase's Cuban branches.

It was not until January, 1974 that Manas, by then residing in the United States, for the first time presented her certificates to Chase's office in New York and demanded payment, which was refused. Manas instituted this action in July, 1974 by motion for summary judgment in lieu of complaint, and Chase cross-moved for summary judgment. Both motions were denied, and the Appellate Division affirmed (52 A.D.2d 794, 383 N.Y.S.2d 357). Chase subsequently removed the case to the United States District Court (for the Southern District of New York, but the action was remanded (443 F.Supp. 418).

* * *

The jury found that the certificates of deposit were repayable in United States dollars, that the certificates could be presented to any Chase branch in the world, including New York and Cuba, and that Manas' funds on deposit in Chase's Marianao branch were confiscated by the Ministry of Misappropriated Funds.

Both parties then moved for judgment. In view of the jury's findings, Trial Term held that Chase's debt to Manas had its situs in Cuba as the certificates were capable of being repaid in Cuba and Chase's Cuban branches were open and operating subject to the laws and jurisdiction of the Cuban government at the time of the September, 1959 confiscation. Trial Term thereupon entered judgment for Chase in December, 1980, concluding:

"In the case at bar, both the persons and the *res* were within the territorial dominion of the acting State at the time of the confiscatory taking. In this court's opinion, under the facts as established at trial, the situs of the debt herein was Cuba. In order for this debt to be beyond Cuban jurisdiction in this case, it would have been necessary for the jury to have found that the place of presentment was only outside of Cuba. The jury finding that payment could be any-where did not change the situs of this debt from Chase in Cuba while it functioned there. It only created an option for plaintiff to collect the debt elsewhere prior to the confiscation. Although it is true, as asserted by plaintiff, that the parent bank is ultimately liable for the obligations of the branch (Sokoloff v. National City Bank of N.Y., 130 Misc. 66, 224 N.Y.S. 102, affd. 223 App.Div. 754, 227 N.Y.S. 907, affd. 8250 N.Y. 69, 164 N.E. 745), such a liability does not alter the situs of the debt. When the branch's liability is extinguished, as under the facts herein, the parent is relieved as well.

"Accordingly, this court holds that the judicial self-limiting act of State doctrine applies herein as the confiscation of plaintiffs funds was an official act of a sovereign government fully executed within its own jurisdiction and whose validity this court must refuse to inquire into, thereby implicitly giving the act ex-traterritorial effect." (106 Misc.2d 660, 666–667, 434 N.Y.S.2d 868.)

* * *

We must first determine whether the property taken by the Cuban government—here, Chase's debt to Manas—was within its borders. For purposes of the Act of State doctrine, a debt is located within a foreign State when that State has the power to enforce or collect it. (Weston Banking Corp. v. Turkiye Garanti Bankasi, A.S., 57 N.Y.2d 315, 324, 456 N.Y.S.2d 684, 442 N.E.2d 1195; Zeevi & Sons v. Grindlays Bank [Uganda], 37 N.Y.2d 220, 228, 371 N.Y.S,2d 892, 333 N.E,2d 168, cert. den. 423 U.S. 866, 96 S.Ct. 126, 46 L.Ed,2d 95; Menendez v. Saks & Co., 485 F.2d 1355, 1364, *supra;* United Bank v. Cosmic Int., 392 F.Supp. 262, affd. 542 F.2d 868, 873 (2nd Cir.).) Since Harris v. Balk, 198 U.S. 215, 222–223,[1] 25 S.Ct 625, 626, 49 L.Ed. 1023, the power to enforce or collect a debt has been dependent on the presence of the debtor. If the debtor is present in the foreign State and the debt is payable there, the foreign sovereign then has power to enforce or collect it, and a confiscation of that debt amounts to a seizure of property within that sovereign's borders.

---

[1]   Although another aspect of *Harris* v. *Balk* has been overruled (see Shaffer v. Heitner, 433 U.S. 186, 97 S.Ct 2569, 53 L.Ed.2d 683).

At the time the Cuban government confiscated Manas' deposits in September, 1959, the debtor (Chase) was present in Cuba. Its Cuban branches were open and operating under Cuban authority, and the debt owed by Chase to Manas—as the jury found—was payable at any Chase bank in the world including the Marianao branch where it was confiscated. While the certificates had by that time matured, and could have been redeemed elsewhere, Manas had taken no steps to redeem them in or out of Cuba. Where, as here, Chase paid over the full amount of its debt pursuant to the direction of the Cuban government, a direction which under the Act of State doctrine is beyond our review, Chase is relieved of liability on any subsequent demand by Manas for the funds. (Trujillo-M v. Bank of Nova Scotia, 51 Misc.2d 689, 692–693, 273 N.Y.S.2d 700, affd. 29 A.D.2d 847, 289 N.Y.S.2d 389, cert. den. 393 U.S. 982, 89 S.Ct. 454, 21 L.Ed.2d 443.)[2]

The fact that Chase's debt to Manas was not exclusively payable in Cuba, but could in addition have been paid in other countries, does not affect this result. Manas bargained for and received the right to collect the debt from Chase at any of its branches throughout the world. While the debt contemplated alternate places of payment and thus had multiple situs, because constituted but a single obligation to pay, payment at one of the places chosen for performance extinguished the debt at all of its situses. Manas herself surely could not have redeemed the certificates of deposit in Cuba and subsequently received payment on those same certificates at a Chase branch in another country. Chase's debt to Manas was satisfied by payment to the Cuban government in response to its confiscation of Manas' accounts, and at that point the debt, wherever else it had been payable, was extinguished.

Only when a debt or other obligation is not payable at all in the confiscating State would the Act of State doctrine be inapplicable. In such situations, the foreign sovereign has no power to enforce or collect the debt. (Zeevi & Sons v, Grindlays Bank [Uganda], 37 N.Y.2d 220, 371 N.Y.S.2d 892, 333 N.E.2d 168, supra; Republic of Iraq v. First Nat. City Bank, 353 F.2d 47, cert. den. 382 U.S. 1027, 86 S.Ct 648, 15 L.Ed.2d 540, supra.) Here, however, as the jury found, Chase's debt to Manas was payable in Cuba, giving Cuba the jurisdiction to collect and enforce it, which the Cuban government exercised. By reason of the Act of State doctrine the legitimacy of the confiscation is beyond our review.

---

   [2]   The Appellate Division's conclusion that "the Act of State doctrine * * * apparently never has been, applied to relieve an American bank of obligations owed by its branches to depositors" (93 A.D.2d, p. 409, 463 N.Y.S.2d 764) ignores the thrust of the decision in Trujillo. While the bank in Trujillo was a Canadian bank, the question presented was the liability of its New York office to repay deposits confiscated from one of its foreign branches pursuant to an order directed at plaintiffs accounts. The court in Trujillo determined that under the Act of State doctrine the bank could not be liable to plaintiff on his subsequent demand for re-payment.

The Hickenlooper amendment (U.S.Code, tit. 22, § 2370, subd. [e], par. [2]), which operates to preclude the application of the Act of State doctrine in certain circumstances, has no effect in this case. * * * Here, Manas was a Cuban citizen at the time of the confiscation and was either present in Cuba or only temporarily absent at the time of confiscation, and the debt, once seized in Cuba, did not come within this country's jurisdiction. Accordingly, the Hickenlooper amendment does not preclude application of the Act of State doctrine in this action.

* * *

In sum, the situs of Manas' property—the debt due from Chase on her certificates—was Cuba at the time of the government's confiscation of her property and Chase's payment. The confiscation was an act of a foreign sovereign affecting the property of one of its own nationals within its own borders, and cannot be examined in this court. Having paid the full amount of the certificates, Chase was relieved of liability to make a second payment on those certificates when Manas presented them some 15 years later.[5]

* * *

WACHTLER, JUDGE (dissenting).

Money deposited in an American bank which is payable at any of its branches, should not be deemed to have its situs in every country in which the bank may have a branch office, so that the debt may be extinguished by any government which decides to confiscate the account "located" within its borders. The concept that a debt may have multiple situses—in every jurisdiction where the debtor has established an office—has never been held by the Supreme Court to be an essential or acceptable ingredient of the Act of State doctrine.

A more conservative application of the Act of State doctrine should not bar the courts of this State from granting the plaintiff any relief in this case. Although the suit is occasioned by the confiscation of bank assets in Cuba, it involves only private litigants and the question as to which of them must bear the loss: the bank whose assets were physically confiscated; or the depositor whose intangible account, payable at any of the bank's worldwide branches, was designated in the Cuban order of confiscation. If the Act of State doctrine requires this court to abstain from considering the legality or illegality of the foreign seizure, and thus from deciding the case

---

[5]   The dissent misapprehends our holding. We hold that in the circumstances disclosed in this record as crystallized by the verdict of the jury, the rights of plaintiff evidenced by the certificates of deposit issued by Chase were located in Cuba at the time of the confiscation specifically directed against Manas' assets, and that this act of the Cuban government is beyond our review. We do not hold that any purported confiscation by a foreign sovereign of deposits at American bank branches would be accorded similar effect. The certificates here were both issued and payable in Cuba, and therefore subject to enforcement and collection by the foreign sovereign. The circumstance that the Chase branch in Cuba was nationalized a year after confiscation of the certificates is irrelevant.

on that ground, it should not preclude the court from resolving this private dispute by consideration of other factors in much the same manner as we would if it had been precipitated by an act of nature.

* * *

The essence of the relationship between the parties is that the bank agreed to safeguard the depositor's money. It did so in the midst of a revolution by accepting deposits from a person whose husband was an official in the government under attack. The bank specifically agreed that the certificates would be redeemed at any of its branches, most of which are in his country, and further agreed to pay in United States currency. Even after the revolution had succeeded, the bank remained in Cuba and maintained assets all of which could have been, and in fact ultimately were, confiscated by the Cuban government. Under these circumstances it could be said that the bank was fully aware of and accepted the risk of confiscation of its assets, and should not be permitted to refuse to honor its commitment to this depositor after her arrival in this country.

* * *

QUESTIONS AND NOTES

1. The *Perez* Court appeared to place no weight on whether or not the U.S. government had recognized the new Castro government; in fact the court concluded that, even if the Act of State doctrine "requires this court to abstain from considering the legality or illegality of the foreign seizure [of plaintiff's deposit by the new Castro" government] "the court could look to other factors." How does the court's reasoning compare to the dissenting opinion in that case?

2. Footnote 5 in the majority opinion concluded that the act of the Cuban government in confiscating the plaintiff's assets was beyond the court's review. Compare this view to the decisions in the Vietnam cases, below.

3. The *Perez* case references the Hickenlooper amendment, 12 U.S.C. § 2370, which provides as follows: "Notwithstanding any other provision of law, no court in the United States shall decline on the ground of the federal act of state doctrine to make a determination on the merits giving effect to the principles of international law in a case in which a claim of title or other right to property is asserted by any party including a foreign state (or a party claiming through such state) based upon (or traced through) a confiscation or other taking after January 1, 1959, by an act of that state in violation of the principles of international law, including the principles of compensation and the other standards set out in this subsection: *Provided,* That his subparagraph shall not be applicable (1) in any case in which an act of a foreign state is not contrary to international law or with respect to a claim of title or other right to property acquired pursuant to an irrevocable letter of credit of not more than 180 days duration issued in good faith prior to the time of the confiscation or other taking, or (2) in any case with respect to which the

President determines that application of the act of state doctrine is required in that *particular* case by the foreign policy interests of the United States and a suggestion to this effect is filed on his behalf in that case with the court."

The Hickenlooper amendment does not apply to confiscations by a foreign State of the property of its own nationals within its borders, since such confiscations are "not contrary to international law." See F. Palicio y Compania, S.A. v. Brash, 256 F.Supp. 481, 486–487, affd. 375 F.2d 1011, cert. den. sub nom Brush v. Republic of Cuba, 389 U.S. 830 (1967), or to expropriated property that remains in the confiscating country without coming within the territorial jurisdiction of the United States. See Banco Nacional de Cuba v. First Nat. City Bank, 431 F.2d 394, 400–402 (2nd Cir.), revd. on other grounds 406 U.S. 759 (1972).

The Vietnam War Cases

VISHIPCO LINE V. THE CHASE MANHATTAN BANK, N.A.

United States Court of Appeals
660 F.2d 854 (2d Cir. 1981)

MANSFIELD, CIRCUIT JUDGE.

* * * Plaintiffs appeal from a judgment of the United States District Court for the Southern District of New York entered after a nonjury trial by Judge Robert L. Carter on December 5, 1980, dismissing their claims against Chase Manhattan Bank, N.A. ("Chase"), for breach of contract. The ten corporate plaintiffs Vishipco Line, Ha Nam Cong Ty, Dai Nam Hang Hai C.T., Rang Dong Hang Hai C.T., Mekong Ship Co. Sarl, Vishipco Sarl, Thai Binh C.T., VN Tau Bien C.T., Van An Hang Hai C.T., and Cong Ty U Tau Sao Mai are Vietnamese corporations which maintained piastre demand deposit accounts at Chase's Saigon branch in 1975. Invoking diversity jurisdiction, they claim that Chase breached its deposit contracts with them when it closed the doors of its Saigon branch on April 24, 1975, to escape from the Communist insurgents and subsequently refused to make payment in New York of the amount owed. The individual plaintiff Ms. Nguyen Thi Cham is a Vietnamese citizen who purchased a six-month two hundred million piastre certificate of deposit ("CD") from Chase's Saigon branch on November 27, 1974, and claims that Chase is in breach for refusing to cash the CD in dollars in New York.

* * *

From 1966 until April 24, 1975, Chase operated a branch office in Saigon. Among its depositors were the ten corporate plaintiffs, which were principally engaged at that time in providing shipping services to the U.S. Government in Southeast Asia, and the individual plaintiff, who owned a 200 million piastre CD issued by Chase's Saigon branch. Chase's operations in Saigon came to an end at noon on April 24, 1975, after Chase officials in New York determined that Saigon would soon fall to the Communists. After closing the branch without any prior notice to depositors, local Chase officials balanced the day's books, shut the vaults and the building itself, and delivered keys and financial records needed to operate the branch to personnel at the French Embassy in Saigon. Saigon fell on April 30th, and on May 1st the new government issued a communique which read as follows:

> All public offices, public organs, barracks, industrial, agricultural and commercial establishments, banks, communication and transport, cultural, educational and health establishments, warehouses, and so forth together with documents, files, property and technical means of U.S. imperialism and the Saigon administration will be confiscated and, from now on, managed by the revolutionary administration.

French gave records to Revolutionary

Shortly thereafter, the French embassy turned over records from the Chase branch to the new government.

* * *

Chase next argues that under Vietnamese law its failure to repay plaintiffs' deposits in the period prior to May 1, 1975, was not a breach of its deposit contract, because the conditions prevailing in Saigon at the time rendered payment impossible. In support of this argument, Chase cites various sections of the South Vietnamese Civil Code which excuse performance under various extenuating circumstances, as well as the provisions included in the deposit contracts used by the Saigon branch which purported to discharge the bank's responsibility for losses to depositors resulting from a variety of unexpected and uncontrollable sources.

Rendered Payment impossible under Vietnamese law/ discharge duty due to acts of god

BUT while impossible in Saigon not impossible elsewhere

This argument must be rejected for the reasons that impossibility of performance in Vietnam did not relieve Chase of its obligation to perform elsewhere. By operating in Saigon through a branch rather than through a separate corporate entity, Chase accepted the risk that it would be liable elsewhere for obligations incurred by its branch. As the official referee in the Sokoloff case (Harrison Tweed, of the Milbank Tweed firm) summarized the law:

Using a branch made them liable

> (W)hen considered with relation to the parent bank, (foreign branches) are not independent agencies; they are. what their name imports, merely branches, and are subject to the supervision and control of the parent bank, and are instrumentalities whereby the parent bank carries on its business. . . . Ultimate liability for a debt of a branch would rest upon the parent bank. Sokoloff v. National City Bank, 130 Misc. 66, 73, 224 N.Y.S. 102, 114 (Sup,Ct.N,Y.Cty. 1927) (emphasis added).

[handwritten margin note: Reason U.S. banks safer]

[handwritten margin note: No waiver of rights so imp. & FM don't apply]

U.S. banks, by operating abroad through branches rather than through subsidiaries, reassure foreign depositors that their deposits will be safer with them than they would be in a locally incorporated bank. Heininger, supra, at 911–12. Indeed, the national policy in South Vietnam, where foreign banks were permitted to operate only through branches, was to enable those depositing in foreign branches to gain more protection than they would have received had their money been deposited in locally incorporated subsidiaries of foreign banks. Chase's defenses of impossibility and force majeure might have succeeded if the Saigon branch had been locally incorporated or (more problematically) if the deposit contract had included an explicit waiver on the part of the depositor of any right to proceed against the home office. But absent such circumstances the Saigon branch's admitted inability to perform did not relieve the Chase of liability on its debts in Saigon, since the conditions in Saigon were no bar to performance in New York or at other points outside of Vietnam. Nor has Chase shown that the Vietnamese government took steps to assume or cancel its branch liabilities. The May 1st decree nationalizing the Vietnamese banking industry only provided that "(a)ll . . . banks . . . will be confiscated and from now on managed by the revolutionary administration." In addition, during discovery Chase, in response to the following interrogatory:

> Interrogatory 4. When the assets were seized did the Government of Vietnam agree to pay the depositors at the Saigon Branch?

replied

> Chase lacks the knowledge necessary to answer this interrogatory.

The evidence therefore can only be read as showing that the Vietnamese government confiscated the assets abandoned by Chase in Saigon, but did not thereby affect Chase's liabilities to its depositors. Under these circumstances, Justice (then Judge) Cardozo's opinion in Sokoloff fifty years ago applies:

> The defendant's liability was unaffected by the attempt to terminate its existence and the seizure of its assets. . . . Plaintiff did not pay his money to the defendant, and become the owner of this chose in action, upon the security of the Russian assets. He paid his money to a corporation organized under our laws upon the security of all its assets, here as well as elsewhere. Everything in Russia might have been destroyed by fire or flood, by war or revolution, and still the defendant would have remained bound by its engagement. Sokoloff v. National City Bank, 239 N.Y. 158, 167, 145 N.E. 917 (1924).

As one commentator has summarized the law: The defenses of frustration and impossibility were . . . rejected at an early stage in the

Sokoloff proceedings, and do not appear to have been successfully raised in subsequent cases involving foreign branches of U.S. banks. Rather, the well-established path from branch to home office has been followed, even if the branch has been closed, to establish an alternative means for performance. Heininger, supra, at 1003–04.

A bank which accepts deposits at a foreign branch becomes *a* debtor, not a bailee, with respect to its depositors. In the event that unsettled local conditions require it to cease operations, it should inform its depositors of the date when its branch will close and give them the opportunity to withdraw their deposits or, if conditions prevent such steps, enable them to obtain payment at an alternative location. See, e. g., Sokoloff v. National City Bank, supra, 130 Misc. at 71, 224 N.Y.S. at 112; Heininger, supra, at 1009–10. In the rare event that such measures are either impossible or only partially successful, fairness dictates that the parent bank be liable for those deposits which it was unable to return abroad. To hold otherwise would be to undermine the seriousness of its obligations to its depositors and under some circumstances (not necessarily present here) to gain a windfall.

Chase's next argument, that under New York law its non-payment must be excused because no demand was ever made prior to the closing of its Saigon branch, must also be rejected. No Vietnamese law was offered on this issue. Nor is Chase's contention supported by New York law. It is not settled that a demand is not necessary where the branch in which the deposit was maintained (or by which the CD was issued) has been closed. 10 Am.Jur.2d Banks & Banking s 450 (1963); Sokoloff v. National City Bank, 250 N.Y. 69, 80–81, 164 N.E. 745 (1928) (where Petrograd branch of National City Bank ceased to exist because of Soviet seizure, this made "demand useless and unnecessary" and no demand was required since it "would manifestly be futile"). Similarly, reliance on New York cases suspending or excusing performance during times of war fails, since Chase, which was ultimately liable for the debt, was never barred by the wartime conditions in Vietnam from making payment outside of Vietnam. Finally, Chase, as a national bank, can find no comfort in the provisions of s 138 of the New York Banking Law, which purport to limit in various ways the liability of state bank and trust companies for deposits made in overseas branches. By its own terms, s 138 is unavailable to Chase in this case, because it only applies to state, not national, banks. If this unavailability has the effect of placing national banks like Chase at a competitive disadvantage vis-a-vis state banks, as Chase alleges, the solution lies with Congress, not the judiciary.

* * *

TRINH V. CITIBANK, N.A.

United States Court of Appeals
850 F.2d 1164 (6th Cir. 1988)

NATHANIEL R. JONES, CIRCUIT JUDGE.

* * * On July 25, 1974, plaintiff's father, Quang Quy Trinh, a retired senator in the South Vietnamese government, opened a joint savings account at Citibank Saigon in his name and that of his son. The account paid annual interest at a rate of 19% compounded daily. At the time Trinh's father opened the account, Trinh was a student residing in Michigan. He became a United States citizen in 1979 and has never returned to Vietnam.

The deposit agreement governing the account provided that "withdrawals [would] be permitted only at Citibank's place of business" which was designated as "28–30 Nguyen Van Thinh, Saigon 1, Republic of Vietnam" and that deposits were payable only in Vietnamese piasters. The agreement further provided as follows:

> Citibank does not accept responsibility for any loss or damage suffered or incurred by any depositor resulting from government orders, laws . . . or from any other cause beyond its control.

J. App. at 126.

In early April 1975, the situation in Saigon was becoming desperate as the North Vietnamese forces closed in on the city. During this period, American embassy officials met often with the branch officers of the American banks in Saigon to consider what actions should be taken to protect the safety of employees, both American and Vietnamese. These meetings produced a contingency plan for emergency evacuation. During this time, the branch bank encouraged concerned depositors to withdraw their money, although the situation did not safely allow for the posting of formal notices suggesting such withdrawals.

On April 24, 1975, on the eve of Saigon's fall to the North Vietnamese, Citibank closed its Saigon branch, and its personnel left the city in conjunction [with the general evacuation of American citizens and Vietnamese employees planned by the United States Embassy. All of the branch's documents, files, records, and books were left in the branch. Cash from the branch, as well as the branch's keys, vault combination, and official documents, were entrusted to embassy officials with a request to turn them over to the National Bank of Vietnam, South Vietnam's central banking authority.

The following day, on April 25, 1975, the South Vietnamese government issued a joint communique stating that Citibank, and two other American banks, had "closed temporarily without asking for permission"; that these banks would be sanctioned; and that the National

Bank and the Finance Ministry guaranteed to return all the money legally deposited.

Less than one week later, on April 30, 1975, the South Vietnamese government in Saigon fell. On May 1, 1975, the new revolutionary administration of Vietnam declared victory and confiscated all banks, Thus, all Saigon banks, including Citibank's branch, were "placed under the management of the Saigon-Gio Dinh Military Management Committee banking committee," and their operations suspended, The National Bank of Vietnam, the central bank, reopened under North Vietnamese control, and over the course of several weeks made a number of announcements concerning its plans for the future. Specifically, the central bank announced:

> The Vietnam National Bank . . . is ready to recover former debts incurred by banks through lending and to conduct settlement of debts, deposits, savings and all other sources of capital in the economy.

> J. App. at 152. It was further announced that: [T]he national bank guarantees that the savings accounts of workers, who legitimately earn their income through their own efforts and labor, will gradually be paid to them. . . .

> As regards banks whose owners have fled the country, the national bank will inventory and re-evaluate their assets and settle their accounts in order to determine their ability to return the savings of account holders. . . .

Shortly after the fall of Saigon, plaintiff's father was placed in a reeducation camp. After his release in 1980, he sent the Citibank Saigon passbook to his son in Michigan. In May 1980, Trinh called the International Division of Citibank in New York to inquire about the deposit. Trinh was told that the National Bank of Vietnam was now responsible for the deposit. On November 5, 1980, Trinh wrote to Walter Wriston, Chairman of Citibank, expressing dissatisfaction with this reply, and was again told that the National Bank was responsible for the deposit. This lawsuit was commenced in the Eastern District of Michigan on June 14, 1984.

* * *

Citibank's primary argument on appeal is that the deposit agreement construed under Vietnamese law[2] places the risk of loss for a political

---

[2]   We agree with the district court that the law of Vietnam applies to this case. Generally, as the lower court explained, a court must apply the law of the forum with the most significant contacts with the case, the law where the contract was made, or the law where the branch was located. See, *e.g.,* Zimmermann v. Sutherland, 274 U.S. 253, 47 S.Ct. 625, 71 L.Ed. 1034 (1927); Aaron Ferer & Sons, Ltd, v. Chase Manhattan Bank, 731 F.2d 112 (2d Cir.1984). Here, all of the

revolution on the depositor not on the domestic home office. In this respect, the bank points to the express terms of the agreement, signed by Trinh's father, which provides both that "Citibank does not accept responsibility for any loss or damage suffered or incurred by any depositor resulting from government orders, laws . . . or from any other cause beyond its control," and that payment on accounts would be made only in Vietnam and only in piasters. In the bank's view, these provisions of the agreement create an implicit distinction between *credit* risk and *sovereign* risk, with the bank bearing only the former. Thus, where a branch is unable to pay its depositors as a result of, for instance, financial mismanagement, robbery, or insolvency the typical kinds of economic or credit risks normally assumed by companies doing business internationally Citibank concedes that the home office would be liable for the deposits because, in such circumstances, payment could nevertheless be made in Vietnam and in piasters. However, where, as here, revolutionary conditions make payment in Vietnam in piasters impossible, Citibank believes that, under the deposit agreement, the depositor, not the domestic home office, must bear the loss.

The bank argues that its intention to create an implicit distinction between credit risk and sovereign risk is suggested, not only by the plain terms of the agreement, but also by a construction of those terms in light of applicable Vietnamese commercial law. More specifically, the bank argues that it should be presumed that the parties intended for their agreement to be consistent with the Vietnamese law of *force majeure*,[3] which, according to the testimony of the bank's Vietnamese law expert, placed the risk of loss on the depositor in the unique circumstances presented here.

* * *

We are not persuaded by the bank's arguments. In the first place, as the district court correctly recognized, it is a general banking principle that the home office is *ultimately liable* on a deposit placed in its foreign branch if, as here, the branch closes or otherwise wrongfully refuses to return a deposit. Sokoloff v. National City Bank, 130 Misc. 66, 73, 224 N.Y.S, 102, 114 (N.Y. Sup.Ct.1927); see also Bluebird Undergarment Corp. v. Gomez, 139 Misc. 742, 249 N.Y.S. 319 (City Ct. N.Y. 1931); Heininger, *Liability of U.S. Banks for Deposits Placed in Their Foreign Branches*, 11 Law & Pol.Int'l Bus. 903, 926 (1979). This well-established general principle of

---

indicators point to a conclusion that Vietnamese law applies. Plaintiffs citizenship was Vietnamese, and his father, Citibank Saigon, the banking relationship, the banking transactions, and the account currency were all located in Vietnam.

3   Article 701 of the Vietnamese Commercial Code (V.C.C.) provided: "The debtor does not have to pay damages if his violation or non-performance of contractual obligations is due to a fortuitous cause or case of *force majeure*."

Article 1206 of the V.C.C. provided: "The depositary is not liable for accidents or risks resulting from *force majeure*, unless previously he had been given notice to return the deposited objects."

ultimate liability is not inconsistent with Citibank's assertion that a branch bank is a separate and distinct business entity. See Brief of Citibank at 30–32. To this end, the bank is surely correct in arguing that absent special circumstances, deposits made in branch banks are payable only there. *Id.* (citing Bluebird Undergarment Corp. v. Gomez, 139 Misc. 742, 249 N.Y.S. 319 (City Ct. N.Y. 1931)). However, as we read *Sokoloff, Bluebird* and similar cases, one of the "special circumstances" triggering liability against the home office *is* the *closing of a branch. Bluebird,* 249 N.Y.S. at 321–22. Thus, while it is true that the payment obligation exists *primarily* between the branch bank and the depositor, the *ultimate* obligation on the deposits remains with the home office. *Id.* ; *Vishipco*, 660 F.2d at 863; see also Annotation, *Branch Banks*, 136 A.L.R. 471, 493–97 (1942).

That the home office of the branch was to be ultimately liable for the deposits of its foreign customers is further suggested, we think, by the Vietnamese laws under which foreign banks operated. These laws permitted foreign banks to operate only through branches, and required the home office of a branch to "clearly earmark *and transfer to the branch in Vietnam*" an amount of capital equal to a certain percentage of the branch's deposits. See *supra* at note 1. The home office was required to maintain this paid-in reserve amount at its proper level, and so as deposits increased, transfers to the branch would increase as well. In our view, by prohibiting foreign banks from operating through locally incorporated subsidiaries, and by requiring parent banks to maintain paid-in capital reserves at their Vietnamese branches, Vietnamese law sought to remove any ambiguity as to where the responsibility would ultimately lie for the liabilities of branch banks. In this respect, South Vietnam furthered its national policy, as recognized by the court in *Vishipco*, of enabling "those depositing in foreign branches to gain more protection than they would have received had their money been deposited in locally incorporated subsidiaries of foreign banks." *Vishipco*, 660 F.2d at 863.

* * *

By operating a branch office in Vietnam, Citibank indicated to its foreign depositors that it accepted the risk that, in at least some circumstances, it would be liable elsewhere for obligations incurred by its branch. *Vishipco*, 660 F.2d at 863. In so doing, it "reassure[d] [those] depositors that their deposits [would] be safer with them than they would be in a locally incorporated bank." *Id.* (citing Heininger, *supra*, at 911–12). With the volatile situation in Vietnam in the early 1970's, this assurance of safety was undoubtedly one of the primary factors motivating Vietnamese depositors, like Trinh, to place their money in Citibank.[4]

---

[4]   That Trinh relied on this safety factor is evidenced by an English translation of the agreement he signed when the account was originally opened on July 25, 1974. The agreement

Certainly, these depositors expected that Citibank, with its worldwide assets and international reputation, would be "good" for the deposits if, for *whatever reason*-whether it be financial mismanagement, insolvency, or political events-Citibank Saigon could not return them. In our view, the deposit agreement did not dispel these expectations. That is, while we recognize that the deposit agreement absolved the *branch office* of responsibility for losses resulting from government orders and "any other cause beyond its control," we do not find in that agreement *any* indication that the depositor could not proceed against the home office if the branch has failed to pay.

Consistent with this, we reject Citibank's argument that the provision of the agreement limiting payment on deposits to Vietnam and to Vietnamese piasters was sufficient to inform depositors that they were to bear the risk of loss, and would have no recourse against the home office, if Citibank Saigon was forced to close due to revolutionary conditions. As we have emphasized, such an allocation of risk is contrary to the depositor's expectations that the bank, by operating through a branch, has consented to be liable elsewhere for the branch's obligation in the event the branch does not meet them. Banks certainly can, and will, seek to limit by contract the extent of their exposure to such liability; however, to be effective, such limitation provisions must be explicit and must clearly and unmistakably inform depositors that they have no right to proceed against the home office. The provision here, specifying the place where the branch will make payment and the currency it will use, is insufficient under this standard. In our view, a person who had signed a deposit agreement containing such a provision would not have been aware that he had given up his right to proceed against the home office in the event the branch was no longer in existence and could not pay its depositors.

* * *

While we do not deny that the closing of a bank by revolutionary forces is the type of fortuitous cause contemplated by the law of *force majeure*, we do not agree that, where a parent/branch relationship is involved, application of that doctrine requires the conclusion that the depositor is to bear the risk of loss. As recognized by both the lower court here and the Second Circuit in *Vishipco*, impossibility of performance in Vietnam did not relieve Citibank of its obligation to perform elsewhere. *Vishipco*, 660 F.2d at 863–64. Citibank had accepted the risk of such an obligation by operating a branch in Vietnam. Since its Vietnamese depositors did not waive their right to proceed against the home office, Citibank cannot be heard to argue that the inability of its Saigon branch to perform relieves

---

contains a section where the depositor is asked to indicate, by checking the relevant box, his reason for opening an account with Citibank. Trinh's reason for banking at Citibank was: "My money is safer with Citibank." See J. App. at 130–31.

the home office of liability for the bank's debts incurred in Saigon. In our view, Citibank, as an ongoing business entity, was able in April 1975, and remains able to this day, to discharge those debts either in New York or at a variety of other points outside of Vietnam.

* * *

Further, and more directly to the point, we are not at all persuaded that, by confiscating the nation's banks, the new government undertook to assume the *liabilities* of foreign banks, like Citibank Saigon, that fled the country in the face of the fall of South Vietnam. As the district court accurately observed, and as evidenced by various statements of the new regime quoted in the court's opinion (623 F. Supp. at 1535), Citibank's proof with regard to the assumption of liabilities of foreign banks was "equivocal at best." For example, in June of 1975, the National Bank issued a communique stating, among other things, that "*all* foreign banks must accept responsibility" for the liquidation of deposits. J. App. at 152. And, a September 7, 1975 newspaper announcement provided as follows:

As regards banks whose owners have fled the country, the national bank will inventory and re-evaluate *their* assets and settle *their* accounts in order to determine *their ability* to return the savings of account holders; the bank will issue a notice concerning these persons.

Id. at 157 (emphasis added). These announcements, and others of similar tone, do *not* as the district court held, "indicate an unqualified assumption of all liabilities" by the new government. Indeed, in our view, the announcements suggest that the new government specifically did *not* intend to assume the liabilities of foreign banks whose "owners fled the country," but instead expected such liability to remain with those banks.

More importantly, the confiscation decree and other decrees of the new government regarding bank deposits would not, in any event, have had any effect on Citibank's debt to Trinh because, as recognized in *Vishipco* and in the court below, the deposits in Citibank Saigon no longer had their "situs" in Vietnam at the time of the decrees.

Generally speaking, an act of state will go unquestioned in United States courts only to the extent that it affects property whose "situs" is within the territorial jurisdiction of the acting state. While this is a relatively simple concept to apply with respect to tangible property, it becomes more difficult with respect to intangible property such as the debts of a bank. As one court has observed: "The situs of intangible property is about as intangible a concept as is known to the law," Tabacalera Severiano Jorge v. Standard Cigar Co., 392 F.2d 706, 714 (5th Cir.), *cert. denied*, 393 U.S. 924, 89 S.Ct. 255, 21 L.Ed.2d 260 (1968). We think the court in *Vishipco* had it right in concluding that, for purposes of the act of state doctrine, a debt does *not* have its "situs" in the foreign state unless the state has the power to enforce or collect it; a power which, the court explained, is dependent upon jurisdiction over the debtor. *Vishipco*, 660 F.2d at 862 (citing Harris v. Balk, 198 U.S. 215, 25 S.Ct. 625, 49 L.Ed. 1023 (1905)). Since in this case, as in *Vishipco*, the debtor (Citibank) abandoned its Saigon branch at the time of the Vietnamese decrees and no longer had any presence in Vietnam which would remain in existence after its departure, the revolutionary government had no jurisdiction over the debtor. Accordingly, the "situs" of the debts was not in Vietnam and the Vietnamese decrees could have no effect on Citibank's debt to Trinh. See *also* Heininger, *Liability of U.S. Banks*, 11 Law & Pol. Int'l Bus. at 975.

* * *

As a final observation, we believe that the result reached by this opinion is fair and equitable under the circumstances. We are, of course, not unmindful of the fact that both Trinh and Citibank are innocent parties and, to a great extent, victims of circumstances beyond their control. However, as with many disputes involving innocent parties, it is our job as a court to determine which of those parties is to suffer the loss. Here, because we are not persuaded that either the deposit agreement or the Vietnamese law of *force majeure* requires a contrary conclusion, we conclude that the loss is to be borne by the bank.

* * *

BAILEY BROWN, SENIOR CIRCUIT JUDGE, dissenting.

* * * I agree with Citibank that Trinh must bear the loss of his savings deposit. I would so hold because believe the deposit agreement so requires. In my view, the agreement's clear and specific provisions limiting payment on the deposit to Vietnam and to Vietnamese currency, and relieving the Saigon branch of liability for damage to a depositor caused by governmental actions or causes beyond the branch's control, create a legal relationship between Citibank's domestic home office and its Saigon branch requiring the domestic home office to rectify the Saigon branch's failure to pay on a deposit only if such rectification can occur in Vietnam and in piasters. In other words, the provision discharging the Saigon branch of liability serves to discharge the domestic home office of liability as well if the governmental action or other cause precludes payment in Vietnam in piasters. Here, the communist overthrow of South Vietnam and subsequent confiscation and nationalization of Citibank's Saigon branch surely falls within the deposit agreement's discharge of liability provision and prevents Citibank's domestic home office from paying Trinh in Vietnam in piasters. Consequently, the deposit agreement calls for Trinh to suffer the loss and, in turn, Trinh's action against Citibank must fail. * * *

NOTES

1.   Are the holdings in the *Vishipco* and *Trinh* consistent? If not, what are the differences?

Government Decrees

WELLS FARGO ASIA V. CITIBANK, N.A.

United States Court of Appeals
936 F.2d 723 (2d Cir. 1991)

Final Submissions After Remand from Supreme Court

I.   BACKGROUND

The background of this action has been recounted in several opinions, including Citibank, N.A. v. Wells Fargo Asia Limited, 495 U.S. 660, 110 S.Ct. 2034 109 L.Ed.2d 677 *("WFAL IV")*; Wells Fargo Asia Limited v. Citibank, N.A., 852 F.2d 657 (2d Cir.1988) *("WFAL III"),* Wells Fargo Asia Limited v. Citibank, N.A., 695 F.Supp. 1450 (S.D.N.Y.1988) *("WFAL II"),* and Wells Fargo Asia Limited v. Citibank, N.A., 660 F.Supp. 946 (S.D.N.Y.1987) *("WFAL I"),* familiarity with which is assumed. Briefly, in 1983, WFAL, a Singapore-chartered bank wholly owned by the United States-chartered Wells Fargo Bank, N.A., placed two six-month nonnegotiable U.S. $1,000,000 deposits with Citibank for its branch in Manila, Philippines ("Citibank/Manila"). The deposit agreement called for WFAL to pay this amount to Citibank in New York for deposit at Citibank/Manila; it called for Citibank to repay Wells Fargo International's New York account for WFAL.

The deposits were to mature in December 1983. In October 1983, however, the Philippine government issued a Memorandum to Authorized Agent Banks ("MAAB 47"). As described in our earlier opinion, MAAB 47 provided, in pertinent part, as follows:

> Any remittance of foreign exchange for repayment of principal on all foreign obligations due to foreign banks and/or financial institutions, irrespective of maturity, shall be submitted to the Central Bank [of the Philippines] thru the Management of External Debt and Investment Accounts Department (MEDIAD) for prior approval.

> As interpreted by the Central Bank of the Philippines, this decree prevented Citibank/Manila, an "authorized agent bank" under Philippine law, from repaying the WFAL deposits with its Philippine assets, *i.e.,* those assets not either deposited in banks elsewhere or invested in non-Philippine enterprises. Citibank/Manila did not repay WFAL's deposits upon maturity.

WFAL III, 852 F.2d at 659. After WFAL commenced the present suit for repayment of the deposited amounts, Citibank/Manila sought and received permission from the Central Bank of the Philippines to repay its foreign depositors to the extent it could do so with non-Philippine assets. Citibank/Manila thereafter repaid WFAL $934,000, leaving $1,066,000 in dispute.

The district court, Honorable Whitman Knapp, *Judge,* entered judgment in favor of WFAL, rejecting Citibank's contention that MAAB 47 made it impossible to repay the WFAL deposits. Noting that MAAB 47 allows obligations to foreign banks to be repaid if the consent of the Central Bank is obtained, and further noting that Citibank had not satisfied its good faith obligation to seek that consent, the court concluded that Citibank's impossibility defense must fail. Though originally making this ruling on the hypothesis that the law of the Philippines applied, see *WFAL I,* 660 F.Supp. at 947, the district court concluded, upon request from this Court for clarification, that New York law, rather than Philippine law, governed the dispute, *WFAL II,* 695 F.Supp. at 1454. It ruled that under New York law, Citibank's worldwide assets were available for satisfaction of WFAL's claim. *Id*

We affirmed. Though the district court had concluded (a) that repayment and collection are independent concepts, and (b) that the parties had not reached an agreement as to the situs of collection, and we did not disturb those rulings, we concluded that the authorities suggest that a debt may be collected wherever it is repayable, *unless* the parties have agreed otherwise. Since the court found here that there was no separate agreement restricting where the deposits could be collected, and we are aware of nothing in the record that contradicts that finding, we conclude that WFAL was entitled to collect the deposits out of Citibank assets in New York.

WFAL III 852 F.2d at 661 (emphasis added).

The Supreme Court vacated our decision, stating that we appeared to have treated the concepts of repayment and collection as interchangeable rather than independent and to have "rel[ied] upon the existence of an agreement between Citibank and WFAL to permit collection in New York." *WFAL IV,* 110 S.Ct. at 2040. The Supreme Court concluded that the district court's finding that there was no agreement as to the situs of collection was not clearly erroneous; it also endorsed "the District Court's conclusion that the parties, in this particular case, failed to establish a relevant custom or practice in the international banking community from which it could be inferred that the parties had a tacit understanding on the point." *Id.* at 2041. Concluding that our decision could not be upheld on the theory that there was an agreement as to the place of collection, the Supreme Court remanded for a determination of whether WFAL's claim is governed by

New York law, Philippine law, or federal common law, and what the content of the governing law is, and directed us to decide the appeal in light of those determinations:

> Given the finding of the District Court that there was no agreement between the parties respecting collection from Citibank's general assets in New York, the question becomes whether collection is permitted nonetheless by rights and duties implied by law. As is its right, . . . WFAL seeks to defend the judgment below on the ground that, under principles of either New York or Philippine law, Citibank was obligated to make its *726 general assets available for collection of WFAL's deposits. . . .
> It is unclear from the opinion of the Court of Appeals which law it found to be controlling; and we decide to remand the case for the Court of Appeals to determine which law applies, and the content of that law.

Id. at 2042.

Accordingly, we proceed to those questions.

II. DISCUSSION

* * *

Regardless of whether the New York or federal test is used, application of these standards leads us to the conclusion that New York law should be used to evaluate Wells Fargo's contention that Citibank's worldwide assets are available for repayment of the deposits. As the New York Court of Appeals has recognized, "New York . . . is a financial capital of the world, serving as an international clearinghouse and market place for a plethora of international transactions . . .[.] In order to maintain its preeminent financial position, it is important that the justified expectations of the parties to the contract be protected." J. Zeevi and Sons, Ltd. v. Grindlays Bank (Uganda) Ltd. (1975) 37 N.Y.2d 220, 227, 371 N.Y.S.2d 892, 898, 333 N.E.2d 168, 172. In our view, these expectations will be best promoted by applying a uniform rule of New York law where, as here, the transactions were denominated in United States dollars and settled through the parties' New York correspondent banks, and where the defendant is a United States bank with headquarters in New York. Since Eurodollar transactions denominated in U.S. dollars customarily are cleared in New York . . ., the rationale for application of New York law becomes even stronger. If the goal is to promote certainty in international financial markets, it makes sense to apply New York law uniformly, rather than conditioning the deposit obligations on the vagaries of local law, and requiring each player in the Eurodollar market to investigate the law of numerous foreign countries in order to ascertain which would limit repayment of deposits to the foreign branch's own assets.

WFAL II, 695 F.Supp. at 1453–54.

As to the content of New York law on the matter, the district court noted that the most recent pronouncement of the New York Court of Appeals, see Perez v. Chase Manhattan National Bank, N.A., 61 N.Y.2d 460, 468, 474 N.Y.S.2d 689, 691, 463 N.E.2d 5, 7, *cert, denied,* 469 U.S. 966, 105 S.Ct. 366, 83 L.Ed.2d 302 (1984), indicated that the parent bank is ultimately liable for the obligations of the foreign branch. Though the district court reasoned that an actual expropriation by the foreign government would be treated differently, it concluded that in the present case, there having been no expropriation and no limitation of the depositor's rights but only action affecting the assets of the branch, New York law would allow collection of the debt in New York:

> [I]f the Philippines had confiscated plaintiffs deposits, New York courts would interpret the expropriation as a compulsory assignment of the depositor's rights, so that payment to the Philippine assignee would discharge the debt. A New York court would further recognize such compulsory assignment as an act of a foreign sovereign unreviewable under the Act of State doctrine. *Perez, supra,* 61 N.Y.2d460, 474 N.Y.S.2d 689, 463 N.E.2d5. We believe New York would take a similar approach in the situation where a foreign government had effected a partial confiscation in the form of a tax on a deposit made at a foreign branch. See, Dunn v. Bank of Nova Scotia (5th Cir.1967) 374 F.2d 876. However, we are aw are of no persuasive authority to tell us to what extent, if any, a New York court would defer to local law in the situation here presented, where the foreign sovereign did not extinguish the branch's debt either in whole or in part but merely conditioned repayment on the obtaining of approval from a government agency. Fortunately, we need not resolve that troublesome question.

WFAL II, 695 F.Supp. at 1454–55. The court found it unnecessary to determine whether New York law would hold that a foreign government's refusal to give the prerequisite consent constitutes an excuse for refusal to make repayment, in light of its earlier finding that Citibank "had not satisfied its good faith obligation to seek the [Philippine] government's consent to use the assets booked at Citibank's non-Philippine offices." *Id* at 1455. The court reaffirmed that finding.

We agree with the district court's analysis, and we conclude, substantially for the reasons that court stated, that New York law governs the present claim and that under New York law, Citibank was not excused from making repayment. In urging that we reach the contrary conclusion, Citibank argues that there is a clear federal policy placing the risk of foreign-law impediments to repayment on the depositor. In so arguing, it

relies on federal banking rules such as 12 U.S.C. § 461(b)(6) (1988), which
provides that banking reserve requirements "shall not apply to deposits
payable only outside the States of the United States and the District of
Columbia," and 12 C.F.R, § 204.128(c) (1990) (issued at 52 Fed. Reg. 47696,
Dec. 16, 1987), which provides that "[a] customer who makes a deposit that
is payable solely at a foreign branch of the depository institution assumes
whatever risk may exist that the foreign country in which a branch is
located might impose restrictions on withdrawals," Citibank's reliance on
these provisions is misplaced. Federal law defines a deposit that is "payable
only at an office outside the United States" as "a deposit . . . as to which the
depositor is entitled, *under the agreement with the institution*, to demand
payment *only* outside the United States." *Id.* § 204.2(t) (emphasis added).
The provisions relied on thus do not reveal a policy allocating the risk to
depositors as a matter of law where there is no such agreement. So long as
state law does not restrict a bank's freedom to enter into an agreement that
allocates the risk of foreign sovereign restrictions, state law does not
conflict with the federal policy reflected in current statutes or regulations.
We see no such restriction in the law of New York, and hence there is no
"'significant conflict'," Miree v. DeKalb County, Georgia, 433 U.S. 25, 31,
97 S.Ct. 2490, 2494–95, 53 L.Ed.2d 557 (1977) (quoting Wallis v. Pan
American Petroleum Corp. 384 U.S. 63, 68, 86 S.Ct. 1301, 1304, 16 L.Ed.2d
369 (1966)), between New York law and federal law such as would be
necessary to justify the creation of a federal common law.

We conclude that under New York law, unless the parties agree to the
contrary, a creditor may collect a debt at a place where the parties have
agreed that it is repayable. In applying this principle to the circumstances
of the present case to affirm the judgment in favor of WFAL, we do not
assume the existence of an agreement between Citibank/Manila and
WFAL to permit collection in New York; rather, in light of the express
finding of the district court that the parties had no agreement as to
permissible situses of collection, we rely on the absence of any agreement
forbidding the collection in New York.

* * *

NOTES

1.   In reviewing the various court decisions in the Chapter, it is
interesting to note that they all stress one or more of the following factors in
reaching their decision: a) the "springing situs" theory of the home country
bank's liability for foreign branch deposits (*Sokoloff*); b) the "voluntary" nature
of branch closings (*Trinh, Vishipco*); c) the role of the Act of State Doctrine
(*Perez, Garcia*); the terms of the deposit agreement: both as to whether it either
specifically 1) *did not* disclaim deposits as being directly payable (*Wells Fargo*),
or 2) *did* disclaim such liability (*Wells Fargo*); d) whether notice was given to
depositors (*Trinh, Vishipco*); e) the role of forum law (*Wells Fargo*); f) equitable

notions of fairness in apportioning political risk (the dissent in *Perez*); g) government nationalization, force majeure and successor in interest issues (*Perez, Sokoloff*); and h) asserted safety and security of deposits (*Garcia*).

2.   The Second Circuit Court of Appeals in the *Wells Fargo* case noted that the U.S. Supreme Court vacated its prior decision in the case, in part, because it relied on "the existence of an agreement between Citibank and WFAL." Did this change the Second Circuit's ultimate holding in the case?

2. IMPLICATIONS OF FEDERAL AND STATE BANKING LAWS

A. U.S. FEDERAL BANKING LAWS

U.S. Federal law contains a sweeping provision regarding payment on deposits in cases of emergency closure. 12 U.S.C. § 633 asserts that Federal Reserve member banks are not liable for deposits made at a foreign branch of a bank if they are unable to repay them as a result of either "an act of war, insurrection, or civil strife" or "an action by a foreign government or instrumentality (whether de jure or de facto) in the country in which the branch is located."[1] An exception is made if "the member bank has expressly agreed in writing to repay the deposit under those circumstances," leaving banks the option of explicitly insuring customer accounts against political risk, but taking from the courts the power to impose an insurance requirement upon them.[2]

The federal statute did not exist prior to its adoption as part of the Riegle Community Development and Regulatory Improvement Act of 1994.[3] After *Vishipco,* the U.S. banking industry sought an addition to 12 U.S.C. § 1828 that would have added a subsection (m) to read as follows:

> (m) In any action or proceeding brought in a state or Federal court in the United States or the District of Columbia, the terms and conditions adopted or made applicable by the parties to any deposit or other obligation of a foreign branch of an insured bank shall be conclusive to establish the place, currency and manner of performance of such deposit or other obligations and the law or custom governing such performance. Notwithstanding any other rules of law, where action or threats on the part of any authority at the place where a foreign branch of an insured bank is located prevents performance at the foreign branch of a deposit or other obligations, in accordance with its terms and conditions

---

[1]   12 U.S.C. § 633 (2012).

[2]   *Id.*

[3]   See generally Riegle Community and Regulatory Development Act of 1994, Pub, L. No. 103–325, 108 Stat. 2160 (1994).

establishing the place, currency, and manner of such performance because of:

(i) seizure, destruction, cancellation, or confiscation by governmental authorities of the branch's assets or business, or assumption of its liabilities;

(ii) other similar governmental decrees or actions, or

(iii) closure of the branch in order to prevent, in the reasonable judgment of the insured bank, harm to the bank's employees or property the deposit or other obligation of the foreign branch will not transfer to and may not be enforce against any other office of the insured bank located outside the country in which the foreign branch is located.

NOTES

1.   The proposed subsection was never introduced in Congress, despite some evidence that regulators at the staff level favored it. See Peter S. Smerdresman & Andreas F. Lowenfeld, Eurodollars, Multinational Banks, and National Laws, 64 N.Y.U.L. REV, 733, 795 n.258 (1989) (citing 12 U.S.C. § 1828).

2.   In the wake of the *Vishipco* case, several U.S. states passed legislation aimed at protecting the interests of U.S. banks abroad. For example, New York banking law provides that banks—including national banks—located in New York and operating a branch abroad "shall be liable for contracts to be performed at such branch office or offices and for deposits to be repaid at such branch office or offices to no greater extent than a bank . . . organized and existing under the laws" of the host country. See N.Y. BANKING LAW § 138 (McKinney 2013). It also holds that if an authority that is not the de jure government of a foreign territory seizes assets of a bank operating in that territory, the liability of that bank "for any deposit theretofore received and thereafter to be repaid by it . . . shall be reduced pro tanto by the proportion" the seized assets bear to the bank's total deposit liabilities. *Id.* Finally, it asserts that a bank located in New York:

shall not be required to repay any deposit made at a foreign branch of any such bank if the branch cannot repay the deposit due to (i) an act of war, insurrection, or civil strife; or (ii) an action by a foreign government or instrumentality, whether de jure or de facto, in the country in which the branch is located preventing such repayment, unless such bank has expressly agreed in writing to repay the deposit under such circumstances.

Id. Michigan has a similar statute. See MICH. COMP. LAWS ANN. § 487.13714 (West 2013).

New York's law did not cover national banks until the 1984 amendments; prior to that, it applied only to banks with state charters, which greatly limited its usefulness, as most banks operating abroad are nationally chartered.

A portion of Nevada's banking law is dedicated to the emergency closure of banks. It defines "emergency" as "any condition or occurrence which may interfere physically with the conduct of normal business operations at one or more or all of the offices of a bank, or which poses an imminent or existing threat to the safety or security of persons or property." NEV. REV. STAT. ANN § 662.265 (West 2013). According to the law, any day on which an office of a bank is closed for all or part of the day is treated as a bank holiday, and "[n]o liability or loss of rights of any kind on the part of any bank, or director, officer or employee thereof, shall accrue or result by virtue of any" such closing." NEV. REV. STAT. ANN § 662.305.

3. DEPOSITOR PREFERENCE AND DEPOSIT INSURANCE ISSUES

U.K. FINANCIAL SERVICES AUTHORITY: ADDRESSING THE IMPLICATIONS OF NON-EEA NATIONAL DEPOSITOR PREFERENCE REGIMES
September 2012

Introduction

* * * 1.1 We propose that firms from non-[European Economic Area] EEA countries that operate national depositor preference regimes be required to accept deposits in the UK using a UK incorporated subsidiary or they must implement an alternative arrangement that ensures UK depositors are no worse off than the depositors in the home country if the firm fails.

1.2 We propose giving firms two years from when the rules come into effect to take steps and put in place the necessary arrangements to comply.

1.3 During the transition period, we propose that firms be required to disclose information to all the UK branch customers about their home country national depositor preference regimes and highlight the fact that the claims of UK branch depositors would be subordinated to the claims of depositors in the home country in the event that the firm fails.

1.4 These proposals aim to ensure that firms from non-EEA countries with national depositor preference regimes take steps to address the disadvantages that UK branch depositors could face because their claims are subordinated to claims of home country depositors if a firm fails. The potential detriment to UK branch depositors would be eliminated if firms were to establish a UK-incorporated deposit taking subsidiary or undertake equally effective alternative measures.

* * *

Branches of firms from non-EEA countries

2.14 Firms from non-EEA countries with national depositor preference regimes operate both branches and UK-incorporated subsidiaries in the UK.

2.15 When a firm from a non-EEA country with a national depositor preference regime uses a branch to accept deposits in the UK, the UK deposits are effectively placed with the same legal entity as the one accepting deposits in the home country. It is often the financial strength of the firm in the home country that attracts investors and customers to the branch in host countries. UK branch depositors are likely to be under the impression that if the firm fails, they would be entitled to participate equally in the distribution of assets from the insolvent firm's estate.

2.16 When a non-EEA firm fails the assets and liabilities of the UK branch would normally under insolvency proceedings be included in the estate of the firm in the home country. When a firm is insolvent, the existence of national depositor preference exacerbates the position of the UK branch depositors relative to home country depositors. Home country deposits that are preferred have a better chance of participating in the distribution of assets and recovering their proceeds from the estate of the failed firm than the UK branch deposits, which, together with all other unsecured creditors, would participate in assets that remained in the estate after insolvency administrators, secured creditors, home country depositors and any other preferred creditors had been pa*id*. The proposals in this consultation paper highlight the disadvantages that UK branch depositors face relative to home country depositors given such circumstances.

Measures to address national depositor preference

3.1 Legislation on national depositor preference is intended to enhance the protection of home country depositors relative to depositors outside the home country. Preferring home country depositors will result in them being better protected against losses arising from claims made against the estate of a failed firm.

3.2 It is not acceptable that UK branch depositors are more exposed to potential losses than home country depositors if a firm fails especially when both classes of depositors have placed their deposits with the same firm. Furthermore there is the possibility that those UK losses may end up being borne by UK taxpayers if there are insufficient assets to recover from the estate of the failed firm.[7]

---

[7]   The estimated amount of deposits held in the UK branches of firms non-EEA countries with national depositor preference regimes was about £800 billion (as at August 2011).

What we are proposing

3.3 We believe that the firms from non-EEA countries that operate national depositor preference regimes and accept deposits in their UK branches should be required to eliminate the subordination of UK branch depositors compared to home country depositors.

3.4 The intended outcome is that UK branch depositors are not subordinated to home country depositors if such a firm were to become insolvent.

3.5 With one exception, any single measure we propose is unlikely to be applicable across all the different countries that operate national depositor preference regimes.

3.6 Therefore we propose introducing a new rule that will require firms to adopt measures to eliminate the subordination of UK branch depositors so that the UK branch depositors do not face the possibility of there being insufficient assets in the estate of the insolvent firm to meet their claims.

3.7 Firms should be prohibited from accepting deposits using a branch in the UK unless they take steps to rectify the disadvantages that UK branch depositors would face. Some firms would have to establish a UK-incorporated subsidiary for accepting deposits in the UK. This measure is available to all the deposit takers from non-EEA countries that operate national depositor preference regimes. However, firms will be able to adopt other measures provided they can demonstrate that these are equally effective. In our pre-consultation we identified other possible measures that firms could adopt.

3.8 If firms from a non-EEA country that operates national depositor preference place their UK deposits in a UK-incorporated subsidiary, the UK depositors would cease to be subordinated to home country depositors in the event the firms fails. When a UK-incorporated subsidiary is insolvent, all its depositors, including UK depositors would be subject to UK insolvency law, and all its depositors would be treated equally as unsecured creditors in the hierarchy of creditor claims. The result is that no individual class of the unsecured creditors category would be worse off.

3.9 Establishing a subsidiary in the UK is one measure that could be adopted by all the firms from non-EEA countries to address the issue of national depositor preference. We also believe that it could help prevent the misconception that UK branch depositors of a firm from a non-EEA country would be treated equally to home country depositors in the event of the firm's failure.

3.10 We recognise that our proposals will require firms to take steps and evaluate their strategy to maintain a deposit-taking branch in the UK. We do not underestimate the implications this will have for the UK branches and the firms in their home country. However, in the absence of any internationally co-ordinated action or individual countries unilaterally removing preference from their national laws, we believe the issue needs to be addressed. Maintaining the status quo could hinder cross-border co-operation efforts in resolving global firms.

* * *

QUESTIONS AND NOTES

1.   Do you agree that banks should be prohibited from accepting deposits in branches in the U.K. without safeguards to eliminate the subordination of U.K. branch depositors compared to home country depositors?

2.   What steps would you take to eliminate the subordination of U.K. branch depositors compared to home country depositors?

3.   The U.S. response to the U.K. depositor preferences rules by the Federal Deposit Insurance Corporation, the deposit insurance agency for the U.S. banking industry, is set forth below.

FEDERAL DEPOSIT INSURANCE CORPORATION
12 C.F.R. Part 330

Deposit Insurance Regulations; Definition of Insured Deposit

AGENCY: Federal Deposit Insurance Corporation (FDIC)

ACTION: Final Rule

September 2013

SUMMARY: The FDIC is adopting a final rule ("Final Rule") that amends its deposit insurance regulations with respect to deposits in foreign branches of U.S. insured depository institutions ("IDI" or "U.S. bank"). The Final Rule clarifies that deposits in branches of U.S. banks located outside the United States are not FDIC-insured deposits. This would be the case even if they are also payable at an office within the United States ("dual payability"). As discussed further below, a pending proposal by the United Kingdom's Prudential Regulation Authority ("U.K. PRA"), formerly known as the Financial Services Authority, has made it more likely that large U.S. banks will change their U.K. foreign branch deposit agreements to make their U.K. deposits payable both in the United Kingdom and the United States. This action has the potential to expose the Deposit Insurance Fund ("DIF") to expanded deposit insurance liability and create operational complexities if these types of deposits were treated as insured. The purpose of the Final Rule is to protect the DIF against the liability that it would otherwise face as a potential global deposit insurer, preserve confidence in the FDIC deposit insurance system, and ensure that the FDIC can effectively carry out its critical deposit insurance functions.

* * *

The vast majority of deposit agreements governing relationships between U.S. banks and their foreign branch depositors have to date not expressly provided for payment of foreign branch deposits at an office in the United States. Accordingly, these foreign branch deposits would not qualify as "deposits" for any purpose under the FDI Act, including deposit insurance and the priority regime for the distribution of a failed bank's receivership assets, known as "depositor preference," as further discussed below. While "deposit" has a defined legal meaning under the FDI Act, for ease of reference, these obligations in foreign branches will generally be called "foreign branch deposits" in this Final Rule.

B.   National Depositor Preference

When a U.S. bank fails, uninsured depositors share in the proceeds from the liquidation of the failed bank's assets. In 1993, Congress amended the FDI Act to establish a system of depositor preference in failed-bank resolutions.[6] In general, "depositor preference" refers to a resolution distribution regime in which the claims of depositors have priority over (that is, are satisfied before) the claims of general unsecured creditors.

Under this regime, set forth in section 11(d)(11) of the FDI Act, the receiver of a failed bank distributes amounts realized from its liquidation to pay claims in the following order of priority.[7] Administrative expenses of the receiver are reimbursed first.[8] Any "deposit liability" is reimbursed next, followed in order by general or senior liabilities, subordinated liabilities, and obligations to shareholders. The term "deposit liability" in section 11(d)(11) is not defined.

C.   The 1994 Advisory Opinion

Shortly after Congress added the national depositor preference provisions, the FDIC's Acting General Counsel was asked whether the term "deposit liability" would include deposit obligations payable solely at a foreign branch of a U.S. bank.[9] As described in the Acting General Counsel's 1994 Advisory Opinion ("General Counsel Advisory Opinion 94–1"), national depositor preference makes general unsecured creditor claims subordinate to any "deposit liability" of the institution. General Counsel Advisory Opinion 94–1 concluded that the term "deposit liability" should be defined with reference to "deposit" under section 3(1) of the FDI Act,

---

[6]   Omnibus Budget Reconciliation Act of 1993, Public Law 103–66, 107 Stat. 312.

[7]   12 U.S.C. 1821(d)(11).

[8]   Secured creditors' claims are satisfied to the extent of their security.

[9]   See FDIC Advisory Opinion 94–1, Letter of Acting General Counsel Douglas H. Jones (Feb. 28, 1994).

which excluded, for any purpose, any obligation of a bank payable only at an office of that bank located outside the United States.[10]

Under the interpretation set forth in General Counsel Advisory Opinion 94–1, "deposit liability" for purposes of national depositor preference includes only deposits payable in the United States and excludes obligations payable solely at a foreign branch of a U.S. bank. Accordingly, an obligation in a foreign branch of a U.S. bank has not been considered a "deposit liability" for purposes of the national depositor preference provisions of section 11(d)(11) of the FDI Act. Thus, if a U.S. bank were to fail, its foreign branch depositors would share in the distribution of the bank's liquidated assets as general creditors after the claims of uninsured domestic depositors and the FDIC as subrogee of insured depositors have been satisfied.[11] If a foreign branch deposit of a U.S. bank were expressly payable at an office of the bank in the United States, however, that deposit would be treated equally with uninsured domestic deposits in the depositor preference regime.

D.   Foreign Branch Deposits of U.S. Banks

Many U.S. banks currently operate through branches in foreign countries, often to provide banking, foreign currency and payment services to multinational corporations. Foreign branch deposits have doubled since 2001 and total approximately $1 trillion today. In many cases, these branches do not engage in retail deposit taking or other retail banking services. Often, their typical depositors are large businesses that choose to bank in a foreign branch of a U.S. bank under deposit agreements governed by non-U.S. law to take advantage of a large bank's multi-country branch network, which allows the transfer of funds to and from branch offices located in different countries and in different time zones.

Currently, the overwhelming majority of the foreign branch deposits of U.S. banks are payable only outside the United States. In the past, making deposits in foreign branches dually payable would have been costly to U.S. banks for several reasons. First, dually payable deposits would have increased a bank's deposit insurance assessment base (which, in the past, excluded deposits payable solely outside the United States) and, therefore, its deposit insurance assessment. Second, the dually payable deposits

---

[10]   Section 3(*l*) was later amended to specify that an obligation carried on the books and records of a foreign office of a U.S. bank would not be a "deposit" for any purpose unless it were payable at an office located in the United States and the contract evidencing the obligation expressly provided for such payment and met other criteria. Riegle Community Development and Regulatory Improvement Act, Public Law 103–325 (1994), section 326(b)(2).

[11]   While section 41 of the FDI Act, 12 U.S.C. 1831r, generally prohibits the FDIC in its corporate capacity and other agencies from making any payment that would satisfy any claim against a bank for foreign branch deposits, the FDIC as *receiver* of a failed bank may make payments from the receivership estate to satisfy such claims.

would have become subject to the Federal Reserve's Regulation D.[12] Third, U.S. banks may have refrained from making foreign deposits dually payable out of concern that doing so could cause them to lose the protection from sovereign risk accorded them under section 25(c) of the Federal Reserve Act.[13]

Recent events have reduced the cost of making foreign deposits dually payable. First, in section 331(b) of the Dodd-Frank Wall Street Reform and Consumer Protection Act,[14] Congress changed the deposit insurance assessment base so that it now in effect covers all liabilities, including foreign branch deposits. Thus, a U.S. bank's use of dual payability would no longer increase a bank's assessment base or deposit insurance assessment. Second, the Federal Reserve now pays interest on reserves and allows more flexibility with respect to the reserves it requires. Finally, as discussed below, nothing in this Final Rule is intended to preclude a U.S. bank from protecting itself against sovereign risk.

E.   The U.K. PRA Consultation Paper

In September 2012, the U.K. PRA published a Consultation Paper addressing the implications of national depositor preference regimes in countries outside the European Economic Area ("EEA"). The Consultation Paper proposes to prohibit banks from non-EEA countries, including U.S. banks, from operating deposit-taking branches in the United Kingdom unless U.K. depositors in those branches would be on an equal footing in the national depositor preference regime with domestic (uninsured) depositors in a failure resolution of the bank. A significant percentage of foreign branch deposits of U.S. banks are located in the United Kingdom and would be subject to this requirement.

The Consultation Paper proposes several options to ensure that depositors in U.K. branches would be treated equally in the event of a multinational bank's resolution. U.S. banks with branches in the United Kingdom could comply in one of these ways. First, the U.S. bank could accept deposits in the United Kingdom using a U.K.-incorporated subsidiary. Second, U.S. banks could create a trust arrangement to segregate assets of the U.K. branch to meet its deposit liabilities, under which the trust would specify the U.K. branch depositors as beneficiaries of the trust. Third, U.S. banks could take other actions to comply, such as making their U.K. deposits payable both in the United States and in the United Kingdom. The Consultation Paper indicates that dual payability

---

[12]   12 CFR Part 204. Regulation D imposes uniform reserve requirements on all depository institutions with transaction accounts or non-personal time deposits.

[13]   12 U.S.C. 633. This section provides that a member bank is not required to repay a deposit in a foreign branch if it cannot do so because of "war, insurrection, or civil strife" or actions taken by the foreign government, unless the member bank has explicitly agreed in writing to repay foreign deposits in such circumstances.

[14]   Pub. L. No. 111–203, 124 Stat. 1538.

should allow U.K. depositors to participate in the preference given to home country (that is, United States) depositors in the resolution of a U.S. bank. The U.K. PRA is still considering comments on the Consultation Paper and has not provided a date by which the requirements proposed in the Consultation Paper will be implemented.

* * *

* * * The Final Rule clarifies that foreign branch deposits are not insured deposits for purposes of the FDI Act, regardless of the location at which the deposit is payable. The FDI Act defines "insured deposit" as the net amount due any depositor for deposits in an insured depository institution as determined under section 11(a) of the FDI Act.[16] Section 11(a) of the FDI Act,[17] cross-referenced in the definition of "insured deposit," instructs the FDIC to "insure the deposits of all insured depository institutions as provided in this Act," but does not expressly address foreign deposits. The FDI Act definition of "deposit" in section 3(1)(5)(A) makes clear that obligations carried on the books and records of an office located outside the United States shall not be deposits for any purpose under the FDI Act, but it does not address whether they must be considered deposits for all purposes, including for purposes of deposit insurance, if they would qualify as deposits under 3(1)(5)(A) because they are payable at an office within the United States under express contractual terms.

* * *

QUESTIONS AND NOTES

1.   It is possible that risk can be appropriately distributed between banks and their depositors via the language in deposit agreements. There are legitimate questions to be raised, however, about the fairness of this approach given (1) the disparity in bargaining power between some depositors and the depository institutions; and (2) the expectations of depositors—particularly less sophisticated depositors—that their deposits are protected notwithstanding language in an agreement they may or may not have read. Should caveat emptor i.e., "let the buyer beware" be the rule for depositors in these situations?

2.   Whether banks can limit their liability and depositors can clarify their risk through the language of deposit agreements is an open question. Some courts have been unwilling to side against plaintiffs even where it means ignoring the language of the deposit agreement.

Banks may use deposit agreements to create various covenants and clauses spelling out which countries laws would govern disputes, a forum for

---

[16]   FDI Act section 3(m)(1), 12 U.S.C. 1813(m)(1).

[17]   12 U.S.C. 1821(a).

litigation or restricting payment on the deposit to the issuing branch. Courts have upheld such clauses in insurance policies and shipping contracts, and might be willing to do the same in deposit agreements assuming the bank could show that the limitation in the depositor's rights had been freely bargained for. See Ethan W. Johnson, Comment, Reducing Liability of American Banks for Expropriated Foreign Branch Deposits, 34 Emory L.J. 201 (1985), cited in the Comizio and Chiachiere article at the beginning of this chapter.

One author has argued that the explicit terms of the deposit agreement and the reasonable expectations of the parties ought to be the "fundamental issue" in determining whether a bank is required to pay on a deposit that is exposed to political risk, asserting that the *Trinh* court "rewrote the deposit agreement and awarded the plaintiffs something they never had under its terms—a deposit payable in the United States in the event of expropriation." See M. Ann Hannigan, United States Home Bank Liability for Foreign Branch Deposits, 1989 U. Ill. L. Rev. 735, 737 (1987).

3.   Another commentator has suggested that the Federal Reserve Board, the primary U.S. federal banking regulator for international banking regulation (See Chapter 7), adopt a regulation permitting U.S. banks to "partially suspend the operations of a foreign branch during periods of unrest in the host country." See Francis X. Curci, Foreign Branches of United State Banks-A Proposal for Partial Suspension During Periods of Unrest, 7 Fordham Int'l L.J. 118, 131 (1983). This proposal appears to be a response to *Vishipco*, in which the closure of the branch resulted in the debts "springing back" to the home office, where courts held they were payable. As long as the branch stayed open, the debt would presumably remain at the branch office and the home office would not be liable. If the political situation were to become untenable and result in expropriation, the author argued, the home office would not be liable because the debtor branch remained within the jurisdiction of the expropriating power. Given the court's sweeping ruling in *Garcia*, it is not clear that such a regulation would protect banks from liability following expropriation. After all, if courts have made a policy decision that banks are offering political risk insurance to foreign branch deposits, and the legal decision that Act of State Doctrine does not apply to adjudications of contract disputes between private parties, the question is whether keeping the branch partially open will not save the bank from liability.

4.   You are counsel to a client who wants to protect its deposits in foreign branches of a U.S. banking organization. What do you advise? How about if you represent a U.S. based international banking organization; how do you protect your client from undue liability for foreign deposits?

5.   Multiple choice questions:

a.   Under the holding of the *Wells Fargo* case, a large depositor in the foreign branch of the U.S. bank would best protect her foreign deposit by: a) ensuring that the deposit agreement stipulates that New York law applies in interpreting the agreement; b) ensuring the deposit agreement does not explicitly limit payment of the deposit at the foreign branch; or c) assuming that the deposit agreement does not explicitly limit payment of the deposit at the foreign branch, nor does relevant state or federal law, explicitly limit payment to the foreign branch.

b.   Under U.S. federal banking laws, deposits at foreign branches of U.S. banks that are guaranteed by the bank's U.S. offices in the event the foreign branch is precluded from making payment on such deposits are subject to: a) U.S. bank reserve requirements;   b)   U.S.   deposit   insurance   assessment requirements; c) only banking laws in the foreign jurisdiction; d) the same bank regulatory requirements as if the deposit had been made in a U.S. office of the bank; or e) a, b and d only.

c.   Under the holding of the *Vishipco* and *Trinh* cases, a U.S. bank with a foreign branch in a country undergoing a violent revolution can "ring fence" its domestic liability for the deposits in such foreign branch by: a) voluntarily closing the branch; b) making clear in the deposit agreement used for the foreign branch that only the foreign branch is liable for payment of such deposits; or c) arguing that no demands for the deposits were made in the branch prior to its voluntary closure.

d.   Where a foreign branch of a U.S. bank is subject to a government decree in that jurisdiction ("Government Decree") barring payment of all or part of deposits in that foreign branch, the obligation of the U.S. bank's guarantee of such deposits under the Wells Fargo decision is limited by: a) the Government Decree; b) the Government Decree to the extent it prevents repayment of only part of the deposits; the remainder is payable by the U.S. bank; or c) the Government Decree only to the extent that the U.S. bank has not specifically agreed in its deposit agreement for the foreign bank that the U.S. bank will guarantee the foreign branch's deposits in the event of a force majeure.

CHAPTER 5

INTERNATIONAL BANK SUPERVISION: THE BASEL COMMITTEE ON BANK SUPERVISION

■ ■ ■

1. INTRODUCTION

In the wake of over 40 years of notable international banking failures and scandals ranging from the Bank Herstatt failure in 1974 to the 1982 Banco Ambrosiano/Vatican Bank scandal (note: the basis of the movie Godfather III, worst of the movie trilogy in the author's view, but a great plot from an international banking law perspective) to the infamous 1991 BCCI bank failure (both discussed in this Chapter) right through to the recent global financial crisis—the Basel Committed on Bank Supervision has evolved as the primary global standard-setter for the prudential regulation of banks and provides a key forum for international cooperation on banking regulatory matters. With a mandate "to strengthen the regulation, supervision and practices of banks worldwide with the purpose of enhancing financial stability," the Basel Committee, composed primarily of the major banking regulatory agencies in the G20 countries, is widely followed today as the definitive source for minimum standards of effective bank regulation by over 200 countries worldwide. Suffice to say, the work of the Basel Committee is vitally important to a current understanding of international banking law, as well as the banking laws of any particular country.

This Chapter will present and analyze the evolution and major pronouncements of the Basel Committee. An important goal of the Chapter will be to chart and analyze the clear evolution of the Basel Committee's work in reaction to perceived weakness in international bank regulation. In particular, the Chapter explores how the Basel Committee as it has gained credibility over time in establishing sound standards for international banking regulation, has become far more detailed and specific in its guidance as to appropriate minimum standards of bank supervision, while at the same gradually obtaining world-wide "buy-in" to follow these standards—an amazing transition from its modest, limited—and infrequent—proposals regarding banking regulation in the 1970s. This Chapter will also explore the evolving regulatory responsibilities of "home" and "host" countries with the goals of ensuring that 1) there are no gaps in cross-border bank supervision, and 2) supervision is adequate. The repeating cycle of banking failures and scandals and subsequent reform have clearly caused the Basel Committee to evolve into the key player in international bank supervision right through to the recent global financial crisis.

2. INTERNATIONAL BANK FAILURES AND NEED FOR INTERNATIONAL BANKING STANDARDS

BCCI U.S. v. BCCI HOLDINGS

United States District Court, District of Columbia
69 F. Supp. 2d 36 (D.D.C) 1999

JOYCE HENS GREEN, DISTRICT JUDGE.

At last! For nearly eight years I have been presiding over this fascinating, complex, and sobering case arising out of the collapse of Bank of Credit and Commerce International ("BCCI"), the largest bank failure in history. The Order that accompanies this Opinion is the final chapter in the longest-running forfeiture proceeding in the history of federal racketeering law. Against the odds, through the combined efforts of the United States Department of Justice, the Trustees appointed by this Court, the BCCI Court Appointed Fiduciaries, the Board of Governors of the Federal Reserve System, and the District Attorney for New York County, more than $1.2 billion has been realized from BCCI assets in the United States. Most of that sum has been forwarded for distribution to the victims of BCCI's collapse.

The worldwide liquidation proceeding conducted by the BCCI Court Appointed Fiduciaries remains ongoing. To date, the Court Appointed Fiduciaries have distributed approximately $4 billion worldwide to innocent depositors and creditors. In two dividends, they have repaid creditors a total of 46 percent on admitted claims. Additional dividends are expected, although the amounts will depend on future recoveries. In contrast to the pessimistic projections of 1991, creditors will certainly receive more than half of their money back.

But today's Final Order of Forfeiture brings to an end the criminal case against the BCCI corporations and its attendant forfeiture proceeding. This Opinion summarizes the landmark events in this case to explain why terminating the forfeiture proceeding at this juncture is appropriate. The United States Government has located all of the BCCI-related assets in this country that it could, all disputes regarding ownership of those assets have been resolved, and, thus, the Court's task is complete.

The Final Order of Forfeiture, and related orders signed today, accomplish the following: (1) declare that the United States has clear title to all property forfeited during this proceeding; (2) authorize the United States Marshals Service to distribute all the assets they hold; (3) provide for the dissolution of the two trusts created by this Court to aid in the liquidation of forfeited assets; (4) transfer certain default judgments obtained by First American Corporation in civil litigation to the Department of Justice for collection; and (5) transfer the stock of First American Corporation to the Court Appointed Fiduciaries to wind up the corporation as they see fit.

After briefly outlining the events leading up to the seizure of BCCI almost exactly eight years ago July 5, 1991 this Opinion describes how this case came to be filed here and how the parties entered into their unique Plea Agreement, which triggered this unprecedented forfeiture proceeding. The Opinion then describes the two trusts created to aid in the liquidation of forfeited assets, and the BCCI-related civil cases over which this Court also presided. The final section summarizes the novel legal issues procedural and substantive that arose during the course of adjudicating a total of 175 claims by third parties contesting the forfeiture of certain assets. The conclusion acknowledges those individuals singled out by the parties as deserving of recognition for their respective contributions to the recoveries made in this case.

I. BACKGROUND TO THE BCCI CRIMINAL CASE

BCCI was founded in 1972. The moving force behind its establishment was Agha Hasan Abedi ("Abedi"), a Pakistani banker who envisioned BCCI becoming an international Islamic bank. Abedi's chief lieutenant was Saiyid Mohammad Swaleh Naqvi ("Naqvi"). Abedi remained at the helm of BCCI until 1988, when he suffered a heart attack. Naqvi succeeded him for two years, until the sovereigns of Abu Dhabi took formal control of the bank in 1990.

Abedi established the principal BCCI corporations in Luxembourg and the Cayman islands. Although formally separate, the BCCI corporations were under the same management and were closely linked in their operations. At its peak, BCCI's coordinated international banking network had more than 400 branches in 69 countries. BCCI's depositors included large corporate interests as well as numerous small businesses and middle class households, particularly in England.

English workers

The extent of BCCI's presence in the United States was not generally known until after the bank had been seized. It was known that BCCI had accounts with correspondent banks in New York City and in the other major international money centers. Additionally, BCCI had been allowed to establish "depository agencies" in the United States. But, it appeared that BCCI was not providing retail banking services to United States customers in this country. There were, however, signs that BCCI sought to infiltrate the United States market.

Small presence in U.S.

Correspondents + "Depository Agencies"

NO Retail

A. Financial General Bankshares Lawsuit

As early as 1978, a group of shareholders of Financial General Bankshares, Inc. the predecessor of First American Bank in Washington, D.C. sued BCCI, among others, claiming that it was behind a hostile takeover attempt. Judge Oliver Gasch, of this Court, preliminarily enjoined any further stock purchases by BCCI. In the course of that lawsuit, BCCI retained the services of prominent Washington counsel, Clark M. Clifford ("Clifford") and Robert A. Altman ("Altman"). Shortly after an amended complaint was filed in 1980, BCCI and all but one defendant settled the claims; BCCI subsequently entered into a consent judgment with the Securities and Exchange Commission. See Financial General Bankshares, Inc. v. Metzger, 523 F. Supp. 744, 747 & nn. 4–5 (D.D.C.1981), *vacated on jurisdictional grounds*, 680 F.2d 768 (D.C. Cir. 1982).

B. Sale of First American Bank

Not long after BCCI had settled the *Financial General Bankshares* case, a new proposal was made to sell First American to Credit and Commerce American Investment, B.V. ("CCAI"), a Netherlands shell corporation wholly owned by Credit and Commerce American Holdings, N.V. ("CCAH"), a Netherlands Antilles corporation. The record shareholders of CCAH were wealthy individuals from the Persian Gulf. Although not apparent at the time, it now appears that nearly all of the money required for the purchase had been loaned to the investors by BCCI. Some of these loans were actual extensions of credit while others were false loans created to disguise BCCI's takeover of First American Bank.

In 1981, the Board of Governors of the Federal Reserve System held hearings to determine whether to approve the sale. Some of the proposed investors from the Middle East testified. See, e.g., BCCI Holdings (Luxembourg) S.A. v. Khalil, 56 F.Supp.2d 14, 38 (D.D.C.1999). Clifford and Altman appeared as counsel in those proceedings. Ultimately, the Federal Reserve approved the safe. Shortly thereafter, Clifford and Altman were chosen by the shareholders to be Managing Directors of the shell corporations, CCAH and CCAI, as well as directors and senior officers of the re-christened First American Corporation, the holding company that controlled the largest bank in the Washington, D.C. area. See generally First American Corp. v. Al-Nahyan, 17 F.Supp.2d 10, 13–14 (D.D.C. 1998).

C. BCCI's Connection to General Noriega

BCCI again came to the fore in 1987 and 1988 in connection with investigations into narcotics trafficking by Panamanian General Manuel Noriega. It was known that Noriega had a banking relationship with BCCI and First American. Federal prosecutors, and then committees of the United States Senate and House of Representatives, investigated allegations that BCCI was laundering Noriega's drug proceeds. BCCI was indicted in the United States District Court in Tampa, Florida and subsequently pled guilty to federal money laundering charges. Certain BCCI employees also were indicted, tried, and convicted on money laundering charges. See United States v. Awan, 966 F.2d 1415 (11th Cir. 1992) (affirming convictions in large part).

D. Seizure of BCCI

Then in 1990 and early 1991, BCCI became the focus of attention in the United States and abroad. In this country, news reports in 1990, and intensifying in early 1991, indicated that the Federal Reserve was investigating rumors that BCCI had secretly been behind the takeover of First American. In December 1990, the Republic of Panama sued BCCI and First American in the United States District Court for the Southern District of Florida, alleging that BCCI illegally owned First American and that both sets of corporate entities had violated federal racketeering laws in laundering proceeds from narcotics trafficking for the benefit of General Noriega.

Abroad, the Bank of England received troubling information about BCCI's financial condition and integrity. In response, it commissioned a special audit, which "disclosed evidence of a complex and massive fraud at BCCI, including substantial loan and treasury account losses, misappropriation of funds, unrecorded deposits, the creation and manipulation of fictitious accounts to conceal bank losses, and concealment from regulatory authorities of BCCI's mismanagement and true financial position." Corrigan, Mattingly & Taylor, *The Federal Reserve's Views on BCCI*, 26 Int'l Law. 963, 970–71 (1992) (based on testimony before the Committee on Banking, Finance and Urban Affairs of the United States House of Representatives on September 3, 1991).

The results of the audit were shared with regulators in other countries, and, on July 5, 1991, banking regulators in the United Kingdom, Luxembourg and the United States, froze assets owned or controlled by BCCI. This included seizure of BCCI's deposit agencies by the Superintendent of Banks of the State of California (since retitled the Commissioner of Financial Institutions of the State of California and the Superintendent of Banks of the State of New York. In addition, the New York Superintendent of Banks seized BCCI's assets at various New York banks, including those at the Bank of New York ("BNY") and Security Pacific Bank ("SPB"). By July 6th, eighteen countries had shut down BCCI's operations in their jurisdictions, and, as of July 29, 1991, forty-four countries had closed down BCCI branches. Responding to the closure of BCCI and the apparent confirmation of its illegal ownership of First American, depositors in BCCI filed putative class action lawsuits in August 1991 against BCCI's auditors, First American and approximately 70 other parties charging RICO violations.

II. CIVIL CASES

During the same time period in which this Court adjudicated third party claims related to forfeited BCCI assets, five civil cases connected to the BCCI liquidation proceedings became part of this Court's docket. The first of these was initiated in 1993 by First American with the blessing of the First American Trustee. The mammoth lawsuit was filed against thirty defendants alleged to have participated in BCCI's illegal ownership scheme. The named defendants included the former record shareholders of CCAH, including, for example, members of the Abu Dhabi royal family, other prominent persons from the Middle East, including the Rulers of Ajman and Fujeirah and Sheikh Mohammed of Dubai, as well as Clark Clifford and Robert Altman. The complaint asserted RICO claims common law claims for fraud, breach of fiduciary duty and civil conspiracy. See First American Corp. v. Al-Nahyan, 948 F.Supp. 1107, 1112–15 (D.D.C. 1996) (detailing parties and allegations in complaint). Settlements were reached with most defendants relatively early in the case. Under these settlement agreements parties paid First American and/or relinquished their stock in CCAH as well as their sizable claims against, or debts owed by, First American. The action was set for jury trial in October 1998, see First American Corp. v. Al-Nahyan, 17 F.Supp.2d 10, 13 (D.D.C.1998), and was settled with the remaining defendants, including Clifford and Altman, shortly before that date. See BCCI Holdings (Luxembourg) S.A. v. Khalil, 182 F.R.D. 335, 336 (D.D.C.1998).

Soon after the final settlement was concluded, the Court entered twelve separate default judgments against six defendants in that lawsuit. Those default judgments are for (1) compensatory damages of up to $500 million in connection with the common law fraud claims and (2) treble damages in connection with the RICO claims in the maximum amount of $1.5 billion. The Orders signed today distribute the RICO judgments to the Department of Justice for enforcement and collection.

The second civil suit was filed by the Court Appointed Fiduciaries against the partners of Clifford and Altman's law firm, Clifford & Warnke, and others for their role in BCCI's takeover of First American. Although the Court Appointed Fiduciaries had caused the BCCI corporations to plead guilty to criminal charges in this regard, the Plea Agreement was "not intended by the parties hereto to preclude the criminal prosecution or any civil action against any culpable BCCI officers, employees, agents or other entities (other than BCCI) or wrongdoers." Plea Agreement at 6. When defendants in this civil suit sought dismissal, the Court found that it would be "contrary to the intent of the parties and this Court's understanding when she accepted that plea" to preclude the Court Appointed Fiduciaries from bringing actions against alleged third-party wrongdoers. BCCI Holdings (Luxembourg) S.A v. Clifford, 964 F.Supp. 468, 477–478 (D.D.C.1997). The case was settled on confidential terms in 1998.

Two additional civil cases were filed by Clifford and Altman seeking, inter alia, indemnification under Virginia corporate law for millions of dollars in legal fees and expenses incurred in connection with their successful defense against criminal charges in this Court and in New York, their defense against administrative charges filed by the Board of Governors of the Federal Reserve System, their appearances to give congressional testimony, and their defense against the lawsuit filed by First American. These cases were all resolved as part of the settlement of First American's lawsuit. [The Court discussed settlement of a fifth civil case against a wealthy Saudi businessman, a BCCI insider.]

* * *

THOMAS C. BAXTER, JR. AND JET JOSEPH DE SARAM BCCI: THE LESSONS FOR BANKING SUPERVISION, INTERNATIONAL MONETARY FUND, CURRENT LEGAL ISSUES AFFECTING CENTRAL BANKS

Vol. 4 (1997)

Introduction

In July 1991, a consortium of central banks, including the Federal Reserve, the Bank of England, and the Luxembourg Monetary Institute, coordinated the closing of a multinational bank known as the Bank of Credit and Commerce International (BCCI). The discovery of a massive and widespread fraud, perpetrated over several years, precipitated BCCI's closure. At the time of its closure BCCI had become a truly global bank. The fact of its closure and the reasons far it provide a particularly graphic illustration of the special difficulties inherent in supervising complex multinational banks.

* * * It raises the following five questions that may be asked in the aftermath of BCCI What happened? How did it happen? Why is what happened important banking supervisors? What is being done to prevent a recurrence? What lessons can be learned from the failure of BCCI?. Each section addresses one of these questions and provides answers that highlight some of the most important lessons.

What Happened?

In July 1991, when the public first learned of what would come to be known as the BCCI scandal, there was no benchmark for comparison. Although other multinational banks, such as Banco Ambroisiano, had failed, none had the complexity or geographic diversity of BCCI Furthermore, none had assumed the identity of a bank for the so called developing world, as BCCI had. BCCI is the largest banking fraud in history, but to call it thus in view of these special characteristics almost minimize its significance.

When BCCI closed, it boasted $23 billion in assets worldwide. It had a known presence of 380 offices in 72 countries and a covert presence in others. Through a complex web of subsidiaries affiliates branches, and other entities some secretly owned through nominees who acquired and retained control for it, BCCI operated in these varied jurisdiction including the United States.

* * *

Financial Costs

The losses stemming from BCCI's closure were enormous. At first estimated to range anywhere from $4 billion, the losses are known to be approximately $10 billion. Nationals from the so called 'developing nations', who were attracted to BCCI for reasons to be explained later, bore the brunt of those losses. Many developing nations had placed large deposits of national reserves with BCCI, as had some prominent international organizations. Therefore a particularly sad fact of BCCI's failure is that the bulk of its losses have been inflicted on populations and nations who were poorly situated to sustain them.

Human Costs

The existence of this human component means that the cost of BCCI cannot be measured only in money. Many individual victims of the bank's wrongdoing lost lifetime savings that they had entrusted to what they perceived as 'their' bank. Among the hardest bit were members of certain immigrant communities, most visibly in the United Kingdom, on whom the banks failure had a disproportionate impact. That people of these communities had been drawn to BCCI in the belief that the bank would be responsive to their special needs and situations.

* * *

The impact on individuals was exacerbated in several countries where there is no system of deposit insurance or where the coverage provided is paltry. Depositors in these locations, in many cases, lost their personal savings. Small businesses that served these communities also suffered, some to the point of bankruptcy.

Other Nonfinancial Costs

* * *

Corruption was an integral part of BCCI's criminal enterprise worldwide. In several countries, officials of governmental bodies, central bankers even 'buttered their bread' with BCCI offerings. They accepted bribes in return for various forms of official largesse, including privileged treatment, special dispositions, changes in legislation, and the placement of large deposits of national reserves with BCCI. Corruption was key to

BCCI's rapid growth, and, in it, BCCI found a willing and able ally. Not surprisingly, public confidence in government has eroded the wash of perceived corruption.

* * *

How Did It Happen?

All of this leads to the next question, How did it happen? There is no single method by which BCCI was able to accomplish its global scheme. Rather, several factors worked in synergistic tandem. These factors shall be organized into the following six categories; (i) fractured supervision; (ii) irrational, corporate organization; (iii) corporate culture; (iv) authority; (v) representation; and (vi) technology.

Fractured Supervision

The globalization of modern banking raises special concerns about which supervisory authority has control over a banking institution's activities. Proper allocation of supervisory responsibility among the various national authorities is vital. Basic to this is the principle of consolidated supervision that a single supervisory authority should preside over the operations of a single financial organizational top to bottom, wherever those operations are conducted.

* * *

The supervision of BCCI was fractured no one country had a clear picture of BCCI'S worldwide activities on a consolidated basis. This was no accident. To achieve this result, BCCI's organizers and operators carefully designed BCCI's structure to evade consolidated supervision, resorted to a covert presence in several jurisdictions, exploited the existence of secrecy laws and manipulated the bank's audit process.

Structure of BCCI

BCCI's organizational structure was key to its avoiding consolidated supervision by any home country. The apex of the BCCI organizational was the parent holding company. BCCI Holdings (Luxembourg) S.A., which was chartered and headquartered in Luxembourg. Below were two principal banking subsidiaries: BCCI S.A. and BCCI (Overseas) limited. These were chartered in Luxembourg and the Cayman Islands, respectively.

Under Luxembourg law, the holding company was not subject to supervision. The Luxembourg bank (BCCI S.A.), which was subject to some supervision in its home country by the Luxembourg authorities, nonetheless conducted its principal operations in the United Kingdom. BCCI's other bank subsidiary (BCCI (Overseas) Limited) had its base in the Cayman Islands, where supervision was neither rigorous nor very effective. As a result of this structure; BCCI escaped effective consolidated supervision.

In sum, out of the 72 countries in which BCCI maintained offices and did business, no single supervisory authority had an unobstructed view of BCCI's entire landscape. Furthermore because BCCIs operations spanned multiple jurisdictions the supervisors in each assumed that the other would deal with BCCI's problems. In actuality, no one *did*.

Public good problem

* * *

Covert Presence

BCCI had another means for evading supervision; the operation of secret subsidiaries through nominees. BCCI used this technique in countries where supervision and regulation were more rigorous or where, for whatever reason, BCCI's presence was unwelcome. For example, in the United States, BCCI deliberately concealed its ownership and control of several financial institutions, including the First American group of banks. Because banking supervisory authorities in the United States were unaware of BCCI's ownership of these institutions, BCCI was able to evade their attention. Even if BCCI had a single supervisor which it did not the U.S. authorities would not have expected that supervisor to be interested in the operations of these banks because the U.S. authorities did not know that they were a part of the BCCI organization. This demonstrates an important concept for bank supervision, that nominee ownership defeats consolidated supervision. Furthermore, certain corporate structures that facilitate nominee ownership, such as bearer share companies, similarly frustrate consolidated Supervision.

Secrecy Laws

Adequate consolidated supervision of a multinational bank such as BCCI requires a significant amount of cross border information sharing among supervisors. Bank secrecy laws; however, substantially impede the dissemination of information. For example, they make it difficult for a home supervisor to secure from jurisdictions where subsidiaries operate the information needed to understand the condition of the consolidated entity. Furthermore, secrecy laws make the detection of fraudulent activity more difficult and impede its investigation and foreclose the timely initiation of enforcement proceedings or criminal prosecutions.

BCCI skillfully exploited the existence of secrecy laws in certain jurisdictions to conceal the criminal activities of parts of its organization from the authorities who were supervising them.

Auditing of BCCI's Global Operations

For most of its life, BCCI divided auditing responsibility for its global operations between two forms of auditors. One firm had responsibility for the Cayman bank, the other had responsibility for the Luxembourg bank. Because no auditor monitored all of BCCI's global operations, BCCI was able to conceal its true condition.

BCCI derived an added benefit from having separate auditors for the two main divisions of its operations. Year end audits were conducted at different times in the different locations, enabling BCCI to deceive each set of auditors. BCCI did this by booking loans in location X while location Y was being audited and using the proceeds of those loans to cover losses in Y. Later, when location X was being audited by another set of auditors and the loans scrutinized, the loans would be discharged or serviced with the proceeds of new loans in location Y. Because different auditors looked at different locations, this simple deception could be used, and was to great effect. The manipulation of auditors enabled BCCI to escape adequate supervision of its operations.

The class Lucy Football

* * *

Corporate Organization

BCCI's corporate organizational structure was tailor made for its illegal activities. This organizational structure appears rational only if one assumes that the organization has an unlawful objective.

For example, in the Cayman Islands, BCCI had set up a structure at the local level that mirrored its global structure (see above). Why, in an area as small as the Cayman Islands, would BCCI require two banks? It was not as if a large number of island depositors were clamoring for BCCI's banking services: rather, it was booking loans on the books of BCCI, subject to the scrutiny of one set of auditors, and paying down those loans with the proceeds of others on the books of BCCI (Overseas), subject to the scrutiny of another set of auditors.

In Luxembourg, too, BCCI's corporate organization served no apparent legitimate commercial purpose. There, BCCI established its flagship bank, BCCI S.A., as well as a branch of a Swiss banking institution that it controlled Banque de Commerce et de placements. Again, one wonders; why BCCI needed to establish two banks in a location like Luxembourg. Surely BCCI was not seeking to serve the depositor community in Luxembourg.

In hindsight, it is clear that BCCI's unique structure had only an illegitimate purpose it was set up deliberately to further its global criminal scheme undetected.

Corporate Culture

The term "corporate culture" is used here to mean several intangible factors that together played a significant part in ensuring the success of BCCI's criminal scheme. The founder and president of BCCI, Agha Hasan

Abedi was able to extract unquestioning loyally and confidentiality within the bank because he exploited these factors in no small measure.

BCCI's corporate culture flourished in its so called central support office. This support office was the operational center of the bank, located at 100 Leadenhall Street in London. The small band of executives working in the support office were all of South Asian origin. Recruited by BCCI's organizers, these executives had relocated to the United Kingdom to work for BCCI. In many cases, these expatriate bankers had also relocated their families to the United Kingdom and had established new roots in that country.

Throughout their tenure at BCCI, the executives at the central support office had been concerned with losing their jobs in London. If that had happened, they could no longer have continued to live with their families in their adopted county. These bankers also knew that, if they lost their positions at BCCI, they could not hope to match at any other institution the salaries that BCCI paid them. BCCI's executives were, therefore, absolutely dependent on the goodwill of BCCI's leader, Agha Hasan Abedi. If he were crossed, the penalty was certainly loss of livelihood and perhaps repatriation.

In addition to the economic disincentive to stray, Agha Hasan Abedi was able to create an almost blind faith among BCCI's staff. He did this by using his remarkable personal charisma and by emphasizing BCCI's commitment to the Islamic religion and the important mission that it was engaged in as a bank, for the developing world.

Authority

A unique characteristic of BCCI's corporate structure was that those individuals running the organization were difficult to identify. An observer could not tell that the bank's worldwide operations were being run out of the fourth floor of BCCI's London office.

Unlike other banks, which are run as hierarchies, BCCI was seemingly egalitarian. None of the officers had titles or rank; they were characterized by the same generic description, 'executives.' Moreover, these executives did not have private offices; their desks were arranged according to what was known in BCCI as the open plan, in a large, open space in the Leadenhall Street office in London.

As a result of this apparent egalitarianism, no one looking in from the outside could determine the source of authority. This arrangement was in stark contrast to most modem style financial institutions, where the source of authority is clear from the individual's title and even from the location of that individual's office on the floor plan.

Instead of the usual trappings of authority, BCCI resorted to a simple legal device, the power of attorney. Each power of attorney identified the executives authorized to act for BCCI's various constituent banks, thus providing an easy way for a few individuals in the central support office to do whatever was necessary to keep BCCI afloat around the world. For example, if an auditor were questioning a ban that appeared to be past due at the Luxembourg bank, an executive in London could, by using a power of attorney, make loans on the books of the Cayman bank, transfer by wire the proceeds to the Luxembourg branch of the Swiss affiliate, and direct from there another wire transfer to the Luxembourg bank.

Representation

BCCI was able to deceive auditors and regulators around the world because it was represented by believable people and because it used credible nominees to hide its ownership of financial institutions. Representatives of BCCI were believed because of who they were and not because of the inherent truth, if any, in what they said. Usually, they were people with distinguished careers and impeccable reputations for integrity. Often, they had significant ties to the political establishments of their countries. The statements that they made on behalf of BCCI had an effect on regulators that those same statements would not have had if BCCI itself had uttered them. It was no accident that BCCI retained people of such caliber; it understood that its representation would go unchallenged and used this to maximum advantage throughout the world.

In its nominees, too, BCCI chose well. They were credible people of enormous personal wealth who did not appear to be unlikely purchasers of a bank. These were conspicuously wealthy individuals, from prestigious families, who seemed to be the lease likely to sell their names for a fee.

* * *

Technology

Finally, BCCI was able to sustain its global deception over time because the people who acted for BCCI understood how modern technology worked and used it to suit their purpose.

The central support office serves as an illustration of this point. From London, executives were able to operate banks around the world by using modern telecommunications equipment and funds transfer systems. Clearly, they understood the payments system and made it work for them, moving funds rapidly from location to location, as needed, to keep BCCI afloat.

BCCI was able to hide funding transactions between affiliates by using an intermediary financial institution that was willing to cooperate. The Banque de Commerce et de Placements, its Swiss affiliate, often performed this role. The intermediary bank would be asked to omit any reference to BCCI as the originating bank in its wire transfer instruction or supporting documentation. This way, BCCI was able to cut off the audit trail of many of its illegal transactions.

In sum, combining all these factors, BCCI accomplished its global criminal objectives.

* * *

NOTES

1.   The authors of this article also observed that BCCI "is important because its methods and activities mocked the very process of supervision and regulation," noting:

> To be effective, banking authorities must be able to rely on what people tell them. This is particularly important in the United States, where banking organizations must file applications with regulatory authorities to engage in certain banking functions. A bank application is approved not only on the basis of what regulators are able to verify on their own but also on the basis of the applicant's representations. Given the limited resources and the significant number of applications, authorities cannot investigate and verify each representation in each application. Consequently, regulators must be able to rely on such representations as true. For this reason, making false representations to banking authorities is a crime in the United States. The Federal Reserve moves aggressively against anyone who makes deliberate misrepresentations in a bank application, and it has done so with respect to the BCCI nominees. Aggressive enforcement action is designed to deter those who would engage in this type of pernicious behavior, which threatens the integrity of the banking supervisory process.

Are there other ways to prevent submission of fraudulent applications to bank regulators? See, e.g., 12 U.S.C. § 1001 (civil and criminal penalties for making any "false filings" with the U.S. government).

2.   It is interesting that BCCI's management was able to exploit emerging payment systems technologies in the late 1980s i.e., the "modern technology" referenced by the article's authors. Today with payment systems technology firmly embedded in the international financial services system, and well known to regulators worldwide, could this exploitation for illegal purpose still occur? The Basel Committee on Payment and Market Infrastructure ("CPMI") promotes "the safety and efficiency of payment, clearing, and settlement and related arrangements." The CPMI is designed to be a global standard setter in this area, aimed at strengthening regulation, policy and practices regarding such arrangement worldwide. See http://www.bis.org/cpmi/. The CPMI over the years has also periodically published and updated "red books," which are publications on the payment, clearing and settlement systems of various CPMI-member countries. The CPMI also looks at threats to the payment systems infrastructure, including cyber-related threats to the

financial sector. See, e.g., Cyber resilience in financial market infrastructures, CPMI, Basel Committee (November 11, 2014).

3.   In recent years cyber attacks involving data breaches, destructive software and attempts to disable critical segments of the financial sector worldwide have been dramatically increasing. The U.S. reported that there has been a major increase in malicious cyber activity targeting U.S. computers and networks, including more than tripling of the volume of malicious software attacks since 2009. See Director of National Intelligence Statement for the Record on the Worldwide Threat Assessment of the U.S. Intelligence Community, statement before the Senate Select Committee on Intelligence (February 16, 2011). Threats to financial institutions have included attacks from a variety of sources, including criminal groups, hackers, disgruntled employees, foreign governments engaged in espionage and information warfare and terrorist groups. See U.S. General Accounting office, Cyber-Security Guidance, Critical Infrastructure Protection (December 9, 2011) ("GAO Cyber Security Report"). Id. These cyber attacks have included, among other things, attempts by cyber criminals to use online banking and payment systems to transfer money from financial institutions to their own accounts, government and terrorist attacks designed to disrupt or disable key parts of the financial sector and probe infrastructure weaknesses, data breaches of confidential customer data to cause reputational and financial harm, and at times, for extortion. See, e.g., Communications-Electronics Security Group of the UK Government, Common Cyber Attacks: Reducing the Impact (2015); Emily Glazer, J.P. Morgan's Cyber Attack: How the Bank Responded, Wall Street Journal (October 3, 2014); Mike Lennon, Hackers Hit 100 Banks in 'Unprecedented' $1 Billion Cyber Heist: Kaspersky Lab, Security Week (February 15, 2015).

Given the real and rising threats of cyber attacks against major financial institutions and potential for significant impact on the global economy, financial regulation and law enforcement have both heightened their scrutiny of cyber security programs, but are increasingly adopting new laws, regulations and policies that focus on cyber resilience and threat response. The U.S., for example, has in recent years issued hundreds of cybersecurity regulatory guidance documents related to the banking and finance sector, as well as a recent Presidential Executive Order characterizing cyber threats as a "national emergency" and calling for increased cooperation and information sharing on such threat within both the government and private sector, as well as enhanced cyber resilience standards. See GAO Cyber Security Report at Appendix II, Table 7, Cybersecurity Guidance Applicable to the Banking and Finance Sector at 53; Presidential Executive Order 13691, Promoting Private Sector Cybersecurity (February 13, 2015).

4.   The international payment systems and its regulation worldwide is certainly worthy of its own legal casebook. The payment system is an operational network—governed by laws, rules and standards—that links bank accounts and provides the functionality for monetary exchange using bank deposits. The payment system is the infrastructure (consisting of institutions,

instruments, rules, procedures, standards, and technical means) established to effect the transfer of monetary value between parties discharging mutual obligations. See Payment Systems: Design, Governance and Oversight, edited by Bruce J. Summers, Central Banking Publications Ltd, (2012).

What makes it a "system" is that it employs cash-substitutes; traditional payment systems are negotiable instruments such as drafts (e.g., checks) and documentary credits such as letters of credit. With the advent of computers and electronic communications a large number of alternative electronic payment systems have emerged. These include debit cards, credit cards, electronic funds transfers, direct credits, direct debits, internet banking and e-commerce payment systems. Some payment systems include credit mechanisms, but that is essentially a different aspect of payment. Payment systems are used in lieu of tendering cash in domestic and international transactions and consist of a major service provided by banks and other financial institutions.

Payment systems may be physical or electronic and each has its own procedures and protocols. Standardization have allowed some of these systems and networks to grow to a global scale, but there are still many country- and product-specific systems. Examples of payment systems that have become globally available are credit card and automated teller machine networks. Specific forms of payment systems are also used to settle financial transactions for products in the equity markets, bond markets, currency markets, futures markets, derivatives markets, options markets and to transfer funds between financial institutions both domestically using clearing and Real Time Gross Settlement (RTGS) systems and internationally using the SWIFT network. See Biago Bossone and Massimo Cirasino, "The Oversight of the Payment Systems: A Framework for the Development and Governance of Payment Systems in Emerging Economies" The World Bank (July 2001).

For example, The Automated Clearing House ("ACH") is a primary electronic network for financial transactions in the U.S., providing clearing and settlement facilities between participating banks. The National Automated Clearing House Association ("NACHA") governs the ACH, and through the Federal Reserve Banks, which uses the FedACH system, are collectively the largest U.S. ACH operator. In 2014, the ACH network processed approximately 23 billion transactions totaling $40 trillion dollars, constituting over 60% of commercial interbank transactions, with the remaining 40% processed by the Electronic Payments Network ("EPN"), the only private sector ACH in the U.S. See *ACH* Volume Increases to 23 Billion Payments in 2014, National Automated Clearing House Association (NACHA) (April 15, 2015).

A number of countries have taken steps to regulate payment systems.

HM TREASURY, U.K., DESIGNATION OF PAYMENT SYSTEMS FOR REGULATION BY THE PAYMENT SYSTEMS REGULATOR

(October 14, 2014)

* * *

In March 2013 the government published a consultation document, Opening up UK payments, (https://www.gov.uk/government/consultations /opening-up-uk-payments), setting out its proposals to bring payment systems under formal economic regulation. This followed a report published in July 2011 by the Treasury Select Committee, expressing serious concerns about the governance of payment systems, and recommending that the Payments Council be brought into regulation.

The government has considerable concerns about UK payment systems. The combination of strong network effects, and the ownership of many of the key payment systems by overlapping groups of the big incumbent banks, are seen as potentially giving rise to problems in three areas:

1. Competition: the structure of the industry may give the incumbent big banks the opportunity to erect barriers to entry, so that challengers and smaller players find it more difficult to access payment systems on fair and transparent terms. These issues may occur both at the level of direct and indirect access to the payment systems.

2. Innovation: the network nature of payment systems (ie all major banks need to be connected for the system as a whole to be effective) means that innovations in the shared space do not give a competitive advantage to banks individually. The banks also have the ability to slow the pace of development of new innovations if, for example, they are not as well-placed to take advantage of them. There is therefore a concern that new innovations might not be developed where they are in the wider social interest, but not in the narrower interests of individual banks.

3. Service-user responsiveness: the network nature of payment systems means that, if a payment system fails to respond to service-user needs, this does not necessarily give a competitive disadvantage to any individual bank. This may lead to payment systems not being responsive to service-user needs and wishes.

* * *

BASEL COMMITTEE ON BANK SUPERVISION
Working Paper No. 13

BANK FAILURES IN MATURE ECONOMIES

* * *

THE HERSTATT CRISIS IN GERMANY

Summary

The following section focuses on the bank failure of Herstatt in Germany, which has received much attention in international finance because of its regulatory implications. Herstatt was closed by its regulators in 1974. The bank was insolvent and left the dollars owed on its foreign-exchange deals unpa*id*.

Banking industry characteristics

* * *

By international standards, the banking system in Germany has always been characterised by a high degree of stability. However, the German banking system has not been spared entirely from banking crises. Examples of crises in Germany include the large-scale banking crisis of 1931, the collapse of Herstatt in 1974 and the default of Schroeder, Muenchmeyer, Hengst & Co in 1983. This study focuses on the Herstatt failure, which is famous in international finance.

The case of Herstatt

The case of Herstatt was the largest and the most spectacular failure in German banking history since 1945.[5] Herstatt was founded in Cologne in 1956 by Iwan Herstatt. At the end of 1973, Herstatt's total assets amounted to DM 2.07 billion and the bank was the thirty-fifth largest in Germany.

Description of the crisis

Herstatt got into trouble because of its large and risky foreign exchange business. In September 1973, Herstatt became over-indebted as the bank suffered losses four times higher than the size of its own capital. The losses resulted from an unanticipated appreciation of the dollar. For some time, Herstatt had speculated on a depreciation of the dollar. Only late in 1973 did the foreign exchange department change its strategy. The strategy of

---

[5]   The Herstatt crisis is well known in international finance because of 'Herstatt risk'. Herstatt risk refers to risk arising from the time delivery lag between two currencies. Since Herstatt was declared bankrupt at the end of the business day, many banks still had foreign exchange contracts with Herstatt for settlement on that date. Many of those banks were experiencing significant losses. Hence, Herstatt risk represented operational risk for those banks which were exposed to the default of Herstatt. But, Herstatt risk was not a reason for the Herstatt crisis.

the bank to speculate on the appreciation of the dollar worked until mid-January 1974, but then the direction of the dollar movement changed again. The mistrust of other banks aggravated Herstatt's problems.

In March 1974, a special audit authorised by the Federal Banking Supervisory Office (BAKred) discovered that Herstatt's open exchange positions amounted to DM 2 billion, eighty times the bank's limit of DM 25 million. The foreign exchange risk was thus three times as large as the amount of its capital (Blei, 1984). The special audit prompted the management of the bank to close its open foreign exchange positions.

Too much bad trades (like Lloyd's)

When the severity of the situation became obvious, the failure of the bank could not be avoided. In June 1974, Herstatt's losses on its foreign exchange operations amounted to DM 470 million. On 26 June 1974, BAKred withdrew Herstatt's licence to conduct banking activities. It became obvious that the bank's assets, amounting to DM 1 billion, were more than offset by its DM 2.2 billion liabilities.

Causes of the crisis

The Herstatt crisis took place shortly after the collapse of the Bretton Woods System in 1973. The bank had a high concentration of activities in the area of foreign trade payments. Under the Bretton Woods System, where exchange rates were fixed, this area of business tended to carry little risk. In an environment of floating exchange rates, this area of business was fraught with much higher risks.[6]

Loss of fixed exchange made safe business risky

How was risk manifest in the crisis?

The cause of Herstatt's failure was its speculation on the foreign exchange markets. After the collapse of the Bretton Woods System in March 1973, the free floating of currencies provided Herstatt with additional incentives for risky bets on foreign exchange. In the end, its forecasts concerning the dollar proved to be wrong. Additionally, open positions exceeded considerably the DM 25 million limit. The management of the bank significantly underestimated the risks that free-floating currencies carried.

How was the problem resolved?

The three big German banks failed to organise a joint rescue. The reason for the failure of the rescue plan was the lack of transparency about the magnitude of actual losses. In June 1974, the loss from Herstatt's foreign exchange operations amounted to DM 470 million. Within ten days, the Federal Banking Supervisory Office (BAKred) withdrew Herstatt's banking licence.

---

[6]   (Kaserer, 2000).

What were the regulatory responses?

The Herstatt crisis had many implications for the regulatory framework. In 1974, shortly after the crisis, Principle 1a was introduced in order to limit the risk accumulated by a bank on its foreign exchange operations. In 1976, the Second Amendment to the Banking Act (KWG) came into force, which strictly limited risks in credit business and tightened the controls of the Federal Banking Supervisory Office (BAKred). Among other things, the risks in credit business were limited through such important measures as the regulation of large credits and the introduction of the principle of dual control. Furthermore, the Association of German Banks (BdB) decided to set up a deposit protection scheme for German banks.

PAUL LEWIS, ITALY'S MYSTERIOUS, DEEPENING BANK SCANDAL

New York Times (1982)

ROME, July 27—The apparent suicide last month of an Italian financier known as "God's banker," who was found hanged beneath London's Blackfriars Bridge, has added to the mystery of a major Italian financial scandal in which the Vatican appears heavily involved.

The cost to the Roman Catholic Church could amount to several hundred million dollars. The scandal centers on some $1.4 billion in unsecured loans made in Latin America by Banco Ambrosiano, Italy's largest privately owned banking group, and endorsed by the Vatican bank. It is sending shock waves through the world of international finance and raising questions about current efforts to regulate the foreign operations of multinational banks.

It has also strained Italy's relations with the Vatican, an autonomous governing unit in Rome. Under pressure from the Italian Government and concerned church leaders, Pope John Paul II has ordered an unusual outside investigation into the Vatican's finances by three Roman Catholic lay bankers. But the Italian Government wants the Vatican to accept a measure of financial responsibility for Ambrosiano's expected losses.

As usual in such scandals in Italy, there are also unverifiable reports that organized-crime figures and a recently discovered, anti-Government secret Masonic lodge are somehow involved.

There are also reports that Banco Ambrosiano may have been a target of the British secret service, which, is said to suspect it of financing Argentine arms purchases during the war over the Falkland Islands.

The Bank of Italy first became suspicious about Banco Ambrosiano in 1978 during a general crackdown on bank fraud, but immediately ran into a heavy political opposition.

* * *

The hanged banker was Roberto Calvi, 61 years old. He had joined Milan's Banco Ambrosiano as a clerk, worked his way up to become its president and, along the way, through a series of spectacular deals, transformed what had been a modest regional bank into a major financial power, with assets of $18.7 billion in 1981.

Mr. Calvi, who was appealing a four-year jail sentence for illegal currency dealings, disappeared from his Rome apartment on June 10, after failing to block an inquiry by the Italian central bank into some $1.4 billion of loans that banks he controlled had made to obscure companies, most of them Panamanian.

Five days after he vanished, his secretary jumped to her death from a window of the Milan bank. Mr. Calvi's body was found on June 18. Collapse of an Empire

The financial panic caused by news of Mr. Calvi's death and the Bank of Italy's investigation provoked the collapse of his financial empire. Shares of companies his group had interests in fell 30 and 40 percent on the Milan stock exchange. After depositors rushed to withdraw their funds, Banco Ambrosiano itself had to be bailed out by a consoartium of six major Italian banks hurriedly put together by the Bank of Italy.

Earlier this month, Banco Ambrosiano Holdings S.A., a Luxembourg subsidiary two-thirds of which is owned by Banco Ambrosiano, defaulted on some $400 million of foreign loans it had received. It is now in receivership. The Bank of Italy has scheduled a meeting of Ambrosiano creditors in London on Thursday.

Last week, banking authorities in the Bahamas suspended for 30 days the license of Ambrosiano's Bahamas operation, Banco Ambrosiano Overseas Ltd., in order to "restore satisfactory liquidity to its operations," the Bahamian central bank said.

"The Ambrosiano affair makes everyone wonder about the Vatican's finances, but it really illustrates the fragility of the international banking system that we are all trying to preserve," said Guido Carli, a former governor of the Bank of Italy and now a prominent industrialist.

* * *

During 1980 and 1981, investigating officials say, the late Mr. Calvi mounted an extensive lending program to the Peruvian, Nicaraguan and Nassau subsidiaries of the Banco Ambrosiano group, using funds borrowed in the Eurodollar market that eventually totaled some $1.2 billion to $1.4 billion.

[margin note: Cosigned w/o any issues]

Most of this money was then lent to a series of Panamanian companies with names such as Bellatrix Inc., Manic Inc. and Astrolfine Inc., most of which are thought to have no more than mail addresses. The loans were granted roughly evenly by Banco Ambrosiano in Milan and by its Luxembourg subsidiary, Banco Ambrosiano Holdings.

[margin note: Vatican vouched for companies + negotiated out of liability]

But Mr. Calvi lent these funds, investigators say, only after receiving what bankers call "letters of comfort" from the Vatican bank. These letters, though vaguely worded, implied that the Vatican had an interest in the companies and was aware of their borrowing plans. Although such letters do not constitute a legal guarantee that the signatory will repay the loans, they are often issued to reassure lenders that a borrowing company has reputable backing.

But the Vatican bank also demanded and received last August what investigators call a "counter letter" signed by Mr. Calvi and absolving it from all legal and financial responsibility for the loans to the Panamanian companies.

[margin note: Borrowed money went to Calvi]

Investigating officials believe the Vatican did have an interest in the Panamanian companies and probably controlled a number of them. But they are convinced that Mr. Calvi was also part owner and effective manager of most of the companies and used the money they borrowed to buy shares in Banco Ambrosiano and probably in other companies as well. By now, one senior official involved in the investigation estimates, the Panamanian companies own around 20 percent of Banco Ambrosiano, 'A House of Cards'

As interest rates soared last year and the dollar strengthened, the investigators surtnise that Mr. Calvi found it increasingly difficult to service his dollar-denominated borrowings with the dividends from his shares, often paid in weak Italian lire. To remain solvent he was forced to borrow more. "It was a house of cards that was bound to fall down," one official said.

As his financial difficulties mounted, the investigators assume Mr. Calvi needed the Vatican letters of comfort to reassure skeptical directors of his own bank that the lending program was sound and also to satisfy foreign lenders.

The real mystery, these sources say, is why Archbishop Marcinkus agreed to provide the letters of comfort that he knew could be used to make lenders think the Panamanian companies enjoyed Vatican backing, while at the same time demanding a secret letter from Mr. Calvi absolving the Vatican of any financial responsibility for what must have been looking by then like an increasingly risky operation. "The Vatican must have known that the two letters could not be genuine at the same time; the deal was intended to defraud and to lead people astray," argued one senior Italian financial official.

There is speculation that the Archbishop may have agreed to the deal to help out an old colleague and financial adviser since Banco Ambrosiano is regarded as one of Italy's "Catholic" banks with longstanding links to the Vatican. He may also have wished to protect the Vatican's own stake in Banco Ambrosiano, which is assumed to be far more than the 1.8 percent shown by the latest official figures.

There is also evidence, officials say, that Archbishop Marcinkus became alarmed by the arrangements he had made and refused to extend the letters of comfort, which expired in June. Mr. Calvi is believed to have asked him to do so at a meeting on June 8 or 9, just after the Banco Ambrosiano directors voted down their president by 11 to 3 and agreed to cooperate with the Bank of Italy's investigation.

On this occasion, officials say, the Vatican bank also turned down a Calvi plan to ease the Banco Ambrosiano group's mounting liquidity problems by buying a package of bank shares well above the market price.

The Archbishop, according to the Vatican press office, is not available for interviews or comment.

* * *

The Pope has already appointed a three-member lay commission to investigate the Vatican bank. It is made up of an American Roman Catholic, Joseph Brennan, a former chairman of the Emigrant Savings Bank of New York; Phillipe de Wech, a former president of Switzerland's Union Bank, and Carlo Cirutti, an Italian civil servant with strong ties to the Vatican.

* * *

[T]he Bank of Italy has already come under attack from private bankers in Britain and the United States for what they see as a wanton endangering of the international banking system by the central bank's refusal to bail out Banco Ambrosiano's Luxembourg holding company under the central bankers' concordat of 1974. This agreement was reached by major central banks, after the failure of West Germany's Herstatt Bank, at a meeting in Basel, Switzerland, and basically commits them to meet any liquidity shortage in national banks as well as in their overseas branches.

But the Italian central bank argues that Banco Ambrosiano Holdings is not a bank and is not even supervised by Luxembourg's banking authority. It also maintains that the holding company is not facing a temporary liquidity shortage that can be cleared up with a little help, but is fundamentally insolvent. "We are not bound to bail out insolvent banks," an official said.

* * *

QUESTIONS AND NOTES

1.   This Chapter gives just a few notable examples of infamous intentional bank failures and scandals. See also Benton E. Gup, Bank Failures in the Major Trading Countries of the World: Causes and Remedies, Quorum Books (1998); Gerard Caprio, Preventing Bank Crises: Lessons From Recent Global Bank Failures, World Bank Publications (1998); Joan Edelman Spiro, The Failure of the Franklin National Bank: Challenge to the International Banking System, Columbia University Press (1980); Drea Knufken, 25 Biggest Bank Failures in History, Business Pundit Blog (May 7, 2009).

2.   Roberto Calvi's son, who never believed his father committed suicide, hired investigators to find evidence of foul play, and convinced Italian authorities to prosecute certain individuals, albeit unsuccessfully. See Stephen Brown, All Acquitted in Italian Banker's Death, Washington Post (June 6, 2009).

3.   THE BASEL COMMITTEE ON BANKING SUPERVISION

Established on 17 May 1930, the Bank for International Settlements (BIS) is the world's oldest international financial organisation. The BIS has 60 member central banks, representing countries from around the world that together make up about 95% of world GDP.

The head office is in Basel, Switzerland and there are two representative offices: in the Hong Kong Special Administrative Region of the People's Republic of China and in Mexico City.

The mission of the BIS is to serve central banks in their pursuit of monetary and financial stability, to foster international cooperation in those areas and to act as a bank for central banks.

In broad outline, the BIS pursues its mission by:

- fostering discussion and facilitating collaboration among central banks;
- supporting dialogue with other authorities that are responsible for promoting financial stability;
- carrying out research and policy analysis on issues of relevance for monetary and financial stability;
- acting as a prime counterparty for central banks in their financial transactions; and
- serving as an agent or trustee in connection with international financial operations.

In 1974, the BIS established the Basel Committee on Bank Supervision.

BASEL COMMITTEE ON BANKING SUPERVISION, HISTORY OF THE BASEL COMMITTEE AND ITS MEMBERSHIP

(2009)

The Basel Committee on Banking Supervision was established as the Committee on Banking Regulations and Supervisory Practices by the central-bank Governors of the Group of Ten countries at the end of 1974 in the aftermath of serious disturbances in international currency and banking markets (notably the failure of Bankhaus Herstatt in West Germany). The first meeting took place in February 1975 and meetings have been held regularly three or four times a year since.

The Committee's members come from Argentina, Australia, Belgium, Brazil, Canada, China, France, Germany, Hong Kong SAR, India, Indonesia, Italy, Japan, Korea, Luxembourg, Mexico, the Netherlands, Russia, Saudi Arabia, Singapore, South Africa, Spain, Sweden, Switzerland, Turkey, the United Kingdom and the United States. Countries are represented by their central bank and also by the authority with formal responsibility for the prudential supervision of banking business where this is not the central bank.

The Committee provides a forum for regular cooperation between its member countries on banking supervisory matters. Initially, it discussed modalities for international cooperation in order to close gaps in the supervisory net, but its wider objective has been to improve supervisory understanding and the quality of banking supervision worldwide, It seeks to do this in three principal ways: by exchanging information on national supervisory arrangements; by improving the effectiveness of techniques for supervising international banking business; and by setting minimum supervisory standards in areas where they are considered desirable.

The Committee does not possess any formal supranational supervisory authority. Its conclusions do not have, and were never intended to have, legal force. Rather, it formulates broad supervisory standards and guidelines and recommends statements of best practice in the expectation that individual authorities will take steps to implement them through detailed arrangements—statutory or otherwise—which are best suited to their own national systems. In this way, the Committee encourages convergence towards common approaches and common standards without attempting detailed harmonisation of member countries' supervisory techniques. More than 100 documents providing guidance on a wide range of supervisory topics appear on the BIS website.

* * *

NOTES

1.   One important objective of the Basel Committee's work has been to close perceived gaps in international supervisory coverage in pursuit of two basic principles: that no foreign banking establishment should escape supervision; and that supervision should be adequate. In May 1983 the Basil Committee finalised Principles for the Supervision of Banks' Foreign Establishments, which established principles for sharing supervisory responsibility for banks foreign branches, subsidiaries and joint ventures between host and parent (or home) supervisory authorities. This document is a revised version of a paper originally issued in 1975 which came to be known as the "Concordat". The text of the earlier paper was expanded and reformulated to take account of changes in the market and to incorporate the principle of consolidated supervision of international banking groups (which had been adopted in 1978). As such, the original Concordat has been revised and updated a number of times to reflect the Basel Committee's evolving views on bank supervision.

2.   As an outcome of the ongoing collaboration in the supervision of international banks, the Basel Committee has addressed a number of related topics. It has collected information on most national systems for supervising banks' foreign establishments; it has examined the obstacles to effective supervision arising from bank secrecy regulations in different countries; and it has studied authorisation procedures for new foreign banking establishments.

3.   The Basel Committee maintains close relations with a number of fellow bank supervisory groupings. These include the Offshore Group of Banking Supervisors, with members from the principal offshore banking centres; and supervisory groups from the Americas, the Caribbean, from the Arab States, from the SEANZA countries of the Indian sub-continent, South-East Asia and Australasia, from central and eastern European countries, from the African continent and from Central Asia and Transcaucasia. The Basel Committee assists these groups in a variety of ways, by providing suitable documentation, participating as appropriate in the meetings, and hosting meetings between the principals to coordinate future work.

The principles agreed by the Basel Committee have been widely disseminated through these international conferences and supervisory groupings. A large number of countries outside the original "Group of Ten" Basel members have given their support to the fundamental objective of ensuring that no international banking activity should escape supervision. See Basel Committee Core Principles for Effective Banking Supervision. As a result there now remain only a very few territories around the world where banking companies are licensed and allowed to operate without serious efforts to accompany a licence with effective supervision and cooperation with other supervisory authorities. Moreover, the Basel Committee has worked to raise the level of supervisors' consciousness of their mutual interdependence where the international activities of banks within their jurisdictions are concerned. The development of close personal contacts between supervisors in different countries has, by all accounts, greatly helped in the handling and resolution of problems affecting individual banks as they have arisen. This is an important, though necessarily unpublicised, element in the Basel Committee's regular work.

4.   Other Basel Committee groups related to financial services include:

• The Financial Stability Board (FSB) (discussed later in this Chapter), which seeks to enhance global financial stability by developing policies and coordinating the work of national financial authorities and international standard-setting bodies. It operates under a mandate from the G20 heads of state and government.

• The International Association of Insurance Supervisors (IAIS) is the international standard-setting body for the supervision of the insurance sector. Its membership of Insurance supervisors and regulators come from about 140 jurisdictions.

• The International Association of Deposit Insurers (IADI) (discussed in Chapter 1), provides guidance on creating and maintaining effective deposit insurance systems. Its members represent deposit insurance agencies from more than 70 jurisdictions.

PRINCIPLES FOR THE SUPERVISION OF BANKS' FOREIGN ESTABLISHMENTS

The Basel Committee on Banking Supervision (May 1983)

I.   Introduction

This report[1] sets out certain principles which the Committee believes should govern the supervision of banks' foreign establishments by parent and host authorities. It replaces the 1975 "Concordat" and reformulates some of its provisions, most particularly to take account of the subsequent acceptance by the Governors of the principle that banking supervisory authorities cannot be fully satisfied about the soundness of individual banks unless they can examine the totality of each bank's business worldwide through the technique of consolidation.

* * *

The principles set out in the report are not necessarily embodied in the laws of the countries represented on the Committee. Rather they are recommended guidelines of best practices in this area, which all members have undertaken to work towards implementing, according to the means available to them.

---

[1]   This document is known as the Basle Concordat.

Adequate supervision of banks' foreign establishments calls not only for an appropriate allocation of responsibilities between parent and host supervisory authorities but also for contact and cooperation between them. It has been, and remains, one of the Committee's principal purposes to foster such cooperation both among its member countries and more widely. The Committee has been encouraged by the like-minded approach of other groups of supervisors and it hopes to continue to strengthen its relationships with these other groups and to develop new ones. It strongly commends the principles set out in this report as being of general validity for all those who are responsible for the supervision of banks which conduct international business and hopes that they will be progressively accepted and implemented by supervisors worldwide. Where situations arise which do not appear to be covered by the principles set out in this report, parent and host authorities should explore together ways of ensuring that adequate supervision of banks' foreign establishments is effected.

* * *

III. General principles governing the supervision of banks' foreign establishments

Effective cooperation between host and parent authorities is a central prerequisite for the supervision of banks' international operations. In relation to the supervision of banks' foreign establishments there are two basic principles which are fundamental to such cooperation and which call for consultation and contacts between respective host and parent authorities: firstly, that no foreign banking establishment should escape supervision; and secondly, that the supervision should be adequate. In giving effect to these principles, host authorities should ensure that parent authorities are informed immediately of any serious problems which arise in a parent bank's foreign establishment. Similarly, parent authorities should inform host authorities when problems arise in a parent bank which are likely to affect the parent bank's foreign establishment.

Acceptance of these principles will not, however, of itself preclude there being gaps and inadequacies in the supervision of banks' foreign establishments. These may occur for various reasons. Firstly, while there should be a presumption that host authorities are in a position to fulfil their supervisory obligations adequately with respect to all foreign bank establishments operating in their territories, this may not always be the case. Problems may, for instance, arise when a foreign establishment is classified as a bank by its parent banking supervisory authority but not by its host authority. In such cases it is the responsibility of the parent authority to ascertain whether the host authority is able to undertake adequate supervision and the host authority should inform the parent authority if it is not in a position to undertake such supervision.

In cases where host authority supervision is inadequate, the parent authority should either extend its supervision, to the degree that it is practicable, or it should be prepared to discourage the parent bank from continuing to operate the establishment in question.

Secondly, problems may arise where the host authority considers that supervision of the parent institutions of foreign bank establishments operating in its territory is inadequate or non-existent. In such cases the host authority should discourage or, if it is in a position to do so, forbid the operation in its territory of such foreign establishments. Alternatively, the host authority could impose specific conditions governing the conduct of the business of such establishments.

* * *

The implementation of the second basic principle, namely that the supervision of all foreign banking establishments should be adequate, requires the positive participation of both host and parent authorities. Host authorities are responsible for the foreign bank establishments operating in their territories as individual institutions while parent authorities are responsible for them as parts of larger banking groups, where a general supervisory responsibility exists in respect of their worldwide consolidated activities. These responsibilities of host and parent authorities are both complementary and overlapping.

* * *

MINIMUM STANDARDS FOR THE SUPERVISION OF INTERNATIONAL BANKING GROUPS AND THEIR CROSS-BORDER ESTABLISHMENTS

The Basel Committee on Banking Supervision (July 1992)

I.   Introduction

In 1975, the Basle Committee obtained the agreement of the G-10 Governors to a paper setting out principles for the supervision of banks' foreign establishments. These arrangements, revised in 1983 and now better known as the Concordat, took the form of recommended guidelines for best practice, and members of the Committee undertook to work towards their implementation according to the means available to them. Subsequently, in April 1990, certain, practical aspects of these principles were elaborated in a Supplement to the Concordat.

* * *

II.   Minimum standards for supervision

Banking groups are increasingly complex organisations and may have several tiers of ownership within them, In some cases, a banking group's home country consolidated supervisory authority will also be the authority directly responsible for the supervision of the group's lead and subsidiary banks. However, in other cases, there will be one authority responsible for the consolidated supervision of the banking group as a whole (the *banking group's* home country authority) and different authorities responsible for the consolidated supervision of individual banks (and such banks' own subsidiaries) that are owned or controlled by the group (the *bank's* home country authority). This may occur, for example, where a banking subsidiary chartered in one country, which is seeking to create an establishment in a second country, is itself owned by a banking group subject to home country consolidated supervision in a third country. A host country authority must be aware of these distinctions between immediate and higher-level home country authorities. Except where specified, the term home country authority includes both types of authority.

The following four minimum standards are to be applied by individual supervisory authorities in their own assessment of their relations with supervisory authorities in other countries. In particular, a host country authority, into whose jurisdiction a bank or banking group is seeking to expand, is called upon to determine whether that bank or banking group's home country supervisory authority[1] has the necessary capabilities to meet these minimum standards. In making this determination, host country authorities should review the other authority's statutory powers, past experience in their relations, and the scope of the other authority's administrative practices. Some authorities may initially need to make either statutory or administrative changes in order to comply with these new standards; therefore, in cases where an authority fails to meet one or more of these standards, recognition should be given to the extent to which the authority is actively working to establish the necessary capabilities to permit it to meet all aspects of these minimum standards.

1. **All international banking groups and international banks should be supervised by a home country authority that capably performs consolidated supervision**

As a condition for the creation and maintenance of cross-border banking establishments, a host country authority should assure itself that the relevant bank and, if different, the banking group is subject to the authority of a supervisor with the practical capability of performing consolidated supervision. To meet this minimum standard, the home country supervisory authority should (a) receive consolidated financial and prudential information on the bank's or banking group's global operations, have the reliability of this information confirmed to its own satisfaction through on-site examination or other means, and assess the information as

---

[1]   In some countries, supervisory responsibility is shared among two or more authorities. The word "authority" is used to include all relevant authorities in any one country.

it may bear on the safety and soundness of the bank or banking group, (b) have the capability to prevent corporate affiliations or structures that either undermine efforts to maintain consolidated financial information or otherwise hinder effective supervision of the bank or banking group, and (c) have the capability to prevent the bank or banking group from creating foreign banking establishments in particular jurisdictions,

2. **The creation of a cross-border banking establishment should receive the prior consent of both the host country supervisory authority and the bank's and, if different, banking group's home country supervisory authority**

Consent by a host country authority for the inward creation of a cross-border banking establishment should only be considered if the appropriate home country authorities have first given their consent to the bank or banking group's outward expansion. Outward consent by a home country authority should always be made contingent upon the subsequent receipt of inward consent from the host authority. Thus, in the absence of consent by both the host country authority and the bank's home country authority and, if different, the banking group's home country authority, cross-border expansion will not be permitted. As a matter of procedure, a host country authority should seek to assure itself that consent has been given by the supervisory authority directly responsible for the entity seeking to create an establishment; this authority, in turn, should assure itself that consent is given by the next higher tier supervisory authority, if any, which may perform consolidated supervision with respect to the entity as part of a banking group.

* * *

If, as a result of the establishment's proposed activities or the location and structure of the bank's or the banking group's management, either authority concludes that the division of supervisory responsibilities suggested in the Concordat is not appropriate, then that authority has the responsibility to initiate consultations with the other authority so that they reach an explicit understanding on which authority is in the best position to take primary responsibility, either generally or in respect of specific activities. A similar review should be undertaken by all authorities if there is a significant change in the bank's or banking group's activities or structure.

Inaction on the part of either authority will be construed as an acceptance of the division of responsibilities established in the Concordat. Thus, each authority is responsible for making a deliberate choice between accepting its responsibilities under the Concordat or initiating consultations on an alternative allocation of supervisory responsibilities for the case at hand.

3. **Supervisory authorities should possess the right to gather information from the cross-border banking establishments of the banks or banking groups for which they are the home country supervisor**

As a condition for giving either inward or outward consent for the creation of a cross-border banking establishment, a supervisory authority should establish an understanding with the other authority that they may each gather information to the extent necessary for effective home country supervision, either through on-site examination or by other means satisfactory to the recipient, from the cross-border establishments located in one another's jurisdictions of banks or banking groups chartered or incorporated in their respective jurisdictions. Thus, consent for inward expansion by a prospective host country authority should generally be contingent upon there being such an understanding, with the foreign bank's or banking group's home country authority, that each authority may gather such information from their respective bank's and banking group's foreign establishments. Similarly, consent for outward expansion by the home country authority should generally be contingent upon there being such an understanding with the host country authority. Through such bilateral arrangements, all home country authorities should be able to improve their ability to review the financial condition of their banks' and banking groups' cross-border banking establishments.

4. **If a host country authority determines that any one of the foregoing minimum standards is not met to its satisfaction, that authority could impose restrictive measures necessary to satisfy its prudential concerns consistent with these minimum standards, including the prohibition of the creation of banking establishments**

In considering whether to consent to the creation of a banking establishment by a foreign bank or foreign banking group, or in reviewing any other proposal by a foreign bank OR banking group which requires its consent, a host country authority should determine whether the bank or banking group is subject to consolidated supervision by an authority that has—or is actively working to establish—the necessary capabilities to meet these minimum standards. First, the host country authority should determine whether the bank or banking group is chartered or incorporated in a jurisdiction with which the host country authority has a mutual understanding for the gathering of information from cross-border establishments. Secondly, the host country authority should determine whether consent for outward expansion has been given by the appropriate home country authorities. Thirdly, the host country authority should determine whether the bank and, if different, the banking group is supervised by a home country authority which has the practical capability of performing consolidated supervision.

If these minimum standards are not met with respect to a particular bank or banking group, and the relevant home country authorities are unwilling or unable to initiate the effort to take measures to meet these standards, the host country authority should prevent the creation in its jurisdiction of any cross-border establishments by that bank or banking group. However, in its sole discretion, the host country authority may alternatively choose to permit the creation of establishments by such a bank or banking group, subject to whatever prudential restrictions on the scope and nature of the establishment's operations which the host country authority deems necessary and appropriate to address its prudential concerns, provided that the host country authority itself also accepts the responsibility to perform adequate supervision of the bank's or banking group's local establishments on a "stand-alone" consolidated basis.

* * *

NOTES

1.   The Basel Committee has noted that gaps in supervision can arise out of structural features of international banking groups. For example, the existence of holding companies either at the head, or in the middle, of such groups may constitute an impediment to adequate supervision. Furthermore, particular supervisory problems may arise where such holding companies, while not themselves banks, have substantial liabilities to the international banking system. Where holding companies are at the head of groups that include separately incorporated banks operating in different countries, the authorities responsible for supervising those banks should endeavour to coordinate their supervision of those banks, taking account of the overall structure of the group in question. Where a bank is the parent company of a group that contains intermediate holding companies, the parent authority should make sure that such holding companies and their subsidiaries are covered by adequate supervision. Alternatively, the parent authority should not allow the parent bank to operate such intermediate holding companies. See the Basel Committee's 1992 Minimum Standards.

2.   Where groups contain both banks and non-bank organisations, the Basel Committee guidelines require that there should, where possible, be liaison between the banking supervisory authorities and any authorities which have responsibilities for supervising these non-banking organisations, particularly where the non-banking activities are of a financial character. Banking supervisors, in their overall supervision of banking groups, should take account of these groups' non-banking activities; and if these activities cannot be adequately supervised, banking supervisors should aim at minimising the risks to the banking business from the non-banking activities of such groups. *Id.*

THE SUPERVISION OF
CROSS-BORDER BANKING

The Basel Committee on Banking Supervision (October 1996)

* * *

CHECKLIST OF PRINCIPLES FOR EFFECTIVE
CONSOLIDATED SUPERVISION

A.   Powers to exercise global oversight

6.   Does the home country supervisor have adequate powers to enable it to obtain the information needed to exercise consolidated supervision, for example:

- does the bank in question have its own routine for collecting and validating financial information from all its foreign affiliates, as well as for evaluating and controlling its risks on a global basis?

- does the home supervisor receive regular financial information relating both to the whole of the group, and to the material entities in the group (including the head office) individually?

- is the home supervisor able to verify that information (e.g. through inspection, auditors' reports or information received from the host authority)?

- is there access to information on intra-group transactions, not only with downward affiliates but also if appropriate with sister companies or non-bank affiliates?

- does the home supervisor have the power to prohibit corporate structures that deliberately impede consolidated supervision?

B.   Exercise of consolidated supervision

7.   Which of the following procedures does the home country supervisor have in place to demonstrate its ability to capably perform consolidated supervision:

- adequate control of authorisation, both at the entry stage and on changes of ownership?

- adequate prudential standards for capital, credit concentrations, asset quality (i.e. provisioning or classification requirements), liquidity, market risk, management controls, etc?

- off-site capability, i.e. systems for statistical reporting of risks on a consolidated basis and the ability to verify or to have the reports verified?

- the capability to inspect or examine entities in foreign locations?

- arrangements for a frequent dialogue with the management of the supervised entity?

- a track record of taking effective remedial action when problems arise?

* * *

5.   In reaching a decision as to the effectiveness of the consolidated supervision conducted by a home supervisor, the host supervisor will also need to take account of his own supervisory capabilities. If he has limited resources, greater demands will be placed on the home supervisor than if host supervision is strong. The host also has to judge the extent to which its supervision complements that of the home supervisor, or whether there are potential gaps. Accordingly, one host supervisor may decide that a given country is conducting effective consolidated supervision, whereas another host supervisor with different capabilities may decide that it is not.

* * *

CORE PRINCIPLES FOR EFFECTIVE
BANKING SUPERVISION
The Basel Committee on Banking Supervision (September, 1997)

1.   Weaknesses in the banking system of a country, whether developing or developed, can threaten financial stability both within that country and internationally. The need to improve the strength of financial systems has attracted growing international concern. The Communiqué issued at the close of the Lyon G-7 Summit in June 1996 called for action in this domain. Several official bodies, including the Basel Committee on Banking Supervision, the Bank for International Settlements, the International Monetary Fund and the World Bank, have recently been examining ways to strengthen financial stability throughout the world.

2.   The Basel Committee on Banking Supervision has been working in this field for many years, both directly and through its many contacts with banking supervisors in every part of the world. In the last year and a half, it has been examining how best to expand its efforts aimed at strengthening prudential supervision in all countries by building on its relationships with countries outside the G-10 as well as on its earlier work to enhance prudential supervision in its member countries. In particular, the Committee has prepared two documents for release:

- a comprehensive set of Core Principles for effective banking supervision (The Basel Core Principles) and,

- a Compendium (to be updated periodically) of the existing Basel Committee recommendations, guidelines and standards most of which are cross-referenced in the Core Principles document.

Both documents have been endorsed by the G-10 central bank Governors. They were submitted to the G-7 and G-10 Finance Ministers in preparation for the June 1997 Denver Summit in the hope that they would provide a useful mechanism for strengthening financial stability in all countries.

3.   In developing the Principles, the Basel Committee has worked closely with non-G-10 supervisory authorities. The document has been prepared in a group containing representatives from the Basel Committee and from Chile, China, the Czech Republic, Hong Kong, Mexico, Russia and Thailand. Nine other countries (Argentina, Brazil, Hungary, India, Indonesia, Korea, Malaysia, Poland and Singapore) were also closely associated with the work. The drafting of the Principles benefited moreover from broad consultation with a larger group of individual supervisors, both directly and through the regional supervisory groups.

4.   The Basel Core Principles comprise twenty-five basic Principles that need to be in place for a supervisory system to be effective. The Principles relate to:

Preconditions for effective banking supervision—Principle 1

Licensing and structure—Principles 2 to 5

Prudential regulations and requirements—Principles 6 to 15

Methods of ongoing banking supervision—Principles 16 to 20

Information requirements—Principle 21

Formal powers of supervisors—Principle 22, and

Cross-border banking—Principles 23 to 25.

In addition to the Principles themselves, the document contains explanations of the various methods supervisors can use to implement them.

5.   National agencies should apply the Principles in the supervision of all banking organisations within their jurisdictions.[2] The Principles are minimum requirements and in many cases may need to be supplemented

---

[2]   In countries where non-bank financial institutions provide financial services similar to those of banks, many of the Principles set out in this document are also capable of application to such non-bank financial institutions.

by other measures designed to address particular conditions and risks in the financial systems of individual countries.

6.   The Basel Core Principles are intended to serve as a basic reference for supervisory and other public authorities in all countries and internationally. It will be for national supervisory authorities, many of which are actively seeking to strengthen their current supervisory regime, to use the attached document to review their existing supervisory arrangements and to initiate a programme designed to address any deficiencies as quickly as is practical within their legal authority. The Principles have been designed to be verifiable by supervisors, regional supervisory groups, and the market at large. The Basel Committee will play a role, together with other interested organisations, in monitoring the progress made by individual countries in implementing the Principles. It is suggested that the IMF, the World Bank and other interested organisations use the Principles in assisting individual countries to strengthen their supervisory arrangements in connection with work aimed at promoting overall macroeconomic and financial stability. Implementation of the Principles will be reviewed at the International Conference of Banking Supervisors in October 1998 and biennially thereafter.

7.   Supervisory authorities throughout the world are encouraged to endorse the Basel Core Principles. The members of the Basel Committee and the sixteen other supervisory agencies that have participated in their drafting all agree with the content of the document.

8.   The chairpersons of the regional supervisory groups[3] are supportive of the Basel Committee's efforts and are ready to promote the endorsement of the Core Principles among their membership. Discussions are in progress to define the role the regional groups can play in securing the endorsement of the Principles and in monitoring implementation by their members.

9.   The Basel Committee believes that achieving consistency with the Core Principles by every country will be a significant step in the process of improving financial stability domestically and internationally. The speed with which this objective will be achieved will vary. In many countries, substantive changes in the legislative framework and in the powers of supervisors will be necessary because many supervisory authorities do not at present have the statutory authority to implement all of the Principles. In such cases, the Basel Committee believes it is essential that national

---

[3]   Arab Committee on Banking Supervision, Caribbean Banking Supervisors Group, Association of Banking Supervisory Authorities of Latin America and the Caribbean, Eastern and Southern Africa Banking Supervisors Group, EMEAP Study Group on Banking Supervision, Group of Banking Supervisors from Central and Eastern European Countries, Gulf Cooperation Council Banking Supervisors' Committee, Offshore Group of Banking Supervisors, Regional Supervisory Group of Central Asia and Transcaucasia, SEANZA Forum of Banking Supervisors, Committee of Banking Supervisors in West and Central Africa.

legislators give urgent consideration to the changes necessary to ensure that the Principles can be applied in all material respects.

* * *

Preconditions for Effective Banking Supervision

1.   An effective system of banking supervision will have clear responsibilities and objectives for each agency involved in the supervision of banking organisations. Each such agency should possess operational independence and adequate resources. A suitable legal framework for banking supervision is also necessary, including provisions relating to authorisation of banking organisations and their ongoing supervision; powers to address compliance with laws as well as safety and soundness concerns; and legal protection for supervisors. Arrangements for sharing information between supervisors and protecting the confidentiality of such information should be in place.

Licensing and Structure

2.   The permissible activities of institutions that are licensed and subject to supervision as banks must be clearly defined, and the use of the word "bank" in names should be controlled as far as possible.

3.   The licensing authority must have the right to set criteria and reject applications for establishments that do not meet the standards set. The licensing process, at a minimum, should consist of an assessment of the banking organisation's ownership structure, directors and senior management, its operating plan and internal controls, and its projected financial condition, including its capital base; where the proposed owner or parent organisation is a foreign bank, the prior consent of its home country supervisor should be obtained.

4.   Banking supervisors must have the authority to review and reject any proposals to transfer significant ownership or controlling interests in existing banks to other parties.

5.   Banking supervisors must have the authority to establish criteria for reviewing major acquisitions or investments by a bank and ensuring that corporate affiliations or structures do not expose the bank to undue risks or hinder effective supervision.

Prudential Regulations and Requirements

6.   Banking supervisors must set prudent and appropriate minimum capital adequacy requirements for all banks such requirements should reflect the risks that the banks undertake, and must define the components of capital, bearing in mind their ability to absorb losses. At least for internationally active banks, these requirements must not be less than those established in the Basel Capital Accord and its amendments.

7.   An essential part of any supervisory system is the evaluation of a bank's policies, practices and procedures related to the granting of loans and making of investments and the ongoing management of the loan and investment portfolios.

8.   Banking supervisors must be satisfied that banks establish and adhere to adequate policies, practices and procedures for evaluating the quality of assets and the adequacy of loan loss provisions and loan loss reserves.

9.   Banking supervisors must be satisfied that banks have management information systems that enable management to identify concentrations within the portfolio and supervisors must set prudential limits to restrict bank exposures to single borrowers or groups of related borrowers.

10. In order to prevent abuses arising from connected lending, banking supervisors must have in place requirements that banks lend to related companies and individuals on an arm's-length basis, that such extensions of credit are effectively monitored, and that other appropriate steps are taken to control or mitigate the risks.

11. Banking supervisors must be satisfied that banks have adequate policies and procedures for identifying, monitoring and controlling country risk and transfer risk in their international lending and investment activities, and for maintaining appropriate reserves against such risks.

* * *

15. Banking supervisors must determine that banks have adequate policies, practices and procedures in place, including strict "know-your-customer" rules, that promote high ethical and professional standards in the financial sector and prevent the bank being used, intentionally or unintentionally, by criminal elements.

Methods of Ongoing Banking Supervision

16. An effective banking supervisory system should consist of some form of both on-site and off-site supervision.

17. Banking supervisors must have regular contact with bank management and thorough understanding of the institution's operations.

18. Banking supervisors must have a means of collecting, reviewing and analysing prudential reports and statistical returns from banks on a solo and consolidated basis.

19. Banking supervisors must have a means of independent validation of supervisory information either through on-site examinations or use of external auditors.

20. An essential element of banking supervision is the ability of the supervisors to supervise the banking group on a consolidated basis.

Information Requirements

21. Banking supervisors must be satisfied that each bank maintains adequate records drawn up in accordance with consistent accounting policies and practices that enable the supervisor to obtain a true and fair view of the financial condition of the bank and the profitability of its business, and that the bank publishes on a regular basis financial statements that fairly reflect its condition.

Formal Powers of Supervisors

22. Banking supervisors must have at their disposal adequate supervisory measures to bring about timely corrective action when banks fail to meet prudential requirements (such as minimum capital adequacy ratios), when there are regulatory violations, or where depositors are threatened in any other way. In extreme circumstances, this should include the ability to revoke the banking licence or recommend its revocation.

Cross-border Banking

23. Banking supervisors must practise global consolidated supervision over their internationally-active banking organisations, adequately monitoring and applying appropriate prudential norms to all aspects of the business conducted by these banking organisations worldwide, primarily at their foreign branches, joint ventures and subsidiaries.

24. A key component of consolidated supervision is establishing contact and information exchange with the various other supervisors involved, primarily host country supervisory authorities.

25. Banking supervisors must require the local operations of foreign banks to be conducted to the same high standards as are required of domestic institutions and must have powers to share information needed by the home country supervisors of those banks for the purpose of carrying out consolidated supervision.

QUESTIONS AND NOTES

1. <u>Multiple Choice Questions</u>:

a. From an international bank regulatory perspective, the common element(s) of numerous international banking scandals over the last thirty five (35) years that have prompted enhanced concerns about international bank supervision has (have) been: a) failure of host countries to perform adequate supervision; b) failure of home countries to perform consolidated supervision; c) the lax banking laws of certain countries; d) all of the above; or e) a and c only.

b. A concordat is best described as: a) a formal international treaty; b) a device used by United Nations security council members; c) an informal arrangement, not constituting a formal agreement; or d) a form of diplomatic agreement between sovereign governments.

c.   The principles set out in the various Basel Concordats have been described at various times by the Basel Committee as: a) basic standards of international law; b) minimum requirements; c) statements of the "best practice" which all banking regulators of Basel member countries have undertaken to work towards implementing, according to the means available to them; d) externally imposed limits on national sovereignty; or e) b and c only.

d.   The Basel Committee: a) has the primary objective of enhancing understanding of key supervisory issues and improving the quality of banking supervision; b) provides a forum for regular cooperation on banking supervisory matters; c) encourages contacts and cooperation among its members only; or d) a and b only.

e.   To date, none of the Basel Concordats specifically set forth recommendations regarding: a) capital standards for banks; b) apportionment between home and host countries of bank supervision responsibilities; c) ensuring adequate information flows between banking supervisory authorities; or d) the lender-of-last-resort role of central banks.

f.   What best describes the reason for the revised Basel Concordat of 1983 ("1983 Basel Principles")? a) a desire of the "Group of 10" nations to publish a new concordat at least once every eight years; b) predictions about the demise of the Soviet bloc; c) the Banco Ambrosiano banking scandal; or d) public reaction to the Hollywood movie "Godfather III."

g.   In connection with the well publicized failure of the Bank of Credit and Commerce International ("BCCI"), what emerged as the primary reason BCCI was able to avoid consolidated supervision by any one home country regulator was: a) large number of immigrant investors; b) BCCI's complex, multi-jurisdiction organization and structure; c) supervision of BCCI was fractured: no one country had a clear picture of BCCI's worldwide activities; d) the covert activities of Archbishop Marcenkus; or e) b and c only.

4. BASEL CAPITAL STANDARDS

PETER COY, HOW NEW GLOBAL BANKING RULES COULD DEEPEN THE U.S. CRISIS

Bloomberg Business (April 16, 2008)

In 1999, in the aftermath of a financial crisis that spread from East Asia to Brazil, Russia, and beyond, the central bankers and finance ministers of 10 of the world's wealthiest nations sent their deputies to the tidy Swiss city of Basel. Their mission: to begin devising a set of improved banking regulations for their governments to adopt, with the hope of reducing the harm from future financial crises. The world's leading financial regulators labored together to strike a balance between ensuring banks' safety and giving them room to take risks and make money, finally in 2004 producing a recommended rulebook called Basel II (Yes, there was a Basel I. More on that later.)

Now, as another financial crisis unfolds, it would seem that nations are adopting Basel II at just the right time. Europe and Japan have put it into practice over the past year, and the U.S. is set to phase in a modified version starting next year. The start date for American banks to begin submitting their plans for compliance to U.S. regulators was Apr. 1.

But despite all the sober and deep thought that went into them, many regulators, academics, and financial analysts are increasingly concerned that the new regulations will end up making today's financial crisis worse rather than better. Basel II is intended to keep banks safe by requiring them to match the size of their capital cushion to the riskiness of their loans and securities. The higher the odds of default, the less they can lend, all else equal.

Here's the problem. Today, many banks already face so many risks that implementing Basel II as written will put them in a capital squeeze. They will either have to reduce risk by cutting back on lending, or sell more shares to give themselves a bigger capital buffer, or both. If the banks do lend less, it could cause an even steeper economic decline, which would lead to more defaults and cause banks to ratchet back even more, and so on in a downward spiral.

* * *

Basel II has some good points. It's based on the uncontroversial notion that bank shareholders need to have skin, in the game, so if there are big losses, shareholders get wiped out before depositors or taxpayers are harmed. Like any company, a bank dies if its assets are worth less than its liabilities. The shareholders' skin in the game is the surplus of a bank's assets, such as the loans it makes and the securities it holds, over its liabilities, such as borrowings from other banks, savings accounts, and certificates of deposit. Basel II says the riskier the loans a bank makes, the more of a buffer shareholders are required to put up.

What happens, though, if loans and securities held by banks, start to go bad all at once, as they are doing today? Neither of the two options that Basel II offers is satisfactory. The first one—shrinking the loan book— would be economically destructive, since cutting off credit in today's recession could send businesses and households into bankruptcy. Indeed, Federal Reserve Chairman Ben Bernanke has found in his academic research that a drying up of bank lending was a major factor in the Great Depression of the 1930s.

The second possibility—raising more money from shareholders—is better for the economy but extremely difficult in a downturn because no one wants to buy. So some banks will simply be swallowed up by other banks or opportunistic investors. The Washington-based consulting firm Federal Financial Analytics wrote positively about Basel II in a study released last December, but said: "The new rules kick in at a time of major credit-market problems, which will mean a sharp spike in U.S. bank regulatory capital." Said the firm: "Significant amounts of risk-based capital will need to be raised in a hurry, driving a new wave of industry mergers and acquisitions."

"IT'S PRETTY SCARY"

It's still too soon to see any constrictive effect of Basel II. Most European countries did not put the rule into effect until Jan. 1. And housing and mortgage markets are still holding up pretty well in most of Europe, notes Jon Peace, a banking analyst for Lehman Brothers in London. As for the U.S., where the housing slump and the credit crunch, are further along, Basel II won't start to be phased in until 2009.

If the credit crunch gets bad enough, regulators are likely to ease up on enforcement of Basel II's capital rules. But that might not happen until some real economic damage is done. "This cycle is going to turn out to be much more severe than the banks ever expected," says Christopher Whalen, cofounder of Institutional Risk Analytics, a Torrance (Calif.) firm that analyses bank balance sheets. "When you start scoring the risk of this stuff using the Basel n framework, it's pretty scary."

How did we get to the point where an accord that's supposed to avoid trouble could potentially make it worse? To understand that, you have to go back to the predecessor accord, Basel I, which financial regulators devised in 1988 to get banks around the world to beef up their capital. It more or less did its job: Unsafe banks got safer. "It was a rough-and-ready thing" recalls Paul Volcker, who as chairman of the Federal. Reserve until 1987 was instrumental in banging the compromise together.

But banks soon learned how to game the system. To avoid having to tie up capital supporting the mortgage loans they made, the banks got those loans off their books by securitizing them. In fact, Basel I was a prime mover in the staggering growth of the mortgage-backed securities market. Basel I didn't require capital backing for lines of credit as long as they lasted less than a year, so banks responded by issuing short-term lines of credit that they rolled over every 364 days.

Alarmed by the "Asian contagion" financial crisis of 1997–98 and tired of being manipulated by the banks, the Basel Committee on Banking Supervision announced in 1999 that it was taking another stab at the problem. The idea was to align the banks' capital more closely with their actual risks, in the process taking away some of the loopholes that let them hold less capital than they really needed. The biggest banks would be required to use their own computerized models to estimate the probability of default on each loan on their books, in keeping with the notion that no one knows a bank's vulnerabilities better than its own managers.

Up until the past year, loan default rates were exceptionally low, so the backward-looking Basel II rules indicated that banks had more than enough capital. That worried U.S. bank examiners, who didn't want banks to shrink their capital cushions in case conditions got worse. While the internationally minded Federal Reserve mainly supported Basel II as written, the domestically focused bank examiners at the FDIC managed to push through some safeguards against undercapitalization. Unlike Europe, the U.S. will retain a crude "leverage ratio" that takes precedence over Basel II if the two measures give different results.

* * *

Basel II is coming online at a time when politicians and economists are debating every aspect of how to regulate financial institutions. In late March, Treasury Secretary Henry Paulson announced a plan for a sweeping reorganization of financial regulation in the U.S., which would give the Federal Reserve new powers as a regulator of market stability. However, the Paulson plan is mainly a set of general guidelines for reform that may or may not happen, while the Basel II rules are about to have an effect.

Calls for more fundamental change are likely to grow if the credit crunch worsens. Basel II itself is a work in progress: On Apr. 16 the Basel committee said it would toughen capital requirements for exotic derivatives and pay more attention to making sure banks have adequate liquidity to pay their bills when money gets tight.

* * *

WHAT MAKES IT DIFFERENT

- Basel I, which was conceived in 1988, made rough estimates of the riskiness of broad categories of loans and other assets. Banks learned how to game the system to minimize their required capital. Basel II forces banks to assess the true risks to their portfolios and hold an appropriate amount of capital against them. It also requires more regulatory supervision and financial disclosure.

THE CONSEQUENCES

- If the riskiness of a bank's portfolio gets too high, the bank has two choices: Raise more capital to boost the size of its buffer or shed risky assets by, say, setting off loans.

* * *

PRESS RELEASE

GROUP OF GOVERNORS AND HEADS OF SUPERVISION ANNOUNCES HIGHER GLOBAL MINIMUM CAPITAL STANDARDS

Basel Committee on Banking Supervision (September 12, 2010)

At its 12 September 2010 meeting, the Group of Governors and Heads of Supervision, the oversight body of the Basel Committee on Banking Supervision, announced a substantial strengthening of existing capital requirements and fully endorsed the agreements it reached on 26 July 2010. These capital reforms, together with the introduction of a global liquidity standard, deliver on the core of the global financial reform agenda and will be presented to the Seoul G20 Leaders summit in November.

The Committee's package of reforms will increase the minimum common equity requirement from 2% to 4.5%. In addition, banks will be required to hold a capital conservation buffer of 2.5% to withstand future periods of stress bringing the total common equity requirements to 7%. This reinforces the stronger definition of capital agreed by Governors and Heads of Supervision in July and the higher capital requirements for trading, derivative and securitisation activities to be introduced at the end of 2011.

* * *

Increased capital requirements

Under the agreements reached today, the minimum requirement for common equity, the highest form of loss absorbing capital, will be raised from the current 2% level, before the application of regulatory adjustments, to 4.5% after the application of stricter adjustments. This will be phased in by 1 January 2015. The Tier 1 capital requirement, which includes common equity and other qualifying financial instruments based on stricter criteria, will increase from 4% to 6% over the same period. (Annex 1 summarises the new capital requirements.)

The Group of Governors and Heads of Supervision also agreed that the capital conservation buffer above the regulatory minimum requirement be calibrated at 2.5% and be met with common equity, after the application of deductions. The purpose of the conservation buffer is to ensure that banks maintain a buffer of capital that can be used to absorb losses during periods of financial and economic stress. While banks are allowed to draw on the-buffer during such periods of stress, the closer their regulatory capital ratios approach the minimum requirement, the greater the constraints on earnings distributions. This framework will reinforce the objective of sound supervision and bank governance and address the collective action problem that has prevented some banks from curtailing distributions such as discretionary bonuses and high dividends, even in the face of deteriorating capital positions.

A countercyclical buffer within a range of 0%–2.5% of common equity or other fully loss absorbing capital will be implemented according to national circumstances. The purpose of the countercyclical buffer is to achieve the broader macroprudential goal of protecting the banking sector from periods of excess aggregate credit growth. For any given country, this buffer will only be in effect when there is excess credit growth that is resulting in a system wide build up of risk. The countercyclical buffer, when in effect, would be introduced as an extension of the conservation buffer range.

These capital requirements are supplemented by a non-risk-based leverage ratio that will serve as a backstop to the risk-based measures described above, in July, Governors and Heads of Supervision agreed to test a minimum Tier 1 leverage ratio of 3% during the parallel run period. Based on the results of the parallel run period, any final adjustments would be carried out in the first half of 2017 with a view to migrating to a Pillar 1 treatment on 1 January 2018 based on appropriate review and calibration.

Systemically important banks should have loss absorbing capacity beyond the standards announced today and work continues on this issue in the Financial Stability Board and relevant Basel Committee work streams. The Basel Committee and the FSB are developing a well integrated approach to systemically important financial institutions which could include combinations of capital surcharges, contingent capital and bail-in debt. In addition, work is continuing to strengthen resolution regimes. The Basel Committee also recently issued a consultative document proposal to ensure the loss absorbency of regulatory capital at the point of non-viability. Governors and Heads of Supervision endorse the aim to strengthen the loss absorbency of non-common Tier 1 and Tier 2 capital instruments.

Transition arrangements

The Governors and Heads of Supervision also agreed on transitional arrangements for implementing the new standards. These will help ensure that the banking sector can meet the higher capital standards through reasonable earnings retention and capital raising, while still supporting lending to the economy. The transitional, arrangements, which are summarised in Annex 2, include:

- National implementation by member countries will begin on 1 January 2013. Member countries must translate the rules into national laws and regulations before this date. As of 1 January 2013, banks will be required to meet the following new minimum requirements in relation to risk-weighted assets (RWAs):

  — 3.5% common equity/RWAs;

  — 4.5% Tier 1 capital/RWAs, and

  — 8.0% total capital/RWAs.

* * *

Phase-in arrangements for the leverage ratio were announced in the 26 July 2010 press release of the Group of Governors and Heads of Supervision. That is, the supervisory monitoring period will commence 1 January 2011; the parallel run period will commence 1 January 2013 and run until 1 January 2017; and disclosure of the leverage ratio and its components will start 1 January 2015. Based on the results of the parallel run period, any final adjustments will be carried out in the first half of 2017 with a view to migrating to a Pillar 1 treatment on 1 January 2018 based on appropriate review and calibration.

After an observation period beginning in 2011, the liquidity coverage ratio (LCR) will be introduced on 1 January 2015. The revised net stable funding ratio (NSFR) will move to a minimum standard by 1 January 2018. The Committee will put in place rigorous reporting processes to monitor the ratios during the transition period and will continue to review the implications of these standards for financial markets, credit extension and economic growth, addressing unintended consequences as necessary.

* * *

THE BASEL COMMITTEE: BASEL CAPITAL PHASE IN ARRANGEMENTS
(SHADING INDICATES TRANSITION PERIODS)
(ALL DATES ARE AS OF 1 JANUARY)

	2011	2012	2013	2014	2015	2016	2017	2018	As of 1 January 2019
Leverage Ratio	Supervisory monitoring		Parallel run 1 Jan 2013–1 Jan 2017 Disclosure starts 1 Jan 2015					Migration to Pillar 1	
Minimum Common Equity Capital Ratio			3.5%	4.0%	4.5%	4.5%	4.5%	4.5%	4.5%
Capital Conservation Buffer						0.625%	1.25%	1.875%	2.50%
Minimum common equity plus capital conservation buffer			3.5%	4.0%	4.5%	5.125%	5.75%	6.375%	7.0%
Phase-in of deductions from CET1 (including amounts exceeding the limit for DTAs, MSRs and financials)				20%	40%	60%	80%	100%	100%

	2011	2012	2013	2014	2015	2016	2017	2018	As of 1 January 2019
Minimum Tier 1 Capital			4–5%	5.5%	6.0%	6.0%	6.0%	6.0%	6.0%
Minimum Total Capital			8.0%	8.0%	8.0%	8.0%	8.0%	8.0%	8.0%
Minimum Total Capital plus conservation buffer			8.0%	8.0%	8.0%	8.625%	9.25%	9.875%	10.5%
Capital instruments that no longer qualify as no-core Tier 1 Capital or Tier 2 Capital			Phased out over 10-year horizon beginning 2013						
Liquidity coverage ratio	Observation period begins				Introduce minimum standard				
Net stable funding ratio		Observation period begins						Introduce minimum standard	

FINANCIAL STABILITY BOARD
2013–2014 ANNUAL REPORT

* * *

1. Financial Stability Board—Organisation, governance and activities

The Financial Stability Board (FSB) coordinates at the international level the financial stability work of national authorities and international standard-setting bodies; and it develops and promotes financial sector policies to enhance global financial stability.[1]

Its membership consists of finance ministries, central banks[2], and financial supervisory and regulatory authorities in 24 countries and territories;[3] the European Central Bank (ECB) and the European Commission; and international financial institutions and standard-setting bodies.[4]

* * *

To facilitate its interaction with a wider group of countries, the [FSB] has established six regional consultative groups (for the Americas, Asia, the Commonwealth of Independent States, Europe, the Middle East and North Africa, and Sub-Saharan Africa). These groups bring FSB members together with institutions from about 65 non-member jurisdictions to discuss vulnerabilities affecting regional and global financial systems and the current and potential financial stability initiatives of the FSB and member jurisdictions.

* * *

1.1 Reducing the moral hazard posed by systemically important financial institutions (SIFIs)

Endorsed by the G20 Leaders at their 2010 Seoul Summit, the FSB's framework to address the systemic risks and moral hazard associated with [Systemically Important Financial Institutions] SIFIs contains three key elements:

---

[1]   The FSB is a not-for-profit association under Swiss law and is hosted by the BIS under a five-year renewable service agreement. The BIS provides financial and other resources for the FSB Secretariat, which currently comprises 30 staff members.

[2]   Including a central bank group, the CGFS. The list of Plenary representatives of the FSB Members is accessible at: http://www.financialstabilityboard.org/wp-content/uploads/plenary.pdf ?page_moved=1

[3]   The country members of the G20 plus Hong Kong SAR, the Netherlands, Singapore, Spain and Switzerland.

[4]   The international financial institutions are the BIS, IMF, OECD and World Bank; the international standard-setting bodies are the BCBS, the International Accounting Standards Board, the IAIS and the International Organization of Securities Commissions.

A resolution framework to ensure that all financial institutions can be quickly resolved without destabilising the financial system and exposing the taxpayer to risk of loss;

higher loss absorbency for SIFIs to reflect the greater risks they pose for the global financial system; and

more intense supervisory oversight for SIFIs.

Resolution of SIFIs. In July 2013, the FSB published *Guidance on recovery triggers and stress scenarios* covering three key aspects of recovery and resolution planning: (i) developing the scenarios and triggers that should be used in recovery plans for global SIFIs (G-SIFIs); (ii) developing resolution strategies and associated operational resolution plans tailored to different group structures; and (iii) identifying the functions that should remain in operation during resolution to maintain systemic stability.

* * *

1.8 Monitoring implementation and strengthening adherence to international standards

The FSB's Coordination Coordination Framework for Implementation Monitoring (CFIM) mandates that implementation of reforms in priority areas (those deemed by the FSB to be particularly important for global financial stability) should be subject to more intensive monitoring and detailed reporting. Current priority areas are the Basel II, Basel 2.5 and Basel III frameworks [* * *].

NOTES

1.   The Basel Committee continues to be a work in progress as it seeks to establish global "buy-in" on a wide range of ever evolving international banking regulatory standards, taking into account new forms of banking technologies such as payment systems discussed earlier in this Chapter, and more recently, corporate governance matters. See, e.g., Basel Committee on Banking Supervision, Guidelines: Corporate governance principles for banks (October 2014).

CHAPTER 6

THE GLOBAL FINANCIAL CRISIS:
MELTDOWN, BAILOUTS AND REFORM

∎ ∎ ∎

1. INTRODUCTION

Suffice to say, any textbook on international banking law would not be complete if it doesn't cover the recent financial crisis. The biggest banking crisis since the Great Depression in 1933, it raised profound bank regulatory and public policy issues and challenges regarding the nature and scope of banking regulation, and the role of government in the context of the near implosion of the international financial system in 2008. This Chapter explores the major causes of the crisis and government actions in response, particularly in the U.S. This Chapter also highlights international regulatory reform efforts in the wake of the financial crisis.

2. CAUSES OF THE FINANCIAL CRISIS

A. FORESHADOWING IN THE EU

HOUSE OF COMMONS, TREASURY COMMITTEE, THE RUN ON THE ROCK, VOLUME I
(26 January 2008)

* * *

1.   Introduction

The run on the Rock

1.   At 8.30 pm on the evening of Thursday 13 September 2007 the BBC reported that Northern Rock plc had asked for and received emergency financial support from the Bank of England.* The terms of the funding facility were finalised in the early hours of Friday 14 September and announced at 7.00 am that day.* That day, long queues began to form outside some of Northern Rock's branches; later, its website collapsed and

---

*   http://news.bbc.co.uk/2/hi/business/6994099.stm.

*   Qq 580,1668.

its phone lines were reported to be jammed.* The first bank run in the
United Kingdom since Victorian times was underway.

* * *

The events of 2007

The Increase in Northern Rock's market share in the first half of 2007

18. In the first half of 2007, Northern Rock continued to expand its
business at a rapid rate. In that period, its loans to cutomers underwent a
net increase of £10.7 billion.[67] The Chancellor of the Exchequer
characterised this period as one in which Northern Rock "had aggressively
expanded its market share."[68] Professor Willem Buiter of the London
School of Economics was critical of this expansion:

> I like healthy growth but it is hard to believe that the quality of
> the asset portfolio and the ability to vet the credit-worthiness of
> your borrowers does not suffer when you take 20% of the net
> incease and 40% to 50% of the gross increase in activity in this
> half year period, so I think they were an organisation that was
> clearly engaged in high-risk behaviour.[69]

* * *

Northern Rock's change of strategy

20. Northern Rock's continued expansionary lending policy required the
continued success of its funding strategy at a time when there were
indications of potential problems on the funding side. In its April 2007
Financial Stability Report, Sir John Gieve told us that the Bank of England
had "identified the increasing wholesale funding of banks as a potential
risk if markets became less liquid".[72] When questioned as to whether
Northern Rock had acknowledged those warnings, Dr Ridley told us that
both the FSR and similar warnings in the Financial Service Authority's
Financial Risk Outlook had influenced Northern Rock's board decisions.[73]
Mr Applegarth also told us that in March 2007 the company had "picked
up the warning signs that the US sub-prime position was meaning a
tightening in pricing and therefore we slowed down the rate of growth and

---

* Qq 345,678.

[67] Q 244.

[68] Q 749.

[69] Q 854.

[72] Q 37.

[73] Qq 412–413.

we gave new guidance against our profits for the year, recognising the tightening in pricing".[74]

*   *   *

[handwritten: ⌐ U.S. situation caused them to not be able to set lending at good rates, Stopped asset creation]

Northern Rock's funding crisis

23. In the middle of this change of strategy, on 9 August 2007, Northern Rock's traders noted a "disclosure in the market" for its funding.[79] This dislocation was the result of a global shock to the financial system, with the American sub-prime mortgage market as its centre. We will examine the causes of this dislocation, and its wider effects beyond the direct impact on Northern Rock, in our forthcoming Report on Financial Stability and Transparency.

24. Two aspects of this worldwide liquidity squeeze appared to surprise Northern Rock, and overcome the attempts highlighted above to combat the tightenting in credit markets. One was the absence of a so-called "flight to quality".

*   *   *

25. Secondly, Northern Rock had not foreseen all its funding markets closing simultaneously, as happened after 9 August. Dr Ridley explained:

> We deliberately diversified our funding platform so that we would have . . . three different types of funding and indeed a diversified programme within the wholesale funding, and geographically we had programmes in the United States, Europe, the Far East, Canada and Australia. That was deliberately so that if one market closed we would still have access to others. The idea that all markets would close simultaneously was unforeseen by any major authority.[83]

The idea of all markets closing to Northren Rock was repeatedly characterised to us by Northern Rock officials as "unforeseeable".[84]

26. One aspect of Norther Rock's financing raised by the Governor of the Bank of England in a speech was Northern Rock's lack of insurance against the troubles it faced. He referred to Countrywide, a bank in the United States that had faced difficulties due to the United States sub-prime crisis:

> Countrywide had paid millions of dollars each year to big banks as a liquidity insurance policy so that, in the event of difficulty, they would provide it with long-term loans. So on August 17

---

[74]   Q 427.

[79]   Q 429.

[83]   Q 403.

[84]   Q 648, 656.

Countrywide was able to claim on that insurance and draw down $11.5bn of committed credit lines. Northern Rock had not taken out anything like that level of liquidity insurance. So when it came to the Bank of England for support, it was important that liquidity was not provided free.[85]

Mr Applegarth explained that Northern Rock had taken out insurance, but that he felt its wide funding base did not merit purchasing too much insurance:

* * *

27.   Northern Rock continued to find some funding, even after 9 August. Mr Applegarth told us that "we were actually still funding—not fully funding, and duration was noticeably shorter, but we were still funding until 13 September".[88] In fact, Mr Applegarth told us that Northern Rock had, before 13 September, "two or three months' worth of liquidity".[89] Despite this, on 16 August, the possibility of the Bank of England giving emergency support was first discussed as a "theoretical" possibility by the Governor of the Bank of England in conversation with Dr R0idley.[90] At this point, the intention of Northern Rock was not to use such a Bank of England facility, but to have it as a "backstop".[91] Mr Applegarth explained that "The problem we had was you could not tell how long the markets were going to be closed and it was a reasonable and propr thing to do to put a backstop facility in place".[92] We consider later the negotiations on the support facility "backstop" and the attempts to find a "safe haven" or buyer which were made at the same time. We also consider later the causes of the retail run on the bank, but one consequence of that run was set out by Mr Applegarth: "Ironically, it was the announcements and the leaking of the backstop that caused the retail run and it was the retail run that reduced our liquidity".[93] The run thus created a situation in which State support for Northern Rock was not a backstop, but an everyday necessity, and where Northern Rock had become reliant on exceptional, State-backed financing.

---

[85]   Speech by Mervyn King, Governor of the Bank of Eng;land at the Northern Ireland Chamber of Commerce and Industry, Belfast on Tuesday 9 October 2007.

[88]   Q 585.

[89]   Q 488.

[90]   Qq 574–575.

[91]   Q 585.

[92]   Q 490.

[93]   Q 529.

RESPONSIBILITY FOR THE PROBLEMS AT NORTHERN ROCK

RESPONSIBILITY OF THE BOARD OF NORTHERN ROCK

* * *

31. The directors of Northern Rock were the principal authors of the difficulties that the company has faced since August 2007. It is right that members of the Board of Northern Rock have been replaced, though haphazardly, since the company became dependent on liquidity support from the Bank of England. The high-risk, reckless business strategy of Northern Rock, with its reliance on short- and medium-term wholesale funding and an absence of sufficient insurance and a failure to arrange standby facility or cover that risk, meant that it was unable to cope with the liquidity pressures placed upon it by the freezing of international capital markets in August 2007. Given that the formulation of that strategy was a fundamental role of the Board of Northern Rock, overseen by some directors who had been there since its demutualisation, the failure of that strategy must also be attributed to the Board. The non-executive members of the Board, and in particular the Chairman of the Board, the Chairman of the Risk Committee and the senior non-executive director, failed in the case of Northern Rock to ensure that it remained liquid as well as solvent, to provide against the risks that it was taking and to act as an effective restraining force on the strategy of the executive members.

* * *

The Regulation of Northern Rock

42. The FSA has acknowledged that there were clear warning signals about the risks associated with Northern Rock's business model, both from its rapid growth as a company and from the falls in its share price from February 2007 onwards. However, insofar as the FSA undertook greater "regulatory engagement" with Northern Rock, this failed to tackle the fundamental weakness in its funding model and did nothing to prevent the problems that came to the fore from August 2007 onwards. We regard this as a substantial failure of regulation.

* * *

[The report discussed testimony that the FSA had conducted regulatory stress testing of Northern Rock's business model and the FSA's "unhappiness" with certain stress test models used by Northern Rock. Stress testing is a regulatory tool designed to test the preparedness of financial institutions for "shocks" to their business model. The object of the test is to understand the sensitivity of the institution's portfolio to changes in various risk factors.]

* * *

Conclusions

66. The FSA did not supervise Northern Rock properly. It did not allocate sufficient resources or time to monitoring a bank whose business model was so clearly an outlier; its procedures were inadequate to supervise a bank whose business grew so rapidly. We are concerned about the lack of resources within the Financial Services Authority solely charged to the direct supervision of Northern Rock. The failure of Northern Rock, while a failure of its own Board, was also a failure of its regulator. As the Chancellor notes, the Financial Services Authority exercises a judgement as to which 'concerns' about financial institutions should be regarded as systematic and thus require action by the regulator. In the case of Northern Rock, the FSA appears to have systematically failed in its duty as a regulator to ensure Northern Rock would not pose such a systematic risk, and this failure contributed significantly to the difficulties, and risks to the public purse, that have followed.

NOTES

1.   Due to perceived regulatory failures that arose during the financial crisis in 2007–2008, the U.K. government decided to restructure its financial regulation system, and abolished the FSA in April 2013 pursuant to the Financial Services Act of 2012. Passed December 19, 2012, the Act created a new "twin peaks" system of financial regulation: 1) The Prudential Regulation Authority, a subsidiary of the Bank of England, to regulate financial firms, including banks, investment banks and insurance companies, and 2) the Financial Conduct Authority, to regulate the activities and conduct of financial firms to ensure the integrity of the financial markets for consumers. See Gonzalo Vina, UK Scraps FSA in Biggest Bank Regulation Overhaul Since 1997, Bloomberg (June 16, 2010); George Parker and Brooke Masters, Osborne abolishes FSA and boosts Bank, Financial Times (June 16, 2010).

B. THE U.S. SUBPRIME CRISIS

FINAL REPORT OF THE NATIONAL COMMISSION ON THE CAUSES OF THE FINANCIAL AND ECONOMIC CRISIS IN THE UNITED STATES

(January 2011)

* * *

1. BEFORE OUR VERY EYES

In examining the worst financial meltdown since the Great Depression, the Financial Crisis Inquiry Commission reviewed millions of pages of documents and questioned hundreds of individuals—financial executives, business leaders, policy makers, regulators, community leaders, people from all walks of life—to find out how and why it happened.

In fact, there were warning signs. In the decade preceding the collapse, there were many signs that house prices were inflated, that lending practices had spun out of control, that too many homeowners were taking on mortgages and debt they could ill afford, and that risks to the financial system were growing unchecked. Alarm bells were clanging inside financial institutions, regulatory offices, consumer service organizations, state law enforcement agencies, and corporations throughout America, as well as in neighborhoods across the country. Many knowledgeable executives saw trouble and managed to avoid the train wreck. While countless Americans joined in the financial euphoria that seized the nation, many others were shouting to government officials in Washington and within state legislatures, pointing to what would become a human disaster, not just an economic debacle.

* * *

Unlike so many other bubbles—tulip bulbs in Holland in the 1600s, South Sea stocks in the 1700s, Internet stocks in the late 1990s—this one involved not just another commodity but a building block of community and social life and a cornerstone of the economy: the family home. Homes are the foundation upon which many of our social, personal, governmental, and economic structures rest. Children usually go to schools linked to their home addresses; local governments decide how much money they can spend on roads, firehouses, and public safety based on how much property tax revenue they have; house prices are tied to consumer spending. Down-turns in the housing industry can cause ripple effects almost everywhere.

When the Federal Reserve cut interest rates early in the new century and mortgage rates fell, home refinancing surged, climbing from $460 billion in 2000 to $2.8 trillion in 2003, allowing people to withdraw equity built up over previous decades and to consume more, despite stagnant wages. Home sales volume started to increase, and average home prices nationwide climbed, rising 67% in eight years by one measure and hitting a national high of $227,100 in early 2006.

* * *

Money washed through the economy like water rushing through a broken dam. Low interest rates and then foreign capital helped fuel the boom. Construction workers, landscape architects, real estate agents, loan brokers, and appraisers profited on Main Street, while investment bankers and traders on Wall Street moved even higher on the American earnings pyramid and the share prices of the most aggressive financial service firms reached all-time highs. Homeowners pulled cash out of their homes to send their kids to college, pay medical bills, install designer kitchens with granite counters, take vacations, or launch new businesses. They also paid off credit cards, even as personal debt rose nationally. Survey evidence shows that about 5% of homeowners pulled out cash to buy a vehicle and over 40% spent the cash on a catch-all category including tax payments, clothing, gifts, and living expenses. Renters used new forms of loans to buy homes and to move to suburban subdivisions, erecting swing sets in their backyards and enrolling their children in local schools.

* * *

But underneath, something was going wrong. Like a science fiction movie in which ordinary household objects turn hostile, familiar market mechanisms were being transformed. The time-tested 30-year fixed-rate mortgage, with a 20% down payment, went out of style. There was a burgeoning global demand for residential mortgage-backed securities that offered seemingly solid and secure returns. Investors around the world clamored to purchase securities built on American real estate, seemingly one of the safest bets in the world.

Wall Street labored mightily to meet that demand. Bond salesmen earned multi-million-dollar bonuses packaging and selling new kinds of loans, offered by new kinds of lenders, into new kinds of investment products that were deemed safe but possessed complex and hidden risks. Federal officials praised the changes—these financial innovations, they said, had lowered borrowing costs for consumers and moved risks away from the biggest and most systemically important financial institutions. But the nation's financial system had become vulnerable and interconnected in ways that were not understood by either the captains of finance or the systems public stewards. In fact, some of the largest institutions had taken on what would prove to be debilitating risks. Trillions of dollars had been wagered on the belief that housing prices would always rise and that borrowers would seldom default on mortgages, even as their debt grew. Shaky loans had been bundled into investment products in ways that seemed to give investors the best of both worlds—high-yield, risk-free—but instead, in many cases, would prove to be high-risk and yield-free.

The securitization machine began to guzzle these once-rare mortgage products with their strange-sounding names: Alt-A, subprime, I-O (interest-only), low-doc, no-doc, or ninja (no income, no job, no assets) loans; 2–28s and 3–27s; liar loans; piggyback second mortgages; payment-option or pick-a-pay adjustable rate mortgages. New variants on adjustable-rate mortgages, called "exploding" ARMs, featured low monthly costs at first, but payments could suddenly double or triple, if borrowers were unable to refinance. Loans with negative amortization would eat away the borrower's equity. Soon there were a multitude of different kinds of mortgages available on the market, confounding consumers who didn't examine the fine print, baffling conscientious borrowers who tried to puzzle out their implications, and opening the door for those who wanted in on the action.

* * *

At first not a lot of people really understood the potential hazards of these new loans. They were new, they were different, and the consequences were uncertain. But it soon became apparent that what had looked like newfound wealth was a mirage based on borrowed money. Overall mortgage indebtedness in the United States climbed from $5.3 trillion in 2001 to $10.5 trillion in 2007. The mortgage debt of American households rose almost as much in the six years from 2001 to 2007 as it had over the course of the country's more than 200-year history. The amount of mortgage debt per household rose from $91,500 in 2001 to $149,500 in 2007. With a simple flourish of a pen on paper, millions of Americans traded away decades of equity tucked away in their homes.

Under the radar, the lending and the financial services industry had mutated. In the past, lenders had avoided making unsound loans because they would be stuck with them in their loan portfolios. But because of the growth of securitization, it wasn't even clear anymore who the lender was. The mortgages would be packaged, sliced, repackaged, insured, and sold as incomprehensibly complicated debt securities to an assortment of hungry investors. Now even the worst loans could find a buyer.

* * *

Most home loans entered the pipeline soon after borrowers signed the documents and picked up their keys. Loans were put into packages and sold off in bulk to securitization firms—including investment banks such as Merrill Lynch, Bear Stearns, and Lehman Brothers, and commercial banks and thrifts such as Citibank, Wells Fargo, and Washington Mutual. The firms would package the loans into residential mortgage-backed securities that would mostly be stamped with triple-A ratings by the credit rating agencies, and sold to investors. In many cases, the securities were repackaged again into collateralized debt obligations (CDOs)—often composed of the riskier portions of these securities—which would then be sold to other investors. Most of these securities would also receive the coveted triple-A ratings that investors believed attested to their quality and safety. Some investors would buy an invention from the 1990s called a credit default swap (CDS) to protect against the securities' defaulting. For every buyer of a credit default swap, there was a seller: as these investors made opposing bets, the layers of entanglement in the securities market increased.

* * *

In Washington, four intermingled issues came into play that made it difficult to acknowledge the looming threats. First, efforts to boost homeownership had broad political support—from Presidents Bill Clinton and George W. Bush and successive Congresses—even though in reality the homeownership rate had peaked in the spring of 2004. Second, the real estate boom was generating a lot of cash on Wall Street and creating a lot of jobs in the housing industry at a time when performance in other sectors of the economy was dreary. Third, many top officials and regulators were reluctant to challenge the profitable and powerful financial industry. And finally, policy makers believed that even if the housing market tanked, the broader financial system and economy would hold up.

In an environment of minimal government restrictions, the number of nontraditional loans surged and lending standards declined. The companies issuing these loans made profits that attracted envious eyes. New lenders entered the field. Investors clamored for mortgage-related securities and borrowers wanted mortgages. The volume of subprime and nontraditional lending rose sharply. In 2000, the top 25 nonprime lenders originated $105 billion in loans. Their volume rose to $188 billion in 2002, and then $310 billion in 2003.

* * *

As home prices shot up in much of the country, many observers began to wonder if the country was witnessing a housing bubble. On June 18, 2005, the *Economist* magazine's cover story posited that the day of reckoning was at hand, with the head-line "House Prices: After the Fall." The illustration depicted a brick plummeting out of the sky. "It is not going to be pretty," the article declared. "How the current housing boom ends could decide the course of the entire world economy over the next few years."

* * *

By the end of 2007, most of the subprime lenders had failed or been acquired, including New Century Financial, Ameriquest, and American Home Mortgage. In January 2008, Bank of America announced it would acquire the ailing lender Countrywide. It soon became clear that risk— rather than being diversified across the financial system, as had been thought—was concentrated at the largest financial firms. Bear Stearns, laden with risky mortgage assets and dependent on fickle short-term lending, was bought by JP Morgan with government assistance in the spring. Before the summer was over, Fannie Mae and Freddie Mac would be put into conservatorship. Then, in September, Lehman Brothers failed and the remaining investment banks, Merrill Lynch, Goldman Sachs, and Morgan Stanley, struggled as they lost the market's confidence. AIG, with its massive credit default swap portfolio and exposure to the subprime mortgage market, was rescued by the government. Finally, many commercial banks and thrifts, which had their own exposures to declining mortgage assets and their own exposures to short-term credit markets, teetered. IndyMac had already failed over the summer; in September, Washington Mutual became the largest bank failure in U.S. history. In October, Wachovia struck a deal to be acquired by Wells Fargo. Citigroup and Bank of America fought to stay afloat. Before it was over, taxpayers had committed trillions of dollars through more than two dozen extraordinary programs to stabilize the financial system and to prop up the nation's largest financial institutions. [Footnotes omitted].

* * *

NOTES

1.   The Financial Crisis Inquiry Commission's Report also discussed, among other things, the fact that potential breakdowns in the enforcement of federal consumer financial laws helped fuel the fire underlying the subprime mortgage loan meltdown. In discussing the efforts of state regulators and attorney generals to enforce consumer lending laws against certain lenders, the Report stated that two former senior federal banking regulators told the Commission that they were defending the agency's constitutional obligation to block state efforts to impinge on federally created banks i.e. national banks. Financial Crisis Report at 13. Because state-chartered lenders had more lending problems, they said, the states should have been focusing there rather than looking to involve themselves in federally chartered institutions, an arena where they had no jurisdiction. *Id.* However, state regulators testified to the Commission that national banks funded 21 of the 25 largest subprime loan issuers operating with state charters, and that those banks were the end market for abusive loans originated by the state-chartered firms. *Id.*

Many states nevertheless pushed ahead in enforcing their own lending regulations, as did even some cities. In 2003, Charlotte, North Carolina-based Wachovia Bank told state regulators that it would not abide by state laws, because it was a national bank and fell under the supervision of the Office of Comptroller of the Currency ("OCC"), the primary federal regulator of national banks; virtually all of the largest banks in the U.S. fell under their supervision. Michigan protested Wachovia's announcement, and Wachovia sued Michigan. The OCC, the American Bankers Association, and the Mortgage Bankers Association entered the fray on Wachovia's side; the other 49 states, Puerto Rico, and the District of Columbia aligned themselves with Michigan. The legal battle lasted four years. In Watters v. Wachovia Bank, N.A., 550 U.S. 1 (2007) the Supreme Court ruled 5–3 in Wachovia's favor, "leaving the OCC its sole regulator for mortgage lending." For years, increasing tensions arose between state and federal bank regulators over the preemption of state consumer financial laws by the OCC under its authority to administer and enforce a single uniform set of banking laws nationwide over national banks under the

National Bank Act (NBA). See Lissa L. Broome and Jerry W. Markham, *Regulation of Bank Financial Service Activities* (West 2011) at 206–228.

As the preemption debate escalated in 2008 and 2009 amid allegations of mortgage and credit card lending abuses during the financial boom, national banks and the OCC received a significant and, by all accounts, unexpected surprise on the preemption issue from an unlikely source: the U.S. Supreme Court. In Cuomo v. Clearing House Association LLC, 129 S.Ct. 2710 (2009), the Court revisited the preemption issue as it applied to the New York state attorney general, who sought certain non-public information "in lieu of [a] subpoena" from national banks to determine whether they had violated New York's fair lending laws. *Id.* at 2714–15. In the courts below, the District Court enjoined the attorney general from enforcing state fair-lending laws through demands for records or judicial proceedings, and the Second Circuit affirmed, citing the preemptive effect of the NBA and OCC regulations. In its review of *Cuomo*, the Court reversed its long standing judicial support for the preemption doctrine in the context of the OCC's visitorial powers, ruling that state attorney generals are not preempted by federal banking laws from bringing lawsuits against national banks for violations of state fair lending and consumer laws. *Id.* at 2721. See also V. Gerard Comizio and Helen Y. Lee, Understanding the Federal Preemption Debate and a Potential Uniformity Solution, 6 Amer. Bus. L. Brief 2 (Spring/Summer 2010).

The Obama administration lost no time reacting to the *Cuomo* decision, with the U.S. Treasury Department introducing legislation the very next day to accomplish the administration's goal of establishing a Consumer Financial Protection Agency. See generally U.S. Dept. of the Treasury, Financial Regulatory Reform: A New Foundation, at 14 (June 17, 2009). In the ensuing months, both the Senate and House of Representatives in the Congress introduced their own proposals for financial regulatory reform that included the establishment of the CFPA, or a variation of such agency. See, e.g., Staff of S. Comm. on Banking, Housing, & Urban Affairs, 111th Cong. Restoring American Financial Stability Act of 2009 (Comm. Print 2009) (introduced by Sen. Dodd), available at http://www.banking.senate.gov/public/_files/AYO09D44_xml.pdf (last visited Nov. 16, 2009). On March 15, 2010 Senate Banking Chairman Chris Dodd (D-Conn) released a Committee Print of proposed legislation, "Restoring American Financial Stability Act of 2010." Among other things, the bill would create a new Consumer Board Financial Protection Bureau that would be housed in the Federal Reserve but would not report to the Federal Reserve. See also The Wall Street Reform and Consumer Protection Act of 2009, H.R. 4173, 111th Cong. (2009), as passed by the House, Dec. 12, 2009, and referred to S. Comm. on Banking, Housing, and Urban Affairs, Jan. 20, 2010. These executive and legislative branch proposals ultimately became the Dodd-Frank Act.

3. GOVERNMENT INTERVENTION

PRESIDENT BUSH'S SPEECH TO THE NATION ON THE ECONOMIC CRISIS
(September 24, 2008)

Good evening. This is an extraordinary period for America's economy.

Over the past few weeks, many Americans have felt anxiety about their finances and their future. I understand their worry and their frustration.

We've seen triple-digit swings in the stock market. Major financial institutions have teetered on the edge of collapse, and some have failed. As uncertainty has grown, many banks have restricted lending, credit markets have frozen, and families and businesses have found it harder to borrow money.

We're in the midst of a serious financial crisis, and the federal government is responding with decisive action.

* * *

Financial assets related to home mortgages have lost value during the house decline, and the banks holding these assets have restricted credit. As a result, our entire economy is in danger. So I propose that the federal government reduce the risk posed by these troubled assets and supply urgently needed money so banks and other financial institutions can avoid collapse and resume lending.

This rescue effort is not aimed at preserving any individual company or industry. It is aimed at preserving America's overall economy.

* * *

[What followed was a discussion of causes of the financial crisis]

With the situation becoming more precarious by the day, I faced a choice, to step in with dramatic government action or to stand back and allow the irresponsible actions of some to undermine the financial security of all.

I'm a strong believer in free enterprise, so my natural instinct is to oppose government intervention. I believe companies that make bad decisions should be allowed to go out of business. Under normal circumstances, I would have followed this course. But these are not normal circumstances. The market is not functioning properly. There has been a widespread loss of confidence, and major sectors of America's financial system are at risk of shutting down.

The government's top economic experts warn that, without immediate action by Congress, America could slip into a financial panic and a distressing scenario would unfold.

* * *

Many Americans are asking, how would a rescue plan work? After much discussion, there's now widespread agreement on the principles such a plan would include.

It would remove the risk posed by the troubled assets, including mortgage-backed securities, now clogging the financial system. This would free banks to resume the flow of credit to American families and businesses.

* * *

In close consultation with Treasury Secretary Hank Paulson, Federal Reserve Chairman Ben Bernanke, and SEC Chairman Chris Cox, I announced a plan on Friday.

First, the plan is big enough to solve a serious problem. Under our proposal, the federal government would put up to $700 billion taxpayer dollars on the line to purchase troubled assets that are clogging the financial system.

In the short term, this will free up banks to resume the flow of credit to American families and businesses, and this will help our economy grow.

Second, as markets have lost confidence in mortgage-backed securities, their prices have dropped sharply, yet the value of many of these assets will likely be higher than their current price, because the vast majority of Americans will ultimately pay off their mortgages.

The government is the one institution with the patience and resources to buy these assets at their current low prices and hold them until markets return to normal.

And when that happens, money will flow back to the Treasury as these assets are sold, and we expect that much, if not all, of the tax dollars we invest will be paid back.

* * *

NOTES

1.   After a political and ideological battle in the U.S. Congress, and original rejection by the House, the Emergency Economic Stabilization Act of 2008 ("EESA") was passed by the Congress and signed into law by President George W. Bush on October 3, 2008, weeks before the 2008 U.S. presidential elections. See Pub. L. 110–343. In response to the subprime mortgage crisis and near implosion of the U.S.—and international—economy, it was designed to restore liquidity to credit markets by authorizing the Secretary of the Treasury to purchase up to $700 billion in mortgage-backed securities and other troubled assets from the country's banks, as well as any other financial instrument the Secretary deemed necessary "to promote financial market stability" Section 101. The EESA also included, among other things, provisions

to minimize foreclosures on federally owned mortgages (Section 109), to recover possible future losses on the government's mortgage investments (Section 134), to prevent windfalls for executives of banks that benefit from the act (Section 111), to monitor the investments of the Treasury Department through reports to Congress (Section 105), a specially created oversight board (Section 104) and a Congressional oversight panel (Section 125). The EESA also temporarily increased deposit insurance coverage from $100,000 to $250,000 per account (Section 136), a change that became permanent pursuant to the Dodd-Frank Act, discussed infra.

The EESA authorized the U.S. Secretary of the Treasury to establish a Troubled Asset Relief Program (TARP) to protect the ability of consumers and businesses to secure credit (Section 101). The EESA featured a graduated release of funds to the Treasury Department. The Treasury Secretary was immediately authorized to spend up to $250 billion; an additional $100 billion would become available if the President confirmed that the funds were needed, and a further $350 billion would be authorized upon confirmation by the President and approval by Congress (Section 115).

In an interesting twist, it become increasingly—and quickly—apparent that the purchase of mortgage backed assets and other troubled assets would not restore liquidity to the credit market soon enough to avert further bank failures and a potential collapse of the economy. As a result, the White House and Treasury changed plans, and announced plans to use $250 billion immediately to purchase stock in troubled banks; this plan also included injection of $125 billion into 10 of the largest banks in the U.S. See Andrew Clark, Paulson abandons plans to buy up toxic mortgages, The Guardian (November 13, 2008). David Lauder, U.S. backs away from plan to buy bad assets, Reuters (November 12, 2008).

The EESA legislation was controversial, as was its implementation. Supporters argued the law was necessary to restore confidence to the financial markets, while detractors considered it a government "bailout" of the private sector banking industry. See, e.g., Luke Mullins, Sen. Jim Bunning: The Bailout is Un-American, U.S. News & World Report (September 23, 2008); Steven Hurst (AP), McCain, Obama raise doubts about bailout plan, USA Today, (September 22, 2008); Paul Krugman, Cash for Trash, N.Y. Times (September 21, 2008).

CONCLUSIONS OF THE FINANCIAL CRISIS INQUIRY COMMISSION
(January 2011)

* * *

- **We conclude over-the-counter derivatives contributed significantly to this crisis**. The enactment of legislation in 2000 to ban the regulation by both the federal and state

governments of over-the-counter (OTC) derivatives was a key
turning point in the march toward the financial crisis.

* * *

OTC derivatives contributed to the crisis in three significant ways.
First, one type of derivative—credit default swaps (CDS)—fueled the
mortgage securitization pipeline. CDS were sold to investors to protect
against the default or decline in value of mortgage-related securities
backed by risky loans. Companies sold protection—to the tune of $79
billion, in AIG's case—to investors in these newfangled mortgage
securities, helping to launch and expand the market and, in turn, to further
fuel the housing bubble.

Second, CDS were essential to the creation of synthetic CDOs. These
synthetic CDOs were merely bets on the performance of real mortgage-
related securities. They amplified the losses from the collapse of the
housing bubble by allowing multiple bets on the same securities and helped
spread them throughout the financial system. Goldman Sachs alone
packaged and sold $73 billion in synthetic CDOs from July 1, 2004, to May
31, 2007. Synthetic CDOs created by Goldman referenced more than 3,400
mortgage securities, and 610 of them were referenced at least twice. This
is apart from how many times these securities may have been referenced
in synthetic CDOs created by other firms.

Finally, when the housing bubble popped and crisis followed,
derivatives were in the center of the storm. AIG, which had not been
required to put aside capital reserves as a cushion for the protection it was
selling, was bailed out when it could not meet its obligations. The
government ultimately committed more than $180 billion because of
concerns that AIG's collapse would trigger cascading losses throughout the
global financial system. In addition, the existence of millions of derivatives
contracts of all types between systemically important financial
institutions—unseen and unknown in this unregulated market—added to
uncertainty and escalated panic, helping to precipitate government
assistance to those institutions.

* * *

[W]e examined the role of the GSEs, with Fannie Mae serving as the
Commission's case study in this area. These government-sponsored
enterprises had a deeply flawed business model as publicly traded
corporations with the implicit backing of and subsidies from the federal
government and with a public mission. Their $5 trillion mortgage exposure
and market position were significant. In 2005 and 2006, they decided to
ramp up their purchase and guarantee of risky mortgages, just as the
housing market was peaking. They used their political power for decades
to ward off effective regulation and oversight—spending $164 million on

lobbying from 1999 to 2008. They suffered from many of the same failures of corporate governance and risk management as the Commission discovered in other financial firms. Through the third quarter of 2010, the Treasury Department had provided $151 billion in financial support to keep them afloat.

* * *

The GSEs participated in the expansion of subprime and other risky mortgages, but they followed rather than led Wall Street and other lenders in the rush for fool's gold. They purchased the highest rated non-GSE mortgage-backed securities and their participation in this market added helium to the housing balloon, but their purchases never represented a majority of the market. Those purchases represented 10.5% of non-GSE subprime mortgage-backed securities in 2001, with the share rising to 40% in 2004, and falling back to 28% by 2008. They relaxed their underwriting standards to purchase or guarantee riskier loans and related securities in order to meet stock market analysts' and investors' expectations for growth, to regain market share, and to ensure generous compensation for their executives and employees—justifying their activities on the broad and sustained public policy support for homeownership.

The Commission also probed the performance of the loans purchased or guaranteed by Fannie and Freddie. While they generated substantial losses, delinquency rates for GSE loans were substantially lower than loans securitized by other financial firms. For example, data compiled by the Commission for a subset of borrowers with similar credit scores—scores below 660—show that by the end of 2008, GSE mortgages were far less likely to be seriously delinquent than were non-GSE securitized mortgages: 6.2% versus 28.3%.

We also studied at length how the Department of Housing and Urban Development's (HUD's) affordable housing goals for the GSEs affected their investment in risky mortgages. Based on the evidence and interviews with dozens of individuals involved in this subject area, we determined these goals only contributed marginally to Fannie's and Freddie's participation in those mortgages.

* * *

In conducting our inquiry, we took a careful look at HUD's affordable housing goals, as noted above, and the Community Reinvestment Act (CRA). The CRA was enacted in 1977 to combat "redlining" by banks—the practice of denying credit to individuals and businesses in certain neighborhoods without regard to their creditworthiness. The CRA requires banks and savings and loans to lend, invest, and provide services to the communities from which they take deposits, consistent with bank safety and soundness.

The Commission concludes the CRA was not a significant factor in subprime lending or the crisis. Many subprime lenders were not subject to the CRA. Research indicates only 6% of high-cost loans—a proxy for subprime loans—had any connection to the law. Loans made by CRA-regulated lenders in the neighborhoods in which they were required to lend were half as likely to default as similar loans made in the same neighborhoods by independent mortgage originators not subject to the law.

* * *

NOTES

1. For a further discussion of the CRA, see Chapter 7. There was a strong dissent to the Financial Crisis Inquiry Commission Report, attributing larger blame for the financial crisis to the GSEs and government affordable housing policies such as the CRA. See Dissenting Views, Financial Crisis Report at pp. 411–538.

2. The Financial Crisis Inquiry Commission noted the role of U.S. insurance giant AIG, Inc. in the subprime meltdown with respect to its sales of credit default swaps (CDS) in the run up to the financial crisis. The company nearly collapsed just days after the collapse of Lehman Brothers. While the U.S. government did not come to the aid of Lehman, in the following months AIG received more than $180 billion of taxpayer assistance in one of the biggest single U.S. financial rescue packages in history, drawing criticism. See Luke Mullins, Why Did the Feds Bail Out AIG but Not Lehman?, U.S. News & World Report (September 18, 2008); Ronald D. Orol, Geithner, Paulson defend $182 billion AIG bailout, Market Watch (January 27, 2010).

Interestingly enough, AIG was able to repay the government by late 2012. See Zachary Tracer, AIG Stock Sale Repays Bailout as U.S. Government Profits, Bloomberg Business (September 10, 2012), even as AIG shareholders won approval of a $970 million settlement, which resolved various claims that the company misled them about the subprime mortgage exposure. See Erik Holm and Serena Na, AIG Sets $725 Million Settlement, Wall Street Journal (July 17, 2010) (settling the last of a total of approximately $1 billion in claims).

3. The U.S. subprime meltdown, its U.S. and global impact, and the U.S. government's intervention have been the subject of a number of outstanding movies and documentaries on the topic. See e.g., Inside the Meltdown, Frontline, PBS; Too Big to Fail, HBO Movies (based on the book of the same name by Andrew Ross Sorkin) (2011); Margin Call, Lionsgate (2011); Inside Job, Charles Ferguson (2010); The Warning, Frontline, PBS (2009); American Casino, Argot Pictures (2009).

STARR INTERNATIONAL COMPANY, INC. v. UNITED STATES

United States Court of Federal Claims (2015)
121 Fed.Cl. 428 (2015)

WHEELER, JUDGE.

Plaintiff Starr International Company, Inc. ("Starr") commenced this lawsuit against the United States on November 21, 2011. Starr challenges the Government's financial rescue and takeover of American International Group, Inc. ("AIG") that began on September 16, 2008. Before the takeover, Starr was one of the largest shareholders of AIG common stock. Starr alleges in its own right and on behalf of other AIG shareholders that the Government's actions in acquiring control of AIG constituted a taking without just compensation and an illegal exaction, both in violation of the Fifth Amendment to the U.S. Constitution. The controlling shareholder of Starr is Maurice R. Greenberg, formerly AIG's Chief Executive Officer until 2005, and one of the key architects of AIG's international insurance business. Starr claims damages in excess of $40 billion.

On the weekend of September 13–14, 2008, known in the financial world as "Lehman Weekend" because of the impending failure of Lehman Brothers, U.S. Government officials feared that the nation's and the world's economies were on the brink of a monumental collapse even larger than the Great Depression of the 1930s. While the Government frantically kept abreast of economic indicators on all fronts, the leaders at the Federal Reserve Board, the Federal Reserve Bank of New York, and the U.S. Treasury Department began focusing in particular on AIG's quickly deteriorating liquidity condition. AIG had grown to become a gigantic world insurance conglomerate, and its Financial Products Division was tied through transactions with most of the leading global financial institutions. The prognosis on Lehman Weekend was that AIG, without an immediate and massive cash infusion, would face bankruptcy by the following Tuesday, September 16, 2008. AIG's failure likely would have caused a rapid and catastrophic domino effect on a worldwide scale.

On that following Tuesday, after AIG and the Government had explored other possible avenues of assistance, the Federal Reserve Board of Governors formally approved a "term sheet" that would provide an $85 billion loan facility to AIG. This sizable loan would keep AIG afloat and avoid bankruptcy, but the punitive terms of the loan were unprecedented and triggered this lawsuit. Operating as a monopolistic lender of last resort, the Board of Governors imposed a 12 percent interest rate on AIG, much higher than the 3.25 to 3.5 percent interest rates offered to other troubled financial institutions such as Citibank and Morgan Stanley. Moreover, the Board of Governors imposed a draconian requirement to take 79.9 percent equity ownership in AIG as a condition of the loan. Although it is common in corporate lending for a borrower to post its assets as collateral for a loan, here, the 79.9 percent equity taking of AIG ownership was much different. More than just collateral, the Government would retain its ownership interest in AIG even after AIG had repaid the loan.

The term sheet approved by the Board of Governors contained other harsh terms. AIG's Chief Executive Officer, Robert Willumstad, would be forced to resign, and he would be replaced with a new CEO of the Government's choosing. The term sheet included other fees in addition to the 12 percent interest rate, such as a 2 percent commitment fee payable at closing, an 8 percent undrawn fee payable on the unused amount of the credit facility, and a 2.5 percent periodic commitment fee payable every three months after closing. Immediately after AIG began receiving financial aid from the Government on September 16, 2008, teams of personnel from the Federal Reserve Bank of New York and its advisers from Morgan Stanley, Ernst & Young, and Davis Polk & Wardwell, descended upon AIG to oversee AIG's business operations. The Government's hand-picked CEO, Mr. Edward Liddy, assumed his position on September 18, 2008. Although the AIG Board of Directors approved the Government's harsh terms because the only other choice would have been bankruptcy, the Government usurped control of AIG without ever allowing a vote of AIG's common stock shareholders.

* * *

The main issues in the case are: (1) whether the Federal Reserve Bank of New York possessed the legal authority to acquire a borrower's equity when making a loan under Section 13(3) of the Federal Reserve Act, 12 U.S.C. § 343 (2006); and (2) whether there could legally be a taking without just compensation of AIG' s equity under the Fifth Amendment where AIG's Board of Directors voted on September 16, 2008 to accept the Government's proposed terms. If Starr prevails on either or both of these questions of liability, the Court must also determine what damages should be awarded to the plaintiff shareholders.

* * *

The weight of the evidence demonstrates that the Government treated AIG much more harshly than other institutions in need of financial assistance. In September 2008, AIG's international insurance subsidiaries were thriving and profitable, but its Financial Products Division experienced a severe liquidity shortage due to the collapse of the housing market. Other major institutions, such as Morgan Stanley, Goldman Sachs, and Bank of America, encountered similar liquidity shortages. Thus, while the Government publicly singled out AIG as the poster child for causing the September 2008 economic crisis (Paulson, Tr. 1254-55), the evidence supports a conclusion that AIG actually was *less* responsible for the crisis than other major institutions. The notorious credit default swap transactions were very low risk in a thriving housing market, but they quickly became very high risk when the bottom fell out of this market. Many entities engaged in these transactions, not just AIG. The Government's justification for taking control of AIG's ownership and running its business operations appears to have been entirely misplaced. The Government did not demand shareholder equity, high interest rates, or voting control of any entity except AIG. Indeed, with the exception of AIG, the Government has never demanded equity ownership from a borrower in the 75-year history of Section 13(3) of the Federal Reserve Act.

The Government did realize a significant benefit in nationalizing AIG. Since most of the other financial institutions experiencing a liquidity crisis were counterparties to AIG transactions, the Government was able to minimize the ripple effect of an AIG failure by using AIG's assets to make sure the counterparties were paid in full on these transactions.[1] What is clear from the evidence is that the Government carefully orchestrated its takeover of AIG in a way that would avoid any shareholder vote, and maximize the benefits to the Government and to the taxpaying public, eventually resulting in a profit of $22.7 billion to the U.S. Treasury. AIG's benefit was to avoid bankruptcy, and to "live to fight another day." PTX 195 at 8; see also testimony of AIG Board member Morris Offit, Tr. 7392 ("we were giving AIG the opportunity to, in effect, live, that the shareholder would still have a 20 percent interest rather than being wiped out by a bankruptcy.").

The Government's unduly harsh treatment of AIG in comparison to other institutions seemingly was misguided and had no legitimate purpose, even considering concerns about "moral hazard."[2] The question is not whether this treatment was inequitable or unfair, but whether the Government's actions created a legal right of recovery for AIG's shareholders.

Having considered the entire record, the Court finds in Starr's favor on the illegal exaction claim. With the approval of the Board of Governors, the Federal Reserve Bank of New York had the authority to serve as a lender of last resort under Section 13(3) of the Federal Reserve Act in a time of "unusual and exigent circumstances," 12 U.S.C. § 343 (2006), and to establish an interest rate "fixed with a view of accommodating commerce

---

[1] According to a chart available to the Government on September 16, 2008, the following financial institutions were among those with significant economic exposure to AIG: ABN AMRO, Banco Santander, Bank of America, Barclays, BNP, Calyon, Citigroup, Credit Suisse, Danske Bank, Deutsche Bank, Goldman Sachs, HSBC, ING, JP Morgan, Merrill Lynch, Morgan Stanley, Rabobank, Société Générale, and UBS.

[2] "Moral hazard" refers to the Government's concern that the availability of Federal Reserve bailout loans might motivate private companies to accept risky propositions, knowing that the Government will extend credit to them if they fail. The Government's policy is to discourage such corporate thinking. Geithner.

and business," 12 U.S.C. § 357. However, Section 13(3) did not authorize the Federal Reserve Bank to acquire a borrower's equity as consideration for the loan. Although the Bank may exercise "all powers specifically granted by the provisions of this chapter and such incidental powers as shall be necessary to carry on the business of banking within the limitations prescribed by this chapter," 12 U.S.C § 341, this language does not authorize the taking of equity. The Court will not read into this incidental powers clause a right that would be inconsistent with other limitations in the statute. Long ago, the Supreme Court held that a federal entity's incidental powers cannot be greater than the powers otherwise delegated to it by Congress. See Fed. Res. Bank of Richmond v. Malloy, 264 U.S. 160, 167 (1924) ("[A]uthority to do a specific thing carries with it by implication the power to do whatever is necessary to effectuate the thing authorized – not to do another and separate thing, since that would be, not to carry the authority granted into effect, but to add an authority beyond the terms of the grant."); see also First Nat'l Bank in St. Louis v. Missouri, 263 U.S. 640, 659 (1924) ("Certainly, an incidental power can avail neither to create powers which, expressly or by reasonable implication, are withheld nor to enlarge powers given; but only to carry into effect those which are granted."); Suwannee S.S. Co. v. United States, 150 Ct. Cl. 331, 336, 279 F.2d 874, 876 (1960) ("No statute should be read as subjecting citizens to the uncontrolled caprice of officials.").

Moreover, there is nothing in the Federal Reserve Act or in any other federal statute that would permit a Federal Reserve Bank to take over a private corporation and run its business as if the Government were the owner. Yet, that is precisely what FRBNY did. It is one thing for FRBNY to have made an $85 billion loan to AIG at exorbitant interest rates under Section 13(3), but it is quite another to direct the replacement of AIG's Chief Executive Officer, and to take control of AIG's business operations. A Federal Reserve Bank has no right to control and run a company to whom it has made a sizable loan. As FRBNY's outside counsel from Davis Polk & Wardwell observed on September 17, 2008 in the midst of the AIG takeover, "the [government] is on thin ice and they know it. But who's going to challenge them on this ground?" PTX 3283, Davis Polk email. Answering this question, the "challenge" has come from the AIG shareholders, whom the Government intentionally excluded from the takeover process.

A ruling in Starr's favor on the illegal exaction claim, finding that the Government's takeover of AIG was unauthorized, means that Starr's Fifth Amendment taking claim necessarily must fail. If the Government's actions were not authorized, there can be no Fifth Amendment taking claim. See Alves v. United States, 133 F.3d 1454, 1456–58 (Fed. Cir. 1998) (Taking must be based on authorized government action); Figueroa v. United States, 57 Fed. Cl. 488, 496 (2003) (If the government action complained of is unauthorized, "plaintiffs takings claim would fail on that basis."); see also Short v. United States, 50 F.3d 994, 1000 (Fed. Cir. 1995) (same). Thus, a claim cannot be both an illegal exaction (based upon unauthorized action), and a taking (based upon authorized action).

The Government defends on the basis that AIG voluntarily accepted the terms of the proposed rescue, which it says would defeat Starr's claim regardless of whether the challenged actions were authorized or unauthorized. While it is true that AIG's Board of Directors voted to accept the Government's proposed terms on September 16, 2008 to avoid bankruptcy, the board's decision resulted from a complete mismatch of negotiating leverage in which the Government could and did force AIG to accept whatever punitive terms were proposed. No matter how rationally AlG's Board addressed its alternatives that night, and notwithstanding that AIG had a team of outstanding professional advisers, the fact remains that AlG was at the Government's mercy. Case law is divided on whether the death knell of bankruptcy represents a real board of directors' choice in such circumstances. Compare Swift & Courtney & Beecher Co. v. United States, 111 U.S. 22, 28–29 (1884) ("The parties were not on equal terms .... The only alternative was to submit to an illegal exaction or discontinue its business.") and In re Consolidated Pretrial Proceedings in Air West Securities Litig., 436 F. Supp. 1281, 1290 (N.D. Cal. 1977) ("[D]efendants' claim that Trustees should be denied recovery . . . because they had an alternative source of recovery (bankruptcy) has never been held to be an adequate alternative under the law of business compulsion.") with Starr Int'l Co. v. Fed. Reserve Bank of N.Y., 906 F. Supp. 2d 202, 219 n.13 (S.D.N.Y. 2012) ("Even a choice between a rock and a hard place is still a choice.") and FDIC v. Linn, 671 F. Supp. 547, 560 (N.D. Ill. 1987) ("Threatened bankruptcy is insufficient to create economic duress."). Voluntary acceptance, however, is not a defense to an illegal exaction claim. * * *

NOTES

1. Interestingly enough, on the issue of damages the *Starr* court concluded that, "if not for the Government's intervention," AIG would have filed for bankruptcy. *Id.* at 9. The court concluded that in a bankruptcy proceeding, AIG's shareholders "would most likely have lost 100% of their stock value." As a result, in applying the "economic loss doctrine" used in assessing damages, the plaintiff was awarded no damages. *Id.* at 9–10. Thus, the plaintiff won a pyrrhic victory. The court's findings, however, that the Federal Reserve Board violated the 5th amendment of the U.S. Constitution in structuring the AIG bailout in the midst of the financial crisis—arguably to prevent a further implosion of the U.S. and international economy due to the significant economic exposure to AIG of the major international financial institutions referenced in footnote 2 of the case—may have important implications in future financial crisis situations.

2.   Prior to 2010, section 13(3) of the Federal Reserve Act ("FRA"), 12 U.S.C. § 343, provided that the Board could authorize any Federal Reserve Bank to extend credit to any corporation in "unusual and exigent circumstances," subject to certain conditions. 12 U.S.C. § 343(A)(3). Effective July 2, 2010, Section 1101 of the Dodd-Frank Act (Pub. L. 111–203, 124 Stat. 1376) made extensive amendments to sections 13(3) of the FRA designed to limit the Board's emergency lending authority, designed to prevent future government "bailouts." See 79 Fed. Reg. 3 (January 6, 2014) (proposing rules implementing Section 1101 of the Dodd-Frank Act designed to ensure that any emergency lending program or facility undertake by the Board is for the purpose of providing liquidity to the financial system, and not to an individual failing financial company). The Dodd-Frank Act is discussed later in this Chapter.

G20 DECLARATION: SUMMIT ON FINANCIAL MARKETS AND THE WORLD ECONOMY
(November 15, 2008)

1.   We, the Leaders of the Group of Twenty, held an initial meeting in Washington on November 15, 2008, amid serious challenges to the world economy and financial markets. We are determined to enhance our cooperation and work together to restore global growth and achieve needed reforms in the world's financial systems.

* * *

Root Causes of the Current Crisis

3.   During a period of strong global growth, growing capital flows, and prolonged stability earlier this decade, market participants sought higher yields without an adequate appreciation of the risks and failed to exercise proper due diligence. At the same time, weak underwriting standards, unsound risk management practices, increasingly complex and opaque financial products, and consequent excessive leverage combined to create vulnerabilities in the system. Policy-makers, regulators and supervisors, in some advanced countries, did not adequately appreciate and address the risks building up in financial markets, keep pace with financial innovation, or take into account the systemic ramifications of domestic regulatory actions.

* * *

Common Principles for Reform of Financial Markets

8.   In addition to the actions taken above, we will implement reforms that will strengthen financial markets and regulatory regimes so as to avoid future crises. Regulation is first and foremost the responsibility of national regulators who constitute the first line of defense against market instability. However, our financial markets are global in scope. Therefore,

intensified international cooperation among regulators and strengthening of international standards, where necessary, and their consistent implementation is necessary to protect against adverse cross-border, regional and global developments affecting international financial stability. Regulators must ensure that their actions support market discipline, avoid potentially adverse impacts on other countries, including regulatory arbitrage, and support competition, dynamism and innovation in the marketplace. Financial institutions must also bear their responsibility for the turmoil and should do their part to overcome it including by recognizing losses, improving disclosure and strengthening their governance and risk management practices.

9. We commit to implementing policies consistent with the following common principles for reform.

* * *

Enhancing Sound Regulation: We pledge to strengthen our regulatory regimes, prudential oversight, and risk management, and ensure that all financial markets, products and participants are regulated or subject to oversight, as appropriate to their circumstances. We will exercise strong oversight over credit rating agencies, consistent with the agreed and strengthened international code of conduct. We will also make regulatory regimes more effective over the economic cycle, while ensuring that regulation is efficient, does not stifle innovation, and encourages expanded trade in financial products and services. We commit to transparent assessments of our national regulatory systems.

* * *

Reinforcing International Cooperation: We call upon our national and regional regulators to formulate their regulations and other measures in a consistent manner. Regulators should enhance their coordination and cooperation across all segments of financial markets, including with respect to cross-border capital flows. Regulators and other relevant authorities as a matter of priority should strengthen cooperation on crisis prevention, management, and resolution.

* * *

G20 LEADERS STATEMENT: THE PITTSBURGH SUMMIT
(September 24–25, 2009)

* * *

Strengthening the International Financial Regulatory System

10. Major failures of regulation and supervision, plus reckless and irresponsible risk taking by banks and other financial institutions, created

dangerous financial fragilities that contributed significantly to the current crisis. A return to the excessive risk taking prevalent in some countries before the crisis is not an option.

* * *

13. Our reform is multi-faceted but at its core must be stronger capital standards, complemented by clear incentives to mitigate excessive risk-taking practices. Capital allows banks to withstand those losses that inevitably will come. It, together with more powerful tools for governments to wind down firms that fail, helps us hold firms accountable for the risks that they take. Building on their Declaration on Further Steps to Strengthen the International Financial System, we call on our Finance Ministers and Central Bank Governors to reach agreement on an international framework of reform in the following critical areas:

- *Building high quality capital and mitigating pro-cyclicality:* We commit to developing by end-2010 internationally agreed rules to improve both the quantity and quality of bank capital and to discourage excessive leverage. These rules will be phased in as financial conditions improve and economic recovery is assured, with the aim of implementation by end-2012. The national implementation of higher level and better quality capital requirements, counter-cyclical capital buffers, higher capital requirements for risky products and off-balance sheet activities, as elements of the Basel II Capital Framework, together with strengthened liquidity risk requirements and forward-looking provisioning, will reduce incentives for banks to take excessive risks and create a financial system better prepared to withstand adverse shocks. We welcome the key measures recently agreed by the oversight body of the Basel Committee to strengthen the supervision and regulation of the banking sector.

* * *

GLOBAL SYSTEMICALLY IMPORTANT BANKS

Basel Committee on Banking Supervision (July 2013)

* * *

I.   Introduction

* * *

3.   The negative externalities associated with institutions that are perceived as not being allowed to fail due to their size, interconnectedness, complexity, lack of substitutability or global scope are well recognised. In

maximising their private benefits, individual financial institutions may rationally choose outcomes that on a system-wide level, are suboptimal because they do not take into account these externalities. Moreover, the moral hazard costs associated with implicit guarantees derived from the perceived expectation of government support may amplify risk-taking, reduce market discipline and create competitive distortions, and further increase the probability of distress in the future. As a result, the costs associated with moral hazard add to any direct costs of support that may be borne by taxpayers.

4.   In addition, given the potential cross-border repercussions of a problem in any of the G-SIBs on the financial institutions in many countries and on the global economy at large, this is not uniquely a problem for national authorities, and therefore requires a global minimum agreement.

* * *

8.   The work of the Committee forms part of a broader effort by the FSB to reduce the moral hazard of G-SIFIs [global systemically important financial instutitions]. Additional measures by the FSB on recovery and resolution address and the second broad objective, which is reduce the impact of failure of a G-SIB.[5] These policies will serve to reduce the impact of a G-SIB's failure and will also help level the playing field by reducing too-big-to-fail (TBTF) competitive advantages in funding markets. These policies have been developed in close coordination with the Committee, and were published by the FSB concurrently with the November 2011 version of this document.

* * *

1.   Cross-jurisdictional activity

21.   Given the focus on G-SIBs, the objective of this indicator is to capture banks' global footprint. Two indicators in this category measure the importance of the bank's activities outside its home (headquarter) jurisdiction relative to overall activity of other banks in the sample: (i) cross-jurisdictional claims; and (ii) cross-jurisdictional liabilities. The idea is that the international impact of a bank's distress or failure would vary in line with its share of cross-jurisdictional assets and liabilities. The greater a bank's global reach, the more difficult it is to coordinate its resolution and the more widespread the spillover effects from its failure.

---

[5]   See Financial Stability Board, *Key attributes of effective resolution regimes for financial institutions* (November 2011) at http://www.financialstabilityboard.org/wp-content/uploads/r_111104cc.pdf?page_moved=1.

2. Size

22. A bank's distress or failure is more likely to damage the global economy or financial markets if its activities comprise a large share of global activity. The larger the bank, the more difficult it is for its activities to be quickly replaced by other banks and therefore the greater the chance that its distress or failure would cause disruption to the financial markets in which it operates. The distress or failure of a large bank is also more likely to damage confidence in the financial system as a whole. Size is therefore a key measure of systemic importance. One indicator is used to measure size: the measure of total exposures used in the Basel III leverage ratio.

* * *

4. THE DODD-FRANK ACT

STATE NATIONAL BANK OF BIG SPRING ET AL. V. JACOB J. LEW ET AL.

958 F.Supp.2d 127 (D.C.D.C.) (August 1, 2013)

* * *

ELLEN SEGAL HUVELLE, DISTRICT JUDGE.

Plaintiffs State National Bank of Big Spring ("SNB" or the "Bank"), the 60 Plus Association ("60 Plus"), the Competitive Enterprise Institute ("CEI") (collectively the "Private Plaintiffs"), and the States of Alabama, Georgia, Kansas, Michigan, Montana, Nebraska, Ohio, Oklahoma, South Carolina, Texas, and West Virginia (collectively "the States") have sued to challenge the constitutionality of Titles I, II, and X of the Dodd-Frank Wall Street Reform and Consumer Protection Act, Pub. L. No. 111–203 (July 21, 2010) (the "Dodd-Frank Act")[.] [Plaintiffs also challenged the constitutionality of Richard Cordray's appointment as director of the Consumer Financial Protection Bureau]. * * * Defendants, who include more than a dozen federal government officials and entities, have filed a motion to dismiss pursuant to Fed. R. Civ. P. 12(b)(1) on the grounds that plaintiffs lack Article III standing, or, in the alternative, that their claims are not ripe for review. For the reasons stated below, the Court will grant defendants' motion.

BACKGROUND

On July 21, 2010, Congress enacted the Dodd-Frank Act as "a direct and comprehensive response to the financial crisis that nearly crippled the U.S. economy beginning in 2008." S. Rep. No. 111–176, at 2 (2010). The purpose of the Act was to "promote the financial stability of the United States . . . through multiple measures designed to improve accountability, resiliency, and transparency in the financial system[.]"*Id.* Those measures included "establishing an early warning system to detect and address emerging threats to financial stability and the economy, enhancing consumer and investor protections, strengthening the supervision of large complex financial organizations and providing a mechanism to liquidate such companies should they fail without any losses to the taxpayer, and regulating the massive over-the-counter derivatives market." *Id.* The Act "creat[ed] several new governmental entities, eliminate[ed] others, and transferr[ed] regulatory authority among the agencies." (See Defendants' Motion to Dismiss [ECF No. 26–1] ("Def. Mot.") at 6.)

In this suit, plaintiffs challenge Title I of Dodd-Frank, which established the Financial Stability Oversight Council ("FSOC" or the "Council"), see 12 U.S.C. § 5321; Title II, which established the Orderly Liquidation Authority ("OLA"), see 12 U.S.C. § 5384; and Title X, which established the CFPB. See 12 U.S.C. §§ 5491, 5511.[3] Specifically, in Count III, the Private Plaintiffs challenge the constitutionality of Title I on separation-of-powers grounds, alleging that the FSOC "has sweeping and unprecedented discretion to choose which nonbank financial companies to designate as 'systematically important' " and that such "powers and discretion are not limited by any meaningful statutory directives." (Second Am. Compl. ¶ 8.) In Count I, the Private Plaintiffs challenge Title X on the grounds that it violates the separation of powers by "delegat[ing] effectively unbounded power to the CFPB, and coupl[ing] that power with provisions insulating the CFPB against meaningful checks by the Legislative, Executive, and Judicial Branches[.]" (*Id.* ¶ 6.)

All plaintiffs challenge Title II on three separate grounds. In Count IV, they allege that Title II violates the separation of powers because it "empowers the Treasury Secretary to order the liquidation of a financial company with little or no advance warning, under cover of mandatory

---

[3] In several unrelated cases, Plaintiffs have mounted challenges to regulations promulgated pursuant to authority delegated by Dodd-Frank. Judge Howell recently held that a plaintiff lacked standing to challenge a CFTC regulation setting minimum liquidation times for swaps and future contracts, which was promulgated, in part, pursuant to Dodd-Frank's DCO Core Principles. See *Bloomberg L.P. v. CFTC*, No. 13–523, 2013 WL 2458283, at *26 (D.D.C. June 7, 2013). The D.C. Circuit also affirmed Judge Howell's ruling in yet another suit challenging CFTC rulemaking in the wake of Dodd-Frank. See Inv. Co. Inst. v. CFTC, 12–5413, 2013 WL 3185090, at *1 (D.C. Cir. June 25, 2013). In Am. Petroleum Inst. v. SEC, No. 12–1668, 2013 WL 3307114, at 1 (D.D.C. July 2, 2013), the plaintiff challenged a provision of Dodd-Frank now codified at section 13(q) of the Securities Exchange Act of 1934, 15 U.S.C. § 78m(q), on First Amendment grounds, and regulations promulgated pursuant to the statute under the Administrative Procedure Act, 5 U.S.C. § 706. Judge Bates vacated the challenged rule, while declining to reach the constitutional challenge as premature in view of the fact that the SEC "has yet to interpret section 13(q) in light of its discretionary authority, and the interpretation it adopts could alter the First Amendment analysis." Id. at *15. See also Am. Petroleum Inst. v. SEC, 714 F.3d 1329 (D.C. Cir. 2013) (Court of Appeals dismissing simultaneously filed suit for lack of subject matter jurisdiction and leaving plaintiff to pursue its claims in the district court). And, in Nat'l Ass'n of Mfrs. v. SEC, No. 13–0635, 2013 WL 3803918, at *1, 31 (D.D.C. July 23, 2013), Judge Wilkins held that section 1502 of the Dodd-Frank Act and a rule promulgated under that authority did not violate the First Amendment.

secrecy, and without either useful statutory guidance or meaningful legislative, executive, or judicial oversight." (Second Am. Compl. ¶ 9.) In Count V, they allege that Title II violates the due process clause of the Fifth Amendment, because the "[t]he forced liquidation of a company with little or no advance warning, in combination with the FDIC's virtually unlimited power to choose favorites among similarly situated creditors in implementing the liquidation, denies the subject company and its creditors constitutionally required notice and a meaningful opportunity to be heard before their property is taken—and likely becomes unrecoverable[.]"

Defendants have moved to dismiss the complaint on the grounds that plaintiffs lack Article III standing to pursue their claims, or, in the alternative, that their claims are not ripe. (See Def. Mot. at 4–5.) This is an unusual case, as plaintiffs have not faced any adverse rulings nor has agency action been directed at them. Most significantly, no enforcement action—"the paradigm of direct governmental authority"—has been taken against plaintiffs. FEC v. NRA Political Victory Fund, 6 F.3d 821, 824 (D.C. Cir. 1993). As a result, plaintiffs' standing is more difficult to parse here than in the typical case. See, e.g., Noel Canning v. NLRB, 705 F.3d 490, 492–93 (D.C. Cir. 2013) (employer challenged NLRB decision finding that it had violated the National Labor Relations Act).

* * *

I.   TITLE 1: FINANCIAL STABILITY OVERSIGHT COUNCIL ("FSOC")

A.   The Statutory Provision

Title I of Dodd-Frank Act established the FSOC. See 12 U.S.C. § 5321. The purposes of the Council are

> to identify risks to the financial stability of the United States that could arise from the material financial distress or failure, or ongoing activities, of large, interconnected bank holding companies or nonbank financial companies, or that could arise outside the financial services marketplace; to promote market discipline, by eliminating expectations on the part of shareholders, creditors, and counterparties of such companies that the Government will shield them from losses in the event of failure; and to respond to emerging threats to the stability of the United States financial system.

12 U.S.C. § 5322(a)(1). The Council has ten voting members: the Secretary of the Treasury, who serves as the Council Chairperson; the Chairman of the Federal Reserve Board; the Comptroller of the Currency; the Director of the CFPB; the Chairperson of the Securities and Exchange Commission ("SEC"); the Chairperson of the Federal Deposit Insurance Corporation ("FDIC"); the Chairperson of the Commodity Futures Trading Commission

("CFTC"); the Director of the Federal Housing Finance Agency ("FHFA"); the Chairman of the National Credit Union Administration ("NCUA") Board; and an independent member with insurance expertise appointed by the President with the advice and consent of the Senate. See 12 U.S.C. § 5321(b)(1). The Council also includes five nonvoting members. See *id.* § 5321(b)(3).

Title I authorizes the Council, upon a two-thirds vote of its voting members, including the affirmative vote of the Treasury Secretary, to designate certain "nonbank financial companies" as "systematically important financial institutions" or SIFIs.[6] 12 U.S.C. §§ 5323(a)(1), (b)(1), 5365, 5366. SIFI designation is based on consideration of eleven enumerated factors leading to a determination that "material financial distress at the U.S. nonbank financial company, or the nature, scope, size, scale, concentration, interconnectedness, or mix of the activities of the U.S. nonbank financial company, could pose a threat to the financial stability of the United States." 12 U.S.C. § 5323(a)(1). See *id.* (a)(2), (b)(2). If an entity is designated as a SIFI, it "will be subject to supervision by the Federal Reserve Board and more stringent government regulation in the form of prudential standards and early remediation requirements established by the Board." Before designating any company as a SIFI, the Council must give written notice to the company of the proposed determination. See 12 U.S.C. § 5323(e)(1). The company is entitled to a hearing at which it may contest the proposed determination. See *id.* § 5323(e)(2). Additionally, once the Council makes a final decision to designate a company as a SIFI, that company may seek judicial review of the determination, and a court will determine whether the decision was arbitrary and capricious. See *id.* § 5323(h). There is no provision for third-party challenges to SIFI designation under Title I. (See Second Am. ¶ 157.)

On April 11, 2012, following a notice-and-comment period, the Council published a "final rule and interpretive guidance . . . describ[ing] the manner in which the Council intends to apply the statutory standards and considerations, and the processes and procedures that the Council intends to follow, in making determinations under section 113 of the Dodd-Frank Act." Authority to Require Supervision and Regulation of Certain Nonbank Financial Companies, 77 Fed. Reg. 21637 (Apr. 11, 2012). On June 3, 2013, while this motion was pending, the Council voted to make proposed determinations regarding a set of nonbank financial companies but did not release the names of the designated companies. (See Second Supplemental Declaration of Gregory Jacob [ECF No. 34–1] ("Second Jacob Decl.") ¶ 5; *id.*, Exs. 3–4.) Those companies then had thirty days to request a hearing

---

[6] A "nonbank financial company" is defined as a company "predominately engaged in financial activities," other than bank holding companies and certain other entities. 12 U.S.C. § 5311(a)(4). The term "systematically important financial institution" does not actually appear in the Dodd-Frank Act, but because it has come into common parlance (see Def. Mot. At 3 n.2), and the parties have used the term throughout their briefs, the Court will do so as well.

before a final determination would be made. (See Second Jacob Decl. ¶ 5.) American International Group, Inc. ("AIG"), Prudential Financial Inc., and the GE Capital Unit of General Electric have confirmed that they are among the designated companies. (See *id.* ¶ 6; *id.*, Ex. 4.) AIG and GE Capital have chosen not to contest their designations, but Prudential has announced that it will appeal. See Danielle Douglas, *Prudential enters uncharted legal realm by appealing its regulatory label*, WASH. POST, July 3, 2013, at A14.

II. TITLE II: THE ORDERLY LIQUIDATION AUTHORITY ("OLA")

A. The Statutory Provision

Pursuant to the OLA of Title II, the Treasury Secretary may appoint the FDIC as receiver of failing "financial company."[9] The purpose of Title II of Dodd-Frank is "to provide the necessary authority to liquidate failing financial companies that pose a significant risk to the financial stability of the United States in a manner that mitigates such risk and minimizes moral hazard." 12 U.S.C. § 5384(a). Title II is viewed as providing "the U.S. government a viable alternative to the undesirable choice it faced during the financial crisis between bankruptcy of a large, complex financial company that would disrupt markets and damage the economy, and bailout of such financial company that would expose taxpayers to losses and undermine market discipline." S. Rep. No. 111–176, at 4. The statute provides that this authority

> shall be exercised in the manner that best fulfills such purpose, so that creditors and shareholders will bear the losses of the financial company; management responsible for the condition of the financial company will not be retained; and the [FDIC] and other appropriate agencies will take all steps necessary and appropriate to assure that all parties . . . having responsibility for the condition of the financial company bear losses consistent with their responsibility, including actions for damages, restitution, and recoupment of compensation and other gains not compatible with such responsibility.

12 U.S.C. § 5384(a).

The OLA replaces, in limited instances, the liquidation and reorganization mechanisms of Chapters 7 and 11 of the Bankruptcy Code. (See State Plaintiffs' Opposition to Defendants' Motion to Dismiss [ECF No. 28] ("States' Opp.") at 5.) Traditionally, bankruptcy proceedings begin

---

[9] "Financial company" is defined under Title II as any company that is a bank holding company, a "nonbank financial company supervised by the Board of Governors," a "company predominately engaged in activities that the Board of Governors has determined are financial in nature", or any subsidiary of any of the above, except not insured depository institutions or insurance companies. 12 U.S.C. § 5381(a)(11). Title II also exempts from coverage insured depository institutions, see *id.* § 5381(a)(8), for which the FDIC already had authority to serve as receiver under the Federal Deposit Insurance Act. See *id.* § 1821.

with the filing of a petition by either the debtor company or the company's creditors in federal bankruptcy court. (See *id.* (citing 11 U.S.C. §§ 301, 303).) A trustee elected by the creditors' committee and the United States trustee act, under court supervision, to ensure that creditors' rights are protected. (See *id.* (citing 11 U.S.C. §§ 307, 341, 702, 704, 705, 1102, 1104, 1106, 1129).) Central to this dispute is the principle under bankruptcy law that "similarly situated creditors are entitled to equal treatment [in the form of] the pro rata payment on their claims." (See *id.* at 6 (citing 11 U.S.C. §§ 726(b), 1123(a)(4)).) The "automatic stay" provided by bankruptcy proceedings "reinforces that right, by preventing individual creditors and other stakeholders from seeking preferential treatment from the company." (See *id.* (citing 11 U.S.C. § 362).)

"There is a strong presumption that the bankruptcy process will continue to be used to close and unwind failing financial companies, including large, complex ones," as the "orderly liquidation authority could be used if and only if the failure of the financial company would threaten U.S. financial stability." S. Rep. No. 111–176, at 4. "Therefore the threshold for triggering the [O]rderly [L]iquidation [A]uthority is very high." *Id.* In order to activate the OLA, two-thirds of the Federal Reserve Board and two-thirds of the FDIC Board provide a written recommendation to the Treasury Secretary. See 12 U.S.C. § 5383(a). The recommendation must include an evaluation of eight statutory factors: [1] "whether the financial company is in default or in danger of default"; [2] "the effect that the default . . . would have on financial stability in the United States"; [3] "the effect that the default . . . would have on economic conditions or financial stability for low income, minority, or underserved communities"; [4] "the nature and extent of actions to be taken"; [5] "the likelihood of a private sector alternative to prevent the default"; [6] "why a case under the Bankruptcy Code is not appropriate"; [7] "the effects on creditors, counterparties, and shareholders of the financial company and other market participants"; and [8] "whether the company satisfies the definition of a financial company" under the statute. *Id.*

Before the Treasury Secretary can authorize use of the OLA, he must make seven findings: [1] that the company is "in default or in danger of default"; [2] that "the failure of the financial company . . . would have serious adverse effects on financial stability in the United States"; [3] that "no viable private sector alternative is available to prevent the default"; [4] that "any effect on the claims or interests of creditors, counterparties, and shareholders of the financial company and other market participants . . . is appropriate"; [5] that "any action taken [under this authority] would avoid or mitigate such adverse effects"; [6] that "a Federal regulatory agency has ordered the financial company to convert all of its convertible debt instruments that are subject to the regulatory order"; and [7] that "the

company satisfies the definition of a financial company" under the statute.
Id. § 5383(b).

If the financial company "does not acquiesce or consent to the appointment of the [FDIC] as receiver, the Secretary shall petition the United States District Court for the District of Columbia for an order authorizing the Secretary to appoint the [FDIC] as receiver." *Id.* § 5382(a)(1). The Secretary's petition is filed under seal. See *id.* The Court "[o]n a strictly confidential basis, and without any prior public disclosure . . . after notice to the covered financial company and a hearing in which the company may oppose the petition, shall determine whether the determination of the Secretary that the covered financial company is in default or in danger of default and satisfies the definition of a financial company under section 5381(a)(11) is arbitrary and capricious." *Id.* § 5382(a)(1)(A)(iii). The Secretary's other findings are not subject to review. See *id.* Additionally, the Act establishes criminal penalties for any "person who recklessly discloses" the Secretary's determination or petition, or the pendency of court proceedings. See *id.* § 5382(a)(1)(C).

A court must make a decision within twenty-four hours of receiving the Secretary's petition; if it does not, the government wins by default. See *id.* § 5382(a)(1)(A)(v). The Court of Appeals reviews the district court's determination under the arbitrary and capricious standard. See *id.* § 5382(a)(2). Once the district court affirms the Secretary's determination, or fails to issue a decision within 24 hours, the Secretary may begin the liquidation by appointing the FDIC as receiver, and the liquidation "shall not be subject to any stay or injunction pending appeal." *Id.* § 5382(a)(1)(A)(v), (B). This judicial review process does not include creditors. (See States' Opp. at 9–10.)

After the FDIC is appointed as receiver, it "succeed[s] to . . . all rights, titles, powers, and privileges of the covered financial company and its assets, and of any stockholder, member, officer, or director[.]" 12 U.S.C. § 5390(a)(1)(A). Under Title II, the FDIC has a broad range of tools available to it. It may merge the company with another, sell its assets, transfer assets and claims to a "bridge financial company" owned and controlled by the FDIC, and repudiate "burdensome" contracts or leases. See *id.* § 5390(a)(1)(G), (h)(1)(A), (c)(1).

Once appointed as receiver, the FDIC must provide notice to the failing company's creditors. See *id.* § 5390(a)(2)(B). Those creditors may file claims, which the FDIC as receiver may pay "in its discretion" and "to the extent that funds are available." *Id.* § 5390(a)(7). The FDIC is required to treat all similarly situated creditors in a similar manner unless it determines that differential treatment is "necessary to maximize the value of the assets of the covered financial company; to initiate and continue operations essential to the implementation of the receivership of any bridge financial company; to maximize the present value return from the sale or other disposition of the assets of the . . . company; or to minimize the amount of any loss realized upon the sale or other disposition of the assets of the covered financial company." *Id.* § 5390(b)(4). "A creditor shall, in no event, receive less than the amount" that it would have received if the FDIC "had not been appointed receiver" and the company instead "had been liquidated under chapter 7 of the Bankruptcy Code." *Id.* § 5390(a)(7)(B), (d)(2). A creditor may seek judicial review on any disallowed claim in federal district court. See *id.* § 5390(a)(4). To date, the OLA has not been invoked. (See Def. Mot. at 14 (citing GAO, "Agencies Continue Rulemakings for Clarifying Specific Provisions of Orderly Liquidation Authority," at 2 (July 2012), at http://www.gao.gov/assets/600/ 592318.pdf).)

[The court grants defendants' motion to dismiss concluding that plaintiffs lack standing since they are unable to demonstrate concrete or actual injury "necessary to establish Article III standing." *Id.* at 25]

* * *

With sixteen titles and almost 900 pages long, the Dodd-Frank Act constitutes landmark financial reform legislation, representing one of the most profound restructuring of U.S. financial regulation since the Great Depression. Significantly, the Dodd-Frank Act also provides broad and substantial delegations to various U.S. federal regulatory agencies the task of implementing its many provisions through regulation. Hundreds of new federal regulations, studies and reports addressing all of the major areas of the new law were required, ensuring that federal rules and policies in this area will be developing for years to come. Suffice to say, the Dodd-Frank Act will continue to have broad impact on the financial services industry.

NOTES

1.   The Dodd-Frank Act is composed of a series of new laws that, in the aggregate, is breathtaking in its scope. In addition to the FSOC and OLA provisions discussed in the *Big Spring* case, the Dodd-Frank Act, among other things, 1) created the Consumer Financial Protection Bureau ("CFPB"), a new federal independent consumer watchdog agency housed within the Federal Reserve Board ("Board"), 4) restructured and consolidated the federal regulatory supervision of banks and their parent companies, 5) adopted new federal oversight of the U.S. insurance industry, 6) adopts new standards and rules for the mortgage industry, 7) adopted new bank and holding company regulation, 8) adopted new federal regulation of the derivatives market, 9) adopted the so-called Volcker Rule, substantially restricting proprietary trading by depository institutions and their holding companies, 10) imposed requirements for "funeral plans" by large, complex financial companies, 11) established new regulation of the securitization market through "skin in the

game" rules and enhanced disclosure requirements, 12) established new regulation of debit card interchange fees, 13) established new and enhanced compensation and corporate governance oversight for the U.S. financial services industry, 14) provided enhanced oversight of municipal securities, 15) provided a specific framework for payment, clearing and settlement regulation, 16) adopted new federal hedge fund regulation, 17) adopted new fiduciary duties and regulation of broker dealers, investment companies and investment advisors, 18) tasked the federal banking agencies with adopting new and enhanced capital standards for all depository institutions, and 19) significantly narrowed the scope of federal preemption of state consumer financial laws.

Some of its major provisions are summarized as follows:

Section 604—Enhanced Board Consolidated Supervision Authority

A common theme of the Dodd-Frank Act is to provide federal regulators with information to monitor and understand the various risks inherent in the financial system so as to permit the regulators to control such risks. Prior to the Dodd-Frank Act, federal regulators only had direct supervisory powers over depository institutions, their holding companies, and certain non-depository institution subsidiaries of the holding companies. Significant nonbank financial companies ("SNBFCs") generally were not subject to any form of federal supervision, although certain of their functionally-regulated subsidiaries might have been. This lack of federal supervision over SNBFCs created unique challenges in the fall of 2008 and is often cited as a reason for why the government was not able to intervene prior to the collapse of Lehman Brothers.

To address these inadequacies, the Dodd-Frank Act makes significant changes to such paradigm by empowering the Board under 604 to have supervisory and enforcement authority over all entities within a holding company structure including all functionally-regulated subsidiaries of such holding companies. Moreover, the Dodd-Frank Act sets forth a procedure for determining that certain companies are SNBFCs and authorizes the Board to supervise and regulate such entities.

Section 616—Regulations Regarding Capital Levels

Section 616 of the Dodd-Frank Act imposes capital requirements on all depository institutions and their holding companies with greater than $500 million in assets. Like bank capital, BHC capital requirements will be countercyclical, so that the amount of capital required to be maintained by a BHC "will increase in times of economic expansion and decrease in times of economic contraction, consistent with the safety and soundness of the company." Section 616(a)(2).

Section 616 of the Dodd-Frank Act also codifies the Board's long-standing "source of strength" doctrine in a new Section 38A of the BHC Act, requiring that any BHC that controls an insured depository institution must serve as a source of financial strength for its depository institution subsidiary. The phrase "source of financial strength" is defined in the statute as "the ability of a company that directly or indirectly owns or controls an insured depository institution to provide financial assistance to such insured depository institution in the event of the financial distress of the insured depository institution." The Board is authorized, however, to adopt regulations further implementing this requirement. See Section 38A(d) of the BHC Act.

Section 606—New Requirements for BHCs to Engage in Financial Activities

Section 4(k) of the Bank Holding Company Act of 1956, as amended ("BHC Act") permits qualifying bank holding companies ("BHCs") to elect financial holding company status in order to engage in an expanded array of financial activities, such as securities underwriting and dealing, insurance underwriting and merchant banking.

Section 606 of the Dodd-Frank Act imposes additional requirements at the BHC level, requiring that BHCs (after July 2015) themselves be well capitalized and well managed in order to engage in nonbank financial activities. Noncompliance with these provisions would trigger remedial restrictions, including limitations on the commencement of new financial activities, restrictions on acquisitions of new subsidiaries engaged in Section 4(k) activities and potential divestiture of either non-banking activities or the depository institution subsidiaries of a BHC.

Section 626—Intermediate Holding Companies

To avoid potential overreach in supervision of non-financial activities, Section 626 of the Dodd-Frank Act permits SNBFCs to form intermediate holding companies ("IHCs"), through which financial activities can be conducted. Generally, only this will be subject to Board supervision. Large foreign banking organizations will also be subject to IHC requirements in the U.S. See Chapter 7, *infra*.

Section 622—Concentration Limits on Large Financial Firms

Consistent with a theme of the Dodd-Frank Act that no institution should be deemed "too big to fail," Section 622 of the Dodd-Frank Act seeks to limit the size of any one banking organization or nonbank financial company. Specifically, in the context of a merger or acquisition, the Board is now prohibited under Section 14 of the BHC Act from approving a transaction involving a financial company (which includes insured depository institutions and holding companies), if the total consolidated liabilities of the resulting financial company would exceed 10% of the aggregated consolidated liabilities of all financial companies as of the end of the preceding calendar year, subject to certain supervisory exceptions or *de minimis* increases. See Section 14(b) of the BHC Act.

Moreover, the Dodd-Frank Act expands the current 10% nationwide deposit concentration limit on certain interstate mergers and acquisitions to include all types of depository institutions, rather than only banks. Section 14(a)(2)

Section 619—Limits on Proprietary Trading—the Volcker Rule

Through the so-called Volcker Rule, Section 619 of the Dodd-Frank Act amends Section 13 of the BHC Act by generally prohibiting a "banking entity" from: (A) engaging in proprietary trading; and (B) investing in or sponsoring a private equity or hedge fund. The term "banking entity" covers insured depository institutions, their holding companies, and any company that is treated as a BHC under Section 8 of the International Banking Act of 1978, and any affiliate or subsidiary of any such entity. SNBFCs engaging in such generally prohibited activities for banking entities will be subject to additional capital requirements and qualitative limits for such activities.[3]

For foreign-based banking entities that engage in proprietary trading outside of the U.S., exceptions are provided for such activities that are conducted under Sections 4(c)(9) or 4(c)(13) of the BHC Act, subject to restrictions that the trading occurs solely outside of the U.S. and that the banking entity is not directly or indirectly controlled by a banking entity that is organized under U.S. law. Investing in or sponsoring a private equity or hedge fund is similarly permitted for activities conducted under the same provisions of the BHC Act, provided that such investment or sponsorship takes place solely outside of the U.S., and that no ownership interest in such hedge fund or private equity fund is offered for sale or sold to a U.S. resident, and that the banking entity is not directly or indirectly controlled by a banking entity that is organized under U.S. law.[4]

All permitted activities are subject to applicable federal or state laws, any restrictions or limitations that may be imposed by the applicable regulator (including capital and quantitative limitations as well as diversification requirements), and must not: (i) present a material conflict of interest between

---

[3] Exceptions to the general prohibition on proprietary trading are provided for certain permitted activities that include:

purchasing, selling, acquiring or disposing of U.S. government or agency securities, including obligations or instruments issued by Fannie Mae, Freddie Mac, Ginnie Mae and the Federal Home Loan Banks, and state, municipal and other political subdivision obligations;

purchasing, selling, acquiring or disposing of securities in connection with underwriting or market-making type activities, but only to the extent reasonably expected to fulfill near term customer demand;

risk-mitigating hedging transactions designed to reduce specific risks to the banking entity in connection with holding such positions; and

engaging in such other activities the regulators (federal banking agencies, SEC or CFTC, as appropriate) determine, by rule, would promote/protect the safety and soundness of the banking entity and U.S. financial stability.

[4] With respect to the general prohibition on investing in a hedge fund or private equity fund, exceptions are provided for: "seed" investments, whereby a banking entity may make and retain an investment in a hedge fund or private equity fund that the banking entity organizes or offers for the purpose of establishing the fund and providing the fund with sufficient initial equity for investment to permit the fund the attract unaffiliated investors; and *de minimis* investments.

In each case, the banking entity's investment must: (i) be reduced to less than 3% of fund ownership within 1 year after the fund is established (which may be extended an additional 2 years); (ii) must be "immaterial" (to be defined by rulemaking) to the banking entity; and (iii) the aggregate of the banking entity's investments in all such funds may not exceed 3% of the banking entity's Tier 1 capital. See Section 13(d)(4) of the BHC Act.

the banking entity and its clients, customers or counterparties; (ii) result in a material exposure by the banking entity to high-risk assets or high-risk trading strategies (as such terms will be defined by rulemaking); or (iii) pose a threat to the safety and soundness of the banking entity or the financial stability of the U.S. See Section 13(d)(2) of the BHC Act.

An important aspect of the Volcker Rule is its "anti-evasion" authority, which requires the appropriate regulators to include in their implementing regulations internal controls and recordkeeping requirements to insure compliance with the rule. See Section 13(e) of the BHC Act. Further, the regulators are authorized to require termination of activities and investments of a banking entity, subject to due notice and an opportunity for a hearing, that are not in compliance with, or that the appropriate regulator determines is an evasion of, the requirements of the Volcker Rule. *Id.* at Section 13(e)(2).

Section 165—Enhanced Prudential Regulation of SIFIs

Companies that have $50 billion or more in assets and that are, or are designated by the FSOC as SIFIs, will be subjected to enhanced supervision and prudential requirements to be administered by the Board. Under Section 165, the Board has independent authority to establish enhanced supervision and prudential standards (which may also be recommended by the FSOC) for SIFIs.

The standards and requirements recommended by the FSOC or undertaken independently by the Board for SIFIs will be more stringent that those applicable to other BHCs and nonbank financial companies that do not present similar risks to the financial stability of the U.S., and may increase in stringency based on consideration of statutory factors.[5]

---

[5] The Board is required to establish the following prudential standards for SIFIs:

(a) Risk-based capital requirements, unless the FRB, in consultation with the FSOC, determines that such requirements are not appropriate for the particular company, in which case the FRB will apply other standards that result in similarly stringent risk controls;

(b) Leverage limits, unless the FRB, in consultation with the FSOC, determines that such requirements are not appropriate for the particular company, in which case the FRB will apply other standards that result in similarly stringent risk controls;

(c) Liquidity requirements;

(d) Overall risk management requirements;

(e) Resolution plan and credit exposure report requirements; and

(f) Concentration limits.

See Section 165(b).

The Board is empowered, but not required, to establish the following additional prudential standards for large BHCs and SNBFCs:

(i)   A contingent capital requirement (subject to a FSOC study), under which the FRB may require a BHC or SNBFC to maintain a minimum amount of contingent capital that is convertible to equity in times of financial stress;

(ii) Enhanced public disclosures;

(iii) Short-term debt limits; and

(iv) Such other prudential standards as the FRB, on its own or pursuant to a recommendation made by the FSOC, determines to be appropriate.

Before applying the prudential standards to a foreign-based SIFI or SNBFC, the Board (or the FSOC in making a recommendation) is directed to give due regard to the principle of national treatment and equality of competitive opportunity, and take into account the extent to which the foreign-based SIFI or SNBFC is subject on a consolidated basis to home country standards that are comparable to those applied to financial companies in the U.S. Section 165(b)(2)(A)-B.

SIFIs and SNBFCs are also be subject to enhanced reporting requirements which include:

(i) The periodic submission of a resolution plan (commonly known as a "funeral plan" or "living will") to the FSOC, Board and the FDIC, which details the company's plan for "rapid and orderly resolution in the event of material financial distress or failure;"[6]

(ii) Periodic reports to be submitted to the FSOC, Board and the FDIC concerning the nature and extent to which the company has credit exposure to other SNBFCs and "significant" BHCs, and the nature and extent to which other SNBFCs and "significant" BHCs have credit exposure to that company.

BHCs with at least $10 billion in assets but less than $50 billion, while not subject to the same prudential standards and enhanced supervision as SIFIs and SNBFCs, are also on the Board's radar screen and are subject to enhanced requirements by virtue of their asset size.[7]

In addition to the OLA powers, if the Board determines that a SIFI poses a "grave threat to the financial stability" of the U.S., the Board Is empowered, upon an affirmative vote of at least 2/3 of the voting members of the FSOC then serving, to limit the ability of the company to merge with, acquire, consolidate with, or otherwise become affiliated with another company, and otherwise limit its activities.[8]

These limitations may also be applied to foreign SIFIs, provided that any regulations give due regard to the principle of national treatment and equality of competitive opportunity, and take into account the extent to which the

---

Id.

[6] The resolution plan will bo subject to review and determination by the Board and FDIC with respect to whether the plan is "credible" and whether it would facilitate an orderly resolution of the company pursuant to the U.S. bankruptcy laws. If deficiencies in the plan are cited, and a large BHC or SIMBFC fails to resubmit a credible plan as required, the BHC or SNBFC may be subject to more stringent capital, leverage, or liquidity requirements, or restrictions on the growth, activities, or operations of the company, or any subsidiary thereof, until such time as the company resubmits a plan that remedies the deficiencies. Section 165(d).

[7] For example, the Board is required to issue regulations requiring each BHC with at least $10 billion in total consolidated assets that is a publicly traded company to establish a risk committee that, in addition to meeting certain requirements with respect to the committee's composition, will be responsible for the oversight of the enterprise-wide risk management practices of the BHC. The Board has discretion with respect to whether to also impose the requirement for a risk committee on publicly traded BHCs with less than $10 billion in assets. Additionally, all financial companies that are regulated by a primary federal financial regulatory agency with total consolidated assets of $10 billion or more conduct self-administered annual stress tests, subject to parameters set forth by regulations. Section 165(i).

[8] *Id.*

foreign SIFI is subject on a consolidated basis to home country standards that are comparable to those applied to U.S. financial companies.[9]

Section 1075—Durbin Interchange Fees

Under the so-called Durbin Amendment, Section 1075 of the Dodd-Frank Act, effective July 21, 2011, a new Section 920 was added to the Electronic Fund Transfer Act, 15 U.S.C. § 1693 et seq; regarding interchange transaction fees and rules for payment card transactions. Section 920(a)(3) requires the Board to establish rules regarding interchange fees charged by payment card issuers for electronic debit transactions and regarding implementation of a new statutory requirement that such fees be reasonable and proportional to the actual cost of a transaction to the issuer, with specific allowances for the costs of fraud prevention. It also restricts the ability of payment card networks to attempt to limit the ability of any person to offer discounts or incentives for the use of a competing network or an alternative form of payment and requires the Board to issue rules barring issuers or payment card networks from placing certain restrictions on the number of payment card networks over which an electronic debit transaction may be processed or inhibiting the ability of a person which accepts debit cards from directing the routing of electronic debit transactions. Section 920(b) There are statutory exemptions to the interchange fee limits for issuers with assets of less than $10 billion and for fees for transactions involving government-issued debit or prepaid cards. Section 920(a)(6).

On June 30, 2011, the Board issued a final rule, 12 CFR Part 235, Regulation II, to implement both Section 920(a) and Section 920(b) effective October 1, 2011. See 76 Fed. Reg. 139 (July 20, 2011). The final rule establishes among other things, standards for assessing whether debit card interchange fees received by debit card issuers are reasonable and proportional to the costs incurred by issuers for electronic debit transactions.[10]

Title X—The CFPB

Title X of the Dodd-Frank Act, entitled the "Consumer Financial Protection Act of 2010" (the "CFPA"), created the CFPB, which is nominally housed within the Board but functions as an autonomous agency. The CFPB is responsible for most of the consumer financial services regulatory authority previously administered by the federal banking regulators and other agencies. The CFPB's primary functions include the supervision of "covered persons" for compliance with "federal consumer financial law" and the promulgation of regulations implementing those laws. The CFPB has broad authority to issue rules to implement, and to enforce, the federal consumer financial laws. The Act includes several specific grants of authority to the CFPB relating to particular consumer protections. The CFPB also has the power to prohibit the marketing, sale or enforcement of the terms of a consumer financial product

[9] *Id.*
[10] *Id.*

that does not conform to the CFPB's rules on unfair, abusive or deceptive acts and practices.

Section 1044—Limits on Preemption of State Consumer Laws

Section 1044 of Title X sets forth new preemption standards for national banks that will have far reaching implications. Specifically, rather than being able to draw from the range of U.S. Supreme Court precedent finding that state laws do not apply to national banks where they impermissibly impair or otherwise restrict a bank's exercise of a federally authorized power, under the preemption standard prescribed by the Act, preemption of a state consumer financial law is permissible only if: (1) application of the state law would have a discriminatory effect on national banks as compared to state banks; (2) the state law is preempted under the standard articulated in by the U.S. Supreme Court in Barnett Bank of Marion County v. Nelson, 517 U.S. 25 (1996), with such preemption determination being made either by the OCC (by regulation or order) or by a court, in either case on a "case-by-case" basis; or (3) the state law is preempted by another provision of federal law other than the Act.

Section 1044 also specifies that, with respect to preemption determinations made by the OCC on a case-by-case by regulation or order, such determination must be limited to a particular state law, as it impacts any national bank that is subject to that law, or the law of any other state with "substantively equivalent" terms. The OCC is required to consult with the CFPB on any determination regarding whether a state law is "substantively equivalent" to a law that is the subject of an OCC preemption determination. In addition, OCC preemption determinations made based on the Barnett Bank standard would not be valid unless the record supporting the determination includes "substantial evidence" that preemption is consistent with that standard.

Section 941—Risk Retention Rules for Securitizers and Originators of Asset-Backed Securities

Title IX to the Dodd-Frank Act provides reforms to the asset-backed securitization process and calls for joint rulemaking by the OCC, Board, FDIC ("Federal banking agencies"), the Securities and Exchange Commission ("SEC"), the Secretary of HUD and the Federal Housing Finance Agency ("FHFA") that, among other things, will most significantly require "any securitizer to retain an economic interest in a portion of the credit risk for any residential mortgage asset that the securitizer, through the issuance of an asset-backed security, transfers, sells, or conveys to a third party." See Section 941(b) (amending Section 15G of the Securities Exchange Act of 1934, 15 U.S.C. § 78a et seg.). Where a securitizer purchases assets from an originator, the federal banking agencies and the SEC will have the discretion to allocate risk retention requirements between a securitizer and an originator.

Section 941 prescribes certain minimum guidelines and standards for the agencies in their tasked rulemaking. Most significantly, Section 941 imposes on the agencies a minimum standard—so-called "skin in the game" rules—to require by rulemaking, a securitizer to retain not less than 5% of the credit risk for any asset that is not a qualified residential mortgage that is transferred, sold, or conveyed through the issuance of an asset-backed security by the securitizer. *Id.*

Section 214—Prohibition on Taxpayer Funding of OLA Transactions

Consistent with the mantra leading up to the enactment of the Dodd-Frank Act of "no future government bailouts," Section 214 of the Dodd-Frank Act provides that no U.S. taxpayer funds may be used to prevent the liquidation of systemically significant financial institutions. All losses must be borne by creditors and shareholders and in the event the FDIC incurs a loss, such loss must be recouped by assessments on other financial companies. Section 214(a). Accordingly, the competitors of a failed SIFI or SNBFC could ultimately be on the hook for the resolution of their competitor.

Suffice to say, the foregoing is intended to be only a brief summary of the most significant of the major provisions of a massive law, subject, as noted, to hundreds of rulemakings designed to implement and clarify this seminal reform legislation. Furthermore, numerous provisions have been controversial within the financial services industry insofar as they constitute new and unprecedential regulation, with some being challenged in the courts. In addition to the Big Spring challenge to the Dodd-Frank Act FSOC and OLA provisions, there have also been challenges to the Durbin interchange fee rules; see NACS et al v. Board of Governors of the Federal Reserve System 746 F.3d 474 (D.C. Cir. March 21, 2014); cert denied, Docket No. 14–200 (January 20, 2015), (ruling in favor of the Board's interpretation of "fair and proportional" fees that banks may charge participating merchants on debit card transactions) (discussed below); Canning v. NLRB, 705 F.3d 490 (D.C. Cir. January 25, 2013) (challenging recess appointment to the NLRB where similar recess appointment authority used to appoint Richard Cordray as the first director of the CFPB), and MetLife, Inc. v. Financial Stability Oversight Council.), Civil Action Complaint No. 15–45 (D.D.C. January 13, 2015).

MetLife, a major U.S. insurance company that owned a national bank at the time the Dodd-Frank Act was passed in 2010, and thus, was a bank holding company, subsequently sold its banking operations and sought to deregister as a bank holding company. Notwithstanding its exit from the banking industry, the FSOC designated MetLife as a systemically important nonbank financial institution pursuant to its authority under 12 U.S.C. 5323(a)1(b)(1). The FSOC based its decision on, among other things, that, "[b]ecause MetLife, Inc. . . . is a significant participant in the U.S. economy and in financial markets" and "is interconnected to other financial firms through its insurance products and capital market activities," "material financial distress at MetLife could lead to an impairment of financial intermediation or of financial market activity function that would be sufficiently severe to inflict significant damage on the broader economy". See Basis for the Financial Stability Oversight Council's Final Determination Regarding MetLife, Inc. (December 18, 2014). MetLife filed a complaint in U.S. District Court challenging the FSOC's determination, alleging, among other things, that FSOC failed to comply with the statutory requirements and its own rules governing designation, and that, contrary to FSOC's conclusions, MetLife's life insurance business does not pose risks to the broader economy comparable to those of a large bank. See MetLife Complaint at 1–3. In so doing, MetLife undertook its challenge pursuant to Section 113 (h) of the Dodd-Frank Act, codified at 12 U.S.C. § 5323(h), which specifically provides for judicial challenges to a FSOC systemic risk determination regarding nonbank financial companies, provided such challenge is filed in U.S. District Court in either the judicial district in which the challenging party is located, or U.S. District Court for the District of Columbia, Id.

2.   The Dodd-Frank Act also provides for enhanced standards for prudential oversight of foreign banking organizations, discussed in Chapter 7.

3.   Under the so-called "Hotel California Provision," any company having total consolidated assets equal to or greater than $50 billion as of January 1, 2010 and that participated in the TARP will automatically be subject to regulation as a SNBFC even if the company ceases to remain a BHC by engaging in a "de-banking" transaction i.e., selling or otherwise transferring control over a despository institution. See Section 117(b). Accordingly, current SIFIs that received TARP will be prohibited from evading the enhanced prudential supervision requirements of the Dodd-Frank Act, including the Volcker Rule.

NACS v. BOARD OF GOVERNORS OF FEDERAL RESERVE SYSTEM

United States Court of Appeals
746 F.3d 474 (D.C. Cir 2014)

* * *

TATEL, CIRCUIT JUDGE.

Combining features of credit cards and checks, debit cards have become not just the most popular noncash payment method in the United States but also a source of substantial revenue for banks and companies like Visa and MasterCard that own and operate debit card networks. In 2009 alone, debit card holders used their cards 37.6 billion times, completing transactions worth over $1.4 trillion and yielding over $20 billion in fees for banks and networks. Concerned that these fees were excessive and that merchants, who pay the fees directly, and consumers, who pay a portion of the fees indirectly in the form of higher prices, lacked any ability to resist them, Congress included a provision in the Dodd-Frank financial reform act directing the Board of Governors of the Federal Reserve System to address this perceived market failure. In response, the Board issued regulations imposing a cap on the per-transaction fees banks receive and, in an effort to force networks to compete for merchants' business, requiring that at least two networks owned and operated by different companies be able to process transactions on each debit card. Merchant groups challenged the regulations, seeking lower fees and even more network competition. The district court granted summary judgment to the merchants, concluding that the rules violate the statute's plain language. We disagree. Applying traditional tools of statutory interpretation, we hold that the Board's rules generally rest on reasonable constructions of the statute, though we remand one minor issue—the Board's treatment of so-called transactions-monitoring costs—to the Board for further explanation.

I.

Understanding this case requires looking under the hood—or, more accurately, behind the teller's window—to see what really happens when customers use their debit cards. After providing some background about debit cards and the debit card marketplace, we outline Congress's effort to solve several perceived market failures, the Board's attempt to put Congress's directives into action, and the district court's rejection of the Board's approach.

A.

We start with the basics. For purposes of this case, the term "debit card" describes both traditional debit cards, which allow cardholders to deduct money directly from their bank accounts, and prepaid cards, which come loaded with a certain amount of money that cardholders can spend down and, in some cases, replenish. Debit card transactions are typically processed using what is often called a "four party system." The four parties are the cardholder who makes the purchase, the merchant who accepts the debit card payment, the cardholder's bank (called the "issuer" because it issues the debit card to the cardholder), and the merchant's bank (called the "acquirer" because it acquires funds from the cardholder and deposits those funds in the merchant's account). In addition, each debit transaction is processed on a particular debit card "network," often affiliated with MasterCard or Visa. The network transmits information between the cardholder/issuer side of the transaction and the merchant/acquirer side. Issuers activate certain networks on debit cards, and only activated networks can process transactions on those cards.

* * *

Along the way, and central to this case, the parties charge each other various fees. The issuer charges the acquirer an "interchange fee," sometimes called a "swipe fee," which compensates the issuer for its role in processing the transaction. The network charges both the issuer and the acquirer "network processing fees," otherwise known as "switch fees," which compensate the network for its role in processing the transaction. Finally, the acquirer charges the merchant a "merchant discount," the difference between the transaction's face value and the amount the acquirer actually credits the merchant's account. Because the merchant discount includes the full value of the interchange fee, the acquirer's portion of the network processing fee, other acquirer and network costs, and a markup, merchants end up paying most of the costs acquirers and issuers incur. Merchants in turn pass some of these costs along to consumers in the form of higher prices. In contrast to credit card fees, which generally represent a set percentage of the value of a transaction, debit card fees change little as price increases. Thus, a bookstore might pay the same fees to sell a $25 hardcover that Mercedes would pay to sell a $75,000 car.

* * *

Seeking to correct the market defects that were contributing to high and escalating fees, Congress passed the Durbin Amendment as part of the 2010 Dodd-Frank Wall Street Reform and Consumer Protection Act, Pub.L. No. 111–203, 124 Stat. 1376 (2010). The amendment, which modified the Electronic Funds Transfer Act (EFTA), Pub.L. No. 95–630, 92 Stat. 3641 (1978), [* * *] EFTA section 920(a), restricts the amount of the interchange fee. Specifically, it instructs the Board of Governors of the Federal Reserve System to promulgate regulations ensuring that "the amount of any interchange transaction fee . . . is reasonable and proportional to the cost incurred by the issuer with respect to the transaction." 15 U.S.C. § 1693o–2(a)(3)(A); see also *id.* § 1693o–2(a)(6)–(7)(A) (exempting debit cards issued by banks that, combined with all affiliates, have assets of less than $10 billion and debit cards affiliated with certain government payment programs from interchange fee regulations). To this end, section 920(a)(4)(B), in language the parties hotly debate, requires the Board to "distinguish between . . . the incremental cost incurred by an issuer for the role of the issuer in the authorization, clearance, or settlement of a particular debit transaction, which cost shall be considered . . ., [and] other costs incurred by an issuer which are not specific to a particular electronic debit transaction, which costs shall not be considered." *Id.* § 1693o–2(a)(4)(B)(i)–(ii). Like the parties, we shall refer to the costs of "authorization, clearance, and settlement" as "ACS costs." In addition, section 920(a) "allow[s] for an adjustment to the fee amount received or charged by an issuer" to compensate for "costs incurred by the issuer in preventing fraud in relation to electronic debit transactions involving that issuer," so long as the issuer "complies with the fraud-related standards established by the Board." *Id.* § 1693o–2(a)(5)(A).

* * *

In late 2010, the Board proposed rules to implement sections 920(a) and (b). As for section 920(a), the Board proposed allowing issuers to recover only "incremental" ACS costs and interpreted "incremental" ACS costs to mean costs that "vary with the number of transactions" an issuer processes over the course of a year. NPRM, 75 Fed. Reg. at 81,735. Issuers would thus be unable to recover "costs that are common to all debit card transactions and could never be attributed to any particular transaction (i.e., fixed costs), even if those costs are specific to debit card transactions as a whole." *Id.* at 81,736. The Board "recognize[d]" that this definition would "impose a burden on issuers by requiring issuers to segregate costs that vary with the number of transactions from those that are largely invariant to the number of transactions" and "that excluding fixed costs may prevent issuers from recovering through interchange fees some costs associated with debit card transactions." The Board nonetheless determined that other definitions of "incremental cost" "do not appropriately reflect the incremental cost of a particular transaction to which the statute refers." *Id.* at 81,735. Limiting the interchange fee to average variable ACS costs, the Board proposed allowing issuers to recover at most 12 cents per transaction—considerably less than the 44 cents issuers had previously received on average. *Id.* at 81,736–39.

After evaluating thousands of comments, the Board issued a Final Rule that almost doubled the proposed cap. The Board abandoned its proposal to define "incremental" ACS costs to mean average variable ACS costs, deciding instead not to define the term "incremental costs" at all. Debit Card Interchange Fees and Routing, Final Rule ("Final Rule"), 76 Fed.Reg. 43,394, 43,426–27 (July 20, 2011). Observing that "the requirement that one set of costs be considered and another set of costs be excluded suggests that Congress left to the implementing agency discretion to consider costs that fall into neither category to the extent necessary and appropriate to fulfill the purposes of the statute," the Board allowed issuers to recover all costs "other than prohibited costs." *Id.* Thus, in addition to average variable ACS costs, issuers could recover: (1) what the proposed rule had referred to as "fixed" ACS costs; (2) costs issuers incur as a result of transactions-monitoring to prevent fraud; (3) fraud losses, which are costs issuers incur as a result of settling fraudulent transactions; and (4) network processing fees. *Id.* at 43,429–31. The Board prohibited issuers from recovering other costs, such as corporate overhead and debit card production and delivery costs, that the Board determined were not incurred to process specific transactions. *Id.* at 43,427–29. Accounting for all permissible costs, the Board raised the interchange fee cap to 21 cents plus an ad valorem component of 5 basis points (.05 percent of a transaction's value) to compensate issuers for fraud losses. *Id.* at 43,404.

* * *

Upset that the Board had nearly doubled the interchange fee cap (as compared to the proposed rule) and had selected the less restrictive anti-exclusivity option, several merchant groups, including NACS, the organization formerly known as the National Association of Convenience Stores, filed suit in district court. The merchants argued that both rules violate the plain terms of the Durbin Amendment: the interchange fee cap because the statute allows issuers to recover only average variable ACS costs, not "fixed" ACS costs, transactions-monitoring costs, fraud losses, or network processing fees; and the anti-exclusivity rule because the statute requires that all merchants—even those who refuse to accept PIN debit—be able to route each debit transaction on multiple unaffiliated networks. Several financial services industry groups, which during rulemaking had urged the Board to set an even higher interchange fee cap and adopt an even less restrictive anti-exclusivity rule, participated as amici curiae in support of neither party.

The district court granted summary judgment to the merchants. The court began by observing that "[a]ccording to the Board, [the statute contains] ambiguity that the Board has discretion to resolve. How convenient." NACS v. Board of Governors of the Federal Reserve System, 958 F.Supp.2d 85, 101 (D.D.C.2013). Rejecting this view, the district court determined that the Durbin Amendment is "clear with regard to what costs the Board may consider in setting the interchange fee standard: Incremental ACS costs of individual transactions incurred by issuers may be considered. That's it!" Id. at 105. The district court thus concluded that the Board had erred in allowing issuers to recover "fixed" ACS costs, transactions-monitoring costs, fraud losses, and network processing fees. Id. at 105–09. The court also agreed with the merchants that section 920(b) unambiguously requires that all merchants be able to route every transaction on at least two unaffiliated networks. Id. at 109–14. The Board's final anti-exclusivity rule, the district court held, "not only fails to carry out Congress's intention; it effectively countermands it!" Id. at 112. Concluding that "the Board completely misunderstood the Durbin Amendment's statutory directive and interpreted the law in ways that were clearly foreclosed by Congress," the district court vacated and remanded both the interchange fee rule and the anti-exclusivity rule. Id. at 114. But because regulated parties had already "made extensive commitments" in reliance on the Board's rules, the district court stayed vacatur to provide the Board a short period of time in which to promulgate new rules consistent with the statute. Id. at 115. Subsequently, the district court granted a stay pending appeal.

The Board now appeals, arguing that both rules rest on reasonable constructions of ambiguous statutory language. Financial services amici, urging reversal but still ostensibly appearing in support of neither party, filed a brief and participated in oral argument—though we have considered only those arguments that at least one party has not disavowed. See Eldred v. Reno, 239 F.3d 372, 378 (D.C.Cir.2001) (noting that arguments "rejected by the actual parties to this case" are "not properly before us"); Eldred v. Ashcroft, 255 F.3d 849, 854 (D.C.Cir.2001) (Sentelle, J., dissenting from denial of rehearing en banc) ("Under the panel's holding, it is now the law of this circuit that amici are precluded both from raising new issues and from raising new arguments."). In a case like this, "in which the District Court reviewed an agency action under the [Administrative Procedures Act], we review the administrative action directly, according no particular deference to the judgment of the District Court." In re Polar Bear Endangered Species Act Listing and Section 4(d) Rule Litigation, 720 F.3d 354, 358 (D.C.Cir.2013) (internal quotation marks omitted). Because the Board has sole discretion to administer the Durbin Amendment, we apply the familiar two-step framework set forth in Chevron U.S.A. Inc. v. Natural Resources Defense Council, Inc., 467 U.S. 837, 104 S.Ct. 2778, 81 L.Ed.2d 694 (1984). At Chevron's first step, we consider whether, as the district court concluded, Congress has "directly spoken to the precise question at issue." *Id.* at 842, 104 S.Ct. 2778. If not, we proceed to Chevron's second step where we determine whether the Board's rules rest on "reasonable" interpretations of the Durbin Amendment. *Id.* at 844, 104 S.Ct. 2778.

Before addressing the parties' arguments, we think it worth emphasizing that Congress put the Board, the district court, and us in a real bind. Perhaps unsurprising given that the Durbin Amendment was crafted in conference committee at the eleventh hour, its language is confusing and its structure convoluted. But because neither agencies nor courts have authority to disregard the demands of even poorly drafted legislation, we must do our best to discern Congress's intent and to determine whether the Board's regulations are faithful to it.

[The Court of Appeals overruled the district court, and upheld the Board's authority to issue the regulations based on the Board's interpretation of Section 920(a).]

* * *

NOTES

1.   Note that the interchange fee rules (adopted under Section 920(a) of the EFTA) that were at issue in the *NACS v. Board of Governors* case govern regulation of *debit* card fees only. In contrast, the European Parliament recently voted to adopt a European Commission proposal to cap interchange fees on *both* credit and debit cards. See press release, Successful vote in European Parliament to cap interchange fees on credit and debit cards, European Commission (March 10, 2015).

2.   The Dodd-Frank Act continues to general controversy and debate, with Congressional criticism that the law either is not tough enough on Wall Street, or arguing for regulatory relief from various of its provisions. See, e.g., Congress Enacts Changes to Dodd-Frank: Potential for More Changes in 114th Congress, National Law Review (January 9, 2015) (As part of $1.1 trillion appropriations bill signed by President Obama on December 16, 2014 Congress passing the first changes to the Dodd-Frank Act: 1) partially repealing Section 716 of the Dodd-Frank Act requiring banks to wall off certain derivatives

sweep trading activities from its banking operations, and 2) clarifying capital requirements for SIFI insurance companies under Section 171(c)(1) by permitting insurance based—not bank—capital standards.)

5. LIABILITY IN THE WAKE OF THE CRISIS

U.S. v. BANK OF AMERICA CORP. ET AL.
CONSENT JUDGMENT
(U.S.D.C., DC April 4, 2012)

Whereas, Plaintiffs, the United States of America and [all 50 states and the District of Columbia] filed their complaint on March 12, 2012, alleging that Bank of America Corporation, Bank of America, N.A., BAC Home Loans Servicing, LP f/k/a Countrywide Home Loans Servicing, LP, Countrywide Home Loans Inc., Countrywide Financial Corporation, Countrywide Mortgage Ventures, LLC, and Countrywide Bank, FSB (collectively, for the sake of convenience only, "Defendant") violated, among other laws, the Unfair and Deceptive Acts and Practices laws of the Plaintiff States, the False Claims Act, the Financial Institutions Reform. Recovery, and Enforcement Act of 1989, the Servicemembers Civil Relief Act, and the Bankruptcy Code and Federal Rules of Bankruptcy Procedure;

* * *

NOW THEREFORE, without trial or adjudication of issue of fact or law, without this Consent Judgment constituting evidence against Defendant, and upon consent of Defendant, the Court finds that there is good and sufficient cause to enter this Consent Judgment, and that it is therefore ORDERED, ADJUDGED, AND DECREED:

* * *

II. SERVICING STANDARDS

1.   Bank of America, N.A. shall comply with the Servicing Standards, attached hereto as Exhibit A, in accordance with their terms and Section A of Exhibit E, attached hereto. [Attachment A set forth detailed servicing standards for mortgages]

III. FINANCIAL TERMS

2.   *Payment Settlement Amounts.* Bank of America Corporation and/or its affiliated entities shall pay or cause to be paid into an interest bearing escrow account to be established for this purpose the sum of $2,382,415,075, which sum shall be added to funds being paid by other institutions resolving claims in this litigation (which sum shall be known as the "Direct Payment Settlement Amount") and which sum shall be distributed in the manner and for the purposes specified in Exhibit B. Payment shall be made by electronic funds transfer no later than seven

days after the Effective Date of this Consent Judgment, pursuant to written instructions to be provided by the United States Department of Justice. After the required payment has been made, Defendant shall no longer have any property right, title, interest or other legal claim in any funds held in escrow. The interest bearing escrow account established by this Paragraph 3 is intended to be a Qualified Settlement Fund within the meaning of Treasury Regulation Section 1.468B–1 of the U.S. Internal Revenue Code of 1986, as amended. The Monitoring Committee established in Paragraph 8 shall, in its sole discretion, appoint an escrow agent ("Escrow Agent") who shall hold and distribute funds as provided herein. All costs and expenses of the Escrow Agent, including taxes, if any, shall be paid from the funds under its control, including any interest earned on the funds.

3. *Payments to Foreclosed Borrowers.* In accordance with written instructions from the State members of the Monitoring Committee, for the purposes set forth in Exhibit C, the Escrow Agent shall transfer from the escrow account to the Administrator appointed under Exhibit C $1,489,813,925.00 (the "Borrower Payment Amount") to enable the Administrator to provide cash payments to borrowers whose homes were finally sold or taken in foreclosure between and including January 1, 2008 and December 31, 2011; who submit claims for harm allegedly arising from the Covered Conduct (as that term is defined in Exhibit G hereto); and who otherwise meet criteria set forth by the State members of the Monitoring Committee. The Borrower Payment Amount and any other funds provided to the Administrator for these purposes shall be administered in accordance with the terms set forth in Exhibit C.

4. *Consumer Relief.* Defendant shall provide $7,626,200,000 of relief to consumers who meet the eligibility criteria in the forms and amounts described in Paragraphs 1–8 of Exhibit D, and $948,000,000 of refinancing relief to consumers who meet the eligibility criteria in the forms and amounts described in Paragraph 9 of Exhibit D, to remediate harms allegedly caused by the alleged unlawful conduct of Defendant. Defendant shall receive credit towards such obligation as described in Exhibit D.

* * *

DEPARTMENT OF JUSTICE

Office of Public Affairs

FOR IMMEDIATE RELEASE   Thursday, February 9, 2012

Federal Government and State Attorneys General Reach $25 Billion Agreement with Five Largest Mortgage Servicers to Address Mortgage Loan Servicing and Foreclosure Abuses

WASHINGTON—U.S. Attorney General Eric Holder, Department of Housing and Urban Development (HUD) Secretary Shaun Donovan, Iowa Attorney General Tom Miller and Colorado Attorney General John W. Suthers announced today that the federal government and 49 state attorneys general have reached a landmark $25 billion agreement with the nation's five largest mortgage servicers to address mortgage loan servicing and foreclosure abuses. The agreement provides substantial financial relief to homeowners and establishes significant new homeowner protections for the future.

The unprecedented joint agreement is the largest federal-state civil settlement ever obtained and is the result of extensive investigations by federal agencies, including the Department of Justice, HUD and the HUD Office of the Inspector General (HUD-OIG), and state attorneys general and state banking regulators across the country. The joint federal-state group entered into the agreement with the nation's five largest mortgage servicers: Bank of America Corporation, JPMorgan Chase & Co., Wells Fargo & Company, Citigroup Inc. and Ally Financial Inc. (formerly GMAC).

"This agreement—the largest joint federal-state settlement ever obtained—is the result of unprecedented coordination among enforcement agencies throughout the government," said Attorney General Holder. "It holds mortgage servicers accountable for abusive practices and requires them to commit more than $20 billion towards financial relief for consumers. As a result, struggling homeowners throughout the country will benefit from reduced principals and refinancing of their loans. The agreement also requires substantial changes in how servicers do business, which will help to ensure the abuses of the past are not repeated."

* * *

The joint federal-state agreement requires servicers to implement comprehensive new mortgage loan servicing standards and to commit $25 billion to resolve violations of state and federal law. These violations include servicers' use of "robo-signed" affidavits in foreclosure proceedings; deceptive practices in the offering of loan modifications; failures to offer non-foreclosure alternatives before foreclosing on borrowers with federally insured mortgages; and filing improper documentation in federal bankruptcy court.

Under the terms of the agreement, the servicers are required to collectively dedicate $20 billion toward various forms of financial relief to borrowers. At least $10 billion will go toward reducing the principal on loans for borrowers who, as of the date of the settlement, are either delinquent or at imminent risk of default and owe more on their mortgages than their homes are worth. At least $3 billion will go toward refinancing loans for borrowers who are current on their mortgages but who owe more on their mortgage than their homes are worth. Borrowers who meet basic criteria will be eligible for the refinancing, which will reduce interest rates for borrowers who are currently paying much higher rates or whose adjustable rate mortgages are due to soon rise to much higher rates. Up to $7 billion will go towards other forms of relief, including forbearance of principal for unemployed borrowers, anti-blight programs, short sales and transitional assistance, benefits for service members who are forced to sell their home at a loss as a result of a Permanent Change in Station order, and other programs. Because servicers will receive only partial credit for every dollar spent on some of the required activities, the settlement will provide direct benefits to borrowers in excess of $20 billion.

Mortgage servicers are required to fulfill these obligations within three years. To encourage servicers to provide relief quickly, there are incentives for relief provided within the first 12 months. Servicers must reach 75 percent of their targets within the first two years. Servicers that miss settlement targets and deadlines will be required to pay substantial additional cash amounts.

In addition to the $20 billion in financial relief for borrowers, the agreement requires the servicers to pay $5 billion in cash to the federal and state governments. $1.5 billion of this payment will be used to establish a Borrower Payment Fund to provide cash payments to borrowers whose homes were sold or taken in foreclosure between Jan. 1, 2008 and Dec. 31, 2011, and who meet other criteria. This program is separate from the restitution program currently being administered by federal banking regulators to compensate those who suffered direct financial harm as a result of wrongful servicer conduct. Borrowers will not release any claims in exchange for a payment. The remaining $3.5 billion of the $5 billion payment will go to state and federal governments to be used to repay public funds lost as a result of servicer misconduct and to fund housing counselors, legal aid and other similar public programs determined by the state attorneys general.

* * *

The joint federal-state agreement requires the mortgage servicers to implement unprecedented changes in how they service mortgage loans, handle foreclosures, and ensure the accuracy of information provided in federal bankruptcy court. The agreement requires new servicing standards which will prevent foreclosure abuses of the past, such as robo-signing, improper documentation and lost paperwork, and create dozens of new consumer protections. The new standards provide for strict oversight of foreclosure processing, including third-party vendors, and new requirements to undertake pre-filing reviews of certain documents filed in bankruptcy court.

The new servicing standards make foreclosure a last resort by requiring servicers to evaluate homeowners for other loss mitigation options first. In addition, banks will be restricted from foreclosing while the homeowner is being considered for a loan modification. The new standards also include procedures and timelines for reviewing loan modification applications and give homeowners the right to appeal denials. Servicers will also be required to create a single point of contact for borrowers seeking information about their loans and maintain adequate staff to handle calls.

The agreement will also provide enhanced protections for service members that go beyond those required by the Servicemembers Civil Relief Act (SCRA). In addition, the four servicers that had not previously resolved certain portions of potential SCRA liability have agreed to conduct a full review, overseen by the Justice Department's Civil Rights Division, to determine whether any servicemembers were foreclosed on in violation of SCRA since Jan. 1, 2006. The servicers have also agreed to conduct a thorough review, overseen by the Civil Rights Division, to determine whether any servicemember, from Jan. 1, 2008, to the present, was charged interest in excess of 6% on their mortgage, after a valid request to lower the interest rate, in violation of the SCRA. Servicers will be required to make payments to any servicemember who was a victim of a wrongful foreclosure or who was wrongfully charged a higher interest rate. This compensation for servicemembers is in addition to the $25 billion settlement amount.

* * *

The agreement resolves certain violations of civil law based on mortgage loan servicing activities. The agreement does not prevent state and federal authorities from pursuing criminal enforcement actions related to this or other conduct by the servicers. The agreement does not prevent the government from punishing wrongful securitization conduct that will be the focus of the new Residential Mortgage-Backed Securities Working Group. The United States also retains its full authority to recover losses and penalties caused to the federal government when a bank failed to satisfy underwriting standards on a government-insured or government-guaranteed loan. The agreement does not prevent any action by individual borrowers who wish to bring their own lawsuits. State attorneys general also preserved, among other things, all claims against the Mortgage

Electronic Registration Systems (MERS), and all claims brought by borrowers.

Investigations were conducted by the U.S. Trustee Program of the Department of Justice, HUD-OIG, HUD's FHA, state attorneys general offices and state banking regulators from throughout the country, the U.S. Attorney's Office for the Eastern District of New York, the U.S. Attorney's Office for the District of Colorado, the Justice Department's Civil Division, the U.S. Attorney's Office for the Western District of North Carolina, the U.S. Attorney's Office for the District of South Carolina, the U.S. Attorney's Office for the Southern District of New York, SIGTARP and FHFA-OIG. The Department of Treasury, the Federal Trade Commission, the Consumer Financial Protection Bureau, the Justice Department's Civil Rights Division, the Board of Governors of the Federal Reserve System, the Federal Deposit Insurance Corporation, the Office of the Comptroller of the Currency, the Department of Veterans Affairs and the U.S. Department of Agriculture made critical contributions.

* * *

DEPARTMENT OF JUSTICE

Office of Public Affairs

FOR IMMEDIATE RELEASE   Tuesday, February 3, 2015

Justice Department and State Partners Secure $1.375 Billion Settlement with S&P for Defrauding Investors in the Lead Up to the Financial Crisis

Attorney General Eric Holder announced today that the Department of Justice and 19 states and the District of Columbia have entered into a $1.375 billion settlement agreement with the rating agency Standard & Poor's Financial Services LLC, along with its parent corporation McGraw Hill Financial Inc., to resolve allegations that S&P had engaged in a scheme to defraud investors in structured financial products known as Residential Mortgage-Backed Securities (RMBS) and Collateralized Debt Obligations (CDOs). The agreement resolves the department's 2013 lawsuit against S&P, along with the suits of 19 states and the District of Columbia. Each of the lawsuits allege that investors incurred substantial losses on RMBS and CDOs for which S&P issued inflated ratings that misrepresented the securities' true credit risks. Other allegations assert that S&P falsely represented that its ratings were objective, independent and uninfluenced by S&P's business relationships with the investment banks that issued the securities.

The settlement announced today is comprised of several elements. In addition to the payment of $1.375 billion, S&P has acknowledged conduct associated with its ratings of RMBS and CDOs during 2004 to 2007 in an agreed statement of facts. It has further agreed to formally retract an allegation that the United States' lawsuit was filed in retaliation for the defendant's decisions with regard to the credit of the United States. Finally, S&P has agreed to comply with the consumer protection statutes of each of the settling states and the District of Columbia, and to respond, in good faith, to requests from any of the states and the District of Columbia for information or material concerning any possible violation of those laws.

* * *

Half of the $1.375 billion payment—or $687.5 million—constitutes a penalty to be paid to the federal government and is the largest penalty of its type ever paid by a ratings agency. The remaining $687.5 million will be divided among the 19 states and the District of Columbia. The allocation among the states and the District of Columbia reflects an agreement between the states on the distribution of that money.

In its agreed statement of facts, S&P admits that its decisions on its rating models were affected by business concerns, and that, with an eye to business concerns, S&P maintained and continued to issue positive ratings on securities despite a growing awareness of quality problems with those securities. S&P acknowledges that:

- S&P promised investors at all relevant times that its ratings must be independent and objective and must not be affected by any existing or potential business relationship;

- S&P executives have admitted, despite its representations, that decisions about the testing and rollout of updates to S&P's model for rating CDOs were made, at least in part, based on the effect that any update would have on S&P's business relationship with issuers;

- Relevant people within S&P knew in 2007 many loans in RMBS transactions S&P were rating were delinquent and that losses were probable;

- S&P representatives continued to issue and confirm positive ratings without adjustments to reflect the negative rating actions that it expected would come.

* * *

"S&P played a central role in the crisis that devastated our economy by giving AAA ratings to mortgage-backed securities that turned out to be little better than junk," said Acting U.S. Attorney Yonekura. "Driven by a desire to increase profits and market share, S&P blessed innumerable securitizations that were used by aggressive lenders to offload the risks of billions of dollars in mortgage loans given to homeowners who had no ability to pay them off. This conduct fueled the meltdown that ultimately led to tens of thousands of foreclosures in my district alone. This historic settlement makes clear the consequences of putting corporate profits over honesty in the financial markets."

* * *

QUESTIONS AND NOTES

1.   Commentators continue to debate the merits of financial reform in the wake of the financial crisis. See Joe Nocera, Did Dodd Frank Work? New York Times (July 21, 2014) (did not end "too big to fail" banks); Mike Konczal, Does Dodd-Frank Work, Washington Post (July 20, 2013) (16 experts debate two questions regarding the Dodd Frank Act: 1) What has gone better than you had expected? 2) What has gone worst?); Ted Kaufman, Happy Birthday to Dodd-Frank, a Law that Isn't Working (July 21, 2013) (criticism of pressing reform issues left unaddressed by the Dodd-Frank Act on its third anniversary of passage); Stephanie Armour and Ryan Tracy, Fed Sets Rules for Foreign Banks, Wall Street Journal (February 18, 2014) (foreign banks criticize new capital, debt level and stress test rules).

Commentators have also debated the perceived failure of the government to more aggressively prosecute banks and their management in the wake of the financial crisis, See, e.g., Jed S. Rakoff, The Financial Crisis: Why Have No High-Level Executives Been Prosecuted, The New York Review of Books (January 9, 2014), while other see bank regulators as too tough in the wake of the crisis. See Richard Blackden, Are US regulators too tough on the UK?, the Telegraph (May 2, 2013).

2.   Note the materials covered in Chapter 5 on the Based Committee's work in establishing regulatory capital standards in Basel I, Basel II and Basel III.

3.   <u>Multiple Choice Questions</u>:

a.   The biggest policy concern(s) expressed about the Basel II capital standards in light of the global financial crisis are: a) concerns that banks have the primary role in assessing their operational and lending risk to determine appropriate capital levels; b) the unintended result that large complex banking organizations using sophisticated risk models would be able to justify lower capital levels than community banks; c) the elimination of Tier 1 capital requirements; or d) only a and b, above.

b.   The G20 Finance Ministers and Central Bank Governors ("G20") concluded in 2008 that the major root causes of the recent global financial crisis were caused by, among other things: a) market participants seeking higher yields without an adequate appreciation of the risks and failure to exercise due diligence; b) failure of the IMF to add new members; c) need for bank supervisors to periodically meet in different countries; d) failure to address the need for more cultural diversity in international bank supervision; or e) the Basel Committee's need to revisit its conclusions on the root causes of the Banco Ambrosiano failure.

c. The G20 recently concluded that one of the important ways to strengthen the international financial system is through enhanced financial regulation, including by the following means: a) financial regulation should amplify economic cycles; b) systematically important financial institutions, markets and instruments should be subject to an appropriate degree of regulation and oversight; c) stronger regulation should be mitigated by less macro-prudential oversight to enhance future economic cycles; or d) capital standards should remain unchanged once the global economy fully recovers.

d. In reaction to the global financial crisis, the G20 countries concluded that, with respect to proposed reforms that will strengthen regulatory regimes so as to avoid future crises, financial regulation is first and foremost the responsibility of regulators in each country, not international organizations. a) True or b) False.

CHAPTER 7

U.S. REGULATION OF FOREIGN BANKING ORGANIZATIONS

■ ■ ■

1. INTRODUCTION

This Chapter is designed to provide a basic understanding of the U.S. laws governing foreign banking organizations ("FBOs") operating in the U.S. The Chapter will primarily focus on the statutory, regulatory and policy standards governing FBOs operating in the U.S., including the regulatory oversight of the Federal Reserve Board ("FRB" or "Board"), which is, by law, the key U.S. regulatory player in U.S. foreign bank supervision. The Chapter will also introduce students to Regulation K, the Board's FBO regulations, and the issues that arise in complying with the standards set forth in those regulations.

There are a number of reasons for this Chapter. First, the U.S. has one of the largest concentrations of foreign banks operating within its borders. Further, the U.S., as a preeminent world economic power, has a large number of the world's major banking institutions headquartered in the U.S., all with substantial operations abroad. Finally, the U.S. is also a key member of the Basel Committee; thus, the study of U.S. foreign bank supervision should be viewed as an important case study in how a key Basel member implements the Basel consolidated supervision standards.

RANDALL D. GUYNN, MARK E. PLOTKIN, AND RALPH REISNER, REGULATION OF FOREIGN BANKS & AFFILIATES IN THE UNITED STATES[*]

(6th Edition, Westlaw 2012)

* * *

Over the past 35 years, foreign banks have grown from a small presence in the United States into a major component of the U.S. commercial banking market. Despite somewhat adverse changes in the U.S. regulatory climate for foreign banks—including a sustained increase in the degree of federal supervision to which they are subject—foreign

---

[*] Reprinted with permission from Regulation of Foreign Banks & Affiliates in the United States, 6th Edition. © 2012 Thomson Reuters.

banks have significantly increased their share of the U.S. banking market during this period.[1] The 1999 passage of the Gramm-Leach-Bliley Act (GLB Act)[2] removed a number of federal restrictions on nonbanking activities for both foreign and domestic banking organizations.

The legal framework applicable to foreign banks operating in the United States is in many ways the framework applicable to domestic banks.[3] This reflects the guiding principle of "national treatment," or parity of treatment between domestic and foreign banks, that has informed U.S. legislation affecting foreign banks since the International Banking Act of 1978 (IBA).[4] Although the IBA has been amended numerous times, it continues to provide the general legal framework under which foreign banks operate in the United States.[5]

Foreign banks conduct their U.S. operations through a variety of forms, including federal or state-licensed branches (the predominant form), agencies, commercial bank subsidiaries, commercial lending companies, and representative offices. The choice of form affects the foreign bank's regulatory treatment, its permissible scope of activities, its opportunities for geographic expansion within the U.S., and determines the identity of its regulators. Thus, the selection of an appropriate vehicle for U.S. banking is a crucial strategic decision for a foreign bank.

---

[1]   The share of total assets of U.S. offices of foreign banks rose from 3.8% in 1973 to 22.0% in 2011. Foreign banks achieved similar market-share increases in total loans, business loans, and total deposits. See Federal Reserve Board, Share Data for U.S. Offices of Foreign Banking Organizations (as of September 2011), available at (Board Share Data) [http://www.federalreserve.gov/releases/iba/default.htm]. *Board Share Data* is a report prepared by the Board and updated quarterly. It provides dollar volume and market-share information of the assets, loans, and deposits of all foreign bank offices in the United States and, separately, of those m New York and California. Unless otherwise indicated, citations are to the *Share Data Report* updated in September 2011. Likewise, unless otherwise indicated, citations to the Federal Reserve's quarterly *Structure Data Report* on the number and type of foreign bank operations in the U.S. (see discussion later in this section) are to the most recent version, which was published September 2011.

[2]   The Gramm-Leach-Bliley Act of 1999, Pub. L. No. 106–102, 113 Stat. 1338 (GLB Act).

[3]   As used in the IBA and this chapter, the term "foreign bank" means "any company organized under the laws of a foreign country . . . which engages in the business of banking." 12 U.S.C.A. § 3101(7).

[4]   The International Banking Act of 1978, Pub. L. No. 95–369, 92 Stat. 607 (codified at 12 U.S.C.A. §§ 3101 to 3108 and in scattered sections of 12 U.S.C.A.).

[5]   The IBA has been amended by: Act of Sept. 14, 1979, Pub. L. No. 96–64, S3 Stat. 412' the Garn-St. Germain Depository Institutions Act of 1982, Pub. L. No 97–320 §§ 704 to 705, 96 Stat, 1469, 1539 to 1640; the Competitive Equality Banking Act of 1987, Pub. L. No. 100–86, § 204, 101 Stat. 552, 584 (CEBA), the Foreign Bank Supervision Enhancement Act of 1991, tit. II, subtit. A of the Federal Deposit Insurance Corporation Improvement Act of 1991, Pub. L. No. 102–242, §§ 201 to 215, 105 Stat. 2286 223 to 305 (FBSEA), the Riegle-Neal Interstate Banking and Brandling Efficiency Act of 1994, Pub. L. No. 103–328, 108 Stat. 2338 (Riegle-Neal Act); and the Economic Growth and Regulatory Paperwork Reduction Act of 1996, div. A, tit. II of the Omnibus Consolidated Appropriations Act, 1997, Pub. L. No. 104–208, 110 Stat. 3009–499 (EGRPRA). The IBA was further amended by the Financial Services Regulatory Relief Act of 2006, Pub. L. No, 109–351, 120 Stat. 1966 § 709 and the Dodd-Frank Act.

* * *

At the time of the IBA's passage in 1978, there were 268 U.S. operations of foreign banks[6] with assets of $109.1 billion.[7] As of September 30, 2011, 316 operations of foreign banks controlled approximately $3.35 trillion in assets.[8] The table below shows the growth of foreign banks' U.S. operations since 1978 based on information from the Board of Governors of the Federal Reserve System (the Board). As the table demonstrates, while the number of U.S. operations has declined in recent years, the volume of assets, deposits, and loans controlled by U.S. offices of foreign banks has risen steadily since 1978.

Selected Assets and Liabilities of U.S. Offices of Foreign Banks[9]

(Figures are in billions of dollars, except Number of Operations)

Year (Year-End, Unless Noted)	Number of Operations*	Total Assets**	Business Loans	Total Loans
1978	268	$109.1	$32.7	$65.3
1983	557	328.8	84.5	192.4
1988	675	650.6	167.3	338.8
1993	704	855.7	195.6	379.6
1998	538	1,117.9	280.2	494.2
June 2002	396	1,373.2	252.8	492.3
June 2006	320	2,193.9	294.1	807.0
March 2008	318	2,754.3	391.6	985.7
December 2010	313	2,944.2	326.6	960.5
September 2011	316	3,398.7	363.9	1,598.7

[6] See International Banking Act of 1978: Hearings Before the Subcomm. on Financial Institutions of the Senate Comm. on Banking, Housing, and Urban Affairs, 95th Cong., 2d Sess. 46 (Table 22) (1978) (IBA Senate Hearings).

[7] Federal Reserve Board, Share Data for U.S. Offices of Foreign Banks (as of September 2002), available at http://www.federalreserve.gov/.

[8] Federal Reserve Board, Structure Data for U.S. Offices of Foreign Banks (as of September 30, 2011), available at http://www.federalreserve.gov/.

[9] Federal Reserve Board, Share Data for U.S. Offices of Foreign Banks (as of September 30, 2011), available at http://www.federalreserve.gov/.

* The Board's data cover foreign bank branches and agencies in 50 states and the District of Columbia, New York investment companies (through 1996), U.S. commercial banks that are more than 25% owned by foreign banks and International Banking Facilities. Representative offices and Edge Act corporations are excluded.

** Adjusted to exclude net claims on own foreign offices.

As a percentage of the entire U.S. banking market, the U.S. operations of foreign banks grew steadily from 1978 until the early 1990s, at which point they stabilized and then declined modestly. The table below shows the share of the entire U.S. banking market (including domestic and foreign-owned banking operations) attributable to U.S. operations of foreign banks.

Ratio of Foreign Banks' U.S. Operations to all Banks in the United States[11]

(Figures are in percentages)

Year (Year-End, Unless Noted)	Total Assets*	Business Loans	Total Loans
1978	8.0%	13.1%	8.8%
1983	14.6	18.3	15.6
1988	19.6	28.2	16.9
1993	21.2	33.8	17.0
1998	19.1	28.5	14.6
June 2002	19.6	25.6	12.4
June 2006	22.4	26.0	14.4
March 2008	23.7	27.2	15.0
December 2010	20.5	25.1	13.7
September 2011	22.0	25.7	14.9

As the table shows, foreign banks account for a significant share of the U.S. banking market, particularly with respect to commercial lending. Foreign banks historically have participated more in wholesale banking than retail banking in the U.S. Overall, however, foreign banks have become fully assimilated in virtually every area of U.S. banking. By all accounts, foreign banks have contributed to meeting the credit needs of the U.S. economy, financing foreign investment, maintaining the pace of financial innovation, and globalizing the U.S. banking markets.[13]

---

[11]   Federal Reserve Board, Share Data for U.S. Offices of Foreign Banks (as of September 2011), available at http://www.federalreserve.org.

*   Adjusted to exclude net claims on own foreign offices.

[13]   See, e.g., Institute of International Bankers, ECONOMIC BENEFITS TO THE UNITED STATES FROM THE ACTIVITIES OF INTERNATIONAL BANKS: FINANCIAL SERVICES IN A GLOBAL ECONOMY (1998); Foreign Banks—Assessing Their Role in the U.S. Banking System, (GAO/GGD-96-26) (Feb. 1996).

2. THE IBA AND FBSEA: THE STATUTORY FRAMEWORK

U.S. GENERAL ACCOUNTING OFFICE: FOREIGN BANKS
(February, 1996)

* * *

REGULATION OF FOREIGN BANK ACTIVITIES IN THE UNITED STATES AND THE CONCEPT OF NATIONAL TREATMENT

The [International Banking Act] IBA of 1978 stands as the landmark federal legislation affecting foreign bank operations in the United States. In passing the IBA, the United States adopted a policy of national treatment governing the activities of foreign banks. The goal of national treatment is to allow foreign banks to operate in the United States without incurring either significant advantage or disadvantage compared with U.S. banks. To implement this policy, the IBA brought U.S. branches and agencies of foreign banks under federal banking laws and regulations. The Federal Reserve [Board] was given regulatory authority for all U.S. international banking laws, which it administers through regulation K.

Before passage of the IBA, foreign branches and agencies operating in the United States enjoyed many regulatory advantages compared with U.S. banks. They were not subject to reserve requirements or deposit interest-rate ceilings, they could operate full-service branches in any state that allowed them to enter, and they could offer both commercial and investment banking services. The 1978 act was designed to eliminate these advantages and to place foreign banks on an equal footing with U.S. banks. The act required foreign banks to choose a home state and prohibited them from establishing full-service branches in states outside the home state. The IBA also limited foreign bank involvement in U.S. securities and other nonbanking markets by restricting them to those activities that could be done by U.S. bank holding companies (BHC).

The act also expanded the options of foreign banks. Prior to the IBA, only states could license foreign branches and agencies. Foreign banks were subject to the laws of the states in which they were licensed, and, in some cases, these laws were more restrictive than federal law for national banks. The act made federal licenses available to foreign banks. It also allowed foreign branches to obtain federal deposit insurance, requiring it for any branch with a significant amount of retail deposits. The act permitted foreign banks to establish Edge Act Corporations[13] and it

---

[13] Edge Act Corporations can engage in international transactions free of U.S. restrictions. U.S. banks can also establish these offices. [U.S. Edge Act Corporations are discussed below].

granted foreign branches and agencies access to the Federal Reserve's discount window.

Although the IBA eliminated many of the advantages that foreign branches and agencies had over U.S. banks, those foreign branches and agencies that were already engaged in interstate branching or securities activities were allowed to continue these activities under the grandfathering provisions of the act.[14] Restrictions, however, were applied to their growth. Foreign banks with interstate branches were only allowed to establish new full-service branches in their home state. They could not establish full-service branches in other states, even in those states where they were already located. Similarly, foreign banks with grandfathered securities activities were limited to those activities in which they were engaged (or had applied to engage) on the grandfather date. In addition, securities firms owned by foreign banks could only expand by internal growth—they were restricted from acquiring or merging with other securities firms or from expanding by hiring significant numbers of employees from other securities firms. Foreign banks that acquire U.S. banks lose their grandfathered securities rights.

With the exception of the grandfathered activities, the IBA and subsequent laws and regulations brought foreign banks under the same restrictions as those governing U.S. banks with some adaptations. The application of U.S. laws and regulations to foreign banks reflects the fact that structural and organizational differences exist between foreign and U.S. banks. For example, foreign banks are not generally organized under the holding company structure, as are most U.S. banks.

Because of these differences, subjecting foreign banks with branches and agencies in the United States to all U.S. laws and regulations without adaptation would likely violate the policy of national treatment. While this policy tries to ensure equal treatment of U.S. and foreign banks in the United States, it recognizes that equal treatment does not necessarily mean the same treatment. Similarly, the United States seeks to have the policy of national treatment applied to U.S. banks operating abroad.[16]

In 1991, Congress passed the Foreign Bank Supervision Enhancement Act (FBSEA). This act, which amended the IBA, authorized federal oversight of all foreign bank operations in the United States and vested this responsibility with the Federal Reserve. It also established uniform standards for all U.S. offices of foreign banks, generally requiring them to

---

[14]   The practice of grandfathering activities is not unique to legislation affecting foreign banks. For example, when the Bank Holding Company Act was passed in 1956, it allowed BHCs that were operating interstate banking networks to retain them. More than 60 foreign banks had interstate branches and were grandfathered under the act. In addition, 17 foreign banks claimed grandfather rights for their securities firms.

[16]   A study by the Department of the Treasury indicated that U.S. banks have not always received such treatment abroad.

meet financial, management, and operational standards equivalent to those required of U.S. banking organizations.[17] Finally, the act prohibited foreign branches from accepting retail deposits, although it grandfathered the branches that already offered insured deposits.

FBSEA increased the Federal Reserve's supervisory and regulatory power over foreign banks by (1) requiring Federal Reserve approval for all foreign banks seeking to establish U.S. offices, whether licensed by state or federal authorities, (2) permitting the Federal Reserve to terminate the activities of a state-licensed branch or agency, or to recommend that OCC terminate the license of a federally licensed branch or agency, and (3) clarifying and strengthening the Federal Reserve's authority to ensure that foreign bank operations in the United States are examined in a comprehensive and coordinated manner.

The act required the Federal Reserve to approve all applications for entry or expansion of foreign bank activities in the United States. The Federal Reserve may not approve such applications unless it determines that the applicant bank engages directly in banking outside the United States and is subject to comprehensive supervision on a consolidated basis by home country authorities.[18] In coordination with the OCC, FDIC, or the state bank regulator, the Federal Reserve was given authority to examine all records pertaining to the foreign bank's activities in the United States. The act required that branches and agencies be examined at least once a year. It gave the Federal Reserve the power to order a foreign bank that operates a state-licensed branch or agency in the United States to terminate its activities (1) if the Federal Reserve finds that the foreign bank is not subject to comprehensive consolidated supervision by its home country supervisor or (2) if it has reasonable cause to believe that the foreign bank or an affiliate has committed a violation of law or engaged in an unsafe or unsound banking practice in the United States. If the Federal Reserve finds these problems in a federally licensed branch or agency, it may transmit a recommendation to OCC for such action.

The Riegle-Neal Interstate Banking and Branching Efficiency Act of 1994 also amended the IBA and gave foreign banks the same interstate branching rights as U.S. banks were granted under the act. Under Riegle-Neal, foreign banks will be allowed to establish de novo full-service branches across state lines whenever U.S. banks are allowed to establish de novo branches across state lines. Riegle-Neal will also allow foreign

---

[17]   The act required the Federal Reserve to establish guidelines for converting data on the capital of foreign banks to the equivalent risk-based capital requirements for U.S. banks for purposes of determining whether a foreign bank's capital level is equivalent to that imposed on U.S. banks.

[18]   A bank is subject to comprehensive consolidated supervision if the supervisor in the bank's home country receives information on the bank's worldwide operations that the Federal Reserve considers sufficient to assess its overall financial condition and compliance with laws and regulations.

banks to expand across state lines by acquiring an existing bank or branch provided that the state also allows U.S. banks to expand in such a manner.

* * *

NOTES

1.   Interestingly enough, Section 613 of the Dodd-Frank Act repealed the Riegle-Neal Act restrictions on the ability of both U.S banks and foreign banks with branches in the U.S. to establish de novo branches across state lives. As such Section, 613 repealed the prior Riegle-Neal Act restrictions permitting de novo branching only if a state had elected to pass laws that "opted-in" to such branching. See 12 U.S.C. §§ 36(g)(1)A and 1828(d)(4)(A).

2.   Generally, U.S. branches of foreign banks cannot accept retail deposits (i.e. deposits with an initial amount of less than $250,000, or offer U.S. federal deposit insurance to depositors (other than certain grandfathered branches pursuant to FBSEA of 1991). Section 335 of The Dodd-Frank Act permanently raised the FDIC deposit insurance limits from $100,000 to $250,000. See FDIC Press Release, Basic FDIC Insurance Coverage Permanently Increased to $250,000 per Depositor (July 21, 2010) (there had been two prior temporary increases in 2008 and 2009—see Chapter 6.

3.   As the GAO report indicates, FBO branch offices, similar to U.S. banks, are subject to the Community Reinvestment Act ("CRA"), P.L. 95–128, 91 state 1147, adopted as title VIII of the Housing and Community Development Act of 1977, 12 USC § 2901. In response to perceived concerns about the practice of "redlining" certain lower income areas from any lending or other banking products and services, the CRA is designed to encourage banks to help meet the needs of borrowers in all segments of the communities banks serve, including low and moderate income neighborhoods, and to deter redlining practices in such areas. See Bernanke, Ben S., "The Community Reinvestment   Act: Its   Evolution   and   New   Challenges"   (http://www.federalreserve.gov/newsevents/speech/Bernanke20070330a.htm).
Prepared Speech by the Chairman of the Federal Reserve System before the Community Affairs Research Conference (March 30, 2007).

The CRA instructs the appropriate federal banking agencies ("AFBA") to encourage regulated financial institutions to help meet the credit needs of the local communities in which they are chartered, consistent with safe and sound operation (Section 802). See 12 CFR Part 25 et seq. (OCC); 12 CFR Parts 203 and 228 et seq. (Board); and 12 CFR Part 345 et seq. (FDIC) for the CRA regulations of each AFBA. To enforce the statute, federal regulatory agencies examine banking institutions for CRA compliance and take this information into consideration when approving applications for new bank branches or for mergers or acquisitions (Section 804).

4.   The FBSEA of 1991 was adopted in response to the BCCI failure and accompanying adverse publicity and political impact in the U.S. regarding BCCI's alleged covert ownership of First American Bank in Washington, D.C.

through Washington lawyer and former U.S. defense secretary Clark Clifford and his law partner Robert C. Altman, who were removed as officers and subsequently prosecuted. See Sara Fritz and James Bates, BCCI Maybe History's Biggest Bank Fraud Scandal, Los Angeles Times (July 11, 1991). The BCCI failure is more fully discussed in Chapter 5.

5. Edge Act and Agreement Corporations are generally financial institutions authorized under U.S. law to conduct business internationally. They can be a subsidiary of a U.S. bank, bank or financial holding company, or branches of foreign banks operating in the U.S.

The Edge Act, adopted in 1919 (sponsored by Senator Walter E. Edge of New Jersey) was originally designed to permit U.S. banks to conduct international banking and finance operations, including equity investment and other activities that were not permissible for U.S. banks and to authorize for the first time U.S. banking activities outside the U.S.

Edge corporations are authorized pursuant to Section 25A of the Federal Reserve Act, 12 U.S.C. § 611, and Regulation K. They may engage in a broad range of international banking and financial activities. 12 U.S.C. § 615.

Section 611 of the FRA authorizes the federal incorporation of financial institutions organized "for the purpose of engaging in international or foreign banking or other international or foreign financial operations. . . ." An Edge Act Corporation is empowered to provide, on an interstate basis, general banking services for international customers, to receive deposits in the United States in the course of international business, and to establish foreign branches. 12 U.S.C. § 615(a)–(b). Also, Edge Corporations may invest in the stock of other corporations. 12 U.S.C. § 615(c) (1976). Those corporations, however, must be organized under the laws of a foreign state, or if organized in the United States, the corporations may only conduct domestic operations incidental to foreign or international business. For a discussion of the history of the Edge Act generally, see James T. Tynion III, New Rules for Edge Act Corporations, Vol. 3 Fordham L.J. 2 (1979).

The IBA also authorizes an Edge Act corporation to be held by a foreign bank. See 12 C.F.R. § 211.5(d) (ownership of Edge corporations by foreign or foreign controlled domestic banking institutions). Edge Act corporations may also establish branches in the U.S. § 211.5(f). Further, under strictly prescribed condition and incidental to their main purpose, Edge corporations may do limited businesses within the U.S., and may even establish a U.S. branch. However, the U.S. branch may only conduct transactions directly linked to international trade. 12 CFR § 211.6. 12 CFR § 211.5(f). Edge and Agreement corporations must comply with U.S. laws addressing, among other things, protecting customer and consumer information, Bank Secrecy Act compliances and customer identification programs. 12 CFR § 211.5(l)–(m). Bank Secrecy Act compliance issues are more fully discussed in Chapter 8.

Banking Edges extended the geographical reach of their parents because an Edge was not considered a bank and hence was not subject to the same interstate banking prohibitions. Thus in the 1960s, the trend was for banks from outside the state of New York to form Banking Edges and locate them in New York City for conducting international banking and for trading in foreign exchange. In the 1970s and 1980s, the trend was toward expansion into regional financial centers, such as Miami, Chicago, and San Francisco.

Investment Edges can engage in a wide range of non-financial investments and related activities.

An Agreement Corporation is chartered by a state to engage in international banking, so named because the corporation enters into an "agreement" with the Fed's Board of Governors to limit its activities to those of an Edge Act Corporation, as if organized under Section 25A of the Federal Reserve Act.

The Board's Regulation K governs the establishment, permissible activities, stock ownership structure, compliance and other conditions and requirements for Edge corporations, 12 CFR § 211.5(a), and also similar requirements for agreement corporations. 12 CFR § 211.5(g)–(m).

The increase in authority under U.S. banking law for international banking, removal of restrictions on interstate branching and restrictions on the size of lending and other activities restricted by an Edge corporations' capital base, have led to a decline in the formation and maintenance of Edge corporations.

3. ESTABLISHING FOREIGN BANKING ORGANIZATIONS IN THE U.S.: REGULATION K

The international operations of FBOs in the U.S. are governed by the Board's Regulation K, 12 CFR § 211 et seq. pursuant to the authority under the Bank Holding Company Act of 1956 (12 U.S.C. § 1841 et seq.). Regulation K was substantially revised as a result of the FBSEA to recognize the primary role the FBSEA gave the Board as the home country consolidated regulator of all FBOs in the U.S. While state bank regulatory authorities and the OCC maintain a primary role in chartering, regulation and oversight of FBOs, the FBSEA gave the Board the role of primary home country supervisor. As a result, establishment of FBOs in the U.S. typically require prior regulatory approvals of both a FBO's primary state regulator, or if it opts to pursue a federally chartered office, the OCC. Historically, choice of regulator has been somewhat driven by regulatory "arbitrage" *i.e.*, a perceived competition among state and federal regulators to provide "user friendly" laws and supervision. This arbitrage was somewhat neutralized for FBOs by the FBSEA's grant of consolidated authority to the Board.

As to choosing a federal versus state chartered office, these decisions are otherwise based on factors similar to those that have faced U.S. banks, ranging from a unified set of federal banking laws and the perceived advantages of preemption of state banking laws favoring the federal charter, to a favorable and asserted knowledge of local markets by state regulators favoring a state charter. See, e.g., V. Gerard Comizio and Helen Lee, Understanding the Federal Preemption Debate and a Case for Uniformity, 6 Am. U. Bus. L. Brief 51 (Spring/Summer 2010). However, the Dodd-Frank Act, in reaction to perceived concerns about the potential for federal preemption to unduly limit state consumer financial protection laws, has placed limits on the scope of federal preemption of such state laws. See Comizio and Lee at 55. (Dodd-Frank Act's creation of the Consumer Financial Protection Bureau, new limits on judicial deference to OCC's decision on the scope of federal preemption, limit on ability of OCC to preempt state consumer financial laws, new empowerment of state attorneys general to enforce state consumer "financial" laws against national banks). See also preemption discussion in Chapter 5, *supra*, regarding the Dodd-Frank Act.

Pursuant to 211.24(a), prior Board approval is required for a FBO to establish a branch, agency or representative office in the U.S. An application is required to be filed with the Board meeting the Board's requirements. 12 CFR § 211.24(b)(1). The applicant is required to file notice of the application in a newspaper of general circulation in the community in which the applicant proposes to engage in business. 12 CFR § 211.24(b)(2). The Board must act on application within 180 days of after receipt of the application, but may be extended for an additional 180 days, after providing notice and reason(s) for the extension. 12 CFR § 211.24(b)(4). In same circumstances, the applicant may voluntarily waive these time periods, typically to avoid the possibility of a denial by the Board where the Board has requested and is waiting for additional information relevant to its decision on the application from either the applicant or its home country supervisor. 12 CFR §§ 211.24(b)(4)/(A)(B) (extension of time periods for Board review); § 211.24(b)(4)(c) (waiver of time frames); § 211.24(c)(ii) (The Board may request additional information in addition to that supplied in the application when the Board believes it necessary for its decision).

NOTES

1.   In the wake of passage of the FBSEA, the Board was criticized for its perceived slow time frames for reviewing and acting on FBO applications. See U.S. General Accounting Office Report, Foreign Banks: Implementation of the Foreign Bank Supervision and Enhancement Act of 1991 (September 1996). The GAO report noted that processing foreign bank applications took the Board more than a year on average. The Board staff advised GAO that the length of time it took to process applications was attributable to the need for additional time to complete background checks and to review issues related to comprehensive supervision, bank operations, and internal controls. They also cited difficulties in obtaining translated information from some applicant

banks, a lack of understanding by some applicants about the level of detail required to review comprehensive consolidated supervision, and some applicants' unfamiliarity with FBSEA requirements as causes of delays.

After the Board issued its March 1993 guidelines, the GAO report noted that there was a decrease in the amount of time taken to process branch, agency, and representative office applications. On average, the total time it took to process such applications (from date of initial filing to disposition) dropped from 574 days to 293 days. Of this, the average time between the date that applications were initially filed and the date they were accepted decreased from 170 days to 130 days, and the average time between acceptance and approval decreased from 404 days to 163 days. The Board's staff attributed this decline to a number of reasons, including commitment to meet the guidelines, experience with the process, and improvements in the name check process. See GAO Report at 9–10.

2.   In addition to required approval of representation, agency and branch offices, the Board must also approve under Regulation K establishment of any commercial lending company. As the name implies, a commercial lending company is defined to mean any organization organized under the laws of any U.S. state, that engages in the commercial lending business and maintain credit balances permissible for an agency office. See 12 CFR §§ 211.21(g) (definition of commercial lending company) and 211.21(b) (definition of, and permissible activities). Interestingly enough, foreign commercial lenders that lend in the U.S. without having a physical presence in the U.S. are not generally subject to Regulation K, but may be subject to state lending laws. See, e.g., The California Finance Lender Law, Cal. Fin. Code, Section 22050 et. Seq.

Sec. 211.23   Nonbanking activities of foreign banking organizations.

(a) Qualifying foreign banking organizations. Unless specifically made eligible for the exemptions by the Board, a foreign banking organization shall qualify for the exemptions afforded by this section only if, disregarding its United States banking, more than half of its worldwide business is banking; and more than half of its banking business is outside the United States.[10] In order to qualify, a foreign banking organization shall:

(1) Meet at least two of the following requirements:

    (i) Banking assets held outside the United States exceed total worldwide nonbanking assets;

    (ii) Revenues derived from the business of banking outside the United States exceed total revenues derived from its worldwide nonbanking business; or

---

[10]   None of the assets, revenues, or net income, whether held or derived directly or indirectly, of a subsidiary bank, branch, agency, commercial lending company, or other company engaged in the business of banking in the United States (including any territory of the United States, Puerto Rico, Guam, American Samoa, or the Virgin Islands) shall be considered held or derived from the business of banking "outside the United States".

(iii) Net income derived from the business of banking outside the United States exceeds total net income derived from its worldwide nonbanking business; and

(2) Meet at least two of the following requirements:

(i) Banking assets held outside the United States exceed banking assets held in the United States;

(ii) Revenues derived from the business of banking outside the United States exceed revenues derived from the business of banking in the United States; or

(iii) Net income derived from the business of banking outside the United States exceeds net income derived from the business of banking in the United States.

(b) Determining assets, revenues, and net income. (1)(i) For purposes of paragraph (a) of this section, the total assets, revenues, and net income of an organization may be determined on a consolidated or combined basis.

NOTES

1. Section 211.23 of Regulator K generally exempts the nonbanking activities of FBOs conducted outside of the U.S. provided: 1) more than half of its worldwide business is banking, and 2) more than half of its banking business is outside the U.S. § 211.23(a).

Section 211.23 essentially exempts the parent companies and other affiliates of FBOs operating in the U.S. from the prohibition under 4(k) of the Bank Holding Company Act on U.S. bank and financial holding companies engaging in non-financial activities. The Gramm-Leach-Bliley Act of 1999 had previously limited the restrictions on U.S. bank holding companies engaging in insurance, merchant banking and securities activities. See 12 USC 1841(k), although the so-called Volcker Rule provisions of the Dodd-Frank Act imposed restrictions on proprietary trading, private equity, and investment activities. See Priyank Gandhi and Patrick C. Kiefer, The Volcker Rule, Center for the Study of Financial Regulation, Issue 10 (Winter 2013). The Volcker Rule provisions are discussed in Chapter 6.

2. The series of Board orders below show an interesting progression in the ability of Chinese Banks to operate in the U.S, based on the degree of home country supervision.

FEDERAL RESERVE BOARD

INDUSTRIAL AND COMMERCIAL BANK OF CHINA
BEIJING, PEOPLE'S REPUBLIC OF CHINA

ORDER APPROVING ESTABLISHMENT OF A
REPRESENTATIVE OFFICE
(January 27, 1997)

Industrial and Commercial Bank of China ("Bank"). Beijing, People's Republic of China, a foreign bank within the meaning of the International Banking Act ("IBA"), has applied under section 10(a) of the IBA (12 U.S.C. § 3107(a)) to establish a representative office in New York, New York. The Foreign Bank Supervision Enhancement Act of 1991, which amended the IBA, provides that a foreign bank must obtain the approval of the Board to establish a representative office in the United States.

* * *

As of June 30, 1996, Bank had total assets of approximately $400 billion. Bank is the largest of four specialized banks in the People's Republic of China and is wholly owned by the Chinese government. Bank operates more than 32,000 offices and a number of subsidiaries in China. Outside China, Bank operates bank subsidiaries in Kazakhstan and Hong Kong, branches in Singapore and Hong Kong, and representative offices in Seoul, Korea; Tokyo, Japan; and London, England.

Massive for then

* * *

The activities of Bank's representative office would include general marketing or promotional activities, research and consulting, and acting as liaison between Bank's customers and correspondent and investment banks. In addition, the representative office would engage in certain loan solicitation and servicing activities. All decisions regarding such loans would be made by Bank's head office and the representative office would not act as payment or collection agent in connection with its loan servicing activities.

Typical rep. office activities

In acting on an application to establish a representative office, the IBA and Regulation K provide that the Board shall take into account whether the foreign bank engages directly in the business of banking outside of the United States, has furnished to the Board the information it needs to assess the application adequately, is subject to comprehensive supervision or regulation on a consolidated basis by its home country supervisor, and has provided adequate assurances of access to information on the operations of the bank and its affiliates to determine compliance with U.S. laws. (12 U.S.C. § 3107(a); 12 C.F.R. 211.24(d)). The Board also may take into account additional standards as set forth in the IBA (12 U.S.C. § 3105(d)(3)–(4)) and Regulation K (12 C.F.R. 211.24(c)).

The Board previously has stated that the standards that apply to the establishment of a branch or agency need not in every case apply to the establishment of a representative office, because representative offices do not engage in a banking business and cannot take deposits or make loans.[1] In evaluating an application to establish a representative office under the IBA and Regulation K, the Board will take into account the standards that apply to the establishment of branches and agencies, subject generally to the following considerations. With respect to supervision by home country authorities, a foreign bank that proposes to establish a representative office should be subject to a significant degree of supervision by its home country supervisor.[2] A foreign bank's financial and managerial resources will be reviewed to determine whether its financial condition and performance demonstrate that it is capable of complying with applicable laws and has an operating record that would be consistent with the establishment of a representative office in the United States. Finally, all foreign banks, whether operating through branches, agencies or representative offices, will be required to provide adequate assurances of access to information on the operations of the bank and its affiliates necessary to determine compliance with U.S. laws.

The Board has considered the following information with respect to home country supervision of Bank. The People's Bank of China (the "PBOC") is the licensing, regulatory, and supervisory authority for banks and all other financial institutions in China and, as such, is the home country supervisor of Bank. Although regulation of the specialized banks by the PBOC historically has focused on the banks' compliance with state economic and financial goals, in the last several years the Chinese authorities have taken steps to develop a more market-oriented bank supervisory program placing greater emphasis on prudential standards. Under the new supervisory regime currently being implemented, the PBOC establishes capital, liquidity and asset quality requirements, regulates the investments of banks in other companies, establishes internal auditing standards for Chinese banks, and monitors Chinese banks for adherence to Chinese laws and regulations. The PBOC, which has authorized Bank to establish the proposed representative office, supervises the foreign and domestic activities of Bank and its subsidiaries.

* * *

---

[1]   See 58 *Federal Register* 6348, 6351 (1993).

[2]   See *Citizens National Bank*, 79 Federal Reserve Bulletin 805 (1993). *See also Promstroybank of Russia*, 82 Federal Reserve Bulletin 599 (1996) (addressing standards applicable to representative offices with limited activities).

Finally, with respect to access to information on Bank's operations, the Board has reviewed the relevant provisions of law in China and has communicated with appropriate government authorities regarding access to information. Bank has committed to make available to the Board such information on the operations of Bank and any of its affiliates that the Board deems necessary to determine and enforce compliance with the IBA, the Bank Holding Company Act of 1956, as amended, and other applicable federal law. To the extent that the provision of such information to the Board may be prohibited or impeded by law, Bank has committed to cooperate with the Board to obtain any necessary consents or waivers that might be required from third parties in connection with disclosure of such information. In addition, subject to certain conditions, the PBOC may share information on Bank's operations with other supervisors, including the Board. In light of the commitments provided by Bank and other facts of record, and subject to the condition described below, the Board concludes that Bank has provided adequate assurances of access to any necessary information the Board may request.

On the basis of all the facts of record, and subject to the commitments made by Bank, as well as the terms and conditions set forth in this order, the Board has determined that Bank's application to establish a representative office should be, and hereby is, approved.

NOTES

1.   Notably, in the ICBC Board order the Board stated that, while it will "take into account the standards that apply to the establishment of branches and agencies [offices]"—a reference primarily to the comprehensive consolidated home country supervision standards set forth in 12 CFR § 211.24(c) (but see exception in the ICBC Board order below regarding the establishment of a branch office)—those standards "need not in every case apply to the establishment of a representative office, because representative offices do not engage in a banking business and cannot take deposits or make loans." Rather, the order specifies that, with respect to supervision by home country authorities, a FBO that proposes to establish a representative office should be subject to "a significant degree of supervision" by it home country supervisor, citing among other things, the Board's prior order in Promstroybank of Russia, 82 Fed. Res. Bull. 599 (1996).

It is interesting to note that, while Chinese banks have been able since then to establish representative and branch offices, and acquire U.S. banks (discussed below) based ultimately on a finding by the Board in 2012, discussed below, that Chinese banks are subject to consolidated and comprehensive supervision by Chinese regulatory authorities, Russian banks have not been able to establish that they are subject to similar supervision. See Putin signs law banning opening of foreign branches in Russian Federation, Tass Russian News Agency (March 15, 2013) (The ban on foreign banks explained by the "unpossibility" by Russian regulatory authorities to fully supervise their operations). To date, no foreign banks have been able to establish offices in Russia.

2.   While representative offices are prohibited from engaging in bank deposit and lending activities, they may engage in a wide range of activities designed to both facilitate existing bank relationships outside the U.S., and faster new relationship in the U.S. These activities may include: soliciting new business for the foreign bank; conducting research; acting as liaison between the foreign bank's head office and customers in the United States; performing preliminary and servicing steps in connection with lending; or performing back-office functions; but may not include contracting for any deposit or deposit-like liability, lending money, or engaging in any other banking activity for the foreign bank. See 12 CFR § 211.24(d)(1); see also 12 CFR § 250.141(h) (activities that constitute permissible "preliminary and servicing steps" in connection with lending).

3.   In its order, the Board also noted that its authority to approve the establishment of the proposed representative office "parallels the continuing authority of the State of New York to license offices of a foreign bank. The Board's approval of this application does not supplant the authority of the State of New York and its agent, the New York State Banking Department (Department), to license the proposed representative office of Bank in accordance with any terms or conditions that the Department may impose." *Id.* at 12.

4.   Approval of representative, agency and branch office applications are also specifically conditioned on compliance with certain commitments required by the Board to be made in connection with the application and with the conditions of the Board order. These commitments are conditions imposed in writing by the Board in connection with its decision, and may be enforced in proceedings under 12 U.S.C. § 1818 (which provides enforcement penalties, including civil money penalties) against a FBO and its affiliates.

FEDERAL RESERVE SYSTEM

INDUSTRIAL AND COMMERCIAL BANK OF CHINA LIMITED BEIJING, PEOPLE'S REPUBLIC OF CHINA

ORDER APPROVING ESTABLISHMENT OF A BRANCH
(August 5, 2008)

Industrial and Commercial Bank of China Limited ("ICBC"), Beijing, People's Republic of China, a foreign bank within the meaning of the International Banking Act ("IBA"), has applied under section 7(d) of the IBA[1] to establish a branch in New York, New York. The Foreign Bank Supervision Enhancement Act of 1991, which amended the IBA, provides

---

[1]   12 U.S.C. § 3105(d).

that a foreign bank must obtain the approval of the Board to establish a branch in the United States.

* * *

ICBC, with total assets of approximately \$1.3 trillion, is the largest bank in China.[2] The government of China owns approximately 74.8 percent of ICBC's shares.[3] No other shareholder owns more than 5 percent of ICBC's shares.[4]

ICBC engages primarily in corporate and retail banking and treasury operations throughout China, including Hong Kong and Macau. Outside China, ICBC operates subsidiary banks in Almaty, Jakarta, London, Luxembourg, and Moscow and branches in a number of countries, including Japan, Indonesia, Korea, Germany, and the United Kingdom. In the United States, ICBC operates a representative office in New York. ICBC would meet the requirements for a qualifying foreign banking organization under Regulation K.[5]

The proposed New York branch would engage in wholesale deposit-taking, lending, trade finance, and other banking services.

Under the IBA and Regulation K, in acting on an application by a foreign bank to establish a branch, the Board must consider whether (1) the foreign bank engages directly in the business of banking outside the United States; (2) has furnished to the Board the information, it needs to assess the application adequately; and (3) is subject to comprehensive supervision on a consolidated basis by its home country supervisors.[6] The

---

[2]   Asset and ranking data are as of March 31, 2008.

[3]   The government of China directly owns approximately 35.3 percent of ICBC's shares through its Ministry of Finance. Central SAFE Investments Limited (also known as "Huijin") and the Social Security Fund of the People's Republic of China hold approximately 35.3 and 4.2 percent of ICBC's shares, respectively. Huijin is currently owned directly by the government of China and was formed to assist in the restructuring of major Chinese banks. The government transferred shares of several Chinese banks, including ICBC, to Huijin at the time of the recapitalization and restructuring of these banks between 2004 and 2006. In addition to its interest in ICBC, Huijin also owns a majority interest in Bank of China Limited, which operates three branches in the United States. The government of China intends to transfer the ownership of Huijin to China Investment Corporation ("CIC"), a recently created investment fund that is also wholly owned by the government of China. * * *

[4]   Goldman Sachs and American Express own 4.9 percent and less than 1 percent of ICBC's shares, respectively.

[5]   12 CFR 211.23(a).

[6]   12 U.S.C. § 3105(d)(2); 12 CFR 211.24. In assessing this standard, the Board considers, among other indicia of comprehensive, consolidated supervision, the extent to which the home country supervisors: (i) ensure that the bank has adequate procedures for monitoring and controlling its activities worldwide; (ii) obtain information on the condition of the bank and its subsidiaries and offices through regular examination reports, audit reports, or otherwise; (iii) obtain information on the dealings with and relationship between the bank and its affiliates, both foreign and domestic; (iv) receive from the bank financial reports that are consolidated on a worldwide basis or comparable information that permits analysis of the bank's financial condition on a worldwide consolidated basis; (v) evaluate prudential standards, such as capital adequacy

Board also considers additional standards as set forth in the IBA and Regulation K.[7]

The IBA includes a limited exception to the general standard relating to comprehensive, consolidated supervision.[8] This exception provides that; if the Board is unable to find that a foreign bank seeking to establish a branch, agency, or commercial lending company is subject to comprehensive supervision or regulation on a consolidated basis by the appropriate authorities in its home country, the Board may nevertheless approve the application provided that: (i) the appropriate authorities in the home country of the foreign bank are actively working to establish arrangements for the consolidated supervision of such bank; and (ii) all other factors are consistent with approval.[9] In deciding whether to exercise its discretion to approve an application under authority of this exception, the Board must also consider whether the foreign bank has adopted and implemented procedures to combat money laundering.[10] The Board also may take into account whether the home country of the foreign bank is developing a legal regime to address money laundering or is participating in multilateral efforts to combat money laundering.[11] This is the standard applied by the Board in this case.

* * *

Based on all the facts of record, the Board has determined that ICBC's home country supervisory authority is actively working to establish arrangements for the consolidated supervision of the bank and that considerations relating to the steps taken by ICBC and its home jurisdiction to combat money laundering are consistent with approval under this standard. The China Banking Regulatory Commission ("CBRC") is the principal supervisory authority of ICBC, including its foreign subsidiaries and affiliates, for all matters other than laws with respect to anti-money laundering. The CBRC has the authority to license banks, regulate their activities, and approve expansion, both domestically and abroad. It supervises and regulates ICBC, including its subsidiaries and foreign operations, through a combination of targeted on-site examinations and continuous consolidated off-site monitoring. Since its establishment in 2003, the CBRC has enhanced existing supervisory programs and developed new policies and procedures designed to create a framework for the consolidated supervision of banks in China.

---

and risk asset exposure, on a worldwide basis. No single factor is essential, and other elements may inform the Board's determination.

[7]   12 U.S.C. § 3105(d)(3)–(4); 12 CFR 211.24(c)(2)–(3).

[8]   12 U.S.C. § 3105(d)(6).

[9]   12 U.S.C. § 3105(d)(6)(A).

[10]   12 U.S.C. § 3105(d)(6)(B).

[11]   *Id.*

* * *

NOTES

1.   Please note that ICBC received Board approval under U.S. banking law for a branch office—the fullest extension of a home country's banking activities in a host country—despite *not* meeting the consolidated comprehensive supervision standards. See 12 U.S.C. 3105(d)(6). How is this consistent with the Basel Committee's 25 Core Principles for Effective Banking Supervision discussed in Chapter 5? At the time the Board approved the ICBC branch application in August 2008, the global financial crises was occurring, amid charges that U.S. and EU banking regulators had not effectively regulated banks under their supervision, discussed in Chapter 6.

2.   Before April 2003, the People's Bank of China ("PBOC") acted as both China's central bank and primary banking supervisor, including with respect to anti-money laundering matters. In April 2003, the CBRC was established as the primary banking supervisor and assumed the majority of the PBOC's regulatory functions. The PBOC maintained its roles as China's central bank and primary supervisor for anti-money laundering matters. An Anti-Money Laundering Bureau ("AML Bureau") was established within the PBOC in 2003. The AML Bureau coordinates anti-money laundering efforts at the PBOC and among other agencies. The AML Bureau also supervised the creation in September 2004 of the China Anti-Money Laundering Monitoring and Analysis Center ("AML Center"). The AML Center collects, monitors, analyzes, and disseminates suspicious transaction reports and large-value transaction reports. The AML Center sends suspicious transaction reports to the AML Bureau for further investigation. The PBOC issued additional rules in June 2007 providing clarification on reporting suspicious transactions to the AML Center and on customer due diligence and recordkeeping.

3.   China participates in international fora that address the prevention of money laundering and terrorist financing. Joining in 2007, China is a member of the Financial Action Task Force ("FATF") and is a party to the 1988 U.N. Convention Against the Illicit Traffic of Narcotics and Psychotropic Substances, the U.N. Convention Against Transnational Organized Crime, the U.N. Convention Against Corruption, and the U.N. International Convention for the Suppression of the Financing of Terrorism.

FEDERAL RESERVE BOARD

LEGAL INTERPRETIVE LETTER

REQUEST FOR EXEMPTION UNDER SECTION 4(C) 9 OF THE BANK HOLDING COMPANY ACT

(August 5, 2008)

* * *

This letter is in response to the requests by China Investment Corporation ("CIC") and Central SAFE Investments Limited ("Huijin"), both of Beijing, People's Republic of China, for exemptions under section 4(c)(9) of the Bank Holding Company Act ("BHC Act" or "Act") (12 U.S.C. § 1843(c)(9)) from the nonbanking restrictions of the Act.

CIC was incorporated by order of the State Council of the People's Republic of China[1] on September 29, 2007, for the purpose of investing the foreign reserves of the Chinese government. CIC is wholly owned by the government of China and operates under the direct supervision and control of the State Council. Huijin is a limited liability investment holding company that is also wholly owned and controlled by the Chinese government. Huijin was established by the State Council on December 16, 2003, to invest in Chinese financial institutions and to implement and execute government policy with respect to those institutions. It has been represented that Huijin does not engage in any other commercial activities. Once governmental formalities are completed, Huijin will become a wholly owned subsidiary of CIC.

Huijin currently owns controlling interests in the Bank of China Limited ("BOC"), Industrial and Commercial Bank of China Limited ("ICBC"), and China Construction Bank ("CCB"), all also of Beijing. BOC operates two insured branches in New York and one uninsured branch in California. ICBC and CCB have each filed an application under section 7(d) of the International Banking Act ("IBA")[2] to establish a branch in New York, New York.[3] Under section 8 of the IBA, any foreign bank that operates a branch, agency, or commercial lending company in the United States and any company that controls the foreign bank is subject to the BHC Act as if the foreign bank or company were a bank holding company.[4] Consequently, Huijin, through its control of BOC, is subject to the BHC Act, and CIC would become subject to the Act upon its acquisition of more

---

[1]　The State Council is the highest executive body in the Chinese government.

[2]　12 U.S.C. § 3105(d).

[3]　The Foreign Bank Supervision Enhancement Act of 1991, which amended the IBA, provides that a foreign bank must obtain the approval of the Board to establish a branch in the United States.

[4]　12 U.S.C. § 3106.

than 25 percent of the voting shares of Huijin. Thereafter, both CIC and Huijin would be subject to the nonbanking limitations and other requirements of the BHC Act.

CIC and Huijin have requested an exemption from the requirements of the BHC Act, based on their status as wholly state-owned vehicles.

The Board has previously considered the issues that arise when a foreign government-owned company seeks to conduct banking operations indirectly in the United States through foreign bank subsidiaries or through the acquisition of U.S. banks. In June 1982, in connection with an application by a foreign government-owned bank to acquire a U.S. bank, the Board noted that a number of significant policy issues were raised by the ownership of a U.S. bank by a foreign government or a foreign government agency, including in particular issues related to the mixing of banking and commerce and to interstate banking in the United States.[5] At that time, the Board noted that its practice was not to apply the provisions of the BHC Act to the foreign government owners of the foreign bank but that the issues raised by such ownership deserved further consideration.

The Board revisited the issues raised by foreign government ownership in 1988 in connection with an application by an Italian bank that was owned by Istituto per la Ricostruzione Industriale ("IRI"), a wholly government-owned financial public corporation. In reviewing this case, the Board determined that, as a legal matter, foreign governments were not themselves "companies" for purposes of the BHC Act, and so were not covered by the Act. However, the Board found that the investment vehicle used by the Italian government, IRI, was structured as a corporate vehicle and was, therefore, a company under the BHC Act.[6]

In making this determination, the Board stated that broad public policy issues are raised by applying the restrictions of the BHC Act to foreign government-owned companies. The Board noted that the Congress had been mindful of these concerns and had provided the Board with broad authority to exempt foreign companies from the nonbanking restrictions of the BHC Act where the Act has the effect of extending the impact of the U.S. regulatory framework to economic transactions and relationships that take place entirely overseas. The Board stated it was particularly appropriate to exercise the express authority of section 4(c)(9) of the Act in the case of foreign government-owned companies to ameliorate restrictions of the Act in the public interest.

The Board has considered the current exemption requests by CIC and Huijin in the context of this background.

---

[5]   See 68 Federal Reserve Bulletin 423, 425 (1982).

[6]   See Board letter to Patricia Skigen, Esq., dated August 19, 1988.

Section 4(c)(9) of the BHC Act provides that the Board may exempt from the restrictions of the Act:

> shares held or activities conducted by any company organized under the laws of a foreign country the greater part of whose business is conducted outside the United States, if the Board by regulation or order determines that, under the circumstances and subject to the conditions set forth in the regulation or order, the exemption would not be substantially at variance with the purposes of [the Act] and would be in the public interest.[7]

[handwritten margin note: Authority]

The Board has reviewed information you have provided regarding CIC and Huijin and, based on its review, has determined that CIC and Huijin are companies under the Act. The Board has further determined that it would be in the public interest and not substantially at variance with the purposes of the Act to grant to CIC and Huijin exemptions from the nonbanking restrictions of the BHC Act under the authority of section 4(c)(9) of the Act.

Under the exemptions, and subject to the conditions described below, CIC would be permitted to make investments in any company, including a U.S. company or a foreign company with U.S. operations, without regard to the nonbanking restrictions of the BHC Act.

[handwritten margin note: Non banking don't apply]

* * *

NOTES

1.   In granting the Section 4(c)(9) exemption, the Board conditioned compliance by CIC and Huijin with several limitations (that are standard for Section 4(c)(9) exemptive orders) designed to "minimize the potential for conflicts of interests, concentration of resources, and unsound banking practices, as well as to mitigate any potential competitive advantage that may accrue to CIC, Huijin, and their subsidiaries from the exemptions":

> First, all transactions by a U.S. branch or agency of any foreign bank subsidiary of CIC or Huijin with a company in which CIC or Huijin (either separately or in combination) has made a controlling investment (a "controlled company") would be limited. Transactions by the U.S. branch or agency with a single controlled company are limited to 10 percent of the branch's or agency's lending base, as described below, and transactions with all controlled companies in the aggregate are limited to 20 percent of the branch's or agency's lending base, and all such transactions must be fully collateralized. Any transaction between the U.S. branch or agency and a controlled company must be on market terms. The U.S. branches and agencies of foreign bank subsidiaries of CIC and Huijin may not cross-market

---

[7]   12 U.S.C. § 1843(c)(9).

goods and services in the United States with such controlled companies.

Second, each of CIC and Huijin must continue to conduct a majority of its business outside the United States, consistent with the requirement of section 4(c)(9) of the Act.

Third, CIC and Huijin may not directly or indirectly (including in combination) acquire control of or exercise a controlling influence over a securities company, an insurance company, or any other company that engages in activities in the United States that are permitted only to a financial holding company under section 4(k) of the BHC Act, 12 U.S.C. § 1843(k) unless CIC and Huijin meet the standards of, and elect to be treated as, financial holding companies.

Fourth, consistent with the requirements of the BHC Act and the Federal Reserve Act, CIC and Huijin and any company, including any foreign bank, that is controlled by CIC or Huijin (either separately or in combination) are required to obtain prior Board approval to make a direct or indirect investment in 5 percent or more of the voting shares of a bank holding company or U.S. bank, 12 U.S.C. § 1842(a) or to make a controlling investment in a corporation organized under section 25A of the Federal Reserve Act (an Edge corporation). 12 U.S.C. §§ 611 and 619. In addition, prior Board approval is required for the acquisition of a controlling interest in a U.S. insured depository institution.

2.   For purposes of the first condition, the "lending base" of a U.S. branch or agency must equal 5 percent of the branch's or agency's third party assets. "Third party assets" is defined to mean the amount of total claims on nonrelated entities as reported on the regulatory report of condition required to be filed with the Board by the branch or agency.

3.   The Board's rationale in providing an exemption letter of this type is typically based on all the facts presented, and representations by the applicant made in connection with the requests. The Board specifically reserves the right to revisit its determination should there be a "material change" in the facts presented to the Board. *CIC Letter* at p. 6.

4.   A foreign bank subsidiary of any FBO granted an exemption under Section 4(c)(9) that currently does not operate a branch, agency, or commercial lending company in the United States would be entitled to take advantage of this exemption. If, however, such foreign bank were subsequently to establish a banking office in the United States, it would be required to conform its activities and investments in the United States to the requirements of Regulation K. 12 CFR Parts 211 and 225.

FEDERAL RESERVE SYSTEM

INDUSTRIAL AND COMMERCIAL BANK OF CHINA LIMITED, BOARD ORDER NO. 2012–4

(May 9, 2012)

Industrial and Commercial Bank of China Limited ("ICBC"), China Investment Corporation ("CIC"), and Central Huijin Investment Ltd. ("Huijin"), all of Beijing, People's Republic of China (collectively, "Applicants"), have requested the Board's approval to become bank holding companies under section 3 of the Bank Holding Company Act of 1956, as amended ("BHC Act"), by acquiring up to 80 percent of the voting shares of The Bank of East Asia (U.S.A.) National Association ("BEA-USA"), New York, New York.

* * *

ICBC, with total assets of approximately $2.5 trillion, is the largest bank in China. The government of China owns approximately 70.7 percent of ICBC's shares through the Ministry of Finance and CIC and Huijin. No other shareholder owns more than 5 percent of ICBC's shares.

* * *

CIC is an investment vehicle organized by the Chinese government for the purpose of investing its foreign exchange reserves. CIC controls Huijin, a Chinese government-owned investment company organized to invest in Chinese financial institutions.[7] In addition to ICBC, Huijin owns controlling interests in two Chinese banks that operate banking offices in the United States: Bank of China Limited and China Construction Bank Corporation, both also of Beijing.[8] Under the International Banking Act, any foreign bank that operates a branch, agency, or commercial lending company in the United States, and any company that controls the foreign bank, is subject to the BHC Act as if the foreign bank or company were a bank holding company.[9] As a result, CIC and Huijin are subject to the BHC

---

[7]   CIC also owns a noncontrolling interest in Morgan Stanley, New York, New York. See China Investment Corporation, 96 Federal Reserve Bulletin B31 (2010) ("CIC Order").

[8]   Bank of China Limited operates two grandfathered insured federal branches in New York City and a limited uninsured federal branch in Los Angeles and has received Board approval to establish an additional uninsured federal branch in Chicago. Bank of China Limited, Board Order No. 2012–6 (May 9, 2012). Bank of China Limited also controls a wholly owned subsidiary bank, Nanyang Commercial Bank, Limited, Hong Kong SAR, People's Republic of China, that operates an uninsured federal branch in San Francisco. China Construction Bank Corporation operates an uninsured state-licensed branch and a representative office in New York City. Huijin also owns a controlling interest in Agricultural Bank of China Limited, Beijing, People's Republic of China, which operates a representative office in New York City and has received Board approval to establish an uninsured state-licensed branch in New York City. *Agricultural Bank of China Limited*, Board Order No. 2012–5 (May 9, 2012).

[9]   12 U.S.C. § 3106.

Act as if they were bank holding companies.[10] Through the proposed acquisition of BEA-USA, Applicants would become bank holding companies under the BHC Act.

BEA-USA, with total consolidated assets of approximately $780 million and deposits of approximately $621 million,[11] engages in retail and commercial banking in the United States. BEA-USA operates 13 branches in New York and California.

Competitive Considerations

The Board * * * considered the competitive effects of the proposal in light of all the facts of the record. Section 3 of the BHC Act prohibits the Board from approving a proposal that would result in a monopoly or would be in furtherance of any attempt to monopolize the business of banking in any relevant banking market. The BHC Act also prohibits the Board from approving a proposal that would substantially lessen competition in any relevant banking market, unless the anticompetitive effects of the proposal clearly are outweighed in the public interest by the probable effect of the proposal in meeting the convenience and needs of the community to be served.

* * *

Supervision or Regulation on a Consolidated Basis

In evaluating this application, and as required by section 3 of the BHC Act, the Board has considered whether Applicants are subject to comprehensive supervision or regulation on a consolidated basis by appropriate authorities in their home country.[22] The Board has long held

---

[10]   The Board previously provided certain exemptions to CIC and Huijin under section 4(c)(9) of the BHC Act, which authorizes the Board to grant to foreign companies exemptions from the nonbanking restrictions of the BHC Act when the exemptions would not be substantially at variance with the purposes of the act and would be in the public interest. See 12 U.S.C. § 1843(c)(9). The exemptions provided to CIC and Huijin do not extend to ICBC, Bank of China Limited, China Construction Bank Corporation, or any other Chinese banking subsidiary of CIC or Huijin that operates a branch or agency in the United States. See Board letter dated August 5, 2008, to H. Rodgin Cohen, Esq.

[11]   Deposit data are as of December 31, 2011.

[22]   12 U.S.C. § 1842(c)(3)(B). As provided in Regulation Y, the Board determines whether a foreign bank is subject to consolidated home country supervision under the standards set forth in Regulation K. See 12 CFR 225.13(a)(4). Regulation K provides that a foreign bank is subject to consolidated home country supervision if the foreign bank is supervised or regulated in such a manner that its home country supervisor receives sufficient information on the worldwide operations of the foreign bank (including the relationships of the bank to any affiliate) to assess the foreign bank's overall financial condition and compliance with law and regulation. 12 CFR 211.24(c)(l)(ii). In assessing this standard under section 211.24 of Regulation K, the Board considers, among other indicia of comprehensive, consolidated supervision, the extent to which the home country supervisors: (i) ensure that the bank has adequate procedures for monitoring and controlling its activities worldwide; (ii) obtain information on the condition of the bank and its subsidiaries and offices through regular examination reports, audit reports, or otherwise; (iii) obtain information on the dealings with and relationship between the bank and its affiliates, both foreign and domestic; (iv) receive from the bank financial reports that are Consolidated on a

that "the legal systems for supervision and regulation vary from country to country, and comprehensive supervision or regulation on a consolidated basis can be achieved in different ways."[23] In applying this standard, the Board has considered the Basel Core Principles for Effective Banking Supervision ("Basel Core Principles"),[24] which are recognized as the international standard for assessing the quality of bank supervisory systems, including with respect to comprehensive, consolidated supervision ("CCS").[25]

ICBC: For a number of years, authorities in China have continued to enhance the standards of consolidated supervision to which banks in China are subject, including through additional or refined statutory authority, regulations, and guidance; adoption of international standards and best practices; enhancements to the supervisory system arising out of supervisory experiences; upgrades to the CBRC in the areas of organization, technological capacity, staffing, and training; and increased coordination between the CBRC and other financial supervisory authorities in China.[26]

The Board has reviewed the record in this case and has determined that the enhancements to standards of bank supervision in China warrant a finding that ICBC is subject to CCS by its home country supervisors. In making this determination, the Board has considered that the CBRC is the principal supervisory authority of ICBC, including its foreign subsidiaries and affiliates, for all matters other than money laundering.[27] The CBRC has primary responsibility and authority for regulating the establishment and activities and the expansion and dissolution of banking institutions,

---

worldwide basis or comparable information that permits analysis of the bank's financial condition on a worldwide consolidated basis; (v) evaluate prudential standards, such as capital adequacy and risk asset exposure, on a worldwide basis. No single factor is determinative, and other elements may inform the Board's determination.

[23]   57 Federal Register 12992, 12995 (April 15, 1992).

[24]   Bank for International Settlements, Basel Committee on Banking Supervision, *Core Principles for Effective Banking Supervision* (October 2006), available at http://www.bis.org/publ/bcbs129.pdf.

[25]   See, e.g., 93rd Annual Report of the Board of Governors of the Federal Reserve System (2006), at 76 ("The Core Principles, developed by the Basel Committee in 1997, have become the de facto international standard for sound prudential regulation and supervision of banks.").

[26]   The Board has previously approved applications from Chinese banks, including ICBC, to establish U.S. branches under a lower standard than the CCS standard. See *China Merchants Bank Co., Limited*, 94 Federal Reserve Bulletin C24 (2008); *Industrial and Commercial Bank of China Limited*, 94 Federal Reserve Bulletin C114 (2008); *China Construction Bank Corporation*, 95 Federal Reserve Bulletin B54 (2009); and *Bank of Communications Co., Ltd.* (order dated April 8, 2011), 97 Federal Reserve Bulletin 49 (2nd Quar. 2011). In each case, the Board made a determination that the bank's home country supervisors were actively working to establish arrangements for the consolidated supervision of the bank. 12 U.S.C. § 3105(d)(6).

[27]   Before April 2003, the People's Bank of China ("PBOC") acted as both China's central bank and primary banking supervisor, including with respect to anti-money-laundering matters. In April 2003, the CBRC was established as the primary banking supervisor and assumed the majority of the PBOC's bank regulatory functions. The PBOC maintained its roles as China's central bank and primary supervisor for anti-money-laundering matters.

both domestically in China and abroad. The CBRC monitors Chinese banks' consolidated financial condition, compliance with laws and regulations, and internal controls through a combination of on-site examinations, off-site surveillance through the review of required regulatory reports and external audit reports, and interaction with senior management.

Since its establishment in 2003, the CBRC has augmented its supervisory structure, staffing, and internal operations; enhanced its existing supervisory programs; and developed new policies and procedures to create a framework for the consolidated supervision of the largest banks in China. The CBRC also has strengthened its supervisory regime related to accounting requirements and standards for loan classification, internal controls, risk management, and capital adequacy, and it has developed and implemented a risk-focused supervisory framework.

Created better consolidated framework [handwritten margin note]

* * *

Banks must report to the CBRC their unconsolidated capital adequacy ratios quarterly and their consolidated ratios semiannually. China's bank capital rules are based on the Basel I Capital Accord, while taking into account certain aspects of the Basel II Capital Accord. In addition, the CBRC, as a member of the Basel Committee on Banking Supervision, has supported the Basel III Capital Accord framework and implementation time frame. The CBRC can take enforcement actions when capital ratios or other financial indicators fall below specified levels. These actions may include issuing supervisory notices, requiring the bank to submit and implement an acceptable capital replenishment plan, restricting asset growth, requiring reduction of higher-risk assets, restricting the purchase of fixed assets, and restricting dividends and other forms of distributions. Significantly undercapitalized banks may be required to make changes in senior management or restructure their operations.

CBRC working to incorporate new Basel [handwritten margin note]

ICBC, like other large Chinese banks, is required to be audited annually by an external accounting firm that meets the standards of Chinese authorities, including the Ministry of Finance, PBOC, and CBRC, and the audit results are shared with the CBRC and PBOC. The scope of the required audit includes a review of ICBC's financial statements, asset quality, capital adequacy, internal controls, and compliance with applicable laws. At its discretion, the CBRC may order a special audit at any time. In addition, in connection with its listing on the Shanghai and Hong Kong stock exchanges, ICBC is required to report financial statements under both International Financial Reporting Standards ("IFRS") and Chinese Accounting Standards ("CAS").[28] These financial

---

[28] Based primarily on newspaper reports, several commenters criticized the reliability and accuracy of Chinese accounting methods. These newspaper articles focus on Chinese firms that are listed on U.S. exchanges through a process called "reverse mergers" whereby the Chinese firm

statements are audited by an international accounting firm under applicable IFRS auditing standards.[29]

* * *

Chinese law imposes various prudential limitations on banks, including limits on transactions with affiliates and on large exposures.[30] Related-party transactions include credit extensions, asset transfers, and the provision of any type of services. Chinese banks are required to adopt appropriate policies and procedures to manage related-party transactions and the board of directors must appoint a committee to supervise such transactions and relationships. Applicable laws require all related-party transactions to be conducted on an arm's-length basis.

* * *

The CBRC is authorized to require any bank to provide information and to impose sanctions for failure to comply with such requests. If the CBRC determines that a bank is not in compliance with banking regulations and prudential standards, it may impose various sanctions

---

acquires a listed U.S. firm and thereby becomes a listed firm. These articles allege that the listed Chinese firms have reported unreliable financial statements audited by Chinese auditing firms. China's largest banks, such as ICBC, use the "Big Four" accounting firms. There is no evidence that Chinese accounting methods or practices at the large Chinese banks, such as ICBC, are unreliable. The International Monetary Fund's ("IMF") financial system stability assessment report and the accompanying detailed assessment report of observance with the Basel Core Principles, discussed in detail below, both found that "[s]ince 2005, [CAS] have substantially converged with [IFRS] and International Standards on Auditing, respectively." IMF, *People's Republic of China, Financial System Stability Assessment* at 57 (June 24, 2011); IMF and World Bank, *People's Republic of China: Detailed Assessment Report of Observance with Basel Core Principles for Effective Banking Supervision* at 9 (April 2012). In addition, the World Bank Report on Observance of Standards and Codes determined that CAS and IFRS are basically compatible and that the Chinese authorities and the International Accounting Standards Board have established a continuing convergence mechanism designed to achieve full convergence in 2012. World Bank, *Report on Observance of Standards and Codes (ROSC) Accounting and Auditing— People's Republic of China* at Executive Summary and at 12 (October 2009), available at http://www.worldbank.org/ifa/rosc_aa_chn.pdf.

[29] The commenters also asserted that the "Big Four" accounting firms in the United States, including the parent company of ICBC's auditor, Ernst & Young, were substantially fined for departing from U.S. generally accepted accounting principles ("U.S. GAAP"). The commenters argued, without providing any supporting data, that any operational deficiencies in the United States by Ernst & Young should be imputed to ICBC's auditor and financial statements, and they requested that the Board require ICBC to submit financial data audited by a fully independent auditing firm that has not been the subject of substantial criticisms by the Public Company Oversight Accounting Board ("PCAOB") or other regulatory body. The Board notes that the PCAOB did sanction Ernst & Young for failing to properly evaluate a specific company's sales returns reserves, which the PCAOB found were both a material component of that company's financial statements and not in conformity with U.S. GAAP. The PCAOB did not find that this was a widespread practice by Ernst & Young or indicative of behavior by any of its foreign accounting operations.

[30] The CBRC definition of an "affiliate" or a "related party" of a bank includes subsidiaries, associates/joint ventures, shareholders holding 5 percent or more of the bank's shares, and key management personnel (and immediate relatives) and those individuals' other business affiliations.

depending upon the severity of the violation. The CBRC may suspend approval of new products or new offices, suspend part of the bank's operations, impose monetary penalties, and in more serious cases, replace management of the bank. The CBRC also has authority to impose administrative penalties, including warnings and fines for violations of applicable laws and rules. Criminal violations are transferred to the judicial authorities for investigation and prosecution.

* * *

Authorities in China also have increased cooperation with international groups and supervisory authorities in other countries regarding bank supervision. In particular, the CBRC has established mechanisms to cooperate with supervisory authorities in at least 25 other countries for the supervision of cross-border banking. In addition, the PBOC and CBRC officially joined the Basel Committee on Banking Supervision on behalf of China and since their accession, have actively participated in the revision of the Basel II Capital Accord, in the formulation of the Basel III Capital Accord, and in other working groups, China also is active in the ongoing work of the Financial Stability Board. In addition, the PBOC, CBRC, other financial supervisory agencies, and other agencies in China have taken joint measures to maintain financial stability.[31] Moreover, authorities in the United States and China that are responsible for the oversight of auditing services for public companies are engaged in continuing discussions with respect to enhancing cross-border cooperation, and the Board looks forward to timely negotiation of an agreement relating to cooperative actions by these authorities.

The IMF recently concluded a financial system stability assessment of China ("FSSA"), including an assessment of China's compliance with the Basel Core Principles.[32] The FSSA determined that China's overall regulatory and supervisory framework adheres to international

---

[31] China has established a system of preliminary indicators for monitoring financial stability, developed methodology and operational frameworks for monitoring financial risks, and published an annual *China Financial Stability Report* since 2005.

[32] The assessment reflects the regulatory and supervisory framework in place as of June 24, 2011. IMF, *People's Republic of China, Financial System Stability Assessment* (June 24, 2011), available at http://www.imf.org/external/pubs/ft/scr/2011/cr11321.pdf. The FSSA covers an evaluation of three components: (1) the source, probability, and potential impact of the main risks to macro financial stability in the near term; (2) the country's financial stability policy framework; and (3) the authorities' capacity to manage and resolve a financial crisis should the risks materialize. The FSSA is a key input to IMF surveillance. The FSSA is a forward-looking exercise, unlike the Board's assessment of the comprehensive, consolidated supervision of an applicant.

The IMF and World Bank separately publish a detailed assessment of the country's observance of the Basel Core Principles that discusses the country's adherence to the Basel Core Principles in much greater detail. See IMF and World Bank, *People's Republic of China: Detailed Assessment Report of Observance with Basel Core Principles for Effective Banking Supervision* (April 2012) ("DAR"), available at http://www.imf.org/external/pubs/ft/scr/2012/cr1278.pdf.

standards.[33] The FSSA found that "[t]he laws, rules and guidance that CBRC operates under generally establish a benchmark of prudential standards that is of high quality and was drawn extensively from international standards and the [Basel Core Principles] themselves."[34] The FSSA additionally noted that "[c]onsolidated supervision of banks and their direct subsidiaries and branches on the mainland or offshore is of high quality."[35] With respect to the CBRC, the FSSA found as follows:

> All the banks, auditors, ratings agencies and other market participants that the mission interacted with were unhesitating in their regard for the role that the CBRC has played in driving professionalism, risk management and international recognition of the Chinese banking system. In particular, the mission observed that [the CBRC] has been the key driving force in driving improvements in risk management, corporate governance and internal control and disclosure in Chinese banks.[36]

Based on its review, the FSSA rated China's overall compliance with the Basel Core Principles as satisfactory. In giving this overall rating, the FSSA noted several areas that merited improvement and made specific recommendations for continued advances in supervision and regulation. The Chinese authorities noted that some of the recommendations of the FSSA are already being implemented, and others will be taken into account in the CBRC's plans to improve supervisory effectiveness.

The Board has taken into account the FSSA's views that China is, overall, in satisfactory compliance with the Basel Core Principles and that there are areas for further improvement. The Board has also taken into account the responses by Chinese authorities to the FSSA report and the progress made by Chinese authorities to address the issues raised in that report.

Based on all the facts of record, including its review of the supervisory framework implemented by the CBRC for ICBC, the Board has determined that ICBC is subject to comprehensive supervision on a consolidated basis by its home country supervisors. This determination is specific to ICBC. By statute, the Board must review this determination in processing future applications involving ICBC and also must make a determination of comprehensive, consolidated supervision in other applications involving different applicants from China.

---

[33]   FSSA at 39.

[34]   FSSA at 59; DAR at 12.

[35]   FSSA at 64; DAR at 16.

[36]   DAR at 7.

NOTES

1. Any company that seeks to own or control, as defined, a U.S. banking organization must apply to the Board for its approval to become a bank holding company under Section 3 of the Bank Holding Company Act of 1956, as amended. 12 U.S.C. § 1842. In addition to the anti-competitive standards under Section 3 of the BHC Act cited in the Board's ICBC Order 2012–4, 12 other standards apply to such transactions. Section 3 of the BHC Act requires the Board to consider the financial and managerial resources and future prospects of the companies and depository institutions involved in the proposal as well as the effectiveness of these companies in combatting money-laundering activities 12 U.S.C § 1842(c)(3)(A). Section 3 of the BHC Act also requires the Board to determine that an applicant has provided adequate assurances that it will make available to the Board such information on its operations and activities and those of its affiliates that the Board deems appropriate to determine and enforce compliance with the BHC Act. _Id._

2. Bank acquisitions that involve the merger of a U.S. bank may also be subject to the requirements under the Bank Merger Act pursuant to Section 18(c) of the Federal Deposit Insurance Act (FDIA), as amended (12 U.S.C. § 1828(c), and for national banks regulated by the OCC, 12 U.S.C. § 215, 215a. Further, when individuals seek to acquire, own or acquire control of a U.S. banking organization, the requirements of the Change in Bank Control Act under Section 7(j) of the FDIA, 12 U.S.C.1817(j) and the regulations thereunder, 12 CFR § 303.80.

3. For acquisitions of control by either companies, or individuals, or both, the control thresholds are quite complicated. Generally, acquisition of ownership of, or the power to vote 25 percent or more of any class of voting securities, or the power, directly or indirectly to direct the management or polices of a U.S. banking organization is conclusively presumed to constitute control. See e.g., 12 CFR § 303.81(c) (FDIC Control Act Rules) 12 U.S.C § 1841(a)(2) (Board control definition). Further, there may be a regulatory presumption of control for ownership of 5 percent or greater of voting common stock, subject to rebuttal by the applicant in writing. See, e.g., 12 CFR § 330.82(b)(2) (10 percent); 12 CFR § 225.41 (Board rules regarding rebuttal of presumptions of control); See also Federal Reserve Board Policy Statement Concerning Minority Equity Investments (September 22, 2008); FDIC Proposed Policy Statement on Investments by Private Capital Investors, 74 Fed. Reg. 32931 (July 9, 2009).

Finally, proposed stock investments by both individuals and corporate entities may be aggregated to reach the control thresholds when parties are deemed to be engaging in "action in concert" for purposes of the control rules. See, e.g., 12 CFR § 330.81(b) (action in concerts defined to mean "knowing participation in a joint activity or parallel action towards a common goal of acquiring control" of a banking organization); 12 CFR § 225.41(b)(2) (Board "action in concert" definition).

Suffice to say, there is a premium on successful planning to identity all regulatory requirements applicable to either establishing a foreign bank office in the U.S., or a foreign banking organization acquiring a U.S. bank.

4.   The Board's 2012 approval of ICBC's acquisition of a small U.S. bank raised issues of compliance with the Foreign Investment and National Security Act of 2007 ("FINSA") Public Law 110-49, 121 Stat. 246 in the context of other recent Chinese acquisitions of U.S. businesses. FINSA, signed into law on July 26, 2007, with an effective date of October 24, 2007, codifies aspects of the structure, role, process, and responsibilities of the Committee on Foreign Investments in the United States ("CFIUS"), and the role of executive branch departments, agencies, and offices in CFIUS's review of transactions for national security concerns. Previously, the sole basis for the existence of CFIUS had been Executive Order 11858 of May 7, 1975, 40 FR 20263, 3 CFR, 1971-1975 Compilation, p. 990. FINSA specifies the following as members of CFIUS: The Secretary of the Treasury (who serves as chairperson), the Attorney General, and the Secretaries of Homeland Security, Commerce, Defense, State, and Energy. FINSA also provides that CFIUS may include, generally or on a case-by-case basis as the President deems appropriate, the heads of any other executive department, agency or office. See 70702 Fed. Reg. 70702 (November 21, 2008) (adopting final U.S. Department of Treasury rules amending 31 CFR Part 800 to implement the FINSA.

Section 721 of the FINSA authorizes the President to review mergers, acquisitions, and takeovers by or with any foreign person which could result in foreign control of any person engaged in interstate commerce in the United States, to determine the effects of such transactions on the national security of the United States. The CFIUS has recently reviewed a number of proposed acquisitions of U.S. companies, including, notably, ICBC's 2012 bank acquisition. See Lingling Wei, China Bank Moves to Buy U.S. Branches, The Wall Street Journal (January 11, 2011) (ICBC's proposed acquisition of Bank of Asia's U.S. bank subsidiary expected to be "carefully scrutinized" by U.S. regulators, including the CFIUS); see also The Committee on Foreign Investment in the United States (CFIUS), Congressional Research Service, (March 6, 2014) (report to Congress analyzing CFIUS review of foreign investment transactions, including those by Chinese entities).

4. "DEATH PENALTY" PROVISION

Sec. 211.25 Termination of offices of foreign banks.

(a) Grounds for termination—General. Under sections 7(e) and 10(b) of the IBA (12 U.S.C. 3105 (d), 3107(b)), the Board may order a foreign bank to terminate the activities of its representative office, state branch, state agency, or commercial lending company subsidiary if the Board finds that:

> (i) The foreign bank is not subject to comprehensive consolidated supervision in accordance with Sec. 211.24(c)(1), and the home country supervisor is not making demonstrable

progress in establishing arrangements for the consolidated supervision of the foreign bank; or

(ii) Both of the following criteria are met:

(a) There is reasonable cause to believe that the foreign bank, or any of its affiliates, has committed a violation of law or engaged in an unsafe or unsound banking practice in the United States; and

(b) As a result of such violation or practice, the continued operation of the foreign bank's representative office, state branch, state agency, or commercial lending company subsidiary would not be consistent with the public interest, or with the purposes of the IBA, the BHC Act, or the FDIA.

* * *

(c) Consultation with relevant state supervisor. Except in the case of termination pursuant to the expedited procedure in paragraph (d)(3) of this section, the Board shall request and consider the views of the relevant state supervisor before issuing an order terminating the activities of a state branch, state agency, representative office, or commercial lending company subsidiary under this section.

(d) Termination procedures—(1) Notice and hearing. Except as otherwise provided in paragraph (d)(3) of this section, an order issued under paragraph (a)(1) of this section shall be issued only after notice to the relevant state supervisor and the foreign bank and after an opportunity for a hearing.

NOTES

1.   Note that Section 211.25(a)(1) references grounds for termination of *state* chartered offices of foreign banks. As such, the Board has sole authority to order termination of state offices upon notice and hearing. 12 CFR § 211.25(d). For termination of a *federally* chartered office or branch, however, termination is under the jurisdiction of the OCC, which, as noted in Chapter 6, charters and regulates national banks. Thus, under Regulation K, the Board's authority is generally limited to, in its discretion, transmitting a recommendation that the license of a federal branch or agency office be terminated if the Board has reasonable cause to believe that the foreign bank or any affiliate of the foreign bank has engaged in conduct for which the activities of a state branch or any office may be terminated pursuant Section 211.25. 12 CFR § 211.25(e).

2.   A foreign bank may voluntarily terminate the activities of any U.S. office upon 30 days' notice to the Board, 12 CFR § 211.25(f). Notice does not satisfy any other relevant state or federal requirements for prior notice of the

closing of a branch office. See, e.g., 12 U.S.C. 1831p (prior notice of closing of a branch office required under Section 39 of the FDIA).

3.   The Board may act to terminate an office without providing an opportunity for a hearing if it determines that "expeditious action is necessary in order to protect the public interest." 12 CFR § 211.25(f)(3)(i)–(iii). Notwithstanding the Board must still provide notice of the intended termination order and grant the foreign bank an opportunity to present a written submission opposing issuance of the order, or take any other actions designed to provide the bank with notice and "an opportunity to present its views" concerning the order. *Id.*

THARAK CHACKO, CASE STUDY: DAIWA BANK

Introduction

On July 13, 1995, Daiwa Bank's Toshihide Iguchi confessed, in a 30-page letter to the president of his bank in Japan, that he had lost around $1.1 billion while dealing in US Treasury bonds.

The executive vice president of Daiwa's New York branch had traded away the bank's money over 11 years—an extraordinarily long period for such a fraud to run—while using his position as head of the branch's securities custody department to cover up the loss by selling off securities owned by Daiwa and its customers.

The trading loss was one of the largest of its kind in history. But it was the cover-ups by Iguchi over a period of years, and then by senior managers at Daiwa between July 13 and September 18 1995, when the bank eventually reported the loss to the US Federal Reserve Board, that did the real damage. These led to criminal indictments against the bank and its officers and, eventually, to one of Japan's largest commercial banks being kicked out of the US markets.

* * *

The Story

Toshihide Iguchi, a Kobe, Japan-born US citizen who majored in psychology at Southwest Missouri State University, Springfield, joined Daiwa's New York branch in 1977. There he learned how to run the small back office of the branch's securities business. Opened as an office in the 1950s, the Daiwa New York branch began dealing in US Treasury securities as part of Daiwa's services to its pension fund customers. During the 1980s the New York desk became a significant force in the US government debt market and was designated as a primary market dealer in 1986.

When Iguchi was promoted to become a trader in 1984, he did not relinquish his back-office duties. All in all, he supervised the securities custody department at the New York branch from approximately 1977 right through to 1995. This lack of segregation, a relatively common feature of small trading desks in the early 1980s but already a discredited practice by the early 1990s, led to Daiwa's downfall.

Daiwa's New York branch managed the custody of the US Treasury bonds that it bought, and those that it bought on behalf of its customers, via a sub-custody account held at Bankers Trust. Through this account, interest on the bonds was collected and dispersed, and bonds were transferred or sold according to the wishes of either customers or the bank's own managers. Daiwa and its customers kept track of what was happening in this account through transaction reports from Bankers Trust that flowed through Iguchi, in his role as head of the back office.

When Iguchi lost a few hundred thousand dollars early on in his trading activities, he was tempted into selling off bonds in the Bankers Trust sub-custody account to pay off his losses. Then, in the words of the FBI agents who investigated the case: "He concealed his unauthorised sales from the custody account . . . by falsifying Bankers Trust account statements so that the statements would not indicate that the securities had been sold."

As he lost more money trying to trade his way back into the black, it became hard work keeping alive this parallel series of reports. But luckily for him, Daiwa and its internal auditors never independently confirmed the custody account statements.

* * *

Later on, while he served his sentence, Iguchi was asked by Time magazine whether his early actions felt like a crime. "To me, it was only a violation of internal rules," he said. "I think all traders have a tendency to fall into the same trap. You always have a way of recovering the loss. As long as that possibility is there, you either admit your loss and lose face and your job, or you wait a little—a month or two months, or however long it takes."

In Iguchi's case it took 11 years, during which time he is said to have forged some 30,000 trading slips, among other documents. When customers sold off securities that Iguchi had, in fact, already sold off on his own behalf, or when customers needed to be paid interest on long-gone securities, Iguchi settled their accounts by selling off yet more securities and changing yet more records. Eventually about $377 million of Daiwa's customers' securities and about $733 million of Daiwa's own investment securities had been sold off by Iguchi to cover his trading losses.

As Iguchi's apparent success grew—he later said that at one point his desk produced half the New York branch's nominal profits—he became something of a golden boy at Daiwa. But the losses accumulated until by the early 1990s it was difficult for Iguchi to continue to hide them, particularly after 1993 when Daiwa made some limited efforts to split up its trading and back-office functions. Yet he managed to survive for another two years before engineering his own day of reckoning.

Iguchi's survival wasn't entirely down to luck. Subsequent investigation showed that risk control lapses and cover-ups were part of the culture of Daiwa's New York operation in the 1980s and early 1990s, to a farcical degree. For example, during the 1995 investigation of the Iguchi affair, the bank was also charged with operating an unauthorised trading area for securities between 1986 and 1993.

* * *

Following a regulatory rebuff in 1993, the bank had assured regulators that traders would no longer report to Iguchi while he occupied his role as head of the securities custody department. In fact, the branch continued to operate without a proper division of responsibilities. Furthermore, during the 1995 investigation Iguchi revealed that between 1984 and 1987, other Daiwa traders had suffered major losses; these had apparently been concealed from regulators by shifting the losses to Daiwa's overseas affiliates (FDIC, 1995).

In Iguchi's confessional letters to Daiwa in mid-summer 1999 (he sent a stream of letters and notes to the bank after that initial July 13 letter) the rogue custody officer suggested that his superiors keep the losses secret until "appropriate measures" could be taken to stabilise the situation. It was a suggestion that was taken up. In the period after July 13 and before about September 18, when Daiwa belatedly advised the Federal Reserve Board of the loss, certain of Daiwa's managers connived with Iguchi to prevent the losses being discovered, despite a legal requirement to report misdoings immediately to the US regulators.

* * *

After Daiwa told regulators about the loss on September 18, Iguchi was taken to a motel and questioned directly by the US Federal Bureau of Investigation. He told FBI agents about what had gone on in the months following his initial confession to Daiwa, and the bank was shocked to find itself facing a 24-count indictment for conspiracy, fraud, bank exam obstruction records falsification and failure to disclose federal crimes.

Daiwa argued, rightly, that not a single customer of the bank had lost any money. At the time of the incident, Daiwa was one of Japan's top 10 banks and one of the top 20 banks in the world in terms of asset size. Like most other Japanese, and some European, banks, it had massive "hidden profits" on its balance sheet that were not accounted for due to the legitimate historical accounting method that it employed. That gave Daiwa's management considerable freedom of action if unexpected problems arose. One of the bank's crisis management actions after Iguchi confessed was to pump back into the defrauded account securities equivalent to those that their New York head of custody had sold off.

But the US regulators were deeply unhappy at the attempted cover-up, and at the way Daiwa had seemed to ignore regulatory warnings over a number of years. They were also unhappy that at least one senior member of Japan's ministry of finance knew about the Daiwa scandal in early August and had not informed his US regulatory counterpart.

This pushed the Daiwa scandal onto the international political stage and led to a telephone conversation in which Japan's finance minister, Masayoshi Takemura, was obliged to make apologetic noises to US Treasury secretary Robert Rubin for his staff's failure to pass on the information. (The call was made only after Takemura had annoyed US officials by denying at an earlier press conference that his ministry had failed in its duties; his aides later denied that any formal apology had been made to Rubin.)

* * *

NOTES

1.   The Daiwa scandal received extensive media coverage. While financial scandals don't always make headlines due to sometimes complex financial issues, the Daiwa situation seemed to make for an easy narrative. See, e.g., AsiaWeek, Japan's $1-Billion Scam, October 27, 1995; *Time* magazine, A Blown Billion, October 9, 1995; *Time* magazine, "I Didn't Set Out to Rob a Bank" (interview with Iguchi), February 1997.

2.   Daiwa bank executives at the time of the scandal in 1995 found that it dogged them into the new millennium. The BBC reported that a Japanese court had ordered 11 current and former board members and executives from the bank to pay the bank $775 million in damages, much of it awarded against the president of Daiwa's New York branch during the Iguchi period. Judge Mitsuhiro Ikeda made it clear that the award was compensation to the bank's shareholders for the fact that "the risk management mechanism at the [New York] branch was effectively not functioning", as well as for management's failure to report the incident promptly, and failures in oversight. See Bank bosses pay $775m fraud charge, BBC News (September 28, 2000).

IN THE MATTER OF DAIWA BANK, LTD. OSAKA, JAPAN AND DAIWA BANK, LTD. NEW YORK BRANCH NEW YORK, NEW YORK

Board of Governors of Federal Reserve System Docket No. 95-028-B-FB (1995)
1995 WL 580439 (F.R.B.)

Notice of Charges and of Hearing Issued Pursuant to the Federal Deposit Insurance Act.

The Board of Governors of the Federal Reserve System (the "Board of Governors") is of the opinion or has reasonable cause to believe that Daiwa Bank Ltd., Osaka, Japan ("Daiwa"), a foreign bank doing business in the United States, and its New York, New York branch (the "New York Branch") have engaged in unsafe and unsound practices and violations of law and regulation in conducting the business of the New York Branch which resulted in approximately $1.1 billion in trading losses and that the unsafe and unsound practices and violations have had, and could in the future continue to have, adverse effects on Daiwa's operations in the United States.

Accordingly, in conjunction with the Superintendent of Banks of the State of New York (the "Superintendent"), the Board of Governors hereby institutes this proceeding by issuing this Notice of Charges and of Hearing (the "Notice") for the purpose of determining whether an appropriate order to cease and desist should be issued by the Board of Governors against Daiwa and the New York Branch requiring them to cease and desist the unsafe and unsound practices and violations and to take affirmative action to correct the unsafe and unsound practices and violations of law and regulation, pursuant to the provisions of section 8 (b) of the Federal Deposit Insurance Act, as amended (the "FDI Act") (12 U.S.C. 1818 (b)).

In support of this Notice, the Board of Governors alleges the following:

Jurisdiction

Daiwa is a foreign bank that is incorporated and doing business in Japan. The New York Branch is licensed by the State of New York and supervised by the Superintendent and the Board of Governors.

At all times pertinent to the charges herein, Daiwa, as a foreign bank, and the New York Branch, as an uninsured branch of a foreign bank, are and each have been, respectively, subject to section 8 of the FDI Act and the rules and regulations of the Board of Governors.

Allegations

Daiwa has informed the Federal Reserve Bank of New York (the "Reserve Bank") that a senior official of the New York Branch, Toshihide Iguchi ("Iguchi"), submitted a written confession to the President of Daiwa. The written confession detailed Iguchi's unauthorized trading of U.S.

Treasury securities in which, over an 11-year period, he lost approximately $1.1 billion. The written confession detailed how he secretly traded U.S. Treasury securities in an unauthorized manner and then misappropriated securities from Daiwa, as well as from customers of the branch for whom the New York Branch was acting as custodian, in order to cover the losses. The confession also described how Iguchi falsified branch records and lied to examiners and auditors in order to hide the trading losses.

* * *

Unsafe and Unsound Practices and Violations of Law

As set forth in this Notice, Daiwa and the New York Branch have engaged in unsafe and unsound practices in conducting the business of the New York Branch. In particular, Daiwa and the New York Branch permitted an official to engage in the trading of U.S. Treasury securities without adequate supervision. Moreover, contrary to safe and prudent banking practices, Daiwa and the New York Branch did not adequately separate the trading function from the backroom operations; thereby permitting Iguchi to influence the performance of record-keeping and internal controls over his own trades. In contravention of safe and prudent banking practices, Daiwa and the New York Branch permitted Iguchi to oversee the branch's custodial operations, thereby giving him unlimited access to Daiwa's, as well as customers', securities held in custody. As a result of these unsafe and unsound practices, Iguchi was able to engage in unauthorized trading activities that resulted in loss of approximately $1.1 billion and was able to hide the losses by misappropriating securities from Daiwa and its customers, by falsifying the branch's records, and by lying to the Reserve Bank, the Superintendent and auditors.

Section 211.24(f) of Regulation K of the Board of Governors (12 C.F.R. 211.24(f)) requires foreign banks operating in the United States and their agencies and branches to file with the appropriate law enforcement authorities and the Federal Reserve reports of suspected criminal activity within 30 days of learning of such activity. See Chapter 8, infra, for a discussion of the requirements for the filing of Suspicious Activity Reports. Notwithstanding this regulatory requirement, neither Daiwa nor the New York Branch filed the appropriate criminal referral form, thereby delaying informing U.S. law enforcement and bank regulatory authorities about a matter that materially impacts on the safety and soundness of the operations of Daiwa and the New York Branch.

Enforcement Proceedings

Notice is hereby given that a hearing will be held on December 27, 1995 in New York, New York, or any other place designated by the presiding administrative law judge, for the purpose of taking evidence on the charges hereinbefore specified in order to determine whether an appropriate order should be issued under the FDI Act requiring Daiwa and the New York Branch to cease and desist from the unsafe or unsound practices and violations of law herein specified and to take affirmative action to correct the conditions resulting from such practices and violations.

* * *

NOTES

1.   On November 1, 1995, Daiwa consented to the issuance by the Board of Governors, the N.Y. Banking Superintendent and several other state banking departments of an Order to Terminate United States Banking Activities (the "Termination Order") against Daiwa, which, among other things, ordered the termination of Daiwa's U.S. banking activities by February 2, 1996, and, as of February 2, 1996, Daiwa did terminate its U.S. banking activities. As it turns out, it was not a permanent ban. Please note footnote 4 in the following Board order.

THE DAIWA BANK, LIMITED
OSAKA, JAPAN
Federal Reserve Board (February 28, 2003)

Order Approving Establishment of a Representative Office

The Daiwa Bank, Limited ("Bank"), Osaka, Japan, a foreign bank within the meaning of the International Banking Act ("IBA"), has applied under section 10(a) of the IBA (12 U.S.C. § 3107(a)) to establish a representative office in New York, New York. The Foreign Bank Supervision Enhancement Act of 1991, which amended the IBA, provides that a foreign bank must obtain the approval of the Board to establish a representative office in the United States.

* * *

The proposed representative office would provide liaison services for Bank's head office and engage in limited marketing activities directed at U.S. subsidiaries and offices of Bank's Japanese corporate clients. The proposed representative office would also be involved in administrative activities related to the closing of Asahi's former branch office.

* * *

With respect to the financial and managerial resources of Bank, taking into consideration Bank's record of operations in its home country, its overall financial resources, and its standing with its home country supervisor, financial and managerial factors are consistent with approval of the proposed representative office.[4]

[Discussion of Regulation K factors for consolidated home country supervision.]

* * *

On the basis of all the facts of record, and subject to the commitments made by Bank and the terms and conditions set forth in this order, Bank's application to establish the representative office is hereby approved. Should any restrictions on access to information on the operations or activities of Bank or any of its affiliates subsequently interfere with the Board's ability to obtain information to determine and enforce compliance by Bank or its affiliates with applicable federal statutes, the Board may require or recommend termination of any of Bank's direct and indirect activities in the United States.

5. ENHANCED PRUDENTIAL STANDARDS FOR FOREIGN BANKING ORGANIZATIONS

Among its many new requirements for the banking industry, the Dodd-Frank Act (discussed more fully in Chapter 6) significantly increases regulatory requirements imposed on foreign banking organizations ("FBOs") and their U.S. and non-U.S. operations. The increased supervision and oversight is based on a broad mandate to U.S. financial regulators to oversee the activities and operation of foreign firms that participate in, benefit from, and pose risks to the U.S. financial system as a result of such activities and operations. Examples of Dodd-Frank Act requirements with far-reaching implications affecting FBOs include the Volcker Rule and its reach to the proprietary trading and covered fund activities of FBOs, discussed below, and imposition of the time-and-resource intensive resolution planning requirement on FBOs. Prudential supervision standards for FBOs with total consolidated assets of $10 billion or more, recently adopted by the Board, are the latest and arguably most significant requirements imposed on foreign participants in the U.S. banking market.

---

[4]   In 1995, the Federal Reserve and other federal and state banking regulators issued a series of orders terminating the U.S. operations of Bank and Daiwa Bank Trust Company in connection with Bank's failure to disclose to regulators and law enforcement authorities trading losses of more than $1 billion. The prohibition against Bank's re-entry into the United States ended in 1998. Since the termination of its U.S. operations, Bank has provided information about reforms to its internal controls and reporting systems. The proposal to maintain the representative office in New York arises from a reorganization of the Japanese operations of Resona and no change or expansion of U.S. operations is contemplated.

The Board's recently adopted rules ("Final Rule")[1] implementing the FBO enhanced prudential standards of Section 165 of the Dodd-Frank Act,[2] impose a tiered system of regulation for FBOs, applying an escalating and more stringent series of requirements based on asset size, beginning with small FBOs (holding total consolidated assets ("TCA") between $10 billion and $50 billion ("Small FBOs")), medium-sized FBOs (holding TCA of at least $50 billion and U.S.-based assets ("USA") of less than $50 billion ("Medium FBOs")), and large FBOs (holding TCA and USA of $50 billion or greater ("Large FBOs")).

In explaining the basis for the FBO provisions of the Final Rule, the Board noted that the requirements of the rule are designed—like many other provisions of the DFA—to prevent another financial crisis. The FBO prudential supervision standards arise out of, and are a response to, the reliance of FBOs operating in the U.S. on the Board for funding at the onset of the most recent financial crisis. The preamble to the Final Rule notes that, "the profile of foreign bank operations in the United States changed substantially in the period preceding the financial crisis. U.S. branches and agencies of foreign banking organizations as a group moved from a position of receiving funding from their parent organizations on a net basis in 1999 to providing significant funding to non-U.S. affiliates by the mid-2000s."[3] According to the Board, "[i]n 2008, U.S. branches and agencies [of FBOs] provided more than $600 billion on a net basis to non-U.S. affiliates."[4]

The FBO prudential supervision standards are a response, in part, to the Board's observation that, as FBOs received less funding from their parent companies, they became "more reliant on less stable, short-term U.S. dollar wholesale funding, contributing in some cases to a buildup in maturity mismatches."[5] Of particular concern to the Board in developing the prudential standards was that, "[t]rends in the global balance sheets of [FBOs leading into the financial crisis] reveal that short-term U.S. dollar funding raised in the United States was used to provide long-term U.S. dollar-denominated project and trade finance around the world as well as to finance non-U.S. affiliates' investments in U.S. dollar-denominated asset-backed securities."[6] Recognizing that "U.S. supervisors, as host

---

[1]   The Final Rule, with portions applicable to FBOs adopted as subparts L through O to Board Regulation YY, was issued by the Board on Feb. 18, 2014. In significant part, the Final Rule is similar to proposed regulations issued in December 2012, with certain changes addressing public comments and with an enhanced phase-in schedule for FBOs to become fully compliant, and a 2018 implementation date for certain obligations. See also Lawrence D. Kaplan, Enhanced Prudential Standards for Foreign Banking Organizations, Paul Hastings Stay Current (March 2014).

[2]   Codified at 12 U.S.C. § 5365.

[3]   Preamble to the Final Rule, at 90.

[4]   Id.

[5]   Id.

[6]   Id.

authorities, have more limited access to timely information on the global operations of [FBOs] than to similar information on U.S.-based banking organizations, [the Board notes that] the totality of the risk profile of the U.S. operations of the [FBOs] can be obscured when these U.S. entities fund activities outside the United States."[7]

Effective July 1, 2016, Medium FBOs (*i.e.*, FBOs having TCA of at least $50 billion and USA of less than $50 billion)[8] will become subject to various enhanced prudential requirements targeted at reducing the aggregate risk these institutions pose to the U.S. financial system. These requirements include:

- **Capital Requirements**—Medium FBOs must meet capital adequacy standards, on a consolidated basis, established by their respective home-country supervisors, consistent with the regulatory capital framework published by the Basel Committee on Banking Supervision, as amended from time to time ("Basel Framework"), including any minimum risk-based capital ratios and minimum leverage ratio.[9]

  > A Medium FBO that does not meet the general minimum capital adequacy standards described above that are consistent with the Basel Framework may be subject to alternative requirements, conditions, or restrictions as may be imposed by the Board in coordination with "any relevant State or Federal regulator."[10]

- **Risk Management/Committee Requirements**—Similar to the requirement applicable to a publicly-traded Small FBO, a Medium FBO must annually certify to the Board that it maintains a committee of its global board of directors (or its equivalent), on a standalone basis or as part of its enterprise-wide risk committee, that oversees risk management policies of the FBO's U.S. operations, and that includes at least one member having experience in identifying, assessing, and managing risk at large, complex firms.[11]

- **Capital Stress Testing**—Also similar to the requirement applicable for a Small FBO, each Medium FBO must be subject, on a consolidated basis, to a capital stress testing regime by its home-country supervisor meeting certain

---

[7]   *Id.*

[8]   Based on TCA as of June 30, 2015 (or the first day of the ninth quarter after exceeding the asset threshold). 12 C.F.R. § 252.152. See generally 12 C.F.R. Part 252, Subpart O (§§ 252.150 *et seq.*).

[9]   12 C.F.R. § 252.143.

[10]   12 C.F.R. § 252.143(c).

[11]   12 C.F.R. § 252.144.

> minimum requirements, and conduct such stress tests (or be subject to a supervisory stress test) and meet any minimum standards set by its home-country supervisor with respect to the stress tests.[12]

- **Liquidity Risk Management Requirements**—A Medium FBO must certify annually to the Board the results of an internal liquidity stress test for either the consolidated operations of the FBO, or the combined U.S. operations of the FBO.[13] Such liquidity stress testing must be conducted consistently with the Basel Committee's liquidity risk management principles.[14]

Large FBOs

Beginning on July 1, 2016, Large FBOs (i.e., FBOs having TCA and USA of $50 billion or more)[15] will become subject to the following prudential requirements targeted at reducing the aggregate risk these institutions pose to the U.S. financial system:

- **Capital Requirements**—Large FBOs must meet capital adequacy standards, on a consolidated basis, established by their respective home-country supervisors, consistent with the Basel Framework, including any minimum risk-based capital ratios and minimum leverage ratio.[16]

  A Large FBO that does not meet the general minimum capital adequacy standards described above that are consistent with the Basel Framework may be subject to alternative requirements, conditions, or restrictions as may be imposed by the Board in coordination with "any relevant State or Federal regulator."[17]

- **Capital Stress Testing**—Similar to the capital stress testing requirements for Small and Medium FBOs, Large FBOs must

---

[12]   12 C.F.R. § 252.146(b)(1). A Medium FBO that does not meet the general minimum capital stress testing standard described above must comply with alternative requirements under the Final Rule. 12 C.F.R. § 252.146(c). Effective on July 1, 2016, Small FBOs (i.e., having TCA of between $10 billion and $50 billion will be subject to capital stress testing and risk committee requirements. 12 C.F.R. § 252.122(a)(1)–(2).

[13]   12 C.F.R. § 252.145(a).

[14]   12 C.F.R. § 252.145(a). A Medium FBO that does not comply with the annual liquidity testing and certification requirement must limit the net aggregate amount that is owed by the FBO's non-U.S. offices and its non-U.S. affiliates to the FBO's combined U.S. operations to a maximum of 25% of the third party liabilities of the FBO's combined U.S. operations, on a daily basis. 12 C.F.R. § 252.145(b).

[15]   Based on TCA as of June 30, 2015 (or the first day of the ninth quarter after exceeding the asset threshold). 12 C.F.R. § 252.152. See generally 12 C.F.R. Part 252, Subpart O (§§ 252.150 *et seq.*).

[16]   12 C.F.R. § 252.154.

[17]   12 C.F.R. § 252.154(c).

be subject, on a consolidated basis, to a capital stress testing regime by its home-country supervisor meeting certain minimum requirements, and conduct such stress tests (or be subject to a supervisory stress test) and meet any minimum standards set by its home-country supervisor with respect to the stress tests.[18] To comply with this requirement, the capital stress testing regime of the Large FBO must include: (i) an annual supervisory capital stress test or an annual evaluation and review by the home-country supervisor of an internal capital adequacy stress test conducted by the Large FBO; and (ii) requirements for governance and controls of stress testing practices by relevant management and the board of directors (or its equivalent).[19]

• **Risk Management/Committee Requirements**—Large FBOs must establish and maintain a risk committee that approves and periodically reviews the risk management policies of the FBO's combined U.S. operations and oversees the risk management framework for such operations, which must be commensurate with the structure, risk-profile, complexity, activities, and size of the FBO, and meet certain minimum requirements under the Final Rule.[20] If the Large FBO is required to have a U.S. intermediate holding company (discussed below), the FBO must maintain its U.S. risk committee as a committee of the board of directors of its U.S. intermediate holding company.[21]

In addition, a Large FBO must appoint a U.S. chief risk officer with experience in identifying, assessing, and managing risk exposures of large, complex financial firms.[22] The U.S. chief risk officer must fulfill certain responsibilities and comply with certain corporate governance and reporting requirements.[23]

---

[18] 12 C.F.R. § 252.158(b)(1).

[19] 12 C.F.R. § 252.158(b)(2).

[20] 12 C.F.R. § 252.155(a).

[21] 12 C.F.R. § 252.155(a)(3). Among other requirements, the risk committee must meet at least quarterly, have at least one member with experience in identifying, assessing, and managing risk exposures of large, complex financial firms, and have at least one member who is not, and was not, an officer or employee (or a member of the immediately family of an executive officer) of the FBO or its affiliates during the last three years. 12 C.F.R. § 252.155(a)(5).

[22] 12 C.F.R. § 252.155(b)(1).

[23] 12 C.F.R. § 252.155(b)(2) and (3). A Large FBO that does not meet the general minimum risk management standards described above may be subject to alternative requirements, conditions, or restrictions as may be imposed by the Board in coordination with "any relevant State or Federal regulator." 12 C.F.R. § 252.155(d).

- **Liquidity Risk Management**—In addition to the above noted risk management and risk committee requirements, a Large FBO is required to maintain a robust liquidity risk management program that includes, among other things, active involvement by the Large FBO's U.S. risk committee, responsibilities for the U.S. chief risk officer, and an independent review component.[24]

- **Liquidity Stress Testing Requirement**—On at least a monthly basis, a Large FBO must conduct stress testing to separately assess the potential impact of liquidity stress scenarios on the cash flows, liquidity position, profitability, and solvency of: (i) the FBO's combined U.S. operations as a whole; (ii) its U.S. branches and agencies on an aggregate basis; and (iii) any U.S. intermediate holding company (discussed below).[25]

  > A Large FBO must maintain a liquidity "buffer" for its U.S. intermediate holding company (if any), as discussed below, and a separate liquidity buffer for its U.S. branches and agencies (if any), both of which are to be calculated according to minimum standards set forth in the Final Rule.[26]

- **Intermediate Holding Company Requirement**—A Large FBO with U.S. non-branch assets of $50 billion or more is required to establish a U.S. intermediate holding company ("IHC"), or designate one from an existing subsidiary that meets the requirements for an IHC.[27] The IHC must then hold all of the Large FBO's ownership interests in any U.S. subsidiaries.[28] Each IHC will be subject to enhanced prudential standards generally consistent with the requirements applicable to Large FBOs, but focused on the FBO's U.S. activities. The IHC structure will facilitate

---

[24]   12 C.F.R. § 252.156(c)(1).

[25]   12 C.F.R. § 252.157(a)(1). The stress testing requirement is subject to a number of minimum requirements, including having in place appropriate policies and procedures, management information systems, as well as control and oversight procedures. 12 C.F.R. § 252.157(a)(6) and (7). Stress tests must take into account various considerations including balance sheet exposures, off-balance sheet exposures, size, risk profile, complexity, business lines, organizational structure, and other characteristics of the FBO and its combined U.S. operations affecting its liquidity risk profile in the U.S. 12 C.F.R. § 252.157(a)(1). The stress tests must also address various scenarios that include adverse market conditions and idiosyncratic stress events for U.S. branches, agencies, and/or any intermediate holding company, and address various planning horizons that include overnight, 30-day, 90-day, and one-year planning scenarios. 12 C.F.R. § 252.157(a)(3) and (4).

[26]   12 C.F.R. § 252.157(c).

[27]   12 C.F.R. § 252.153(a)(1).

[28]   12 C.F.R. § 252.153(b).

supervision and oversight by the Board akin to the agency's treatment of bank holding companies ("BHCs"), including with respect to examination and inspection by the Board.[29] Prudential standards applicable to an IHC include the following:

— *Capital and Leverage Requirements*: Subject to transition provisions for leverage,[30] an IHC is required to calculate and meet all capital adequacy standards set forth in the Board's capital adequacy rules for BHCs, savings and loan holding companies, and state member banks,[31] and comply with all restrictions associated with applicable capital buffers, in the same manner as a BHC.[32] An IHC is also subject to the capital planning requirements generally applicable to BHCs with average total consolidated assets of $50 billion or more.[33]

— *Risk Management and Risk Committee Requirements*: An IHC is also required to establish and maintain a risk committee that approves and periodically reviews the risk management policies and oversees the risk management framework of the IHC, which risk management framework shall have the same required contents as discussed above for Large FBOs.[34] The risk committee must be a committee of the board of directors of the IHC (or equivalent thereof), and may also serve as the Large FBO's U.S. risk committee for its combined U.S. operations.[35]

— *Liquidity Requirements*: An IHC is required to comply with the liquidity risk management requirements, conduct liquidity stress tests, and hold a liquidity buffer pursuant to the same requirements as discussed above that are applicable to Large FBOs.[36]

---

[29] 12 C.F.R. § 252.153(b)(3) and (e).

[30] An IHC that is required to be established by July 1, 2016 must comply with the leverage capital requirements beginning on January 1, 2018, provided that each subsidiary BHC and insured depository institution controlled by the Large FBO immediately prior to the establishment or designation of the IHC, and each BHC and insured depository institution acquired by the FBO after establishment of the IHC, is subject to leverage capital requirements under 12 CFR Part 217 until December 31, 2017. 12 C.F.R. § 252.153(e)(ii)(B).

[31] 12 C.F.R. § 252.153(e)(2)(i), *referencing* 12 CFR Part 217 and any successor regulation.

[32] 12 C.F.R. § 252.153(e)(2)(i).

[33] 12 C.F.R. § 252.153(e)(2)(ii) *referencing* 12 C.F.R. § 225.8.

[34] 12 C.F.R. § 252.153(e)(2)(ii).

[35] 12 C.F.R. § 252.153(e)(3).

[36] 12 C.F.R. § 252.153(e)(4) *referencing* 12 C.F.R. §§ 252.156 and 252.157.

— *Stress Test Requirements*: Subject to transition provisions for
stress testing,[37] an IHC is required to comply with the
prudential supervision requirements for supervisory and
company-run stress tests in the same manner as applicable to
U.S. BHCs.[38]

While affected Large FBOs have until July 1, 2016 to establish the IHC,
Large FBOs with U.S. non-branch assets of $50 billion or more as of June
30, 2014 were required to submit an implementation plan by January 1,
2015 outlining the Large FBO's proposed process to come into compliance
with the IHC requirement and certain other minimum requirements.[39]

NOTES

1.   To understand the Board's perspective, it is important to understand
how the Board approached the FBO funding issue during the recent financial
crisis. As noted by the Board, the agency extended credit to FBOs during the
financial crisis because "[c]onsistent with provisions in the Federal Reserve
Act, branches and agencies of foreign banks operating in the United States
have the same access as domestic banks to the [Board's] discount window,
which is used for borrowing short-term funds." Board Current FAQs, available
at: http://www.federalreserve.gov/faqs/banking_12843.htm. Noting that many
FBOs operating in the U.S. experienced funding problems similar to those
experienced by domestic institutions, the Board observed, "[a]ddressing the
funding problems of both domestic and foreign-owned financial institutions
operating in the United States was essential to restore the flow of credit to U.S.
households and businesses and to encourage a stronger economic recovery and
a return to full employment." *Id.*

According to an analysis of information released by the Board under the
DFA and pursuant to various Freedom of Information Act requests, it appears
that FBOs were significant recipients of Board emergency liquidity funding,
which was provided for a number of reasons, including to avert cash shortfalls
and to "keep the credit markets from grinding to a halt" (See "The Fed's
Liquidity Lifelines," Bloomberg News, available at: http://
www.bloomberg.com/data-visualization/federal-reserve-emergency-lending/#/
overview/?sort=nomPeakValue&group=none&view=peak&position=0&
comparelist=&search). Based on the compiled data, slightly more than half of
the 50 largest borrowers were foreign banks. Thus, it appears that the Board
is relying, in part, on its experience during the financial crisis to support its

---

[37]   An IHC that is required to be established by July 1, 2016 must comply with the stress test
requirements beginning on October 1, 2017, provided that each subsidiary BHC and insured
depository institution controlled by the Large FBO immediately prior to the establishment or
designation of the IHC, and each BHC and insured depository institution acquired by the FBO
after establishment of the IHC, must comply with the stress test requirements in 12 C.F.R. Part
252, Subparts B, E, or F, as applicable, until September 30, 2017. 12 C.F.R. § 252.153(e)(ii)(C).

[38]   12 C.F.R. § 252.153(e)(4) *referencing* 12 C.F.R. Part 252, Subparts E (§§ 252.40–252.47)
and F (§§ 252.50–252.58).

[39]   12 C.F.R. § 252.153(d).

exercise of authority for the issuance of enhanced prudential standards for FBOs.

2.   A significant portion of the Final Rule's requirements imposed on Small and Medium FBOs involve providing the Board with information on policies and procedures an FBO has prepared or is compliant with in connection with its home-country supervision. In contrast, many of the requirements imposed on Large FBOs under the Final Rule will exceed those imposed by their home-country supervisors, and will also involve additional and significant Board oversight. However, it is important to highlight that these Large FBO requirements are substantially similar to the requirements that the Board imposes on similarly-sized U.S.-based bank holding companies. Thus, the asserted effect of the Final Rule with respect to Large FBOs is to level the playing field among large providers of financial services in the United States. In effect, the Board has imposed a regulatory regime that is intended to treat FBOs that have the same access to the benefits of U.S. jurisdiction as domestic banks (via the discount window, etc.) to the same oversight and supervision as comparably sized U.S. banks. In this manner, the Board intends to exercise its oversight of FBOs, generally, and Large FBOs, in particular, to perceived aggregate risk these institutions pose to the U.S. financial system. FBOs, however, have reacted negatively to increased regulatory requirements in the U.S., and their home countries, particular the EU, have threatened significantly increased requirements for U.S. banks operating in their countries. See, e.g., Foreign Banks Brace for Fed Stress Tests, the Wall Street Journal (March 3, 2015).

3.   Another issue that the Board referenced in its justification for the FBO enhanced standards is the increasing concentration, complexity and interconnectedness of the largest FBOs operating in the U.S. According to the Board, as of 2007, "the top ten foreign banking organizations accounted for over 60 percent of foreign banking organizations' U.S. assets, up from 40 percent in 1995."[11] In contrast, commercial and industrial lending originated by FBOs' U.S. operations as a share of their third-party U.S. liabilities dropped after 2003.[12] Thus, FBO enhanced prudential standards are as much a reaction to greater exposure and vulnerability in the U.S. to the U.S. operations of FBOs as to potential funding exposure. As articulated by the Board, at the core of the agency's concern is the notion that, "[d]uring periods of financial stress, subsidiaries of [FBOs] may not be able to rely on support from their home-country parent, and therefore, these subsidiaries should have the ability to absorb losses and maintain ready access to funding, meet obligations to creditors and other counterparties, and continue to serve as credit intermediaries without assuming such support."[13] In other words, the Board wants an FBO's U.S. operations to be self-sufficient and, to the extent possible, self-contained.

---

[11]   Preamble to the Final Rule at 91.

[12]   *Id.*

[13]   *Id.* at 239.

CHAPTER 8

THE EUROPEAN UNION: SINGLE MARKET BANKING REGULATION

■ ■ ■

1. INTRODUCTION

With 28 member states having a combined population of over 500 million people, or 7.3% of the world's population, and constituting 20%—16,584 trillion U.S. dollars—of the global gross domestic product in 2012, the EU is the world's preeminent political and economic union. Operating through a system of supranational institutions, the EU, among other things, has recently created a unique system of unified banking regulations throughout the EU. As part of an effort to develop, in the European Commission's own words, "a single rulebook for financial services in the EU"—known as the Single Supervisory Mechanism ("SSM"), SSM is designed to address "[s]upervisory failings" in the EU related to the global financial crisis.

A study of EU banking regulation is important for a number of reasons. First, a number of the major EU members (e.g., Great Britain, Germany, France, Italy and Switzerland) are also Basel Committee members (discussed in Chapter 6) and the ramifications of cross-border financial service regulation certainly impacts the work of the Basel Committee. Second, many EU members have large and developed banking systems and related regulatory regimes that make the EU influential in the area of banking regulation, with attendant world-wide impact on international banks operating within the EU.

Finally, the precedent of a system of cross-border banking regulation—impacting many of the world's major banking organizations—and potentially enforced by a supranational banking authority—is certainly an important area for consideration in studying international banking law.

This chapter examines the EU's cross border banking regulation among its members, and the recently created European Banking Authority EU's ("EBA"). Unlike the work of the Basel Committee discussed in Chapter 5, which has no inherent cross-border legal authority, the EBA is intended to provide cross border bank regulatory authority over banking organizations located within the EU.

As such, the EBA is a truly significant development in international banking regulation. The recognition of such transnational authority on banking regulatory matters through treaty and the political bodies of the EU, the EU Commission and Parliament is a quantum leap in addressing uniform banking regulation on a global basis. While the EU is certainly a unique transnational federation, it is certainly worthwhile to study the work of the EU in this area due to its potential impact on international banking regulation.

This is particularly important since one of the primary goals of international banking regulation since the inception of the Basel Committee in 1974 has been to adopt international banking regulatory standards that ensure that no banking organization operating on a cross border basis escapes supervision, and that supervision is adequate. These goals are in essence a quest to both avoid so-called regulatory arbitrage i.e., banks gravitating toward jurisdictions that may provide lax regulation, and enhancing international cooperation and cooperation in regulating banks that operate on an international basis.

2. BRIEF HISTORY OF THE EUROPEAN UNION

The European Union (EU) is a politico-economic union of 28 member states that are located primarily in Europe. The EU operates through a system of supranational institutions and intergovernmental negotiated decisions by the member states. The institutions are: the European Commission, the Council of the European Union, the European Council, the Court of Justice of the European Union, the European Central Bank, the Court of Auditors, and the European Parliament. The European Parliament is elected every five years by EU citizens.

The EU traces its origins from the European Coal and Steel Community (ECSC) and the European Economic Community (EEC), formed by the so-called Inner Six countries in 1951 and 1958, respectively. In the intervening years, the community and its successors have grown in size by the accession of new member states and in power by the addition of policy areas to its remit. The Maastricht Treaty established the European Union under its current name in 1993 and introduced the European Citizenship. The latest major amendment to the constitutional basis of the EU, the Treaty of Lisbon, came into force in 2009.

The EU has developed a single market through a standardised system of laws that apply in all member states. Pursuant to the Schengen Agreement, when traveling within the Schengen Area—comprising 26 EU countries—passport controls have been abolished. EU policies aim to ensure the free movement of people, goods, services, and capital, enact legislation in justice and home affairs, and maintain common policies on trade, agriculture, fisheries, and regional development.

Through the Common Foreign and Security Policy, the EU has developed a role in external relations and defence. The union maintains permanent diplomatic missions throughout the world and represents itself at the United Nations, the WTO, the G8, and the G-20. The monetary union was established in 1999 and came into full force in 2002. It is currently composed of 19 member states that use the euro as their legal tender.

NOTES

1.   The European Union has seven institutions: the European Parliament, the Council of the European Union, the European Commission, the European Council, the European Central Bank, the Court of Justice of the European Union and the European Court of Auditors. Competencies in scrutinizing and amending legislation are divided between the European Parliament and the Council of the European Union while executive tasks are carried out by the European Commission and in a limited capacity by the European Council (not to be confused with the aforementioned Council of the European Union). The monetary policy of the eurozone is governed by the European Central Bank. The interpretation and the application of EU law and the treaties are ensured by the Court of Justice of the European Union. There are also a number of ancillary bodies which advise the EU or operate in a specific area.

The European Council gives direction to the EU, and convenes at least four times a year. It comprises the President of the European Council, the President of the European Commission and one representative per member state; either its head of state or head of government. The European Council has been described by some as the Union's "supreme political authority." It is actively involved in the negotiation of the treaty changes and defines the EU's policy agenda and strategies.

The European Council uses its leadership role to sort out disputes between member states and the institutions, and to resolve political crises and disagreements over controversial issues and policies. It acts externally as a "collective head of state" and ratifies important documents (for example, international agreements and treaties).

The European Commission acts as the EU's executive arm and is responsible for initiating legislation and the day-to-day running of the EU. The Commission is also seen as the motor of European integration. It operates as a cabinet government, with 28 Commissioners for different areas of policy, one from each member state, though Commissioners are bound to represent the interests of the EU as a whole rather than their home state.

Relevant to cross border regulations, the legal authority of the EU is based on a series of treaties. These first established the European Community and the EU, and then made amendments to those founding treaties. These are power-giving treaties which set broad policy goals and establish institutions with the necessary legal powers to implement those goals. These legal powers include the ability to enact legislation which can directly affect all member states and their inhabitants. The EU has legal personality, with the right to sign agreements and international treaties.

Under the principle of supremacy, national courts are required to enforce the treaties that their member states have ratified, and thus the laws enacted under them, even if doing so requires them to ignore conflicting national law, and (within limits) even constitutional provisions.

2.   The creation of a European single currency became an official objective of the European Economic Community in 1969. In 1992, after having negotiated the structure and procedures of a currency union, the member states signed the Maastricht Treaty and were legally bound to fulfill the agreed-on rules including the convergence criteria if they wanted to join the monetary union. The states wanting to participate had first to join the so-called European Exchange Rate Mechanism.

In 1999 the currency union started, first as an accounting currency with eleven member states joining. In 2002, the currency was fully put into place, when euro notes and coins were issued and national currencies began to phase out in the eurozone, which by then consisted of 12 member states. The eurozone (constituted by the EU member states which have adopted the euro) has since grown to 19 countries, the most recent being Lithuania which joined in January 2015. Denmark, the United Kingdom, and Sweden decided not to join the euro.

Since its launch the euro has become the second reserve currency in the world with a quarter of foreign exchanges reserves being in euro. The euro, and the monetary policies of those who have adopted it in agreement with the EU, are under the control of the European Central Bank (ECB).

The ECB is the central bank for the eurozone, and thus controls monetary policy in that area with an agenda to maintain price stability. It is at the centre of the European System of Central Banks, which comprehends all EU national central banks and is controlled by its General Council, consisting of the President of the ECB, who is appointed by the European Council, the Vice-President of the ECB, and the governors of the national central banks of all 28 EU member states.

The European System of Financial Supervision is an institutional architecture of the EU's framework of financial supervision composed by three authorities: the European Banking Authority ("EBA"), the European Insurance and Occupational Pensions Authority and the European Securities and Markets Authority. To complement this framework, there is also a European Systemic Risk Board under the responsibility of the ECB. The aim of this financial control system is to ensure the economic stability of the EU. Our focus will be on the EBA as the EU's primary bank regulatory agency.

To prevent the joining states from getting into financial trouble or crisis after entering the monetary union, they were obliged in the Maastricht treaty to fulfill important financial obligations and procedures, especially to show budgetary discipline and a high degree of sustainable economic convergence, as well as to avoid excessive government deficits and limit government debt to a sustainable level.

The Maastricht treaty has been tested in the context of the recent economic and financial problems faced by some members. See, e.g., Jack Ewing, European Central Bank Could Be Power Broker in Greek Debt Crisis, N.Y. Times February 18, 2015; Keiligh Baker and James Chapman, Eurozone finance ministers agree to extend Greece financial rescue package for another four months, Daily Mail (February 21, 2015). Even though the Maastricht treaty generally forbids eurozone states to assume the debts of other states, various emergency rescue funds had been created by the members to support the recent debt crisis of certain EU numbers to meet their financial obligations and buy time for reforms that those states can gain back their competitiveness. *Id.*

3. THE EUROPEAN BANKING AUTHORITY

A. ESTABLISHMENT OF THE EBA

REGULATION (EU) NO 1093/2010 OF THE EUROPEAN PARLIAMENT AND OF THE COUNCIL OF 24 NOVEMBER 2010

establishing a European Supervisory Authority (European Banking Authority), amending Decision No 716/2009/EC and repealing Commission Decision 2009/78/EC

THE EUROPEAN PARLIAMENT AND THE COUNCIL OF THE EUROPEAN UNION,

* * *

Whereas,

(1) The financial crisis in 2007 and 2008 exposed important shortcomings in financial supervision, both in particular cases and in relation to the financial system as a whole. Nationally based supervisory models have lagged behind financial globalisation and the integrated and interconnected reality of European financial markets, in which many financial institutions operate across borders. The crisis exposed shortcomings in the areas of cooperation, coordination, consistent application of Union law and trust between national supervisors.

(2) Before and during the financial crisis, the European Parliament has called for a move towards more integrated European supervision in order to ensure a true level playing field for all actors at the level of the Union and to reflect the increasing integration of financial markets in the Union [* * *].

* * *

(5) The European Council, in its conclusions of 19 June 2009, confirmed that a European System of Financial Supervisors, comprising three new European Supervisory Authorities, should be established. The system should be aimed at upgrading the quality and consistency of national supervision, strengthening oversight of cross-border groups and establishing a European single rule book applicable to all financial institutions in the internal market. It emphasised that the European Supervisory Authorities should also have supervisory powers in relation to credit rating agencies and invited the Commission to prepare concrete proposals on how the European System of Financial Supervisors could play a strong role in crisis situations, while stressing that decisions taken by the European Supervisory Authorities should not impinge on the fiscal responsibilities of Member States.

* * *

(8) The Union has reached the limits of what can be done with the present status of the Committees of European Supervisors. The Union cannot remain in a situation where there is no mechanism to ensure that national supervisors arrive at the best possible supervisory decisions for cross-border financial institutions; where there is insufficient cooperation and information exchange between national supervisors; where joint action by national authorities requires complicated arrangements to take account of the patchwork of regulatory and supervisory requirements; where national solutions are most often the only feasible option in responding to problems at the level of the Union, and where different interpretations of the same legal text exist. The European System of Financial Supervision (hereinafter 'the ESFS') should be designed to overcome those deficiencies and provide a system that is in line with the objective of a stable and single Union financial market for financial services, linking national supervisors within a strong Union network.

(9) The ESFS should be an integrated network of national and Union supervisory authorities, leaving day-to-day supervision to the national level. Greater harmonisation and the coherent application of rules for financial institutions and markets across the Union should also be achieved. In addition to the European Supervisory Authority (European Banking Authority) (hereinafter 'the Authority'), a European Supervisory Authority (European Insurance and Occupational Pensions Authority) and a European Supervisory Authority (European Securities and Markets Authority) as well as a Joint Committee of the European Supervisory Authorities (hereinafter 'the Joint Committee') should be established. A European Systemic Risk Board (hereinafter 'the ESRB') should form part of the ESFS for the purposes of the tasks as specified in this Regulation and in Regulation (EU) No 1092/2010 of the European Parliament and of the Council.

* * *

(11) Authority should act with a view to improving the functioning of the internal market, in particular by ensuring a high, effective and consistent level of regulation and supervision taking account of the varying interests of all Member States and the different nature of financial institutions. The Authority should protect public values such as the stability of the financial system, the transparency of markets and financial products, and the protection of depositors and investors. The Authority should also prevent regulatory arbitrage and guarantee a level playing field, and strengthen international supervisory coordination, for the benefit of the economy at large, including financial institutions and other stakeholders, consumers and employees. Its tasks should also include promoting supervisory convergence and providing advice to the Union institutions in the areas of banking, payments, e-money regulation and supervision, and related corporate governance, auditing and financial reporting issues. The Authority should also be entrusted with certain responsibilities for existing and new financial activities.

* * *

NOTES

1.   EU Regulation 1093/2010 also provided, in paragraph 2D that:

It is desirable that the Authority promote a consistent approach in the area of deposit guarantees to ensure a level playing field and the equitable treatment of depositors across the Union. As deposit guarantee schemes are subject to oversight in their Member States rather than regulatory supervision, the Authority should be able to exercise its powers under this Regulation in relation to the deposit guarantee scheme itself and its operator.

See the materials in Chapter 1 regarding deposit insurance schemes.

2.   In November 2008, the European Commission mandated a High-Level Group chaired by Jacques de Larosière to make recommendations on how to strengthen European supervisory arrangements with a view to better protecting the citizen and rebuilding trust in the financial system. In its final report presented on 25 February 2009 (the 'de Larosière Report'), the High-Level Group recommended that the supervisory framework be strengthened to reduce the risk and severity of future financial crises. It recommended reforms to the structure of supervision of the financial sector in the Union. The group also concluded that a European System of Financial Supervisors should be created, comprising three European Supervisory Authorities, one for the banking sector, one for the securities sector and one for the insurance and occupational pensions sector, and recommended the creation of a European Systemic Risk Council. The report represented the reforms the experts considered were needed and on which work had to begin immediately. See The

High-Level Group on Financial Supervision in the ELL, Chair, Jacques de Larosière (February 25, 2009).

In its Communication of March 4, 2009 entitled 'Driving European Recovery', the Commission proposed to put forward draft legislation creating a European system of financial supervision and a European systemic risk board. In its Communication of May 27, 2009 entitled 'European Financial Supervision', it provided more detail about the possible architecture of such a new supervisory framework reflecting the main thrust of the de Larosière Report.

$$* * *$$

PROPOSAL FOR A REGULATION OF THE EUROPEAN PARLIAMENT AND OF THE COUNCIL

amending Regulation (EU) No 1093/2010 establishing a European Supervisory Authority (European Banking Authority) as regards its interaction with Council Regulation (EU) (Brussells 12.9.2012)

EXPLANATORY MEMORANDUM

1.   CONTEXT OF THE PROPOSAL

Today, the solidity of the banking sector is in many instances still closely linked to the Member State in which they are established. Doubts about the sustainability of public debt, economic growth prospects, and the viability of credit institutions have been creating negative, mutually reinforcing market trends. This may lead to risks for the viability of some credit institutions as well as for the stability of the financial system, and may impose a heavy burden for already strained public finances of the Member States concerned.

The situation poses specific risks within the euro area, where the single currency increases the likelihood that developments in one Member State can create risks for economic development and the stability of the Euro area as a whole. Furthermore, the current risk of financial disintegration along national borders significantly undermines the Single Market for financial services and prevents it from contributing to economic recovery.

The establishment of the European Banking Authority (EBA) by Regulation (EU) No. 1093/2010 of the European Parliament and the Council of 24 November 2010 establishing a European Supervisory Authority (European Banking Authority), and of the European System of Financial Supervision (ESFS) already contributed to improved cooperation between national supervisors and to the development of a single rulebook for financial services in the EU. However, supervision of banks remains to a large extent within national boundaries and thereby fails to keep up with integrated banking markets. Supervisory failings have, since the onset of the banking crisis, significantly eroded confidence in the EU banking sector and contributed to an aggravation of tensions in euro area sovereign debt markets.

The Commission has therefore called in May 2012, as part of a longer term vision for economic and fiscal integration, for a banking union to restore confidence in banks and in the euro. One of the key elements of the banking union should be a Single Supervisory Mechanism (SSM) with direct oversight of banks, to enforce prudential rules in a strict and impartial manner and perform effective oversight of cross border banking markets. Ensuring that banking supervision across the Euro area abides by high common standards will contribute to build the necessary trust between Member States, which is a pre-condition for the introduction of any common backstops.

* * *

Under this new mechanism, the ECB will carry out a wide range of key supervisory tasks over credit institutions in the Euro area Member States. With a view to maintaining and deepening the internal market, other Member States will be allowed to enter into close collaboration with the ECB.

To avoid fragmentation of the internal market following the establishment of the single supervisory mechanism, the proper functioning of the EBA needs to be ensured. The role of the EBA should therefore be preserved in order to further develop the single rulebook and ensure convergence of supervisory practices over all EU.

* * *

EUROPEAN BANKING AUTHORITY
2013 ANNUAL REPORT

* * *

Mandate, tasks and governance

The European Banking Authority (EBA) is part of the European System of Financial Supervision (ESFS), which is helping to rebuild trust in the financial sector in the EU. The EBA promotes supervisory convergence across the EU and provides advice to EU institutions in the areas of banking, payments and e-money regulation, as well as on issues related to corporate governance, auditing and financial reporting.

Through the development of its single rulebook for banking, the single set of harmonized prudential rules that institutions throughout the EU must respect, the EBA helps guarantee financial stability and a level playing field across financial markets.

The EBA is one of three new European supervisory authorities (ESAs) created as a response to shortcomings in the supervision of increasingly interconnected international financial markets, as well as of institutions such as those affected by the financial crisis of 2007/08. The EBA is accountable to both the European Parliament and Council of the European Union. It has the power to temporarily prohibit or restrict financial activities that threaten the orderly functioning and integrity of financial markets or the stability of the financial system.

Together with EIOPA [European Insurance and Pensions Authority] and ESMA [European Securities and Market Authority], the EBA is charged with:

- improving the functioning of the internal financial market by means of ensuring a high, effective and consistent level of prudential regulation and supervision;

- protecting depositors and investors, as well as the integrity, efficiency and orderly functioning of financial markets;

- maintaining the stability of the financial system and strengthening international supervisory coordination.

The EBA works to improve the quality and consistency of national supervision and to strengthen oversight of cross-border groups, and acts as an independent advisory body to the Parliament, the Council and the Commission on banking issues.

One of the EBA's key tasks is to harmonise regulatory technical standards (RTS) in financial services into the single rulebook in order to create a level playing field and adequate protection of depositors, investors and consumers across the EU. All concerned parties contribute to the definition of the EBA's technical standards through participation in the EBA's BSG, which is not only consulted on proposed measures, but also on the impact studies on the effect the proposed new standards will have on the sector.

The EBA has the power to investigate the incorrect or insufficient application of Union law by an NSA, can compel that authority to take the actions necessary to become compliant and can require it to take specific courses of action in emergency situations.

The principal decision-making body of the EBA is its Board of Supervisors, which is composed of the heads of the relevant competent authorities in each EU Member State and is chaired by the chairperson of the EBA. Representatives of the Commission, the ESRB, the ECB, EIOPA and ESMA also participate as observers in the meetings of the EBA Board of Supervisors.

* * *

B. THE SINGLE RULEBOOK

EUROPEAN BANKING AUTHORITY, THE SINGLE RULEBOOK

The Single Rulebook aims to provide a single set of harmonised prudential rules which institutions throughout the EU must respect. The term Single Rulebook was coined in 2009 by the European Council in order to refer to the aim of a unified regulatory framework for the EU financial sector that would complete the single market in financial services. This will ensure uniform application of Basel III in all Member States. It will close regulatory loopholes and will thus contribute to a more effective functioning of the Single Market.

Why do we need a Single Rulebook?

European banking legislation is currently based on a Directive which leaves room for significant divergences in national rules. This has created a regulatory patchwork, leading to legal uncertainty, enabling institutions to exploit regulatory loopholes, distorting competition, and making it burdensome for firms to operate across the Single Market.

Moreover, the financial crisis has shown that in integrated financial markets, these divergences can have very disruptive effects. Once risks generated under the curtain of minimum harmonisation materialise, the impact is surely not contained within national boundaries but spread across the EU single market.

It is, therefore, crucial to use exactly the same definition of regulatory aggregates and the same methodologies for the calculation of key requirements, such as the capital ratio.

A Single Rulebook for a more resilient, transparent and efficient banking sector

A Single Rulebook based on a regulation will address these shortcomings and will thereby lead to a more resilient, more transparent, and more efficient European banking sector:

- A more resilient European banking sector: A Single Rulebook will ensure that prudential safeguards are, wherever possible, applied across the EU and not limited to individual Member States as the crisis highlighted the extent to which Member States' economies are interconnected.

- A more transparent European banking sector: A Single Rulebook will ensure that institutions' financial situation is more transparent and comparable across the EU for supervisors, deposit-holders and investors. The financial crisis has demonstrated that the opaqueness of regulatory requirements in different Member States was a major cause of financial instability. Lack of transparency is an obstacle to effective supervision but also to market and investor confidence.

- A more efficient European banking sector: A Single Rulebook will ensure that institutions do not have to comply with 27 differing sets of rules.

Single Rulebook and flexibility

Although a Single Rulebook is a key for Europe, it is true that the new regulatory framework has to be shaped in such a way to leave a certain degree of national flexibility in the activation of macro prudential tools, as credit and economic cycles are not synchronised across the EU.

For this reason, Member States will retain some possibilities to require their institutions to hold more capital. For example, Member States will retain the possibility to set higher capital requirements for real estate lending, thereby being able to address real estate bubbles. If they do, this will also apply to institutions from other Member States that do business in that Member State. Moreover, each Member State is responsible for adjusting the level of its countercyclical buffer to its economic situation and to protect economy/banking sector from any other structural variables and from the exposure of the banking sector to any other risk factors related to risks to financial stability.

Furthermore, Member States would naturally retain current powers under "pillar 2", i.e. the ability to impose additional requirements on a specific bank following the supervisory review process.

EBA's role in building of the Single Rulebook

The European Banking Authority plays a key role in building up of the Single Rulebook in banking.

The EBA is mandated to produce a number of Binding Technical Standards (BTS) for the implementation of the CRD IV package and the BRRD. BTS are legal acts which specify particular aspects of an EU legislative text (Directive or Regulation) and aim at ensuring consistent harmonisation in specific areas. BTS are always finally adopted by the European Commission by means of regulations or decisions. At that point they become legally binding and directly applicable in all Member States. This means that, on the date of their entry into force, they become part of the national law of the Member States and their implementation into national law is not only unnecessary but also prohibited.

* * *

C. THE EBA AT WORK

EUROPEAN BANKING AUTHORITY, EBA OPINION ON VIRTUAL CURRENCIES

(4 July 2014)

Executive summary

One of the tasks of the EBA is to monitor new and existing financial activities and to adopt guidelines and recommendations with a view to promoting the safety and soundness of markets and convergence of regulatory practice. In September 2013, 'virtual currencies' emerged on the EBA's radar as one of the many innovations to monitor. Following three months of analysis, the EBA issued a public warning on 13 December 2013, making consumers aware that VC are not regulated and that the risks are unmitigated as a result.

The question that remained unaddressed at the time was whether VCs should or can be regulated. This EBA Opinion sets out the result of this assessment and is addressed to EU legislators as well as national supervisory authorities in the 28 Member States.

VCs are a digital representation of value that is neither issued by a central bank or a public authority, nor necessarily attached to a FC, but is accepted by natural or legal persons as a means of payment and can be transferred, stored or traded electronically. The main actors are users, exchanges, trade platforms, inventors, and e-wallet providers.

While there are some potential benefits of VCs, for example, reduced transaction costs, faster transaction speed and financial inclusion, these benefits are less relevant in the European Union, due to the existing and pending EU regulations and directives that are explicitly aimed at faster transactions speeds and costs and at increasing financial inclusion.

The risks, by contrast, are manifold. More than 70 risks were identified across several categories, including risks to users; risks to non-user market participants; risks to financial integrity, such as money laundering and other financial crime; risks to existing payment systems in conventional FCs, and risks to regulatory authorities.

Numerous causal drivers for these risks were identified too, as these indicate the regulatory measures that would be required to mitigate the risks. The risks include the fact that a VC scheme can be created, and then its function subsequently changed, by anyone, and in the case of decentralised schemes, such as Bitcoins, by anyone with a sufficient share of computational power; that payer and payee can remain anonymous; that VC schemes do not respect jurisdictional boundaries and may therefore undermine financial sanctions and seizure of assets; and that market participants lack sound corporate governance arrangements.

A regulatory approach that addresses these drivers comprehensively would require a substantial body of regulation, some components of which are untested. It would need to comprise, amongst other elements, governance requirements for several market participants, the segregation of client accounts, capital requirements and, crucially, the creation of 'scheme governing authorities' that are accountable for the integrity of a VC scheme and its key components, including its protocol and transaction ledge.

* * *

A potential regulatory approach for the long term

152. This section addresses each of the risk drivers separately and, in aggregate, specifies a potential comprehensive regulatory approach for the long term.

Scheme governance authority

153. To address risk driver a)—i.e. that anyone, including criminals, can anonymously create a VC without being held responsible for any changes made to the VC protocol, or other core elements of the VC scheme by others at a later stage—the creation of an entity that is accountable to the regulator would need to be a mandatory requirement for a VC scheme to be regulated as a financial service and for it to be allowed to interact with existing regulated financial services.

* * *

Customer due diligence (CDD) requirements

156. The risk driver b), which concerns the anonymity of payers and payees could be addressed, at least within the EU, by requiring exchanges, and any other non-user market participants that interact with FC, to comply with CDD requirements. CDD requirements include the collection and verification of basic identity information; matching names against lists of known parties (such as 'politically exposed persons'); determining the customer's risk in terms of likeliness to commit money laundering, terrorist finance or identity theft; and monitoring a customer's transactions against their expected behaviour and recorded profile, as well as that of the customer's peers.

157. With transfers and exchanges of VC units (other than person-to-person transactions between wallets), information on the payer and the payee has to be exchanged with the relevant scheme governance authority. These transactions are then not only traceable but can also be linked to an individual's identity. KYC requirements would need to be imposed on exchanges, scheme governing authorities and potentially on some other market participants too.

* * *

Authorisation and corporate governance

162. To address risk driver p), market participants such as scheme governance authorities and exchanges (and perhaps others) would need to be registered and authorised before beginning to provide VC services. An authorisation should only be granted to a legal person established in a Member State. The authorisation requirements would need to be tailored to address the risks specific to each type of market participants, such as accreditation of IT security with international standards certified by an independent third party and periodic assessments, to mitigate IT security vulnerabilities.

163. In addition, information on the identity of persons who ultimately own or control the legal entity would need to be provided, including evidence of their being fit and proper persons, and that they are capable to run these businesses.

* * *

Separation of VC schemes from conventional payment systems

169. Risk driver r) regarding the interconnectivity between VC and FC schemes should mainly be addressed by the mitigation measures in pre-existing oversight requirements for payment systems. However, complete mitigation can only be assured by requiring regulated financial institutions that decide to provide VC services to establish a separate entity for the VC-related business. This is to make sure that VC activities do not impair the financial soundness and settlement obligations of the regulated financial entity.

* * *

A global regulatory approach

173. As expressed in risk driver c), the global, internet-based nature of VCs would require a regulatory approach to strive for an international, and ideally global, coordination, otherwise it will be difficult achieve a successful regulatory regime. In the absence of a global approach, national regulators will be required to issue continued warnings to potential users to make them aware of the risks of VC schemes that do not comply with the regulatory regime.

NOTES

1.   The concept of governance authority in the EBA virtual currency opinion is derived from the European Central Bank. See Harmonised oversight approach and oversight standards for payment instruments, European Banking Authority (February 2009). There, the governance authority is described as being accountable for the overall functioning of the scheme that promotes the (initiation of the) payment instrument in question and for

ensuing that all the actors involved comply with the scheme's rules. Moreover, it is responsible for ensuring the scheme's compliance with oversight standards. *Id.*

EUROPEAN BANKING AUTHORITY, WARNING TO CONSUMERS ON VIRTUAL CURRENCIES

(12 December 2013)

Summary

The European Banking Authority (EBA) is issuing this warning to highlight the possible risks you may face when buying, holding or trading virtual currencies such as Bitcoin. Virtual currencies continue to hit the headlines and are enjoying increasing popularity.

However, you need to be aware of the risks associated with virtual currencies, including losing your money. No specific regulatory protections exist that would cover you for losses if a platform that exchanges or holds your virtual currencies fails or goes out of business.

While the EBA is currently assessing all relevant issues associated with virtual currencies, in order to identify whether virtual currencies can and should be regulated and supervised, you are advised to familiarize yourself with the risks associated with them.

What are virtual currencies?

A virtual currency is a form of unregulated digital money that is not issued or guaranteed by a central bank and that can act as means of payment. Virtual currencies have come in many forms, beginning as currencies within online computer gaming environments and social networks, and developing into means of payment accepted 'offline' or in 'real life'. It is now increasingly possible to use virtual currencies as a means to pay for goods and services with retailers, restaurants and entertainment venues. These transactions often do not incur any fees or charges, and do not involve a bank.

More recently, the virtual currency 'Bitcoin' has set the scene for a new generation of decentralised, peer-to-peer virtual currencies—often also referred to as crypto currencies. Following the currency's recent growth, dozens of other virtual currencies have followed in Bitcoin's wake.

How does it work?

Using Bitcoin as an example, virtual currencies can be bought at an exchange platform using conventional currency. They are then transferred to a personalised Bitcoin account known as a 'digital wallet'. Using this wallet, consumers can send Bitcoins online to anyone else willing to accept them, or convert them back into a conventional fiat currency (such as the Euro, Pound or Dollar).

New Bitcoins are created online using computer-intensive software known as 'Bitcoin miners'. This software allows consumers to 'mine' small amounts of the currency through solving deliberately complex algorithms. However, the increase in the money supply is fixed so only small amounts are released over time.

What are the risks you need to be aware of?

The EBA has identified several characteristics and risks that you should be aware of when buying, holding, or trading virtual currencies.

You may lose your money on the exchange platform

In order to purchase virtual currencies, you may buy currency directly from someone who owns them or through an exchange platform. These platforms tend to be unregulated. In a number of cases, exchange platforms have gone out of business or have failed—in some instances due to hacking by third parties. The EBA is aware of consumers permanently losing significant amounts of money held on these platforms.

You should be aware of the fact that exchange platforms are not banks that hold their virtual currency as a deposit. If an exchange platform loses any money or fails, there is no specific legal protection—for example through a deposit guarantee scheme—that covers you for losses arising from any funds you may have held on the exchange platform, even when the exchange is registered with a national authority.

Your money may be stolen from your digital wallet

Once you have bought virtual currency it is stored in a 'digital wallet', on a computer, laptop or smart phone. Digital wallets have a public key, and a private key or password that allows you to access them. However, digital wallets are not impervious to hackers. Similar to conventional wallets, money may therefore be stolen from your wallet. Cases have been reported of consumers losing virtual currency in excess of US $1 million, with little prospect of having it returned.

In addition, if you lose the key or password to your digital wallet, your virtual currency may be lost forever. There are no central agencies that record passwords or issue replacement ones.

You are not protected when using virtual currencies as a means of payment

When using virtual currencies as a means to pay for goods and services you are not protected by any refund rights under EU law offered, for example, for transfers from a conventional bank or other payment account. Unauthorised or incorrect debits from digital wallet can therefore not usually be reversed. Acceptance of virtual currencies by retailers is also not permanently guaranteed and is based on their discretion and/or contractual agreements, which may cease at any point and with no notice period.

The value of your virtual currency can change quickly, and could even drop to zero

The price of Bitcoins and other virtual currencies has risen sharply. This has prompted some consumers to choose to invest in them. However, you need to be aware that the value of virtual currencies has been very volatile and can easily go down as well as up. Should the popularity of a particular virtual currency go down, for example if another virtual currency becomes more popular, then it is quite possible for their value to drop sharply and permanently.

The currencies' price volatility affects you if you buy virtual currencies as a means of payment: unlike money paid into a traditional bank or payment account denominated in a fiat currency, you cannot be assured that the value of your virtual currency funds remains largely stable.

Transactions in virtual currency may be misused for criminal activities, including money laundering

Transactions in virtual currencies are public, but the owners and recipients of these transactions are not. Transactions are largely untraceable, and provide virtual currency consumers with a high degree of anonymity. It is therefore possible that the virtual currency network will be used for transactions associated with criminal activities, including money laundering. This misuse could affect you, as law enforcement agencies may decide to close exchange platforms and prevent you from accessing or using any funds that the platforms may be holding for you.

You may be subject to tax liabilities

You should be aware that holding virtual currencies may have tax implications, such as value added tax or capital gains tax. You should consider whether tax liabilities apply in your country when using virtual currencies.

What can you do to protect yourself?

We recommend that, if you buy virtual currencies, you should be fully aware and understand their specific characteristics. You should not use 'real' money that you cannot afford to lose.

You should also exercise the same caution with your digital wallet as you would do with your conventional wallet or purse. You should not keep large amounts of money in it for an extended period of time, and ensure you keep it safe and secure. You should also familiarise yourself with the ownership, business model, transparency, and public perception of the exchange platforms that you are considering using.

NOTES

1.   Bitcoin has attracted the attention of banking and law enforcement authorities in a number of countries. See, e.g., China Bans Financial Companies From Bitcoin Transactions, Bloomberg News (December 5, 2013); FinCEN Guidance: Application of FinCEN's Regulations to Persons Administering, Exchanging or Using Virtual Currencies (March 28, 2013); James Ball, Charles Arthur and Adam Gabbatt, FBI claims largest Bitcoin seizure after arrest of Silk Road Founder, The Guardian, October 2, 2013; Pete Rizzo, UK Eliminates Tax on Bitcoin Trading, Publishes Official Guidance, Coin Desk, (March 2, 2014); press release, NY DFS Releases Proposed Bitcoin Regulatory Framework For Virtual Currency Firms, New York Department of Financial Services (July 17, 2014).

4. CROSS BORDER COOPERATION

COMMISSION DELEGATED REGULATION (EU) NO 524/2014
(12 March 2014)
supplementing Directive 2013/36/EU of the European Parliament and of the Council with regard to regulatory technical standards specifying the information that competent authorities of home and host Member States supply to one another

* * *

Whereas:

(1) In order to ensure efficient cooperation between competent authorities of home and host Member States information exchange should be two-way, within the respective supervisory competences of those authorities. It is therefore necessary to specify which information concerning institutions, and where relevant, concerning the functioning of their branches, should be provided by the competent authorities of the home Member State to the competent authorities of the host Member State, as well as which information regarding branches needs to be provided by competent authorities of host Member States to the competent authorities of the home Member State.

(2) Exchange of information between competent authorities of home and host Member States should be seen in a wider context of supervision of cross-border banking groups and, were relevant, information could be provided at the consolidated level. In particular, if an institution has an ultimate parent undertaking in the Member State where it has its head office, and the competent authority concerned is also the consolidating supervisor, possibilities should be made available to provide information at the consolidated level rather than at the level of an institution operating through a branch. However, in this case the competent authority should notify competent authorities of host Member States that the information is provided at the consolidated level.

* * *

(4) * * * In order to facilitate the monitoring of institutions, the competent authorities of host and home Member States should keep each other informed about situations of non-compliance with national or Union law as well as about supervisory measures and sanctions imposed on institutions.

* * *

(7) To ensure that the relevant information is exchanged within reasonable limits while avoiding situations where the competent authorities of a home Member State are obliged to forward any information about an institution, regardless of its nature and importance, to all competent authorities of host Member States, in specific cases, only information that is relevant to a particular branch should be transmitted exclusively to the competent authorities in charge of supervising this branch. For similar purposes, in a number of specific areas, only information revealing situations of non-compliance should be exchanged between competent authorities of home and host Member States, meaning that no information should be exchanged where the institution is in conformity with national and Union law.

(8) This Regulation should also address exchange of information in relation to the carrying out of activities in a host Member State by way of the provision of cross-border services. Given the nature of cross-border services, competent authorities of host Member States are confronted with a lack of information regarding operations being conducted in their jurisdictions, and therefore it is essential to specify in detail what information needs to be exchanged for the purposes of safeguarding financial stability and monitoring conditions of authorisations, in particular monitoring whether the institution provides services in accordance with the notifications provided. * * *

* * *

NOTES

1.   How do the cross border cooperation standards of EU Regulation No. 524/2014 compare to the Basle standards? See 25 Core Principles for Effective Banking Supervision discussed in Chapter 5. Does Regulation No. 524/2014 go beyond the Basle standards or are they less comprehensive? It should be assumed that Basle member countries are following the Basle Standards generally; the EBA's mission is cross-border regulatory guidance that is binding on member countries.

2.   In paragraph (7), why are limits placed in exchange of information between authorities of home and host member states?

Bank of England, The Prudential Regulation Authority's Approach to Bank Supervision
(June 2014)

Foreword

The Prudential Regulation Authority (PRA) is the United Kingdom's prudential regulator of deposit-takers, insurers and major investment firms. As part of the Bank of England, the PRA makes an important contribution to the Bank's financial stability objective of protecting and enhancing the stability of the UK financial system, and likewise supports the objective of the Monetary Policy Committee to maintain price stability in the United Kingdom. In the same way, the work of the Bank of England as a whole supports the PRA in delivering its objectives.

* * *

Reflecting the international nature of the banking industry and capital markets, and in particular the United Kingdom's membership of the single market in EU financial services, the PRA plays a full and active role with its counterparts globally and in the European Union. The PRA, at times as part of the wider Bank, also actively participates in global forums like the G20, Financial Stability Board, Basel, International Association of Insurance Supervisors etc., in developing and implementing prudential standards and in supervising international firms.

The PRA's approach to banking supervision

International approach

Banking is an international industry. Supervision of overseas firms operating in the United Kingdom, and consolidated supervision of international groups operating in the United Kingdom via supervisory colleges, are therefore important parts of the PRA's work.

The PRA's legal powers and responsibilities vary depending on the location of the parent and the legal form of its operations in the United Kingdom. Regardless of this, the PRA's supervisory approach is to assess all firms to the same prudential standards. Where the PRA does not have direct powers against such firms, it will raise any concerns that it has with the firm's home state supervisor or at the appropriate international forum.

Supervision of overseas firms operating in the United Kingdom

* * *

For subsidiaries of overseas firms the PRA has full powers and responsibilities and so its approach is to treat such firms equivalently to UK-owned firms (applying its full prudential requirements, including for example stress testing for the most significant firms). Consistent with its objective the PRA assesses, and limits as necessary, the (potentially complex) interlinkages with the rest of the group.

For UK branches of EEA [European Economic Area] firms, the PRA's powers and responsibilities are limited under European law. In order to assure itself that risks to the UK financial system from such branches are adequately managed, the PRA focuses on resolution planning (along with the RD) and on ensuring that it has access to relevant information on the safety and soundness of the parent firm via collaboration with home regulators. In particular the PRA engages in supervisory and resolution colleges, including Crisis Management Groups (CMGs) where applicable. The PRA takes a close interest in liquidity, focusing, in collaboration with the home regulator, on the position of the whole firm of which the branch is a part.

* * *

Where the PRA is not satisfied regarding the safety and soundness of the branch and the parent firm, it works with the home authority and promotes public understanding of the limits of its powers, and uses whatever tools it can to reduce the impact of these limitations. In emergency situations, consistent with European law, the PRA will take any precautionary measures necessary to protect the interests of depositors, and will inform the home authority of such measures at the earliest opportunity.

* * *

For UK branches of non-EEA firms, the PRA's authorisation applies to the whole firm. At the point at which a non-EEA branch seeks initial authorisation in the United Kingdom, the PRA will, as a first step, form a judgement on the adequacy of the home regulator, including its ability and willingness to share confidential information. Where it considers the home supervisor not to have a regime broadly equivalent to that of the United Kingdom, the PRA will refuse authorisation of the branch. It may instead decide to authorise a stand-alone subsidiary, in which case it may limit the interlinkages with the rest of the group or ring-fence the subsidiary (for example if it considers the home supervisor not to deliver effective consolidated supervision).

* * *

For existing UK branches of non-EEA firms where the home regime is not considered to be equivalent, the PRA's supervisory work is aimed at mitigating the risks of non-equivalence in the relevant areas. * * *

For UK branches of non-EEA firms where the PRA is satisfied that the home regulatory regime is equivalent, and where the PRA has assured itself over resolution plans and the home regulator's supervisory approach, the PRA relies where possible on the home regulator's prudential supervision. In these cases, the PRA focuses on collaboration with home regulators (including via supervisory colleges) and on resolution plans. In addition, the PRA takes a close interest in liquidity and ensures that there are senior individuals in the United Kingdom that are clearly responsible for management of both the UK operations and business booked in the United Kingdom. The PRA discusses and agrees with the home regulator the areas in which it will seek to rely on the home regulator's supervision.

Supervisory colleges

The PRA is an active participant in international co-ordination of supervision for major firms. Where invited to do so, it participates in supervisory colleges for all firms with significant operations in the United Kingdom, whether a legal entity or a branch.

NOTES

1. The U.K. is not within the eurozone and has made a decision to not have its banks subject to the EBA. See Ian Traynor, David Cameron blocks EU treaty with veto casting Britain adrift in Europe, The Guardian (December 9, 2011) (among other things, U.K. Prime Minister Cameron "demanded that any transfer of power from national regulators to an EU regulator on financial services be subject to a veto"): See also, Huw Jones, Bank of England seeks to opt out from EU bank stress tests, Reuters (December 5, 2013). The U.K. agreed to establishment of the EBA stress tests on eurozone banks after reassurances from EU government ministers that the EBA "would not interfere with U.K. control of its financial centre."). Nonetheless, as the foreword to the Bank of England/PRA paper states the PRA "plays a full and active role with its counterparts globally and in the European Union."

2. The PRA, which is part of the U.K.'s central bank, the Bank of England, was established in 2013 in the wake of the financial crisis, pursuant to the Financial Services Act of 2012. The PRA and its governing board are accountable to the British Parliament. See Bank of England, A framework for stress testing the U.K. bank system (October 2013).

3. How does the PRA's regulatory approach synch with Basel Committee standards?

ANDREA ENRIA, CHAIRMAN, EUROPEAN BANKING AUTHORITY, CHALLENGES FOR THE FUTURE OF EU BANKING

Banking Forum of IESE Busiess School, Barcelona, Spain (November 26, 2014)

* * *

Challenges for the future

[after a discussion of a) bank restructuring and debt overhang resulting from the global financial crisis, and b) bank's internal models and risk weighted assets.]

c.   Conduct issues

Finally, I would like to address the third major challenge confronting banks and regulators: making sure that episodes of the conduct failure such as those experienced in recent years are effectively eradicated from bank practices.

We have seen cases of manipulation of market benchmarks, mis-selling of financial products to consumers, circumvention of anti-money laundering and counter terrorist financing regulation, and support to tax evasion on an unprecedented scale. The first and most relevant adverse effect has been on the reputation of the banks involved and of the banking sector as a whole. The confidence of consumers and users of banking services in the integrity of bank behaviour has been seriously compromised. It will take time and effort to gain it back. The banking sector used to be perceived as the "intelligent plumbing" of our economies, facilitating commercial transactions, ensuring that financial resources could flow efficiently to the best investment opportunities, protecting today's savings for tomorrow's needs. Now, it is more frequently considered a bloated sector, distracting resources from other parts of the economy, often in pursuance of the individual interests of the bankers themselves. The second adverse effect is on financial stability, as the scale of conduct failure is such that very material sanctions have been applied or onerous settlements have been achieved, which had a relevant impact on banks—according to some estimates, the costs of conduct failure accruing to a small sample of major EU and US major banks alone since the beginning of the financial crisis in 2007 have exceeded EUR 200 bn, [billion] with additional EUR 70 bn expected in the near future (* * *). The costs tend to arise as a result of compensation paid out by banks, regulatory fines as well as litigation payments.

I believe that the relevant primary legislation to deal with conduct issues is in place in the EU. The key issue is effective application and enforcement. Most importantly, we need to dispel the impression that competent authorities across the Single Market attach different priorities to addressing conduct issues, sometimes also as a consequence of inconsistencies in RWAs across Member States. We have a duty to iron out these differences and promote rigorous and convergent supervisory practices.

QUESTIONS AND NOTES

1. The Basel Committee on Banking Supervision has sought to define corporate governance standards for banks. See the Basel Committee's, Corporate governance principles for banks—consultative documents (October, 2014).

2. What were the reason(s) for the European Commission establishing the European Banking Authority pursuant to EU Regulation No. 1093–2010?

3. What are the legal elements of the Single Supervisory Mechanism ("SSM") for oversight of banking institutions operating within the EU?

4. What impact, if any, does/will the SSM have on future actions of the Basel Committee?

5. What purposes did the Banking Advisory Committee serve, as established by the First Banking Directive of the EC? Have these purposes been served?

CHAPTER 9

ANTI-MONEY LAUNDERING, ANTI-TERRORISM AND BANK SECRECY LAWS

■ ■ ■

1. INTRODUCTION

The U.S. Bank Secrecy Act, The USA PATRIOT Act, anti-terrorism, anti-money laundering and Office of Foreign Asset Control ("OFAC") and Suspicious Activity Report ("SAR") rules have emerged over the last 10 years as one of the major practice areas in banking law. Particularly for large banks operating on international basis, compliance with thee laws—and severe civil and criminal penalties for violating them—are a major concern.

This chapter analyzes the development of anti-money laundering, terrorism and embargo rules, including the post September 11, 2001 adoption of the USA PATRIOT Act. The chapter will explore the progression of these laws over the years in imposing increasing levels of "know your customer," currency transaction reporting, suspicious activities report filing obligations, compliance policies and procedures, "prohibited party" transactions and potentially significant civil and criminal liability for violating these rules.

2. THE BANK SECRECY ACT

During the late 1960s a number of foreign bank accounts had been employed to finance criminal activity or "launder" criminal proceeds.[1] The United States money service business industry remained susceptible to such activity, which prompted a congressional response. In 1970 the United States Congress passed the Bank Records and Foreign Transaction Act also known as the Bank Secrecy Act (BSA) to combat the growing concern of money laundering occurring among banks and financial service providers.[2] These institutions were being used as intermediaries to further criminal activity such as drug trafficking, tax evasion and terrorism.[3]

The need to monitor financial transactions raised privacy concerns. The Right to Financial Privacy Act (RFPA) sought to address these

---

[1]   See H.R. Rep. No. 975, 91st Cong., 2d Sess.

[2]   http://www.fincen.gov/statutes_regs/bsa/ See Pub. L. No. 91–508 Stat. 1114 (1970).

[3]   See H.R. Rep. No. 975, 91st Cong., 2d Sess.

concerns; however, criticism of the BSA remained. An examination of the constitutional challenges, liability for noncompliance and the lack of proper agency wide technological safeguards to secure private financial records illustrate the anti-money laundering provisions have taken precedence over financial privacy concerns. This is particularly evidenced by the expansion of the BSA.

Money laundering commonly refers to the financial transaction where criminals try to "disguise the proceeds, source or nature of their illicit activities".[4] The BSA requires banks and industries susceptible to money laundering to take precautionary measures against financial crime. Such measures include filing and reporting data on financial transactions that may involve money laundering. Cash transactions over $10,000 and other suspicious transactions must be reported.[5] FinCEN has estimated some 15 million BSA reports are filed each year by approximately 25,000 U.S. financial institutions.[6] The law was amended several times to address new challenges.[7] By 1986 the Money Laundering Control Act of 1986 (MLCA) was enacted, making money laundering a crime in and of itself.[8] The Act also addressed "smurfing" which is the structuring of transactions in smaller denominations in order to evade Currency Transaction Reporting (CTR) by making each transaction less than the $10,000 CTR reporting requirement.[9] CTR is required when an individual or someone acting on the individuals behalf conducts more than one cash transaction in a single day that involves an aggregate of 10,000 dollars into the US or out of the US. Failure to file this report may result in forfeiture of the funds.[10]

The Money Laundering Prosecution Improvement Act of 1988 prohibited financial institutions from issuing cashier's checks, traveler's checks, money order or bank checks to an individual in amounts of more than $3,000 without appropriate customer documentation.[11] The Treasury Department created the Financial Crimes Enforcement Network (FinCEN) in 1990 to monitor money laundering activities as there was "insufficient intelligence analysis and resources to support financial investigations".[12] By 1992 law enforcement urged for more information on suspicious transactions to support financial investigations. Congress responded with

---

[4]   http://www.treasury.gov/resource-center/terrorist-illicit-finance/Pages/Money-Laundering.aspx.

[5]   31 U.S.CA. 5324 and 31 C.F.R 103.53

[6]   http://www.fincen.gov/statutes_regs/bsa/bsa_data.html.

[7]   http://www.fincen.gov/statutes_regs/bsa/bsa_timeline.html.

[8]   *Id.*

[9]   31 U.S.CA. 5324 and 31 C.F.R 103.53. See also Lisa L. Broome and Jerry Markham, *Regulation of Bank Financial Services Activities*, pp. 1015 (West 2008).

[10]   *Id.*

[11]   Pub. L. No. 100–690, 102 Stat. 4354 (1998), Lisa L. Broome and Jerry Markham, *Regulation of Bank Financial Services Activities*, pp. 1015 (West 2008).

[12]   http://www.fincen.gov/statutes_regs/bsa/bsa_timeline.html.

the enactment of the Annunzio-Wylie Money Laundering Suppression Act, which requires suspicious activity reporting (SAR).[13] In addition whistleblower protections were provided to individuals who filed a SAR. The Act increased penalties against noncompliant banks and individuals.[14] By 1994 the Money Laundering Suppression Act required money services businesses (MSB) to report transactions through Currency Transaction Reporting (CTR).[15] MSBs include business that provide money transmission, check cashing, currency transfer and the sale of money orders. These businesses are required to register persons in charge as well as all branches in operation.[16] There was improved cooperation between regulatory, financial and law enforcement communities with the merger of the Treasury's Office of Financial Enforcement with FinCEN.[17] FinCEN's mission was expanded to include regulatory authority.[18]

A nationwide coordinated effort to prevent money laundering with the Department of Treasury and the Department of Justice was initiated in 1998 with the Financial Crimes Strategy Act.[19] In 2000 law enforcement requested more information on money transmitters, issuers, sellers and redeemers of money. Congress required MSBs to file a suspicious activity reports.[20]

The September 11th attack prompted congress to swiftly enact the PATRIOT Act in 2001. President Bush announced a Financial War on Terror at FinCEN. Title III of the Act amended the BSA by expanding record keeping and reporting requirements to encompass specific domestic and international transactions that included nonfinancial trades or businesses. There are special due diligence standards imposed on domestic financial institutions with regards to financial accounts that belong to foreign persons. These institutions are required to report to FinCEN.[21] The PATRIOT Act allowed for information sharing and registration requirements for underground money transmitters. Financial institutions were deemed the front line against money laundering and terrorist financing (Id.). The Secretary of Treasury or Attorney General can issue a summons or a subpoena to a foreign bank with regards to any correspondent account maintained in the United Sates (31 U.S.C.A § 5318(k)(3)). The Act also required banks to identify their customers under the Customer Information Program. Banks are required to gather name,

---

[13]   Id. See also Pub. L. No. 103–325, 108 Stat. 2160.
[14]   http://www.fincen.gov/statutes_regs/bsa/bsa_timeline.html.
[15]   Id.
[16]   Id. See also 31 U.S. Code § 5330.
[17]   http://www.fincen.gov/statutes_regs/bsa/bsa_timeline.html.
[18]   Id.
[19]   Id. See 31 U.S.C.A. § 5340.
[20]   Id.
[21]   Money Laundering Abatement and Financial AntiTerrorism Act of 2001, Pub. L. No. 108–458.

address, tax ID number and proof of identity. Theses due diligence requirement are known as the "Know your Customer" requirements (KYC).

By 2002 most financial institutions received new or amended Anti-Money Laundering program requirements (*Id.*). Section 314(b) of the USA PATRIOT Act allows for financial institutions to share information with each other. These institutions are protected from liability through safe harbor provisions. Sharing information is encourage by FinCEN as it aids in the identification and reporting of potential terrorist or money laundering activity (http://www.fincen.gov/statutes_regs/bsa/bsa_ timeline.html).

* * *

NOTES

1.   Today the BSA has broad statutory coverage regarding financial institutions. The BSA has expanded the definition of a financial institution. Residential mortgage lenders and originators, depository institutions, casinos, money services business, insurance, securities, commodities and futures, mutual funds and correspondent accounts for foreign banks as well as precious metal and jewelry business are all deemed "financial institutions" for the purposes of reporting requirements under the BSA (*Id.*). FinCEN has issued an Anti-Money Laundering Program and SAR filing regulations for these businesses. See http://www.fincen.gov/statutes_regs/bsa/bsa_timeline.html.

2.   The RFPA does not protect a customer's bank records from discovery in a civil action between private parties (see Clayton Brokerage Co., Inc. of St. Louis v. Clement, 87 F.R.D. 569, 571 (D. Md. 1980)). Nor does the RFPA prevent foreign governments from requesting and obtaining customer financial records from financial institutions when it has been enforced by the United States (see 28 U.S.C.A. § 1782(a); Young v. U.S. Dept. of Justice, 882 F.2d 633, 636–39(2d Cir. 1989); In re Letter of Request for Judicial Assistance from Tribunal Civil de Port-au-Prince, Republic of Haiti, 669 F. Supp. 403, 407(S.D. Fla. 1987)). See Patel v. Hayman, 2009 WL 1748964 (D.N.J. 2009). The *Patel* case held that the RFPA "does not limit access to financial institutions records by state employees" (see Patel v. Haymen, 2009 WL 178964 (D.N.J.2009)). Thus, the RFPA is not a panacea for financial privacy. It is designed to prevent the federal government from unencumbered access to financial records. Financial records have to be requested from a government authority in order for the RFPA rules to trigger. Government authority means "any agency or department of the United States, or any officer, employee, or agent thereof" (12 U.S.C.A. § 3401(3) (1988)).

The RFPA accommodates financial institutional reporting under 12 U.S.C 341(d) of the BSA. Financial institutions and their employees are immune from civil liability when they report of known or suspicious activity through the filling of suspicious activity reports with FinCEN. Thus depositors have no recourse against these financial institutions. The RFPA does not overrule the

BSA. Under the RFPA customer must be given notice when their information is transmitted between federal agencies however this is not the case when their information is being transmitted to FinCEN or when FinCEN transmits their information to law enforcement. The need to share information appears to be the overriding principle. Interagency cooperation is said to aid in the identification and reporting of potential terrorist or money laundering activity (http://www.fincen.gov/statutes_regs/bsa/bsa_timeline.html).

There are many exceptions to the RFPA. When a customer is given notice regarding disclosure of her financial records to a federal agency and chooses to object to this disclosure, she does not have much recourse (see Banking Crimes Fraud, Money Laundering and Embezzlement, John K. Villa Vol. 2 October 2014 at § 9:1, 9–7). Studies suggest that there is hardly a legal basis for maintaining a customer's objection unless the government was responsible for technical mistakes in their request for financial documents (*Id.*). Thus customer lawsuits seeking to prevent disclosure have been mostly unsuccessful and it appears that the RFPA is merely a way to deter government form free access to financial records (*Id.*).

3.   Congress responded to financial privacy concerns by creating a statutory Fourth Amendment protection for bank records in its enactment of the Right to Financial Privacy Act (Right to Financial Privacy Act of 1978 12 U.S.C.A §§ 3401 et seq.). Under the RFPA financial institutions have to protect the privacy of their customer's financial records or related information. However this right is limited. The RFPA prevents unregulated access to those private financial records by government authorities while protecting government's interest in attaining disclosure of records that are useful to a reasonable law enforcement investigation or financial supervisory activity (Richard Cordero, Annotation, *Construction and application of Right to Financial Privacy Act of 1978*, at § 1[a], 112 A.L.R. Fed 295 (1993)). Government agencies are required to provide notice and an opportunity to object before a bank discloses one's financial records to a federal agency (Right to Financial Privacy Act, 12 U.S.C §§ 3401–342). However the RFPA was amended by the USA Patriot Act of 2001 to allow the disclosure of financial information to any intelligence or counterintelligence agency in any investigation related to international terrorism (U.S.A Patriot Act of 2001 §§ 358). See Section 5 of this Chapter on RFPA issues.

3.   U.S. CONSTITUTIONAL ISSUES

CALIFORNIA BANKERS ASSOCIATION v. SCHULTZ

Supreme Court of the United States
416 U.S. 21 (1974)

MR. JUSTICE REHNQUIST delivered the opinion of the Court.

These appeals present questions concerning the constitutionality of the so-called Bank Secrecy Act of 1970 (Act), and the implementing regulations promulgated thereunder by the Secretary of the Treasury. The Act, Pub.L. 91–508, 84 Stat. 1114, 12 U.S.C. ss 1730d, 1829b, 1951–1959, and 31 U.S.C. ss 1051–1062, 1081–1083, 1101–1105, 1121–1122, was enacted by Congress in 1970 following extensive hearings concerning the unavailability of foreign and domestic bank records of customers thought to be engaged in activities entailing criminal or civil liability. Under the Act, the Secretary of the Treasury is authorized to prescribe by regulation certain recordkeeping and reporting requirements for banks and other financial institutions in this country. Because it has a bearing on our treatment of some of the issues raised by the parties, we think it important to note that the Act's civil and criminal penalties attach only upon violation of regulations promulgated by the Secretary; if the Secretary were to do nothing, the Act itself would impose no penalties on anyone.

The express purpose of the Act is to require the maintenance of records, and the making of certain reports, which 'have a high degree of usefulness in criminal, tax, or regulatory investigations or proceedings.' 12 U.S.C. ss 1829b(a)(2), 1951; 31 U.S.C. s 1051. Congress was apparently concerned with two major problems in connection with the enforcement of the regulatory, tax, and criminal laws of the United States.[1]

First, there was a need to insure that domestic banks and financial institutions continue to maintain adequate records of their financial transactions with their customers. Congress found that the recent growth of financial institutions in the United States had been paralleled by an increase in criminal activity which made use of these institutions. While many of the records which the Secretary by regulation ultimately required to be kept had been traditionally maintained by the voluntary action of many domestic financial institutions, Congress noted that in recent years some larger banks had abolished or limited the practice of photocopying checks, drafts, and similar instruments drawn on them and presented for payment. The absence of such records, whether through failure to make them in the first instance or through failure to retain them, was thought to seriously impair the ability of the Federal Government to enforce the myriad criminal, tax, and regulatory provisions of laws which Congress had enacted. At the same time, it was recognized by Congress that such required records would 'not be made automatically available for law enforcement purposes (but could) only be obtained through existing legal process.' H.R.Rep.No. 91–975, p. 10 (1970); see S.Rep.No. 91–1139, p. 5 (1970).

---

[1]   See generally S.Rep.No.91–1139 (1970); H.R.Rep.No.91–975 (1970), U.S.Code Cong. & Admin.News 1970, p. 4394; Hearings on Foreign Bank Secrecy and Bank Records (H.R. 15073) before the House Committee on Banking and Currency, 91st Cong., 1st and 2d Sess. (1969–1970); Hearings on Foreign Bank Secrecy (S. 3678 and H.R. 15073) before the Subcommittee on Financial Institutions of the Senate Committee on Banking and Currency, 91st Cong., 2d Sess. (1970).

In addition, Congress felt that there were situations where the deposit and withdrawal of large amounts of currency or of monetary instruments which were the equivalent of currency should be actually reported to the Government. While reports of this nature had been required by previous regulations issued by the Treasury Department, it was felt that more precise and detailed reporting requirements were needed. The Secretary was therefore authorized to require the reporting of what may be described as large domestic financial transactions in currency or its equivalent.

Second, Congress was concerned about a serious and widespread use of foreign financial institutions, located in jurisdictions with strict laws of secrecy as to bank activity, for the purpose of violating or evading domestic criminal, tax, and regulatory enactments. The House Report on the bill, No. 91–975, supra, at 12–13, described the situation in these words:

'Considerable testimony was received by the Committee from the Justice Department, the United States Attorney for the Southern District of New York, the Treasury Department, the Internal Revenue Service, the Securities and Exchange Commission, the Defense Department and the Agency for International Development about serious and widespread use of foreign financial facilities located in secrecy jurisdictions for the purpose of violating American law. Secret foreign bank accounts and secret foreign financial institutions have permitted proliferation of 'white collar' crime; have served as the financial underpinning of organized criminal operations in the United States; have been utilized by Americans to evade income taxes, conceal assets illegally and purchase gold; have allowed Americans and others to avoid the law and regulations governing securities and exchanges; have served as essential ingredients in frauds including schemes to defraud the United States; have served as the ultimate depository of black market proceeds from Vietnam; have served as a source of questionable financing for conglomerate and other corporate stock acquisitions, mergers and takeovers; have covered conspiracies to steal from the U.S. defense and foreign aid funds; and have served as the cleansing agent for 'hot' or illegally obtained monies.

'The debilitating effects of the use of these secret institutions on Americans and the American economy are vast. It has been estimated that hundreds of millions in tax revenues have been lost. Unwarranted and unwanted credit is being pumped into our markets. There have been some cases of corporation directors, officers and employees who, through deceit and violation of law, enriched themselves or endangered the financial soundness of their companies to the detriment of their stockholders. Criminals engaged in illegal gambling, skimming, and narcotics traffic are operating their financial affairs with an impunity that approaches statutory exemption.

'When law enforcement personnel are confronted with the secret foreign bank account or the secret financial institution they are placed in an impossible position. In order to receive evidence and testimony regarding activities in the secrecy jurisdiction they must subject themselves to a time consuming and of times fruitless foreign legal process. Even when procedural obstacles are overcome, the foreign jurisdictions rigidly enforce their secrecy laws against their own domestic institutions and employees.

'One of the most damaging effects of an American's use of secret foreign financial facilities is its undermining of the fairness of our tax laws. Secret foreign financial facilities, particularly in Switzerland, are available only to the wealthy. To open a secret Swiss account normally requires a substantial deposit, but such an account offers a convenient means of evading U.S. taxes. In these days when the citizens of this country are crying out for tax reform and relief, it is grossly unfair to leave the secret foreign bank account open as a convenient avenue of tax evasion. The former U.S. Attorney for the Southern District of New York has characterized the secret foreign bank account as the largest single tax loophole permitted by American law.' U.S.Code Cong. & Admin.News 1970, p. 4397.

* * *

Plaintiffs urge that when the bank makes and keeps records under the compulsion of the Secretary's regulations it acts as an agent of the Government, and thereby engages in a 'seizure' of the records of its customers. But all of the records which the Secretary requires to be kept pertain to transactions to which the bank was itself a party. See United States v. Biswell, 406 U.S. 311, 316, 92 S.Ct. 1593, 32 L.Ed.2d 87 (1972). The fact that a large number of banks voluntarily kept records of this sort before they were required to do so by regulation is an indication that the records were thought useful to the bank in the conduct of its own business, as well as in reflecting transactions of its customers. We decided long ago that an Internal Revenue summons directed to a third-party bank was not a violation of the Fourth Amendment rights of either the bank or the person under investigation by the taxing authorities. See First National Bank v. United States, 267 U.S. 576, 45 S.Ct. 231, 69 L.Ed. 796 (1925), aff'g 295 F. 142 (SD Ala. 1924); Donaldson v. United States, supra, 400 U.S., at 522, 91 S.Ct., at 538. '(I)t is difficult to see how the summoning of a third party, and the records of a third party, can violate the rights of the taxpayer, even if a criminal prosecution is contemplated or in progress.' Id., at 537, 91 S.Ct. at 545 (Douglas, J., concurring).

Plaintiffs nevertheless contend that the broad authorization given by the Act to the Secretary to require the maintenance of records, coupled with the broad authority to require certain reports of financial transactions, amounts to the power to commit an unlawful search of the banks and the customers.

* * *

[In Fourth Amendment Challenge to the foreign reporting requirements, the Court upholds the Treasury regulations as reasonable in light of the statutory purpose of the BSA, and consisted with the Fourth Amendment]

* * *

B. FOURTH AMENDMENT CHALLENGE TO THE DOMESTIC REPORTING REQUIREMENTS

The District Court examined the domestic reporting requirements imposed on plaintiffs by looking to the broad authorization of the Act itself, without specific reference to the regulations promulgated under its authority. The District Court observed:

'(A)lthough to date the Secretary has required reporting only by the financial institutions and then only of currency transactions over $10,000, he is empowered by the Act, as indicated above, to require, if he so decides, reporting not only by the financial institution, but also by other parties to or participants in transactions with the institutions and, further, that the Secretary may require reports, not only of currency transactions but of any transaction involving any monetary instrument—and in any amount—large or small.' 347 F.Supp., at 1246.

The District Court went on to pose, as the question to be resolved, whether 'these provisions, broadly authorizing an executive agency of government to require financial institutions and parties (thereto) . . . to routinely report . . . the detail of almost every conceivable financial transaction . . . (are) such an invasion of a citizen's right of privacy as amounts to an unreasonable search within the meaning of the Fourth Amendment.' Ib*id*.

Since, as we have observed earlier in this opinion, the statute is not self-executing, and were the Secretary to take no action whatever under his authority there would be no possibility of criminal or civil sanctions being imposed on anyone, the District Court was wrong in framing the question in this manner. The question is not what sort of reporting requirements might have been imposed by the Secretary under the broad authority given him in the Act, but rather what sort of reporting requirements he did in fact impose under that authority.

'Even where some of the provisions of a comprehensive legislative enactment are ripe for adjudication, portions of the enactment not immediately involved are not thereby thrown open for a judicial determination of constitutionality. 'Passing upon the possible significance of the manifold provisions of a broad statute in advance of efforts to apply the separate provisions is analogous to rendering an advisory opinion upon a statute or a declaratory judgment upon a hypothetical case.' Watson v. Buck, 313 U.S. 387, 402, 61 S.Ct. 962, 967, 85 L.Ed. 1416.' Communist Party v. SACB, 367 U.S., at 71, 81 S.Ct., at 1397.

The question for decision, therefore, is whether the regulations relating to the reporting of domestic transactions, violations of which could subject those required to report to civil or criminal penalties, invade any Fourth Amendment right of those required to report. To that question we now turn.

* * *

We have no difficulty then in determining that the Secretary's requirements for the reporting of domestic financial transactions abridge no Fourth Amendment right of the banks themselves. The bank is not a mere stranger or bystander with respect to the transactions which it is required to record or report. The bank is itself a party to each of these transactions, earns portions of its income from conducting such transactions, and in the past may have kept records of similar transactions on a voluntary basis for its own purposes. See United States v. Biswell, 406 U.S., at 316, 92 S.Ct., at 1596. The regulations presently in effect governing the reporting of domestic currency transactions require information as to the personal and business identity of the person conducting the transaction and of the person or organization for whom it was conducted, as well as a summary description of the nature of the transaction. It is conceivable, and perhaps likely, that the bank might not of its own volition compile this amount of detail for its own purposes, and therefore to that extent the regulations put the bank in the position of seeking information from the customer in order to eventually report it to the Government. But as we have noted above, 'neither incorporated nor unincorporated associations can plead an unqualified right to conduct their affairs in secret.' United States v. Morton Salt Co., supra, 338 U.S., at 652, 70 S.Ct., at 368.

The regulations do not impose unreasonable reporting requirements on the banks. The regulations require the reporting of information with respect to abnormally large transactions in currency, much of which information the bank as a party to the transaction already possesses or would acquire in its own interest. To the extent that the regulations in connection with such transactions require the bank to obtain information from a customer simply because the Government wants it, the information is sufficiently described and limited in nature, and sufficiently related to a tenable congressional determination as to improper use of transactions of that type in interstate commerce, so as to withstand the Fourth Amendment challenge made by the bank plaintiffs. '(T)he inquiry is within the authority of the agency, the demand is not too indefinite and the information sought is reasonably relevant. 'The gist of the protection is in the requirement, expressed in terms, that the disclosure sought shall not be unreasonable.'' United States v. Morton Salt Co., supra, at 652–653, 70 S.Ct., at 369; see Oklahoma Press Publishing Co. v. Walling, 327 U.S. 186, 208, 66 S.Ct. 494, 505, 90 L.Ed. 614 (1946).

In addition to the Fourth Amendment challenge to the domestic reporting requirements made by the bank plaintiffs, we are faced with a similar challenge by the depositor plaintiffs, who contend that since the reports of domestic transactions which the bank is required to make will include transactions to which the depositors were parties, the requirement that the bank make a report of the transaction violates the Fourth Amendment rights of the depositor. The complaint filed in the District Court by the ACLU and the depositors contains no allegation by any of the individual depositors that they were engaged in the type of $10,000 domestic currency transaction which would necessitate that their bank report it to the Government. This is not a situation where there might have been a mere oversight in the specificity of the pleadings and where this Court could properly infer that participation in such a transaction was necessarily inferred from the fact that the individual plaintiffs allege that they are in fact 'depositors.' Such an inference can be made, for example, as to the recordkeeping provisions of Title I, which require the banks to keep various records of certain transactions by check; as our discussion of the challenges by the individual depositors to the recordkeeping provisions, supra, implicitly recognizes, the allegation that one is a depositor is sufficient to permit consideration of the challenges to the recordkeeping provisions, since any depositor would to some degree be affected by them. Here, however, we simply cannot assume that the mere fact that one is a depositor in a bank means that he has engaged or will engage in a transaction involving more than $10,000 in currency, which is the only type of domestic transaction which the Secretary's regulations require that the banks report. That being so, the depositor plaintiffs lack standing to challenge the domestic reporting regulations, since they do not show that their transactions are required to be reported.[28]

Plaintiffs in the federal courts 'must allege some threatened or actual injury resulting from the putatively illegal action before a federal court may assume jurisdiction.' Linda R. S. v. Richard D., 410 U.S. 614, 617, 93 S.Ct. 1146, 1148, 35 L.Ed.2d 536 (1973). There must be a 'personal stake in the outcome' such as to 'assure that concrete adverseness which sharpens the presentation of issues upon which the court so largely depends for illumination of difficult constitutional questions.' Baker v.

---

[28]   We hold here and in other parts of this opinion that certain of the plaintiffs did not make the requisite allegations in the District Court to give them standing to challenge the Act and the regulations issued pursuant to it. In so holding, we do not, of course, mean to imply that such claims would be meritorious if presented by a litigant who has standing.

Carr, 369 U.S. 186, 204, 82 S.Ct. 691, 703, 7 L.Ed.2d 663 (1962). . . . Abstract injury is not enough. It must be alleged that the plaintiff 'has sustained or is immediately in danger of sustaining some direct injury' as the result of the challenged statute or official conduct. Massachusetts v. Mellon, 262 U.S. 447, 488, 43 S.Ct. 597, 601, 67 L.Ed. 1078 (1923). The injury or threat of injury must be both 'real and immediate,' not 'conjectural' or 'hypothetical.' Golden v. Zwickler, 394 U.S. 103, 109–110, 89 S.Ct. 956, 960, 22 L.Ed.2d 113 (1969); Maryland Casualty Co. v. Pacific Coal & Oil Co., 312 U.S. 270, 273, 61 S.Ct. 510, 512, 85 L.Ed. 826 (1941); United Public Workers v. Mitchell, 330 U.S. 75, 89–91, 67 S.Ct. 556, 564– 565, 91 L.Ed. 754 (1947).' O'Shea v. Littleton, 414 U.S. 488, 493–494, 94 S.Ct. 669, 695, 38 L.Ed.2d 674 (1974) (footnote omitted).

We therefore hold that the Fourth Amendment claims of the depositor plaintiffs may not be considered on the record before us. Nor do we think that the California Bankers Association or the Security National Bank can vicariously assert such Fourth Amendment claims on behalf of bank customers in general.

* * *

MR. JUSTICE DOUGLAS, dissenting.

* * *

I

Customers have a constitutionally justifiable expectation of privacy in the documentary details of the financial transactions reflected in their bank accounts. That wall is not impregnable. Our Constitution provides the procedures whereby the confidentiality of one's financial affairs may be disclosed.

A

First, as to the recordkeeping requirements,[3] their announced purpose is that they will have 'a high degree of usefulness in criminal, tax, or regulatory investigations or proceedings,' 12 U.S.C. ss 1829b(a)(2), 1953(a). The duty of the bank or institution is to microfilm or otherwise copy every check, draft, or similar instrument drawn on it or presented to it for payment and to keep a record of each one 'received by it for deposit or collection,' 12 U.S.C. ss 1829b(d)(1) and (2). The retention is for up to six years unless the Secretary determines that 'a longer period is necessary,'

---

[3]   The Act authorizes the Secretary to issue regulations to carry out its purposes, 12 U.S.C. s 1829b(b). It empowers him to define institutions or persons affected, 12 U.S.C. ss 1953(a), (b)(5), to make exceptions, exemptions, or other special arrangements, 12 U.S.C. ss 1829(c), (f); to seek injunctions, 12 U.S.C. s 1954; and to assess and collect civil penalties, 12 U.S.C. s 1955.

12 U.S.C. s 1829b(g). The regulations[4] issued by the Secretary show the depth and extent of the quicksand in which our financial institutions must now operate.[5]

---

[4]　　Title 31 CFR s 103.34 at the time this litigation was commenced provided that banks shall:

'(a) . . . secure and maintain a record of the taxpayer identification number of the person maintaining the account; or in the case of an account of one or more individuals, such bank shall secure and maintain a record of the social security number of an individual having a financial interest in that account.

'(b) Each bank shall, in addition, retain either the original or a microfilm or other copy or reproduction of each of the following:

'(1) Each document granting signature authority over each deposit or share account;

'(2) Each statement, ledger card or other record on each deposit or share account, showing each transaction in, or with respect to, that account;

'(3) Each check, clean draft, or money order drawn on the bank or issued and payable by it, except those drawn on accounts which can be expected to have drawn on them an average of at least 100 checks per month over the calendar year or on each occasion on which such checks are issued, and which are (i) dividend checks, (ii) payroll checks, (iii) employee benefit checks, (iv) insurance claim checks, (v) medical benefit checks, (vi) checks drawn on governmental agency accounts, (vii) checks drawn by brokers or dealers in securities, (viii) checks drawn on fiduciary accounts, (ix) checks drawn on other financial institutions, or (x) pension or annuity checks;

'(4) Each item other than bank charges or periodic charges made pursuant to agreement with the customer, comprising a debit to a customer's deposit or share account, not required to be kept, and not specifically exempted, under subparagraph (b)(3) of this section;

'(5) Each item, including checks, drafts, or transfers of credit, of more than $10,000 remitted or transferred to a person, account or place outside the United States;

'(6) A record of each remittance or transfer of funds, or of currency, other monetary instruments, checks, investment securities, or credit, of more than $10,000 to a person, account or place outside the United States;

'(7) Each check or draft in an amount in excess of $10,000 drawn on or issued by a foreign bank, purchased, received for credit or collection, or otherwise acquired by the bank;

'(8) Each item, including checks, drafts or transfers of credit, of more than $10,000 received directly and not through a domestic financial institution, by letter, cable or any other means, from a person, account or place outside the United States;

'(9) A record of each receipt of currency, other monetary instruments, checks, or investment securities, and of each transfer of funds or credit, of more than $10,000 received on any one occasion directly and not through a domestic financial institution, from a person, account or place outside the United States; and

'(10) Records prepared or received by a bank in the ordinary course of business, which would be needed to reconstruct a demand deposit account and to trace a check deposited in such account through its domestic processing system or to supply a description of a deposited check. This subparagraph shall be applicable only with respect to demand deposits.' 37 Fed.Reg. 6914.

During this litigation the above provision was amended by the Secretary making it unnecessary to microfilm copies of checks 'drawn for $100 or less,' 31 CFR s 103.34(b)(3) (1973). Since banks must copy all checks it is hard to see how this new exemption is meaningful.

[5]　　Like requirements are placed on brokers and dealers in securities, 31 CFR s 103.35.

It is estimated that a minimum of 20 billion checks—and perhaps 30 billion—will have to be photocopied and that the weight of these little pieces of paper will approximate 166 million pounds a year.[6]

It would be highly useful to governmental espionage to have like reports from all our bookstores, all our hardware and retail stores, all our drugstores. These records too might be 'useful' in criminal investigations.

One's reading habits furnish telltale clues to those who are bent on bending us to one point of view. What one buys at the hardware and retail stores may furnish clues to potential uses of wires, soap powders, and the like used by criminals. A mandatory recording of all telephone conversations would be better than the recording of checks under the Bank Secrecy Act, if Big Brother is to have his way. The records of checks—now available to the investigators—are highly useful. In a sense a person is defined by the checks he writes. By examining them the agents get to know his doctors, lawyers, creditors, political allies, social connections, religious affiliation, educational interests, the papers and magazines he reads, and so on ad infinitum. These are all tied to one's social security number; and now that we have the data banks, these other items will enrich that storehouse and make it possible for a bureaucrat—by pushing one button— to get in an instant the names of the 190 million Americans who are subversives or potential and likely candidates.

It is, I submit, sheer nonsense to agree with the Secretary that all bank records of every citizen 'have a high degree of usefulness in criminal, tax, or regulatory investigations or proceedings.' That is unadulterated nonsense unless we are to assume that every citizen is a crook, an assumption I cannot make.

Since the banking transactions of an individual give a fairly accurate account of his religion, ideology, opinions, and interests, a regulation impounding them and making them automatically available to all federal investigative agencies is a sledge-hammer approach to a problem that only a delicate scalpel can manage. Where fundamental personal rights are involved—as is true when as here the Government gets large access to one's beliefs, ideas, politics, religion, cultural concerns, and the like—the Act should be 'narrowly drawn' (Cantwell v. Connecticut, 310 U.S. 296, 307, 60 S.Ct. 900, 905, 84 L.Ed. 1213) to meet the precise evil.[7] Bank accounts at

---

[6]   Hearings on Foreign Bank Secrecy and Bank Records (H.R. 15073) before the House Committee on Banking and Currency, 91st Cong., 1st and 2d Sess., 320 (1969–1970).

[7]   And see Roe v. Wade, 410 U.S. 113, 155, 93 S.Ct. 705, 728, 35 L.Ed.2d 147; Police Dept. of Chicago v. Mosley, 408 U.S. 92, 101, 92 S.Ct. 2286, 2293, 33 L.Ed.2d 212; Gooding v. Wilson, 405 U.S. 518, 522, 92 S.Ct. 1103, 1106, 31 L.Ed.2d 408; Shuttlesworth v. Birmingham, 394 U.S. 147, 151, 89 935, 938, 22 L.Ed.2d 162; Cameron v. Johnson, 390 U.S. 611, 617, 88 S.Ct. 1335, 1338, 20 L.Ed.2d 182; Zwickler v. Koota, 389 U.S. 241, 250, 88 S.Ct. 391, 396, 19 L.Ed.2d 444; Whitehill v. Elkins, 389 U.S. 54, 62, 88 S.Ct 184, 188, 19 L.Ed.2d 228; Ashton v. Kentucky, 384 U.S. 195,

times harbor criminal plans. But we only rush with the crowd when we vent on our banks and their customers the devastating and leveling requirements of the present Act. I am not yet ready to agree that America is so possessed with evil that we must level all constitutional barriers to give our civil authorities the tools to catch criminals.

* * *

We said in Katz v. United States, 389 U.S. 347, 351–352, 88 S.Ct. 507, 511, 19 L.Ed.2d 576: 'What a person knowingly exposes to the public, even in his own home or office, is not a subject of Fourth Amendment protection. . . . But what he seeks to preserve as private, even in an area accessible to the public, may be constitutionally protected.' As stated in United States v. White, 401 U.S. 745, 752, 91 S.Ct. 1122, 1126, 28 L.Ed.2d 453, the question is 'what expectations of privacy' will be protected by the Fourth Amendment 'in the absence of a warrant.' A search and seizure conducted without a warrant is per se unreasonable, subject to 'jealously and carefully drawn' exceptions, Jones v. United States, 357 U.S. 493, 499, 78 S.Ct. 1253, 1257, 2 L.Ed.2d 1514. One's bank accounts are within the 'expectations of privacy' category. For they mirror not only one's finances but his interests, his debts, his way of life, his family, and his civic commitments. There are administrative summonses for documents, cf. Camara v. Municipal Court, 387 U.S. 523, 87 S.Ct. 1727, 18 L.Ed.2d 930; See v. City of Seattle, 387 U.S. 541, 87 S.Ct. 1737, 18 L.Ed.2d 943. But there is a requirement that their enforcement receive judicial scrutiny and a judicial order, United States v. United States District Court, 407 U.S. 297, 313–318, 92 S.Ct. 2125, 2134–2137, 32 L.Ed.2d 752. As we said in that case, 'The Fourth Amendment does not contemplate the executive officers of Government as neutral and disinterested magistrates. Their duty and responsibility are to enforce the laws, to investigate, and to prosecute. . . . But those charged with this investigative and prosecutorial duty should not be the sole judges of when to utilize constitutionally sensitive means in pursuing their tasks. The historical judgment, which the Fourth Amendment accepts, is that unreviewed executive discretion may yield too readily to pressures to obtain incriminating evidence and overlook potential invasions of privacy and protected speech.' *Id.* , at 317, 92 S.Ct., at 2136.

Suppose Congress passed a law requiring telephone companies to record and retain all telephone calls and make them available to any federal agency on request. Would we hesitate even a moment before

---

201, 86 S.Ct. 1407, 1410, 16 L.Ed.2d 469; Elfbrandt v. Russell, 384 U.S. 11, 18, 86 S.Ct. 1238, 1241, 16 L.Ed.2d 321.

The same view is often expressed in concurring opinions. See Doe v. Bolton, 410 U.S. 179, 216, 93 S.Ct. 739, 760, 35 L.Ed.2d 201 (Douglas, J., concurring); Gregory v. Chicago, 394 U.S. 111, 119, 89 S.Ct. 946, 950, 22 L.Ed.2d 134 (Black, J., concurring); United States v. Robel, 389 U.S. 258, 270, 88 S.Ct. 419, 427, 19 L.Ed.2d 508 (Brennan, J., concurring in result).

striking it down? I think not, for we condemned in United States v. United States District Court 'the broad and unsuspected governmental incursions into conversational privacy which electronic surveillance entails.' *Id.* , at 313, 92 S.Ct., at 2135.

A checking account, as I have said, may well record a citizen's activities, opinion, and beliefs as fully as transcripts of his telephone conversations.

The Fourth Amendment warrant requirements may be removed by constitutional amendment but they certainly cannot be replaced by the Secretary of the Treasury's finding that certain information will be highly useful in 'criminal, tax, or regulatory investigations or proceedings.' 12 U.S.C. s 1951(b).

We cannot avoid the question of the constitutionality of the reporting provisions of the Act and of the regulations by saying they have not yet been applied to a customer in any criminal case. Under the Act and regulations the reports go forward to the investigative or prosecuting agency on written request without notice to the customer. Delivery of the records without the requisite hearing of probable cause[17] breaches the Fourth Amendment.

* * *

[JUSTICES BRENNAN and MARSHALL also separately dissented]

UNITED STATES V. MILLER
United States Supreme Court
425 U.S. 435 (1976)

MR. JUSTICE POWELL delivered the opinion of the Court.

Respondent was convicted of possessing an unregistered still, carrying on the business of a distiller without giving bond and with intent to defraud the Government of whiskey tax, possessing 175 gallons of whiskey upon which no taxes had been paid, and conspiring to defraud the United States of tax revenues. 26 U.S.C. ss 5179, 5205, 5601 Et seq.; 18 U.S.C. s 371. Prior to trial respondent moved to suppress copies of checks and other bank records obtained by means of allegedly defective subpoenas duces tecum served upon two banks at which he had accounts. The records had been

---

[17]   A criminal prosecution in this country for not reporting an overseas transaction is still a criminal prosecution under the Bill of Rights; and to these the Fourth Amendment has been applicable from the beginning. Cases of immigration officers stopping people at the border who are leaving or entering the country are obviously inapposite and certainly the Court cannot be serious in saying that the monetary value of the article being seized is relevant to whether the search and seizure without a warrant was constitutional. As said in Katz it is 'persons' not 'places' that the Fourth Amendment protects; and it would labor the point to engage in lengthy argument that 'things' as well as 'places' are not the object of the Fourth Amendment's concerns.

maintained by the banks in compliance with the requirements of the Bank Secrecy Act of 1970, 84 Stat. 1114, 12 U.S.C. s 1829b(d).

The District Court overruled respondent's motion to suppress, and the evidence was admitted. The Court of Appeals for the Fifth Circuit reversed on the ground that a depositor's Fourth Amendment rights are violated when bank records maintained pursuant to the Bank Secrecy Act are obtained by means of a defective subpoena. It held that any evidence so obtained must be suppressed. Since we find that respondent had no protectable Fourth Amendment interest in the subpoenaed documents, we reverse the decision below.

I

On December 18, 1972, in response to an informant's tip, a deputy sheriff from Houston County, Ga., stopped a van-type truck occupied by two of respondent's alleged co-conspirators. The truck contained distillery apparatus and raw material. On January 9, 1973, a fire broke out in a Kathleen, Ga., warehouse rented to respondent. During the blaze firemen and sheriff department officials discovered a 7,500-gallon-capacity distillery, 175 gallons of non-tax-paid whiskey, and related paraphernalia.

Two weeks later agents from the Treasury Department's Alcohol, Tobacco and Firearms Bureau presented grand jury subpoenas issued in blank by the clerk of the District Court, and completed by the United States Attorney's office, to the presidents of the Citizens & Southern National Bank of Warner Robins and the Bank of Byron, where respondent maintained accounts. The subpoenas required the two presidents to appear on January 24, 1973, and to produce

"all records of accounts, i.e., savings, checking, loan or otherwise, in the name of Mr. Mitch Miller (respondent), 3859 Mathis Street, Macon, Ga. and/or Mitch Miller Associates, 100 Executive Terrace, Warner Robins, Ga., from October, 1972, through the present date (January 22, 1973, in the case of the Bank of Byron, and January 23, 1973, in the case of the Citizens & Southern National Bank of Warner Robins)."

The banks did not advise respondent that the subpoenas had been served but ordered their employees to make the records available and to provide copies of any documents the agents desired. At the Bank of Byron, an agent was shown microfilm records of the relevant account and provided with copies of one deposit slip and one or two checks. At the Citizens & Southern National Bank microfilm records also were shown to the agent, and he was given copies of the records of respondent's account during the applicable period. These included all checks, deposit slips, two financial statements, and three monthly statements. The bank presidents were then told that it would not be necessary to appear in person before the grand jury.

The grand jury met on February 12, 1973, 19 days after the return date on the subpoenas. Respondent and four others were indicted. The overt acts alleged to have been committed in furtherance of the conspiracy included three financial transactions the rental by respondent of the van-type truck, the purchase by respondent of radio equipment, and the purchase by respondent of a quantity of sheet metal and metal pipe. The record does not indicate whether any of the bank records were in fact presented to the grand jury. They were used in the investigation and provided "one or two" investigatory leads. Copies of the checks also were introduced at trial to establish the overt acts described above.

* * *

The Government contends that the Court of Appeals erred in three respects: (i) in finding that respondent had the Fourth Amendment interest necessary to entitle him to challenge the validity of the subpoenas duces tecum through his motion to suppress; (ii) in holding that the subpoenas were defective; and (iii) in determining that suppression of the evidence obtained was the appropriate remedy if a constitutional violation did take place.

We find that there was no intrusion into any area in which respondent had a protected Fourth Amendment interest and that the District Court therefore correctly denied respondent's motion to suppress. Because we reverse the decision of the Court of Appeals on that ground alone, we do not reach the Government's latter two contentions.

II

In Hoffa v. United States, 385 U.S. 293, 301–302, 87 S.Ct. 408, 413, 17 L.Ed.2d 374, 382 (1966), the Court said that "no interest legitimately protected by the Fourth Amendment" is implicated by governmental investigative activities unless there is an intrusion into a zone of privacy, into "the security a man relies upon when he places himself or his property within a constitutionally protected area." The Court of Appeals, as noted above, assumed that respondent had the necessary Fourth Amendment interest, pointing to the language in Boyd v. United States, supra, 116 U.S., at 622, 6 S.Ct., at 528, 29 L.Ed., at 748, which describes that Amendment's protection against the "compulsory production of a man's private papers."[1] We think that the Court of Appeals erred in finding the subpoenaed documents to fall within a protected zone of privacy.

On their face, the documents subpoenaed here are not respondent's "private papers." Unlike the claimant in Boyd, respondent can assert neither ownership nor possession. Instead, these are the business records

---

[1]   The Fourth Amendment implications of Boyd as it applies to subpoenas duces tecum Have been undercut by more recent cases. Fisher v. United States, 425 U.S. 391, at 407–409, 96 S.Ct. 1569, at 1578–1580, 48 L.Ed.2d 39, 53–55 (1976). See Infra, at 1625.

of the banks. As we said in California Bankers Association v. Shultz, supra, 416 U.S., at 48–49, 94 S.Ct., at 1511, 39 L.Ed.2d, at 833, "(b)anks are . . . not . . . neutrals in transactions involving negotiable instruments, but parties to the instruments with a substantial stake in their continued availability and acceptance." The records of respondent's accounts, like "all of the records (which are required to be kept pursuant to the Bank Secrecy Act,) pertain to transactions to which the bank was itself a party." *Id.,* at 52, 94 S.Ct., at 1513, 39 L.Ed.2d, at 835.

Respondent argues, however, that the Bank Secrecy Act introduces a factor that makes the subpoena in this case the functional equivalent of a search and seizure of the depositor's "private papers." We have held, in California Bankers Association v. Shultz, supra, at 54, 94 S.Ct., at 1514, 39 L.Ed.2d, at 836, that the mere maintenance of records pursuant to the requirements of the Act "invade(s) no Fourth Amendment right of any depositor." But respondent contends that the combination of the recordkeeping requirements of the Act and the issuance of a subpoena[2] to obtain those records permits the Government to circumvent the requirements of the Fourth Amendment by allowing it to obtain a depositor's private records without complying with the legal requirements that would be applicable had it proceeded against him directly.[3] Therefore, we must address the question whether the compulsion embodied in the Bank Secrecy Act as exercised in this case creates a Fourth Amendment interest in the depositor where none existed before. This question was expressly reserved in *California Bankers Assn., supra,* at 53–54, and n. 24, 94 S.Ct., at 1513–1514, 39 L.Ed.2d, at 835–836.

Even if we direct our attention to the original checks and deposit slips, rather than to the microfilm copies actually viewed and obtained by means of the subpoena, we perceive no legitimate "expectation of privacy" in their contents. The checks are not confidential communications but negotiable instruments to be used in commercial transactions. All of the documents obtained, including financial statements and deposit slips, contain only information voluntarily conveyed to the banks and exposed to their employees in the ordinary course of business. The lack of any legitimate expectation of privacy concerning the information kept in bank records was assumed by Congress in enacting the Bank Secrecy Act, the expressed purpose of which is to require records to be maintained because they "have

---

[2]   Respondent appears to contend that a depositor's Fourth Amendment interest comes into play only when a defective subpoena is used to obtain records kept pursuant to the Act. We see no reason why the existence of a Fourth Amendment interest turns on whether the subpoena is defective. Therefore, we do not limit our consideration to the situation in which there is an alleged defect in the subpoena served on the bank.

[3]   It is not clear whether respondent refers to attempts to obtain private documents through a subpoena issued directly to the depositor or through a search pursuant to a warrant. The question whether personal business records may be seized pursuant to a valid warrant is before this Court in No. 74–1646, Andresen v. Maryland, cert. granted, 423 U.S. 822, 96 S.Ct. 36, 46 L.Ed.2d 39.

a high degree of usefulness in criminal tax, and regulatory investigations and proceedings," 12 U.S.C. s 1829b(a)(l). Cf. Couch v. United States, supra, at 335, 93 S.Ct., at 619, 34 L.Ed.2d, at 558.

The depositor takes the risk, in revealing his affairs to another, that the information will be conveyed by that person to the Government. United States v. White, 401 U.S. 745, 751–752, 91 S.Ct. 1122, 1125–1126, 28 L.Ed.2d 453, 458–459 (1971). This Court has held repeatedly that the Fourth Amendment does not prohibit the obtaining of information revealed to a third party and conveyed by him to Government authorities, even if the information is revealed on the assumption that it will be used only for a limited purpose and the confidence placed in the third party will not be betrayed. *Id.*, at 752, 91 S.Ct., at 1126, 28 L.Ed.2d, at 459; Hoffa v. United States, 385 U.S. at 302, 87 S.Ct., at 413, 17 L.Ed.2d, at 382; Lopez v. United States, 373 U.S. 427, 83 S.Ct. 1381, 10 L.Ed.2d 462 (1963).[4]

This analysis is not changed by the mandate of the Bank Secrecy Act that records of depositors' transactions be maintained by banks. In California Bankers Assn. v. Shultz, 416 U.S., at 52–53, 94 S.Ct., at 1512–1513, 39 L.Ed.2d, at 835–836, we rejected the contention that banks, when keeping records of their depositors' transactions pursuant to the Act, are acting solely as agents of the Government. But, even if the banks could be said to have been acting solely as Government agents in transcribing the necessary information and complying without protest[5] with the requirements of the subpoenas, there would be no intrusion upon the depositors' Fourth Amendment rights. See Osborn v. United States, 385 U.S. 323, 87 S.Ct. 429, 17 L.Ed.2d 394 (1966); Lewis v. United States, 385 U.S. 206, 87 S.Ct. 424, 17 L.Ed.2d 312 (1966).

* * *

MR. JUSTICE MARSHALL, dissenting.

In California Bankers Assn. v. Shultz, 416 U.S. 21, 94 S.Ct. 1494, 39 L.Ed.2d 812 (1974), the Court upheld the constitutionality of the recordkeeping requirements of the Bank Secrecy Act. 12 U.S.C. s 1829b(d). I dissented, finding the required maintenance of bank customers' records to be a seizure within the meaning of the Fourth Amendment and unlawful in the absence of a warrant and probable cause. While the Court in California Bankers Assn. did not then purport to decide whether a customer could later challenge the bank's delivery of his records to the Government pursuant to subpoena, I warned:

---

[4]   We do not address here the question of evidentiary privileges, such as that protecting communications between an attorney and his client. Cf. Fisher v. United States, 425 U.S., at 403–405, 96 S.Ct., at 1577, 48 L.Ed.2d, at 51–53.

[5]   Nor did the banks notify respondent, a neglect without legal consequences here, however unattractive it may be.

"(I)t is ironic that although the majority deems the bank customers' Fourth Amendment claims premature, it also intimates that once the bank has made copies of a customer's checks, the customer no longer has standing to invoke his Fourth Amendment rights when a demand is made on the bank by the Government for the records . . . By accepting the Government's bifurcated approach to the recordkeeping requirement and the acquisition of the records, the majority engages in a hollow charade whereby Fourth Amendment claims are to be labeled premature until such time as they can be deemed too late." 416 U.S., at 97, 94 S.Ct., at 1535, 39 L.Ed.2d, at 861.

Today, not surprisingly, the Court finds respondent's claims to be made too late. Since the Court in California Bankers Assn. held that a bank, in complying with the requirement that it keep copies of the checks written by its customers, "neither searches nor seizes records in which the depositor has a Fourth Amendment right," *Id.* , at 54, 94 S.Ct., at 1514, 39 L.Ed.2d, at 836, there is nothing new in today's holding that respondent has no protected Fourth Amendment interest in such records. A fortiori, he does not have standing to contest the Government's subpoena to the bank. Alderman v. United States, 394 U.S. 165, 89 S.Ct. 961, 22 L.Ed.2d 176 (1969).

I wash my hands of today's extended redundancy by the Court. Because the recordkeeping requirements of the Act order the seizure of customers' bank records without a warrant and probable cause, I believe the Act is unconstitutional and that respondent has standing to raise that claim. Since the Act is unconstitutional, the Government cannot rely on records kept pursuant to it in prosecuting bank customers. The Government relied on such records in this case and, because of that, I would affirm the Court of Appeals' reversal of respondent's conviction. I respectfully dissent.

UNITED STATES V. FITZGIBBON

United States Court of Appeals
576 F.2d 279 (10th Cir. 1978)

LOGAN, CIRCUIT JUDGE.

Kenneth C. Fitzgibbon appeals his conviction by a jury of knowingly and willfully making a false statement in violation of 18 U.S.C. s 1001, in connection with bringing foreign currency through U.S. Customs.

On appeal the appellant makes a number of claims: the indictment was defective; he was charged under the wrong statute; the evidence was insufficient to support the verdict; he was the victim of an illegal search; the jury was improperly instructed; and the Act involved here is unconstitutional.

Defendant-appellant Fitzgibbon entered the United States at Denver on a flight from Calgary, Canada. Upon arrival at U.S. Customs Fitzgibbon tendered to the official on duty, Joseph Lockhart, the "Customs Declaration" Form 6059-B, which is given during flight to all passengers coming into the United States from abroad. A question on the form asks "Are you or anyone in your party carrying over $5,000.00 in coin, currency, or monetary instruments?" Fitzgibbon had checked a "no" answer to that question. The official asked Fitzgibbon that question again orally during his inspection, as is apparently done routinely. Fitzgibbon's answer again was "no."

Fitzgibbon had come under suspicion on a tip, the investigation of which showed he had purchased a ticket from Denver to Calgary, Canada, and a return on the same flight forty minutes later. He had in fact returned the following morning, Lockhart testified that he did not recognize Fitzgibbon's name or appearance as one for whom he was to watch, but noticed Fitzgibbon was hesitant in answering "no" to the question about money. He stated that he then asked Fitzgibbon if he acquired anything in Canada and again the answer was "no." As Lockhart examined Fitzgibbon's baggage, his testimony was that the defendant appeared nervous. Lockhart then motioned to a supervisor for a secondary examination. Fitzgibbon was taken to a search room and, in the presence of another Customs official, Lockhart "padded down" Fitzgibbon as a safety precaution and requested that the defendant empty his pockets. In Fitzgibbon's wallet was a relatively small amount of Canadian and Mexican money. Lockhart asked Fitzgibbon if this was the only currency the defendant had on his person and Fitzgibbon answered "yes." Defendant was then asked to remove his boots. In doing so he mumbled something about "investment," and as he removed each boot he reached into it and pulled out a bundle of Canadian currency, amounting in total to approximately $9,800.00 Canadian (worth slightly more than that total in U.S. dollars).

Fitzgibbon was then read his Miranda rights and taken to another room where he volunteered to Customs Agent H. R. King that he had acquired the money in Canada and wanted to avoid a hassle with the United States Internal Revenue Service because part of the money was not his; he was to send $5,410.72 of the money to an attorney in New Jersey. The remainder he said he earned in doing some construction work on a home in Washington state belonging to a Canadian resident. Fitzgibbon produced a slip of Canadian hotel notepaper from an envelope with the figure 5410.72 written on it.

* * *

Appellant contends that the portions of the Bank Secrecy Act, 84 Stat. 1114, involved here (31 U.S.C. ss 1101–1105) violate his First, Fourth and Fifth Amendment rights and should be declared unconstitutional.

The contentions regarding the First and Fourth Amendments have been rejected by the U. S. Supreme Court in *California Bankers Ass'n v. Shultz,* 416 U.S. 21, 94 S.Ct. 1494, 39 L.Ed.2d 812 (1974) and *United States v. Miller,* 425 U.S. 435, 96 S.Ct, 1619, 48 L.Ed,2d 71 (1976).

Fitzgibbon's Fifth Amendment objection is directed to the power of the government to compel persons crossing our national borders to file reports of information which might later be used as incriminating evidence in a criminal prosecution. The constitutional issues raised by appellant here have been considered and resolved against appellant's position in *United States v. San Juan,* 405 F.Supp. 686 (D.Vt.1975), rev'd on other grounds, (without discussion of these constitutional issues) 545 F.2d 314 (2d Cir. 1976). We do not here decide the constitutional questions raised because they are not properly before us. Fitzgibbon was convicted of filing a false statement, under 18 U.S.C. § 1001. The Supreme Court has held in several cases "that one who furnishes false information to the Government in feigned compliance with a statutory requirement cannot defend against prosecution for his fraud by challenging the validity of the requirement itself." *United States v. Knox,* 396 U.S. 77, 79, 90 S.Ct. 363, 365, 24 L.Ed.2d 275 (1969).

* * *

NOTES

1.   Please note that in the *Fitzgibbon* case, the court avoided the appellant's Fifth Amendment objections to the BSA currency transaction reporting requirements, basing its holding on 18 U.S.C. § 1001, which generally prohibits the filing of false information on government applications and forms.

UNITED STATES V. THOMPSON
United States Court of Appeals
603 F.2d 1200 (5th Cir. 1979)

CHARLES CLARK, CIRCUIT JUDGE.

On March 12, 1979, George Thompson, III was found guilty of unlawfully causing the Ridglea Bank of Fort Worth, Texas, to fail to file a currency transaction report (CTR), 31 U.S.C. §§ 1059, 1081, with the knowledge that this violation was committed in the furtherance of violations of other federal laws, in that Thompson, in violation of 18 U.S.C. s 2(b), aided and abetted Michael E. Welch in knowingly and intentionally possessing with the intent to distribute, and in distributing, cocaine in violation of 21 U.S.C. § 841(a)(1). Thompson was sentenced to three years imprisonment and fined $20,000.00. He appeals his conviction arguing first that the statute and regulations under which he was prosecuted are unconstitutionally vague as applied to him, second that he is entitled to structure a single transaction in currency as multiple loans so as to avoid reporting requirements, and third that the evidence is insufficient to establish that he caused the bank to fail to file the CTR. We reject appellant's arguments and affirm his conviction.

I.   STATEMENT OF FACTS

George Thompson, III was Chairman of the Board of Ridglea Bank. The evidence presented at trial established that beginning in 1974, Thompson authorized a series of loans to Michael E. Welch. These loans were to enable Welch, an aspiring jazz musician, to purchase musical instruments. Welch experienced difficulty in repaying these loans and in April 1976 approached Thompson with a plan by which Thompson would arrange for additional loans to Welch. Welch proposed using the proceeds of these loans to purchase marijuana that he would in turn resell, utilizing the profits derived from the venture to repay the initial indebtedness. A series of loans followed, all approved by Thompson and disbursed in cash to Welch.[1] Welch testified that Thompson knew at the time these loans were made that the proceeds would be used to purchase marijuana. Thompson denied such knowledge, claiming that he did not know nor did he want to know what the loans were to be used for. Some time prior to March 9, 1977, Welch approached Thompson and proposed a plan whereby the proceeds of additional loans would be used to purchase cocaine which, when sold, would generate a much greater profit than had the sales of marijuana. Again, Welch planned to use the profits to discharge his indebtedness at the Ridglea Bank. Previously having become aware of currency transaction reporting requirements, Thompson advised Welch that any future monies loaned by Ridglea Bank would be in amounts of less than $10,000 in order to avoid filing a currency transaction report. On March 9, 1977, Welch met with Thompson at Ridglea Bank in order to obtain $45,000.00. Welch again testified that Thompson knew at the time of the loan transaction that the proceeds would be used to purchase cocaine. Thompson again denied having such knowledge, claiming that he did not know nor did he want to know what the loans would be used for. Thompson had five notes prepared, each in the amount of $9,000.00 and each bearing a different maturity date. He admitted intentionally structuring the transaction in such a manner to avoid filing a currency transaction report. Thompson personally processed the notes by receiving five cash tickets from the bank's Loan and Discount Department and, upon presentation to a commercial teller, receiving $45,000.00 in cash in five separate $9,000.00 bundles. Thompson immediately transferred the entire $45,000.00 in cash to Welch at one time. Welch testified that after obtaining the $45,000.00 he purchased almost two pounds of cocaine.

---

[1]   The record discloses that Welch received loans of $17,600.00 on April 23, 1976, $24,800.00 on May 7, 1976, and $7,500.00 on November 9, 1976.

No CTR was filed by the Ridglea Bank for the March 9, 1977, transaction. The commercial teller who disbursed the $45,000.00 in cash to Thompson, and whose responsibility it was to file a CTR, testified that Thompson provided him no information from which a report could be filed. The teller further testified that Thompson was the only person who could have provided the information necessary to enable a CTR to be filed as there was no information on the loan application and Welch had no accounts with the bank. The teller explained his failure to file a CTR as based on a reliance on Thompson's authority as Chairman of the Board and on an assumption that Thompson would tell him to file a CTR were one needed.

II.   VAGUENESS CHALLENGE

[1]   Appellant contends that the statute and regulations under which he was prosecuted are unconstitutionally vague as applied to him in that the terms "transaction" and "currency transaction" are nowhere defined. We reject this argument.

Congress enacted the Currency and Foreign Transactions Reporting Act "to require certain reports or records where such reports or records have a high degree of usefulness in criminal, tax, or regulatory investigations or proceedings." 31 U.S.C. § 1051. The Act provides that:

Transactions involving any domestic institution shall be reported to the Secretary (of the Treasury) at such time, in such manner, and in such detail as the Secretary may require if they involve the payment, receipt, or transfer of United States currency, or such other monetary instruments as the Secretary may specify, in such amounts, denominations, or both, or under such circumstances, as the Secretary shall by regulation prescribe. 31 U.S.C. § 1081. The pertinent regulation requires that:

Each financial institution shall file a report of each deposit, withdrawal, exchange of currency or other payment or transfer, by, through, or to such financial institution which involves a Transaction in currency of more than $10,000.

31 C.F.R. § 103.21(a) (emphasis added). The regulations expressly define a "transaction in currency" as being "(a) transaction involving the physical transfer of currency from one person to another." 31 C.F.R. s 103,11.[2] The regulation's definition of "transaction in currency" is reprinted in its entirety on the reverse side of Form 4789, which is utilized by

---

²   The regulation provides:

Transaction in currency. A transaction involving the physical transfer of currency from one person to another. A transaction which is a transfer of funds by means of bank check, bank draft, wire transfer, or other written order, and which does not include the physical transfer of currency is not a transaction in currency within the meaning of this part.

31 C.F.R. s 103.11.

financial institutions in filing CTRs. The terms "currency" and "person" also are defined in the regulations with similar specificity.[3]

The "void for vagueness" doctrine requires that a law give a person of ordinary intelligence a reasonable opportunity to know what is prohibited so that he may act accordingly. Grayned v. City of Rockford, 408 U.S. 104, 108, 92 S.Ct. 2294, 33 L.Ed.2d 222 (1972). A statute is fatally vague only when it exposes a potential actor to some risk or detriment without giving him fair warning of the proscribed conduct. Rowan v. United States Post Office Dep't, 397 U.S. 728, 740, 90 S.Ct. 1484, 25 L.Ed.2d 736 (1970). While criminal statutes must fairly apprise those who are subject to them as to the conduct that is proscribed, no more than a reasonable degree of certainty can be demanded. Boyce Motor Lines, Inc. v. United States, 342 U.S. 337, 340, 72 S.Ct. 329, 96 L.Ed. 367 (1952); United States v. Barnett, 587 F.2d 252, 256 (5th Cir. 1978). See also United States v. Griffin, 589 F.2d 200, 207 (5th Cir. 1979), Petition for cert. filed, 47 U.S.L.W. 3763 (U.S. May 22, 1979) (No. 78–1518).

With reference to the above authorities, we cannot say that the applicable statute and regulations as defined failed to afford appellant fair notice of what constitutes a "transaction in currency of more than $10,000." Rather, the government's proof at trial clearly established a violation of the reporting requirements as defined, in that an unreported physical transfer of $45,000.00 in cash from the Ridglea Bank to Welch occurred on March 9, 1977. The mere fact that appellant intentionally structured the $45,000.00 transfer as five $9,000.00 loans with different maturity dates does not remove the transaction from the ambit of the reporting requirements, where these loans were executed by the same borrower, on the same day, in the same bank, and where the proceeds of the loans totalling in excess of $10,000.00 were physically transferred by the financial institution to the borrower at the same time and place.

III. AVOIDANCE ISSUE

[2] Appellant argues that he was entitled to structure a single transaction in currency as multiple loans, thus avoiding the obligation to report pursuant to § 1081 and the relevant regulations. Appellant analogizes this to a taxpayer structuring a financial transaction in a

---

[3]   The regulation provides:

Currency. The coin and currency of the United States or of any other country, which circulate in and are customarily U.S.ed and accepted as money in the country in which issued. It includes U.S. silver certificates, U.S. notes and Federal Reserve notes, but does not include bank checks or other negotiable instruments not customarily accepted as money.

Person. An individual, a corporation, a partnership, a trust or estate, a joint stock company, an association, a syndicate, joint venture, or other unincorporated organization or group, and all entities cognizable as legal personalities.

31 C.F.R. s 103.11.

certain manner to avoid, rather than evade, the payment of taxes. The analogy is inapposite, Congress has lawfully required reporting of transactions in currency of more than $10,000.00 as an aid to criminal, tax, or regulatory investigations or proceedings.[4] In the instant case, appellant intentionally sought to defeat the statutory requirements by engaging in an unreported transaction in currency of more than $10,000.00. Appellant cannot flout the requirements of s 1081 with impunity. The decision to structure a $45,000.00 transaction in currency as five $9,000.00 loans with the intent to annul the reporting requirements does not equate to a decision to structure a financial transaction in a lawful manner so as to minimize or avoid the applicability of a tax covering only specific activity.

* * *

QUESTIONS AND NOTES

1.   Under FinCEN's CTR rules, 31 C.F.R. § 1010.311 (see also FinCEN Form 104, Currency Transactions Report), Federal law prohibits "structuring," making it a crime to break up transactions into smaller amounts for the purpose of evading the CTR reporting requirement and this may lead to a required disclosure from the financial institution to the government. Structuring transactions to prevent a CTR from being reported can result in imprisonment for not more than five years and/or a fine of up to $250,000. If structuring involves more than $100,000 in a twelve month period or is performed while violating another law of the United States, the penalty is doubled. See Notice to Customers: A CTR Reference Guide, http://www.fincen.gov/.

2.   Consider the following situations—do these constitute illegal "structuring?"

a.   A married couple, John and Jane, sell a vehicle for $15,000 in cash. To evade the CTR reporting requirement, John and Jane structure their transactions using different accounts. John deposits $8,000 of that money into his and Jane's joint account in the morning. Later that day, Jane deposits $1,500 into the joint account, and then $5,500 into her sister's account, which is later transferred to John and Jane's joint account.

b.   Bob wants to place $24,000 cash he earned from his illegal activities into the financial system by using a wire transfer. Bob knows his financial institution will file a CTR if he purchases a wire with over $10,000 currency in one day. To evade the CTR reporting requirement, Bob wires the $24,000 by purchasing wires with

---

[4]   There can be no doubt that Congress enacted the reporting provisions as an aid to criminal, tax, or regulatory investigations and proceedings. See 31 U.S.C. s 1051; H.R.Rep. No. 91–975 (1970) Reprinted in (1970) 2 U.S.Code Cong. & Admin.News, pp. 4394, 4396; 31 C.F.R. s 103.21. The United States Supreme Court recognized this purpose when it rejected various constitutional challenges raised against the reporting requirements. See California Bankers Ass'n v. Shultz, 416 U.S. 21, 37–38, 63–78, 94 S.Ct. 1494, 39 L.Ed.2d 812 (1974).

currency in $6,000 increments over a short period of time, occasionally skipping days in an attempt to prevent the financial institution from filing a CTR.

See CTR Reference Guide at 2 (both fact patterns constitute illegal structuring).

3.   Do you think law enforcement authorities that brought charges against the bank president in the *Thompson* case were motivated by the fact that he actively assisted in structuring loans (and currency transactions) that were used in illegal sale of narcotics? Would there be a different result if it occurred in a jurisdiction where the possession and sale of marijuana is legal? See FinCEN Guidance, BSA Expectations Regarding Marijuana-Related Businesses (February 14, 2014) (requirements for "Marijuana Priority" SAR filings when a financial institution customer is engaged in a marijuana-related business in a state where such business is permissible under state law).

4. BANK CIVIL LIABILITY FOR BSA COMPLIANCE

LEE V. BANKERS TRUST

United States Court of Appeals
166 F.3d 540 (2d Cir. 1999)

BACKGROUND

MCLAUGHLIN, CIRCUIT JUDGE.

In 1990, Bankers Trust Company ("Bankers Trust"), hired Let W. Lee as a Vice President for Global Retirement and Security Services. Later it promoted him to Managing Director. In April 1994, Bankers Trust asked Lee to work in its Global Security Services practice, and he agreed. Lee always worked in the New Jersey offices of Bankers Trust.

In Spring 1995, Lee asked two Bankers Trust employees, Harvey Plante and Gerard Callaghan, to look into Bankers Trust's older "custody credit" accounts. These accounts had been languishing unclaimed for long periods, and Lee asked Plante and Callaghan to determine whether Bankers Trust could properly keep some of this money rather than letting it escheat to the state. Plante told Callaghan and Lee that Bankers Trust had more than $3.9 million in the accounts that did not have to be escheated. Lee and Callaghan then told Plante that any non-escheatable funds that were properly documented should be transferred to a reserve account at Bankers Trust.

Plante was placed in charge of the reserve account. Lee maintains that he told Plante: (1) to clear all dealings with Bankers Trust's compliance department; (2) not to transfer any money that was not properly documented; (3) not to transfer any funds that might possibly be escheatable; and (4) to keep a detailed list of funds in the reserve account.

In March 1996, Bankers Trust became troubled by Plante's activities and questioned him about the reserve account. Shortly thereafter, Bankers Trust let Lee know that Plante claimed that Lee had told him to transfer *escheatable* funds into the reserve account. Lee denied this claim.

On March 21, 1996, Lee met with John Foos, John Peters and Elizabeth Hughes, all of whom worked in Bankers Trust's Securities Services practice. After meeting with this trio for over five hours, Lee signed a statement prepared by Bankers Trust. Bankers Trust then ordered Lee to stay out of his office while it conducted an investigation. Lee claims that by the end of March 21st, everyone at Bankers Trust was discussing his involvement in some kind of wrongdoing.

In early June 1996, Lee claims that Richard Coffina, Head of Human Resources at Bankers Trust, told him that the firm would like him to resign. Lee did resign on June 6, 1996. The press reported that Lee left Bankers Trust amid allegations of wrongdoing. Bankers Trust never made any public statement regarding Lee's activities or the reason for his departure.

Lee claims that after his resignation, Bankers Trust filed a "Suspicious Activity Report" ("SAR") with the United States Attorney's Office for the Southern District of New York. This claim is curious because an SAR is a confidential report that financial firms are required by law to file when they suspect illegal activities by their employees. Disclosure of even the filing of an SAR, let alone disclosure of its substance, is prohibited by law. Thus, it remains a mystery as to how Lee knows that Bankers Trust filed an SAR.

On October 30, 1996, Lee filed suit in the United States District Court for the Southern District of New York (Batts, J.), alleging that Bankers Trust defamed him through its *conduct* in investigating the reserve accounts. His complaint focuses on Bankers Trust's search of his office and its alleged filing of an SAR. He also asserted a claim for false imprisonment.

Bankers Trust moved to dismiss the complaint for failure to state a claim. Judge Batts granted the motion, finding that the defendant is immune from a defamation claim based on the alleged filing of an SAR, and that the other actions by Bankers Trust were not "statements" that could support a claim for defamation. She also dismissed the false imprisonment claim as frivolous. Lee now appeals, arguing that: (1) Bankers Trust does not enjoy absolute immunity from liability for statements in the SAR that it purportedly filed; (2) its other actions can support a claim for defamation; and (3) Judge Batts should have applied New York, not New Jersey law in assessing his defamation claims. Lee does not appeal the dismissal of his false imprisonment claim.

DISCUSSION

I.   *Defamatory Statements in the SAR*

In his complaint, Lee alleged that Bankers Trust defamed him in an SAR filed with the United States Attorney for the Southern District of New York. While refusing to confirm or deny the filing of an SAR, Bankers Trust counters that it has immunity for any allegedly defamatory statements made in such a filing. Lee recognizes that Bankers Trust enjoys some immunity for statements in an SAR, but argues that this immunity extends only to statements made in good faith. Lee is incorrect.

This Court reviews *de novo* a district court's decision to dismiss a complaint for failure to state a claim, taking all factual allegations as true and construing all reasonable inferences in the plaintiff's favor. See Jaghory v. New York State Dep't of Educ., 131 F.3d 326, 329 (2d Cir. 1997). Dismissal is proper only "if 'it appears beyond doubt that the plaintiff can prove no set of facts in support of his claim which would entitle him to relief.'" Valmonte v. Bane, 18 F.3d 992, 998 (2d Cir. 1994) (quoting Conley v. Gibson, 355 U.S. 41, 45–46, 78 S.Ct. 99, 2 L.Ed.2d 80 (1957)).

The regulations promulgated under the Annunzio-Wylie Act (the "Act"), 31 U.S.C. § 5318(g), require financial institutions like Bankers Trust to file an SAR "no later than thirty (30) days after the initial detection of a known or suspected violation of federal law, a suspected transaction related to money laundering activity, or a violation of the Bank Secrecy Act." 12 C.F.R. § 208.20(d) (1997). Institutions are prohibited from acknowledging filing, or commenting on the contents of, an SAR unless ordered to do so by the appropriate authorities. See 12 C.F.R. § 208.20(j) & (g).

SAR filers are protected from civil liability by the "safe harbor" provision of the Act, which provides:

> Liability for disclosures. Any financial institution that makes a disclosure of any possible violation of law or regulation or a disclosure pursuant to this subsection or any other authority, and any director, officer, employee, or agent of such institution, shall not be liable to any person under any law or regulation of the United States or any constitution, law, or regulation of any State or political subdivision thereof, for such disclosure or for any failure to notify the person involved in the transaction or any other person of such disclosure.

31 U.S.C. § 5318(g)(3) (Supp.1998). The safe harbor provision applies, regardless of whether the SAR is filed as required by the Act or in an excess of caution. See 12 C.F.R. § 208.20(k) (1998) (to be recodified at 12 C.F.R. 208.62(k) (1999)).

Although the regulation does not say so, Lee argues that there is immunity only where the disclosures in the SAR were made in good faith. We disagree.

It is axiomatic that the plain meaning of a statute controls its interpretation, see Greenery Rehabilitation Grp., Inc. v. Hammon, 150 F.3d 226, 231 (2d Cir. 1998), and that judicial review must end at the statute's unambiguous terms. See Rubin v. United States, 449 U.S. 424, 430, 101 S.Ct. 698, 66 L.Ed.2d 633 (1981). Legislative history and other tools of interpretation may be relied upon only if the terms of the statute are ambiguous. See Aslanidis v. United States Lines, Inc., 7 F.3d 1067, 1073 (2d Cir, 1993).

The plain language of the safe harbor provision describes an unqualified privilege, never mentioning good faith or any suggestive analogue thereof. The Act broadly and unambiguously provides for immunity from *any* law (except the federal Constitution) for *any* statement made in an SAR by *anyone* connected to a financial institution. There is not even a hint that the statements must be made in good faith in order to benefit from immunity. Based on the unambiguous language of the Act, Bankers Trust enjoys immunity from liability for its filing of, or any statement made in, an SAR.

Our conclusion based on the language of the Act is bolstered by a common sense appraisal of the safe harbor provision's place within the Act. Financial institutions are required by law to file SARs, but are prohibited from disclosing either that an SAR has been filed or the information contained therein. See 12 C.F.R. § 208.20(k) (1998). Thus, even in a suit for damages based on disclosures allegedly made in an SAR, a financial institution cannot reveal what disclosures it made in an SAR, or even whether it filed an SAR at all.

Under plaintiff's theory, he can allege, on information and belief, that a bank filed an SAR containing allegedly defamatory statements that were not made in good faith. If the bank sought summary judgment, it would then have to establish that the statements in the SAR were made in good faith, but it would be prohibited by law both from disclosing the filing or the contents of an SAR. It flies in the face of common sense to assert that Congress sought to impale financial institutions on the horns of such a dilemma.

Finally, although the safe harbor provision is unambiguous, and does not require resort to legislative history, the history of the Act demonstrates that Congress did not intend to limit protection to statements made in good faith. An earlier draft of the safe harbor provision included an explicit good faith requirement for statements made in an SAR. See 137 Cong. Rec. S16,642 (1991). However, the requirement was dropped in later versions of the bill, and was not included in the bill that was eventually enacted by

Congress. See 137 Cong. Rec. S17,910, S17,969 (1991); 31 U.S.C. § 5318(g)(3).

Lee urges us to ignore the plain meaning of the Act, the "common sense" argument, and the legislative history, and to accept the analysis suggested by the Eleventh Circuit in Lopez v. First Union Nat'l Bank, 129 F.3d 1186 (11th Cir.1997). In *Lopez,* the court stated that the safe harbor provision protects institutions only if they have "a good faith suspicion that a law or regulation may have been violated." *Lopez,* 129 F.3d at 1192–93. *Lopez* did not explain where the requirement of a "good faith suspicion" came from, or why it was necessary to its decision.

We decline to import a good faith requirement into the statute. The Act provides immunity for "disclosure of *any possible* violation of law or regulation." 31 U.S.C. § 5318(g)(3) (emphasis added). We conclude that the safe harbor provision does not limit protection to disclosures based on a good faith belief that a violation has occurred.

[The court dismissed the defamation by conduct and choice of law claims]

* * *

NOTES

1.   The *Lee* case makes clear that neither the filing of a SAR or its contents with FinCEN may be disclosed to either the party who is the subject of the SAR, or any third parties. 31 U.S.C. § 5318(g)(3). The SAR filer has the option of providing a copy of a SAR to its primary regulator. *Id.*

2.   A financial institution is required to file a SAR no later than 30 calendar days after the date of initial detection of facts that may constitute a basis for filing a suspicious activity report. If no suspect was identified on the date of detection of the incident requiring the filing, a financial institution may delay filing a SAR for an additional 30 calendar days to identify a suspect. In no case shall reporting be delayed more than 60 calendar days after the date of initial detection of a reportable transaction. See 31 C.F.R. § 103.

3.   FinCEN requires that any SAR filers must disclose to FinCEN any request for a SAR or "SAR-related information" by any third party. FinCEN has concluded that SAR information should not be disclosed to judicial discovery, even pursuant to a request for in camera inspection. See Hasie Financial Group v. OCC, No. 08–10642 (5th Cir. 2011).

4.   The Government Accountability Office (GAO) conducted an audit from March 2008 to January 2009. http://www.gao.gov/assets/290/285430.pdf. It concluded that FinCEN, the Treasury Communication System (TCS) and the Internal Revenue Services (IRS) had "significant weaknesses . . . that impaired [the] ability to ensure the confidentiality, integrity and availability of these information systems". *Id.* at page 26. The GAO detailed sensitive information

shared amongst these agencies, which include, transactions, Social Security numbers and account numbers. There were egregious security weaknesses reported, with the GAO report alleging, among other things, that user authentication was not always implemented when accessing the data, encryption was not always implemented, laptop computer use was not controlled when exiting and entering FinCEN and key systems were missing critical patches. *Id.* at pages 9–14.

5. RIGHT TO PRIVACY

BERGER v. INTERNAL REVENUE SERVICE

United States District Court, D. New Jersey
487 F.Supp 2d 482 (2007)

ACKERMAN, SENIOR DISTRICT JUDGE.

This matter comes before the Court on the motion for summary judgment (Docket No. 10) filed by Defendants Internal Revenue Service and the Department of the Treasury (collectively "IRS" or "Defendants"). Plaintiffs Lawrence S. Berger and Realty Research Corporation ("RRC") brought this action under the Freedom of Information Act ("FOIA"), 5 U.S.C. § 552, and the Privacy Act, 5 U.S.C, § 552a, to compel disclosure of certain documents from the IRS relating to the civil and criminal tax investigation of which Plaintiffs were the subjects. For the following reasons, Defendants' motion for summary judgment will be granted.

Background

Plaintiffs were the subject of a civil Trust Fund Recovery Penalty ("TFRP") investigation and related criminal investigation ("Cl") by the IRS.[1] Berger resides in Morristown, New Jersey, and RRC is a New Jersey corporation with its principal place of business at Berger's address in Morristown. Revenue Officer Mary M. Williams handled the civil TFRP inquiry in the IRS's small business/self-employed field office in Parsippany, New Jersey, and Special Agent Eric Rennert handled the CI in the IRS's criminal investigation field office in Springfield, New Jersey. No charges were ever brought against Plaintiffs as a result of these investigations.

* * *

The IRS initially withheld 1 page in full and 64 pages in part of the Cl file pursuant to 31 U.S.C. § 5319 and Exemption 3. These pages—pages

---

[1] "The Internal Revenue Code . . . requires employers to withhold from their employees' paychecks funds representing the employees' personal income and Social Security taxes. Because employers must hold these funds in 'trust' for the United States, the taxes are commonly referred to as 'trust fund' taxes. Should employers fail to turn over the trust fund taxes, the IRS may collect a Trust Fund Recovery Penalty, equal to the sum of the unpaid taxes, directly from the officers or other persons within the company who are responsible for collecting the taxes." Ruggiero v. United States, 242 F.R.D. 437, 438, 2007 WL 1119200, at *1 (N.D.III.2007) (citations omitted).

515–17, 547, 568–72, 578–79, 584–600, 820–25, 831, 1634–35, 1643, and 2038–64—contain information regarding certain cash transactions made by Plaintiffs, including Currency and Banking Retrieval System ("CBRS") summary information and CBRS CTRs. Section 5319 provides that CTRs and other "report[s] and record[s] of reports" of transactions prepared pursuant to the Bank Secrecy Act (Title 31, Chapter 53, Subchapter II) "are exempt from disclosure under section 552 of title 5." 31 U.S.C. § 5319. Thus, Congress explicitly precluded disclosure of CTRs and similar reports ("Bank Secrecy Act reports") under § 5319 and expressly stated that covered reports would be exempt from disclosure under FOIA. Plaintiffs agree that § 5319 meets the criteria of Exemption 3 because it mandates withholding in such a manner as to leave no discretion on the issue to the agency. The few courts to address the issue have reached the natural conclusion that § 5319 qualifies as an exempting statute under Exemption 3. See *Small,* 820 F.Supp. at 166 (describing reports exempt from FOIA disclosure pursuant to § 5319 as "financial institution reports and records of reports of transactions involving the payment, receipt or transfer of United States coins and currency"); see also Sciba v. Bd. of Governors of Fed. Reserve Sys., Civil Action No. 04–1011, 2005 WL 3201206, at *3 (D.D.C. Nov.4, 2005); Linn v. U.S. Dep't of Justice, Civil Action No. 92–1406, 1995 WL 631847, at *30 (D.D.C. Aug. 22, 1995).

After considering Plaintiffs' response to Defendants' summary judgment motion and re-reviewing the withheld material, the IRS disclosed all or part of 22 pages which were initially withheld pursuant to § 5319. The IRS determined that information in those 22 pages not derived or extracted directly from Bank Secrecy Act reports could be segregated from exempt information, and the IRS therefore disclosed portions of Cl file pages 516–17, 547, 568–72, 578–79, 820–25, 831, 1634–35, 1643, and 2038–39. Defendants therefore have conceded Plaintiffs' argument that certain information not extracted from Bank Secrecy Act reports should be disclosed, and have in fact disclosed such information. The remaining information withheld pursuant to § 5319, the IRS asserts, constitutes Bank Secrecy Act forms or information derived or extracted from Bank Secrecy Act reports. (Second Keys Decl, at ¶¶ 14–22.) Based on its review of the Second Keys Declaration and the *Vaughn* Index, the Court accepts the IRS's representation.

This Court rejects Plaintiffs' other arguments for disclosure of information covered by § 5319. Plaintiffs contend that Exemption 3 does not cover CBRS information because, "in other contexts," the IRS has some discretion, based on the Internal Revenue Manual, to release CBRS information. (Pls.1 Br. at 9.) This Court finds that CBRS reports qualify as reports under the Bank Secrecy Act that are exempt from disclosure under FOIA. Section 5319 provides that Bank Secrecy Act reports and records of reports are "exempt from disclosure under section 552 of title 5." 31 U.S.C.

§ 5319. This explicit statement of congressional intent to exempt reports such as CBRS reports outweighs the strained reading Plaintiffs offer based on the thin reed of an asserted section of the Internal Revenue Manual.[7] "The absolute language of section 5319 eliminates any possibility of agency discretion," *Linn,* 1995 WL 631847, at ***30**; see also *Sciba,* 2005 WL 3201206, at *6 ("A fair reading of section 5319 leads to the conclusion that it explicitly exempts financial institution reports from public disclosure under the FOIA."). Furthermore, a court in this District has held that CBRS information is covered by § 5319 and exempt from disclosure under FOIA Exemption 3. See *Small,* 820 F.Supp. at 166 (discussing "information from the . . . Currency and Banking Retrieval System" and holding that because § 5319 "explicitly restricts the release of this information, the IRS must withhold this information from [plaintiff] under FOIA"). This Court similarly concludes that the IRS properly withheld documents pursuant to Exemption 3 and § 5319.

C. Privacy Act

[17] Plaintiffs also argue that even if the IRS properly withheld information pursuant to FOIA and § 5319, the Privacy Act nonetheless allows disclosure where the information concerns transactions by Plaintiff Berger himself, The Privacy Act provides that "[e]ach agency that maintains a system of records shall . . . (1) upon request by any individual to gain access to his record or to any information pertaining to him which is contained in the system, permit him and upon his request, a person of his own choosing to accompany him, to review the record and have a copy made of all or any portion thereof in a form comprehensible to him." 5 U.S.C, § 552a(d). Plaintiffs stress that the Privacy Act applies even if FOIA

---

[7]   Plaintiffs cite an Internal Revenue Manual ("I.R.M.") provision which states, according to Plaintiffs, that with regard to the contents of a CBRS report, "the examiner may disclose to the examined entity that a currency report was or was not filed and the contents of the report if any." (Pls.' Br. at 9 (quoting Internal Revenue Manual § 4.26.4.9 (Jan. 1, 2003)).) Plaintiffs argue that under this asserted I.R.M, section, the IRS has some discretion to disclose CBRS information. Therefore, according to Plaintiffs, such information cannot be exempt under Exemption 3 because that exemption only covers statutes which provide that "matters be withheld from the public in such a manner as to leave no discretion on the issue." 5 U.S.C. § 552(b)(3)(A).

Defendants do not address Plaintiffs' Internal Revenue Manual argument. After its own search, the Court could not find the language quoted by Plaintiffs in the current version of I.R.M. § 4.26.4.9, effective November 17, 2006, or indeed anywhere else in the current version of the Internal Revenue Manual. Of course, the applicable Internal Revenue Manual would be the January 1, 2003 version in effect when Plaintiffs made their initial request. Even if the provision Plaintiffs quote was in effect at that time, this Court finds, for the reasons stated in this Opinion and Order, that CBRS reports qualify as reports exempt from disclosure under FOIA and § 5319.

Furthermore, while the current version of the Internal Revenue Manual is not directly applicable here, this Court's independent review of the current Internal Revenue Manual bolsters the Court's view that § 5319 covers this information. The current Internal Revenue Manual provides that "Examiners must not disclose CBRS information to the public." I.R.M. § 4.26.4.10 (Nov. 17, 2006). Another current Internal Revenue Manual provision states that "Form 8300 reports filed after December 31, 2001 and accessed through the Currency and Banking Retrieval System (CBRS) are Title 31 information subject to Bank Secrecy Act disclosure standards and are not subject to release under FOIA." I.R.M. § 11.3.13.7.6(4) (Jan. 1, 2006). Much of the information withheld by the IRS are Form 8300s or information derived from Form 8300s.

exempts disclosure, as the Privacy Act specifically states that "[n]o agency shall rely on any exemption contained in section 552 of this title to withhold from an individual any record which is otherwise accessible to such individual under the provisions of this section." 5 U.S.C. § 552a(t).

However, Plaintiffs ignore the exceptions to the Privacy Act. Section 552a(j)(2) authorizes an agency to promulgate rules to exempt any system of records from disclosure under § 552a(d) if the system of records is maintained by an agency which "performs as its principal function any activity pertaining to the enforcement of criminal laws" and "which consists of (A) information compiled for the purpose of identifying individual criminal offenders and alleged offenders . . . (B) information compiled for the purpose of a criminal investigation . . . or (C) reports identifiable to an individual compiled at any stage of the process of enforcement of the criminal laws." 5 U.S.C. § 552a(j)(2). Section 552a(k)(2) similarly authorizes an agency to promulgate rules to exempt any system of records from disclosure under § 552a(d) if the system of records includes "investigatory material compiled for law enforcement purposes, other than material within the scope of subsection (j)(2) of this section." 5 U.S.C. § 552a(k)(2).

Pursuant to these explicit statutory exceptions to Privacy Act disclosure, the IRS has issued a rule exempting its system of records encompassing CTRs and other Bank Secrecy Act reports from disclosure under subsection (d) of the Privacy Act. Internal Revenue Service, Privacy Act of 1974, System of Records Notice, Treasury/IRS 46.050, 66 Fed.Reg. 63784, 63847 (Dec. 10, 2001). Thus, the IRS has elected, in its statutorily-granted rulemaking authority, to exempt from the Privacy Act the same records exempted from FOIA under Exemption 3 and § 5319. (Keys Decl at ¶¶ 12–13.) The IRS properly withheld Bank Secrecy Act report information under both FOIA and the Privacy Act.

* * *

6. OFAC AND FINANCIAL EMBARGOS

The Office of Foreign Assets Control (OFAC) is a financial intelligence and enforcement organization of the U.S. government charged with planning and execution of economic and trade sanctions in support of U.S. national security and foreign policy objectives. Acting under Presidential national emergency powers, OFAC carries out its activities against problematic foreign states, organizations and individuals alike.[22]

---

[22] Involvement of the U.S. Department of the Treasury in economic sanctions against foreign states dates to the War of 1812, when Secretary Albert Gallatin administered sanctions against Great Britain in retaliation for the harassment of American sailors. The Division of Foreign Assets Control was established in the Office of International Finance by a Treasury Department order in 1950, following the entry of the People's Republic of China into the Korean War; President Harry

A component of the U.S. Treasury Department, OFAC operates under the auspices of the Office of Terrorism and Financial Intelligence and is primarily composed of intelligence targeters and lawyers. While many of OFAC's targets are broadly set by the White House, most individual cases are developed as a result of lengthy investigations by OFAC's Office of Global Targeting (OGT).

Often described as one of the most powerful yet unknown government agencies. OFAC has been in existence for more than half-century and is playing an increasingly significant role as a foreign policy lever of the U.S. government. The agency is empowered to levy significant penalties against entities that defy it, including imposing colossal fines, freezing assets, and altogether barring parties from operating in the U.S. Notably, in 2014 OFAC reached a record $1 billion settlement with the French bank BNP Paribas, discussed below, which was a portion of approximately $9 billion penalty imposed in relation to the case as whole.

In addition to the Trading with the Enemy Act and the various national emergencies currently in effect, OFAC derives its authority from a variety of U.S. federal laws regarding embargoes and economic sanctions.

In enforcing economic sanctions, OFAC acts to prevent "prohibited transactions," which are described by OFAC as trade or financial transactions and other dealings in which U.S. persons may not engage unless authorized by OFAC or expressly exempted by statute. OFAC has the authority to grant exemptions to prohibitions on such transactions, either by issuing a general license for certain categories of transactions, or by specific licenses issued on a case-by-case basis. OFAC administers and enforces economic sanctions programs against countries, businesses or groups of individuals, using the blocking of assets and trade restrictions to accomplish foreign policy and national security goals.

OFAC is responsible for administering the Specially Designated Nationals (SDN) List. The list is a publication of OFAC which lists individuals and organizations with whom United States citizens and permanent residents are prohibited from doing business.

NOTES

1.   When an entity or individual is placed on the SDN list it can petition OFAC to reconsider, but OFAC is not required to remove an individual or entity from the SDN list. Some federal courts have found the current Treasury/OFAC process to be constitutionally deficient. In KindHearts v. Treasury, 463 F.Supp.2d 1049 (C.D. Cal. 2006) a federal court found that

---

S Truman declared a national emergency and blocked all Chinese and North Korean assets subject to U.S. jurisdiction. In addition to blocking Chinese and North Korean assets, the Division administered certain regulations and orders issued under the amended Trading with the Enemy Act. On October 15, 1962, by a Treasury Department order, the Division of Foreign Assets Control became the Office of Foreign Assets Control.

Treasury's seizure of assets without notice or means of appeal is a violation of the Fourth and Fifth Amendments. In Al Haramain v. U.S. Department of the Treasury, No. 10–35032 (9th Cir. 2011) the Ninth Circuit Court of Appeals upheld a lower court's ruling that procedures used by Treasury to shut down the Al Haramain Islamic Foundation of Oregon in 2004 was unconstitutional. The court said the Fifth Amendment's guarantee of due process requires Treasury to give adequate notice of the reasons it puts a group on the terrorist list, as well as a meaningful opportunity to respond. In addition, the court ruled that freezing the groups assets amounts to a seizure under the Fourth Amendment, so that a court order is required. See also Tanzanian Bank Scores Rare Win Against Fincen, American Banker, August 28, 2015 (Tanzanian bank wins preliminary injunction against the U.S. Treasury Department for being designated as a "primary money laundering concern").

22 U.S.C. § 234 AA–9. BAN ON IMPORTING GOODS AND SERVICES FROM COUNTRIES SUPPORTING TERRORISM

(a) Authority

The President may ban the importation into the United States of any good or service from any country which supports terrorism or terrorist organizations or harbors terrorists or terrorist organizations.

(b) Consultation

The President, in every possible instance, shall consult with the Congress before exercising the authority granted by this section and shall consult regularly with the Congress so long as that authority is being exercised.

(c) Reports

Whenever the President exercises the authority granted by this section, he shall immediately transmit to the Congress a report specifying—

   (1) the country with respect to which the authority is to be exercised and the imports to be prohibited;

   (2) the circumstances which necessitate the exercise of such authority;

   (3) why the President believes those circumstances justify the exercise of such authority; and

   (4) why the President believes the prohibitions are necessary to deal with those circumstances.

* * *

PROCLAMATION 3447—EMBARGO ON ALL TRADE WITH CUBA

February 3, 1962

By the President of the United States of America

A Proclamation

* * *

Whereas the United States, in accordance with its international obligations, is prepared to take all necessary actions to promote national and hemispheric security by isolating the present Government of Cuba and thereby reducing the threat posed by its alignment with the communist powers;

Now, Therefore, I, John F. Kennedy, President of the United States of America, acting under the authority of section 620(a) of the Foreign Assistance Act of 1961 (75 Stat. 445), as amended, do

1.   Hereby proclaim an embargo upon trade between the United States and Cuba in accordance with paragraphs 2 and 3 of this proclamation.

2.   Hereby prohibit, effective 12:01 A.M., Eastern Standard Time, February 7, 1962, the importation into the United States of all goods of Cuban origin and all goods imported from or through Cuba; and I hereby authorize and direct the Secretary of the Treasury to carry out such prohibition, to make such exceptions thereto, by license or otherwise, as he determines to be consistent with the effective operation of the embargo hereby proclaimed, and to promulgate such rules and regulations as may be necessary to perform such functions.

3.   AND FURTHER, I do hereby direct the Secretary of Commerce, under the provisions of the Export Control Act of 1949, as amended (50 U.S.C. App. 2021–2032), to continue to carry out the prohibition of all exports from the United States to Cuba, and I hereby authorize him, under that Act, to continue, make, modify, or revoke exceptions from such prohibition.

* * *

NOTES

1.   The United States embargo against Cuba (in Cuba *el bloqueo*) is a commercial, economic, and financial embargo imposed on Cuba. It began on October 19, 1960 (almost two years after the Batista regime was deposed by the Cuban Revolution) when the US placed an embargo on exports to Cuba except for food and medicine. On February 7, 1962 this was extended to include almost all imports.

Currently, the Cuban embargo is enforced mainly with six statutes: the Trading with the Enemy Act of 1917, the Foreign Assistance Act of 1961, the

Cuba Assets Control Regulations of 1963, the Cuban Democracy Act of 1992, the Helms—Burton Act of 1996, and the Trade Sanctions Reform and Export Enhancement Act of 2000. The Cuban Democracy Act was signed into law in 1992 with the stated purpose of maintaining sanctions on Cuba so long as the Cuban government refuses to move toward "democratization and greater respect for human rights" (see Section 6002(6) Statement of Policy, 22 U.S.C. § 6002(6)). In 1996, Congress passed the Helm-Burton Act, which further restricted United States citizens from doing business in or with Cuba, and mandated restrictions on giving public or private assistance to any successor government in Havana unless and until certain claims against the Cuban government are met. In 1999, U.S. President Clinton expanded the trade embargo even further by also disallowing foreign subsidiaries of U.S. companies to trade with Cuba. In 2000, Clinton authorized the sale of "humanitarian" U.S. products to Cuba.

The United States does not generally block Cuba's trade with third parties. Cuba can, and does, conduct international trade with many third-party countries. These countries are not under the direct jurisdiction of U.S. domestic laws, although foreign countries that trade with Cuba could be potentially penalised by the U.S.. Thus, the Cuban Democracy Act has been condemned as an "extraterritorial" measure that contravenes "the sovereign equality of States, non-intervention in their internal affairs and freedom of trade and navigation as paramount to the conduct of international affairs." See Speakers Denounce Cuban Embargo as 'Sad Echo' of Failed Cold War Policies; General Assembly for Twentieth Year, Demands Lifting of Economic Blockade, United Nations General Assembly Meeting Coverage (October 25, 2011).

Beyond criticisms of human rights in Cuba and its state sponsored terrorism designation, the United States holds $6 billion worth of financial claims against the Cuban government. The pro-embargo position is that the U.S. embargo is, in part, an appropriate response to these unaddressed claims. At present, the embargo, which limits American businesses from conducting business with Cuban interests, is still in effect and is the most enduring trade embargo in modern history.

2. The U.S. maintains embargos and sanctions against a number of governments worldwide. See, e.g., 31 CFR Part 360 (Iranian embargo regulations implementing Executive Order 13059).

THE WHITE HOUSE OFFICE
OF THE PRESS SECRETARY
December 17, 2014

For Immediate Release

FACT SHEET: Charting a New Course on Cuba

Today, the United States is taking historic steps to chart a new course in our relations with Cuba and to further engage and empower the Cuban people. We are separated by 90 miles of water, but brought together through the relationships between the two million Cubans and Americans of Cuban descent that live in the United States, and the 11 million Cubans who share similar hopes for a more positive future for Cuba.

It is clear that decades of U.S. isolation of Cuba have failed to accomplish our enduring objective of promoting the emergence of a democratic, prosperous, and stable Cuba. At times, longstanding U.S. policy towards Cuba has isolated the United States from regional and international partners, constrained our ability to influence outcomes throughout the Western Hemisphere, and impaired the use of the full range of tools available to the United States to promote positive change in Cuba. Though this policy has been rooted in the best of intentions, it has had little effect— today, as in 1961, Cuba is governed by the Castros and the Communist party.

We cannot keep doing the same thing and expect a different result. It does not serve America's interests, or the Cuban people, to try to push Cuba toward collapse. We know from hard-learned experience that it is better to encourage and support reform than to impose policies that will render a country a failed state. With our actions today, we are calling on Cuba to unleash the potential of 11 million Cubans by ending unnecessary restrictions on their political, social, and economic activities. In that spirit, we should not allow U.S. sanctions to add to the burden of Cuban citizens we seek to help.

* * *

<h3 style="text-align:center">US DEPARTMENT OF THE TREASURY,
THE OFFICE OF FOREIGN ASSETS CONTROLS:
FREQUENTLY ASKED QUESTIONS RELATED TO CUBA</h3>
(January 15, 2015)

V. Banking

30. Are authorized travelers in Cuba permitted to use credit or debit cards issued by a U.S. financial institution?

Yes. Travelers are advised to check with their financial institution before traveling to Cuba to determine whether the institution has established the necessary mechanisms for its credit or debit cards to be used in Cuba. See 31 CFR § 515.560(c)(5) and 515.584(c).

31. Can my bank refuse to allow me to use my credit or debit card in Cuba?

OFAC regulations do not require financial institutions or credit card companies to accept, maintain, or facilitate authorized financial relationships or transactions.

32. Are financial institutions other than banks permitted to open correspondent accounts in Cuba?

Depository institutions, as defined in 31 CFR § 515.333, which include certain financial institutions other than banks, are permitted to open correspondent accounts at banks in Cuba. See 31 CFR § 515.584(a).

33. Are Cuban banks permitted to open correspondent accounts at U.S. banks?

No. U.S. depository institutions are permitted to open correspondent accounts at Cuban banks located in Cuba and in third countries, and at foreign banks located in Cuba, but Cuban banks are not generally licensed to open such accounts at U.S. banks. See note to 31 CFR § 515.584(a).

34. In what ways can Cuban nationals lawfully present in the United States participate in the U.S. financial system?

Certain Cuban nationals who have taken up residence in the United States on a permanent basis and who meet the requirements set forth in 31 CFR § 515.505 are licensed as unblocked nationals, and may participate fully in the U.S. financial system. See 31 CFR § 515.505(a)(1); (d).

Pursuant to 31 CFR § 515.571, Cuban nationals who are present in the United States in a non-immigrant status or pursuant to other non-immigrant travel authorization issued by the U.S. government, such as a non-immigrant visa, may open and maintain bank accounts for the duration of their stay in the United States in such status. Accounts that are not closed prior to the departure of Cuban nationals from the United States must be blocked and reported as such. Section 515.571 also authorizes such Cuban nationals to engage in normal banking transactions involving foreign currency drafts, travelers' checks, or other instruments negotiated incident to travel in the United States.

35. If a Cuban national resident in the United States has applied to become a lawful permanent resident alien of the United States, does that individual have to apply to OFAC to be treated as an unblocked national?

No. If a Cuban national has taken up residence in the United States and has applied to become a lawful permanent resident alien of the U.S. and has an adjustment of status application pending, then the Cuban national is considered unblocked and does not need to apply to OFAC to be treated as an unblocked national, provided that he or she is not a prohibited official of the Government of Cuba or a prohibited member of the Cuban Communist party. See 31 CFR § 515.505(a)(1).

36. What new transactions involving wire transfers to Cuba are authorized?

OFAC has issued a new general license that authorizes U.S. depository institutions to reject funds transfers originating and terminating outside the United States where neither the originator nor the beneficiary is a person subject to U.S. jurisdiction and provided that certain prohibited individuals do not have an interest in the transfer. U.S. depository institutions are authorized to process such funds transfers where they would be authorized pursuant to the CACR if the originator or beneficiary were a person subject to U.S. jurisdiction. For a complete description of what this general license authorizes and the restrictions that apply please see 31 CFR § 515.584(d).

DEPARTMENT OF THE TREASURY

Washington, D.C. 20220
Compl-2013–193659
(June 30, 2014)

SETTLEMENT AGREEMENT

This Settlement Agreement (the "Agreement") is made by and between the U.S. Department of the Treasury's Office of Foreign Assets Control ("OFAC") and BNP Paribas SA ("BNPP").

I.   PARTIES

1.   OFAC administers and enforces economic sanctions against targeted foreign countries, regimes, terrorists, international narcotics traffickers, and persons engaged in activities related to the proliferation of weapons of mass destruction, among others. OFAC acts under Presidential national emergency authorities, as well as authority granted by specific legislation, to impose controls on transactions and freeze assets under U.S. jurisdiction.

2.   BNPP is a bank registered and organized under the laws of France.

II.   FACTUAL STATEMENT

3.   For a number of years, up to and including 2012, BNPP processed thousands of transactions to or through U.S. financial institutions that involved countries, entities, and/or individuals subject to the sanctions programs administered by OFAC. BNPP appears to have engaged in a systematic practice, spanning many years and involving multiple BNPP branches and business lines, that concealed, removed, omitted, or obscured references to, or the interest or involvement of, sanctioned parties in U.S. Dollar ("USD") Society for Worldwide Interbank Financial Telecommunication ("SWIFT") payment messages sent to U.S. financial institutions. While these payment practices occurred throughout multiple branches and subsidiaries of the bank, BNPP's subsidiary in Geneva

("BNPP Suisse") and branch in Paris ("BNPP Paris") facilitated or conducted the overwhelming majority of the apparent violations of U.S. sanctions laws described in this Agreement, The specific payment practices the bank utilized in order to process certain sanctions-related payments to or through the United States included omitting references to sanctioned parties; replacing the names of sanctioned parties with BNPP's name or a code word; and structuring payments in a manner that did not identify the involvement of sanctioned parties in payments sent to U.S. financial institutions.

8.   At a September 23, 2004, meeting, BNPP Suisse decided to shift its USD clearing activity away from BNPP's New York branch ("BNPP New York") to a U.S. bank's New York branch in an apparent effort to shield BNPP New York from liability for violations of U.S. sanctions regulations. A BNPP Suisse Compliance representative present at the meeting stated that he or she believed that the bank made the decision "as a precautionary measure, in case the Bank's interpretation of U.S. sanctions laws might be incorrect."

10. Beginning in or around mid-2005, some BNPP Suisse employees voiced concerns over the use of the Regional Banks' accounts to clear transactions through the United States. On August 5, 2005, a member of BNPP Suisse Compliance warned the bank's Front Office in writing that the Regional Bank transfers could be viewed as an attempt to circumvent or avoid U.S. sanctions: "[t]his practice effectively means that we are circumventing [or avoiding] the US embargo on transactions in USD by Sudan." In September 2005, a meeting took place in Geneva between BNPP Paris' Head Office Management and members of BNPP Suisse. A BNPP Suisse chronology of issues regarding Sudan (drafted several years later by a compliance member) noted that the "meeting had been called to express, to the highest level of the bank, the reservations of the Swiss Compliance office concerning the transactions executed with and for Sudanese customers." Specifically, BNPP Suisse Compliance conveyed its concerns to the former BNPP Group Chief Operating Officer. Based on the compliance member's written chronology of events, the former BNPP Group Chief Operating Officer purportedly asked BNPP Suisse Compliance whether "Switzerland has declared an embargo on Sudan." The chronology then states that the executive subsequently noted that there should be no doubts whatsoever concerning this matter and asked that no minutes be taken for that meeting. BNPP stated to OFAC that "[a]ccording to a handwritten note taken after the meeting, the conclusion reached was that BNPP Geneva could 'continue current operations while respecting embargoes and exercising caution.' "

16. In addition to the above, various BNPP branches routed other USD payments to or through the United States in apparent violation of U.S. sanctions programs, including the following:

a. BNPP Suisse and BNPP Paris negotiated a variety of trade finance instruments on behalf of or that involved parties subject to U.S. sanctions on Sudan, Iran, Cuba, and Burma and routed USD payments to or through the United States pursuant to these instruments;

b. BNPP Suisse, BNPP Paris, BNPP's branch in Rome, and BNPP's branch in Milan all processed correspondent banking or retail banking transactions to or though the United States that involved the interest of a person subject to U.S. sanctions on Sudan, Iran, Cuba, or Burma; and

c. BNPP Suisse processed a number of payments to or though the United States related to syndicated loans involving Iranian parties, and BNPP's branch in Milan processed one transaction pertaining to a corporate and investment banking instrument in which a Cuban party had an interest through the United States.

17. BNPP solicited advice from multiple law firms over a number of years regarding the legality of the types of transactions leading to the apparent violations described in this Agreement. Some of this guidance, and in particular guidance received in September 2006, appears to indicate that BNPP's payment processes could result in apparent violations of U.S. sanctions laws. For example, in September 2006, BNPP received a memorandum from a U.S. law firm that indicated that non-U.S. branches of non-U.S. banks appeared to be prohibited from processing sanctions-related transactions through the United States. The same memorandum contained the following guidance, which appears to describe the potential implications of a non-U.S. bank attempting to shield its own U.S. branch from sanctions-related transactions:

> [W]here a transaction is a prohibited transaction because it is conducted through a bank in the U.S., albeit an unaffiliated bank, if the use of the unaffiliated bank were perceived to result from an effort by the foreign bank to avoid the involvement of its U.S. branch in handling prohibited transactions, there is a substantial risk either that regulators or prosecutors would attempt to make a case that the foreign bank is in some fashion a CACR or ITR Covered Person or that the foreign bank could be considered to be involved in an evasion of the OFAC sanctions. Evasions are specifically prohibited by the CACR sanctions as well as the ITR sanctions.

Notwithstanding this guidance, the bank continued to process hundreds of payments through the United States using practices that did not reveal the interest in those transactions of parties subject to sanctions programs administered by OFAC. The bank's conduct also continued for several years after OFAC contacted the bank directly (in 2007) regarding BNPP Suisse's USD business with Sudan and Iran.

* * *

24. BNPP cooperated with OFAC by conducting an extensive internal investigation, executing a statute of limitations tolling agreement with multiple extensions, and agreeing to a limited waiver of attorney-client privilege in order to provide OFAC with relevant information.

* * *

III. TERMS OF SETTLEMENT

IT IS HEREBY AGREED by OFAC and BNPP that:

26. BNPP has terminated the conduct outlined in paragraphs 3 through 21 above and BNPP has established, and agrees to maintain, policies and procedures that prohibit, and are designed to minimize the risk of the recurrence of, similar conduct in the future.

28. Without this Agreement constituting an admission or denial by BNPP of any allegation made or implied by OFAC in connection with this matter, and solely for the purpose of settling this matter without a final agency finding that a violation has occurred, BNPP agrees to a settlement in the amount of $963,619,900 arising out of the apparent violations by BNPP of IEEPA, TWEA, the Executive orders, and the Regulations described in paragraphs 18–21 of this Agreement. BNPP's obligation to pay OFAC such settlement amount shall be deemed satisfied by its payment of a greater or equal amount in satisfaction of penalties assessed by U.S. federal, state, or county officials arising out of the same pattern of conduct.

* * *

QUESTIONS AND NOTES

1. What does the term "prohibited transactions" and "prohibited persons" mean in the context of the OFAC rules? What are the exceptions?

2. Who must comply with the OFAC regulations? Are foreign affiliates and subsidiaries of U.S. companies included? How about the offices of non-U.S. based corporations?

3. What type of OFAC compliance program should a bank establish? What should be included in an ongoing compliance program checklist?

4. You are outside counsel to a small community bank. The bank's compliance staff calls to get your advice about the fact that the name of a new customer attempting to open a large savings account triggered a "hit" on the OFAC "prohibited persons" list software the bank uses. What steps would you advise them to take to comply with the OFAC rules?

5.   Are banks required to file SARs regarding activity deemed suspicious even when a portion or all of the activity occurred outside the U.S.?

6.   A longtime bank customer engages in activity that the bank's compliance staff in a branch office believes technically trigger the SAR filing requirements. Nonetheless, the compliance staff believes the customer to be basically honest, and a "sweet old gentleman." Can the compliance staff bring the matter to the customer's attention in the hopes that it can, in the bank branch manager's words, be "straightened out?"

7.   The Basel Committee on Bank Supervision has issued guidance for a number of years on anti-money laundering and terrorist financing issues related to the banking system. See Prevention of criminal use of the banking system for the purposes of money laundering (December 1988); Core principles for effective banking supervision (updated September, 2012) (principle No. 29 deals with abuse of financial services); Sound management of risks related to money laundering and financing of terrorism (January 2014).

CHAPTER 10

LEGAL ETHICS: MULTI-NATIONAL PRACTICE OF BANKING LAW

■ ■ ■

1. INTRODUCTION

This Chapter will highlight the particular ethics issues that may arise in the context of multi-jurisdictional banking law practice. With trends toward globalization of the practice of corporate law, it is important to understand cross-border ethics issues, particularly in the context of complex and sophisticated international financial transactions. Such transactions typically involve a wide array of corporate, bank regulatory and other legal issues cutting across many countries and their respective laws.

The chapter will explore issues that arise in multi-jurisdictional practice regarding ethics rules in different jurisdictions, including conflicts of interest and confidentiality rules. Further, the chapter will present and analyze developments regarding efforts to establish an international code of legal ethics, including the efforts of the International Bar Association and the ABA.

As discussed in Prof. Lutz's article below, a U.S. lawyer—and her law firm—engaged in an international corporate practice is called upon to represent banking clients on transactions that involve rendering advice that takes into account a wide range of legal information from a variety of jurisdictions. The nature of legal issues is typically transjurisdictional, involving multiple parties and various foreign languages and cultures. Whether the lawyer is competent to render advice in such situations, or whether the lawyer is obligated when performing services for a client to engage competent foreign counsel, is a central concern. It is important for lawyers to have little doubt about the professional standards to which the public and profession hold them. These standards ultimately involve more than the professional conduct rules of a jurisdiction; they include, inter alia, ethical considerations and malpractice standards.

NOTES

1.   The Annual Law School Survey of Student Engagement recently reported that only half the students responding said their law schools prepared them well to deal with real-world ethical dilemmas and issues that may arise

in law practice. See Evaluating the Value of Law School: Student Perspectives, Law School Survey of Student Engagement, Annual Results (2010). The Survey noted that this is especially true for law students in a classroom (versus clinic) setting. The ABA has prodded law schools to have legal ethics be a central part of the curriculum for all areas of law taught. Particularly in the context of multi-jurisdictional practice such as international banking law, there is a particular need for a practicing lawyer to have a high degree of awareness and sensitivity about ethical issues which may cross cultural and social norms.

2.   Other legal commenters have cited law schools as failing to complement the focus on skill in legal analysis with effective support for developing ethical skills. See, e.g. William M. Sullivan, Anne Colby, Judith Welch Wegner, Lloyd Bond and Lee S. Shulman, Educating Lawyers: Preparation for the Practice of Law, The Carnegie Foundation for the Advancement of Education at 6 (2010).

2. LEGAL ETHICS IN THE GLOBAL CORPORATE LAW FIRM

ROBERT E. LUTZ, ETHICS AND INTERNATIONAL PRACTICE: A GUIDE TO THE PROFESSIONAL RESPONSIBILITY OF PRACTITIONERS
16 Fordham Int'l L.J., 1 (1992)

* * *

The giving of advice on foreign law, as well as the selection and use of foreign counsel, are matters occurring more and more frequently in law practice today.[1] Whether one has a specialty practice or a general one, there is a greater likelihood today that a matter demanding transnational legal expertise will cross a lawyer's desk than there was just a few years ago.

Moreover, with the institutionalization of transnational legal practice—especially through U.S. law firm "mergers," "associations," "affiliations," and "branch offices" with foreign law firms—U.S. lawyers are giving advice on foreign law or using foreign counsel in a great variety of ways.

B.   Special Problem Areas for U.S. Lawyers

1.   Liability for Legal Advice on Foreign Law

The responsibility for the selection and employment of a foreign lawyer usually and most often appropriately falls on the U.S. lawyer: The lawyer is often better equipped than a client to recognize foreign law questions, and normally better able and better positioned to deal with foreign counsel.

---

[1]   In this Article, the use of "foreign" signifies matters or persons outside the United States.

However, the extent to which a court will hold a U.S. lawyer directly responsible for the work of a foreign lawyer may depend on the circumstances of each case.[105]

2. Responsibility for Opinions of Foreign Lawyers

Often, the U.S. lawyer will be justified in assuming the correctness of the advice of foreign legal counsel, after determining the counsel's qualifications and monitoring the counsel's work. If so, the U.S. lawyer may want to incorporate such advice when directly advising the client. However, unless the U.S. lawyer clearly advises the client that the lawyer's advice incorporates foreign counsel's opinions, a court may find that the U.S. lawyer is responsible for the foreign lawyer's advice and, arguably, falls short of the standard of competence owed to the client. Indeed, a lawyer who has no expertise in a specialized matter should not render an opinion in the specialized area, and should refer the matter to a lawyer qualified in that field.[106] The importance of a U.S. lawyer's isolating a foreign lawyer's opinion becomes even greater when the U.S. lawyer anticipates that third parties might rely on the U.S. lawyer's opinion.[107] A type of disclaimer clause could include the following: "In rendering the opinions expressed in paragraphs _____, we have relied [solely] on the opinion of _____ insofar as such opinions relate to _____ law, and we have made no independent examination of the laws of such jurisdiction."[108]

3. Communication Problems

Potential communication problems can arise in several contexts in the U.S. lawyer-client and U.S. lawyer-foreign lawyer relationships. First, in representing a foreign client, the U.S. lawyer may face language barriers in explaining to the foreign client the legal consequences of certain actions, or the substance of a foreign lawyer's advice on foreign law. Second,

---

[105] See, e.g., Tormo v. Yormark, 398 F. Supp. 1159, 1173 (D.N.J. 1975) (discussing possible degreess of inquiry into referred out-of-state lawyer's background for referring lawyer to avoid liability for negligent referral); Bluestein v. State Bar of Cal., 529 P.2d 599, 606–07 (Cal. 1974) (disciplining lawyer for lawyer's aiding and abetting unlicensed person who had practiced abroad to practice in California). In California, the duty to act competently includes the "duty to supervise the work of subordinate attorney and non-attorney employees or agents." *See* California Professional Rules, *supra* note 10, Rule 3–110 cmt.; *see also supra* note 14.

[106] See, e. g., Horne v. Peckham, 158 Cal Rptr. 714, 718 (Ct. App. 1979).

[107] For ethical rules concerning third party evaluations, see MODEL RULES, supra note 10, Rule 2.3 & cmt.

[108] Committee on Corporations of the Business Law Section of the State Bar of California, Report of the Committee on Corporations Regarding Legal Opinions in Business Transactions, reprinted in 14 PAC. LJ. 1001, 1028 (1983). On legal opinions, see, for example, MICHAEL GRUSON ET AL., LEGAL OPINIONS IN INTERNATIONAL TRANSACTIONS: FOREIGN LAWYERS' RESPONSE TO US OPINION REQUESTS (2D ED. 1989); 2A PHILIP WOOD, LAW AND PRACTICE OF INTERNATIONAL FINANCE §§ 18.01[5]–[6] (1990); Committee on Legal Opinions, Third-Party Legal Opinion Report, Including the Legal Opinion Accord, of the Section of Business Law, American Bar Association, 47 BUS. LAW. 167, 195–96 (1991); Neil Flanagin, Opinions on Foreign Law, in NEGOTIATING AND STRUCTURING INTERNATIONAL COMMERCIAL TRANSACTIONS: LEGAL ANALYSIS WITH SAMPLE AGREEMENTS 95–108 (Shelly P. Battram & David N. Goldsweig, eds. 1991).

language problems between the lawyers can impede the U.S. lawyer's supervision and monitoring of the foreign lawyer. Finally, the actual translation of documents and laws can be troublesome.[109] In the words of one commentator, these difficulties "can cause negotiations to collapse, contracts to be drafted incorrectly, transactions to go awry, or for that matter can endanger the long-term viability of a valuable foreign investment."[110]

While communication difficulties can arise in various contexts, there are also a variety of communication levels at which effective communication is at risk. In many transnational trade or investment matters, U.S. lawyers will need to explain the sources of law of and interrelationship of several legal systems for U.S. or foreign clients to appreciate the meaning of any proffered legal advice. "The law professional in international transactions is primarily an interpreter, a channel for communication between and among formally organized legal systems with differing national histories and experiences, traditions, institutions, and customs."[111]

Thus, at various levels and contexts, problems with communication may not only disturb an otherwise successful transnational venture, but also place the U.S. lawyer at risk of violating the duty of competence.

QUESTIONS AND NOTES

1.   In the abstract to the introduction of Professor Lutz's article, he posed a number of important questions about the then-emerging trend toward multi-jurisdictional i.e., global corporate law firms:

> Taking some typical international practice situations, we can highlight the basic professional competence questions posed: (1) ABC Company, located in California, wants to establish a manufacturing facility in Mexico, (2) ABC asks a lawyer to draft a sales agency agreement that it will use in dealing with a French distributor. The lawyer has previously prepared such an agreement for this client for use with respect to distributorships in the United States. These hypothetical situations raise the following professional competence questions: (1) What are the lawyer's professional responsibilities if the lawyer undertakes sole representation of this client in the lawyer's home jurisdiction, for example California, and this representation involves advising on foreign law? In this example, sometimes referred to as the "self-help" option, the lawyer independently, and without foreign expert assistance, counsels the

---

[109]   See Rodolfo Sacco, Legal Formants: A Dynamic Approach to Comparative Law, 39 AM. J. COMP. L. 1, 10–20 (1991).

[110]   See Goebel, supra note 38, at 448.

[111]   Henry P. de Vries, The International Legal Profession—The Fundamental Right of Association, 21 INT'L LAW. 845, 851 (1987).

client. (2) What are the lawyer's professional responsibilities if the lawyer undertakes representation of the client in the foreign country? For example, given the facts above, is the lawyer somehow professionally restricted from going abroad to France or Mexico and doing legal work for a client in those countries? Which country's professional standards would apply to the lawyer's activities? (3) If the lawyer decides that he or she is not competent to advise on foreign law, what are that lawyer's responsibilities with respect to selecting competent local counsel and to-selecting competent counsel who resides and practices in a foreign country? (4) Once the lawyer selects counsel competent to advise on foreign law matters, what are the lawyer's professional obligations as to the counsel's activities? What problems is the lawyer likely to encounter, and how can they best be handled? The following sections will address these concerns and hopefully offer guidance to the U.S. lawyer engaged in international practice. They will also offer suggestions regarding lawyer-client and U.S. lawyer-foreign lawyer communications, and liability for foreign lawyer legal opinions, both of which are relevant to the use and selection of foreign counsel.

2.   Many U.S. law firms operating on an international basis require that all lawyers in their non-U.S. offices have strong English language skills. Also, a number require that partners outside the U.S. are admitted to the bar in the U.S. Can you see ethical reasons for this approach?

3.   The Lutz article notes that problems with communications may not only hamper an international corporate transaction but "also place the U.S. lawyer at risk of violating the duty of competence." What does the author mean by this statement in discerning a lawyer's relevant ethical duties and obligations? In this regard, the California State Bar Standing Committee on Professional Responsibility and Conduct has offered the following guidance:

> If direct communication in a language clearly understood by the client is not possible, the attorney must take into account the fact that means other than direct communication will be required to discuss the client's case and to meet the [attorney's professional] responsibilities. . . . Although relevant, the means used are not controlling with respect to the issue of lawyer competency; however, adequate communication is necessary in order to render "competent" legal services.

> On any matter which requires the client understanding, the attorney must take all reasonable steps to insure that the client comprehends the legal concepts involved and the advice given, irrespective of the mode of communication used, so that the client is in a position to make an informed decision. Appreciation of the client's language may have a substantial bearing on the capability of the attorney to communicate with the client concerning such facts, legal concepts and advice. The attorney may need to communicate in a particular

language or dialect and for this purpose may need to use an interpreter skilled in a particular language or dialect. Other means reasonably available to counsel, such as a person skilled . . . in translating a written document, may need to be used in order for counsel to act competently in a particular case. Another alternative is to refer the case to or associate a bilingual attorney who can assist with the language problem, as is done in other areas when a lawyer is confronted with a matter calling for skills outside his or her personal experience or ability. California State Bar Standing Comm. on Professional Responsibility and Conduct, Formal Op. 1984–77 (1984) (interpreting Rule 6–101 of California Rules of Professional Conduct, predecessor of current Rule 3–110).

Please keep this in mind as you read the following excerpt from an article on legal ethics.

LAURENCE ETHERTINGTON AND ROBERT LEE, ETHICAL CODES AND CULTURAL CONTEXT: ENSURING LEGAL ETHICS IN THE GLOBAL LAW FIRM
14 Indiana Journal of Global Legal Studies, 1 (2007)

* * *

In the world of globalized legal services, we might not be too surprised to find an Australian lawyer working in the Brussels office of a New York law firm on a contract for a Japanese client with a German counterpart, which is governed by English common law, but in which disputes are to be referred to the International Chamber of Commerce's International Court of Arbitration based in Paris. There are doubtless many practical and professional problems that arise in such situations of global legal practice, but, in this paper, we wish to suggest that not least of these are issues of legal ethics,[5] in part generated by the global context and not easily amenable to resolution by reference to any single code within the "home" or "host" jurisdiction. For example, there may be difficulties in isolating precisely what those ethical obligations might comprise. These obligations might be rooted in the requirements of local law, but they might arise equally from the values and expectations of the client, or from other lawyers whether inside or outside of the firm in question. The common expectation of regulatory control exercised by a professional bar may be replaced by a fluidity in which clearly defined rules and duties are not easily discernible. The questions that this paper seeks to answer are: How might lawyers best be provided with and follow ethical approaches

---

[5]   See generally Laurel S. Terry, U.S. Legal Ethics: The Coming of Age of Global and Comparative Perspectives, 4 WASH. U. GLOBAL STUD. L. REV. 463, 470–72, 523–26 (2005) (arguing that theorizing about legal ethics in transnational lawyering has often lagged behind the reality of legal practice).

appropriate to the delivery of global legal services, and what is the role that firms might play in achieving this?

Before addressing these questions it is useful to elaborate a little further on the impact of globalization upon legal ethics. An obvious issue is that a law firm operating in a number of jurisdictions may face problems in accommodating potentially conflicting ethical codes. The problem is not only spatial, but is to some degree temporal.[6] This is because the traditional understandings and values laid down over time and embedded into the very strata of the codes are slowly eroded by the tide of globalization. Globalization is not a neutral force. In pursuit of economic integration, it drives to open up markets and further market choice. Much of what lies within professional conduct rules is antithetical to its purpose, as these rules have been supportive generally of state-sanctioned restrictive practice regulating the delivery of legal services in return for assurances of ethical behavior.[7] Justifications for market intervention and the allowance of a monopoly right to provide legal representation based on arguments of informational asymmetry[8] are less and less persuasive to those supporting the market liberalization agenda inherent in the globalization of services delivery. Threats to legal ethical frameworks under globalization are, therefore, not only confined to a clash of cultures but also include a clash of values.[9]

* * *

---

[6] Disjunctions between space and time are a hallmark of globalization. See generally ANTHONY GIDDENS, MODERNITY AND SELF-IDENTITY 14–21 (1991) (arguing that in the "pre-modern" world, time and space were connected through place, but in the modern world there is a separation of time and space because the global map has no privileging of place); James H. Mittelman, The Dynamics of Globalization, in GLOBALIZATION: CRITICAL REFLECTIONS 1, 3 (James H. Mittelman ed., 1996) (arguing that globalization compresses the time and space aspects of social relations).

[7] Such practices might be under direct threat from the General Agreement on Trade in Services (GATS) of the WTO. See generally Paul D. Paton, Legal Services and the GATS: Norms as Barriers to Trade, 9 NEW ENG. J. INT'L & COMP. L. 361 (2003), available at http://www.nesl.edu/students/student_journals.cfm (discussing the conflict between global and domestic forces in shaping ethical rules for the legal community); Joseph McCahery & Sol Picciotto, Creative Lawyering and the Dynamics of Business Regulation, in PROFESSIONAL COMPETITION AND PROFESSIONAL POWER: LAWYERS, ACCOUNTANTS AND THE SOCIAL CONSTRUCTION OF THE MARKET 238 (Yves Dezalay & David Sugarman eds., 1995) (discussing business regulation and the effect it has on lawyering).

[8] E.g., R. C. O. Matthews, The Economics of Professional Ethics: Should the Professions Be More Like Business?, 101 ECON. J. 737, 739–41 (1991); Anthony Ogus, Rethinking Self-Regulation, 15 O.J.L.S. 97, 97–98 (1995) (U.K.). For a discussion of the changing regulatory schemes governing the legal profession, see Alan A. Paterson, Professionalism and the Legal Services Market, 3 INT'L J. LEGAL PROF. 137, 145–49 (1996).

[9] This is not to underplay the importance of culture clashes, which are considered in detail below, but perhaps the clash of values is indicated by the erosion of professional structures, taking place within jurisdictions as well as across them. For a U.K. perspective, see Andrew M. Francis, Legal Ethics, the Marketplace and the Fragmentation of Legal Professionalism, 12 INT'L J. LEGAL PROF. 173 (2005). For a U.S. perspective, see Herbert M. Kritzer, The Professions Are Dead, Long Live the Professions: Legal Practice in a Postprofessional World, 33 L. & SOC'Y REV. 713 (1999).

For both types of firms, however, globalization will present a context within which issues of ethics arise. These may be somewhat wider than the traditional realm of legal ethics. For example, will the project being financed in a developing country create questions of corporate social responsibility if indigenous people are to be displaced or biodiversity threatened? Even if the lawyers feel unconcerned about providing services to support such activity, they may feel it prudent to point out the legal and other risks that may attach to that activity. Interestingly, this is an area in which international banks have chosen to regulate their own activity by adopting what have become known as the Equator Principles.[18] These voluntary principles are based on the International Finance Corporation (IFC) Environmental and Social Standards and apply globally to development projects in all industry sectors with capital costs of $10 million or more.[19] Given that the banks will look to their lawyers to incorporate the relevant standards within the conditions and covenants of the lending document, it will be necessary for the law firms to develop an understanding of the business ethical requirements of their clients.

II.   CONFLICTS IN ETHICAL DUTIES

The difficulties arising out of this complex layering of professional duties—or "double deontology"[29]—should not be overstated. In general, "there are fundamental principles of legal professional ethics which can be found, in one form or other, in most jurisdictions."[30] There are, however, even significant differences between common law jurisdictions. For example, the "conflict of interests" duty is very different for U.S. lawyers, who enjoy much greater freedom to act where there is client consent than do English lawyers, for whom the situation is also muddied by different requirements under professional regulations and at common law. This reflects a clearer focus on the duty to the client for U.S. lawyers, whereas

---

[18]   Over forty institutions have adopted the principles at the time of writing. International Finance Corporation, Our Approach to Sustainability (2006), http://www.ifc.org/equatorprinciples. For the full text of the revised Equator Principles, see The "Equator Principles": A Financial Industry Benchmark for Determining, Assessing and Managing Social & Environmental Risk in Project Financing, July 6, 2006, available at http://www.commdev.org/userfiles/files/ 1013_file_Equator_Principles.pdf.

[19]   Malcolm Forster, The Equator Principles—Towards Sustainable Banking? 2005 BUTTERWORTHS J. INT'L BANKING & FIN. L. [JIBFL] 217; Paul Watchman, Banks, Business and Human Rights, 2006 JIBFL 46, 50 n.2.

[29]   DONALD NICOLSON & JULIAN WEBB, PROFESSIONAL LEGAL ETHICS: CRITICAL INTERROGATIONS 62 (1999). The basic position is that lawyers practicing as foreign legal advisors are required to comply with the local ethical code as well as their home professional standards (to some degree at least). Council Directive 77/249/EEC, To Facilitate the Effective Exercise by Lawyers of Freedom to Provide Services, arts. 4, 6, 1977 O.J. (L 78) 17, 18 (EC); see Julian Lonbay, Legal Ethics and Professional Responsibility in a Global Context, 4 WASH. U. GLOBAL STUD. L. REV. 609, 611–12 (2005).

[30]   Alison Crawley & Christopher Bramall, Professional Rules, Codes, and Principles Affecting Solicitors (Or What Has Professional Regulation to do With Ethics?), in LEGAL ETHICS AND PROFESSIONAL RESPONSIBILITY, supra note 20, at 99, 99.

lawyers in some other countries have more diverse duties beyond those owed to the client.[31] Similar differences exist in areas such as attorney-client privilege and contingency fees.[32] Differences in practice rules may reflect the local context. For example, advocates involved in conveyancing on the Isle of Man were traditionally allowed to act for both sides in property sale or purchase transactions, a rule which probably reflected the small size of the profession on the Island, but which has been revised recently, reflecting the growth in the profession and burgeoning development on the Island.[33]

III. CULTURAL BASIS OF ETHICS

Professional conduct rules reflect shared values or beliefs about how lawyers ought to behave. It will be clear from the text above that this may be with a view to arriving at a particular end or goal. Thus, the rule may be to respect client confidentiality in order, at least in part, to engender client trust. The value of client trust generates the rule or precept that we should respect and keep confidences. According to Wines and Napier, "[e]thics is the systematic application of moral principles to concrete problems."[40] For instance, when faced with a request for information about the activity of a client for whom the lawyer has worked, the lawyer will need to apply the rule ("respect client confidentiality") in this specific situation. This might not lead, however, to a blanket refusal to make disclosure because other rules, such as "further the administration of justice," might conflict with such action. An ethical standpoint, for example, disclosing only when required to do so by a court order, will be arrived at by the analysis of the application of the rules to the real life problem at hand. Thus, professional ethics involve decisions that will govern conduct in accordance with cultural norms.[41]

---

[31]   Nancy J. Moore, Regulating Law Firm Conflicts in the 21st Century: Implications of the Globalization of Legal Services and the Growth of the "Mega Firm", 18 GEO. J. LEGAL ETHICS 521, 528 (2005) (review essay).

[32]   Mark, supra note 1, at 1185 (discussing Australia in particular). The German Bar has outlawed contingency fees even though they would apparently not be ruled unenforceable as sufficiently immoral (contra bonos mores) by the courts. Detlev F. Vagts, Professional Responsibility in Transborder Practice: Conflict and Resolution, 13 GEO. J. LEGAL ETHICS 677, 683 (2000).

[33]   Compare STEPHEN CROW, ISLE OF MAN: REPORT OF AN INQUIRY INTO PLANNING AND OTHER MATTERS AT MOUNT MURRAY 13, ¶¶ 2.29–2.30 (2000), available at http://www.gov.im/ infocentre/archived_releases/pdfs/Entire_crow_report.pdf (status of regulations in 2000), with J.P. SHIMMIN, A.C. DOUGLAS & E.G. LOWEY, REPORT OF THE SELECT COMMITTEE ON THE COMPENSATION CLAIM—MOUNT MURRAY RESIDENTS 8, ¶¶ 3.12–3.14 (2005), available at http:// www.tynwald.org.im/papers/reports/2004/main.shtml (status of regulations in 2004).

[40]   William A. Wines & Nancy K. Napier, Toward an Understanding of Cross-Cultural Ethics: A Tentative Model, II J. BUS. ETHICS 831, 831 (1992).

[41]   See generally Larry R. Churchill, The Teaching of Ethics and Moral Values in Teaching: Same Contemporary Confusions, 53 J. HIGHER EDUC. 296 (1982) (discussing the misconception concerning the relation between teaching ethics and the way individuals make moral decisions in reality).

It is clear, however, from observation of confidentiality rules in areas such as banking or medicine, that some cultures of confidentiality are stronger than others. It is easy to recognize the broad, shared value of confidentiality, but it may be held with different degrees of commitment in different cultures. Switzerland has historically pursued a very strong line of banking secrecy, and while this may have served its economic interest in attracting deposits to Swiss banks, there is no reason to argue that this stance is morally weaker than that of surrounding countries which more readily disclose banking information. Moreover, a banker preserving absolute client confidentiality in the face of doubts as to the provenance of the money might be viewed in such a culture as a model professional even though such conduct might be castigated as underhanded or ethically dubious according to the professional standards in another cultural setting.

The identification of differing ethical rules and the foundations from which these differences arise demonstrate that professional ethics are culturally distinct. In relation to legal ethics, these cultural differences may reflect aspects of different legal cultures, but they may also reflect differences in wider social structures and values. Indeed, it is possible that the very commitment to, and understanding of, ethical principles is different in different jurisdictions, reflecting differing intellectual traditions or patterns of education. Equally, even when there is a shared commitment to a value, its manifestation in certain forms of conduct may be problematic. By way of illustration, take a series of television advertisements for HSBC Bank shown in the United Kingdom under the strap-line "The World's Local Bank." The purpose of the campaign has been described as follows: "HSBC commercials typically show the effects that different meanings for the same word or gesture have in different countries, which is intended to convey that HSBC's operations in 77 countries prepare the bank for helping customers wherever they are."[42]

One title in the series shows an English businessman being entertained by a group of Chinese businessmen in a Chinese restaurant.[43] The English man struggles to eat the eel served to him but finishes every last bit. This is to the consternation of his Chinese hosts, who then serve an even bigger eel to the alarm of the guest and so on. The voiceover states that: "the English believe that it's a slur on your hosts' food if you don't clean your plate; whereas the Chinese feel you are questioning their generosity if you do."[44] Clearly, both parties share the value and recognize the importance of gratitude, but its expression takes very different forms within the cultures concerned.

---

[42] Stuart Elliot, A Bank That Isn't Your Average New Yorker Is Starting to Spread the News—About Itself, N.Y. TIMES, Apr. 19, 2005, at C5.

[43] Crave Online, Spiked Humor, HSBC Commercial—English Man in Chinese Restaurant.

[44] Id.

As well as culturally derived professional rules and other norms, lawyers and legal professions also operate within differing social and cultural environments, such as social hierarchies. Their ethical behavior is influenced by many contexts, including the type of work they do, their positions within hierarchies, and the nature of their clients.[45] The hierarchies themselves may not be based on the Anglo-American tournament to partnership,[46] especially where firms are historically of a small size, or may be influenced by other prevailing hierarchies in society—as reflected, for example, in Indian society. Values, beliefs, and behavioral norms influence not only group members' behavior, but also their interpretations of the "meaning" of other peoples' behavior.[47] Lawyers working within an increasingly rich cultural environment need to have or to develop intercultural awareness skills, so that they are able to communicate effectively with others who do not share common cultural experiences.[48] One aspect of these necessary skills is an awareness of, and sensitivity to, differences in professional ethics.

The wider world of business has had to grapple with the impact of globalization upon ethical issues, including religious and cultural pluralism, within, as well as between, countries. One strategy is to seek to develop a system of global business ethics, though this is an extremely complex and demanding task.[49] It may also be a problematic approach because of the problems of cultural imperialism, which are particularly stark where harmonized systems, reflecting the economically liberal values of globalization, may be perceived as homogenization based on Western standards.[50] The development of an international code of ethics for lawyers began in the 1950s,[51] though, notwithstanding the significant expansion of

---

[45]   NICOLSON & WEBB, supra note 29, at 51.

[46]   See generally MARC GALANTER & THOMAS PALAY, TOURNAMENT OF LAWYERS: THE TRANSFORMATION OF THE BIG LAW FIRM (1991) (discussing how the structuring of compensation and incentives around a promotion-to-partner contest has transformed the big law firm in the United States).

[47]   Helen Spencer-Oatey, Introduction to CULTURALLY SPEAKING: MANAGING RAPPORT THROUGH TALK ACROSS CULTURES 4 (Helen Spencer-Oatey ed., 2000).

[48]   See generally GEERT HOFSTEDE & GERT JAN HOFSTEDE, CULTURES AND ORGANIZATIONS: SOFTWARE OF THE MIND: INTERCULTURAL COOPERATION AND ITS IMPORTANCE FOR SURVIVAL (2005) (discussing the importance of intercultural cooperation for the survival in the business world); FONS TROMPENAARS & CHARLES HAMPDEN-TURNER, RIDING THE WAVES OF CULTURE: UNDERSTANDING CULTURAL DIVERSITY IN GLOBAL BUSINESS (2d ed. 1998) (discussing cultural differences and the impact those differences have on the process of doing business and managing).

[49]   E.g., Georges Enderle, Business Ethics, in THE BLACKWELL COMPANION TO PHILOSOPHY 531, 531–32, 546 (Nicholas Bunnin & E.P. Tsui-James eds., 2d ed. 2003).

[50]   See Mark, supra note 1 at 1178. For a wider perspective on this issue, see JACQUES ATTALI, MILLENNIUM: WINNERS AND LOSERS IN THE COMING WORLD ORDER 117–30 (Leila Conners & Nathan Gardels trans., Random House 1991) (1990).

[51]   NICOLSON & WEBB, supra note 29, at 62. For a copy of the latest version of this code, see INTERNATIONAL BAR ASSOCIATION, INTERNATIONAL CODE OF ETHICS (1988). SEE COUNCIL OF THE BARS AND LAW SOCIETIES OF THE EUROPEAN UNION, CODE OF CONDUCT FOR LAWYERS IN THE EUROPEAN UNION (2002), available at http://www.idhae.org/pdf/code2002_en.pdf, for the European code that enshrines many similar provisions.

global legal services in the last twenty years, these codes have remained rather static instruments.[52] While harmonized systems might provide the desired efficiency in delivery of legal services, there are a number of problems that might attach to them. There is a great danger that they might erode moral pluralism and fail to adequately reflect local cultures, values, and identities.[53] There is also the risk that such codes are based on compromises around what is easily acceptable from the various jurisdictions and avoid controversy by a minimalist approach to ethics.[54]

* * *

VI. THE ROLE OF THE FIRM

There are a number of mechanisms by which firms can and do establish, maintain, and develop internal guiding norms and values, as well as disseminate legal knowledge and develop practice skills that can be used to develop a professional ethos.[72] The first is the recruitment process. A hiring regime based on a strong behavioral model, that seeks to determine character traits by reviewing actions taken in real life situations, will look to isolate how people might react in a variety of stressful, awkward, or difficult situations, including those involving ethical determinations. This type of recruitment process can consider also the applicant's awareness of, and sensitivity to, different cultural contexts. A second mechanism is likely to be the firm's training program. Formal training may include reflection on, and discussion of, ethical issues, as well as guidance in the firms approach, perhaps through role-play or other simulation.[73] This type of experiential learning in a safe environment,

---

[52] See generally Andrew Boon & John Flood, Globalization of Professional Ethics? The Significance of Lawyers' International Codes of Conduct, 2 LEGAL ETHICS 29, 55–56 (1999) (arguing that the absence of discourse about the international codes is a barrier to the globalization of professional ethics); H. W. Arthurs, A Global Code of Ethics for the Transnational Legal Field, 2 LEGAL ETHICS 59 (1999) (discussing the difficulties of creating a universal or global code of ethics and criticizing such codes as ineffective); Mary C. Daly, The Ethical Implications of the Globalization of the Legal Profession: A Challenge to the Teaching of Professional Responsibility in the Twenty-First Century, 21 FORDHAM INT'L L.J. 1239, 1248–49 (1998) (pointing to the lack of take-up of global ethics issues within the law curriculum).

[53] Ana Marta González, Ethics in Global Business and in a Plural Society, 44 J. BUS. ETHICS 23, 23–24 (2003); Mark, supra note 1, at 1178.

[54] González, supra note 53, at 24; see also Mark, supra note l, at 1187; Spencer-Oatey, supra note 47, at 5. By 'minimalist' we mean that instead of an inclusive set of ethical values, consensus is reached by focusing on a core set of universal values. The advantage might then be to lay the foundations from which further negotiation can proceed. See Sissela Bok, What Basis for Morality? A Minimalist Approach, 76 MONIST 349, 352–53 (1993).

[72] See generally Jeffrey Gandz & Frederick C. Bird, Designing Ethical Organizations, BUS. Q., Autumn 1989, at 108 (discussing the positive steps that organizations must take to ensure that their employees act ethically); Kevin T. Jackson, Globalizing Corporate Ethics Programs: Perils and Prospects, 16 J. BUS ETHICS 1227 (1997) discussing both the difficulties and the possibilities involved in international corporate ethics programs).

[73] See Alan Paterson, Legal Ethics: Its Nature and Place in the Curriculum, in LEGAL ETHICS AND PROFESSIONAL RESPONSIBILITY, supra note 20, at 175, 184–85 (discussing how this is a particularly useful approach for ethics education, though it does have some potential pitfalls);

supported by tutors or mentors, might be particularly well suited to this task. In a sense, such training replaces an apprenticeship model in large firms where access to partners with relevant experience may be limited.[74] To an extent, the elaborate checks made in relation to conflicts in large law firms might be seen as replacing the everyday dialogue that might take place in smaller firms where the entirety of the firms business is known to all staff. Training to ensure that a less experienced lawyer is at least aware of the danger of an ethical trap similarly replaces a model of more direct supervision.

A second element of this kind of training is the softer "socialization" that generally accompanies formal training sessions, where informal peer discussions and observation can be at least as important as formal sessions. Third, there is the kind of "legitimate peripheral participation" that forms part of the development of professional knowledge, particularly for trainees and junior professionals.[75] Observing how peers and more experienced professionals work in their day-to-day practice, together with the undertaking of increasingly less peripheral tasks, is a highly effective method of inculcating the kind of tacit knowledge and skills that are difficult to develop through other means.[76] Socialization can be encouraged outside of formal training sessions through identifying and supporting informal activities so as to develop "communities of practice"[77] and to enhance development of professional moral character. In resolving tensions that do arise, law firms may be in a position to "eclectically integrate the virtues of various cultures and, through the process of mutual consultation and conflict resolution, distribute an ethically sound decision-making procedure."[78]

* * *

Alan Paterson Self-Regulation and the Future of the Profession, in LAW'S FUTURE(S): BRITISH LEGAL DEVELOPMENTS IN THE 21ST CENTURY 29, 49 (David Hayton ed., 2000) (discussing the importance of reflexivity in responsive regulation).

[74] Elizabeth Nosworthy, Ethics and Large Law Firms, in LEGAL ETHICS AND LEGAL PRACTICE: CONTEMPORARY ISSUES, supra note 57, at 57, 65–66.

[75] JEAN LAVE & ETIENNE WENGER, SITUATED LEARNING: LEGITIMATE PERIPHERAL PARTICIPATION 29 (1991).

[76] Id.

[77] See, e.g., ETIENNE WENGER, COMMUNITIES OF PRACTICE: LEARNING, MEANING, AND IDENTITY 6–7 (1998); John Seely Brown & Paul Duguid, Organizational Learning and Communities-of-Practice: Toward a Unified View of Working, Learning, and Innovation, 2 ORG. SCI. 40, 47–48 (1991). The role of a 'community of practice' is similar to the role played by 'quality circles' or 'ethical circles' through which professional moral character can contribute to shared morality within a firm. Sampford & Parker, supra note 57, at 17. In a sense, the former processes of socialization that inculcated ethical norms at the level of the profession may be replaced by these 'varied and contingent' processes at the firm level. See Francis, supra note 9, at 174.

[78] Ashay B. Desai & Terri Rittenburg, Global Ethics: An Integrative Framework for MNEs, 16 J. BUS. ETHICS 791, 797 (1997).

QUESTIONS

1.   In planning your approach to represent a client on an international bank merger transaction how would you address conflicting ethics rules, social norms and laws? How about social responsibility, religious or moral issues?

To: **ABA Entities, Courts, Bar Associations (state, local, specialty and international), Law Schools, Disciplinary Agencies, Individuals, and Entities**

From: ABA Commission on Ethics 20/20 Working Group on Uniformity, Choice of Law, and Conflicts of Interest

Date: January 18, 2011

Re: Issues Paper: Choice of Law in Cross-Border Practice

I.   Introduction

The American Bar Association Commission on Ethics 20/20 is examining a number of legal ethics issues arising from the increasing globalization of law practice. The goal of this paper is to identify ethics-related choice of law problems that have arisen because of this increase in cross-border practice and to elicit comments on possible approaches that the Commission is currently considering.

* * *

II.   Model Rule 8.5: Disciplinary Authority; Choice of Law

Rules of professional conduct vary within the United States and around the world. These variations create problems for lawyers who engage in cross-border practice, especially when they encounter legal ethics issues that could be resolved differently depending on which jurisdiction's rules apply.

Model Rule 8.5 of the Model Rules of Professional Conduct is designed to address this problem. It provides as follows:

(a) Disciplinary Authority. A lawyer admitted to practice in this jurisdiction is subject to the disciplinary authority of this jurisdiction, regardless of where the lawyer's conduct occurs. A lawyer not admitted in this jurisdiction is also subject to the disciplinary authority of this jurisdiction if the lawyer provides or offers to provide any legal services in this jurisdiction. A lawyer may be subject to the disciplinary authority of both this jurisdiction and another jurisdiction for the same conduct.

(b) Choice of Law. In any exercise of the disciplinary authority of this jurisdiction, the rules of professional conduct to be applied shall be as follows:

(1) for conduct in connection with a matter pending before a tribunal, the rules of the jurisdiction in which the tribunal sits, unless the rules of the tribunal provide otherwise; and

(2) for any other conduct, the rules of the jurisdiction in which the lawyer's conduct occurred, or, if the predominant effect of the conduct is in a different jurisdiction, the rules of that jurisdiction shall be applied to the conduct. A lawyer shall not be subject to discipline if the lawyer's conduct conforms to the rules of a jurisdiction in which the lawyer reasonably believes the predominant effect of the lawyer's conduct will occur.

Rule 8.5(a) describes the circumstances under which a lawyer is subject to the disciplinary authority of a jurisdiction, even if the lawyer is licensed in another jurisdiction. Rule 8.5(b) identifies which jurisdiction's rules of professional conduct should be applied to the lawyer's conduct. For example, a lawyer might be subject to the disciplinary authority of New Jersey under Rule 8.5(a) by engaging in law practice there, but Rule 8.5(b) might specify that the New Jersey disciplinary authority should apply the ethics rules of Illinois to determine whether the lawyer should, in fact, be disciplined.

III. Potential Problems and Ambiguities with Model Rule 8.5

Model Rule 8.5 supplies clear answers in some circumstances, but it produces unclear and arguably problematic results in other contexts.

* * *

QUESTIONS AND NOTES

1.   The ABA's Commission on Ethics offered the following fact patterns and questions, among others, in highlighting the potential problems and ambiguities in applying Model Rule 8.5:

* * *

Fact Pattern #3: Conflicts in International Multi-Office Law Firms. Firm JKL has offices in the United States and Country Q. Max in JKL's New York office represents NCO on contract matters. Lia, in JKL's office in Country Q, is asked to undertake an arbitration, litigation, or negotiation against NCO on a matter unrelated to Max's work. Lia's work will be done entirely in Q. Q's rules allow her to do the work. New York's imputation rules treat Max and Lia as one lawyer for conflict purposes, so Lia's clients are imputed to Max. Thus, if Lia were in New York she could not accept the work without informed consent. Can Lia undertake the engagement?

Fact Pattern #4: Choice of Law Provisions in Engagement Letters. Anticipating the inconsistent conflict rules in the prior two fact patterns, the two firms had specified in their original engagement letters with their clients that the conflict rules in a designated jurisdiction (or in the Model Rules) would govern their relationship. The firms wish only, to the extent allowed, to contract for governing conflict rules, not other rules where there might be inconsistency among jurisdictions, because lack of uniformity in conflict rules is where they run into the most difficult problems. The firms reason that conflict rules are nearly always default rules that can be supplanted by private contract (i.e., informed consent as defined in the rules). Can the firms and the clients bind themselves to such a substitution with the result that the firms can safely conform their conduct to the conflict rules identified in the agreement? Would reliance on such a contractual provision give lawyers a reasonable belief that their conduct complied with applicable rules of professional conduct under Model Rule 8.5(b)(2)?

2.   With regard to the foregoing fact patterns, the Commission sought feedback regarding, among other things, the following questions:

- Does Rule 8.5(a) make clear (or as clear as possible) which jurisdictions would have disciplinary authority over the lawyers identified in these fact patterns? If not, how should Rule 8.5(a) be changed?

- Does Rule 8.5(b) enable a lawyer *confidently* to resolve the issues in the above fact patterns? If not, how should Rule 8.5(b) be revised to offer clearer guidance? What should be the answers to the above fact patterns?

- Should the choice of rule provision vary depending on whether the underlying legal service primarily arises under state or federal law, with a greater emphasis on uniformity when the service arises under federal law?

- In those cases where the current rule offers a clear answer, is that answer correct? If not, how should Rule 8.5(b) be changed?

How would you answer these questions?

3.   UNAUTHORIZED PRACTICE OF LAW

AMERICAN BAR ASSOCIATION:
RULE 5.5 UNAUTHORIZED PRACTICE OF LAW;
MULTIJURISDICTIONAL PRACTICE OF LAW

(a) A lawyer shall not practice law in a jurisdiction in violation of the regulation of the legal profession in that jurisdiction, or assist another in doing so.

(b) A lawyer who is not admitted to practice in this jurisdiction shall not:

(1) except as authorized by these Rules or other law, establish an office or other systematic and continuous presence in this jurisdiction for the practice of law; or

(2) hold out to the public or otherwise represent that the lawyer is admitted to practice law in this jurisdiction.

* * *

(d) A lawyer admitted in another United States jurisdiction or in a foreign jurisdiction, and not disbarred or suspended from practice in any jurisdiction or the equivalent thereof, may provide legal services through an office or other systematic and continuous presence in this jurisdiction that:

(1) are provided to the lawyer's employer or its organizational affiliates; are not services for which the forum requires pro hac vice admission; and, when performed by a foreign lawyer and requires advice on the law of this or another jurisdiction or of the United States, such advice shall be based upon the advice of a lawyer who is duly licensed and authorized by the jurisdiction to provide such advice; or

(2) are services that the lawyer is authorized by federal or other law or rule to provide in this jurisdiction.

(e) For purposes of paragraph (d), the foreign lawyer must be a member in good standing of a recognized legal profession in a foreign jurisdiction, the members of which are admitted to practice as lawyers or counselors at law or the equivalent, and are subject to effective regulation and discipline by a duly constituted professional body or a public authority.

AMERICAN BAR ASSOCIATION: *LAW FIRMS AND ASSOCIATIONS*, RULE 5.5 UNAUTHORIZED PRACTICE OF LAW; MULTIJURISDICTIONAL PRACTICE OF LAW—COMMENT

(1) A lawyer may practice law only in a jurisdiction in which the lawyer is authorized to practice. A lawyer may be admitted to practice law in a jurisdiction on a regular basis or may be authorized by court rule or order or by law to practice for a limited purpose or on a restricted basis. Paragraph (a) applies to unauthorized practice of law by a lawyer, whether through the lawyer's direct action or by the lawyer assisting another person. For example, a lawyer may not assist a person in practicing law in violation of the rules governing professional conduct in that person's jurisdiction.

(2) The definition of the practice of law is established by law and varies from one jurisdiction to another. Whatever the definition, limiting the practice of law to members of the bar protects the public against rendition of legal services by unqualified persons. This Rule does not prohibit a lawyer from employing the services of paraprofessionals and delegating functions to them, so long as the lawyer supervises the delegated work and retains responsibility for their work.

* * *

(3) A lawyer may provide professional advice and instruction to nonlawyers whose employment requires knowledge of the law; for example, claims adjusters, employees of financial or commercial institutions, social workers, accountants and persons employed in government agencies. Lawyers also may assist independent nonlawyers, such as paraprofessionals, who are authorized by the law of a jurisdiction to provide particular law-related services. In addition, a lawyer may counsel nonlawyers who wish to proceed pro se.

(4) Other than as authorized by law or this Rule, a lawyer who is not admitted to practice generally in this jurisdiction violates paragraph (b)(1) if the lawyer establishes an office or other systematic and continuous presence in this jurisdiction for the practice of law. Presence may be systematic and continuous even if the lawyer is not physically present here. Such a lawyer must not hold out to the public or otherwise represent that the lawyer is admitted to practice law in this jurisdiction. See also Rules 7.1(a) and 7.5(b).

* * *

(7) Paragraphs (c) and (d) apply to lawyers who are admitted to practice law in any United States jurisdiction, which includes the District of Columbia and any state, territory or commonwealth of the United States. Paragraph (d) also applies to lawyers admitted in a foreign jurisdiction. The word "admitted" in paragraphs (c), (d) and (e) contemplates that the lawyer is authorized to practice in the jurisdiction in which the lawyer is admitted and excludes a lawyer who while technically admitted is not authorized to practice, because, for example, the lawyer is on inactive status.

* * *

(9) Lawyers not admitted to practice generally in a jurisdiction may be authorized by law or order of a tribunal or an administrative agency to appear before the tribunal or agency. This authority may be granted pursuant to formal rules governing admission pro hac vice or pursuant to informal practice of the tribunal or agency. Under paragraph (c)(2), a lawyer does not violate this Rule when the lawyer appears before a tribunal

or agency pursuant to such authority. To the extent that a court rule or other law of this jurisdiction requires a lawyer who is not admitted to practice in this jurisdiction to obtain admission pro hac vice before appearing before a tribunal or administrative agency, this Rule requires the lawyer to obtain that authority.

* * *

(15) Paragraph (d) identifies two circumstances in which a lawyer who is admitted to practice in another United States or a foreign jurisdiction, and is not disbarred or suspended from practice in any jurisdiction, or the equivalent thereof, may establish an office or other systematic and continuous presence in this jurisdiction for the practice of law. Pursuant to paragraph (c) of this Rule, a lawyer admitted in any U.S. jurisdiction may also provide legal services in this jurisdiction on a temporary basis. See also *Model Rule on Temporary Practice by Foreign Lawyers.* Except as provided in paragraphs (d)(1) and (d)(2), a lawyer who is admitted to practice law in another United States or foreign jurisdiction and who establishes an office or other systematic or continuous presence in this jurisdiction must become admitted to practice law generally in this jurisdiction.

* * *

(17) If an employed lawyer establishes an office or other systematic presence in this jurisdiction for the purpose of rendering legal services to the employer, the lawyer may be subject to registration or other requirements, including assessments for client protection funds and mandatory continuing legal education. See *Model Rule for Registration of In-House Counsel.*

(18) Paragraph (d)(2) recognizes that a U.S. or foreign lawyer may provide legal services in a jurisdiction in which the lawyer is not licensed when authorized to do so by federal or other law, which includes statute, court rule, executive regulation or judicial precedent.

* * *

4. INTERNATIONAL CODE OF ETHICS FOR CROSS BORDER PRACTICE OF LAW

ABOUT THE INTERNATIONAL BAR ASSOCIATION
http://www.ibanet.org/

The International Bar Association (IBA) is the world's foremost international association of lawyers. With a membership of some 18,000 individual lawyers in 183 countries, as well as 174 Bar Associations and

Law Societies, it is able to place worldwide experience and a network of personal contacts at the disposal of its members.

The principal aims and objectives of the IBA are to encourage the discussion of problems relating to professional organisation and status; to promote an exchange of information between legal associations worldwide; to support the independence of the judiciary and the right of lawyers to practise their profession without interference; to keep abreast of developments in the law, and to help in improving the law and making new laws.

Above all it seeks to provide a forum in which individual lawyers can contact, and exchange ideas with, other lawyers.

NOTES

1.   The IBA and its Sections publish journals, books and the proceedings of their meetings. An annual Directory of Members gives full details of each member, providing a reference for those seeking contacts with colleagues in other countries. The IBA's conferences and seminars fulfil one of the Association's most important objectives: the promotion of useful contacts and interchange between lawyers throughout the world. Every two years a major conference is held, in which all three Sections of the IBA participate. The individual Sections hold their own conferences in the intervening years. A program of specialised seminars is held throughout the year.

INTERNATIONAL BAR ASSOCIATION, INTERNATIONAL PRINCIPLES ON CONDUCT FOR THE LEGAL PROFESSION
Adopted on 28 May 2011

Lawyers throughout the world are specialized professionals who place the interests of their clients above their own, and strive to obtain respect for the Rule of Law. They have to combine a continuous update on legal developments with service to their clients, respect for the courts, and the legitimate aspiration to maintain a reasonable standard of living. Between these elements there is often tension. These principles aim at establishing a generally accepted framework to serve as a basis on which codes of conduct may be established by the appropriate authorities for lawyers in any part of the world. In addition, the purpose of adopting these International Principles is to promote and foster the ideals of the legal profession. These International Principles are not intended to replace or limit a lawyer's obligation under applicable laws or rules of professional conduct. Nor are they to be used as criteria for imposing liability, sanctions, or disciplinary measures of any kind.

1.   Independence

A lawyer shall maintain independence and be afforded the protection such independence offers in giving clients unbiased advice and representation. A lawyer shall exercise independent, unbiased professional judgment in advising a client, including as to the likelihood of success of the client's case.

2.   Honesty, Integrity and Fairness

A lawyer shall at all times maintain the highest standards of honest, integrity and fairness towards the lawyer's clients, the court, colleagues and all those with whom the lawyer comes into professional contact.

3.   Conflicts of Interest

A lawyer shall not assume a position in which a client's interests conflict with those of the lawyer, another lawyer in the same firm, or another client, unless otherwise permitted by law, applicable rules of professional conduct, or, if permitted, by client's authorisation.

4.   Confidentiality/Professional Secrecy

A lawyer shall at all limes maintain and be afforded protection of confidentiality regarding the affairs of present or former clients, unless otherwise allowed or required by law and/or applicable rides of professional conduct.

5.   Clients' Interest

A lawyer shall treat client interests as paramount, subject always to there being no conflict with the lawyer's duties to the court and the interests of justice, to observe the law, and to maintain ethical standards.

6.   Lawyers' Undertaking

A lawyer shall honour any undertaking given in the course of the lawyer's practice in a timely manner, until the undertaking is performed, released or excused.

7.   Clients' Freedom

A lawyer shall respect the freedom of clients to be represented by the lawyer of their choice. Unless prevented by professional conduct rules or by law, a lawyer shall be free to take on or reject, a case.

8.   Property of Clients and Third Parties

A lawyer shall account promptly and faithfully for and prudently hold any properly of clients or third parties that comes into the lawyer's trust, and shall keep it separate from the lawyer's own property.

9. Competence

A lawyer's work shall be carried out in a competent and timely manner. A lawyer shall not take on work that the lawyer does not reasonably believe can be carried out in that manner.

10. Fees

Lawyers are entitled to a reasonable fee for their work, and shall not charge an unreasonable fee. A lawyer shall not generate unnecessary work.

COMMENTARY ON IBA INTERNATIONAL PRINCIPLES ON CONDUCT FOR THE LEGAL PROFESSION

Adopted by the International Bar Association at the Warsaw Council Meeting
28 May 2011

Introduction

1.   The lawyer's role, whether retained by an individual, a corporation or the state, is as the client's trusted adviser and representative, as a professional respected by third parties, and as an indispensable participant in the fair administration of justice. By embodying all these elements, the lawyer, who faithfully serves a client's interests and protects the client's rights, also fulfils the functions of the lawyer in society—which are to forestall and prevent conflicts, to ensure that conflicts are resolved in accordance with recognised principles of civil, public or criminal law and with due account of rights and interests, to negotiate and draft agreements and other transactional necessities, to further the development of the law, and to defend liberty, justice and the rule of law

* * *

3.   The International Principles express the common ground which underlies all the national and international rules which govern the conduct of lawyers, principally in relation to their clients. The General Principles do not cover in detail other areas of lawyer conduct, for instance regarding the courts, other lawyers or the lawyer's own bar.

4.   The International Principles take into consideration:

- national professional rules from stales throughout the world;

- the Basic Principles on the Role of Lawyers, adopted by the Eighth United Nations Congress on the Prevention of Crime and the Treatment of Offenders, Havana (Cuba), 27 August to 7 September 1990;

- the Universal Declaration of Human Rights.

5.   It is hoped that the Principles and this Commentary will be of help, for instance, to bars that are struggling to establish their independence and that of their members in emerging democracies, and to lawyers and bars to

understand better the issues arising in cross-border situations as a consequence of conflicting national rules and regulations.

6.   It is hoped that the Principles will increase understanding among lawyers, decision makers and the public of the importance of the lawyers role in society, and of the way in which the principles by which the legal profession is regulated support that role.

7.   The IBA urges judges, legislators, governments and international organisations to strive, along with lawyers and bars, to uphold, the principles set out in the International Principles. However, no statement of principles or code of ethics can provide for every situation or circumstance that, may arise. Consequently, lawyers must act not only in accordance with the professional rules and applicable laws in their own state (and maybe also the rules and laws of another slate in which they are practising), but also in accordance with the dictates of their conscience, in keeping with the general sense and ethical culture that inspires these International Principles.

* * *

3.   Conflicts of interest

* * *

Trust and confidence in the legal profession and the rule of law depends upon lawyers' loyalty to clients. Rules regarding conflicts of interest vary from jurisdiction to jurisdiction. The definition of what constitutes a conflict also differs from jurisdiction to jurisdiction, including (but not exhaustively) whether information barriers are permitted at all, and also whether conflict of interest prohibitions cover all the law firm or whether information barriers can help. Generally, a lawyer shall not represent a client if the representation involves a conflict of interest. A conflict of interest exists if the representation of one client will be directly adverse to another client; or there is a significant risk that the representation of one or more clients will be materially limited by the lawyer's responsibilities to another client, a former client, a third person or by a personal interest of the lawyer. Notwithstanding the existence of conflict of interest, in some jurisdictions a lawyer may represent the client if the lawyer reasonably believes that the lawyer will be able to provide competent and diligent representation to each affected client, the representation is not prohibited by law, the representation, does not involve the assertion of a claim by one client against another client represented by the lawyer in the same litigation or other proceeding before a tribunal, and each affected client gives informed consent, confirmed in writing. A lawyer who has formerly represented a client in a matter or whose present or former firm has formerly represented a client in a matter shall not use information relating to the representation to the disadvantage of the former client except when permitted by applicable law or ethics rules.

In some jurisdictions, certain potentially conflicting situations may be permitted subject to proper disclosure to and, to the extent permitted by applicable law or ethics rules, consent by all parties involved, provided always that disclosure may be made without, breaching confidentiality obligations. Without prejudice to additional duties, if a conflict becomes apparent only after the lawyer's work has commenced, some jurisdictions require the conflicted lawyer to withdraw from the case in its entirety and in respect of all clients concerned; others require withdrawal from representing one client only, but not all of them.

In addition, legal and professional conduct conflict of interest must be clearly distinguished from commercial conflict of interest. A lawyer should be entitled to defend the interests of or represent a client in a case even if that client is a competitor or its interests conflict with the commercial interests of another present or former client, not involved or related in that particular case assigned to the lawyer. Also, a lawyer may defend the interests of or represent a client against another client in any circumstance where the latter, whether in negotiating an agreement, or in another legal action or arbitration, has chosen to place its interests for those cases with another lawyer; however, in such cases, the first-mentioned lawyer will have to comply with all other applicable rules of professional conduct, and in particular with rules of confidentiality, professional secrecy and independence.

QUESTIONS AND NOTES

1.   In light of the IBA's guidance on conflicts of interest, how do the differences in national rules on conflicts of interest have to be taken into account in any case of cross-border practice? The IBA stated the following on this issue:

> Every lawyer is called upon to observe the relevant rules on conflicts of interest when engaging in the practice of law outside the jurisdiction in which the lawyer is admitted to practice. Every international law firm will have to examine whether its entire organisation complies with such rules in every jurisdiction in which it is established and engaged in the provision of legal services. A universally accepted framework for determining proper conduct in the event of conflicting or incompatible rules has yet to be developed, although certain jurisdictions have adopted conflict of law principles to determine which rules of professional conduct apply in cross-border practice.

How would a law firm implement policies to comply with this guidance?

5. SPECIAL ISSUES

A. FOREIGN LAWYERS PRACTICING IN THE U.S.

AMERICAN BAR ASSOCIATION SECTION OF LEGAL EDUCATION AND ADMISSIONS TO THE BAR

Proposed Model Rule on Admission of Foreign Educated Lawyers

A lawyer educated at a law school located outside the United States and its territories (a "foreign-educated lawyer") is qualified to take the bar examination in this jurisdiction if the foreign-educated lawyer:

(1) received his or her legal education and graduated from a foreign law school that:

(a) is government sanctioned or recognized, if educational institutions are state regulated within the country; or

(b) is recognized or approved by an evaluation body, if such agency exists within the country; or

(c) is chartered to award first degrees in law by the appropriate authority within the country;

(2) is authorized to practice law in a foreign jurisdiction; and

(3) has been awarded, by a law school fully approved by the Council, an LLM Degree for the Practice of Law in the United States which has been certified by the Council as meeting the criteria established by the Council to qualify a foreign-educated lawyer to sit for the bar examination in a United States jurisdiction.

COMMENT

A. Meaning of "Authorized" to Practice Law

As used in (2) of this rule, the word "authorized" is intended to mean that the applicant has achieved the ability to engage in activities which would be recognized in the United States as the practice of law. Foreign jurisdictions vary in the ways persons acquire the ability to engage in these activities and the labels attached to such authorization. For example some countries in Central and South America, do not issue specific certificates or licenses to practice law. Only the completion of law degree program, at a law school approved by the Ministry of Education to grant the degree, is required. Other South American Countries require the graduate to register with the appropriate Bar Association by presenting the diploma and a police certificate that the law school graduate does not have a criminal record. In general countries assign different labels to approval by the government to practice law. Whatever the label or requirement, a United

States jurisdiction considering an application under this rule should insure that the applicant can, in his or her own country, engage in the activities which are generally considered the practice of law in the United States.

B. The Process of Applying for Admission to a United States Jurisdiction

When an applicant seeks to take a bar examination under this Model Rule, the applicant will have to complete the application required by the jurisdiction. The application should include the following:

(1) Certification by the Law School that

    (i) the applicant was awarded an LL.M. for the Practice of Law in the United States, and

    (ii) that the requirements of the LL.M. were certified by the ABA Council as meeting the criteria established by the Council to qualify the foreign-educated lawyer to sit for a bar examination.

    (iii) that the applicant received his or her foreign law degree at a foreign law school that:

        (a) is government sanctioned or recognized, if educational institutions are state regulated within the country; or

        (b) is recognized or approved by an evaluation body, if such agency exists within the country; or

        (c) is chartered to award first degrees in law by the appropriate authority within the country;

(2) Documentation provided by the applicant that the applicant is authorized to practice law in a foreign jurisdiction.

* * *

Process for an ABA Approved Law School to Obtain Certification From the Council of the ABA Section of Legal Education and Admissions to the Bar.

A law school that is fully approved by the Council of the ABA Section of Legal Education and Admissions to the Bar which seeks certification that an LL.M. Degree for the Practice of Law in the United States satisfies the specified Criteria must submit a written description of the LL.M. program for review by the Consultant on Legal Education of the American Bar Association and submission to the Council for action. The Consultant's Office will notify the school in writing as to whether the proposed LL.M. program satisfies the Criteria and has been certified by the Council during subsequent regularly scheduled site visits, site teams will gather the facts necessary to determine if the LL.M. program continues to satisfy the Criteria.

Many ABA approved law schools have LL.M. programs that are designed to meet educational goals other than preparing students for the practice of law in the United States. The Section of Legal Education and Admission to the Bar does not, through this certification program, exercise any oversight or assessment of other LL.M programs beyond the requirements of Standard 308. The limited purpose of the Model Rule and certification process is to aid the state courts and bars in identifying LL.M programs that meet certain criteria designed to prepare graduates of foreign law schools to take the bar examination and to be prepared to practice law in the United States.

AMERICAN BAR ASSOCIATION SECTION OF LEGAL EDUCATION AND ADMISSIONS TO THE BAR

REPORT

In 2009, the Chair of the Section of Legal Education and Admissions to the Bar, Professor Randy Hertz, appointed the Special Committee on International Issues to undertake a comprehensive review of the Section Council's role in discussions relating to international trade in legal services and in other international legal education issues. In addition to the general initiatives relating to the globalization of the practice of law and legal education, two specific developments impacted that decision. One was the anticipated request from a non-US law school to seek ABA accreditation. The other was a Resolution (attached) adopted by the Conference of Chief Justices urging the Section of Legal Education and Admissions to the Bar to consider implementing a program that would certify the quality of the legal education of foreign trained common law educated applicants seeking permission to take a bar examination and qualify for admission to the bar.

That Committee provided the Council of the Section with a "Report of the Special Committee on International Issues." The report addressed the following areas with respect to accreditation: accreditation of foreign law schools that seek to meet ABA standards; working with jurisdictions that seek assistance in developing a local or regional accreditation system to insure that the process is rigorous and reliable; and developing a range of criteria that would allow the ABA to advise state supreme courts and bar administrators that a graduate meeting the criteria was sufficiently educated in U.S. law that he or she could be allowed to apply to take the state bar exam even though the primary law degree was from another country.

The Report also suggested that the Section establish a permanent committee to address the recommendations in the Committee Report. In Fall 2009, consistent with the Committee's recommendation, the Council created a new standing committee on International Legal Education. Included in the Committee's initial charge was a request that it undertake two tasks on behalf of the Council. The first task was to draft a proposed Model Rule that would establish criteria for an LL.M. program designed to qualify a foreign lawyer from civil or common law jurisdictions to take a bar examination and to prepare the foreign lawyer for the practice of law in the United States. The second task was to explore additional options for admission for foreign lawyers who studied and practiced law in common law jurisdictions to qualify to take a bar examination and to seek admission in a United States jurisdiction without completing a degree program at an ABA accredited law school. The proposed Model Rule on Admission of Foreign Educated Lawyers addresses the first task. The Committee is still discussing the contents and procedures of a Model Rule that would address the second task.

Proposed Model Rule

The purpose of the attached Model Rule is to aid state courts and bar examiners in identifying LL.M. programs that meet specific criteria designed to prepare graduates of foreign law schools to take the bar examination and to practice law in the United States. * * *

* * *

The Model Rule includes a requirement that the applicant be "authorized" to practice law in a foreign jurisdiction. The meaning of "authorized" is discussed in the Comment to the Model Rule. The comment does not resolve the issue of exactly what it means that an "applicant can, in his or her own country, engage in the activities which are generally considered to be the practice of law in the United States". The Proposed Model Rule relies on the appropriate authority of the jurisdiction where the applicant applies to make that decision based on the documents presented by the applicant. The Committee decided against adding a specific number of years of legal practice as a requirement in addition to the applicant being "authorized" to practice.

Proposed Criteria

Under the proposal, the Section's role is limited to "certifying" that a school's LL.M. program meets the Criteria. The Comments to the Model Rule and the discussion of the certification process in the Criteria make it clear that the Council does not intend to establish standards or engage in the oversight of other LL.M. programs for foreign students or domestic students beyond what is currently required by Standard 308.

* * *

After a foreign lawyer completes the LL.M. program and applies to take a bar examination, the proposal requires the law school to certify to the state court that the applicant has completed the "certified" LL.M. degree and that the applicant's foreign law degree was granted by a foreign law school that satisfies the requirements of the Model Rule. Placing the burden on the schools encourages schools to consider whether the applicant's foreign degree satisfies the Model Rule requirements when making a school's admission decision.

* * *

Final Call: Section Won't Accredit Non-US Law Schools, but Foreign Lawyers Can Be Admitted
American Bar Association Journal Online
(October 1, 2012)

It looks as though the ABA Section of Legal Education and Admissions to the Bar won't be accrediting foreign law schools anytime soon.

The council of the legal education section, which is recognized by the Department of Education as the national accrediting body for U.S. law schools, rejected the idea of accrediting foreign law schools by a 15–0 vote (with two abstentions) in August when it met in Chicago during the 2012 ABA Annual Meeting.

But the motion the council approved also acknowledged "the need to address the issue of identifying appropriate standards for licensing foreign lawyers who seek to practice in U.S. jurisdictions."

The section, however, has no specific plans to address that issue, said Barry Currier, the ABA's interim consultant on legal education. "That particular matter is one small piece of a bigger puzzle that will take time to work through in a satisfactory way," he said.

Currently, only graduates of accredited U.S. law schools are entitled to take the bar exam in any state as a key step toward being admitted to practice, but many states also allow graduates of law schools outside the United States to take their bar exams within certain guidelines. In 2011, according to statistics gathered by the National Conference of Bar Examiners, 5,620 graduates of non-U.S. law schools took the bar exam in the District of Columbia and 28 states. Their total bar pass rate was 30 percent, compared to 74 percent for graduates of accredited U.S. law schools. The decision in August capped a four-year debate within the legal education section on whether to accredit foreign law schools that have based their educational programs on the American model, with its emphasis on the substance of U.S. law and professional ethics.

The issue first surfaced in 2008, when the Peking University of Transnational Law, a Chinese law school in Shenzhen that embraces the American model of legal education, announced its intention to seek ABA accreditation (but never did).

In response, the council appointed a special committee to study the issue. In 2010, the committee recommended that the section begin accrediting foreign law schools that meet its standards for U.S. schools. Doing so, the committee said, would give state supreme courts additional guidance in deciding which lawyers trained in other countries should be allowed to sit for a U.S. bar exam and help avoid a system in which the rules vary from state to state.

But the committee's recommendation drew dozens of comments, many of them opposing the idea of accrediting foreign law schools. So the council appointed a second committee to study the matter further with extensive input from key stakeholder groups.

In Chicago, the council considered the second committee's recommendation that the section refrain from accrediting foreign law schools. The committee maintained that doing so would divert the section's attention and resources at a time of significant strain on its finances and personnel, and that it would require the development and implementation of appropriate procedures for monitoring compliance with the accreditation standards. Moreover, the committee said, it would be difficult to acculturate students educated at foreign law schools in the culture, values and ethics of the American legal system.

The committee based its recommendation on a survey of key stakeholder groups—including the Conference of Chief Justices, state bar examiners, bar leaders, law school deans and faculty members—which found little support for the idea of accrediting foreign law schools.

The survey results clearly left an impression on council members. Ruth V. McGregor, the retired chief justice of the Arizona Supreme Court whose term on the council ended Aug. 31, said accrediting foreign law schools would require a broad-based consensus among stakeholder groups in the United States, and "it's clear we don't have any such consensus."

QUESTIONS AND NOTES

1.   You are a U.S. citizen practicing international banking law in the Seoul, South Korea office of a global law firm headquartered in London, U.K. Your banking clients are based in a number of countries, and engage you to advise them on banking transactions in Europe, North America, Africa and Asia. What legal code(s) of ethics do you follow in connection with your representation in these various transactions?

2.   What are areas of ethics are most likely to conflict in various jurisdictions in undertaking international banking practice? Are they easily reconciled?

3.   Is an International Code of Ethics an easy solution for conducting a multi-jurisdictional practice? If not, why not?

4.   What role does a law firm play in fostering—and enforcing—ethics standards in multi-jurisdictional practice?

5.   How much should you know about your international banking clients before undertaking to represent them? How about an ongoing basis once they become your client?

6.   The reading below should be considered in light of the materials presented in Chapter 9.

B. MONEY LAUNDERING AND TERRORIST FINANCING: ETHICAL STANDARDS

AMERICAN BAR ASSOCIATION, VOLUNTARY GOOD PRACTICES GUIDANCE FOR LAWYERS TO DETECT AND COMBAT MONEY LAUNDERING AND TERRORIST FINANCING
(April 23, 2010)

* * *

In 1989, the major industrialized nations formed an intergovernmental body known as the Financial Action Task Force on Money Laundering ("FATF") to coordinate efforts to prevent money laundering in both the international financial system and the domestic financial systems of the member entities. FATF first issued a comprehensive plan, known as the Forty Recommendations, for combating money laundering that was intended to present the basic framework for anti-money laundering ("AML") efforts and be of universal application. The Forty Recommendations are a set of international standards and are not a binding international convention, but many countries (including the United States) have committed to implementing them.

A decade after the creation of FATF, FATF sought to enlist the support of so-called "gatekeepers" to combat money laundering and terrorist financing. "Gatekeepers" include certain designated non-financial businesses and professions ("DNFBPs") such as lawyers, notaries, trust and company service providers ("TCSPs"), real estate agents, accountants, and auditors who assist with transactions involving the movement of money in the domestic and international financial systems. This effort is known as the "Gatekeeper Initiative."

A month after the September 11, 2001 terrorist attacks in the United States, FATF expanded its mandate to address terrorist financing and issued the Special Recommendations on Terrorist Financing. The Special Recommendations, originally comprised of eight recommendations, are intended to supplement the Forty Recommendations and are designed to combat the funding of terrorist acts and terrorist organizations. A ninth special recommendation was added in October 2004 to address concerns with cash couriers, thereby transforming the Special Recommendations into what have become known as the Nine Special Recommendations. The Forty Recommendations and the Nine Special Recommendations are sometimes referred to as the "40+9 Recommendations." In sum, the 40+9 Recommendations, together with their interpretative notes, constitute the international standards for combating money laundering and terrorist financing.

* * *

In June 2007, FATF collaborated with representatives of the international banking and securities industries to formulate risk-based guidance for financial institutions. Known as the "Guidance on the Risk-Based Approach to Combating Money Laundering and Terrorist Financing—High Level Principles and Procedures" ("Financial Institution Guidance"), this document was the first risk-based guidance paper issued by FATF for a specific industry sector.

Shortly after the issuance of the Financial Institution Guidance, FATF met with representatives of the DNFBP sectors, including lawyers, to determine if they would be willing to engage in a similar collaborative effort to develop risk-based guidance for their businesses and professions. The DNFBPs agreed to do so, and following such efforts FATF ultimately issued separate risk-based guidance papers in 2008 for every DNFBP sector, including lawyers.

During the negotiations with FATF over the guidance for lawyers, representatives of the legal profession emphasized to FATF the importance of ensuring that any risk-based approach developed did not undermine the attorney-client privilege or the duty of client confidentiality or otherwise impede the delivery of legal services generally. After over a year of intense debate and discussion, in October 2008 FATF issued risk-based guidance for the legal profession entitled "RBA Guidance for Legal Professionals" ("Lawyer Guidance").[2]

* * *

The Lawyer Guidance is "high level" guidance intended to provide a broad framework for implementing a risk-based approach for the legal profession. It does not offer detailed direction on the application of this approach to specific factual situations, nor does it take into account the practical realities of the practice of law in an increasingly complex environment or attempt to address jurisdictional variations among the FATF member countries. For those reasons, the Lawyer Guidance urges

---

[2]   RBA GUIDANCE FOR LEGAL PROFESSIONALS ("LAWYER GUIDANCE"), adopted October 23, 2008. FATF Recommendations 12 (customer due diligence), 16 (suspicious transaction reports), and 24 (monitoring) and the related Interpretative Notes specifically deal with lawyers.

the legal profession generally, or in different countries, to develop "good practice in the design and implementation of an effective risk-based approach."[3]

To assist practitioners in understanding the practical implications of a particular provision in the Lawyer Guidance, this paper provides various "Practice Pointers." These Practice Pointers are intended to offer insight into the Lawyer Guidance provision in question, especially from the perspective of a practitioner.

* * *

What is Money Laundering?

Money laundering "is the criminal practice of filtering ill-gotten gains, or 'dirty' money, through a series of transactions; in this way the funds are 'cleaned' so that they appear to be proceeds from legal activities."[4] Money laundering was made a federal crime in the U.S. under the Money Laundering Control Act of 1986 and is addressed under 18 U.S.C. § 1956 (laundering of monetary instruments) and § 1957 (engaging in monetary transactions in property derived from specified unlawful activity). Money laundering involves three distinct stages: the placement stage, the layering stage, and the integration stage.[5] The placement stage is the stage at which funds from illegal activity, or funds intended to support illegal activity, are first introduced into the financial system. The layering stage involves further disguising and distancing the illicit funds from their illegal source through the use of a series of frequently complex financial transactions. This stage may include the creation of tiered entities and complicated entity structures designed to conceal the source of the illicit funds. The integration phase of money laundering results in the illicit funds, now laundered, returning to "a status of expendability in the hands of the organized crime group that generated them."[6]

* * *

What is Client Due Diligence?

The 40+9 Recommendations require that lawyers perform CDD when they perform or carry out specified activities.[12] CDD is intended to assist lawyers in forming a reasonable belief that they have appropriate

---

[3]   LAWYER GUIDANCE ¶ 6.

[4]   BANK SECRECY ACT ANTI-MONEY LAUNDERING EXAMINATION MANUAL, Federal Financial Institutions Examination Council at 7 (2007), available at http://www.occ.gov/publications/publications-by-type/comptrollers-handbook/index-comptrollers-handbook.html.

[5]   See http://www.fatf-gati.org/document/29/0,3343,en_32250379_32235720_33659613_1_1_1_1,00.htmll# (explaining three stages of money laundering).

[6]   See http://www.fincen.gov/news_room/aml_history.html. (explaining three stages of money laundering).

[12]   See Recommendation 12.

awareness of the true identity of each client[13] and the true nature of the matter they have been engaged to undertake. CDD is not intended to place the lawyer in an adversarial relationship with the client; rather, the purpose is to make sure the lawyer knows the true identity and business goals of the client.

CDD should be performed at client intake, but it also should be periodically performed during the course of the engagement. The level of required CDD varies depending on the risk profile of the client. For some clients, "basic" CDD may be appropriate. For clients posing a higher risk, "enhanced" CDD may be necessary. At the other end of the spectrum, reduced CDD may be sufficient. The relative levels of CDD are described in greater detail below.

The three (3) steps required to be taken in "basic" CDD are as follows:

- Identify and appropriately verify the identity of each client on a timely basis.[14]

- Identify the beneficial owner,[15] and take reasonable measures to verify the identity of the beneficial owner of the client such that the lawyer is reasonably satisfied that the lawyer knows who the beneficial owner is. Clients generally should be subject to the full range of CDD measures, including the requirement to identify the beneficial owner in accordance with Lawyer Guidance ¶ 114. The purpose of identifying beneficial ownership is to ascertain those natural persons who exercise effective control over a client, whether by means of ownership, voting shares, contract rights, or otherwise. Lawyers may use a risk-based approach when determining the extent to which they are required to identify the beneficial owner, depending on the type of client, suspicious behavior that might suggest someone is seeking to conceal the true party in interest, the difficulty of ascertaining the identity, the business relationship and transaction, and other appropriate factors, including the geographic location of the client.

  The issue of whether a lawyer must, in all cases, identify the beneficial owners of a client was a highly controversial issue in the drafting of the Lawyer Guidance. Although FATF initially sought to adopt a rules-based approach that would require lawyers to always identify the beneficial owners of a client, after strong opposition from representatives of the legal

---

[13]   LAWYER GUIDANCE ¶ 114.

[14]   See Section 6 for a more detailed discussion of this step.

[15]   The Lawyer Guidance defines "beneficial owner" as follows: "*Beneficial owner* refers to the natural person(s) who ultimately owns or controls a client and/or the person on whose behalf a transaction is being conducted. It also incorporates those persons who exercise ultimate effective control over a legal person or arrangement." See LAWYER GUIDANCE Annex 2.

profession, FATF ultimately agreed that this analysis would be subject to a risk-based approach. Consequently, depending on the risks presented by the client, it may be appropriate to identify the beneficial owners of a client. Lawyers should do so only when, from a risk-based standpoint, such an analysis is warranted. It is impractical in some instances for a lawyer to identify the beneficial owners of a client. The cost, time, and effort to undertake such an analysis is typically disproportionate to advancing the goals of detecting and preventing money laundering and terrorist financing unless other factors are present.

Practice pointer: For example, if a lawyer is dealing with a syndication of investors or financiers or an entity that has a large number of owners but is not publicly traded, ascertaining the client's beneficial owners would be extremely time consuming. Unless other facts put the lawyer on notice that something unusual or suspicious were transpiring, the process of determining all the beneficial owners of the client would be disproportionate to the level of risk.

- Obtain information to understand the client's circumstances and business depending on the nature, scope, and timing of the services to be provided. This information may be obtained from clients in the normal course of the lawyers' acceptance of the retention and receipt of instructions from the client.

* * *

QUESTIONS AND NOTES

1. The ABA guidance was a collaborative effort of representatives of the American Bar Association ("ABA") Task Force on Gatekeeper Regulation and the Profession, the ABA Section of Real Property, Trust and Estate Law, the ABA Section of International Law, the ABA Section of Business Law, the ABA Section of Taxation, the ABA Criminal Justice Section, the American College of Trust and Estate Counsel, the American College of Real Estate Lawyers, the American College of Mortgage Attorneys, and the American College of Commercial Finance Lawyers.

Also, the Task Force on Gatekeeper Regulation and the Profession, the ABA Section of Real Property, Trust and Estate Law, the ABA Section of International Law, the ABA Section of Business Law, the ABA Section of Taxation, the ABA Criminal Justice Section, the ABA Law Practice Management Section, the American College of Trust and Estate Counsel, the American College of Real Estate Lawyers, the American College of Mortgage Attorneys, and the American College of Commercial Finance Lawyers have formally endorsed or approved the ABA guidance.

2.   If you are asked to advise a law firm on setting up a program designed to ensure compliance with best practices for complying with international anti-money laundering standards, what would you advise as the primary components of such a program? Would you recommend that an ongoing firm committee be tasked with money laundering oversight and compliance for this program? If so, what would be the responsibilities of the committee?

INDEX

References are to Pages

431